Vice President of Editorial	Melissa Wagner
Director of Acquisitions	Mikaela Felty
Director of Book Development	Jocelynn Hessler
Production Manager	Mike Brehm
Cover Design	Jose Rosado

Published in the United States of America by
IGI Global Scientific Publishing
701 East Chocolate Avenue
Hershey, PA, 17033, USA
Tel: 717-533-8845 | Fax: 717-533-7115
Website: https://www.igi-global.com E-mail: cust@igi-global.com

Library of Congress Cataloging-in-Publication Data

LCCN: 2026011092 (CIP Data Pending)
ISBN13: 9798337385259
Isbn13Softcover: 9798337385266
EISBN13: 9798337385273
British Cataloguing in Publication Data
A Cataloguing in Publication record for this book is available from the British Library.

The Academic Profession and Professorial Appointments in the Age of AI in Higher Education

Rany Sam
https://orcid.org/0000-0003-3266-5974
National University of Battambang, Cambodia

IGI Global
Scientific Publishing
Publishing Tomorrow's Research Today

Editorial Advisory Board

Table of Contents

Detailed Table of Contents

The academic profession, which encompasses teachers, researchers, and personnel in higher education institutions, has been considered a stable and structured profession with well-defined roles, norms, and career paths. However, in the past few decades, there have been some major changes taking place in higher education institutions across the globe due to globalization, technological changes, policy shifts, and changing demands of students. At the same time, there are some features of the profession that remain unchanged, such as the central role of teaching, research, and academic freedom. This chapter discusses how the academic profession is undergoing changes while maintaining its defining features.

Artificial intelligence (AI) is rapidly integrating into higher education and transforming the work of most academics. The chapter examines how different forms of AI are affecting academics' work, professional identities, and trajectories through their academic careers. The chapter approaches AI as part of a broader change in academic governance and how university administrators use data to make decisions. The chapter examines how AI will affect core academic functions, including teaching, research, and service, as well as how universities hire and evaluate faculty for promotion and tenure. This chapter also explores power, ethical, and equity issues in AI, including algorithmic bias, academic monitoring, and the effects of AI on the global higher education system, with respect to gender, career stage, and geographic distribution. This chapter draws on concepts from the sociology of professions and higher education to identify the conflict between traditional academic values and the use of AI governance technologies, driven by the need for greater efficiency.

This chapter examines how artificial intelligence is reshaping the inner landscape of academic life, not merely by changing tasks, but by unsettling how academics understand themselves, their work, and their professional purpose. In AI-mediated universities, teaching, research, assessment, administration, and even hiring increasingly pass through technological systems that promise efficiency while quietly redefining academic value. The chapter argues that academic identity is becoming more negotiated, exposed, and fragile, as professors are asked to work alongside machines while preserving forms of judgment, care, creativity, and ethical responsibility that cannot be reduced to data. It also explores how professorial appointments may need to evolve in response to these shifts, placing renewed emphasis on human discernment, intellectual courage, institutional trust, and the deeper vocation of higher education in a rapidly automated age.

Artificial intelligence (AI) is transforming higher education by influencing teaching, research, governance, and academic labor. This chapter adopts a conceptual review approach using structured narrative synthesis to examine how AI reshapes the professoriate in contemporary universities. Drawing on literature related to digital pedagogy, governance, and human–AI collaboration, the chapter analyzes how AI contributes to pedagogical restructuring, faculty role transformation, and evolving digital scholarly identity. It also discusses concerns related to algorithmic bias, academic integrity, and surveillance-oriented governance. The chapter argues that universities must adopt transparent governance systems and human-centered pedagogical approaches to ensure that AI supports academic autonomy, critical inquiry, and responsible higher education practices.

Artificial intelligence (AI) is reshaping higher education, influencing faculty roles, identities, and career trajectories. This chapter examines the impact of AI on recruitment, evaluation, tenure, promotion, and professional development. Drawing on literature from higher education studies, AI ethics, and the sociology of professions,

This chapter examines the academic promotion system in Cambodian public universities, highlighting national and institutional challenges that hinder merit-based career advancement. Despite rapid expansion in higher education, promotion practices remain inconsistent, with unclear criteria, limited research capacity, and centralized decision-making processes constraining academic development within specialized, relevant ministries and the Council of Ministers. Heavy teaching workloads, insufficient funding, and weak research support further limit faculty productivity and progression. Drawing on comparative insights and policy analysis, the chapter argues for a more transparent, standardized, and performance-oriented promotion framework. It proposes practical reforms, including clearer evaluation criteria, strengthened research infrastructure, and decentralized yet accountable governance mechanisms, to enhance fairness, motivation, and institutional quality in Cambodia's public higher education sector.

The integration of data-driven systems and artificial intelligence in higher education is reshaping academic work in significant ways. This chapter examines how datafication and metric-based evaluation reconfigure the labour, priorities, and identity of the professoriate in India. Drawing on qualitative interviews with 80 faculty members, it shows that administrative demands and performance metrics increasingly dominate academic life, reducing time for sustained research. While AI is widely used for teaching-related efficiency, its impact on research remains limited. The findings also reveal growing inequalities across career stages, particularly affecting early-career

Foreword

It is my great pleasure and honor to introduce *The Academic Profession and Professorial Appointments in the Age of AI in Higher Education*, an important edited volume that addresses one of the most significant transformations confronting universities in the twenty-first century. Artificial intelligence (AI) is rapidly reshaping every dimension of higher education—from teaching and learning to research, governance, academic evaluation, and institutional leadership. As universities around the world are navigating this unprecedented technological revolution, the academic profession itself is undergoing profound changes that require thoughtful reflection, evidence-based policy, and innovative leadership.

This volume arrives at a particularly important moment in the evolution of global higher education. While discussions surrounding AI often focus on technological capabilities and digital innovation, this book reminds us that the future of higher education is ultimately about people. Professors, researchers, teacher educators, academic leaders, and policymakers remain at the heart of knowledge creation, critical inquiry, and societal development. The central question is therefore not whether AI will become part of higher education—it already has—but rather how universities can integrate AI responsibly while preserving the essential values of academic freedom, professional integrity, ethical responsibility, and human judgment.

One of the greatest strengths of this edited volume lies in its international and interdisciplinary perspectives. The contributors represent diverse academic traditions and national contexts, bringing together experiences and insights from Cambodia, India, Vietnam, Indonesia, Morocco, South Africa, Nepal, Cyprus, Syria, and Bangladesh while also drawing upon broader comparative perspectives from North America, Europe, and the Global South. Such diversity enriches the discussion by demonstrating that although higher education systems differ in history, governance, and resources, they share many common opportunities and challenges in response to AI-driven transformation.

The chapters collectively explore a wide range of contemporary issues affecting the academic profession. Readers will find thoughtful discussions on academic identity, faculty recruitment, professorial appointments, promotion and tenure systems, research productivity, digital scholarship, professional development, academic freedom, institutional governance, AI literacy, doctoral supervision, ethics, and policy reforms. Importantly, many contributors move beyond theoretical discussion by offering empirical evidence, systematic reviews, conceptual frameworks, and practical recommendations that can inform institutional decision-making and future research.

I am particularly pleased to see meaningful attention given to developing country perspectives, especially those of Cambodia and other emerging higher education systems. Too often, international scholarship is dominated by experiences from well-resourced institutions, leaving limited space for voices from countries undergoing rapid educational transformation. This volume helps address that imbalance by highlighting local realities while engaging with global debates. It demonstrates that valuable innovations, policy lessons, and scholarly contributions emerge from every region of the world when diverse perspectives are encouraged and respected.

The editors have successfully assembled a coherent collection that balances conceptual scholarship with practical relevance. Rather than viewing AI solely as a technological innovation, the book examines its broader implications for academic careers, institutional culture, leadership, governance, and the future of the professoriate. Throughout the volume, contributors consistently emphasize that technological advancement must remain aligned with the fundamental mission of universities: advancing knowledge, nurturing critical thinking, promoting ethical scholarship, and serving society through education and research.

As Rector of the National University of Battambang, I have witnessed firsthand the growing importance of digital transformation and innovation in strengthening higher education. Universities today are expected not only to produce graduates equipped for rapidly changing labor markets but also to cultivate responsible citizens capable of addressing increasingly complex global challenges. Achieving these goals requires institutions to embrace technological innovation while safeguarding the human values that define academic excellence. AI should therefore be viewed not as a replacement for educators but as a powerful tool that enhances teaching, research, collaboration, and institutional effectiveness when implemented thoughtfully and responsibly.

This volume also has particular significance for academic leaders and policymakers. As universities reconsider promotion criteria, faculty evaluation systems, research assessment, and professional development in response to AI, evidence-informed governance becomes increasingly essential. The chapters presented here offer valuable insights for designing transparent, equitable, and accountable academic systems that recognize both technological competence and enduring scholarly contributions. These discussions undoubtedly stimulate meaningful dialog among university leaders seeking to modernize their institutions without compromising academic quality or integrity.

I would like to commend the editors for their vision, dedication, and scholarly leadership in bringing together this outstanding international collaboration. Coordinating contributions from scholars across multiple countries and disciplinary backgrounds is a considerable achievement that reflects both academic commitment and international partnership. I also extend my sincere appreciation to all contributing authors for sharing their expertise and advancing scholarly understanding of one of the most pressing issues facing higher education today.

I am confident that *the Academic Profession and Professorial Appointments in the Age of AI in Higher Education* will become a valuable reference for university leaders, policymakers, faculty members, researchers, doctoral students, and graduate scholars interested in the future of higher education. More importantly, I hope this volume will encourage continued international collaboration and inspire new research that places human values, academic excellence, and ethical innovation at the center of the digital transformation of higher education.

I warmly congratulate the editors and contributors to this significant scholarly achievement and commend this volume to readers around the world.

H.E. Sok Khorn
National University of Battambang, Cambodia

Preface

Higher education stands at one of the most transformative moments in its history. The rapid emergence and widespread adoption of artificial intelligence (AI) are fundamentally changing how universities teach, conduct research, assess learning, manage institutional operations, and engage with society. Unlike previous technological revolutions, AI has the capacity not only to automate routine tasks but also to influence intellectual work, which is traditionally regarded as the exclusive domain of scholars. Consequently, universities around the world are rethinking the nature of academic work, the future of professorial appointments, the criteria for academic excellence, and the responsibilities of higher education institutions in an increasingly digital world.

The academic profession has historically been built upon principles of intellectual autonomy, academic freedom, peer review, scholarly integrity, and public service. Professors have long served as educators, researchers, mentors, innovators, and leaders who generate and disseminate knowledge to advance society. Today, however, these traditional roles are evolving rapidly. Artificial intelligence involves reshaping classroom instruction through intelligent tutoring systems and adaptive learning platforms; transforming research through data-driven analytics and generative technologies; supporting administrative decision-making through predictive models; and influencing recruitment, promotion, tenure, and performance evaluation through algorithm-assisted systems. These developments offer unprecedented opportunities for innovation while simultaneously raising complex questions concerning ethics, transparency, accountability, equity, academic identity, and professional autonomy.

As AI continues to advance, universities face a critical challenge: How can they harness the benefits of technological innovation while preserving the human values that define higher education? This question lies at the heart of this edited volume, *The Academic Profession and Professorial Appointments in the Age of AI in Higher Education*. Bringing together distinguished scholars from Cambodia, India, Vietnam, Indonesia, Morocco, South Africa, Nepal, Cyprus, Syria, Bangladesh, and other international contexts, this volume offers a comprehensive examination of how AI is redefining academic careers, institutional governance, faculty development, research practices, and the future of the professoriate across diverse higher education systems.

Unlike many existing publications that primarily examine AI from the perspectives of educational technology or computer science, this book places the academic profession itself at the center of scholarly inquiry. It investigates how AI influences not only teaching and learning but also the structures, cultures, policies, and values that shape academic careers. The volume explores pressing issues surrounding faculty recruitment, professorial appointments, promotion and tenure, academic evaluation, professional development, research productivity, institutional governance, academic identity, digital scholarship, ethical leadership, and policy reform. In doing so, it recognizes that technological transformation must be accompanied by thoughtful governance, responsible leadership, and a continued commitment to academic excellence.

One of the defining strengths of this volume is its international scope. The contributors represent a broad range of geographical regions, institutional contexts, and disciplinary perspectives. Their collective expertise demonstrates that while higher education systems vary considerably in their histories, governance structures, and resource capacities, they share common challenges as AI increasingly influences academic work. The inclusion of studies from both developed and developing countries enables meaningful comparisons that enrich the understanding of how local contexts shape institutional responses to global technological change. This diversity of perspectives encourages readers to appreciate both universal trends and context-specific solutions.

The volume is also notable for its methodological diversity. Readers will encounter conceptual analyses, systematic literature reviews, policy analyses, empirical quantitative and qualitative studies, mixed-methods investigations, comparative research, scenario planning, and theoretical frameworks. Together, these approaches provide a multidimensional understanding of the academic profession in the digital era and illustrate the richness of contemporary scholarship on AI and higher education. The contributors not only identify emerging challenges but also propose practical strategies and policy recommendations that can guide universities toward responsible and sustainable AI integration.

The importance of this book extends beyond technological innovation. At its core, it is about people—academics whose professional identities, careers, and daily practices are being transformed by rapidly evolving technologies. It asks fundamental questions that will shape the future of higher education. What qualities should define the professor of the future? How should universities evaluate academic excellence in an AI-supported environment? How can institutions ensure fairness, transparency, and accountability when algorithmic systems become increasingly influential in terms of faculty recruitment, promotion, and performance assessment? What competencies should future academics develop to thrive in digitally transformed universities? How can academic freedom, intellectual creativity, and ethical scholarship be preserved amid growing reliance on automated systems?

These questions are especially relevant for countries that are actively reforming their higher education sectors. Many institutions across Asia, Africa, Latin America, and other developing regions are simultaneously pursuing digital transformation, quality assurance, internationalization, research capacity building, and governance reform. AI offers tremendous opportunities to accelerate these developments, yet it also risks widening inequalities if implementation occurs without adequate infrastructure, policy frameworks, professional development, and ethical safeguards. Several chapters in this volume address these concerns directly, offering valuable lessons for emerging higher education systems while contributing to broader international discussions.

This book is intended for a wide audience. It serves as an important reference for university leaders seeking evidence-informed approaches to institutional transformation; policymakers responsible for higher education reform; faculty members adapting to evolving professional roles; researchers investigating AI, digital governance, educational leadership, and the sociology of the academic profession; doctoral candidates and graduate students exploring contemporary issues in higher education; teacher educators preparing future academics; and practitioners responsible for faculty development and institutional quality assurance. The volume also provides valuable insights for international organizations, accreditation agencies, and research networks interested in the future of higher education in the age of artificial intelligence.

To provide readers with a comprehensive understanding of this rapidly evolving field, the book is organized into twenty-six carefully selected chapters that collectively examine the academic profession from multiple complementary perspectives. While each chapter addresses a distinct dimension of AI and higher education, together, they present a coherent narrative illustrating how technological innovation is reshaping academic careers, institutional governance, professional identity, and scholarly practice. The chapters range from philosophical reflections on academic identity and professional purpose to empirical investigations of AI literacy, faculty commitment, doctoral supervision, policy reform, institutional governance, and future scenarios for higher education leadership. Collectively, they demonstrate that the future of the professoriate depends not only on technological advancement but also on thoughtful leadership, ethical governance, inclusive policy, and continuous professional learning.

The following section introduces each chapter individually, highlighting its unique contribution to advancing the understanding of the academic profession and professorial appointments in the age of artificial intelligence.

ORGANIZATION OF THE BOOK

This edited volume comprises twenty-six chapters that collectively examine the evolving nature of the academic profession and professorial appointments in the era of artificial intelligence. While each chapter explores a distinct dimension of this transformation, together, they provide a comprehensive understanding of how AI is reshaping academic work, institutional governance, professional identity, faculty careers, and higher education policy. The chapters combine conceptual discussions, empirical research, policy analyses, systematic reviews, and comparative perspectives, thereby offering readers both theoretical insights and practical implications.

Chapter 1: Continuity and Change in the Academic Profession

The academic profession, which encompasses teachers, researchers, and personnel in higher education institutions, has been considered a stable and structured profession with well-defined roles, norms, and career paths. However, in the past few decades, there have been some major changes taking place in higher education institutions across the globe due to globalization, technological changes, policy shifts, and changing demands of students. At the same time, there are some features of the profession that remain unchanged, such as the central role of teaching, research, and academic freedom. This chapter discusses how the academic profession is undergoing changes while maintaining its defining features.

Chapter 2: Reconfiguring the Academic Profession in the Age of Artificial Intelligence

Artificial intelligence (AI) is rapidly integrating into higher education and transforming the work of most academics. The chapter examines how different forms of AI are affecting academics' work, professional identities, and trajectories through their academic careers. The chapter approaches AI as part of a broader change in academic governance and how university administrators use data to make decisions. The chapter examines how AI will affect core academic functions, including teaching, research, and service, as well as how universities hire and evaluate faculty for promotion and tenure. This chapter also explores power, ethical, and equity issues in AI, including algorithmic bias, academic monitoring, and the effects of AI on the global higher education system, with respect to gender, career stage, and geographic distribution. This chapter draws on concepts from the sociology of professions and higher education to identify the conflict between traditional academic values and the use of AI governance technologies, driven by the need for greater efficiency.

Chapter 3: Academic Identity and Professional Purpose in AI-Mediated Universities

This chapter examines how artificial intelligence is reshaping the inner landscape of academic life, not merely by changing tasks, but by unsettling how academics understand themselves, their work, and their professional purpose. In AI-mediated universities, teaching, research, assessment, administration, and even hiring increasingly pass through technological systems that promise efficiency while quietly redefining academic value. The chapter argues that academic identity is becoming more negotiated, exposed, and fragile, as professors are asked to work alongside machines while preserving forms of judgment, care, creativity, and ethical responsibility that cannot be reduced to data. It also explores how professorial appointments may need to evolve in response to these shifts, placing renewed emphasis on human discernment, intellectual courage, institutional trust, and the deeper vocation of higher education in a rapidly automated age.

Chapter 4: Reimagining the Professoriate: How AI Is Reshaping Academic Roles and Responsibilities

Artificial intelligence (AI) is transforming higher education by influencing teaching, research, governance, and academic labor. This chapter adopts a conceptual review approach using structured narrative synthesis to examine how AI reshapes the professoriate in contemporary universities. Drawing on literature related to digital pedagogy, governance, and human–AI collaboration, the chapter analyzes how AI contributes to pedagogical restructuring, faculty role transformation, and evolving digital scholarly identity. It also discusses concerns related to algorithmic bias, academic integrity, and surveillance-oriented governance. The chapter argues that universities must adopt transparent governance systems and human-centered pedagogical approaches to ensure that AI supports academic autonomy, critical inquiry, and responsible higher education practices.

Chapter 5: AI and the Academic Profession: Navigating Careers in Higher Education

Artificial intelligence (AI) is reshaping higher education, influencing faculty roles, identities, and career trajectories. This chapter examines the impact of AI on recruitment, evaluation, tenure, promotion, and professional development. Drawing on literature from higher education studies, AI ethics, and the sociology of professions, it explores opportunities such as efficiency, transparency, and data-driven insights, alongside risks including bias, metric-driven cultures, and threats to autonomy and equity. A conceptual framework for the responsible integration of AI emphasizes transparency, human oversight, and alignment with institutional values. Comparative case studies from North America, Europe, and the Global South highlight successes, limitations, and lessons for achieving equitable and accountable academic careers.

Chapter 6: Redefining Professorial Roles and Navigating AI Integration in Academic Careers

This chapter examines how artificial intelligence (AI) is reshaping the academic profession and professorial appointments in contemporary higher education. Situating AI within the historical evolution of academic evaluation—from peer judgment and collegial governance to metricization and algorithmic mediation—the chapter analyzes how AI-driven systems are transforming research, teaching, service, and faculty career pathways. Drawing on the sociology of professions, audit culture, and theories of algorithmic governance, it conceptualizes AI as a sociotechnical force that reconfigures professional authority, autonomy, and notions of academic merit. Particular attention is given to the implications of AI for faculty recruitment, promotion, and tenure, as well as for early-career academics and institutional equity. The chapter argues that while AI offers opportunities for efficiency and innovation, its integration requires robust governance frameworks to safeguard academic freedom, professional judgment, and inclusivity.

Chapter 7: Appointments of Professors in the Age of AI-Driven Hiring, Promotion, and Tenure in Higher Education: Appointment Legitimacy in Academic Careers

This chapter examines professorial hiring, promotion, and tenure as legitimacy-critical sociotechnical regimes under AI-mediated evaluation. It shows how datafication, commensuration, and dashboard governance reconstitute academic merit into machine-legible proxies, amplifying construct drift, proxy sovereignty, and automation bias unless bounded by appointment-grade constraints. Integrating professional jurisdiction, institutional logics, sociotechnical infrastructure, measurement-validity governance, and epistemic justice, it specifies due-process requirements for transparency, explainability, contestability, data minimization, and academic freedom. It proposes auditable governance controls and a capability-building roadmap so committees and leaders retain accountable peer judgment while modernizing evaluation.

Chapter 8: Academic promotion in Cambodian public universities: challenges and moving forward

This chapter examines the academic promotion system in Cambodian public universities, highlighting national and institutional challenges that hinder merit-based career advancement. Despite rapid expansion in higher education, promotion practices remain inconsistent, with unclear criteria, limited research capacity, and centralized decision-making processes constraining academic development within specialized, relevant ministries and the Council of Ministers. Heavy teaching workloads, insufficient funding, and weak research support further limit faculty productivity and progression. Drawing on comparative insights and policy analysis, the chapter argues for a more transparent, standardized, and performance-oriented promotion framework. It proposes practical reforms, including clearer evaluation criteria, strengthened research infrastructure, and decentralized yet accountable governance mechanisms, to enhance fairness, motivation, and institutional quality in Cambodia's public higher education sector.

Chapter 9: Datafying the Professoriate: AI, Metrics, and the Changing Nature of Academic Work

The integration of data-driven systems and artificial intelligence in higher education is reshaping academic work in significant ways. This chapter examines how datafication and metric-based evaluation reconfigure the labour, priorities, and identity of the professoriate in India. Drawing on qualitative interviews with 80 faculty members, it shows that administrative demands and performance metrics increasingly dominate academic life, reducing time for sustained research. While AI is widely used for teaching-related efficiency, its impact on research remains limited. The findings also reveal growing inequalities across career stages, particularly affecting early-career and contractual faculty. The chapter argues that datafication restructures academic work by privileging measurable outputs over intellectual autonomy.

Chapter 10: Digitalization, AI, and the Changing Social Contract of the Professoriate

This chapter examines how digitalization and artificial intelligence are reshaping the social contract of the professoriate in contemporary higher education. The academic profession has long been built around a delicate balance of autonomy, intellectual responsibility, institutional service, and public trust. Yet the growing presence of AI-driven systems, data analytics, automated assessment, digital teaching platforms, and performance-based monitoring is altering how professors teach, research, publish, collaborate, and are evaluated. Rather than treating AI as a purely technical innovation, the chapter considers it as a force that quietly reorganizes academic labor, authority, and identity. It explores the tensions between efficiency and freedom, transparency and surveillance, innovation and precarity. Ultimately, the chapter argues that universities must rethink the social contract of academic work so that technological transformation strengthens, rather than weakens, the human, ethical, and scholarly foundations of the professoriate.

Chapter 11: The Impact of AI on Academic Freedom, Institutional Governance, and Professional Autonomy

AI is transforming education in various ways, as this chapter shows. It examines how algorithmic systems affect research, policy, curriculum, faculty evaluation, and student assessment. This chapter examines how academic administration and institutional governance are increasingly using generative AI tools, AI-driven analytics, and automated decision systems. We examine monitoring, algorithmic bias, openness, intellectual freedom, and the erosion of researchers' and teachers' professional judgement. Academic autonomy is examined in relation to automated performance evaluation, predictive analytics, and AI-assisted monitoring systems. The chapter also discusses university AI ethics and regulation. New ideas include participatory governance models, explainable AI, and human-centered AI frameworks. Balancing technological advancement with ethical governance principles can help universities ensure that AI supports academic honesty, institutional responsibility, and professional independence.

Chapter 12: Future Scenarios for the Professoriate and Higher Education Leadership in 2035

The analysis of 2035 for professors and education leadership is undertaken in this chapter using futures studies, with scenario planning being the focus. A crisis in the academic paradigm, the development of a "research precariat," and the decline of the Humboldtian vision of the scholarly-citizen are recognized. Based on an assessment of present trends, including generative AI, academic de-bundling, and the diffusion of the knowledge authority, four scenarios are derived, namely, the Augmented AI Academy, the Global Knowledge Network, the Corporate Integration of Vocational Education, and the Resilient Human-Centric Organization. These scenarios bring about distinct challenges for the professoriate and its leadership that would require a transition from bureaucratic management toward ecosystem leadership and anticipatory governance. The implications of this foresight exercise indicate a possible evolution in the value proposition of the professoriate, from knowledge diffusion to validation and social innovation by 2035.

CONCLUDING REFLECTIONS

Taken together, the twenty-six chapters in this volume demonstrate that artificial intelligence is far more than a technological innovation. It represents a transformative force that is reshaping the academic profession, redefining professorial appointments, and influencing virtually every aspect of higher education. Across diverse national contexts, institutional settings, and disciplinary traditions, the contributors collectively illustrate how AI is transforming teaching, research, academic leadership, governance, professional development, faculty evaluation, doctoral education, scholarly communication, and institutional decision-making.

A distinguishing characteristic of this volume is its balance between optimism and critical reflection. The contributors acknowledge AI's remarkable potential to enhance educational quality, research productivity, institutional efficiency, and global collaboration. At the same time, they recognize the ethical, social, and professional challenges associated with algorithmic governance, datafication, academic surveillance, digital inequality, and the changing nature of scholarly work. Rather than presenting AI as either a threat or a universal solution, this book advocates thoughtful, evidence-informed, and human-centered approaches that preserve the fundamental values of higher education while embracing responsible innovation.

Another significant contribution of this edited collection is its truly international perspective. The participation of scholars from multiple countries enables meaningful comparisons across diverse higher education systems and enriches understanding of how different institutional, cultural, and policy contexts shape AI adoption. Equally important is the inclusion of perspectives from developing and emerging higher education systems, which remain underrepresented in much of the existing literature. By bringing together voices from both established and rapidly developing academic communities, this volume contributes to a more inclusive and globally relevant understanding of the future of higher education.

This book also advances scholarship by integrating multiple disciplinary perspectives, including higher education studies, educational leadership, educational technology, public policy, sociology of professions, human resource management, digital governance, ethics, teacher education, and futures studies. The diversity of methodologies represented—including conceptual analyses, empirical investigations, systematic reviews, mixed-methods research, policy analyses, scenario planning, and theoretical frameworks—provides readers with a comprehensive understanding of one of the most important developments currently shaping higher education worldwide.

We hope this volume will serve not only as an authoritative academic reference but also as a catalyst for future research, institutional dialogue, and policy innovation. As universities continue to navigate the opportunities and complexities presented by artificial intelligence, sustained collaboration among scholars, university leaders, policymakers, educators, and researchers will be essential for ensuring that technological advancement strengthens rather than diminishes the mission of higher education.

ACKNOWLEDGEMENTS

As editors, we express our deepest gratitude to all contributing authors whose expertise, scholarly commitment, and intellectual generosity made this volume possible. Their willingness to share diverse perspectives and engage in constructive scholarly dialogue has resulted in a collection that reflects both academic excellence and international collaboration.

We sincerely thank the anonymous reviewers for their thoughtful comments and valuable recommendations, which greatly enhanced the quality and rigor of the chapters included in this book. We also acknowledge the editorial and production teams whose professionalism and dedication supported the successful development of this publication.

Finally, we extend our appreciation to our respective universities, colleagues, students, and families for their encouragement and unwavering support throughout the preparation of this volume. Their inspiration and confidence have been invaluable throughout this collaborative journey.

EDITORS' CLOSING REMARKS

The future of higher education will not be determined solely by advances in artificial intelligence but by the collective wisdom with which educators, researchers, university leaders, and policymakers choose to employ these technologies. AI will continue to evolve, yet the enduring purposes of higher education—creating knowledge, cultivating critical thinking, advancing innovation, promoting ethical leadership, and serving society—remain unchanged.

It is our sincere hope that The Academic Profession and Professorial Appointments in the Age of AI in Higher Education will inspire meaningful scholarly conversations, stimulate interdisciplinary research, inform institutional policies, and encourage responsible leadership in universities worldwide. More importantly, we hope this volume will help shape a future in which technological innovation and human values work together to strengthen the academic profession for generations to come.

Acknowledgment

The completion of *The Academic Profession and Professorial Appointments in the Age of AI in Higher Education* has been made possible through the collective efforts, expertise, and commitment of many individuals and institutions. As editors, we are deeply grateful to everyone who contributed to the successful development of this volume.

First and foremost, we extend our sincere appreciation to all chapter authors for their outstanding scholarly contributions. Their willingness to share their expertise, research findings, and diverse perspectives has resulted in a rich and comprehensive collection that advances understanding of the academic profession and professorial appointments in the age of artificial intelligence. The international collaboration represented in this volume reflects the value of scholarly exchange across disciplines, institutions, and countries. We also express our heartfelt gratitude to the anonymous reviewers for their thoughtful evaluations, constructive feedback, and professional recommendations. Their careful review of the submitted chapters has significantly strengthened the academic rigor, quality, and coherence of this publication.

Our sincere thanks are extended to the editorial and production team at IGI Global Scientific Publishing for their professionalism, guidance, and continuous support throughout the publication process. Their commitment to academic excellence has been instrumental in bringing this volume to completion. We would also like to acknowledge our respective universities and affiliated institutions for fostering an environment that encourages research, innovation, and international scholarly collaboration. Their support for academic inquiry and knowledge dissemination has contributed significantly to the realization of this project.

Special appreciation is extended to our colleagues, research collaborators, and students whose discussions, insights, and encouragement have enriched our thinking throughout the development of this book. Their intellectual engagement has inspired many of the ideas explored in these chapters.

Finally, we express our deepest gratitude to our families for their unwavering encouragement, patience, and understanding during the preparation of this volume. Their constant support has been an invaluable source of motivation throughout this scholarly journey.

It is our sincere hope that this book will contribute meaningfully to ongoing discussions on the future of the academic profession, inspire further interdisciplinary research, and support university leaders, policymakers, educators, and researchers in navigating the opportunities and challenges presented by artificial intelligence in higher education.

Chapter 1
Continuity and Change in the Academic Profession

Reetika Ranjan
http://orcid.org/0009-0002-7326-355X
Christ University, India

Pinnika Syam Yadav
http://orcid.org/0000-0003-4954-1273
Christ University, India

ABSTRACT

The academic profession, which encompasses teachers, researchers, and personnel in higher education institutions, has been considered a stable and structured profession with well-defined roles, norms, and career paths. However, in the past few decades, there have been some major changes taking place in higher education institutions across the globe due to globalization, technological changes, policy shifts, and changing demands of students. At the same time, there are some features of the profession that remain unchanged, such as the central role of teaching, research, and academic freedom. This chapter discusses how the academic profession is undergoing changes while maintaining its defining features.

1. INTRODUCTION

Just consider being a professor: teaching students all day long, searching through books and data to uncover new truths, and discussing big concepts with your co-workers. This is what has been at the heart of the academic discipline, the world of universities and academicians, through the centuries. It is not just a job, it is a calling, building society by creating the future generation, breaking the boundaries of

DOI: 10.4018/979-8-3373-8525-9.ch001

what we can do and asking the authorities questions which they would never want to hear. Nevertheless, now at the start of the 2020s and beyond it all appears impetuous and agitated. The question being asked by people inside and outside universities is: Can we preserve the old ways of doing things, or do we need a total overhaul to keep up? We are going to gut what is happening. Firstly, globalization means that the world is increasingly getting smaller than it used to. The ideas, students and researchers transgress the frontiers in a quicker than ever fashion. An Indian student can attend an American university, or European scientists can cooperate with their partners in Africa working on a project. This is eliminating past divisions but it is also a form of competition- who is the hauler of the best talent, the most funding? This suggests that an employee may feel shy and hesitate to discuss some of these matters during the interview process.This implies that an employee might be hesitant to discuss some of these issues during the interviewing process due to feeling really shy. Second, the fact is that technology, or rather digital stuff, is the game-changer. The internet and computers have ceased to be a tool, it changed the manner in which we share knowledge (now we think online journals as opposed to printed books), the manner we instruct (we are in virtual classes in times of pandemic), and even the way we learn (now we have been able to analyze loads of data in just a few seconds). The question, therefore, with the emergence of AI, is: Because a machine can rip through thousands of papers or check essay papers, why are human professors special? And do we not need that thinking ability which is deep? (Borgman, 2015). On top of that business-like universities have turned into businesses. This is termed as marketizing in which the schools are competing to secure customers in the same way businesses do. Decisions are arrived at based on tuition fees, sponsorships and rankings. And the sale of additional bosses and additional rules: administrators, who lay down goals, calculate the costs and cut them (Deem and Brehony, 2005; Teixeira and Korytkowski, 2022; Tight, 2021). Gone have gone the days when professors behaved in a rather consensus driven manner as they were in the small departmental meetings. Measures of success now become the number, which is now measurable: how many papers you published, how much money in grants you managed to attract, how you rated by your students on the internet (Hazelkorn, 2015; Shore & Wright, 2015). And this is that they are not everywhere at the same rate. It depends on your field. A biologist at a laboratory will be operating high-tech machinery and doing research projects with some teamwork, but a professor of literature will be falling over dusty books in a deserted office. High-status universities are associated with various strains, whereas small community colleges focus on teaching. The place is also an issue - education in some countries, like Sweden or Denmark, will be funded by the government, and it appeared less predatory in the market scenario than in the United States, the United Kingdom or Australia (Pedro, 2009; Siekkinen et al., 2020; Valimaa & Nokkala, 2014). And age plays a role: Youngish professors, who just came out of graduate school were exposed to all this technology and numbers and can come to terms with it more easily than older ones who still

could remember a time when publish or perish was not such an aggressive phenomenon (Avramovic, 2024; Jung & Horta, 2019). Despite all this homosexuality, there are some common threads that one feels like pulling wherever he goes. The professors are all groaning about ludicrous workloads, classes at an excess, e-mail messages piling up, grant applications, and time-wasting. The levels of concentration sink as one indulges in one activity after another. The burnout is being paved by the deep research time, which is getting tremendously short and whose pressure is also well above the ceiling. But on the same breath, the great majority of them affirm that they were unable to forfeit it to anything. They are also fond of their topic, the buzz of the discovery, the aha-moments with students. That is the combination of severe reality and massive emotion that allows one to conclude that change and sameness are not antipodes; they are connected and become part of the daily life of academicians (Arimoto, 2009; Leisyte, 2014; McInnis, 2009). To make this realistic, think in day-to-day terms. In the 80s, a professor might spend his days lecturing in the mornings, writing in a library in the afternoons, and eating one evening in a department where professors would talk about any thought they had. Today? On a single day, you wake up and start getting emails that are offered by the admins about a budget cut, then teach a hybrid class (in-person and online), conduct a set of swift lessons with your international partners via Zoom, and finally update your resume to revise it during a performance review. It is a work which is evolving, but the flame, the love of learning, remains the same (Enders & de Wert, 2009; Henkel, 2007).

1.1 Problem Statement

To put the point the most simply, the question that this paper will answer is as follows: How do professors and universities navigate the push -pull of holding on to the thing that is working and adapting to new reality in a world that is changing faster than at any previous time? It is not just about survival, but as to whether in an adaptive process, academia will be capable of surviving to self. The example is at the individual level: A researcher who values the freedom of giving in to bizarre ideas, who has always valued the same. This time you are advised to start searching powerful projects that can earn revenue or relax bosses. The former dream of a job and a career of a safe ten years at the end after prove yourself (you know, lifetime), thinking your niche, and making the decisions with your colleagues, falling apart. Instead, job is unstable, short-term employment, part-time employment, cross-sell to sell services to someone like sales person or become a beggar (Schuster and Finkelstein, 2006). Go college age and you have a bewildering assortment of conflicting messages. The schools must be able to deliver high standards in areas of research during implementation and enrolment of a greater number of students of all backgrounds as well as enhance classes. They go after international celebrities and funds and give back to local work and neighborhood needs. Give facts, but we depress not the free brains that are the founders of real progress. To get invited to conduct a marathon with a torch in your hand that is burning. On the one extreme side, it is about how universities can still be able to provide credible knowledge to the society. When they are acting like corporations and setting the profits and the truth in opposition to one another, they can prevent doubting the government or big business. Will even intelligent people be happy to be employed as a professor when the employment becomes too superficial, and the choice is conducted through score cards? These are the issues that are rife throughout the disciplines of study, as well as on the news report stations on the educational crisis. They are triggering off scandals: Is there a need to reinvent the financing? Protect free speech more? Make jobs fairer? Therefore, the key question that drives this paper is: How do forces of holding things steady and blowing them up perform together in the world of professors and how shall we tell whether these changes are adding vitality to the academy or wereting its very soul? Closely related can be given the instance of a relatively recent situation that can be found in the real world. Due to the COVID-19 pandemic, all over the world business schools switched to online everything overnight. That was great change, professors became familiar with the new technology and students became familiar with screens. But the nature of teaching, getting in touch with the pupils, creating the interest was the same. Or budget cuts in the majority of countries: Colleges lose instructional posts and still professors are taking care of students by tutoring them. It is the conflict in the following stories: Adapt or die, and in the meantime, save your soul (Siekkinen et al., 2020; Schuster and Finkelstein, 2006). 1.2 Research Contribution The paper is not merely focused on laying out problems, but it is also focused on making new thoughts and answers on what to do to rectify the problems. Combining the insights of such disciplines as education policy, organizational dynamics, job theories, and for instance studies of the knowledge as such, it provides the whole picture of the happening in this academic field (Musselin, 2018). It is not fanatical: it does not have to consider that everything is falling and change is always good. Instead, it is a harmonious organization where change and continuity are balling along. First of all, it will alter the concept of being a professional scholar. It is not in its place, but as a tree which is blown in the wind, but whose roots are deep. Old conservative values like seeking the truth without the need to get partisan, and educating with responsibility are not discarded, but adjusted to the new worlds. A professor can be such an example as the research (new) can be shared using social media and yet, the honest comments of peers (old) can be valued. This helps academics to gain a preview of how they can be loyal to their side as well in the event that things go out of control (Leisyte,

2014). Second, it presents different specialists, who have disjointed thoughts in one map. Instead of considering globalization on the one hand and technology on the other hand, it represents how they will mix up in places like how global teams can use digital tools and still resort to trusted networks. Such a holistic approach reveals those trends, including how metrics can affect everybody, yet those in their younger professions disproportionately (Hazelkorn, 2015; Jung and Horta, 2019). Finally, it's practical. It presents such sweet spots of change to leaders and policy-makers: Retain what is strong (like free inquiry) and embrace good upgrades (like open-access publishing). It suggests the way in which the interference can be made as such as through the means of better job or stress relieving programs (Avramovic, 2024). Why does this matter? In a world where knowledge stems economies - be it AI startups, climate solutions and so on, we all sense the impact of academia losing its magic.The paper can be useful in ensuring that universities never lose their magic at the hands of such a framework.

2. LITERATURE REVIEW

This part makes a profound dive into opinions that have been already voiced by experts on the alterations in academia. It is an enormous academic discourse, and it relies on books, articles, and world studies. Our discussion will be based on the main points that will be explained in a simple form via simple examples.

2.1 Globalization and the Academic Metamorphosis

The world has become a global village, and borders are becoming not crucial in the process of the exchange of ideas and people. This interpretation applied on the world of higher education is associated with Chinese students who learn in Canada or professionals who write a paper with a worker in Brazil or universities which open a branch in the foreign country. International mobility of students and educators (due to diversity and profit), collaborative research (to combat the problems of the world like pandemics), internationalizing courses (to be able to teach the world cultures), and inter-school degree programs (including joint degrees) are among the elements that are divided by scholars like Philip Altbach and Jane Knight (Altbach and Knight, 2007). What drives this? Money- foreign students take high prices. Politics- education is one of the soft powers of countries, like establishing alliances. It is simple since Tech supports it using video-calls and sharing databases. And knowledge itself: The problems like climate change are not crossing an edge, and this is why we should be having global intelligence (Altbach and Knight, 2007; Oleksiyenko and Chan, 2020). But not all rosy. Other critics like Simon Marginson point out that there is a center-periphery model where the leading schools are located in the US /UK and dictating the trends and strands being emulated by the poorer nations. Raewyn Connell mentions the Southern theory and says that the notions of westernism (Europe/North America) hold the priority, not considering knowledge of the African or Asian wisdom (Connell, 2007; Marginson, 2016). Using a personal example, it is possible to refer to a young Indian researcher: Globalization enables them to attend Zoom on work with Harvard professors advancing their career. Nevertheless, they can be even forcibly made to write using the English-only journals at the disadvantage of the local languages. Studies have found out that this creates imbalance- the rich countries export the models with models and others obtain the models and localize them unevenly. In general, globalization reshapes the global academia by rendering academia international and by presenting the issue of power disparities that needs to be eliminated (Oleksiyenko & Chan, 2020). To be more precise, recent statistics by UNESO show that in the last 10 years there has been a doubling in the number of international students, which is a source of revenue to the university, but has caused cultural clashes in campuses. The Bologna Process is the process of harmonizing the degrees in Europe so that this will make mobility easier but can be rather overly standardizing and not very national in its nuances. These destinations as Singapore are in Asia and have talent around the world, such incentives in these places make them forms a hub like environment. Nonetheless, brain drain has some adverse effects that reflect on sending countries. According to the scholars, more equitable flows like provision of more scholarships to the Global South students should be encouraged. This process as this literature suggests does not mean globalization is neutral, however, it is shaped by the economics and politics, and in this case, academics walk a borderless world that is not even (Altbach and Knight, 2007).

2.2 Digitalization and Creation of Knowledge

Digitalization indicates that technology is changing our process of creating knowledge and sharing it. Christine Borgman, in the book about the big data, explains how the computers handle large areas of information- consider handling genomes or the trend a social media- people could not process by their own. Such tools as Google Scholar or the artificial intelligence search can help conduct literature reviews quicker, you can publish drafts right away with the assistance of such websites as ResearchGate (Borgman, 2015). But it's a double-edged sword. We are dependent upon the services which privately owned companies (as in the case of Elsevier publications to journals) provide at a high price making access restricted. This is what the open access movement fights- free everything! Yet, who pays? And is it freedom of lesser quality without gatekeepers? AI takes it further. The tools such as ChatGPT can be used to do paper summarizing or even draft writing of grant writing. Optimistic people stand their ground saying it frees human beings in thinking big-picture-AI ticks figures, we read the meaning. Pessimists are fretting this is stealing knowledge: Every robot does the grunt work: In the event that it becomes any robot would we lose the slow, deep knowledge that transforms the scholar into the wise person? (Borgman, 2015). Examples abound. During the lockdown of schools, learning services like Zoom still occurred, which most individuals believed was unreal. On the research aspect, large amounts of data in astronomy have led to the discovery of new galaxies although it is the prejudice of the algorithms that makes ethicists anxious. Studies have shown that it is not digitals and not everybody has fast internet or computer savvy, this will practically cripple low-income students in rural areas. More literature shed light on evolution. The first digital transformations (1990s web) have pertained to access; they are now worrying about integration. Borgman notices that science that consumes much data changes practices - social, repeatable - with the price of privacy of personal information. The field of humanities has seen the implementation of digital humanities to Shakespeare where text-mining is coupled with the emerging technology. Yet there are resellers: But even now there are resisting profs, who like pens and papers to brood. Overall, digitalization brings new opportunities, yet demands new capabilities and principles to ensure that the knowledge production will be human-centered (Borgman, 2015). To make it deeper, environmental impacts: Massive quantities of energy are consumed in data centers, and this has led to climate change, ironic on the case of research on the green. Or equity: Women and minorities are typically put at a disadvantage due to the lack of access to technology. Future research Future-facing research speculates that AI co-authored documents can be produced as early as the year 2030, which brings about the matter of author accountability.

2.3 Governance and Managerialism

Managerialism involves The ivory tower described as the process of transferring the ivory tower to engineering business by transferring business suits to the ivory tower, making universities companies with bosses, plans and scorecard. It is named new managerialism by Rosemary Deem and Kevin Brehany where admins are involved running on such tools as annual reviews, quality checks, HR policies to run it (Deem & Brehany, 2005). This is altered under the influence of neoliberal ideas: Governments invest less, and efficiency makes schools earn money. It possesses greater resource wise beneficence but often tends to come into conflict with the academic freedom. Still further down the line is the concept of a phenomenon by Slaughter and Leslie called academic capitalism: Unis act entrepreneurial, patent idea, partner with corporations (e.g., pharma funds med research). It is great at innovation, but it has a potential to be biased - does industry money give results? This thrived in the US following the US deregulation that followed 1980s (Slaughter & Leslie, 1997). Chris Shore and Susan Wright talk about the culture of auditing where there is no time to lose: Student surveys, number of publications. It aims responsibility yet it leads to execution of doing good with the aim of looking good on paper, rather than doing good in reality. Reports are hours of work without any research by Profs, this creates an anger (Shore & Wright, 2015). Life Real world: Faculty strike on wages: The UK paying actual CEO wages to the vice-chancellors. In Australia, the performance pay is a measurement assumption, in which the bonuses can be seen in order to include motivating some of the people at the expense of others. It has been denounced as the means of compromising the trust - why micromanage the specialists? But its enthusiasts argue that it is revamping the old systems. History Expanding The post-WWII unis was stretched out through expansion by state funding and agreeable cordiality, which encountered a challenge of oil crises in the 1970s, that lured managerial responses. Different studies come up with conflicting findings: respective productivity growth, employee dissatisfaction, and higher number of administrators to the faculty. Gender issues: Women are forced to take the burden of administration without any salary. It is not of management instruments in literature but a balance issue that does not imply over Walking over Autonomy (Deem & Brehony, 2005; Slaughter and Leslie, 1997; Shore and Wright, 2015).

2.4 Precarity and Restructuring of the Labor Market

The meaning of precarity is that the jobs have no security, no good wage, no good pay, and always there is anxiety. Along with what statistics document since the 1970s, Jack Schuster and Martin Finkelstein can trace the disappearance of full-time tenured jobs and the growth of the so-called contingent jobs which are part-time. Why? Budget reductions- reduce the amount spent by the government, they hire on low salary. Managers like managing flexibly to save money. In addition to that, the number of PhDs that seek less jobs is too high (Schuster & Finkelstein, 2006). Difficulties in the world of contingents (adjuncts, temp lecturers) are not any simpler: Poverty wages (some earn below minimum a per-class), no benefits, go gig-hopping. They are denied research grants, conferences and even office space, in short feeling like second class citizens. Lockout of committees will mean lesser sway in changes. It is not even: women and people of color take the most significant share of precarious positions since they are discriminated during hiring/promotion. The proportion of non-tenure-track faculty members is 70 percent in the US. But in Europe zero-hour contracts are adding up to no definite hours. Stories of adjuncts on food stamps bring about human cost. Others, however, can escape in freelancing in alt-ac jobs (non-uni) to adjust to the new circumstances. Reform: Organize contingents, restrict their percentages, raise wages: this is one of the calls made by literature. The studies have linked precarity to the poor quality of teaching/research-stressed employees are not capable of doing their best. On a broader level, it makes one question the future of profession: Who goes to academia, that is a trap? (Schuster & Finkelstein, 2006).

2.5 Performance Indications and Review

Numbers assessing worth Quotas, rankings, awards. Ellen Hazelkorn shows that the rankings (QS, Times Higher Ed) affect how decision-making-unis promotes top place by hiring superstars or developing glitzy campuses, whereby such issues as lackadaisical attitude to teaching are ignored (Hazelkorn, 2015). The REF score scheme carries out a study of quality/impact in the UK, which is open to criticism as too limited to cover the humanities (focusing on hot research). Objectivity Bibliometrics (citation counts) do not work: Self-cites bloat, disciplines vary (humanities citation less). San Francisco Declaration is in the defensive: Judge not journals but people. But measure, that it be easier,--speedy, likewise. Examples: When h-index is bad helps to promote an individual, but not a team. Women/non-whites are discriminated because of student assessments. Literature has indicated the existence of gaming: Publish junk Counts, or salami slicing (division of a single study into many papers). Permanent stress on surveillance. Portfolio: Work portfolios, peer accounts. Growing, history: Metrics usage with increased accountability requirements. Global spread via OECD. Consequences: Revolution in measurable ways, but, destroys daring research. Equity concerns: Global South: The problems of global South are less problematic due to the language barriers (Hazelkorn, 2015; Shore and Wright, 2015).

2.6 Identity and well-being in academics

Academic identity refers to the manner in which you think of yourself as an academic and its relation to your discipline including such values as curiosity. It builds up at school of gradation, life long relationships. However, as they go, there is something that the Newbies lack that their mentors possessed (Leisyte, 2014; McInnis, 2009). Physical state is also damaged: According to academic surveys, 40-50 percent of them are struggling with stress, anxiety, burnout. Reasons: Overwork (60+weeks), feel insecure, work-life (emails at midnight) (Avramovic, 2024). It is non-personal, structure-system demands inexhaustible productivity. Nurturing and prejudice is an added burden of women. Examples: among the young professionals: imposter syndrome. Pros: Community support is good. The literature world is associated with identity resilience, which is driven by impetuses- an intrinsic joy is dominant instead of remuneration. Interventions: Mindfulness, maximum workload. More profound: Generation change - millennials appreciate balance. The dissimilarities in the world: The collectivism societies soften stress with help of family. COVID worsened mental problems. Holistic demands: Therapy, policy changes.

3. METHODOLOGY

The manner in which this research was compiled will be discussed now. A synthesis of both big-picture thinking (the conceptual part) and empirical evidence (the empirical part) shall be applied in this study to simplify it. It was not merely a collection of information in the shape of surveys or interviews but we have collected and researched on what has already been already written on the same by the professionals. This would enable us to identify big patterns that cut across numerous places, including why professors in all universities are under increasing stress, and at the same time spot the small ones, like why a university in the US is different than a university in India. It is expected to keep things grounded and premised on facts, and not to be too fluffy and not to pay attention to the actual evidence (Jung and Horta, 2019; Valimaa and Nokkala, 2014). On the one hand, what is the source of information? We searched different fields of knowledge including treasure hunt using different libraries. They include higher education and studies, sociology of professions, organisational theory, and science and technology studies. The materials that we have received are credible materials: articles in various acclaimed journals, in-depth books published by scholars and works based on real statistical data of different states. To demonstrate that, we had to include the works of the US, Europe, Asia, even such a place as Australia or Africa in order to make sure that we are not viewing things only through one side of the prism. It has now been interpreted by constructing a conceptual framework. Conceive it, as a crass drawing, or a kind of a check sheet, which enables in sorting out this messy world of scholarly activity into readily perceivable categories. These spheres are the most notable aspects of the way in which professors and researchers operate on a day-to-day basis: employment, knowledge production, teaching and learning, governance, and autonomy, and professional identity. In both of those spaces, we dug two sides: what is changing everything (this new technology or cost-saving measures) and what is still constant (this old culture of working together). We sought too the gears by which these changes and these constant elements act upon one another--as links between the old and the new.

4. ANALYSIS

4.1 Dialectic of Continuity and Change

The dialectic is an analysis of continuous transformation rather than merely a form of change. We must stop thinking in black and white connotations that everything is so awful or nothing is ever the same to fully know what is happening in the academia today. Instead, consider picture continuity (the thing that stays) and change (the thing that is new) to be two partners in the dance, where a complex routine is being performed on them - they are mutually necessary, as well as affect the whole performance. This is the one that philosophers call the dialectic. To illustrate, university managers can be establishing more top-down levels of control where managers control what will pass the test and the old system of peer-reviewing of the work of other professors still is at the helm in making decisions on whether a research is good or not. To a great number of people, the employment environment is getting increasingly unstable, but still, being part of a group of professionals in your field of practice is what gives individuals a purpose and a sense of community. The delegation of technological equipment is reversing the working environment, but a face-to-face discussion in conferences or down the hall may yield the most visions (Avramovic, 2024; Pedro, 2009; Siekkinen et al., 2020). The push-and-pull reflects the two-faced character of the academia, one hand it is a gigantic social machine which interacts with the rest of the nature, it is preoccupied by such issues as government regulations, chilly budgets, market competition over money and students, and frenzy technological changes. On the other hand, it is a limited circle of professionals who possess their own sets of rules including the seeking of truth at all costs, adoration of hard evidence and references to the courageous doubts. These internal values serve as stays to the bonkers revisions--they are also wise impulses to the wisdom revisions which make the good stuff alive. Among all that, three general approaches can be differentiated in which continuity and change work in conjunction: adaptation, resilience, and contestation. This dance will make academia alive and kicking since it is not set free or entirely remade.

4.2 Employment Structures: Contingency and Stasis

One example of a change-and-stay-the-same dance in the working environment is the professors. On the change side, there is an enormous shift to the casualization which merely translates to conversion of employment positions to temporary ones. Most of the scholars had acquired a lifetime employment with privileges on passing the examination in the olden times and most had been given secure tenure employment. In our times, in most of the countries, such are a piece of pie. Rather it is a spurt of temporary employment (disposable income adjuncts), non-renewable contracts (one or two years) and postdoc. This splits the profession into two worlds, specifically a small section of the lucked-out full-timers who are stableized and a growing number of outsiders who are unsure and undercompensated with no benefits (Schuster and Finkelstein, 2006). Why is this happening? It is a combination of economic hardship- the governments and schools economize down and therefore employ less permanent employees so as to save money. Employees are easily rented and fired by bosses who like this. Moreover, universities graduate a lot more PhDs than the number of full jobs, and therefore the supply of skilled people that are competing with each other is increasing. Everything is not flipped, but this is where the continuity is introduced. Even to this day, the tenure can still be used in various cases, e.g. the type of safety net which surrounds free speech in that professors can make controversial statements with impunity without being harassed. Your own research quality female audited by peers, and your teaching and service to the community, are to be covered by your promotions. What makes you qualified? Experience in an area, which is heavy and years of experience. And just in case your job is not so secure identity yourself acquires during your stay in grad school awaits. This mixture is literally literal headaches. The schools are ranked among the best research institutes and place the scientists in dead-end jobs without going to the laboratory. They demand great instruction yet they expose the temp teachers to huge classes and have no time to prepare. This creates an environment of anger, protests, solutions like an increased full time work of more wages to the temp. It is merely a labor market which is transforming and leaving a lot of them behind, yet the desire to work makes people stay (Schuster and Finkelstein, 2006).

4.3. Knowledge Production Digital Transformation and Epistemic Continuity

The digital technology has totally overturned the knowledge creation process including giving the scientists the super powers that they never possessed. With the aid of computers, you are able to handle whale loads of data in a couple of seconds. Internet archives have the implication that you can read ancient documents using your laptop. Taking a virtual meeting using applications like Zoom or shared drives can provide an opportunity to make teams work together in real time. These devices not only initiate the doors into the stuff that was not available to us before, but also push the scope of our knowledge to its extremes (Borgman, 2015). Nevertheless, the deep modes of knowing that are referred to as epistemic practices do not fade away. Peer review regulations: your paper can never be published again without being meticulously read by specialists in your field. The human brains are still required to think big: to reconcile theories, to interpret sloppy findings or to construct novel ideas. That is a concern as the traditional methods are interfered by the new technology. Big data can spew out data that seems to be large and has not been stopped by any story. Create papers and publish them online (as open access) allows bypassing reviews that have the ability to propagate junk information, but at the same time, it enables more voices to be added to the discussion. The ace card is AI: the summarizing tools or statystic analysers could change the job forever. On the good, it can serve to get back to tedious things, and abandon humanity to creative leaps. On the dark side, it only takes the deep reading away, leaving it in the hands of machines, that you are an expert in (Borgman, 2015). To put it crudely, it enables creating more and simpler writing (change), although the art of doing it correctly is human (continuity). This contradiction means that scholarship will be compelled to evolve over time to ensure that knowledge is dependable.

4.4 Governance: Managerial Control and Collegial Resilience.

This tension of which university administration is ample evidence. The reform aims at managerialization- introduction of bosses who will take decisions on the highest level. They implement strategy plans, they monitor performances, and they operate employees comparable to the performance in an enterprise. This pushes the previous collegiate model where professors would talk about the things out there in a group to come up with budgets or recruitments (Deem & Brehony, 2005; Slaughter and Leslie, 1997). It is an effect of larger-scale shifts: the introduction of "neoliberalism principles by governments (decreased state funding, enhanced competition in the form of a business), and a promotion of schools competing with each other. It promises to be easy and worth the money, yet it can dig out the freedom of going mad with ideas. Nevertheless there is still the old group style but with some modifications. Professional get-togethers, promotion committees and peer reviews are also carried on despite the chiefdom of bosses. Numbers will not be better than expert judgments in the course of judging research. This portrays the abrasiveness of educational customs. The result? Power is on the line. It might take place that professors are engaged in the elections and they believe that their ideas are not considered in the long run. This attracts grievances but also it attracts the channels of resistance like the unions or petition. Academic freedom is a giant, it has to be discussed by all, but there is no stability in employment of the temp.

4.5 Metrics and Evaluation: Measurement and Verdict

In the academic science there is hardly a point when you can nowadays hear of the numbers being either absent or present- a scorecard in your career and mine almost. Examples of such items are your citation frequencies, impact factor, h- index, grants awarded, or student satisfaction with you as a teacher. It is because of this desire to have clear and swift diagnoses of the brainy stuff which is hard to measure and ultimately makes the difference in how people do their jobs, rewarding what they can learn effortlessly, making fair comparisons between people through bosses (Hazelkorn, 2015; Shore and Wright, 2015). But critics hate them. Figures are deceitful: they add to what is quantifiable and obscure all the others. Journal ratings of your article are based on the magazine, and not the article. Assessment of the students can also be discriminating. However, measures are here to stay as they seem to be fair in the competitions of who is the best, save on reviews and dazzle funders that you are worth it and peers still vote, and they carry their experience to the vote. That is why it makes mixed systems: metrics are not top-down. In order to enhance it, provide the scores stories, implement of any form of evidence and invent a method of focusing on quality not on the amount.

4.6 Disciplinary Cultures: Stasis in the Mid of Interdisciplinarity

The old subjective system of organization persists even after all the screaming about interdisciplinarity. Factions - as physics or psychology - still continue to systematize knowledge, and exist as the pro you are, and schools of construction. Why? They not only show you the explicit charts to study but also train you on the methods, set quality standards, and provide additional contacts with people with whom you may share similar interests (Jung and Horta, 2019). But the stress is on assimilation: the actual problems demand concepts everywhere. Funders enjoy team-ups. But one must meet with impediments everywhere--departments keeping track of the purse, promotions are in paper positions in your own department and training will keep you running along only one logical course. It introduces smart fixes, which include: a cross-work centres that are adjacent to regular departments, mixed-idea journals, and part-field jobs. These portray change to happen through slight adaptation of the old.

4.7 Academic Identity: Change and Stability

The identities of scholars, although very tricky, are changing marginally. Adoring some profound questions, prize smarts, commit to teaching, arrive home in your discipline are the constituent parts of the core. This assumes a form in grad school. It is driven by inner impulse; the eagerness that brings you nights of insomnia, the joy of the learner when you discover the aha-aha eureka, the thrill of the discovery; as it were. more than wealth and even glory. These guarantee that you spring off pressures. but fashions change it: young professors are nurtured in scorecards, and as young professors are prone to talk of any hustle; old professors remember the past times go. Increased work and tensions do not go together and cause stress. This is reflected in health problems: stress, worry, burnout does not belong to individual failures but to personal symptoms that something is wrong with the system with respect to the work principles having a meaning (Avramovic, 2024; Leisyte, 2014; McInnis, 2009).

5. CONCLUSION

The postivation of changes occurring in professor and research world along with the visible resilience are unprecedented. This has made a critical analysis of the interdependence of the stable aspects, and the movable ones, as the fibers in a tapestry, weaving up a fabricated, although so very rich picture. Change and stability, the facade and the foundation sit side by side, new and old passions keep a student fraternity alive and well and new demands are made as the traditions are desperately holding onto (Arimoto, 2009; Enders and de Weert, 2009; Musselin, 2018). What we have found out is that one can never simply simplify academia into simple stories and how things are simply getting worse or they will all turn out fine. No--to-day colleges are all full of pulls and tugs, which must be incessantly consulted and compromised. The jobs are also predisposed to instability, however, such tenure jobs as safe havens do not fade away. The technologically improved knowledge is produced and the crude methods to analyze and reason still exist. Management of schools is bossier, and views of the group are extensive. Following scorecards, actual expert checks keep on growing. Implications of Significance To a common student it does not take much time to see the changes and the constants in order to be a wiser sailer in the tempest. Instead of burying the substantial quantity of chaos, you can use the good you can retain (e.g. peer support), learn on how to recycle traditions without moving away (e.g. through use of technology to create a better teaching) and avail yourself of the chance to create something novel (e.g. online global teams). In the case of the whole university, there should be no update plan replicating the tricks used in the corporate world without giving due respect to the uniqueness of the academia. There should be a balance in the diet of the checks and freedom of decision making. Employments should offer real security of deep study, and not an economical malleability to fry individuals over. Policies governing higher education must be mindful to governments and grand policy makers that the universities do not just deal with businesses of just making money, but are a part of the social good. Schools can do everything: impose knowledge, make good citizens, deal with such phenomena as climate or inequality. Critical Challenges Unstable work is harmful both in terms of the well-being of individuals and the perspectives of the entire horizon. Fix, by establishing more full-time and better opportunities to the temporary workers (Schuster and Finkelstein, 2006). Workloads exploding? That is an organisational issue that needs real changes: create realistic limits and instill cultures that embrace quality and not quantity production. Too many scorecards? Time to rethink: devise ways of judging which would enable people to develop, and discovering all kinds of wins and keeping pro views as their central focus (Hazelkorn, 2015). Digital tech and AI? Quite exciting, but risky. Smartly execute it to increase human intelligence (Borgman, 2015). Future Directions This steady and varies dynamic means that in the future of academia, the future will not be associated with abandonment of the past, or opposition to the novelty in general. Winning just means to make good decisions: resist to what is doing well, change what is not, and embrace the changes that will strengthen the root. The society is becoming increasingly motivated by knowledge, making the health of professors an issue of concern to everyone (Siekkinen et al., 2020). Finally, there is the crossroad of academia. The way forward will be identified through the decisions made by individuals, institutions and society. Through the turns of change, in dignifying the places of resistance, in mutual protection of the essence imperatives, of fair labor and free thought, the universities will be able to ride on the waves preserving their unique luster and enormous contributions to humanity.

6. REFERENCES

Altbach, P. G., & Knight, J. (2007). The internationalization of higher education: Motivations and realities. *Journal of Studies in International Education, 11*(3-4), 290–305. DOI: 10.1177/1028315307303542

Arimoto, A. (2009). Changing academic profession in the world from 1992 to 2007. In *The changing academic profession over 1992–2007: International, comparative, and quantitative perspectives* (RIHE International Publication Series No. 12, pp. 1–25). Research Institute for Higher Education, Hiroshima University.

Avramović, A. (2024). Great expectations: Change and continuity in academic roles and tasks. *Scandinavian Journal of Public Administration, 28*(1), 45–67. DOI: 10.58235/sjpa.2024.13153

Borgman, C. L. (2015). *Big data, little data, no data: Scholarship in the networked world.* MIT Press. DOI: 10.7551/mitpress/9963.001.0001

Connell, R. (2007). *Southern theory: The global dynamics of knowledge in social science.* Allen & Unwin.

Deem, R., & Brehony, K. J. (2005). Management as ideology: The case of 'new managerialism' in higher education. *Oxford Review of Education, 31*(2), 217–235. DOI: 10.1080/03054980500117827

Enders, J., & de Weert, E. (2009). Towards a T-shaped profession: Academic work and career in the knowledge society. In *The changing face of academic life: Analytical and comparative perspectives* (pp. 251–272). Palgrave Macmillan., DOI: 10.1057/9780230242166_13

Hazelkorn, E. (2015). *Rankings and the reshaping of higher education: The battle for world-class excellence* (2nd ed.). Palgrave Macmillan. DOI: 10.1057/9781137446671

Henkel, M. (2007). Shifting boundaries and the academic profession. In Kogan, M., & Teichler, U. (Eds.), *Key challenges to the academic profession* (pp. 93–122). UNESCO/International Centre for Higher Education Research.

Jung, J., & Horta, H. (2019). Changing academic profession in East Asia: Responses to a common challenge. In J. Jung, H. Horta, & A. Yonezawa (Eds.), *The changing academic profession in international and comparative perspectives* (pp. 45–62). Springer. https://doi.org/DOI: 10.1007/978-981-13-9621-2_3

Leisyte, L. (2014). Changing academic identities in the context of a managerial university – Bridging the duality between professions and organizations: Evidence from the US and Europe. In Fumasoli, T., Goastellec, G., & Kehm, B. M. (Eds.), *The relevance of academic work in comparative perspective* (pp. 69–88). Springer., DOI: 10.1007/978-3-319-06185-6_5

Marginson, S. (2016). *The dream is over: The crisis of Clark Kerr's California idea of higher education*. University of California Press.

McInnis, C. (2009). Traditions of academic professionalism and shifting academic identities. In Barnett, R., & Di Napoli, R. (Eds.), *Academic and professional identities in higher education: The changing frame of UK and US academics* (pp. 1–14). Routledge.

Musselin, C. (2018). New forms of competition in higher education. *Socio-economic Review*, *16*(3), 657–683. DOI: 10.1093/ser/mwy033

Oleksiyenko, A., & Chan, S. J. (2020). Internationalization and the academic profession in Asia: Continuity and change. *Higher Education*, *80*(2), 215–230. DOI: 10.1007/s10734-019-00477-2

Pedró, F. (2009). Continuity and change in the academic profession in European countries. *Higher Education in Europe*, *34*(3-4), 393–405. DOI: 10.1080/03797720903356594

Schuster, J. H., & Finkelstein, M. J. (2006). *The American faculty: The restructuring of academic work and careers*. Johns Hopkins University Press.

Shore, C., & Wright, S. (2015). Governing by numbers: Audit culture, rankings and the new world order. *Social Anthropology*, *23*(1), 22–28. DOI: 10.1111/1469-8676.12098

Siekkinen, T., Pekkola, E., & Carvalho, T. (2020). Change and continuity in the academic profession: Finnish universities as living labs. *Higher Education*, *80*(5), 931–948. DOI: 10.1007/s10734-019-00422-3

Slaughter, S., & Leslie, L. L. (1997). *Academic capitalism: Politics, policies, and the entrepreneurial university*. Johns Hopkins University Press.

Teixeira, P., & Korytkowski, P. (2022). The marketization of higher education: Continuity and change in the neoliberal era. *Higher Education Policy*, *35*(1), 1–20. DOI: 10.1057/s41307-021-00247-8

Tight, M. (2021). The neoliberal-turn and the marketization of higher education: The UK experience. *Higher Education*, *82*(4), 711–726. DOI: 10.1007/s10734-020-00619-0 PMID: 33776079

Välimaa, J., & Nokkala, T. (2014). The Finnish academic profession: Continuity and change in a changing world. In Fumasoli, T., Goastellec, G., & Kehm, B. M. (Eds.), *The academic profession in Europe: New tasks and new challenges* (pp. 125–144). Springer., DOI: 10.1007/978-3-319-01028-1_7

Chapter 2
Reconfiguring the Academic Profession in the Age of Artificial Intelligence

Pawan Pant
http://orcid.org/0000-0003-1774-5650
Chandigarh University, India

ABSTRACT

Artificial intelligence (AI) is rapidly integrating into higher education and transforming the work of most academics. The chapter examines how different forms of AI are affecting academics' work, professional identities, and trajectories through their academic careers. The chapter approaches AI as part of a broader change in academic governance and how university administrators use data to make decisions. The chapter examines how AI will affect core academic functions, including teaching, research, and service, as well as how universities hire and evaluate faculty for promotion and tenure. This chapter also explores power, ethical, and equity issues in AI, including algorithmic bias, academic monitoring, and the effects of AI on the global higher education system, with respect to gender, career stage, and geographic distribution. This chapter draws on concepts from the sociology of professions and higher education to identify the conflict between traditional academic values and the use of AI governance technologies, driven by the need for greater efficiency.

DOI: 10.4018/979-8-3373-8525-9.ch002

INTRODUCTION

Globally, university education systems are undergoing significant change driven by the rapid growth of artificial intelligence and related data-intensive technologies (Alenezi et al., 2025; Chih et al., 2024). More and more universities have begun using AI systems to support teaching/learning analytics, research management, performance evaluation, and institutional governance (Selwyn, 2019; Williamson, 2019). As a result, there has been a significant transformation in how academic work is organized, evaluated, and measured in many higher education systems (Selwyn, 2019; Williamson, 2019).

The academic profession has traditionally been regarded as a self-regulating community of scholars, characterized by scholarly expertise, academic freedom, and the capacity to exercise professional judgment (Clark, 1987; Altbach et al., 2000). Over the past few decades, however, universities have increasingly adopted a more managerially oriented, audit-based governance model, with greater attention to accountability, performance metrics, and responsiveness to marketplace demands (Deem et al., 2007; Shore & Wright, 2015). The use of AI technologies will speed up this trend as the use of AI will allow universities to evaluate, surveil, and make decisions about faculty members and students algorithmically, change the roles and identities of faculty members, and shape the professional trajectories of faculty members (Selwyn, 2019; Williamson, 2019).

The current state of AI-assisted support for essential academic functions, such as assessing students, customizing learning, conducting bibliometric analyses, allocating funds for research projects, hiring and promoting faculty, and appointing professors, continues to grow rapidly (Zawacki-Richter et al., 2019; Borenstein & Howard, 2021). Those promoting the use of AI systems contend that these technologies improve efficiency, promote objectivity, and foster evidence-based decision-making. However, critics warn that algorithmic governance has the potential to compromise the autonomy of academia; to maintain, if not widen, disparities among socially disadvantaged communities; and to reduce the diverse ways of contributing to the academic enterprise to simple quantitative measures (Kogan & Teichler, 2007; Noble, 2018). This tension raises important issues around how academic professionalism will be defined in AI-enabled systems of higher education.

In addition, several scholars have pointed out that the effects of Artificial Intelligence (AI) on the academic profession are unevenly distributed depending on where (institutional context), what (discipline), and who (global region) you are. For example, AI-based evaluation systems are likely to have a disproportionate impact on early-career academics, women academics, scholars from the Global South, and academics working in either teaching-heavy or interdisciplinary areas (Morley, 2014; Marginson, 2016). Therefore, to understand how AI will affect the academic profession, a more comprehensive analysis should be developed that incorporates considerations of technological change, power relations, governance structures, and global inequities.

This chapter analyses how Artificial Intelligence affects how people work within universities, how they progress through their careers, and how they create, develop, and maintain their university-provided professional standards. This analysis is underpinned by sociological theories of professions, academic literature on higher education, and critical literature on AI (Zawacki-Richter et al., 2019; Selwyn, 2019). It suggests that the future of the academic profession will be determined by both the technology available to it and by institutional choices, ethical frameworks, and policy interventions that shape how AI is designed, governed, and used (Borenstein & Howard, 2021). This chapter will contribute to the ongoing dialogue on the use of technology in higher education while respecting the core principles of professional integrity.

Research Design and Analytical Framework

A critical conceptual and policy-analytical approach, employing an interdisciplinary literature synthesis, is used to study how AI affects academic work, governing structures, and professional identity in higher education. The authors' primary focus is not on their own original empirical fieldwork; rather, they analyze how AI will reshape academic work at the postsecondary education level and the broader impacts or consequences of that change (as well as the likelihood of such changes) through a critical examination of existing scholarship published in various subject areas with respect to the impact of AI on academic work.

The authors analyse scholarly work concerning the effects of AI on postsecondary education, as it relates to many areas of study, including but not limited to: managerialist approaches to the management of academic institutions; the impact of datafication on the evaluation of academic research; and algorithmic governance (i.e., data-driven decision-making). Further evidence of this analysis will be demonstrated through institutional examples and comparative evidence from policies relative to AI in postsecondary education. Finally, the authors distinguish between AI technology currently in use in academic institutions and future application of AI technology to support the transformation of academic labour.

The chapter is intended primarily as a critical, analytical literature review that synthesizes current theoretical debates on the impact of AI technologies on the academic profession and its future.

CONCEPTUALIZING THE ACADEMIC PROFESSION

The academic job has always existed in a classic form of professionalism, having as its core characteristics: specialized knowledge, relative independence, co-op governing bodies (peer-reviewed), and a normative (functional) commitment to the creation and sharing of knowledge. Academic jobs were developed through peer review and evaluation (though they remain within the academic disciplines) and therefore operate outside bureaucratic or purely market-produced employment. Academics work through the three areas that underpin all academic functions: teaching, research, and service. Using professional judgment, academics create interconnections among their academic communities (i.e., the academic community of all academics of your area of study) and society as a whole.

Sociological perspectives on the academic profession highlight that it can be viewed as both a professional occupation and an institutionalized form of labour within universities. From a professional standpoint, academics control the profession's entrance criteria, established quality standards, peer review, tenure systems, and department-specific codes and rules for discipline. On the other hand, from an organizational perspective, academic professionals have been subjected to increasing managerial control, performance measurement systems, and externally imposed accountability mechanisms from the state, the market, and global ranking systems in recent years.

The conflict between professional independence and institutional regulation has grown in strength over time and is essential to understanding the effects of AI on scholarship (Marginson, 2016). The academic profession has also changed in response to massification, globalization, and neoliberal reforms in postsecondary education (Teichler, 2017). The growth in student numbers, the increasing diversity of postsecondary institutions, and greater competition for funding from external sources have changed how academics work and are rewarded in their careers. Academics were not only expected to engage in teaching and research but also to secure external funding, demonstrate impact, undertake administrative tasks, and meet their university's performance targets (Marginson, 2016). These issues have contributed to the differentiation and stratification of the academic profession, between research-oriented and teaching-oriented positions, and between those with secure and those with insecure employment.

In this context, improvements in digitalization (datafication) have altered how the academic profession is conceptualized and governed (Espeland & Sauder, 2007; Muller, 2018). Digital Technologies Have Enabled the Regular Collection and Analysis of Data on Teaching Performance, Research Output, Citation Rates, and Institutional Rankings. It is Argued that These New Technologies Have Resulted in a Change in Academics from 'Professionals' to 'Measurement Professionals' Since

Their Value is Becoming More and More Based on Measurement Criteria Rather than Delivery by Peers. The applications of artificial intelligence in automating the evaluation process, predicting future performance, and making decisions regarding faculty members have also contributed to blurring the distinction between human expertise and algorithmically driven measures of authority (Williamson, 2019; Selwyn, 2019).

To comprehend the effect that Artificial Intelligence (AI) will have on oneself as a member of the academia, one needs to reconsider their understanding of what constitutes autonomy; moving away from a fixed conception of autonomy toward one based more upon the fluidity created by the ongoing redefinition of your own profession, the academic profession can be seen as an area where you will see clashes between old ways of doing things (i.e., collegiality, academic freedom) and new ways of doing things (i.e., algorithms for governance, managing people instead of encouraging collaboration) (Williamson, 2019; Selwyn, 2019). From this perspective, it is clear that AI is not merely replacing or augmenting academic work but also redefining professional identities, hierarchies, and power relations among those involved in post-secondary education (Arocena & Senker, 2018).

In this regard, a critical and relational approach to understanding and strategically implementing the academic profession over time has shaped it both historically and continuously, as technology, institutions, and politics have rapidly emerged.

To properly evaluate the effects that the use of AI will have on how we define professional judgement (pursuant to specific moral guidelines), accountability, and academic authority, we must also evaluate its potential effects on both the actual structure of future academic work and on what constitutes the core values that underpin higher education as a public good.

Operationalizing Key Concepts

The analytical definition of several core concepts used in this chapter have been established to provide clarity with respect to their conceptual meaning. These core concepts are:

A. Algorithmic Governance - This refers to the increased adoption of AI-enabled systems, predictive analytics and automated decision-support tools as a means of governing institutions including the areas of faculty evaluations, recruitment and academic administration in an institution.

Examples of algorithmic governance indicators include:

- AI-supported recruitment screening,
- Predictive student analytics,
- Digital performance dashboards,

- Bibliometric evaluation systems,
- Automated institutional decision-support systems.

B. Academic Autonomy - This refers to the ability of academic staff members to exercise their own independent professional judgement related to the areas of teaching, research, governance and developing curricula.

Examples of academic autonomy indicators include:

- Faculty involvement in governance,
- Peer review authority,
- Curriculum independence,
- Control of the research agenda,
- Professional discretion.

C. Metric-based Evaluation - This refers to the growing emphasis on using quantitative indicators of performance as a basis for establishing criteria through which to evaluate the academic performance of faculty members.

Examples of metric-based evaluation indicators include:

- Citation counts,
- H-index metrics,
- Publication output per faculty member,
- Student evaluation analytics,
- Grant acquisition metrics,
- Institutional ranking indicators.

The operational definitions outlined above will serve as the analytical framework in order to assess how AI technologies are influencing professional identities, the structures that govern institutions and the academic careers of faculty members.

ARTIFICIAL INTELLIGENCE IN HIGHER EDUCATION

As part of the transition to technology use in higher education and to enable universities to change their teaching and research practices, institutional management, and faculty performance assessment, AI has become an important aspect of digital transformation in recent years.

For this discussion, the term 'artificial intelligence' refers to computer systems that perform tasks typically associated with human intelligence, such as making decisions based on learned experience, recognizing patterns, and predicting events and outcomes (Russell & Norvig, 2021). Higher education employs AI in many ways (e.g., in instructional technologies and throughout university governance, administration, and faculty academic labor).

According to recent global reports (OECD (2021) & EDUCAUSE surveys), colleges and universities continue to use institutionally supported AI Technologies, including AI-based predictive student systems, AI-based learning analytics, Automated Administrative Tools, and AI-generated content for teaching and research support. However, institutionally-supported AI Technologies continue to be adopted at varying levels depending upon the type of institution, geographical area, and academic field. Figure 1 illustrates some of the key domains of higher education where AI Technologies continue to be utilized more heavily by institutions.

Figure 1. Comparative AI Adoption Areas in Higher Education Institutions.

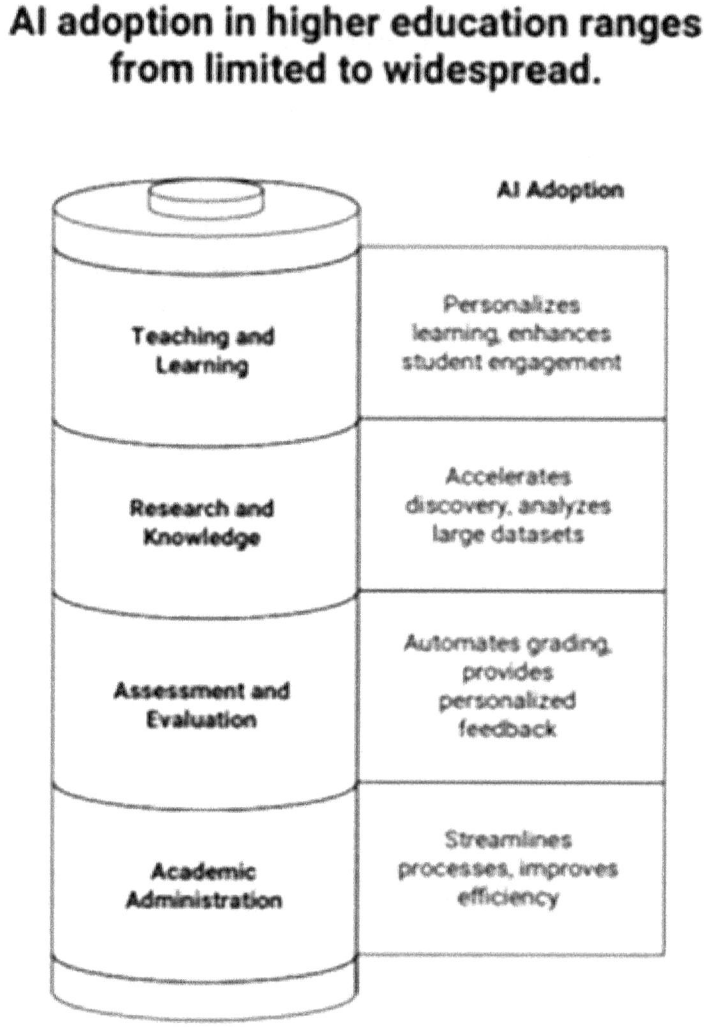

Source: Author's Creation

AI in Teaching and Learning

AI is transforming how educators and learners interact across the higher education system. Increasingly, we are witnessing AI-enabled tools, such as adaptive learning services (including LMSs), intelligent tutoring systems, and others, that help personalize education, assess student performance, and predict success (Zawacki-Richter et al., 2019; Luckin et al., 2016).

Additionally, by using learning analytics and predictive modeling, institutions can use these data to identify students at risk of dropout, automate feedback responses, and enhance curriculum/design (Zawacki-Richter et al., 2019). Although these applications may assist in improving student participation and efficiency, researchers have expressed concern about data privacy, student surveillance, and deskilling of academic instructional positions (Selwyn, 2019).

Arizona State University uses AI-powered adaptive learning systems to personalize the learning experience for students and strengthen retention rates. In the same way, Georgia Tech has tested using AI-supported teaching assistants to help foster student interaction in online educational settings. From these two examples, we can see that although the number of institutions and programs adopting AI continues to grow, the use of AI remains atypical compared with the number of programs that have adopted it.

AI in Assessment and Evaluation

As AI transforms assessment practices in colleges and universities, there has been an increase in the use of automated grading, plagiarism detection, and AI-enhanced feedback systems. This transformation has been achieved by evaluating student work using natural language processing and machine learning methods across various assignment types, including written work, code submissions, and oral presentations (Zawacki-Richter et al., 2019). While these systems are considered objective, scalable, and efficient compared with current assessment methodologies, critics argue that they are overly simplistic for evaluating complex learning objectives and that they perpetuate the inherent biases in the training datasets used to develop them (Borenstein & Howard, 2021). As more institutions adopt algorithms in their assessment processes, the foundational principles of traditional pedagogical approaches grounded in formative assessment and faculty-generated academic judgments will continue to be challenged (Selwyn, 2019).

Examining the growing trend of universities using AI-powered assessment tools, such as Turnitin's AI assessment feedback and automated programming assessment tools for formative assessment, it is clear that most institutions are still using these tools as enhancers rather than as fully autonomous evaluative tools.

AI in Research and Knowledge Production

AI's presence in research is becoming more significant. AI will be used in the future for data analysis, finding relevant literature, simulating data, and assisting with writing. Machine learning technology can help researchers manage large datasets, identify trends in those datasets, and accelerate research across disciplines (Van Dis et al., 2023). Bibliometric & Scientometric systems leveraging AI are widely used to evaluate productivity levels, assess the global impact of researchers, and identify collaborative networks (Hicks et al., 2015). While these tools increase efficiency in the research process, they also foster a culture of metric-based evaluation that affects each publication process, shapes funding allocation across research projects and purposes, and ultimately influences researchers' reputations in academia.

The growth of generative AI systems, such as ChatGPT, Claude and Gemini, has sparked more conversations on fundamental aspects of authorship, academic integrity, knowledge production and labour within academia. Recent research indicates generative AI tools are increasingly being used for synthesis of literature, drafting, programming assistance & communication of research; however, many concerns regarding hallucination, epistemic reliability and dependency will need to be addressed.

AI in Academic Administration and Governance

In addition to teaching and research, universities are using AI across many areas of administration and governance. AI-supported systems support many aspects of enrollment management, resource allocation, campus safety, and long-term strategic planning. AI plays a specific role in faculty recruitment, performance evaluations, promotions, and professorial appointments. While algorithm-based support tools for decision-making can help decision-makers be more consistent and efficient, they may also pose significant challenges for transparency, accountability, and collegial decision-making (Williamson, 2019; Zawacki-Richter et al., 2019).

Universities in the UK, Australia and USA have adopted predictive analytic systems to assist with enrollment management, retention tracking of students and thereby support for institutional decision- making. Nonetheless, fully automated governance systems at this point in time remain rather rare.

Expanding Scope and Uneven Adoption

The application of artificial intelligence to higher education is increasing, but uneven adoption persists across institutions, academic disciplines, and geographic locations. The leading research institutions worldwide currently apply AI most extensively, whereas many institutions in the Global South remain constrained by inadequate infrastructure, limited funding, and restrictive government regulations (Marginson, 2016). AI is also predominantly developed by private firms, raising concerns about commercialization, data ownership, and the growing influence of external entities on academic research (Selwyn, 2022).

In short, while AI is currently used to facilitate pedagogical innovation in higher education, it is also changing how scholars evaluate their research, how institutions govern themselves, and how academic careers are managed. Therefore, understanding the broader application will help reshape academia and redefine how power is distributed within the institution. In an increasingly digital world, the definition of an expert will continue to depend on human-created knowledge, and may now also include algorithmically derived knowledge.

Table 1. AI Applications in Higher Education and Implications for Academic Work

AI Application Area	Institutional Function	Potential Benefits	Risks and Challenges	Implications for Academic Profession
Learning Analytics	Teaching	Personalized learning	Student surveillance	Reduced pedagogical autonomy
Automated Assessment	Evaluation	Faster feedback	Bias and oversimplification	Standardization of evaluation
Bibliometric Systems	Research	Productivity tracking	Metric dependency	Research pressure
Predictive Analytics	Governance	Resource efficiency	Algorithmic opacity	Reduced collegial governance
AI Recruitment Tools	Hiring	Administrative efficiency	Bias and exclusion	Career stratification

Source: Developed by the author based on literature synthesis.

RECONFIGURATION OF ACADEMIC WORK

The introduction of AI in higher education will transform the basic dimensions of academic work: the three major areas: Teaching, Research, and Service; thus, it will redefine the professional roles, responsibilities, and identities. AI is not merely an augmentation of already present forms of labour organization, evaluation, and administration; it introduces new forms of each of these practices and, therefore, fundamentally alters how academic work will be performed and valued. This transformation reflects broader trends toward data-driven management, efficiency-driven governance, and AI-driven decision-making in universities (Williamson, 2019; Selwyn, 2019).

A conceptual framework displaying the influence of AI on the modification of teaching, research, governance and professional persona within universities is illustrated in Figure 2.

Figure 2. Conceptual Framework for the Reconfiguration of Academic Work in AI-Driven Universities.

Source: Author-developed conceptual framework based on Williamson (2019), Selwyn (2019), and Shore & Wright (2015).

Reconfiguring Teaching and Pedagogy

AI-powered technology will revolutionize how we teach in schools. Instructors who were previously at the center of their students' education will now rely heavily on data to provide individualized learning pathways for students and to automate many of the aspects of the teaching-learning process. By providing automated feedback and improving curricular development (Luckin et al., 2016; Zawacki-Richter et al., 2019), instructors will act as mentors who facilitate learning, rather than simply providing students with the knowledge they require.

While AI has great potential to help instructors become more effective educators and to reduce the workload associated with teaching, it can also lead to the deskilling of academic labor and a loss of pedagogical autonomy. Throughout this transition to data-driven education, the effectiveness (or "success") of an instructor's teaching is increasingly monitored by student engagement metrics and learning analytics, potentially restricting available pedagogical options, as what can be measured becomes more tangible than what is pedagogically appropriate (Selwyn, 2019). Thus, teaching is now conducted in a monitored, data-driven environment under the watchful eye of an algorithm.

Reconfiguring Research and Knowledge Production

Artificial intelligence is significantly impacting research methods and the production and organization of scholarly knowledge. Using machine-learning tools, researchers can rapidly analyze large datasets, conduct large-scale literature reviews, generate new hypotheses, and receive support when composing academic articles, among other benefits (Van Dis et al., 2023). Overall, the implementation of these tools leads to much faster completion of research projects and greater breadth of inquiry—especially in fields that rely heavily on data.

As researchers increasingly use AI-driven bibliometric and scientometric systems, this will place greater emphasis on performance-based evaluation of academic research. Projected impact scores based on citation counts and other metrics will affect funding decisions, promotions, and institutional rankings, thereby promoting a metric-based culture of academic research productivity (Hicks et al., 2015). This represents a shift in scholarly research from a primarily curiosity-driven pursuit to one with goals strategically optimized for maximal output, with negative effects on the originality of the work produced, on interdisciplinary connections within the academic community, and on overall diversity in knowledge creation and exploration among researchers across disciplines.

Reconfiguring Service, Administration, and Governance

AI-enabled systems are transforming how academic services and administration are conducted (e.g., scheduling, admissions screening, resource allocation, and institutional planning). As such, AI automation can help alleviate administrative workloads but also repurpose service work and embed the decision-making process within an opaque algorithmic system (Shore & Wright, 2015).

Particularly troubling is AI's use in academic governance, including performance appraisals, workload allocation, and decision-support systems for recruitment and promotion. Through these technologies, authority is removed from collegial groups and shifted to algorithmic processes, thus challenging traditional models of shared governance and peer-review practices (Williamson, 2019; Zawacki-Richter et al., 2019). Now, academic service has been transformed from participation-based governance to compliance with data-driven institutional logics.

Change Academic Identities

AI has fundamentally changed how academic workers do their jobs, with important consequences for how scholars define their identities and boundaries. For example, academic workers must now develop new skills in digital and data literacy, work in a hybrid environment in which humans and machines interact, and contend with increasing algorithmic evaluation of their work. Such changes create significant ambiguity regarding the separation among academic, technical, and administrative roles, thereby altering hierarchies and expectations for professionals (Borenstein & Howard, 2021).

The differential distribution of AI-based responsibilities and benefits will only heighten existing disproportionalities within the academic workforce. Those in the early stages of their careers, as well as teaching-focused faculty and scholars based in low-resourced institutions, may experience heightened surveillance and increased workloads without any concomitant increase in autonomy or recognition (Morley, 2014; Marginson, 2016). Therefore, this transformation of how academic workers do their jobs is not value-free; rather, it is fully embedded within and subject to institutional power relations.

To summarize, AI-based transformations are changing how academia operates with respect to productivity, as well as by creating new standards of practice, evaluating performance, and governing behaviour. To evaluate the future of the academic profession and to develop institutional responses that integrate technology and academic principles, we must better understand these transformations.

ARTIFICIAL INTELLIGENCE AND ACADEMIC CAREERS

The role of AI in shaping and developing academic careers, including recruitment, evaluation, promotion, and retention of academics in higher education institutions, is becoming increasingly important. In the past, academic careers were governed by peer review, discipline-based standards, and collegiality. However, as institutions increasingly rely on AI to evaluate and make decisions about academic careers, the role and importance of AI in these processes have given rise to a new form of algorithmic governance that will change how academics develop their careers.

Figure 3. AI and the Transformation of Academic Career Pathways.

Source: Adapted from literature synthesis on AI governance and academic labor.

AI in Recruitment and Professorial Appointments

AI-based technologies are now being used in academic job placements for pre-screening applicants, reviewing written applications to identify the most qualified candidates, and creating an overall ranking of these candidates using established criteria such as publication productivity, total number of citations, evaluation of teaching, and success with grant proposals. These automated systems offer faster evaluations and more consistent determinations, particularly for universities with large applicant pools and limited administrative resources (Bogen & Rieke, 2018). Increasingly, algorithmic decision support tools are enhancing the evaluation of scientist applicants by providing predictive evaluations of future research productivity and suitability for a given university.

However, researchers warn that such tools may also perpetuate historical biases against women, minorities, interdisciplinary researchers, and scientists from less well-known universities (Noble, 2018; Binns, 2018). As reliance on AI in hiring processes increases, so too does the likelihood that the definition of success is narrowed to quantitative measures easily captured by AI data, thereby limiting overall diversity, innovation, and subjective perceptions of merit in academia.

Performance Evaluation, Promotion, and Tenure

Evaluation systems increasingly driven by artificial intelligence (AI) will continue to play an ever-increasing role in promotion and tenure review at universities. Universities are using algorithmic analyses of metrics such as student evaluations, citation counts, and workload records to measure teaching effectiveness, research impact, and contributions to service, thereby leading to the development of new aid performance evaluation systems. While these instruments facilitate continuous evaluation and comparative benchmarking, they also support the audit culture and the metric-based accountability movement (Shore and Wright, 2015; Muller, 2018).

The automated evaluation of academic performance may minimize the opportunities for qualitative evaluation, contextual assessment, and collegial deliberation. As a result, academic careers are becoming more reliant on compliance with algorithmic performance criteria, rather than on holistic assessments of individual scholarly contributions. This transformation will have serious implications for academic freedom, ingenuity, and the ability to conduct long-lasting, knowledge-producing research.

Precarity, Stratification, and Early-Career Academics

The disproportionate effects of AI on the academic workforce create new forms of stratification across academic careers. Early-career academics and adjunct staff, as well as teaching-focused faculty, are often under increased pressure due to algorithmic scrutiny, performance assessment, and short-term contract reviews (Morley, 2014; Marginson, 2016). This pressure on early-career academics and adjunct staff could increase their precariousness, as the renewal of their contracts and their professional development may depend on narrowly defined metrics based on how workloads are allocated and performance is tracked through AI.

The increasing reliance upon AI-based performance systems may also exacerbate global inequalities in academic career advancement. Scholars from the Global South and those employed at resource-constrained institutions may be disadvantaged by metrics that privilege publication venues, funding sources, and collaboration networks that are primarily populated by elite institutions in the Global North (Altbach, 2015). Therefore, AI not only contributes to career differentiation within institutions but also to the broader global stratification of academic labor.

Changing Career Identities and Professional Expectations

New forms of technical adaptation will also be required to integrate AI into an academic career. Increasingly, scholars are being asked to demonstrate digital capabilities, data literacy, and the ability to adapt to an algorithmic world. Success on an academic career path is no longer only measured by being a leader in one's field but rather through alignment with institutional performance indicators and the technologies that support those institutions (Borenstein & Howard, 2021).

The redefinition of academic identity, which blurs the boundary between scholarly independence and organizational conformity, will further amplify algorithmic power as academic careers are increasingly datafied and standardized, thereby challenging the historical view of the academic profession as an independent, self-regulating community of scholars.

In conclusion, AI is currently reshaping the academic profession by changing hiring, assessment, and promotion processes; increasing stratification; and reshaping professional identity. Understanding how these changes are occurring will better inform our assessment of AI's impact on the academic profession with respect to sustainability, fairness, and integrity in higher education.

Table 2. Comparative Impact of AI Across Academic Functions

Academic Function	AI Tools	Impact on Autonomy	Impact on Workload	Ethical Risks
Teaching	Adaptive learning systems	Reduced instructional discretion	Mixed	Student surveillance
Research	Generative AI and bibliometrics	Metric dependence	Increased productivity pressure	Bias in evaluation
Administration	Predictive analytics	Reduced collegial governance	Administrative automation	Opaque decision-making
Recruitment	AI screening systems	Standardized evaluation	Faster recruitment	Algorithmic bias
Performance Evaluation	Learning analytics dashboards	Continuous monitoring	Audit culture intensification	Data privacy concerns

Source: Author-developed comparative analytical framework.

POWER, ETHICS, AND INEQUALITY IN AI-DRIVEN ACADEMIA

The ethical, political, and social issues prompted by the expanding role of artificial intelligence in the administration of colleges and schools will also change significantly. Artificial intelligence systems are not merely "tools" that are both apolitical and technological; rather, they reflect the values and assumptions of their designers and the power context in which they are created. Noble (2018); Williamson (2019) state that the models used by universities to assess faculty performance, to allocate resources to faculty, and to manage the careers of faculty are increasingly based upon algorithms that will require that the academic community provide consideration for how they may be structured to be unfair, unethical, and oppressive; how they may contribute to inequality among members of the academic workforce; and how they will destroy the aspirational goals of the university's workings.

Power and academic autonomy in the algorithmic era

AI has introduced entirely new forms of power into the university system by removing human judgment and collegial deliberation from final decisions within the university's governance structure, replacing those functions with algorithmic systems. Research produced in the university system, for teaching performance and productivity, as well as research output and the estimation of a faculty member's career path, is increasingly based on data-driven models that may not be easily understood or contested (Beer, 2017). The transformation from academic self-governance and autonomy, which are in part based on academic judgement, to having one's work aligned with and subject to algorithmic criteria has occurred substantially in universities and will continue to do so as these AI systems are continually developed.

In addition to altering decision-making processes, algorithmic governance has reshaped the structure of accountability in higher education. AI systems are often promoted as providing objective, efficient decisions; however, the underlying processes used to develop the decisions are seldom disclosed. As such, there are serious issues with the processes associated with academic evaluations, including responsibility for the evaluation, justification for the evaluation, and adherence to the principles of due process (Binns, 2018). Consequently, scholars may feel that they are losing agency as their perception of judgment and education becomes less important than that of a computer.

Ethical Risks: Bias, Surveillance & Transparency

Using AI in higher education clearly raises ethical concerns relating to bias and surveillance. AI systems trained on historical data will reproduce and exacerbate existing inequalities along gender, race, discipline & institutional prestige (see Noble, 2018). Therefore, recruitment and promotion procedures that privilege these biases perpetuate discrimination through technology, presenting it as neutral.

Furthermore, AI has developed monitoring tools to track learning (learning analytics), productivity, and digital and other forms of academic real work, which means that there is increased scrutiny of academic work conducted through these means. While these tools are presented as quality assurance systems, they reduce trust, increase stress, and erode academic freedom (see Selwyn, 2019). Because of the increased governance that accompanies an emphasis on surveillance, there are fundamental ethical issues concerning privacy, consent, and the boundaries of administrative authority in academics' lives.

Inequalities and Stratification Within Higher Education

The ethical implications of AI cannot be considered in isolation from the broader systems of inequality within the academic profession. AI has created evaluation systems that privilege quantifiable outputs, with or without a standard measure, thereby disadvantaging scholars whose work is primarily teaching, interdisciplinary, or locally based (see Muller, 2018). Individuals in entry-level academic positions, adjunct faculty, and scholars working in precarious employment are particularly susceptible to systems of algorithmic evaluation based on short-term, performance-based measures (see Morley, 2014).

The AI systems developed to date exacerbate existing inequalities in higher education worldwide. Institutions in the Global North are better suited to developing and implementing AI technologies, whereas institutions in the Global South face substantial infrastructural and financial barriers (see Marginson, 2016). In addition, the ranking systems and bibliometrics that are generally part of AI systems have reinforced the hierarchy of knowledge and devalued scholarship and epistemologies from non-Western sources (see Altbach, 2015).

Ethical Governance and Professional Accountability

Addressing the ethical use of AI in higher education requires strong, well-defined governance frameworks built on transparency, accountability, and inclusivity. Academics have advocated a participatory approach to AI Governance that includes academics in the development, implementation, and evaluation of algorithmic governance systems (see Floridi et al., 2018). The participatory approach emphasises explainability, the ability to oversee the human element, and the protection of Academic Freedom as a principle of any system of governance.

Professional accountability is a critical element that informs the ethical use of AI. As academics, administrators, and policymakers engage critically with AI technologies, they must consider their social impact and resist the deterministic view that AI adoption will occur regardless. Ethical AI is not a technical issue; however, it is as much a normative and political project that relates to an individual scholar's professional integrity and the preservation of the public charter of the academic profession.

In short, the transformation of higher education through AI will redistribute power, redefine ethical norms, and exacerbate the systemic nature of inequality within higher education and across higher education systems. Critical engagement with these issues is essential to ensure that AI is used as a tool that enhances equity, autonomy, and professionalism in scholars' lives.

INSTITUTIONAL AND POLICY RESPONSES

As higher educational institutions and policymakers increasingly respond strategically and ethically to the rise in artificial intelligence's impact as it relates to both academic work and career paths, so too will the academic profession be impacted by AI in ways that are not solely determined by technology itself but also by institutional decisions, regulatory systems and professionals' norms (Williamson, 2019; Selwyn, 2020). Therefore, institutional and policy choices will play an important role in determining whether AI is presented as a means of enhancing academics' professionalism or further develops non-hierarchical decision-making around AI use and equality in academia (surface-level).

Institutional AI Integration Strategies

Although many universities globally are developing institutional strategies for integrating AI into their teaching, research and administrative functions, which many would perceive to be primarily data-driven with an focus toward future innovation, technology and process-driven, many of these continued to ignore how they will all impact on how personal academic labour will have been undertaken, professional autonomy and ethical issues (Borenstein & Howard, 2021).

Institutional responses can best embed AI within a framework of shared governance (i.e., joint decision making). Involving faculty in the development, implementation, and evaluation of AI systems will enhance transparency, enable better contextual judgment, and increase the legitimacy of AI use (Shore & Wright, 2015). Utilising a participatory model to govern the integration of AI across all institutional activities will better balance the benefits (e.g., efficiency) that AI provides with participatory decision-making processes, while preserving faculty members' professional autonomy within the institution.

Policy and Regulatory Frameworks

Both national and international level governments and regulatory authorities are developing policy frameworks related to AI in education, with emphasis on data privacy issues, transparency and accountability of algorithms, and ethical use of data (OECD, 2021; European Commission, 2021); however, the implementation of these policies continues to be inconsistent and underdeveloped as it relates to higher education institutions and the academic profession.

Examples of areas where higher education policies will need to focus to achieve gains in AI use include risks associated with evaluation, recruitment, and performance management. Some of the key areas include ensuring that faculty members are aware of and understand how algorithmic systems work; establishing due process in faculty appointments; and ensuring that metrics are not misused in promotions and tenure evaluations (Muller, 2018). Absent the establishment of these safeguards, AI could embed a higher-education culture of "audit" and further diminish faculty members' academic judgment.

Professional Development and AI Literacy

Supporting the development of academics' professional literacy will play an important role in the successful implementation of AI within an institution. All faculty need not only to develop their technical knowledge (i.e., how to operate AI tools) but also to develop critical awareness of how algorithmic and AI systems are used to shape decisions, both direct and indirect, regarding evaluation, governance, and knowledge production (Selwyn, 2019). Professional development and training efforts should focus on ethical considerations to help faculty understand the implications of their actions for others, data governance, and the limitations of AI tools (rather than merely providing an operational understanding).

Developing faculty members' capacity to use AI systems effectively will substantially reduce systemic inequality in the academic profession. If faculty do not have inclusive opportunities to develop their capacity to use AI systems, faculty at all levels (i.e., experienced and early-career) will be disadvantaged. Those working in resource-poor environments will not have access to the advantages that AI use provides (Marginson, 2016).

Academic Voice and Collective Representation

Collective representation through faculty senates, academic professional associations, and academic unions will continue to be an essential means of influencing how academic institutions and policymakers develop policies on the integration and use of AI systems in higher education. Collectively, these three representative bodies can influence and negotiate the terms under which AI will be used within institutions, how academic freedom will be protected, and the development of equitable criteria for evaluating and rewarding faculty (Kogan & Teichler, 2007).

Collective professional associations will have an important role in developing disciplinary standards for ethics and guidelines for the use of AI systems in teaching, research, and evaluation. These collective efforts will enable the academic profession to position itself as proactive and to embrace technological change rather than simply reacting to the emergence of new AI-related technologies. Ultimately, both academic institutions and policymakers need to decide whether AI will be used to achieve managerial efficiencies within higher education institutions, or whether governance should be understood as a socio-technical construct that integrates economic, academic, and social responsibility (i.e., how AI will impact each of these constructs).

GLOBAL AND COMPARATIVE PERSPECTIVES

Higher education systems worldwide vary widely in how they are affected by Artificial Intelligence (AI). Factors such as the economy, governance system, technology, and regulatory structure will affect how AI is used and its impact on an academic's job. AI use also depends on an academic's national policy environment, their position within the school hierarchy, and the extent to which the global knowledge system is developed (Marginson, 2016; Altbach et al., 2009).

National context and institutional diversity

There are significant differences in the extent to which higher education institutions are prepared to integrate AI in their academic and administrative work. The majority of universities in high-income countries (North America, Europe, parts of East Asia) have much greater access to IT infrastructure and research funds, and many more private-sector partnerships that enable large-scale use of AI than universities in low- or middle-income countries. In addition, in environments where AI is commonly found, it is embedded in performance management systems, research evaluation frameworks, and strategic decision-making processes.

Conversely, universities in low- and middle-income countries face numerous structural barriers to AI adoption, including limited funding, connectivity, and regulatory capacity. While AI may create new mechanisms to increase access and efficiency, the development and deployment of AI systems will remain incomplete and driven by external forces. Thus, the transformation of academic practice mediated by AI is significantly different across national contexts (Altbach 2015).

Global Rankings, Metrics, & Academic Stratification

AI-based analysis is closely linked to global ranking systems and bibliometric databases, both of which create academic prestige and facilitate career mobility.

These systems place greater value on research outputs from higher-impact journals indexed in the predominant citation databases, thereby creating hierarchies among institutions and scholars across regions (Hicks et al., 2015). Because of its ability to compare, predict, and benchmark performance globally, AI amplifies these dynamics.

In the Global South, the current emphasis on metrics limits opportunities to recognize research relevant to the region, as well as research published in languages other than English or grounded in alternative knowledge systems. Thus, AI also contributes to what scholars describe as "global stratification of knowledge production," in which academic recognition and career mobility vary greatly by geopolitical boundaries (Marginson, 2016; Connell, 2007).

Comparisons of Academic Work Experiences

Research comparing different forms of academic labor demonstrates that the impact of AI varies across academic labor regimes. In a regime characterized by strong tenure protections and collegial governance, the acceptance of AI as part of academic practice is frequently contested and mediated by professional norms. Conversely, in market-driven and managerial academic labor regimes, AI is often adopted as an efficiency tool, a means of monitoring performance, and a means of optimizing the academic workforce (Teichler, 2017). These types of AI adoption have significant implications for workload allocation, performance evaluation, and job security among academic staff. Commercially based academics at teaching-focused institutions are generally subject to a greater level of algorithmic monitoring and shorter-term metrics than tenured academics at research-intensive institutions.

Towards Context-Sensitive AI Governance

The limitations of universal approaches to AI governance, by providing ethical guidelines that fail to account for the vastly different institutional realities, cultures of scholarship, and regional priorities in the Global North, highlight the need for context-sensitive approaches to govern AI in higher education systems, especially when they do not consider the different epistemologies and goals of development represented by regional contexts. Moreover, inclusive knowledge exchange can enable inclusive AI practice through capacity building and local innovation if it is inclusive, avoids epistemic dominance, and supports pluralised understandings of what constitutes "academic excellence." The transformation of AI's impact on the academic profession remains highly variable globally, politically inflected, and shaped by diverse contexts. Comparative analysis will be critical in developing ethically and equitably appropriate responses to AI beyond a global or regional focus.

REIMAGINING THE FUTURE OF THE ACADEMIC PROFESSION

As artificial intelligence continues to integrate rapidly into higher education, the academic profession needs to be fundamentally rethought. This section redefines the academic profession, arguing that academics should work with AI and apply their expertise to create societal value. The future of academia will depend on how universities, policymakers, and academics themselves negotiate the balance between technological advancements and traditional aspects of academia (Selwyn, 2019; Williamson, 2019).

Collaboration Between Humans and AI in Academic Work

One of the main challenges for the future of the academic profession is redefining the relationship between human expertise and algorithms. Artificial intelligence enhances the efficiency of academic research through two methods: it develops new educational methods and automates basic administrative tasks, while handling advanced data analysis needs (OECD 2021). When AI is used responsibly, it can enable academics to devote more time to higher-order cognitive activities, such as critical inquiry, mentoring, and cross-disciplinary collaboration.

However, to ensure that the use of AI in academic work is beneficial, there must be clear boundaries and meaningful human oversight in all collaboration efforts. Academics must retain their authority to exercise interpretive judgment, make ethical decisions, and assess research quality. If there are no safeguards in place to ensure that the use of AI does not displace professionals' expertise, there is a risk that AI will replace expert judgment rather than complement it (Borenstein & Howard, 2021). Therefore, reimagining academia requires developing algorithms that augment, rather than replace, human judgment.

Redefining Academic Autonomy and Professionalism

The development of AI-mediated governance systems has generally reshaped how academic professionals conceptualize academic autonomy. Traditionally, academic autonomy was based on the ability of academics to depend on self-regulation by their peers through a system of peer review, but now with AI and its application within the academic environment, academic autonomy will be redefined such that autonomy is not simply the absence of oversight; rather, it is a capacity to meaningfully influence the design and use of the evaluative systems (Beer, 2017). In this sense, professional autonomy means that academic professionals should have the authority to determine how data will be used to inform decision-making processes.

In the era of AI development and implementation, academic professionals will need to establish new commitments and considerations grounded in ethical concern. Academic professionals must critically evaluate how well they educate themselves about whether their use of algorithmic tools aligns with their ethical standards, with particular emphasis on the assumptions and inadequacies inherent in contexts with social problems (Floridi et al., 2018).

Towards Inclusive and Sustainable Academic Futures

For academia to be rethought, issues of inequality that predate AI's impact must be addressed, as these inequalities are likely to persist after AI's implementation. Institutional policies that promote the inclusion of early-career academic professionals, support diverse forms of scholarship for all academic professionals, and recognize teaching, service, and community engagement as equally valuable in academic settings and in research metrics are necessary to create an inclusive, effective, long-term future for academia. In addition, AI systems must be designed and governed to recognize and celebrate multiple definitions of excellence in academia, rather than relying solely on a single performance metric.

Long-term sustainability within academia is equally dependent on maintaining fundamental societal values and engaging in behaviors that foster holistic assessment practices that encourage risk-taking by academic professionals and support those committed to knowledge creation from diverse backgrounds, perspectives, and cultural norms. By rethinking academia as a profession, there is potential to both strengthen the profession itself and deepen understanding of its value as a dominant and significant part of broader social institutions and constructs.

Thus, the future of the academic profession will not solely be developed through AI but will also result from the deliberate choices that academic professionals, institutional governing bodies, and society at large make with respect to governance, the ethical implications of AI, and the professional values that will be utilized to govern both academics and academics' use of AI tools. The reimagining of the academic profession's future presents an opportunity to reaffirm its commitment to creating knowledge, achieving autonomy, and serving the public good in an AI-mediated world.

CONCLUSION AND FUTURE RESEARCH DIRECTIONS

This chapter has examined the changes in the academic profession brought about by artificial intelligence. It has focused on how these changes will affect work in higher education and how they may be reflected in academic governance, academic evaluation, and professional identity. Rather than viewing AI simply as a technological advancement, this analysis has explored AI as a socio-technical force within broader societal transformations across politics, economics, and institutional change. AI will drive structural change, blurring the lines of how researchers, professionals, and institutions work together to create it; as such, they will experience extensive new power relationships, norms, and ideas about excellence linked to traditional notions of what constitutes excellence.

As demonstrated in this chapter, AI will have significant implications for academic labor in teaching, research, and service; it will also continue to intensify performance and outcome metrics while providing affirmative managerial control over activities. Additionally, algorithmic evaluation systems will disrupt traditional methods for conducting peer reviews and governing the academic community. Furthermore, there are ethical, transparent, and participatory governance frameworks to ensure that AI supports, rather than erodes, academic judgment. As such, academic institutions must view academics not only as users of AI but also as co-designers of AI-based systems and significant assistants in making AI successful in reforming the academic profession. Without doing so, AI will only serve to reinforce existing inequities, erase non-dominant knowledge systems, and expedite the precarity of academic employment.

Three main areas should be explored in future empirical research. First, there is a need for researchers to find out how academics are experienced AI based evaluations and decision making relative to different governing structures within the institutional context and relative to national context; second, comparisons should be undertaken regarding how AI interacts with different governance models, labour regimes, and academic culture; and finally, there is a need for many different types of disciplines to be brought together to review the ethical, transparent, and participatory use of AI in academia and for the academic profession. A deeper understanding of AI's impact on professional identity, academic freedom, and universities' public mission is needed to ensure the long-term sustainability of the academic profession.

Thus, AI presents both risks and opportunities for the academic profession; consequently, AI will fare well or poorly depending on community-based strategies, institutional leadership, and sustained critical inquiry. Higher education may align human judgment, ethical accountability, and the common good within the sector and the academic profession in ways that make effective use of AI's advantages while preserving the fundamental aspects of life in higher education.

REFERENCES

Alenezi, H., Alenezi, A., Alshahrani, A., & Alenezi, M. (2025). The quiet transformation of higher education in the AI era. PMC, Article PMC12438950. https://pmc.ncbi.nlm.nih.gov/articles/PMC12438950/

Altbach, P. G. (2015). *Global perspectives on higher education*. Johns Hopkins University Press.

Altbach, P. G., Gumport, P. J., & Berdahl, R. O. (2000). *American higher education in the twenty-first century: Social, political, and economic challenges* (2nd ed.). Johns Hopkins University Press., https://www.worldcat.org/title/american-higher-education-in-the-twenty-first-century-social-political-and-economic-challenges/oclc/42682899

Altbach, P. G., Reisberg, L., & Rumbley, L. E. (2009). *Trends in global higher education: Tracking an academic revolution*. UNESCO Institute for Higher Education and Brill.

Beer, D. (2017). The social power of algorithms. *Information Communication and Society*, *20*(1), 1–13. DOI: 10.1080/1369118X.2016.1216147

Binns, R. (2018). Fairness in machine learning: Lessons from political philosophy. *Proceedings of the 1st Conference on Fairness, Accountability and Transparency*, 149–159. DOI: 10.1145/3278721.3278775

Bogen, M., & Rieke, A. (2018). Help wanted: An examination of hiring algorithms, equity, and bias. Upturn. https://www.upturn.org/reports/2018/hiring-algorithms/

Borenstein, J., & Howard, A. (2021). Emerging challenges in AI and the need for AI ethics education. *Professional Ethics Report*, *34*(1), 61–65. https://www.semanticscholar.org/paper/Emerging-challenges-in-AI-and-the-need-for-AI-Borenstein-Howard/c463e0a0b9a4c53ad6a90d5254. DOI: 10.1007/s43681-020-00002-7 PMID: 38624388

Chih, W.-H., Ghasemaghaei, M., & Hassan, S. (2024). Will artificial intelligence drive the advancements in higher education? A tri-phased exploration. *Technological Forecasting and Social Change*, *201*, 123254. Advance online publication. DOI: 10.1016/j.techfore.2024.123254

Clark, B. R. (1987). The academic life: Small worlds, different worlds. Carnegie Foundation for the Advancement of Teaching. https://eric.ed.gov/?id=ED299902

Connell, R. (2007). *Southern theory: The global dynamics of knowledge in social science*. Polity Press.

Deem, R., Hillyard, S., & Reed, M. (2007). *Knowledge, higher education, and the new managerialism: The changing management of UK universities*. Oxford University Press., DOI: 10.1093/acprof:oso/9780199265909.001.0001

Espeland, W. N., & Sauder, M. (2007). Rankings and reactivity: How public measures recreate social worlds. *AJS; American Journal of Sociology*, *113*(1), 1–40. DOI: 10.1086/517897

European Commission. (2021). Proposal for a regulation on artificial intelligence (AI Act). https://digital-strategy.ec.europa.eu/en/library/proposal-regulation-laying-down-harmonised-rules-artificial-intelligence

Floridi, L., Cowls, J., Beltrametti, M., Chatila, R., Chazerand, P., Dignum, V., Luetge, C., Madelin, R., Pagallo, U., Rossi, F., Schafer, B., Valcke, P., & Vayena, E. (2018). AI4People—An ethical framework for a good AI society: Opportunities, risks, principles, and recommendations. *Minds and Machines*, *28*(4), 689–707. DOI: 10.1007/s11023-018-9482-5 PMID: 30930541

Hicks, D., Wouters, P., Waltman, L., de Rijcke, S., & Rafols, I. (2015). Bibliometrics: The Leiden Manifesto for research metrics. *Nature*, *520*(7548), 429–431. DOI: 10.1038/520429a PMID: 25903611

Kogan, M., & Teichler, U. (Eds.). (2007). Key challenges to the academic profession. UNESCO Forum on Higher Education, Research and Knowledge. https://www.academia.edu/75785262/Key_Challenges_to_the_Academic_Profession

Luckin, R., Holmes, W., Griffiths, M., & Forcier, L. B. (2016). Intelligence unleashed: An argument for AI in education. Pearson. https://www.pearson.com/content/dam/one-dot-com/one-dot-com/global/Files/efficacy-and-research/reports/Intelligence-Unleashed-v14-WEB.pdf

Marginson, S. (2016). The worldwide trend to higher participation in higher education: Dynamics of social stratification in inclusive systems. *Journal of Education Policy*, *31*(5), 601–623. DOI: 10.1080/02680939.2016.1171646

Marginson, S. (2016). Globalization in higher education. In Marginson, S. (Ed.), *The good, the bad, and the ugly* (pp. 15–40). Routledge., DOI: 10.4324/9781003207528-2

Morley, L. (2014). *Academic women in neoliberal times*. Palgrave Macmillan.

Muller, J. (2018). *The tyranny of metrics*. Princeton University Press.

Noble, S. U. (2018). *Algorithms of oppression: How search engines reinforce racism*. NYU Press. DOI: 10.18574/nyu/9781479833641.001.0001

OECD. (2021). *Bridging the artificial intelligence divide: Policy options*. OECD Publishing., DOI: 10.1787/6e5f6549-

Russell, S., & Norvig, P. (2021). *Artificial intelligence: A modern approach* (4th ed.). Pearson., https://aima.cs.berkeley.edu/

Selwyn, N. (2019). Should robots replace teachers? AI and the future of education. Polity Press. https://eric.ed.gov/?id=ED599636

Selwyn, N. (2022). Education and technology: Critical approaches. Bloomsbury Academic. https://www.bloomsbury.com/uk/education-and-technology-9781350145559/

Shore, C., & Wright, S. (2015). Audit culture revisited: Rankings, ratings, and the reassembling of society. *Current Anthropology*, *56*(4), 421–444. https://www.jstor.org/stable/2661148. DOI: 10.1086/681534

Teichler, U. (2017). The changing academic profession. In *International higher education* (pp. 12–14). Springer., https://www.scribd.com/document/862316594/Teichler-Academic-Profession

Van Dis, E. A. M., Bollen, J., Zuidema, W., van Rooij, R., & Bockting, C. L. (2023). ChatGPT: Five priorities for research. *Nature*, *614*(7947), 224–226. DOI: 10.1038/d41586-023-00288-7 PMID: 36737653

Williamson, B. (2019). The hidden architecture of higher education: Building a big data infrastructure for the 'smarter university'. *International Journal of Educational Technology in Higher Education*, *16*(1), 50. DOI: 10.1186/s41239-019-0174-1

World Bank. (2025). Artificial intelligence revolution in higher education. https://www.worldbank.org/en/region/lac/publication/ia-educacion-superior-inteligencia-artificial16(1)

Zawacki-Richter, O., Marín, V. I., Bond, M., & Gouverneur, F. (2019). Systematic review of research on artificial intelligence applications in higher education – where are the educators? International Journal of Educational Technology in Higher Education, 16, 39. , Article 50. DOI: 10.1186/s41239-019-0171-06(1)

KEY TERMS AND DEFINITIONS

Academic Autonomy: Professional independence in teaching, research, and governance

Algorithmic Governance: Use of AI systems in institutional decision-making and governance

Datafication: Transformation of activities into measurable digital data

Digital Managerialism: Technology-driven administrative control within institutions

Generative AI: AI systems capable of generating text, code, images, or data

Metricization: Reliance on quantitative indicators for evaluation

Chapter 3
Academic Identity and Professional Purpose in AI-Mediated Universities

Mustafa Kayyali
http://orcid.org/0000-0003-3300-262X
Maaref University of Applied Sciences, Syria

ABSTRACT

This chapter examines how artificial intelligence is reshaping the inner landscape of academic life, not merely by changing tasks, but by unsettling how academics understand themselves, their work, and their professional purpose. In AI-mediated universities, teaching, research, assessment, administration, and even hiring increasingly pass through technological systems that promise efficiency while quietly redefining academic value. The chapter argues that academic identity is becoming more negotiated, exposed, and fragile, as professors are asked to work alongside machines while preserving forms of judgment, care, creativity, and ethical responsibility that cannot be reduced to data. It also explores how professorial appointments may need to evolve in response to these shifts, placing renewed emphasis on human discernment, intellectual courage, institutional trust, and the deeper vocation of higher education in a rapidly automated age.

INTRODUCTION

The academic profession has always been more than a set of duties. To be an academic is not simply to teach classes, publish papers, attend committees, supervise students, and meet institutional expectations. Beneath these visible responsibilities lies something more intimate and more difficult to measure: a sense of intellectual

DOI: 10.4018/979-8-3373-8525-9.ch003

selfhood, a professional identity formed through inquiry, doubt, mentorship, disciplinary belonging, ethical responsibility, and the slow accumulation of scholarly judgment. Academic life is built not only around what professors do, but around who they become through doing it. It is a vocation shaped by ideas, communities, traditions, tensions, and personal commitments. Yet this very sense of academic selfhood is now being unsettled by the rapid rise of artificial intelligence in higher education.

The contemporary university is increasingly mediated by intelligent systems. AI now enters lecture halls, research workflows, assessment practices, administrative processes, student support systems, recruitment procedures, and institutional decision-making (Bhat, 2023). It recommends readings, detects plagiarism, generates feedback, summarizes articles, supports data analysis, predicts student performance, ranks productivity, assists in hiring, and even produces text that resembles academic writing. At first glance, such developments may appear largely technical. They seem to promise efficiency, speed, personalization, and relief from repetitive work. Many academics, exhausted by administrative overload and growing performance pressures, may understandably welcome tools that reduce routine burdens. Yet the deeper issue is not only what AI can do for universities. The more searching question is what AI begins to do to the meaning of academic work itself.

Academic identity is never fixed. It has always changed in response to wider social, political, economic, and technological shifts. The medieval scholar, the public intellectual, the disciplinary expert, the laboratory scientist, the entrepreneurial academic, and the digitally networked researcher all represent different historical formations of academic identity. Still, the current moment carries a special kind of disturbance. AI does not merely provide a new instrument in the academic toolkit. It enters the very spaces where academics have traditionally located their professional worth: knowledge production, interpretation, evaluation, communication, originality, and judgment. When machines can draft essays, generate literature reviews, assist with peer review, simulate tutoring, translate texts, produce research summaries, and identify patterns across vast bodies of data, the academic is forced to ask a difficult question: what remains distinctively human in scholarly work?

This question should not be approached with panic, nor should it be dismissed with naïve optimism. The point is not to romanticize the pre-AI university as if it were a pure realm of intellectual freedom. Academic life before AI was already marked by managerialism, precarious employment, ranking pressures, publication anxiety, bureaucratic expansion, and unequal access to recognition (Ma, 2025). Many academics have long felt that their professional identity was being narrowed by performance indicators and institutional metrics. AI enters this already strained environment. It does not arrive on neutral ground. It is absorbed into universities that are already preoccupied with efficiency, competitiveness, global visibility, and measurable outputs. For this reason, the meaning of AI in higher education cannot be separated from the structures into which it is introduced.

One of the central concerns of this chapter is that AI-mediated universities may intensify a shift from academic identity as vocation to academic identity as performance. When scholarly work is increasingly tracked, optimized, predicted, and compared, the academic may begin to appear less as a reflective professional and more as a data-producing unit within an institutional system. Publications become countable outputs, teaching becomes measurable engagement, supervision becomes completion rates, and professional contribution becomes a dashboard of indicators. AI can make these processes faster and more sophisticated, but not necessarily wiser (Sublime, 2024). It may help institutions see patterns that were previously invisible, yet it may also encourage forms of visibility that flatten the richness of academic life. Not everything meaningful in higher education can be captured as a metric. The quiet encouragement given to a struggling student, the intellectual risk of pursuing an unfashionable question, the moral courage to challenge institutional convenience, or the slow formation of scholarly maturity may resist computational recognition.

At the same time, it would be too simple to present AI only as a threat. AI can support academics in powerful ways. It can assist multilingual scholars, reduce certain barriers to participation, open new possibilities for interdisciplinary research, help students receive timely support, and allow teachers to design more responsive learning environments. It can free academics from some mechanical tasks and create space for deeper intellectual engagement, at least in principle. For researchers working with large datasets, AI can reveal relationships that human analysis alone might miss. For teachers working with diverse student populations, AI can help identify learning gaps and offer adaptive materials. For institutions seeking more inclusive support systems, AI can assist in recognizing students at risk before failure becomes unavoidable. These possibilities should not be ignored.

The problem, then, is not AI itself, but the assumptions that guide its use. If AI is treated as a substitute for academic judgment, it may weaken the profession (Rony et al, 2024). If it is treated as a servant of managerial control, it may deepen alienation. If it is used to standardize intellectual life, it may diminish creativity. But if it is approached as a tool that supports, rather than replaces, human responsibility, it may help academics reclaim parts of their work that have been buried under bureaucracy and exhaustion. The difference depends on institutional culture, ethical governance, professional agency, and the willingness of universities to ask not only what AI can automate, but what it must never be allowed to hollow out.

This chapter focuses particularly on academic identity and professional purpose in relation to professorial appointments. Professorial appointments are not merely employment decisions. They are symbolic acts through which universities declare what they value. Whom a university appoints, promotes, rewards, and recognizes says a great deal about its understanding of scholarship, teaching, service, leadership, and public responsibility. In an AI-mediated university, appointment criteria may be increasingly influenced by data-rich profiles: publication analytics, citation patterns, teaching evaluations, grant histories, collaboration networks, digital visibility, and perhaps even AI-assisted assessments of productivity or impact. Such tools may offer useful information, but they also raise serious questions. Can the promise of a scholar be reduced to measurable patterns? Can intellectual courage be predicted? Can mentorship be quantified? Can ethical leadership be identified by algorithmic systems? Can a professor's future contribution be meaningfully inferred from past data alone?

The danger is not simply that AI may produce biased or incomplete assessments, although that danger is real (Hartung et al, 2025). The deeper concern is that universities may gradually adjust their understanding of academic excellence to fit what AI systems can measure. When this happens, the tool does not merely evaluate the profession; it reshapes the profession's imagination of itself. Academics may begin to internalize algorithmic expectations, selecting research topics, writing styles, publication strategies, and professional behaviors that align with machine-readable success. A subtle narrowing may occur. The professor becomes not only evaluated by the system, but formed by anticipation of the system's judgment.

Professional purpose becomes crucial here. The academic profession needs more than adaptation; it needs self-clarification. What is the purpose of the professor in an age when information is abundant, text can be generated instantly, and expertise is increasingly mediated by platforms? The answer cannot be that academics merely provide content. Content is everywhere. Nor can it be that professors simply certify knowledge through assessment, since assessment itself is being transformed by AI-generated work. The deeper purpose of the academic may lie in cultivating judgment, sustaining intellectual integrity, guiding students through uncertainty, asking questions that are not immediately profitable, preserving spaces for slow thought, and defending the university as a human institution rather than a knowledge factory.

This does not mean rejecting technological change. It means insisting that technological change must be interpreted through the values of higher education, not the other way around. AI can help universities become more responsive, inclusive, and intellectually ambitious (Bong et al, 2025). But without a renewed understanding of academic identity, it can also accelerate the erosion of autonomy, trust, and professional meaning. The task is not to protect academics from change, as if identity were fragile glass. Rather, the task is to help the profession enter this new age with greater clarity about what should change, what should be preserved, and what must be reimagined.

The chapter therefore argues that AI-mediated universities require a renewed theory of academic professionalism. Such a theory must recognize the usefulness of intelligent systems while defending the irreducible human dimensions of academic work. It must take seriously the pressures facing universities without surrendering to a purely instrumental view of knowledge. It must reconsider professorial appointments not only as mechanisms of recruitment and promotion, but as moral and intellectual choices about the future of the university. Above all, it must return to a deceptively simple but urgent question: in a university increasingly shaped by machines, what kind of academic human being do we still need?

THE UNSETTLED SELF: ACADEMIC IDENTITY IN THE SHADOW OF INTELLIGENT SYSTEMS

Academic identity has never been a simple possession, something one carries like a title printed on an office door. It is slower than that, more layered, and often more fragile. It is made through years of reading, teaching, arguing, failing, revising, mentoring, being misunderstood, being challenged, and gradually learning how to stand inside a field of knowledge with both confidence and humility. The academic self is not born at the moment of appointment, nor is it guaranteed by a doctorate, a professorial rank, or a list of publications (Macháček & Melecký, 2025). It is formed in the uneasy space between personal conviction and institutional expectation, between disciplinary inheritance and intellectual restlessness, between the desire to contribute and the fear of becoming irrelevant. In the AI-mediated university, this self is being unsettled in ways that are not always dramatic, but deeply consequential.

The disturbance begins quietly. A professor uses an AI tool to summarize a dense report, then to refine a lecture outline, then to generate possible essay questions, then to compare student responses, then to identify research trends. At first, the machine appears as an assistant, almost invisible, politely efficient, strangely tireless. It removes small burdens. It saves time. It offers language when language is slow to arrive. Yet after repeated use, a more difficult question begins to hover: where does assistance end and substitution begin? At what point does the academic cease to feel like the primary author of an intellectual act and become instead a curator of machine-generated possibilities? The answer is rarely clear. That is precisely the problem.

Academic identity depends heavily on the belief that one's work carries traces of one's judgment. A lecture is not merely information arranged for students; it is a performance of intellectual care. A research article is not only a container of findings; it is a record of decisions, hesitations, exclusions, risks, and interpretive commitments (van den Hoonaard, 2025). Feedback on student writing is not just correction; it is a small ethical encounter in which the teacher recognizes an emerging mind. When intelligent systems enter these spaces, they do not simply make work easier.

They alter the felt relationship between the academic and the work. The professor may still supervise, select, approve, and revise, but the inner texture of authorship changes. Something once experienced as directly crafted may become mediated, assembled, or partially outsourced. This does not make the work meaningless, but it complicates the source of meaning.

The academic profession has, of course, always depended on tools. Books, libraries, laboratories, statistical software, learning management systems, archives, databases, search engines, and citation managers have all reshaped scholarly practice. No serious account of academic identity should pretend that scholars once worked in some pure, unmediated state. The mind has always leaned on instruments. Yet AI differs from earlier tools because it does not merely extend memory, calculation, storage, or communication. It imitates intellectual behavior. It produces prose, generates interpretations, offers arguments, detects patterns, simulates dialogue, and sometimes performs with a fluency that feels disturbingly close to human expression. It does not simply hold the ladder while the academic climbs; it sometimes appears to climb beside them, or even ahead of them.

This creates a peculiar emotional atmosphere inside the contemporary university. There is excitement, certainly, and sometimes genuine relief. But there is also unease, embarrassment, suspicion, and a quiet erosion of confidence. Academics who once built their professional identity around mastery of language may feel disoriented when machines produce elegant paragraphs in seconds (Machajewski, 2026). Researchers trained to spend months mapping a literature may feel unsettled when AI systems generate plausible syntheses almost instantly. Teachers who took pride in designing learning materials may wonder whether their labor now seems unnecessarily slow. Even senior scholars, outwardly secure in reputation, may feel an inward tremor. If the machine can do so much of what once signaled expertise, what exactly remains as the mark of the academic?

The answer cannot simply be "critical thinking," although that phrase is often summoned like a protective charm. Critical thinking is essential, yes, but too often it is invoked vaguely, as though naming it solves the problem. The deeper issue is that academic identity is not built on thinking alone, but on a particular moral and intellectual orientation toward knowledge. It involves the capacity to dwell with uncertainty, to resist premature closure, to distinguish fluency from depth, to recognize the difference between a convincing sentence and a responsible claim. It involves taste, patience, suspicion, generosity, memory, and a sense of proportion. AI may help arrange knowledge, but it does not inhabit the burden of knowing. It does not feel the cost of error. It does not stand before students, colleagues, or society as a responsible subject.

Still, the shadow of intelligent systems falls unevenly across academic life. For some academics, especially those working in under-resourced institutions or in languages marginalized by global publishing systems, AI may offer a new route into scholarly participation (Mutua, 2025). It can help refine academic English, translate ideas, organize references, and reduce some of the hidden inequalities that have long shaped whose knowledge travels and whose remains trapped locally. For early-career academics, it may serve as a companion in navigating unfamiliar genres and institutional demands. For overloaded teachers, it may ease the exhaustion of routine preparation. These benefits are real. They should not be dismissed by those whose own academic identities were secured under more favorable conditions.

Yet even here, the gift is ambiguous. Support can become dependency. Assistance can become normalization. The same tool that helps a marginalized scholar participate may also intensify global expectations of speed, polish, and productivity. If AI makes it easier to produce more, institutions may soon expect more (Davidson, 2024). If it accelerates writing, reviewing, grading, and communication, then academic time itself may be compressed further. The professor who once struggled against bureaucratic overload may discover that technology has not restored contemplative space but filled it with new tasks. Faster systems do not automatically produce freer minds. Sometimes they merely raise the tempo of captivity.

The unsettled academic self is also shaped by surveillance and comparison. Intelligent systems are increasingly woven into institutional analytics: publication tracking, teaching evaluation, student engagement data, grant success prediction, citation mapping, workload measurement, and performance profiling. These systems can reveal patterns, and some patterns matter. They may help institutions identify inequities, support struggling students, or recognize invisible forms of labor. But they can also convert academic identity into a profile of measurable traces. The professor becomes a constellation of outputs, scores, dashboards, and probabilities. A career becomes legible through data points, while the less visible aspects of academic life—intellectual courage, collegial generosity, careful mentorship, principled dissent—remain faint or absent.

Figure 1. AI-Mediated Pressures on Academic Identity

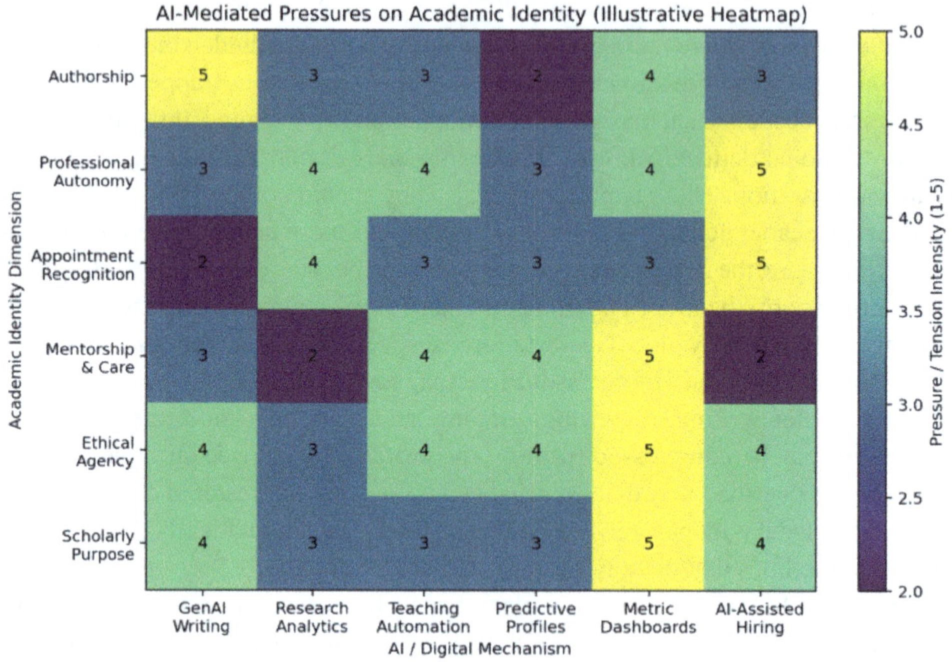

There is a quiet violence in being known too narrowly. When institutions recognize only what systems can count, academics may begin to shape themselves around countable forms of worth. Research topics are chosen because they are publishable, not because they are urgent (Muhammed-Mikaaeel et al, 2025). Writing becomes strategically optimized. Collaboration becomes a visibility tactic. Teaching becomes performance management. Even kindness can be squeezed into institutional language as "student satisfaction." Over time, the academic self learns to anticipate measurement. It becomes watchful. It edits itself before the system does. This is not the old authoritarian control of the university; it is softer, more ambient, and perhaps more difficult to resist because it speaks the language of improvement.

AI deepens this condition by making evaluation appear more objective than it is. An algorithmic recommendation, a predictive score, or an automated assessment may carry an aura of neutrality, even when built on partial data and inherited assumptions. Academic identity is then exposed to a new kind of judgment: impersonal, opaque, and difficult to contest (Wallbank, 2022). A colleague's criticism can be answered. A committee's decision can be debated. But a model's inference often arrives as a technical fact, wrapped in institutional authority. The professor may not know exactly how they have been read, categorized, or compared. This uncertainty can produce a strange professional anxiety: the feeling of being evaluated by something that does not truly understand what it is evaluating.

The implications for professorial appointments are profound. Appointment has always been more than recruitment; it is a ritual of recognition. It tells a scholar, "Your work matters here. Your voice belongs in this community. Your future contribution is worth our trust." In an AI-mediated university, appointment processes may increasingly rely on data-rich evaluations of candidates. Publication trajectories, citation networks, collaboration patterns, teaching feedback, online visibility, and predicted impact may all become part of the decision-making landscape. Used cautiously, such evidence can broaden understanding. Used carelessly, it can narrow the academic imagination. The danger is not that data will be included, but that data will become the grammar through which academic promise is understood.

A promising scholar is not always the most measurable scholar. Some forms of academic potential are awkward, slow-burning, and initially difficult to classify. The best teacher in a department may not generate spectacular evaluation scores because their teaching is demanding rather than pleasing (Uttl, 2024). A researcher working against disciplinary fashion may appear less productive before their work becomes necessary. A scholar from a conflict-affected or underfunded setting may have fewer publications, but a deeper intellectual resilience and a sharper grasp of realities that privileged institutions too easily overlook. An appointments system overly dependent on AI-mediated indicators risks mistaking smoothness for substance, visibility for value, and past legibility for future significance.

The academic self is unsettled, then, not only because AI can perform certain tasks, but because AI participates in redefining recognition (Nelson, 2025). It changes what institutions see, what they reward, and eventually what academics learn to desire. Identity does not collapse all at once. It bends. It adapts. It protects itself. It borrows new language. It says "innovation" when it means fear, "efficiency" when it means exhaustion, "adaptability" when it means compliance. This may sound severe, but universities have long been places where noble vocabulary can cover wounded realities. The AI age simply gives this old problem new machinery.

Table 1. AI-Mediated Academic Identity Tensions and Constructive Responses

AI-Mediated Tension	How It Appears in Academic Work	Professional Risk	Constructive Response
Authorship becomes mediated	AI supports drafting, summarizing, translation, and literature organization	Scholars may become curators of fluent outputs rather than responsible authors	Require disclosure norms, verification routines, and explicit ownership of claims
Identity becomes measurable	Academic worth is read through citations, profiles, dashboards, and digital traces	Invisible labor and slow scholarly growth become undervalued	Balance metrics with narrative evidence, peer judgment, and contextual review
Autonomy becomes algorithmically shaped	AI systems recommend topics, classify student risk, rank visibility, and frame performance	Academics may adapt to what systems reward rather than what scholarship requires	Give faculty governance rights over AI adoption, criteria, and data use
Teaching becomes partially automated	AI generates feedback, quizzes, materials, and learner analytics	Pedagogical care may be replaced by scalable but thin interaction	Keep human oversight in assessment and protect relational teaching time
Appointments become data-rich	Candidates are evaluated through publication analytics, teaching data, digital visibility, and predicted impact	Committees may mistake legibility for promise and prestige for vocation	Use AI as evidence support, not final judgment; read careers contextually
Purpose becomes productivity	Speed, output, responsiveness, and visibility dominate institutional expectations	Academic vocation thins into performance management	Protect meaningful difficulty, slow thought, mentorship, and public responsibility

And yet, there remains room for a more hopeful reading. The unsettled self is not necessarily a defeated self. To be unsettled can also mean to be awakened from habit. AI may force academics to ask questions that should have been asked long ago. Why has academic worth been so closely tied to productivity? Why have institutions undervalued teaching, care, translation, service, and community engagement? Why has academic identity often been built around scarcity, competition, and prestige? Why are so many scholars exhausted in systems that claim to serve knowledge? If intelligent systems expose the fragility of academic identity, perhaps they also reveal how much of that identity had already been distorted by institutional pressures before AI arrived.

The task, then, is not to defend an untouched academic self, because such a self does not exist. The task is to cultivate a more conscious one. Academics need to understand how AI mediates their labor, language, authority, and self-perception (Hu et al, 2025). They need spaces to discuss not only technical skills but professional meaning. They need appointment and promotion systems that value judgment beyond metrics. They need institutional cultures that do not treat slowness as failure, hesitation as weakness, or human limitation as inefficiency. They need the right to use tools without becoming tools themselves.

In the shadow of intelligent systems, academic identity must become more deliberate. The professor of the future may work with AI daily, perhaps intimately, but must still preserve a sense of authorship grounded in responsibility. This authorship will not mean doing everything alone. It will mean knowing what must not be delegated: ethical judgment, intellectual honesty, care for students, courage in inquiry, and the capacity to ask whether a system that works well is also working wisely. The academic self may be unsettled, yes. But it is not erased. It is being asked, rather urgently, to remember its deeper name.

From Professional Autonomy to Algorithmic Mediation: How AI Reframes Academic Work

Professional autonomy has long been one of the quiet pillars of academic life (Hartz, 2024). It is not always visible from the outside, and perhaps that is why it is so easily misunderstood. To many observers, autonomy may look like privilege: the professor choosing research topics, designing courses, assessing students, organizing time, speaking with a degree of institutional protection, sometimes even resisting managerial directives in the name of scholarly judgment. Yet autonomy, at its best, is not a decorative freedom attached to academic status. It is the condition that allows scholarship to remain intellectually honest. It gives the academic room to follow difficult questions, to disagree with fashionable assumptions, to teach beyond narrow utility, to assess with fairness rather than convenience, and to preserve a stubborn loyalty to truth when institutional incentives push elsewhere.

In the AI-mediated university, this autonomy is not simply taken away. That would be too blunt, too obvious. Rather, it is reframed, softened, redirected, and gradually surrounded by systems that claim to support academic work while also influencing its rhythm, boundaries, and acceptable forms. The professor may still appear autonomous. They may still choose readings, write lectures, supervise students, design research projects, attend committees, and publish articles. Yet increasingly these acts are filtered through algorithmic infrastructures: recommendation systems, predictive analytics, automated writing support, plagiarism detectors, citation platforms, research impact dashboards, student-risk models, learning management analytics, AI-assisted peer review, automated feedback engines, and ranking-oriented performance systems. The academic still acts, but now often acts inside a dense field of computational suggestion.

This is the subtlety of algorithmic mediation. It rarely announces itself as control. It arrives as help.

A system recommends which students need attention. Another suggests how a course might be improved. A platform identifies "engagement gaps." A dashboard compares publication performance against departmental benchmarks. An AI assistant proposes lecture activities, rubric language, article titles, references, summaries, and possible research questions (Chen et al, 2025). A recruitment platform filters candidates. A citation database maps scholarly influence. A ranking system translates institutional work into competitive signals. None of these systems, taken alone, necessarily destroys autonomy. Many of them may be useful, even genuinely valuable. Yet together they create a new environment in which academic judgment is increasingly exercised in conversation with algorithmic outputs, and sometimes under their quiet pressure.

Figure 2. Professional Purpose Risk Surface Under AI Mediation

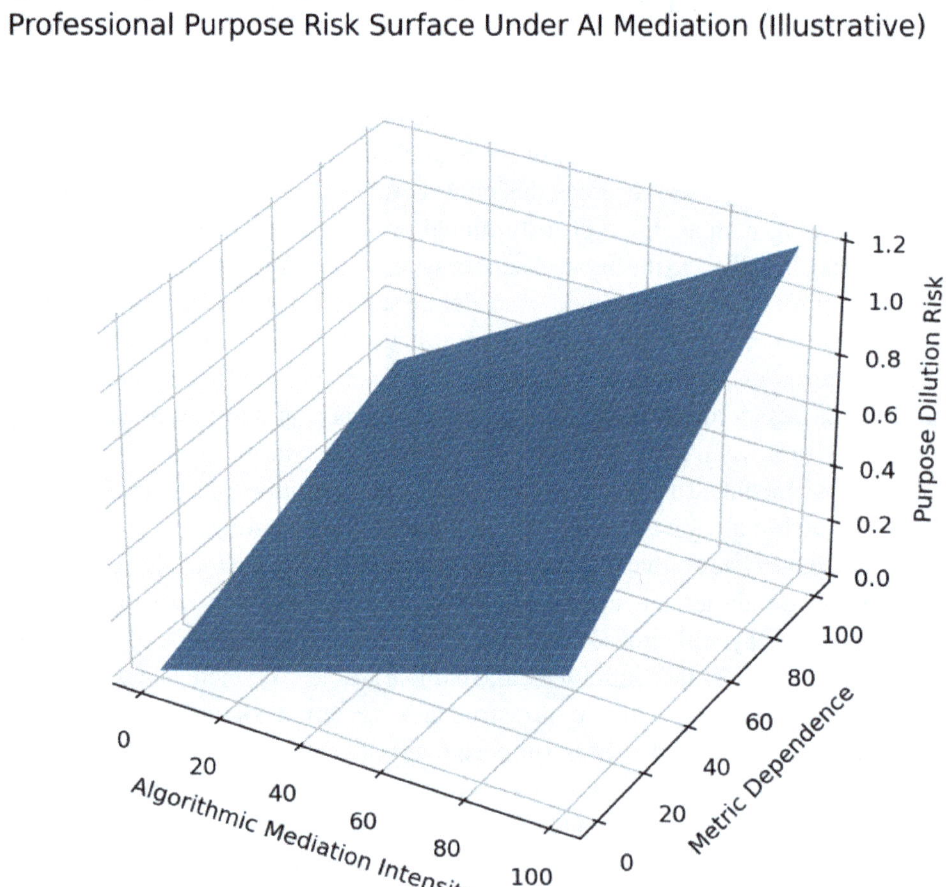

The shift is not from freedom to slavery. It is from professional autonomy to mediated autonomy. That distinction matters.

In traditional academic work, autonomy was linked to disciplinary expertise and professional trust. A professor's authority came from years of study, intellectual formation, peer recognition, and membership in a scholarly community. Of course, this ideal was never perfect. Academic autonomy has always been unevenly distributed. Senior professors often enjoyed more of it than junior academics. Prestigious institutions protected it more than fragile ones. Scholars in dominant languages, wealthy countries, and powerful disciplines moved with more freedom than those working from the margins. Still, the idea carried moral weight: academics were trusted, at least in principle, to make judgments that could not be fully dictated by administrators, markets, or external authorities.

AI complicates this arrangement because it changes the location of judgment. A professor may no longer be the sole interpreter of student performance, research relevance, or academic productivity. Their judgment is accompanied by machine-generated signals that appear precise, timely, and objective. A student is not merely struggling; the system marks them as "at risk." A course is not simply demanding; analytics suggest "low engagement." A scholar is not merely developing slowly; publication metrics imply underperformance. A department is not simply intellectually diverse; dashboards may identify it as strategically misaligned. The vocabulary changes. The atmosphere changes. The academic begins to encounter professional life through categories produced elsewhere.

There is something almost imperceptible but deeply powerful in this shift. Once academic work is translated into data, and once that data is interpreted by systems designed to optimize performance, the academic becomes visible in ways that are not always self-authored (Yamada, 2026). Visibility can be helpful. It may reveal patterns of inequality, highlight neglected students, expose workload imbalances, or challenge complacent assumptions. But visibility also carries a cost. To be seen by systems is to be simplified by them. The fullness of academic labor—its hesitations, relational nuances, ethical tensions, failed experiments, private acts of care, and intellectual risks—cannot easily fit into dashboards. What cannot be fitted may become institutionally faint.

Teaching offers one of the clearest examples. Teaching has always required judgment that is partly technical, partly emotional, partly ethical, and partly theatrical. A teacher reads the room. Notices silence. Senses confusion before it becomes visible. Changes pace. Pushes one student harder and offers another more patience. Decides when to explain, when to wait, when to disturb certainty. No analytic system can fully grasp this living texture. AI tools may support teaching by generating materials, adapting exercises, identifying patterns, and offering feedback at scale (Tang, 2024). They may help overloaded academics respond more quickly to students' needs. Yet they can also reshape teaching into a sequence of measurable interactions: logins, submissions, response times, quiz attempts, participation rates, satisfaction scores, predicted outcomes.

The danger is not that these measures are useless. The danger is that they may become too persuasive.

When teaching is mediated by AI, the professor may begin to orient toward what the system can detect. A course becomes more "successful" when students interact visibly with the platform. Feedback becomes more efficient when automated comments are deployed. Assessment becomes more scalable when rubrics are machine-readable. Learning becomes easier to monitor when it produces data traces. But what about the student who thinks deeply and participates little? What about the uncomfortable conversation that changes a learner's intellectual direction but leaves no analytic footprint? What about the slow, almost invisible formation of confidence? What about the kind of teaching that unsettles students before it helps them grow? A university that relies too heavily on algorithmic mediation may confuse trackable learning with meaningful learning.

Research is undergoing a similar reframing. AI tools now assist with literature reviews, data analysis, drafting, translation, coding, hypothesis generation, and research visualization (Alalaq, 2025). For many scholars, especially those working under severe time pressure or linguistic disadvantage, these tools can feel liberating. They can reduce drudgery, open methodological possibilities, and allow researchers to move through vast bodies of literature with greater speed. But speed has its own politics. Once research can be accelerated, the institutional expectation of productivity may rise. A paper that once took months to prepare may now be expected sooner. A grant proposal may be drafted faster, reviewed faster, revised faster. The machine saves time, and then the institution quietly reclaims that time.

This is one of the strangest paradoxes of academic technology: tools designed to reduce burden often become mechanisms for expanding workload. The academic is told that AI will free them from repetitive tasks, but the freed hours do not necessarily become contemplative hours (McGeorge, 2023). They become additional outputs, more emails, more revisions, more reports, more grant applications, more responsiveness, more institutional agility. Autonomy is then reframed not as the freedom to think slowly, but as the responsibility to manage oneself efficiently within accelerated systems. The professor becomes an entrepreneur of their own cognitive bandwidth.

There is an almost tragic irony here. Academic autonomy was once defended because knowledge needed time: time to read, to doubt, to test, to misunderstand, to return, to change one's mind (Rider, 2022). AI-mediated work, however, often rewards immediacy. The first draft arrives quickly. The summary appears instantly. The data visualization is generated in seconds. The temptation is obvious. Why linger? Why struggle? Why sit with the discomfort of an incomplete thought when a polished formulation is already available? Yet some forms of scholarship are born precisely from delay. Not every difficulty is inefficiency. Sometimes difficulty is the mind doing its necessary work.

This does not mean that academics should reject AI assistance in research or teaching. That would be both unrealistic and intellectually lazy. The issue is not whether AI should be used, but who defines the terms of its use. Does AI remain a tool under academic judgment, or does academic judgment become an adjustment to AI-generated norms? Does the professor decide when automation serves learning, or does the platform gradually decide what learning should look like? Does the researcher use AI to deepen inquiry, or does AI-supported productivity become another expectation in already crowded professional lives? These questions are not technical footnotes. They go to the heart of academic professionalism.

Administrative work reveals another layer of the problem. Universities are increasingly governed through data systems that promise transparency, accountability, and strategic planning. AI may help allocate resources, forecast enrollment, detect risk, evaluate performance, and support decision-making (Koukaras et al, 2025). In principle, this could lead to more informed governance. In practice, the same systems can intensify managerial oversight. Academic departments may be judged through predictive models of growth, employability, grant capture, citation influence, and student satisfaction. Professors may find their work interpreted through institutional metrics they did not design and may not fully trust. The language of academic judgment is then displaced by the language of optimization.

Optimization is seductive because it sounds neutral. Who would oppose improvement? Who would argue against better performance, stronger outcomes, more efficient processes? Yet optimization always assumes a target. It asks: better according to what? Efficient for whom? Productive toward which vision of the university? An AI system can optimize scheduling, assessment, publication strategy, student retention, or resource allocation, but it cannot decide whether the optimized future is educationally humane. That decision belongs to people. Or at least it should.

Algorithmic mediation also affects collegial life, though this is less frequently discussed (Monteiro-Krebs et al, 2023). Academic communities depend on trust, informal judgment, conversation, disagreement, and shared responsibility. When more aspects of work become measurable and comparable, colleagues may increasingly encounter one another through performance signals. Who publishes more? Who attracts more grants? Who receives better student evaluations? Who has stronger digital visibility? AI-enhanced analytics may sharpen these comparisons, making professional identity more competitive and less communal. The collegial gaze can become managerial even when no manager is present. People begin to measure themselves against one another through the eyes of systems.

This is where autonomy becomes psychological as well as institutional. A professor may technically retain freedom, yet feel inwardly governed by algorithmic expectations (Donoghue, 2025). They may choose research topics with citation potential. They may design assessments that are easier to process. They may write in ways that fit searchable patterns. They may cultivate online presence because visibility feeds professional recognition. They may avoid risky intellectual paths because risk is not easily rewarded by data-driven systems. No one has commanded them directly. Still, the field has been arranged. The choices are free, but not innocent.

The matter becomes especially sensitive in relation to professorial appointments. Hiring and promotion have always involved imperfect judgments, shaped by reputation, networks, disciplinary politics, institutional needs, and sometimes plain human bias. AI might help reduce certain forms of arbitrariness by providing broader evidence and identifying overlooked patterns. It could support fairer processes if used carefully, transparently, and critically. But it could also intensify existing inequities by privileging candidates whose careers already produce clean, abundant, machine-readable data. Scholars from elite institutions, well-funded systems, dominant languages, and highly indexed fields may appear stronger simply because their work is more visible to the infrastructures that count.

A truly wise appointments process should resist the temptation to let algorithmic mediation become intellectual destiny (Beer, 2022). It should ask what the data misses. It should notice interrupted careers, fragile institutions, multilingual labor, public engagement, mentorship, social courage, and the difficult work of building academic life under constrained conditions. It should treat AI-generated evidence as partial, not prophetic. The professoriate cannot be renewed by selecting only those who already resemble the system's preferred image of excellence. Universities need scholars who trouble systems, not merely those who score well inside them.

Professional autonomy in the AI age must therefore be reimagined rather than nostalgically defended. The older model of the isolated academic sovereign is no longer sufficient, and perhaps it never was. Autonomy today must include the capacity to understand, question, and negotiate the systems that mediate academic work. It must involve algorithmic literacy, but not in the thin sense of knowing which buttons to press. Academics need to know how data is produced, how models classify, how bias travels, how platforms shape behavior, and how institutional incentives hide inside technical tools. They need a voice in AI governance. They need the authority to refuse inappropriate automation. They need collective protections against systems that convert professional judgment into procedural compliance.

This kind of autonomy is relational and political. It is not the freedom of the lone professor behind a closed office door. It is the shared capacity of academic communities to decide how technology enters their work and what values it must serve. It requires universities to trust academics not as nostalgic defenders of tradition, but as ethical stewards of knowledge. It requires administrators to resist the fantasy that every academic problem can be solved through better analytics. It requires technology developers to recognize that education is not merely a design challenge. And it requires academics themselves to be honest about their own temptations: the temptation to use AI unreflectively, to chase speed, to outsource judgment, to accept convenience as wisdom.

The movement from professional autonomy to algorithmic mediation is not necessarily a story of decline. It could become a story of renewal, but only if universities are brave enough to name what is at stake. AI can support academic work. It can enrich teaching, expand research possibilities, and reduce some unnecessary burdens (Hashem et al, 2024). Yet it must remain answerable to academic purpose. The professor should not become a technician supervising automated processes, nor a data profile optimized for institutional goals. The professor should remain a person entrusted with judgment, interpretation, care, and intellectual responsibility.

Perhaps the central question is not whether AI will reframe academic work; it already has. The question is whether academics will participate in that reframing as authors or merely as subjects of systems designed elsewhere. If autonomy is to survive in any meaningful form, it cannot mean freedom from mediation. That world is gone, if it ever existed. It must mean freedom within mediation: the ability to think with tools without being thought by them, to use systems without becoming system-shaped, and to defend the human seriousness of academic work in a university increasingly enchanted by intelligent machines.

PROFESSORIAL PURPOSE IN AN AGE OF ACCELERATION, MEASUREMENT, AND MACHINE ASSISTANCE

The question of professorial purpose has become strangely urgent. For much of modern academic history, the professor's role seemed, at least on the surface, reasonably stable: to teach, to research, to supervise, to examine, to serve the institution, and to contribute to the wider life of knowledge. These functions were never simple, and they were never equally valued, but they formed a recognizable professional grammar. A professor was someone entrusted with intellectual authority and educational responsibility. Someone expected to know deeply, judge carefully, speak with some courage, and guide others into disciplined forms of thought. That image still survives, but it now stands in a climate that feels less patient, less trusting, and far more crowded with instruments that claim to know, measure, predict, and assist.

The contemporary professor works in an age of acceleration. Academic time has been tightened almost beyond recognition. Emails arrive with the nervous rhythm of emergency. Deadlines multiply. Students expect faster feedback. Journals expect quicker revisions. Institutions demand strategic responsiveness. Grant cycles, ranking cycles, accreditation cycles, performance-review cycles, and digital reporting cycles compress the academic year into a sequence of barely digested obligations. The old fantasy of the professor as a contemplative figure surrounded by books and long afternoons of thought has become, for many, almost comic. There are still books, yes. There is still thought. But both are often squeezed between forms, meetings, metrics, and the soft tyranny of permanent availability.

AI enters this accelerated environment not as a pause, but as an amplifier. It promises to help academics keep up (Youvan, 2024). It can draft, summarize, classify, translate, compare, generate, check, and reformat with uncanny speed. In one sense, this is a relief. Anyone who has carried the weight of academic overwork can understand the appeal of a tool that reduces the friction of routine tasks. A professor may use AI to prepare teaching materials, organize references, improve the clarity of a document, create examples for students, design assessment rubrics, explore research angles, or respond more efficiently to administrative demands. Such assistance is not trivial. It can make academic work more manageable, especially in institutions where staff are overburdened, resources are thin, and expectations are constantly rising.

Yet there is a quiet trap hidden in the word "assistance." Assistance to what end? If AI simply helps academics do more of what already exhausts them, then the technology may become less a liberation than a velvet extension of pressure. A professor who can produce lecture materials faster may soon be expected to redesign courses more often. A scholar who can summarize literature faster may be expected to publish more frequently. A supervisor who can generate feedback templates more quickly may be assigned more students. A department that can analyze performance data more efficiently may be required to report more often, in greater detail, with sharper targets. Time saved by technology does not automatically become time restored to thought. Very often, institutions quietly absorb it.

This is where professorial purpose must be distinguished from academic productivity. Productivity is about outputs. Purpose is about orientation (Ali & Ali, 2022). Productivity asks how much has been produced, how quickly, how visibly, and with what measurable effect. Purpose asks why the work matters, whom it serves, what kind of human formation it supports, and what forms of truth, justice, understanding, or imagination it keeps alive. The two are not enemies. A professor cannot simply retreat from productivity, and serious academic work does require evidence of contribution. But when productivity becomes the dominant language through which academic life is understood, purpose begins to thin out. The professor may become busy without being intellectually alive, visible without being meaningful, efficient without being wise.

Measurement deepens this tension. Universities now inhabit dense cultures of evaluation. Research is measured through publications, citations, journal rankings, impact factors, grant income, h-indexes, database presence, and international collaboration scores (Goyanes et al, 2025). Teaching is measured through student evaluations, completion rates, engagement analytics, employability outcomes, learning indicators, and satisfaction surveys. Institutional service is increasingly documented, benchmarked, audited, and translated into performance language. Some of this is understandable. Public institutions need accountability. Students deserve quality. Research funding should be responsibly used. Academic privilege should not hide behind vague claims of excellence. Measurement, when handled with humility, can reveal neglect, challenge complacency, and support improvement.

The problem begins when measurement forgets its own limits. A number may illuminate, but it can also distort. It may show what is countable while concealing what is formative. It may reward what is visible while neglecting what is quietly transformative. It may encourage academics to perform value rather than inhabit it. A professor who mentors a first-generation student through years of doubt may alter a life in ways no dashboard can adequately register. A teacher who introduces intellectual discomfort into a classroom may receive lower satisfaction scores precisely because the learning was demanding. A scholar who spends years building a difficult conceptual argument may appear less productive than another who produces frequent but forgettable publications (Cameron, 2024). A senior academic who protects younger colleagues, defends ethical standards, or resists institutional shortcuts may leave few measurable traces, though the university may depend on such people more than it knows.

AI intensifies measurement because it makes data easier to gather, process, and interpret. It can identify patterns across student behavior, research output, institutional performance, and professional trajectories. It can rank, cluster, predict, and recommend. Used responsibly, this may help universities make fairer and better-informed decisions. But the professoriate must be careful. The danger is not merely that AI systems might be inaccurate or biased, though they certainly can be. The deeper danger is that universities may slowly adapt their definition of academic worth to fit what AI can measure well. Once that happens, professorial purpose risks being pulled toward machine-readable performance. The professor becomes not only a teacher, scholar, and mentor, but a producer of data signals.

In such a setting, it is tempting to ask: what is the professor for? Not in the narrow institutional sense, but in the deeper moral and intellectual sense. If AI can generate summaries, explain concepts, translate texts, draft feedback, produce examples, detect patterns, support writing, and provide students with instant responses, then the professor's value cannot rest simply on delivering information (Zhao, 2025). Information delivery was never the highest form of teaching anyway. Good teaching has always involved selection, framing, timing, provocation, care, and judgment. It is not the pouring of content into empty minds, but the cultivation of attention, discipline, curiosity, and intellectual conscience. AI can provide answers, sometimes useful ones. But the professor helps students learn what makes a question worth asking, what counts as a responsible answer, and why easy fluency may hide shallow understanding.

This may become one of the most important professorial purposes in the AI age: to defend depth against the seductions of instant articulation. AI can make language arrive before thought has matured. It can produce the appearance of comprehension without the struggle that often gives comprehension its roots. Students may submit polished work without having passed through confusion. Academics themselves may be tempted by the same shortcut. The danger is not only plagiarism or dishonesty; those are surface concerns compared with the larger intellectual hazard. The real risk is the weakening of the inner apprenticeship through which people learn to think. Thought often needs resistance. It needs the sentence that refuses to come, the paragraph that collapses, the argument that embarrasses its author, the awkward draft, the slow recognition that one has been wrong. A university that removes too much difficulty in the name of efficiency may unintentionally impoverish learning.

The professor's purpose, then, includes preserving meaningful difficulty. Not cruelty. Not elitist obscurity. Not the old habit of making learning unnecessarily painful. Meaningful difficulty is different. It is the kind of challenge that invites students into intellectual adulthood. It says: this matters enough to require effort from you. In a culture increasingly shaped by automation and speed, the professor may need to become a guardian of productive slowness. A strange role, perhaps. But an essential one. To ask students to read carefully when summaries are available, to write honestly when generated prose is effortless, to argue from evidence when opinion can be instantly decorated with citations, to sit with ambiguity when the machine offers a neat answer—these are not nostalgic gestures. They are acts of educational seriousness.

Research, too, demands a renewed sense of purpose. Machine assistance may transform the mechanics of scholarly work, but it cannot determine the ethical direction of inquiry. AI can reveal patterns, generate hypotheses, process language, and assist with analysis (Lado, 2025). It can support interdisciplinary exploration and widen access to complex methods. Yet it cannot decide which questions deserve attention in a wounded world. It cannot feel the injustice of neglected topics. It cannot understand why certain silences in a field are morally troubling. It cannot know what it means for a community to be misrepresented, or for a discipline to forget its own exclusions. The professor's research purpose is not merely to produce findings, but to bring judgment, context, courage, and responsibility to the pursuit of knowledge.

This matters especially because acceleration can make scholarship reactive. Academics may chase emerging trends, funding priorities, citation opportunities, and institutional strategies (Oyedokun, 2025). AI can make that chase more efficient. It can identify hot topics, map gaps, propose titles, locate target journals, and assist in producing work aligned with current visibility structures. There is nothing inherently wrong with relevance. Scholarship should not be indifferent to contemporary concerns. But when relevance becomes trend-following, the professor's deeper responsibility is endangered. Some of the most important academic work begins before the world recognizes its importance, or after the world has decided to look away. Professorial purpose requires the freedom, and the courage, to work outside immediate applause.

There is also a pastoral dimension to professorial purpose, though universities often avoid that language because it sounds too intimate, too old-fashioned, maybe too soft. But students do not arrive as abstract learners. They arrive as anxious, hopeful, distracted, wounded, ambitious, uncertain human beings. AI-supported systems may identify risk factors and recommend interventions, and this can be useful. Still, care cannot be fully automated. A student may need feedback, but they may also need recognition. They may need someone to notice that their silence is not laziness, that their confidence is performative, that their anger hides fear, that their brilliance is being suffocated by circumstances outside the classroom. The professor is not a therapist, nor should the role be romanticized into endless emotional labor. Yet education without human recognition becomes cold very quickly.

Machine assistance may help professors respond to students more consistently, but it cannot replace the moral texture of presence. Presence is not merely being physically or digitally available. It is the capacity to attend. To listen beyond the formal question. To sense when explanation is not enough. To invite a student into seriousness without humiliating them. To say, sometimes gently and sometimes firmly, that they are capable of more. In an AI-mediated university, this kind of presence may become more valuable, not less. The more automated the educational environment becomes, the more students may need encounters with teachers who are unmistakably human in their judgment and care.

Professorial purpose is also connected to institutional conscience. Universities, like all institutions, are capable of self-deception. They can speak of excellence while exhausting their staff (Gibbs, 2022). They can celebrate innovation while neglecting justice. They can praise inclusion while rewarding only those who fit old patterns of prestige. They can adopt AI in the language of transformation while using it mainly to intensify control. Professors, particularly those with secure positions, have a responsibility to question these contradictions. Not performatively. Not as habitual opposition. But as part of the ethical labor of academic life. A university without internal critics becomes a polished machine for reproducing its own assumptions.

This is why professorial appointments in the AI age should not focus only on technological adaptability. Universities certainly need academics who can engage intelligently with AI, redesign curricula, understand new research tools, and prepare students for changing professional worlds. But if appointment criteria become too fascinated with digital fluency, they may overlook deeper qualities: judgment, patience, integrity, intellectual generosity, independence of mind, and the ability to protect educational purpose under pressure. The professor of the future should not simply be the most AI-ready candidate. They should be someone capable of asking what AI readiness is for.

There is a danger that "future-ready" academic profiles will become another narrow template: internationally published, digitally visible, metrics-rich, grant-active, platform-literate, flexible, fast, and endlessly responsive. Such scholars may indeed be valuable. But a university also needs those who think against speed, who cultivate neglected traditions, who mentor carefully, who build community, who ask inconvenient questions, who refuse to confuse technological sophistication with wisdom. Professorial purpose cannot be reduced to institutional agility. The university needs agile people, yes, but also rooted people. People with memory. People with intellectual stubbornness. People who know that not every old thing is obsolete and not every new thing is progress.

The age of acceleration, measurement, and machine assistance therefore requires a more deliberate understanding of professorial purpose. The professor is not merely a content expert, not merely a research producer, not merely a facilitator of learning, not merely a manager of academic processes, and certainly not merely a human supervisor of intelligent systems. The professor is a custodian of judgment within a knowledge environment increasingly crowded by speed and simulation. This custodianship is not passive. It involves designing meaningful learning, conducting responsible inquiry, mentoring emerging thinkers, challenging institutional simplifications, and translating knowledge into forms that preserve complexity without making it inaccessible.

Perhaps the word "purpose" itself needs rescuing. It should not be turned into motivational ornament, the kind of language used in strategic plans and leadership workshops until it loses all salt. Purpose is heavier than that. It carries obligation. It asks what one is willing to protect when protection is inconvenient. For professors, purpose may lie in defending the conditions under which truth can still be pursued with seriousness: time, trust, dialogue, intellectual freedom, ethical restraint, and human care. AI can assist many academic tasks, but it cannot supply these conditions by itself. In some cases, it may even threaten them if adopted without reflection.

The professor's task in this new age is not to compete with machines on speed, memory, or fluency. That contest would be both exhausting and absurd. The task is to deepen the forms of human academic work that machines can mimic but not truly own: discernment, responsibility, wisdom, imagination, moral courage, and the slow formation of minds. The professor may use AI, and in many cases should use it (Kumar, 2023). But the professor must also remain capable of stepping back from the glittering convenience of assistance and asking the older, harder questions: What is being learned? What is being lost? Who benefits? Who becomes invisible? What kind of university are we building when we allow speed and measurement to define excellence?

In the end, professorial purpose in the AI-mediated university may be less about preserving old authority and more about renewing academic humanity under new conditions. The professor no longer stands at the front of knowledge as its sole gatekeeper. That world has faded, and perhaps it deserved to fade. But the professor can still stand as a guide to meaning, a critic of shallow certainty, a witness to intellectual seriousness, and a defender of those forms of learning that require more than access to information. The machines may assist. The metrics may inform. The pace may quicken. Yet the deeper work remains stubbornly human: to help knowledge become understanding, to help understanding become judgment, and to help judgment become a responsible way of being in the world.

HUMAN JUDGMENT, ETHICAL AGENCY, AND THE FRAGILE CORE OF ACADEMIC PROFESSIONALISM

Academic professionalism has always rested on a fragile center (Schleck, 2022). It is easy to mistake that center for expertise, because expertise is the most visible part of the academic role: the degree, the publications, the lectures, the citations, the disciplinary vocabulary, the authority to examine and supervise. Yet expertise alone has never been enough to make someone a true academic professional. A professor may know much and still judge poorly. A researcher may produce endlessly and still act without ethical depth. A teacher may master every technical aspect of instruction and still fail to recognize the human being sitting before them. The deeper core of academic professionalism lies elsewhere: in judgment, in ethical agency, in the capacity to decide responsibly when rules are incomplete, data is ambiguous, and institutional pressures are pulling in the wrong direction.

This core is fragile because it cannot be fully standardized. It cannot be written once in a policy document and then mechanically applied to every situation. Academic judgment lives in difficult particulars. It appears when a professor decides whether a student's weak performance reflects laziness, fear, illness, poor preparation, or a temporary collapse of confidence. It appears when a supervisor must tell a doctoral candidate that an argument is not yet mature, without extinguishing the very courage needed to continue. It appears when a researcher chooses not to exaggerate findings, even though stronger claims would bring greater attention. It appears when a hiring committee recognizes promise in an unconventional candidate whose path does not fit the polished grammar of prestige. These moments rarely look heroic from the outside. They are small, often private, sometimes uncomfortable. Still, they are the substance from which academic integrity is made.

The arrival of AI in universities has made this fragile core more visible, precisely because so many academic tasks can now be assisted, accelerated, or partially simulated by intelligent systems. AI can generate feedback, summarize articles, propose research questions, detect patterns, evaluate textual similarity, predict student risk, support grading, help draft reports, and produce language that sounds alarmingly competent. It can do many things that once appeared to belong securely to academic labor (Bauer et al, 2023). This creates a temptation, almost a whisper in the institutional ear: if machines can help with so much, perhaps academic judgment itself can be made more efficient, more consistent, more scalable. Perhaps ethical decision-making can be supported by clearer rules and better data. Perhaps professionalism can be translated into procedures.

There is some truth in this. Human judgment is not magically pure. Academics can be biased, tired, defensive, impatient, elitist, careless, or unfair. A professor may misread a student. A reviewer may dismiss unfamiliar work. A committee may reproduce old hierarchies while speaking the language of excellence. AI systems, if carefully designed and critically governed, may help expose patterns that human actors overlook. They may identify inequities in assessment, reveal gaps in student support, or reduce some arbitrary inconsistencies in administrative decisions. It would be foolish to pretend that human judgment is always noble and machine mediation always corrupting. The matter is more tangled than that.

Yet the danger begins when support becomes substitution, or when the appearance of objectivity weakens the felt burden of responsibility. Ethical agency requires someone to answer for a decision. Not just to process it. Not simply to justify it through policy language. To answer for it. A machine can recommend, classify, calculate, and compare, but it cannot bear responsibility in the human sense (Coeckelbergh, 2023). It does not lie awake after a harmful decision. It does not feel shame when a student is treated unjustly. It does not know what it means to betray a colleague, neglect a duty, or protect a vulnerable person at personal cost. Responsibility belongs to subjects who can be called to account, who can reflect, regret, revise, and learn. Academic professionalism depends on that capacity.

This is why human judgment remains indispensable in AI-mediated universities. Judgment is not merely choosing between options. It is the art of interpreting situations in light of values. It asks not only, "What does the evidence show?" but also, "What does this evidence fail to show?" It asks, "What kind of harm might be hidden behind procedural correctness?" It asks, "What would fairness mean here, in this actual case, with these actual people?" AI can help organize information, but it cannot determine the moral weight of context. It cannot decide whether an exception should be made for a student whose life has been disrupted by war, poverty, illness, or family collapse. It cannot fully grasp why a rigidly applied rule may become unjust in a particular circumstance. It cannot understand the difference between consistency and fairness unless humans define, interpret, and sometimes contest that difference.

The distinction matters. Universities often confuse fairness with sameness. A machine can apply the same rule to everyone with impressive consistency. But academic justice sometimes requires unequal attention (Gbadamosi, 2025). A first-generation student struggling to decode academic culture may need forms of guidance that a more privileged student does not. A scholar from an underfunded institution may have fewer indexed publications but a richer record of intellectual and civic contribution. A candidate who has worked under conflict, displacement, or institutional collapse may not display the conventional signs of smooth academic progression. To judge such cases well requires more than metrics. It requires historical imagination. It requires humility before lives not easily captured by forms.

AI-mediated evaluation systems are especially risky when they treat academic worth as a pattern to be inferred from past data. Past data is never innocent. It carries the marks of exclusion, uneven opportunity, disciplinary fashion, linguistic hierarchy, geopolitical privilege, and institutional wealth. If such data is used uncritically in appointment, promotion, funding, or performance review, the system may reproduce inherited inequalities while appearing modern and neutral. Worse still, it may make injustice harder to challenge because the decision no longer looks like prejudice. It looks like analysis. It arrives wrapped in numbers, probabilities, rankings, and confident visualizations. The old bias wears a new suit.

Here the ethical agency of academics becomes vital. Professors and academic leaders must learn to ask uncomfortable questions of AI systems: What data trained this judgment? Whose work is visible to the system, and whose is missing? Which languages, journals, regions, institutions, and research traditions are privileged? What forms of contribution disappear because they are not easily indexed? What assumptions about excellence are being quietly embedded? And perhaps most importantly: who benefits when a decision is delegated to technical infrastructure? These questions are not expressions of technological hostility (JAYARON, 2024). They are acts of professional care.

There is a tendency in contemporary institutional culture to treat ethics as compliance. Complete the training. Follow the protocol. Declare the conflict. Use the approved platform. Insert the required statement. Compliance matters, of course; without procedures, ethical talk can become decorative. But academic ethics cannot be reduced to rule-following. Some of the most serious ethical failures occur inside technically compliant systems. A research project may pass formal review and still exploit a community. A promotion process may follow regulations and still reward shallow productivity over meaningful contribution. A classroom policy may be applied consistently and still humiliate students who needed understanding. A university may adopt AI governance guidelines and still cultivate a culture in which academics feel unable to question algorithmic decisions.

Ethical agency is more demanding. It requires the capacity to interrupt procedure when procedure becomes morally thin. It requires academics to notice when institutional convenience is masquerading as necessity. It requires the courage to say no, or at least not yet. This courage is not always grand. Sometimes it means refusing to use an AI detection tool as definitive proof of student misconduct, because such tools can be uncertain and because accusation itself can wound. Sometimes it means questioning a performance dashboard that reduces teaching to satisfaction scores. Sometimes it means resisting pressure to produce research outputs that are technically acceptable but intellectually hollow. Sometimes it means admitting that an AI-generated text, however polished, has not yet passed through sufficient human understanding.

The issue of authorship is particularly revealing. AI unsettles authorship because it can produce language without lived accountability. Academic writing is not merely the arrangement of sentences; it is a public act of responsibility (Mulenga & Shilongo, 2024). The author stands behind claims, evidence, interpretations, and omissions. When AI contributes to drafting or analysis, the academic must decide what it means to own the final work. This is not simply a technical question of disclosure, though disclosure matters. It is an ethical question about intellectual presence. Has the scholar genuinely understood what is being claimed? Have they verified the evidence? Have they shaped the argument through their own judgment? Or have they allowed machine fluency to cover a deficit of thought?

There is no need for puritanism here. Scholars have always received help: from editors, colleagues, translators, research assistants, software, reviewers, and students. Academic work is rarely solitary in any pure sense. But AI assistance can obscure the boundary between support and substitution because the system produces seemingly complete intellectual forms. A paragraph appears. A literature review appears. A conceptual framework appears. The temptation is not only to use these outputs, but to trust their surface. Ethical professionalism requires a slower relation to such assistance. It asks academics to treat AI output not as finished knowledge, but as material requiring suspicion, correction, contextualization, and ownership.

In teaching, the fragile core of professionalism becomes even more delicate. AI can help design lessons, create examples, produce quizzes, and provide immediate feedback (Mondal et al, 2023). These uses may enrich learning when guided by thoughtful pedagogy. Yet teaching is never only design and delivery. It is a moral relation. The teacher holds power over students' confidence, progress, evaluation, and sometimes their sense of belonging in the university. To teach ethically is to use that power with restraint and attention. It means refusing to reduce students to data profiles. It means seeing beyond predictive categories. A student flagged as "low engagement" may be exhausted from work. A student with AI-polished writing may be hiding insecurity rather than dishonesty. A student who performs poorly in standardized assessment may think with originality in conversation. The professor must read these situations with care.

There is a danger that AI systems will make academics less patient with ambiguity. When dashboards offer classifications and tools provide rapid answers, the messy work of interpretation may feel inefficient. But ambiguity is not a defect in academic life; it is often where the most important professional judgment begins. A teacher who never tolerates ambiguity becomes a functionary. A researcher who never questions the frame becomes a technician. A leader who never looks beyond indicators becomes a manager of surfaces. Academic professionalism requires living with incomplete knowledge while still acting responsibly. That is not weakness. It is maturity.

This is also why the ethical agency of academics must be collective, not only individual. A single professor may act responsibly in their classroom, but if the institution imposes AI systems without transparency, consultation, or appeal, individual ethics will not be enough. Universities need cultures where academics can question tools without being dismissed as resistant or outdated (Rosenberg, 2023). They need governance structures that include faculty, students, technical experts, ethicists, and affected communities. They need clear mechanisms for contesting AI-assisted decisions. They need appointment and promotion practices that recognize the limits of metrics. They need workload models that do not use machine efficiency as an excuse to increase human exhaustion. In short, they need an institutional ethics worthy of the technologies they adopt.

The fragile core of academic professionalism is also threatened by fatigue. This point should not be underestimated. Ethical judgment requires time, attention, and emotional energy. Exhausted academics are more likely to rely on shortcuts, templates, automated recommendations, and institutional defaults. Not because they are careless people, but because they are human. A university that demands ethical excellence while overloading its staff is indulging in hypocrisy. If institutions want academics to exercise judgment in AI-rich environments, they must protect the conditions under which judgment remains possible. Time to read. Time to meet students. Time to discuss difficult cases. Time to reflect before acting. These are not luxuries; they are ethical infrastructure.

Professionalism in the age of AI should therefore be understood as a disciplined refusal to abandon responsibility. It is not anti-technological. It is not sentimental.

It does not imagine professors as sacred figures untouched by tools. It recognizes that AI can strengthen academic work when placed under human purposes. But it also insists that no system, however intelligent, can replace the human obligation to judge, care, answer, and sometimes dissent. The professor remains necessary not because machines are weak, but because academic life involves decisions whose meaning exceeds computation.

This has major implications for professorial appointments. Universities should not appoint professors merely for their productivity, digital fluency, or ability to operate efficiently in AI-supported environments. They should look for evidence of judgment. How does the candidate handle complexity? How do they speak about students? Do they understand the ethical dimensions of their research? Can they recognize the limits of data? Are they capable of intellectual independence, or do they merely reproduce fashionable vocabularies? Do they show care for the academic community? Can they be trusted with power? These questions are slower than metric-based assessment, and they are more difficult to answer. But they are closer to the heart of what a professor is.

The future university will need academics who can work with intelligent systems without surrendering their ethical agency to them (Andoniou, 2025). It will need professors who understand that a recommendation is not a verdict, that a score is not a soul, that a pattern is not a person, and that efficiency is not the same as wisdom. It will need scholars who can teach students to question machine-generated certainty, to examine evidence carefully, to write with integrity, and to remain morally alert in a world where polished language can be produced without understanding. It will need academic leaders who refuse the comfort of purely technical solutions to deeply human problems.

Human judgment is fragile, yes. It is vulnerable to bias, fatigue, pride, fear, and institutional pressure. But its fragility is also what makes it precious. It can be educated. It can be corrected. It can be humbled. It can learn from those it has harmed. It can become more generous, more exacting, more awake. Machines may assist judgment, but they cannot undergo moral growth. They cannot become wise through remorse. They cannot acquire integrity. Academic professionalism, at its deepest, is built on this human possibility: the possibility that those entrusted with knowledge can also become more responsible in how they use it.

In AI-mediated universities, then, the task is not to protect human judgment from every form of technological influence (Ciasullo et al, 2026). That would be impossible and undesirable. The task is to keep judgment answerable to ethical agency rather than algorithmic convenience. The task is to ensure that professors do not become mere operators of intelligent systems, and that universities do not mistake automated coherence for moral clarity. The task is to preserve the fragile core: the human capacity to decide, to care, to doubt, to resist, to repair, and to stand behind one's work with intellectual and ethical seriousness. Without that core, academic professionalism may remain administratively functional, perhaps even impressively efficient, but it will lose the very quality that makes it worthy of trust.

RECLAIMING THE ACADEMIC VOCATION: TOWARD MEANINGFUL PROFESSORIAL APPOINTMENTS IN AI-MEDIATED UNIVERSITIES

To speak of academic vocation today may sound almost naïve. The word itself carries an older music, a trace of seriousness that does not sit easily inside the contemporary university's preferred vocabulary of productivity, competitiveness, employability, innovation, impact, and strategic alignment. Vocation suggests calling. It suggests commitment before calculation, responsibility before visibility, service before self-branding. It evokes the scholar who teaches not merely because teaching is assigned, researches not merely because publication is required, and serves not merely because a workload model demands it, but because academic life has become bound to a larger moral and intellectual purpose. Yet in the AI-mediated university, this older language may be precisely what needs to be recovered, not as nostalgia, and certainly not as romantic decoration, but as a necessary corrective to the growing temptation to define professors through measurable performance and technological adaptability alone.

The academic vocation has never been pure. It has been entangled with hierarchy, exclusion, vanity, institutional politics, disciplinary gatekeeping, and the uneven privileges of class, language, gender, geography, and race (Benzecry & Smith, 2024). There is no need to pretend otherwise. Some invocations of vocation have even been used to exploit academics, especially younger and precariously employed scholars, by asking them to sacrifice endlessly for the "love" of knowledge while institutions benefit from their exhaustion. So reclaiming vocation cannot mean asking professors to endure more, give more, publish more, mentor more, and quietly accept impossible working conditions because academic life is supposedly noble. That would be cruel. A meaningful academic vocation must be protected by fair structures, humane workloads, transparent governance, and institutional respect. Without these, vocation becomes a polite word for burnout.

Still, if the concept is handled carefully, it remains indispensable. The university needs more than competent knowledge workers. It needs people capable of carrying intellectual responsibility across time. It needs professors who understand that teaching is not content delivery, that research is not output production, that mentorship is not administrative supervision, and that academic service is not merely committee attendance. It needs academics who can hold together expertise and humility, authority and care, freedom and accountability. In an age when AI systems can generate text, analyze data, recommend decisions, personalize learning, map scholarly influence, and imitate forms of academic reasoning, the human vocation of the professor must be articulated with greater clarity, because what is left unnamed is easily absorbed by systems that speak louder, faster, and with more institutional confidence.

Professorial appointments are one of the most important places where this clarity must appear. Appointment is never merely a staffing procedure. It is an act of institutional imagination. Every professorial appointment answers, whether openly or not, a question about the kind of university being built. Is the university seeking a producer of ranked outputs? A grant-winning academic entrepreneur? A teacher with deep commitment to students? A public scholar? A disciplinary guardian? A technological innovator? A moral voice? A builder of academic communities? Ideally, the answer should not be singular, because universities require diverse forms of excellence. Yet the danger in AI-mediated systems is that appointment processes may drift toward what can be captured, compared, scored, and predicted. The candidate becomes a profile. The profile becomes a pattern. The pattern becomes a proxy for worth.

This is not to argue that data has no place in appointments. That would be neither realistic nor wise. Publication records, citation patterns, teaching evaluations, research grants, supervision experience, collaboration networks, and professional service can provide useful evidence. AI tools may help committees organize large bodies of information, detect inconsistencies, widen searches, identify overlooked candidates, and reduce some forms of procedural bias (Schwartz, 2022). Used carefully, such tools may strengthen rather than weaken academic decision-making. The problem begins when evidence hardens into destiny, when data ceases to support judgment and begins to replace it, when committees mistake the measurable part of a career for the whole human and scholarly story.

A meaningful professorial appointment process in AI-mediated universities must therefore ask not only "What has this candidate produced?" but "What kind of academic presence might this person bring into the institution?" That question is slower, more difficult, and less comfortable than counting outputs. It requires attention to the texture of a career: the risks taken, the students supported, the intellectual communities built, the ethical choices made, the neglected problems pursued, the conditions under which work was produced. A scholar who has published fewer articles from a fragile institution may have shown more courage, resilience, and originality than someone whose career has unfolded inside a well-funded academic machine. A teacher whose evaluations are mixed may have challenged students more deeply than a colleague who mastered the art of pleasing them. A researcher whose work does not yet attract high citation counts may be opening a path that others have not learned to recognize.

Appointment committees need to recover the art of reading academic lives. Not scanning them. Reading them.

This kind of reading is not sentimental. It does not ignore quality, rigor, or achievement. On the contrary, it demands a richer understanding of them. Rigor is not always visible as prestige. Originality is not always immediately rewarded. Ethical leadership does not always produce glamorous metrics. Mentorship may leave its deepest traces in other people's confidence, not in institutional dashboards. Public service may matter profoundly even when it does not translate neatly into citations. In AI-mediated universities, where systems may privilege what is cleanly indexed and easily compared, human committees must become more alert to the forms of academic value that remain stubbornly irregular (Hutson, 2025).

Figure 3. Professorial Appointment Criteria: Machine Readability vs Human Value

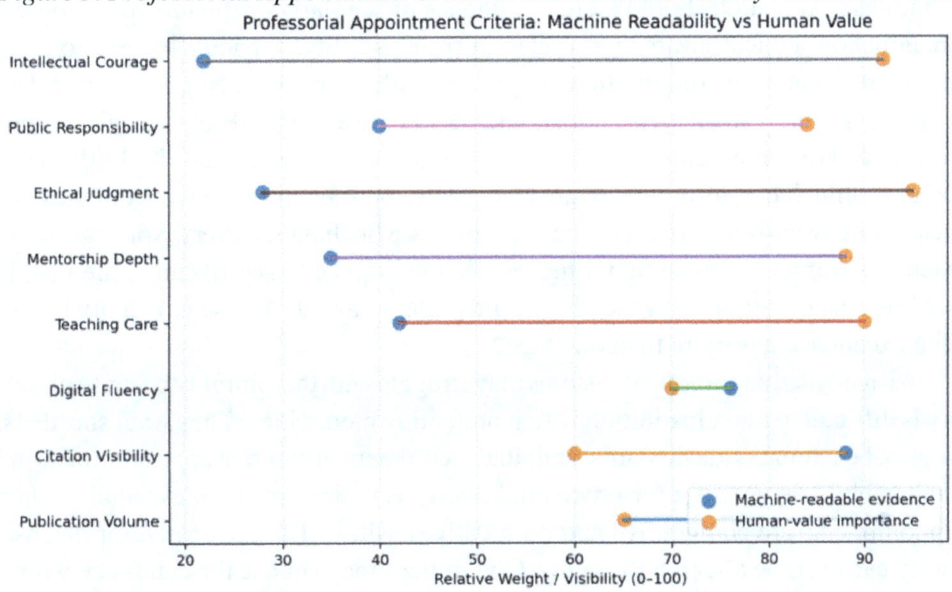

The question of AI competence also needs careful handling. Professors appointed in the coming years will certainly need to understand AI. They should be able to engage with its possibilities, risks, and implications for teaching, research, assessment, authorship, and governance. A professor who simply refuses to understand AI will be poorly equipped to serve students and institutions shaped by it. But AI competence should not be reduced to tool proficiency. Knowing how to prompt a system, automate a task, or generate materials is useful, but it is not enough. The deeper competence is interpretive and ethical. Can the candidate distinguish machine fluency from intellectual depth? Can they design learning experiences that preserve student agency? Can they guide students in using AI without surrendering the struggle of thought? Can they question algorithmic outputs rather than merely consume them? Can they see who is advantaged and who is made invisible by digital systems?

A university that appoints professors only because they are technologically agile may end up hiring efficient operators rather than academic stewards. The future professor should not be imagined as a person who simply works faster with machines. Speed is not wisdom. Responsiveness is not depth. Digital fluency is not moral seriousness. The professor needed in AI-mediated universities is someone who can work with intelligent systems while protecting the human purposes those systems cannot define: judgment, responsibility, understanding, care, and intellectual freedom.

This has implications for appointment criteria. Universities may need to move beyond narrow lists of publications, grants, teaching scores, and service roles toward more integrative portraits of academic contribution (Buch-Hansen et al, 2025). Candidate evaluation should include evidence of scholarly originality, pedagogical imagination, ethical awareness, collegial responsibility, capacity for mentorship, public relevance, and thoughtful engagement with technology. Not every candidate will excel equally in all areas, nor should they be expected to. Professorial communities need different temperaments and strengths. Some academics build theories; others build laboratories, programs, journals, partnerships, student cultures, or bridges between university and society. Some are brilliant lecturers. Some are quiet mentors. Some are institutional healers. Some are necessary irritants, the people who ask the question everyone else would prefer to avoid. A wise university knows that excellence has more than one face.

AI-mediated appointment systems may struggle with this plurality because plurality is difficult to rank. Institutions often prefer tidy hierarchies. They want shortlists, scores, benchmarks, dashboards, and final recommendations that appear rational and defensible. The pressure for procedural clarity is understandable, especially when appointments are competitive and politically sensitive. But the search for defensibility can become a search for safety. Committees may choose the candidate whose metrics are easiest to justify rather than the candidate whose contribution may be most transformative. This is one reason human judgment must remain central. The appointment of a professor is not simply a risk-management exercise. It is a wager on intellectual and human possibility.

There is also a need to reclaim trust. AI-mediated universities often expand because institutions no longer fully trust human judgment (Keen, 2025). They want systems to monitor, verify, predict, and standardize. Some of this distrust has been earned; academic decisions have not always been fair, transparent, or free from favoritism. Yet replacing flawed human judgment with opaque technical systems does not automatically create justice. Trust must be rebuilt through better human processes: diverse committees, transparent criteria, reflective deliberation, conflict-of-interest safeguards, external review, and a willingness to discuss what cannot be quantified. AI can assist such processes, but it cannot supply trust by itself. Trust grows when people believe that decisions have been made with seriousness, care, and openness to complexity.

The academic vocation also requires institutions to appoint professors who can resist the narrowing of university purpose. In many systems, professors are increasingly expected to align with employability agendas, funding priorities, ranking strategies, market visibility, and digital transformation plans. These demands are not always illegitimate. Universities do operate within social and economic realities. They must prepare students for changing worlds, secure resources, and demonstrate relevance. But if every academic appointment is shaped primarily by immediate strategic utility, the university loses its longer memory. It forgets that some knowledge matters before it is profitable, that some questions are valuable because they disturb consensus, and that some forms of teaching serve society not by producing immediate skills but by forming judgment, conscience, and imagination.

AI may sharpen this tension because it makes strategic alignment easier to model. Institutions may increasingly ask which candidates are likely to raise rankings, secure grants, attract students, expand digital programs, or enhance institutional visibility. Again, these are not trivial concerns. But professorial appointments should also ask: Who will help the university remain intellectually honest? Who will protect students from shallow certainty? Who will pursue inconvenient knowledge? Who will build academic communities rather than merely personal careers? Who will help colleagues think, not just perform? Who will remember that the university is not only an engine of innovation, but also a shelter for difficult reflection?

Reclaiming vocation means treating professors as bearers of responsibility, not just performers of tasks. It also means refusing to reduce academic identity to individual achievement. The professor's work is profoundly relational. Professors shape students, departments, disciplines, institutions, and public conversations (Diamond & Adam, 2023). They inherit traditions and revise them. They open doors or close them. They can create climates of fear, generosity, arrogance, curiosity, competition, or trust. A single appointment can change the moral weather of a department. This is not easily measurable, but anyone who has lived inside a university knows it is true. Some academics make those around them smaller. Others make intellectual life feel possible again.

AI cannot detect all of this. Not fully. Perhaps not even close.

A more meaningful appointment process would therefore include serious attention to academic character, though that phrase must be used carefully. Character should not become a vague moral test or a cover for personal preference. It should refer to observable patterns of professional conduct: fairness in collaboration, respect for students, integrity in research, generosity in peer work, courage in difficult situations, openness to criticism, and the ability to use authority without theatrical self-importance. Universities often appoint for brilliance and later suffer because brilliance arrived without humility. The AI age, with all its speed and polish, may make humility even more necessary. The professor who believes that technological mastery makes them superior is dangerous. So is the professor who hides behind tradition to avoid learning. The better figure is neither technophile nor technophobe, but a reflective academic who can ask, with some seriousness, what tools are doing to the soul of the work.

This also requires attention to early-career scholars. If universities want future professors with vocation, they must stop training them only for survival in metric-saturated systems. Doctoral education and academic development should include reflection on purpose, ethics, pedagogy, public responsibility, AI use, and institutional citizenship (Usher, 2025). Young academics should not learn that the only path to professorship is relentless output, strategic branding, and permanent availability. They should see models of academic life that are intellectually ambitious but not spiritually depleted. Otherwise, appointment committees will later lament the very professional culture their institutions helped create.

Reclaiming academic vocation in AI-mediated universities is not a call to return to some imagined golden age. That age did not exist. It is a call to build a more conscious future, one in which intelligent systems serve academic purposes rather than quietly redefining them. Professorial appointments are a crucial starting point because they determine who will carry the university forward. If universities appoint only for productivity, they will get productivity, perhaps in abundance, but may lose wisdom. If they appoint only for technological fluency, they may gain innovation while losing judgment. If they appoint only for prestige, they will reproduce prestige. If they appoint for vocation—understood as disciplined commitment to knowledge, students, ethics, and public responsibility—they may still produce excellent research and teaching, but with a deeper center of gravity.

The challenge is not simple. Meaningful appointments take time. They require committees willing to read deeply, deliberate honestly, and resist the seductions of easy comparison. They require criteria that welcome evidence without becoming enslaved to it. They require courage to recognize unconventional excellence and humility to admit uncertainty. They require universities to ask what kind of professors their students and societies actually need, not merely what kind of profiles their systems most easily reward.

In the AI-mediated university, the academic vocation will not survive by accident. It must be named, defended, revised, and built into institutional practice (Rao, 2025). Professors will use machines. They will work through platforms, analytics, automated systems, and intelligent assistants. That is now part of the landscape. But the appointment of a professor should still mark the arrival of a human being entrusted with more than tasks. It should recognize someone capable of judgment, care, intellectual courage, and responsibility before knowledge. Someone who can help a university remain a university, even as its tools become more powerful than anything earlier generations could have imagined.

Table 2. Professorial Appointment Framework for AI-Mediated Universities

Appointment Criterion	What Committees Should Look For	Evidence Sources	AI-Era Caution
Scholarly Originality	Work that opens questions, challenges assumptions, or develops a distinctive intellectual direction	Publications, research statement, external letters, sample work	Do not reduce originality to citation velocity or fashionable keywords
Pedagogical Judgment	Capacity to teach beyond content delivery and cultivate discernment, difficulty, and student agency	Teaching portfolio, sample syllabus, peer observation, student learning evidence	Student ratings and platform analytics are partial signals, not the whole picture
Ethical Agency	Ability to handle ambiguity, data limits, authorship, fairness, and human responsibility in AI-rich settings	Ethics statement, case discussion, research practice, governance participation	Tool fluency is not the same as moral seriousness
Mentorship and Care	Evidence of supporting students and early-career colleagues with attention, fairness, and professional generosity	Supervision record, mentoring narratives, testimonies, advising examples	Mentorship depth is often poorly captured by dashboards
Technological Discernment	Thoughtful use of AI without surrendering judgment, originality, or academic responsibility	AI-use statement, course design examples, research workflow explanation	Avoid appointing for speed alone; ask what technology is for
Public and Institutional Responsibility	Contribution to university culture, public knowledge, equity, and intellectual community	Service record, public engagement, program building, community projects	Public value may be less machine-readable than grants or metrics
Intellectual Courage	Willingness to pursue difficult, unfashionable, or ethically necessary questions	Research trajectory, references, interview discussion, public work	Risk-taking may look less efficient in performance systems

The future of professorial appointments, then, should not be a contest between human judgment and artificial intelligence (Xu, 2022). It should be a disciplined partnership in which AI informs but does not decide, supports but does not define, accelerates but does not hollow out, and reveals patterns without flattening persons into patterns. The professoriate of the AI age must be selected not only for what it can produce, but for what it can protect. And perhaps that is the simplest way to understand academic vocation now: the commitment to protect the human, ethical, and intellectual seriousness of higher education when everything around it is becoming faster, smoother, and easier to measure.

CONCLUSION

The rise of AI in higher education does not mark the end of the academic profession, but it does mark the end of any simple understanding of it. The professor can no longer be imagined only as a disciplinary expert who transmits knowledge, produces research, and participates in institutional service. That image was already incomplete, yet AI has made its limitations impossible to ignore. In a world where information can be generated, reorganized, translated, summarized, and circulated at astonishing speed, the value of the academic can no longer rest primarily on access to knowledge. The university must now look more carefully at the forms of human presence, judgment, responsibility, and imagination that remain essential when knowledge itself becomes technologically abundant.

This chapter has argued that academic identity in AI-mediated universities is becoming more exposed, more contested, and perhaps more fragile. AI enters the academic world not as a neutral machine, but as a force that interacts with existing pressures: marketization, managerialism, ranking cultures, precarious labor, publication demands, and institutional obsession with measurable performance. For this reason, the impact of AI cannot be understood only through discussions of innovation, productivity, or digital transformation. These are important, but they do not reach the heart of the matter. The deeper issue concerns meaning. What does it mean to be a scholar when machines can imitate scholarly language? What does it mean to be a teacher when automated systems can deliver feedback and personalize learning pathways? What does it mean to be a professor when appointment, promotion, and recognition may increasingly be influenced by algorithmic readings of academic worth?

The answer is not found in denial. Universities cannot pretend that AI is a passing trend or a minor technical addition to established practice. AI will continue to shape research, teaching, administration, and governance. It will become more embedded, more subtle, and more difficult to separate from everyday academic work. Nor is the answer found in surrender. To accept AI uncritically as the inevitable logic of the future would be to give up one of the university's most important responsibilities: the responsibility to think before adapting. Higher education should not merely absorb technological systems because they are available, efficient, or fashionable. It should ask what kinds of academic life these systems encourage, what kinds they weaken, and what kinds they make almost impossible.

At the center of this discussion is the question of professional purpose. AI may assist academics in many valuable ways, but it cannot decide what academic work is for. It cannot determine the moral direction of a university. It cannot replace the difficult human act of weighing evidence, context, consequence, and care. It cannot mentor a student in the full sense of the word, because mentorship is not only guidance; it is relationship, recognition, patience, and trust. It cannot carry the ethical burden of scholarship, because responsibility cannot be outsourced to a system. It cannot defend intellectual freedom, because freedom requires a subject who can risk something. It cannot fully understand the meaning of a question, because the most important questions in academic life are often born from human vulnerability, historical memory, injustice, curiosity, and hope.

This is why academic identity must be renewed rather than merely protected. There is little value in nostalgia for an earlier university that was itself unequal, hierarchical, and often exclusionary. The academic profession has never been pure. It has always been shaped by power, privilege, institutional politics, and uneven access to recognition. Yet the answer to these imperfections is not to hand the future of academic life to automated systems of evaluation and control. Instead, AI should push universities to revisit the foundations of academic professionalism with greater honesty. What qualities should define a professor in the coming decades? What forms of excellence are worth rewarding? What kinds of intellectual labor have been ignored because they are difficult to measure? What does responsible scholarship look like when machines can accelerate both discovery and distortion?

Professorial appointments are especially important in this regard. They are among the most consequential decisions a university makes, because they shape not only departments, but institutional memory, intellectual culture, student experience, and future research directions. In AI-mediated universities, appointment processes may benefit from richer data and more systematic analysis. However, they must not become captive to what is easiest to quantify. A professor is not simply a bundle of outputs. A scholar's worth cannot be fully read through citation counts, publication frequency, grant income, student ratings, or digital visibility. These indicators may tell part of the story, but they do not tell the whole story. Sometimes they do not even tell the most important part.

A future-oriented appointments system should therefore combine evidence with discernment. It should use data without worshipping it. It should welcome technological support without allowing technology to define excellence on its own terms. It should recognize research productivity, but also intellectual originality. It should value teaching effectiveness, but also the quiet art of forming minds. It should reward public engagement, but not reduce it to online visibility. It should notice leadership, but distinguish genuine academic stewardship from administrative performance. Most importantly, it should preserve room for human judgment, because appointing a professor is not merely an act of selection; it is an act of trust.

The AI-mediated university will also need to rethink academic autonomy. Autonomy should not be understood as isolation or resistance to accountability. Rather, it is the professional space required for academics to pursue truth, exercise judgment, challenge assumptions, and act according to scholarly and ethical standards.

When AI systems are used to monitor, rank, nudge, and predict academic behavior, autonomy may slowly contract. The danger is not always dramatic. It may happen quietly, through dashboards, automated recommendations, productivity analytics, and institutional norms that encourage academics to become legible to systems rather than faithful to their deepest intellectual responsibilities. A professor may remain formally free while becoming practically governed by invisible expectations.

For this reason, universities must cultivate what might be called critical technological professionalism. Academics should not be passive users of AI tools, nor should they be forced into the role of reluctant resisters. They need the knowledge, confidence, and institutional voice to question how AI is designed, adopted, and evaluated. They should participate in decisions about AI governance, assessment policy, research ethics, workload models, student support, and appointment criteria. AI literacy should not be reduced to technical training. It must include ethical, pedagogical, epistemological, and professional reflection. Academics need to understand not only how to use AI, but how AI changes the conditions under which they teach, think, judge, and belong.

The future of academic identity will depend heavily on whether universities treat academics as replaceable knowledge workers or as reflective professionals whose humanity remains central to the mission of higher education. If the former view prevails, AI may accelerate the transformation of universities into automated knowledge enterprises, efficient but spiritually thin. Teaching may become content delivery plus analytics. Research may become output generation plus visibility management. Appointments may become predictive selection. Academic purpose may shrink into compliance with institutional metrics. Such a university might be productive, perhaps even globally competitive, but it would risk losing the qualities that make higher education worthy of public trust.

A different future is possible. AI could be used to reduce unnecessary burdens, expand access, support multilingual scholarship, strengthen student care, and open new paths for inquiry. It could help academics spend less time on mechanical tasks and more time on interpretation, dialogue, creativity, and mentorship. It could expose hidden inequalities and support more thoughtful institutional decisions. It could enrich academic work rather than diminish it. But this better future will not emerge automatically. It requires governance, imagination, ethical restraint, and a renewed commitment to the human purposes of the university.

The academic profession now stands at a delicate threshold. The question is not whether professors will use AI; they already do, and they will do so more extensively. The real question is whether they will be allowed, encouraged, and trusted to remain professors in the deepest sense: people who think with care, teach with responsibility, judge with humility, research with integrity, and serve institutions without becoming absorbed by them. Academic identity in the age of AI must therefore be neither defensive nor careless. It must be reflective, courageous, and morally awake.

In the end, AI forces higher education to confront a truth it has sometimes neglected. The worth of the university does not lie only in the knowledge it stores, produces, or distributes. It lies in the human beings it forms, the questions it keeps alive, the freedoms it protects, and the responsibilities it refuses to abandon. Professorial appointments in the AI age should be guided by this larger vision. Universities should appoint not only those who can produce measurable outputs, but those who can carry the intellectual and ethical weight of academic life in uncertain times. The future professor will need technological competence, certainly. But even more, they will need judgment, generosity, courage, imagination, and purpose.

AI may change the tools of academic work. It may change its pace, its methods, and its visible forms. But it should not be allowed to empty the academic vocation of its human center. The task ahead is not to choose between professors and machines. It is to build universities in which intelligent technologies serve humane intelligence, where data informs but does not dominate, and where academic identity remains rooted in the difficult, beautiful, unfinished work of thinking with and for others.

REFERENCES

Alalaq, A. S. (2025). AI Tools for Data and Academic Content Analysis. *Authorea Preprints.*

Ali, W., & Ali, W. (2022). How to Improve Productivity through a Goal-Oriented Approach? Journal of Economics, Management &. *Business Administration (London), 1*(1), 55–67.

Andoniou, C. (2025). Rewiring Education for a Super-Smart Society: Cognitive Integrity, AI Ethics, and the Future of Knowledge. *Computing&AI Connect*, *2*(1), 1–10. DOI: 10.69709/CAIC.2025.112122

Bauer, E., Greisel, M., Kuznetsov, I., Berndt, M., Kollar, I., Dresel, M., Fischer, M. R., & Fischer, F. (2023). Using natural language processing to support peer-feedback in the age of artificial intelligence: A cross-disciplinary framework and a research agenda. *British Journal of Educational Technology*, *54*(5), 1222–1245. DOI: 10.1111/bjet.13336

Beer, D. (2022). *The tensions of algorithmic thinking: Automation, intelligence and the politics of knowing*. Policy Press.

Benzecry, G., & Smith, D. J. (2024). A Critical Analysis of Academia. Available at *SSRN* 4803139.

Bhat, J. (2023). Automating Higher Education Administrative Processes with AI-Powered Workflows. *International Journal of Emerging Trends in Computer Science and Information Technology*, *4*(4), 147–157. DOI: 10.63282/3050-9246.IJETCSIT-V4I4P116

Bong, Y., Yunus, S., Weerawarna, R., Senkerik, R., Tan, R., Masood, T., ... & Camilleri, V. (2025). Universities' role in the artificial intelligence innovation system for sustainable development.

Buch-Hansen, H., Nesterova, I., & Nielsen, P. (2025). Envisioning an academia for degrowth transformations. *Globalizations*, *22*(6), 1050–1067. DOI: 10.1080/14747731.2025.2480527

Cameron, L. D. (2024). The making of the "good bad" job: How algorithmic management manufactures consent through constant and confined choices. *Administrative Science Quarterly*, *69*(2), 458–514. DOI: 10.1177/00018392241236163

Chen, H., Van Reyk, D., & Oliver, B. G. (2025). The use of AI large language models by university students for assignment preparation. *Advances in Physiology Education*, *49*(2), 517–525. DOI: 10.1152/advan.00181.2024 PMID: 40131177

Ciasullo, A., Santoianni, F., & Manfredini, A. (2026). Rethinking Human Agency in AI-Mediated Education. *Journal of Inclusive Methodology and Technology in Learning and Teaching*, *6*(1).

Coeckelbergh, M. (2023). Narrative responsibility and artificial intelligence: How AI challenges human responsibility and sense-making. *AI & Society*, *38*(6), 2437–2450. DOI: 10.1007/s00146-021-01375-x

Davidson, S. (2024). The economic institutions of artificial intelligence. *Journal of Institutional Economics*, *20*, e20. DOI: 10.1017/S1744137423000395

Diamond, R. M., & Adam, B. E. (Eds.). (2023). *The disciplines speak I: Rewarding the scholarly, professional, and creative work of faculty*. Taylor & Francis. DOI: 10.4324/9781003447764

Donoghue, R. (2025). Freedom under algorithms: How unpredictable and asocial management erodes free choice. *Frontiers in Artificial Intelligence*, *8*, 1582085. DOI: 10.3389/frai.2025.1582085 PMID: 40860718

. Gbadamosi, G. G. (2025). Unequal Academy: The Struggle and Challenges of Token Black Academics in the United Kingdom. "Unequal Academy: The Struggle and Challenges of Token Black Academics in the UK".

Gibbs, P. (2022). Self-Deception and the Duty of the Truth-Teller in the University–A Values Perspective. In *Trusting in Higher Education: A multifaceted discussion of trust in and for higher education in Norway and the United Kingdom* (pp. 173–183). Springer International Publishing.

Goyanes, M., Domínguez-Díaz, A., Jordá, B., & de-Marcos, L. (2025). Gender gap in citations, h-index, and representation: Examining the highly cited authors across continents and disciplines in Google Scholar. *PLoS One*, *20*(11), e0334690. DOI: 10.1371/journal.pone.0334690 PMID: 41231907

Hartung, T., Hoffmann, S., & Whaley, P. (2025). Assessing risk of bias in toxicological studies in the era of artificial intelligence. *Archives of Toxicology*, *99*(8), 3065–3090. DOI: 10.1007/s00204-025-03978-5 PMID: 40615561

Hartz, R. (2024). Demeaning, depriving, and isolating the academic subject: A case study of the degradation of professional autonomy. *Management Learning*, *55*(5), 703–719. DOI: 10.1177/13505076231207938

Hashem, R., Ali, N., El Zein, F., Fidalgo, P., & Khurma, O. A. (2024). AI to the rescue: Exploring the potential of ChatGPT as a teacher ally for workload relief and burnout prevention. *Research and Practice in Technology Enhanced Learning*, •••, 19.

Hu, H., Zhou, Q., & Hashim, H. (2025). Negotiating identity in the age of ChatGPT: Non-native English researchers' experiences with AI-assisted academic writing. *Humanities & Social Sciences Communications*, *12*(1), 1–11. DOI: 10.1057/s41599-025-05351-4

. Hutson, J. (2025). From Prohibition to Preparation: Reframing Academic Integrity in the Age of AI. MRS Journal of Arts, Humanities and Literature, 2(11).

JAYARON, B. (2024). Educators' academic insights on artificial intelligence: Challenges and opportunities. Electronic Journal of eLearning.

. Keen, J. (2025). Human Agency in Algorithmic Universities: Student Leadership and Ethical Governance in AI-Mediated Universities.

Koukaras, C., Hatzikraniotis, E., Mitsiaki, M., Koukaras, P., Tjortjis, C., & Stavrinides, S. G. (2025). Revolutionising educational management with AI and wireless networks: A framework for smart resource allocation and decision-making. *Applied Sciences (Basel, Switzerland)*, *15*(10), 5293. DOI: 10.3390/app15105293

Kumar, R. (2023). Faculty members' use of artificial intelligence to grade student papers: A case of implications. *International Journal for Educational Integrity*, *19*(1), 9. DOI: 10.1007/s40979-023-00130-7

. Lado, M. J. (2025). Data Modeling and Process Analysis: Essential for Technology Analysts and AI Experts: How Can Diagrams Solve Challenges in AI and Process Analysis?. Amazon Digital Services LLC-Kdp, 2025.

Ma, Y. (2025). AI, Education, and Academic Publishing in between Knowledge Capitalism and Socialism. *Beijing International Review of Education*, *7*(4), 351–374. DOI: 10.1177/25902547251390638

Macháček, M., & Melecký, A. (2025). To be a professor: Academic mobility and publishing performance. *PLoS One*, *20*(11), e0336133. DOI: 10.1371/journal.pone.0336133 PMID: 41248149

Machajewski, S. (2026). *The Learn-It-All Educator: A Guidebook for Training Brains*. Not Replacing Them with AI.

McGeorge, D. (2023). *The ChatGPT revolution: How to simplify your work and life admin with AI*. John Wiley & Sons.

Mondal, H., Marndi, G., Behera, J. K., & Mondal, S. (2023). ChatGPT for teachers: Practical examples for utilizing artificial intelligence for educational purposes. *Indian Journal of Vascular and Endovascular Surgery*, *10*(3), 200–205. DOI: 10.4103/ijves.ijves_37_23

Monteiro-Krebs, L., Zaman, B., Geerts, D., & Caregnato, S. E. (2023). Every word you say: Algorithmic mediation and implications of data-driven scholarly communication. *AI & Society*, *38*(2), 1003–1012. DOI: 10.1007/s00146-022-01468-1

. Muhammed-Mikaaeel, A. A., Hassan, S. K., & Salman, K. O. (2025). EXPLORING CONSIDERABLE FACTORS TOWARDS CHOOSING A GOOD RESEARCHABLE LEGAL TOPIC.

Mulenga, R., & Shilongo, H. (2024). Academic integrity in higher education: Understanding and addressing plagiarism. *Acta Pedagogia Asiana*, *3*(1), 30–43. DOI: 10.53623/apga.v3i1.337

Mutua, S. N. (2025). Decolonizing Knowledge Production: Barriers and Strategies for African Scholars in Academic Publishing. *Multidisciplinary Journal of Technical University of Mombasa*, *4*(1), 93–104. DOI: 10.48039/mjtum.v4i1.92

. Nelson, R. (2025). Academic Identity in the AI Era. AI-Powered Pedagogy and Curriculum Design: Practical Insights for Educators.

Oyedokun, T. T. (2025). Navigating the dynamics of present-day academic libraries: An in-depth analysis of strategies, challenges, and emerging trends. *IFLA Journal*, *51*(2), 470–489. DOI: 10.1177/03400352241291907

Rao, S. (2025). Universities in Ruins or on the Cusp of Renewal? Dark Academia, Global Data, Liberal Arts, and the Coming AI Shock. *INNOVAPATH*, *1*(9), 7–7. DOI: 10.63501/s9xyhj53

Rider, S. (2022). Autonomy for Whom? Governance of What? The Rationality of Academic Freedom. In *Academic Freedom in the European Context: Legal, Philosophical and Institutional Perspectives* (pp. 117–148). Springer International Publishing. DOI: 10.1007/978-3-030-86931-1_6

Rony, M. K. K., Parvin, M. R., Wahiduzzaman, M., Debnath, M., Bala, S. D., & Kayesh, I. (2024). "I wonder if my years of training and expertise will be devalued by machines": Concerns about the replacement of medical professionals by artificial intelligence. *SAGE Open Nursing*, *10*, 23779608241245220. DOI: 10.1177/23779608241245220 PMID: 38596508

Rosenberg, B. (2023). *"Whatever it is, I'm against it": Resistance to change in higher education.* Harvard Education Press.

Schleck, J. (2022). *Dirty knowledge: Academic freedom in the age of neoliberalism*. U of Nebraska Press. DOI: 10.2307/j.ctv21v2b0c

. Schwartz, R. (2022). Towards a standard for identifying and managing bias in artificial intelligence.

Sublime, J. (2024). The AI race: Why current neural network-based architectures are a poor basis for artificial general intelligence. *Journal of Artificial Intelligence Research*, *79*, 41–67. DOI: 10.1613/jair.1.15315

Tang, K. H. D. (2024). Implications of artificial intelligence for teaching and learning. *Acta Pedagogia Asiana*, *3*(2), 65–79. DOI: 10.53623/apga.v3i2.404

Usher, M., Barak, M., & Erduran, S. (2025). What role should higher education institutions play in fostering AI ethics? Insights from science and engineering graduate students. *International Journal of STEM Education*, *12*(1), 51. DOI: 10.1186/s40594-025-00567-x

Uttl, B. (2024). Student evaluation of teaching (SET): Why the emperor has no clothes and what we should do about it. *Human Arenas*, *7*(2), 403–437. DOI: 10.1007/s42087-023-00361-7

van den Hoonaard, D. K. (2025). Doing it right? Interpretive research in an era of research ethics review. In *Handbook of Interpretive Research Methods in the Social Sciences* (pp. 456–470). Edward Elgar Publishing. DOI: 10.4337/9781803926391.00038

Wallbank, A. J. (2022). Academic writing and student identity: Helping learners write in an age of massification, metrics and consumerism. In *Student support services* (pp. 203–222). Springer Nature Singapore. DOI: 10.1007/978-981-16-5852-5_10

Xu, Z. (2022). Human judges in the era of artificial intelligence: Challenges and opportunities. *Applied Artificial Intelligence*, *36*(1), 2013652. DOI: 10.1080/08839514.2021.2013652

Yamada, K. (2026). Structural failures in AI safety: A cross-system comparative analysis with educational impact observations. Available at *SSRN* 6285340. DOI: 10.2139/ssrn.6285340

. Youvan, D. C. (2024). Amplification Through Progression: From Analog Signals to Artificial Intelligence.

Zhao, D. (2025). The impact of AI-enhanced natural language processing tools on writing proficiency: An analysis of language precision, content summarization, and creative writing facilitation. *Education and Information Technologies*, *30*(6), 8055–8086. DOI: 10.1007/s10639-024-13145-5

KEY TERMS AND DEFINITIONS

Academic Identity: the professional selfhood academics develop through inquiry, teaching, research, mentorship, disciplinary belonging, and ethical responsibility.

Academic Vocation: the sense of calling that frames professorial work as a commitment to knowledge, students, ethics, and public responsibility.

AI-Mediated University: a university where teaching, research, assessment, appointments, and governance are increasingly shaped by intelligent systems.

Algorithmic Mediation: the filtering of academic work through AI tools, analytics, dashboards, recommendation systems, and machine-readable indicators.

Ethical Agency: the human capacity to make responsible academic decisions when data, rules, and automated systems are incomplete or morally insufficient.

Professional Purpose: the deeper reason for academic work beyond productivity, including judgment, mentorship, integrity, public responsibility, and intellectual formation.

Professorial Appointment: a symbolic and institutional decision through which universities declare what kinds of academic excellence, values, and futures they recognize.

Chapter 4
Reimagining the Professoriate:
How AI Is Reshaping Academic Roles and Responsibilities

Ranjit Singha
http://orcid.org/0000-0002-3541-8752
Christ University, India

Surjit Singha
http://orcid.org/0000-0002-5730-8677
Kristu Jayanti (Deemed to be University), India

ABSTRACT

Artificial intelligence (AI) is transforming higher education by influencing teaching, research, governance, and academic labor. This chapter adopts a conceptual review approach using structured narrative synthesis to examine how AI reshapes the professoriate in contemporary universities. Drawing on literature related to digital pedagogy, governance, and human–AI collaboration, the chapter analyzes how AI contributes to pedagogical restructuring, faculty role transformation, and evolving digital scholarly identity. It also discusses concerns related to algorithmic bias, academic integrity, and surveillance-oriented governance. The chapter argues that universities must adopt transparent governance systems and human-centered pedagogical approaches to ensure that AI supports academic autonomy, critical inquiry, and responsible higher education practices.

DOI: 10.4018/979-8-3373-8525-9.ch004

INTRODUCTION

Higher education institutions have historically evolved alongside technological transformations that reshape how knowledge is produced, communicated, and institutionalized within society. Universities adapted to earlier technological developments such as the printing press, industrial scientific infrastructure, digital computing, and the expansion of the internet, each of which altered pedagogical practices, scholarly communication, and academic organization. In the twenty-first century, artificial intelligence (AI) has emerged as another major technological development influencing universities across teaching, research, administration, and institutional governance. The increasing integration of AI technologies into higher education environments is reshaping academic labor, decision-making processes, and the professional identity of the professoriate (Zawacki-Richter et al., 2019).

The professoriate has traditionally been structured around three interconnected responsibilities: teaching, research, and institutional service. Professors have historically functioned not only as educators and researchers but also as participants in governance systems that shape curriculum development, academic standards, and institutional policy. These professional roles have long been influenced by disciplinary traditions, scholarly norms, and broader social expectations associated with higher education institutions (Marginson, 2016). However, the rapid expansion of AI-supported systems has begun to challenge several assumptions underlying traditional academic work by introducing technologies capable of performing tasks previously associated primarily with human intellectual activity.

AI technologies are now increasingly integrated into multiple dimensions of higher education. Universities employ generative AI systems, adaptive learning platforms, predictive analytics tools, intelligent tutoring systems, automated grading applications, and AI-assisted research technologies to support educational and administrative functions. Institutions such as Arizona State University have explored AI-supported tutoring and personalized learning systems to improve student engagement. At the same time, Georgia State University has utilized predictive analytics systems to identify students at risk of academic underperformance and support retention initiatives. These developments illustrate how AI adoption is increasingly becoming embedded within institutional decision-making and pedagogical practices rather than remaining limited to experimental technological applications.

Supporters of AI integration argue that these technologies may enhance instructional efficiency, improve access to personalized learning, and expand research capabilities. Adaptive learning systems can provide individualized educational feedback based on student performance patterns, while AI-supported analytical tools may assist researchers in organizing large datasets and identifying emerging research trends (Crompton et al., 2023). Research-intensive institutions such as

Massachusetts Institute of Technology and Stanford University have increasingly incorporated AI-supported computational systems into interdisciplinary research initiatives involving medicine, engineering, economics, and data science. These developments suggest that AI is influencing not only teaching practices but also the broader organization of knowledge production within universities.

At the same time, the educational implications of AI remain contested and unevenly understood. Although AI technologies may improve efficiency in some institutional contexts, concerns persist about algorithmic bias, data privacy, academic integrity, surveillance-oriented governance, and the reduction of complex academic practices to quantifiable metrics. Universities increasingly rely on data-driven systems to evaluate student engagement, faculty productivity, and institutional performance, raising important questions regarding transparency, accountability, and academic autonomy (Williamson & Eynon, 2020). Consequently, AI integration should be understood not only as technological progress but also as a broader institutional transformation reshaping relationships among governance, academic labor, and knowledge production.

The emergence of generative AI technologies has further intensified debates surrounding authorship, originality, and intellectual authenticity within higher education. Students and researchers now have access to systems capable of generating essays, research summaries, coding outputs, and analytical interpretations that closely resemble human-produced academic work. While these technologies may support learning and research processes, they also complicate conventional assessment methods and raise unresolved questions regarding ethical AI use and scholarly integrity (Selwyn, 2019). In response, institutions such as the University of Cambridge and the University of Melbourne have introduced guidance on the responsible use of generative AI in teaching and assessment practices. These developments reflect broader efforts within higher education to establish governance frameworks that can respond to rapidly evolving technological environments.

The growing influence of AI has also changed expectations regarding academic professionalism and digital competence. Faculty members are increasingly expected to engage with digital pedagogy, AI-supported research systems, data interpretation tools, and technology-mediated forms of scholarly communication. Universities such as the University of Michigan and the National University of Singapore have developed faculty development initiatives focused on generative AI, digital scholarship, and responsible integration of technology. These institutional responses indicate that AI adoption in higher education requires not only technological infrastructure but also professional adaptation and institutional support mechanisms.

Rather than portraying AI as either inherently beneficial or fundamentally disruptive, this chapter approaches AI integration as a complex institutional phenomenon shaped by pedagogical, technological, ethical, and governance-related tensions.

The concept of human–AI collaboration suggests that AI systems may increasingly serve as supportive tools in academic environments, augmenting rather than fully replacing human intellectual activity (Brynjolfsson & McAfee, 2017). However, the consequences of such collaboration remain uneven across disciplines, institutions, and educational systems.

This chapter adopts a conceptual review approach using structured narrative synthesis to examine how AI is reshaping the professoriate in higher education. Drawing on literature on digital pedagogy, academic governance, technological transformation, and human–AI collaboration, the chapter critically analyzes how AI integration contributes to pedagogical restructuring, faculty role transformation, governance pressures, and evolving forms of digital scholarly identity. Rather than presenting deterministic conclusions regarding technological change, the chapter highlights both opportunities and unresolved challenges associated with AI integration in universities. Through this analysis, the chapter aims to contribute to ongoing scholarly discussions regarding the future of academic work, institutional governance, and human-centered higher education in increasingly AI-mediated academic environments.

BACKGROUND

The relationship between technological innovation and higher education has evolved continuously across different historical periods, shaping how universities organize teaching, research, and knowledge dissemination. Earlier technological developments, such as the printing press, expanded access to scholarly materials and enabled universities to standardize curricula and scholarly communication. Later developments associated with industrialization and scientific modernization contributed to the growth of research universities, laboratories, and specialized academic disciplines. These transformations illustrate that universities have historically adapted to technological shifts while simultaneously redefining academic roles and institutional structures (Castells, 2010).

The emergence of digital computing technologies during the late twentieth century marked another important transition in higher education. Computer-assisted instruction systems and early educational software introduced new forms of technology-supported learning, although these systems primarily functioned as supplementary tools rather than transformative institutional mechanisms. The expansion of the internet during the 1990s and early 2000s significantly accelerated digital transformation within universities by enabling online communication, virtual learning environments, and distance education programs. Learning management systems such as Blackboard, Moodle, and Canvas allowed institutions to centralize course materials, monitor student participation, and facilitate online interaction between instructors and learners (Bates, 2019).

These digital platforms also contributed to the growth of learning analytics within higher education. Universities increasingly collect data related to student attendance, online engagement, assignment submission patterns, and academic performance. Initially, these systems were primarily designed to support administrative efficiency and course organization. Over time, however, data-driven educational technologies evolved into more sophisticated analytical systems capable of supporting predictive monitoring, adaptive instruction, and institutional decision-making.

The rapid advancement of artificial intelligence has significantly accelerated this transformation. Unlike earlier digital tools that primarily supported information delivery and communication, AI systems can perform more complex cognitive functions, such as natural language processing, predictive modeling, machine learning, automated classification, and data interpretation. These capabilities have enabled universities to implement intelligent tutoring systems, automated assessment tools, adaptive learning environments, and AI-assisted research applications that increasingly influence both pedagogical and administrative practices (Wang et al., 2024).

Several higher education institutions have already begun integrating AI-supported systems into teaching and student support initiatives. For example, Arizona State University has explored AI-enhanced tutoring and personalized learning systems designed to improve student engagement and retention. Similarly, Georgia State University has utilized predictive analytics systems to identify students at risk of academic underperformance and support early intervention strategies. These developments demonstrate how AI technologies are increasingly embedded within institutional approaches to student success and academic support.

AI integration has also become increasingly significant within academic research environments. Research-intensive institutions such as the Massachusetts Institute of Technology and Stanford University have expanded interdisciplinary AI research initiatives that involve medicine, engineering, economics, computational science, and social research. Machine learning systems are increasingly used to analyze large datasets, support computational modeling, conduct bibliometric analysis, and accelerate literature synthesis processes. These technologies allow researchers to address complex scientific and interdisciplinary problems that require large-scale analytical capacity and advanced computational infrastructure.

The COVID-19 pandemic further accelerated the adoption of digital and AI-supported technologies across higher education systems worldwide. Universities were compelled to transition rapidly to remote and hybrid learning environments, increasing institutional reliance on online learning platforms, video conferencing technologies, digital collaboration tools, and AI-supported educational systems. While this transition enabled academic continuity during the crisis, it also exposed major inequalities related to digital access, technological infrastructure, and institutional preparedness. The pandemic, therefore, highlighted both the opportunities and the structural limitations of technology-mediated higher education environments.

At the same time, the growing integration of AI into higher education has generated important ethical, institutional, and governance-related concerns. Universities increasingly utilize learning analytics systems, predictive monitoring tools, and performance dashboards to evaluate student engagement, faculty productivity, and institutional performance indicators. Although such systems may improve administrative efficiency and support evidence-based decision-making, scholars have raised concerns regarding data privacy, algorithmic bias, surveillance-oriented governance, and the reduction of academic work into quantifiable performance metrics (Williamson & Eynon, 2020).

Institutional responses to these challenges have begun to emerge across universities globally. Institutions such as the University of Cambridge and the University of Melbourne have introduced guidance on responsible use of generative AI in teaching and assessment. Similarly, UNESCO has emphasized the importance of ethical AI governance, transparency, and human-centered educational approaches in its policy recommendations concerning AI and education. These developments indicate that AI integration within universities is increasingly recognized not only as a technological issue but also as a governance and policy challenge requiring institutional oversight and ethical regulation.

The transformation associated with AI adoption is therefore not merely technological but also organizational, pedagogical, and professional. As universities increasingly incorporate AI-supported systems into teaching, research, governance, and assessment processes, the professoriate must adapt to changing expectations for digital literacy, interdisciplinary collaboration, algorithmic awareness, and technology-mediated scholarship. Consequently, the growing integration of AI into higher education is reshaping not only institutional operations but also the broader culture and professional identity of academic work within contemporary universities.

THEORETICAL FRAMEWORK

Understanding how artificial intelligence (AI) reshapes the professoriate requires a theoretical framework capable of explaining not only technological innovation but also the institutional, organizational, and professional transformations emerging within higher education. This chapter adopts a conceptual perspective grounded in three complementary theoretical approaches: Technological Determinism, Academic Capitalism Theory, and Human–AI Collaboration Theory. These perspectives were selected because they collectively explain how AI influences institutional restructuring, academic labor, governance systems, and evolving relationships between human expertise and computational technologies.

The selection of these theories was guided by the chapter's central objective of examining AI not merely as a technological tool but as a broader institutional force that reshapes teaching practices, research processes, governance mechanisms, and professional identity within universities. Although alternative frameworks such as Sociotechnical Systems Theory, Institutional Theory, and Professional Identity Theory also provide valuable insights into technological change, the present chapter prioritizes theories that more directly explain the interaction between technological transformation, managerial governance, and academic labor restructuring in AI-mediated higher education environments.

Technological Determinism provides the first analytical foundation for this chapter. This perspective suggests that technological innovation plays a significant role in shaping institutional structures, social practices, and professional relationships (Castells, 2010). Within higher education, AI technologies increasingly influence how knowledge is generated, evaluated, and disseminated. The relevance of Technological Determinism in this chapter lies in its ability to explain how emerging technologies alter the organization of academic work and institutional processes. AI-supported learning systems, predictive analytics platforms, automated grading tools, and generative AI applications introduce new forms of pedagogical organization and decision-making that gradually reshape traditional academic practices. However, this chapter does not adopt a purely deterministic interpretation that portrays technology as an autonomous force operating independently of social and institutional contexts. Instead, the theory is used critically to explain how technological capabilities create pressures for institutional adaptation while recognizing that universities retain agency in determining how AI systems are implemented and governed.

Academic Capitalism Theory provides a second important analytical lens for understanding AI integration within universities. This perspective emphasizes how higher education institutions increasingly operate within market-oriented environments shaped by competition, performance metrics, commercialization, and managerial accountability (Marginson, 2016). The theory is particularly relevant for analyzing the growing reliance on AI-supported governance systems within contemporary universities. Learning analytics platforms, publication tracking systems, citation metrics, and predictive performance dashboards reflect broader institutional trends toward quantification and data-driven management. AI technologies may intensify these tendencies by enabling universities to monitor faculty productivity, student performance, and institutional outcomes more efficiently and continuously. Within this framework, AI is not viewed simply as an educational innovation but also as a managerial instrument that may reinforce audit cultures, metric-driven evaluation systems, and competitive institutional behavior. Academic Capitalism

Theory, therefore, helps explain tensions between technological efficiency and academic autonomy, particularly in contexts where quantitative performance indicators increasingly shape academic careers and institutional priorities.

Human–AI Collaboration Theory offers a complementary perspective that moves beyond narratives of technological replacement. Rather than assuming that AI will substitute human expertise, this perspective emphasizes cooperative relationships between humans and intelligent systems (Brynjolfsson & McAfee, 2017). The theory is especially useful for understanding how professors increasingly interact with AI technologies as supportive tools in teaching, research, and governance. AI systems may assist with tasks such as data analysis, literature synthesis, adaptive instruction, administrative monitoring, and predictive modeling. At the same time, human academics continue to provide ethical judgment, disciplinary interpretation, creativity, mentorship, and contextual understanding. This perspective aligns with the chapter's argument that the future professoriate will likely operate within hybrid academic environments characterized by continuous interaction between computational systems and human intellectual labor. Human–AI Collaboration Theory, therefore, helps explain the transformation of academic roles from traditional knowledge transmission toward facilitation, interpretation, critical evaluation, and interdisciplinary collaboration.

While these three theories form the primary analytical foundation of the chapter, alternative theoretical perspectives were also considered. Sociotechnical Systems Theory emphasizes the mutual interaction between technology and social structures and could provide valuable insights into institutional adaptation processes. Institutional theory may explain how universities respond to external pressures, legitimacy concerns, and policy expectations surrounding AI adoption. Similarly, Professional Identity Theory could deepen analysis of how academics negotiate changes in scholarly identity, authority, and professional values within digitally mediated environments. However, these perspectives were not adopted as primary frameworks because the chapter focuses more specifically on the structural transformation of academic labor, governance systems, and human–technology interaction in relation to AI integration.

Together, Technological Determinism, Academic Capitalism Theory, and Human–AI Collaboration Theory provide an integrated conceptual foundation for examining the transformation of the professoriate in the age of AI. The theories collectively explain how technological innovation reshapes pedagogical structures, influences governance mechanisms, alters professional expectations, and redefines relationships between human scholars and intelligent systems. Rather than viewing AI integration as inherently beneficial or disruptive, the combined theoretical framework enables this chapter to critically examine the opportunities, tensions, and institutional contradictions emerging within increasingly AI-mediated higher education environments.

Methodological Approach

This chapter adopts a conceptual review approach using a structured narrative synthesis to examine how artificial intelligence (AI) is reshaping the professoriate in higher education institutions. The purpose of the chapter is not to conduct empirical testing but to critically synthesize existing scholarly literature on the institutional, pedagogical, governance-related, and professional implications of AI integration within academic environments.

A structured literature search was conducted using major academic databases, including Scopus, Web of Science, ERIC, and Google Scholar. The literature search focused primarily on peer-reviewed journal articles, scholarly books, review studies, and higher education policy literature published between 2018 and 2026. This timeframe was selected because it captures the rapid expansion of generative AI systems, learning analytics, adaptive educational technologies, and AI-supported governance mechanisms in higher education following the acceleration of digital transformation during and after the COVID-19 pandemic.

The search process utilized combinations of keywords such as "artificial intelligence in higher education," "AI and professoriate," "digital pedagogy," "generative AI in universities," "academic governance and AI," "learning analytics," "human–AI collaboration," "digital scholarly identity," and "AI-supported research." Boolean operators and database-specific filters were applied to refine search results and ensure relevance to higher education contexts.

The inclusion criteria for literature selection consisted of:

- peer-reviewed academic publications;
- higher education-focused studies;
- conceptual, empirical, and review-based scholarly works related to AI integration in universities;
- English-language publications; and
- studies addressing teaching, research, governance, ethics, or academic identity in relation to AI technologies.

The exclusion criteria included:

- non-academic opinion articles and blogs;
- Industry reports are lacking methodological transparency.
- studies unrelated to higher education contexts;

- duplicate publications; and
- sources focused exclusively on primary or secondary education without broader relevance to university systems.

The selected literature was analyzed through thematic synthesis. During the synthesis process, recurring themes related to AI-augmented teaching, AI-enhanced research productivity, algorithmic governance, academic integrity, digital scholarly identity, and human–AI collaboration were identified and comparatively examined across studies. These thematic patterns informed the conceptual framework proposed in this chapter.

Rather than attempting to provide exhaustive systematic review coverage, this chapter aims to develop a theoretically informed conceptual understanding of how AI technologies are transforming academic roles and institutional structures within higher education. The chapter, therefore, combines insights from digital pedagogy, academic governance studies, and technology-society scholarship to critically interpret emerging developments in AI-supported higher education environments critically.

The methodological approach adopted in this chapter acknowledges the rapidly evolving nature of AI technologies and recognizes that many institutional practices surrounding generative AI and algorithmic governance are still emerging. Consequently, the chapter emphasizes analytical interpretation and conceptual integration rather than definitive causal claims.

CONCEPTUAL FRAMEWORK

The conceptual framework proposed in this chapter moves beyond a descriptive categorization of teaching, research, governance, and professional identity by emphasizing the relational and transformative mechanisms through which artificial intelligence (AI) reshapes the professoriate in higher education. Rather than treating these dimensions as isolated domains, the framework conceptualizes AI integration as a dynamic institutional process that produces interconnected pedagogical, organizational, and professional transformations.

At the foundational level, AI integration within universities introduces technological systems such as generative AI tools, adaptive learning platforms, predictive analytics systems, automated assessment technologies, and AI-supported research applications into academic environments. The adoption of these technologies initiates a process of pedagogical restructuring in which traditional lecture-centered instructional models gradually shift toward personalized, data-driven, and technology-mediated learning environments. Learning analytics, intelligent tutoring systems, and adaptive educational platforms alter how educational content is delivered, monitored, and evaluated, thereby changing the pedagogical architecture of higher education.

These pedagogical transformations subsequently contribute to a transformation of the faculty role. As AI systems increasingly automate routine academic tasks such as grading, content summarization, data analysis, and administrative monitoring, professors transition from conventional knowledge transmitters toward facilitators of learning, interdisciplinary collaborators, digital mentors, and ethical interpreters of AI-generated information. Academic work increasingly requires competencies related to digital pedagogy, data literacy, algorithmic awareness, and responsible technology use. Consequently, the professional responsibilities of academics become more technologically mediated and institutionally adaptive.

Simultaneously, expanding AI integration generates governance pressures within universities. Data-driven management systems, performance analytics, predictive monitoring tools, and algorithmic evaluation mechanisms increasingly influence institutional decision-making across faculty assessment, research productivity, student performance monitoring, and resource allocation. These developments intensify tensions surrounding academic autonomy, surveillance, metric-driven evaluation cultures, and institutional accountability. The framework, therefore, recognizes governance transformation as a mediating institutional mechanism through which AI reshapes power relations and administrative structures within higher education.

These cumulative transformations ultimately contribute to the adaptation of digital identity among academics. As teaching practices, research processes, and governance systems become increasingly AI-mediated, professors are compelled to renegotiate their scholarly identities within digitally networked academic environments. Academics increasingly engage with AI-supported research tools, online dissemination platforms, interdisciplinary collaborations, and digitally mediated forms of scholarly communication. This adaptation process reshapes how professors understand professional expertise, intellectual authority, academic labor, and ethical responsibility in technologically evolving institutional contexts.

The framework, therefore, conceptualizes AI integration not as a singular technological intervention but as a cascading institutional process in which technological adoption triggers interconnected pedagogical restructuring, faculty role transformation, governance pressures, and adaptation of digital scholarly identity. These dimensions interact continuously rather than sequentially, creating feedback loops among institutional governance systems, academic labor practices, and evolving forms of human–AI collaboration in higher education.

TRANSFORMATION OF TEACHING ROLES

Artificial intelligence (AI) is increasingly transforming teaching practices in higher education by reshaping how educators design, deliver, and evaluate learning experiences. Traditional models of teaching, which often relied on lecture-based instruction and one-directional knowledge transmission, are gradually evolving toward more interactive, personalized, and technology-supported approaches. AI-enabled tools provide educators with new opportunities to analyze student learning patterns, personalize instructional content, and support student engagement in more dynamic ways. As a result, the role of professors is shifting from that of information providers to facilitators of learning environments that integrate both human expertise and technological capabilities.

One of the most significant contributions of AI in teaching is the development of intelligent tutoring systems. These systems use machine learning algorithms and natural language processing to analyze student responses and adapt instructional materials based on individual learning needs. By continuously monitoring student progress, intelligent tutoring systems can identify areas where learners struggle and provide targeted feedback or additional learning resources. This adaptive approach helps create personalized learning pathways that accommodate diverse student abilities and learning styles (Wang et al., 2024). For example, a student who demonstrates difficulty understanding a particular concept may receive supplementary explanations, practice exercises, or multimedia learning materials designed to reinforce that topic.

AI-driven learning platforms also support the concept of adaptive learning environments. Adaptive systems dynamically modify course content and learning sequences based on students' performance data, ensuring that learners receive appropriate levels of challenge and support. These technologies can enhance student motivation and improve academic outcomes by enabling learners to progress at their own pace while receiving immediate feedback on their performance. In this way, AI helps shift higher education toward more student-centered pedagogical models.

Despite these potential advantages, the growing reliance on AI-supported teaching systems also introduces important pedagogical concerns. Generative AI tools and automated tutoring systems may occasionally produce inaccurate or misleading responses, commonly referred to as "hallucinated" outputs, which can create confusion among students if information is accepted without critical verification. Excessive reliance on AI-generated explanations may also foster passive learning, with students prioritizing convenience and quick answers over deeper analytical engagement and independent reasoning. Furthermore, while adaptive learning systems may perform effectively in structured, skills-oriented disciplines, their application in humanities and interpretive social science contexts remains more limited because many forms of learning in these disciplines involve ambiguity, contextual interpretation, ethical reflection, and open-ended discussion that are difficult to quantify algorithmically. AI-supported tutoring environments may also lack the emotional sensitivity, mentorship capacity, and relational understanding that characterize meaningful human educational interactions. Consequently, although AI technologies can support instructional efficiency and personalized learning, they cannot fully replace the intellectual, emotional, and ethical dimensions of human-centered pedagogy within higher education.

Another important aspect of AI integration in teaching is automating routine administrative and assessment tasks. AI-powered grading systems can evaluate objective assessments such as multiple-choice tests, quizzes, and coding exercises with high accuracy and efficiency. Automated grading tools reduce the time faculty members spend on repetitive evaluation tasks, allowing them to dedicate more time to meaningful interactions with students. For instance, professors can focus on mentoring students, facilitating discussions, and guiding collaborative learning activities rather than managing large volumes of grading work.

AI technologies also support instructors in designing more engaging and interactive learning experiences. Learning analytics tools provide insights into student engagement patterns, attendance behavior, and assignment performance. By analyzing these data, instructors can identify students who may be at risk of academic difficulties and intervene early with additional guidance or support. These insights enable educators to make informed pedagogical decisions that improve the effectiveness of their teaching strategies.

The integration of AI into teaching practices also creates new pedagogical roles for professors. Rather than functioning solely as content experts who deliver lectures, educators increasingly act as learning designers, mentors, and facilitators of collaborative knowledge creation. Professors curate digital learning resources, design problem-based learning activities, and guide students in critically evaluating information generated by AI systems. This shift reflects a broader transformation in higher education, where the emphasis moves from memorization and content delivery toward analytical thinking, creativity, and problem-solving skills.

Despite these advantages, the transformation of teaching roles also introduces new challenges for educators. Professors must develop digital literacy and technological competencies to integrate AI tools into their instructional practices effectively. They must also consider ethical issues related to data privacy, algorithmic bias, and the appropriate use of AI in educational contexts. Additionally, educators must ensure that technology enhances rather than replaces meaningful human interactions in the learning process.

Overall, the integration of AI into higher education is redefining professors' roles as facilitators of technology-enhanced learning environments. By combining human expertise with intelligent digital tools, educators can create more personalized, inclusive, and effective educational experiences that prepare students for the evolving demands of the knowledge economy.

AI IN RESEARCH PRODUCTIVITY

Artificial intelligence (AI) is increasingly influencing academic research by transforming how knowledge is collected, analyzed, interpreted, and disseminated within higher education institutions. Research activities that previously depended heavily on time-intensive manual processes—such as literature screening, data organization, coding, transcription, and statistical analysis—are now increasingly supported by machine learning systems, natural language processing tools, and automated analytical platforms. These technologies enable researchers to process large volumes of information more rapidly and identify patterns that may be difficult to detect through conventional methods alone (Long & Aleven, 2025). As a result, AI is reshaping research productivity, interdisciplinary collaboration, and the organization of scholarly work across multiple academic disciplines.

One major area in which AI influences research productivity involves literature synthesis and knowledge discovery. AI-supported research tools can scan large collections of journal articles, conference proceedings, and bibliographic databases to identify thematic patterns, citation relationships, and emerging research trends. Such tools may help scholars locate relevant literature, organize references, and identify research gaps more efficiently than traditional manual review processes. Bibliometric analysis platforms supported by AI can also map citation networks and scholarly collaborations, allowing researchers to examine the evolution of research domains and identify influential publications or institutions. These capabilities may be particularly useful in fields characterized by rapidly expanding bodies of literature where manual review alone becomes increasingly difficult.

AI technologies are also widely used for large-scale data analysis and predictive modeling. In disciplines such as medicine, economics, psychology, environmental science, and computational social science, researchers increasingly rely on machine learning systems to process extensive datasets and identify statistical relationships. Predictive algorithms can support pattern recognition, forecasting, image analysis, and behavioral modeling, thereby expanding researchers' analytical capacity. For example, AI-assisted systems may help medical researchers identify disease patterns within diagnostic datasets. In contrast, environmental researchers may use computational models to examine climate-related variables across long-term datasets. Such applications illustrate how AI can enhance computational efficiency and facilitate interdisciplinary research that requires advanced analytical infrastructure.

At the same time, the growing integration of AI into research environments has generated important methodological and epistemological concerns. Increased computational efficiency does not necessarily guarantee stronger conceptual rigor or more reliable scientific interpretation. AI systems frequently operate through algorithmic processes that are not fully transparent to users, creating what scholars often describe as "black box" decision-making systems. Researchers may therefore struggle to fully understand how certain outputs, classifications, or predictive relationships are generated. This lack of interpretive transparency can complicate reproducibility, methodological accountability, and scholarly verification, particularly when researchers rely heavily on proprietary AI tools without critically evaluating the underlying algorithms or datasets.

The increasing use of generative AI in academic writing has also intensified debates surrounding authorship, originality, and intellectual responsibility. AI systems are now capable of generating summaries, analytical interpretations, coding suggestions, and literature overviews that resemble human-written scholarly text. While such tools may improve drafting efficiency and information organization, they also pose risks of superficial synthesis, fabricated citations, inaccurate interpretations, and overreliance on automated outputs. In some cases, generative AI systems may produce persuasive but factually incorrect content, commonly referred to as "hallucinated" information. If researchers fail to verify AI-generated outputs critically, inaccurate information may enter scholarly discourse and compromise research quality.

Another important concern is algorithmic bias in AI-assisted research systems. Machine learning models are shaped by the datasets they are trained on. If those datasets contain historical biases, disciplinary biases, or unrepresentative sampling, AI systems may reproduce or amplify distorted interpretations. In research involving social, demographic, or behavioral data, biased algorithms may generate discriminatory outcomes or misleading analytical conclusions. Consequently, scholars must critically examine both the quality of training data and the assumptions embedded within computational models before integrating AI-generated findings into academic research.

The growing use of AI in research productivity also raises questions regarding academic labor and professional expectations within universities. Institutions increasingly emphasize research output, publication metrics, citation impact, and grant acquisition as indicators of scholarly productivity. AI-supported systems may intensify these pressures by accelerating publication processes and enabling faster production of research materials. While some scholars view these technologies as opportunities to enhance efficiency and collaboration, others caution that excessive emphasis on productivity may encourage quantity-oriented research cultures at the expense of originality, critical reflection, and intellectual depth. The acceleration of research workflows through AI, therefore, introduces tensions between efficiency and scholarly rigor in contemporary academic environments.

Despite these concerns, AI technologies continue to offer significant opportunities for advanced interdisciplinary collaboration and expand analytical capabilities in higher education research. AI-supported systems may assist researchers in addressing complex scientific and social problems that require large-scale computational analysis and cross-disciplinary collaboration. However, the effective integration of AI into academic research depends on maintaining strong standards of methodological transparency, ethical accountability, and critical human oversight. Rather than replacing scholarly expertise, AI tools are most effective when used as supportive instruments that complement human interpretation, theoretical reasoning, and disciplinary judgment.

Overall, AI is reshaping research productivity by altering how scholars conduct literature synthesis, analyze data, collaborate across disciplines, and disseminate knowledge. Nevertheless, the long-term implications of AI-assisted research remain contested and context-dependent. The challenge for universities and researchers is therefore not simply adopting AI technologies but developing governance frameworks and research cultures that balance computational efficiency with intellectual rigor, methodological transparency, and ethical responsibility.

ACADEMIC GOVERNANCE AND DATA ANALYTICS

The integration of artificial intelligence (AI) and advanced data analytics into university governance systems has significant implications for the structure and functioning of higher education institutions. Traditionally, academic governance relied heavily on collegial decision-making processes involving faculty committees, academic senates, and administrative leadership. These systems emphasized peer evaluation, professional judgment, and disciplinary expertise in decisions related to curriculum design, faculty promotion, research funding, and institutional planning. However, the growing availability of institutional data and analytical technologies has introduced new mechanisms for monitoring performance and guiding decision-making within universities.

Universities increasingly employ learning analytics platforms, research management systems, and performance dashboards to evaluate teaching effectiveness, track research productivity, and allocate institutional resources. These systems collect and analyze large volumes of data related to student engagement, course completion rates, publication outputs, citation metrics, and grant funding. Institutional leaders can use these data to identify trends, assess institutional performance, and develop strategies to improve academic outcomes and organizational efficiency. As a result, data-driven governance has become an important component of modern university administration (Williamson & Eynon, 2020).

Learning analytics systems are particularly influential in monitoring teaching performance and student engagement. These platforms collect detailed information about student participation in online learning environments, including login frequency, assignment submissions, discussion forum activity, and assessment results. By analyzing these data, universities can identify patterns in student learning behavior and evaluate the effectiveness of instructional methods. Administrators and faculty members can use this information to design targeted interventions that support student success and reduce dropout rates. For example, predictive analytics models can identify students at risk of academic failure and recommend early support measures, such as tutoring or mentoring.

AI-supported governance systems also play an important role in evaluating faculty performance and research productivity. Many universities now rely on digital research management platforms that track publication records, citation impact, grant applications, and collaborative research activities. These systems provide administrators with comprehensive data about faculty achievements and research outputs, enabling institutions to measure academic performance more systematically. In some cases, such data are used to inform promotion decisions, tenure evaluations, and resource allocation strategies.

The use of AI and data analytics in academic governance can offer several advantages. Data-driven decision-making can improve transparency and accountability by providing objective evidence to support administrative decisions. Universities can also use analytics tools to identify areas of institutional strength and weakness, enabling them to develop strategic plans that enhance educational quality and research impact. Furthermore, predictive analytics can help institutions anticipate future challenges, such as declining enrollment trends or emerging research opportunities.

Despite these benefits, the growing reliance on AI and data analytics in academic governance also raises important concerns regarding academic autonomy and professional identity. Scholars have argued that data-driven evaluation systems may introduce new forms of managerial oversight within universities, potentially shifting power away from faculty-led governance structures toward administrative decision-making processes (Williamson & Eynon, 2020). When academic performance is evaluated primarily through quantitative metrics such as publication counts, citation indices, and student evaluation scores, there is a risk that complex scholarly contributions may be reduced to simplified numerical indicators.

Another concern relates to the potential biases embedded in algorithmic decision-making systems. Data analytics tools depend on the quality and representativeness of the data used to train their algorithms. If institutional datasets reflect existing inequalities or disciplinary biases, AI systems may inadvertently reinforce those patterns in faculty evaluations or resource allocation decisions. For instance, disciplines with traditionally higher publication rates or greater access to research funding may receive disproportionate recognition within data-driven evaluation systems.

Privacy and surveillance are also important issues associated with the use of learning analytics technologies. The collection of detailed data on student and faculty activities raises questions about consent, data ownership, and the ethical use of personal information. Universities must therefore establish clear policies governing data collection, storage, and usage to ensure that analytics systems respect the rights and privacy of academic community members.

In response to these challenges, many scholars emphasize the importance of maintaining a balanced approach to data-driven governance in higher education. While AI and analytics tools can provide valuable insights for institutional decision-making, they should complement rather than replace traditional forms of academic judgment and peer evaluation. Faculty participation in governance processes remains essential to ensure that institutional policies reflect the values and priorities of the academic community.

Overall, integrating AI and data analytics into university governance systems represents a significant transformation in the management of higher education institutions. By combining data-driven insights with collegial decision-making, universities can harness the benefits of technological innovation while preserving the intellectual autonomy and collaborative governance traditions that define academic life.

ETHICAL AND INTEGRITY CHALLENGES

The rapid advancement of generative artificial intelligence technologies has introduced significant ethical and academic integrity challenges within higher education. Generative AI systems, capable of producing human-like text, code, images, and analytical summaries, have become increasingly accessible to students and educators. Tools based on advanced language models can generate essays, research summaries, programming scripts, and even complex problem-solving responses within seconds. While these technologies offer valuable educational support, they also complicate the traditional methods universities use to evaluate authentic learning and academic honesty. As a result, academic institutions are facing new challenges in maintaining standards of integrity and intellectual accountability.

One of the primary concerns associated with generative AI in education is the potential for academic misconduct. Students may rely on AI tools to produce assignments, essays, and examination responses that appear original but are actually generated by automated systems. This situation makes it more difficult for instructors to determine whether submitted work genuinely reflects a student's understanding and intellectual effort. Traditional plagiarism detection tools, designed to identify copied text from existing sources, are often less effective at detecting AI-generated content because it may be newly generated rather than copied from previous publications.

The availability of generative AI tools also raises questions about the boundaries between legitimate academic assistance and unethical academic behavior. For example, students frequently use technological tools such as grammar checkers, citation managers, and statistical software to support their learning. Generative AI may be viewed as an extension of these digital aids, providing writing suggestions, summarizing academic texts, or assisting with coding tasks. However, the extent to which students can rely on AI-generated content without compromising academic integrity remains a topic of ongoing debate among educators and policymakers. Establishing clear guidelines regarding acceptable AI use is therefore essential for maintaining academic standards.

In response to these challenges, many educators emphasize the need to redesign assessment methods to evaluate higher-order cognitive skills better. Traditional assessment formats, such as take-home essays or standardized written examinations, may be more vulnerable to AI-assisted responses. To address this issue, instructors are increasingly exploring alternative evaluation approaches that emphasize analytical reasoning, critical reflection, and creative problem-solving (Selwyn, 2019). For instance, oral presentations, in-class discussions, project-based learning assignments, and collaborative research projects can provide opportunities for students to demonstrate their understanding in ways that are more difficult to replicate through automated tools.

Another ethical concern involves the transparency and accountability of AI-generated information. Generative AI systems often produce responses based on patterns learned from large datasets rather than verified factual knowledge. Consequently, AI-generated outputs may contain inaccuracies, biased interpretations, or fabricated references. If students or researchers rely on such outputs without critical evaluation, there is a risk that misinformation may enter academic discourse. Educators, therefore, play an important role in teaching students how to critically assess AI-generated content and verify information using reliable academic sources.

The use of AI in academic contexts also raises broader ethical questions related to intellectual property and authorship. When AI tools contribute to the creation of written content or analytical insights, determining the extent of human contribution becomes complex. Scholars must consider whether AI-assisted work should be disclosed, how such contributions should be acknowledged, and whether existing authorship conventions adequately reflect the role of AI technologies in scholarly production.

Furthermore, ethical challenges are not limited to student use of AI tools. Faculty members and researchers also increasingly employ AI technologies for tasks such as data analysis, literature reviews, and content generation. While these tools can enhance research efficiency, they require careful oversight to ensure methodological transparency and ethical research practices. Institutions must therefore develop policies that guide responsible AI use across both teaching and research activities.

Ultimately, addressing the ethical and integrity challenges associated with generative AI requires a balanced, proactive approach. Universities must combine clear institutional policies, updated assessment strategies, and comprehensive digital literacy education to ensure that AI technologies support learning rather than undermine academic integrity. By fostering a culture of ethical technology use and critical engagement with AI systems, higher education institutions can maintain academic standards while embracing the opportunities presented by technological innovation.

PROFESSIONAL IDENTITY OF THE PROFESSORIATE

The rapid integration of artificial intelligence (AI) into higher education is transforming not only institutional practices but also the professional identity of the professoriate. Traditionally, professors have been recognized as subject-matter experts responsible for teaching, conducting research, and contributing to academic governance. Their authority was largely derived from disciplinary expertise, scholarly publications, and mentorship within academic communities. However, as AI technologies increasingly shape how knowledge is created, disseminated, and evaluated, the roles and identities of professors are evolving in response to new technological and institutional demands.

One of the most notable changes in academics' professional identity is the shift toward interdisciplinary collaboration. Contemporary research challenges—such as climate change, public health crises, digital transformation, and social inequality—require expertise from multiple disciplines. AI technologies further encourage such collaboration by enabling researchers from diverse fields to work with shared datasets, computational models, and analytical tools. As a result, professors are increasingly required to work across disciplinary boundaries and collaborate with experts in fields such as data science, computer science, engineering, and social sciences. This shift encourages a more networked, collaborative form of academic identity, in which knowledge creation is often the result of collective intellectual effort rather than individual scholarly contributions.

Another important dimension of the evolving professoriate is the role of academics as facilitators of technology-enhanced learning environments. With the growing use of AI-driven educational tools, professors are no longer limited to delivering lectures and grading assignments. Instead, they act as learning designers who curate digital resources, integrate intelligent tutoring systems, and guide students in navigating complex digital information environments. This role requires educators to develop competencies in digital pedagogy, instructional design, and educational technology management. Professors must understand how AI tools operate, how they can be integrated effectively into course structures, and how they influence student learning behaviors.

The emergence of AI technologies also requires academics to act as ethical stewards of digital innovation. As AI systems become increasingly embedded in teaching, research, and institutional governance, professors play an essential role in evaluating the ethical implications of these technologies. Issues such as algorithmic bias, data privacy, intellectual property, and responsible AI use require careful consideration within academic settings. Scholars must critically assess the reliability and fairness of AI-driven systems while also guiding students in understanding the ethical dimensions of technology use. In this sense, professors serve as guardians of academic integrity and ethical scholarship in an increasingly digital academic environment.

The evolving professional identity of the professoriate also involves developing digital literacy and technological competence. Digital literacy extends beyond basic technology use; it includes the ability to critically evaluate digital information, understand algorithmic processes, and effectively use computational tools for teaching and research. Professors must remain informed about emerging technologies that influence their disciplines and continuously update their skills to remain effective educators and researchers. Professional development programs and institutional support mechanisms are therefore essential in helping faculty members adapt to rapidly changing technological environments.

Furthermore, the increasing reliance on digital platforms for academic communication and collaboration has transformed how scholars engage with global academic communities. Professors now disseminate their research through online repositories, digital journals, and academic networking platforms, enabling broader visibility and international collaboration. These digital platforms also allow scholars to engage with public audiences, policymakers, and industry partners, thereby expanding the societal impact of academic research.

The transformation of academic identity in AI-mediated environments may also contribute to new forms of professional pressure and labor precarity within higher education. Faculty members are increasingly expected to adapt to emerging digital technologies continuously, integrate AI-supported systems into teaching and research, and maintain productivity within rapidly evolving institutional environments. These expectations may intensify workload pressures, particularly for academics who already face heavy teaching responsibilities, administrative obligations, and performance evaluation demands. Furthermore, the growing reliance on digital platforms and data-driven performance systems may contribute to anxiety surrounding professional visibility, publication metrics, and technological competence. In some cases, academics may feel pressured to adopt AI tools not because of pedagogical value but because of institutional expectations related to efficiency, innovation, and competitiveness. Consequently, the transformation of scholarly identity should not be interpreted solely as a process of technological empowerment but also as a negotiation involving adaptation pressures, institutional surveillance, and changing expectations surrounding academic labor.

Despite these opportunities, the transformation of professional identity also presents challenges. Some academics may experience concerns regarding technological displacement, increased workload associated with learning new technologies, or the potential erosion of traditional academic values. Addressing these concerns requires institutions to provide adequate support, training, and governance frameworks that ensure technology enhances rather than undermines the academic profession.

In conclusion, the professional identity of the professoriate is undergoing a significant transformation as AI technologies reshape higher education. Professors increasingly function as interdisciplinary collaborators, technology facilitators, and ethical guardians of digital innovation. By cultivating digital literacy, critical awareness of algorithmic systems, and a commitment to responsible technology use, the professoriate can continue to play a central role in advancing knowledge and guiding the future of higher education in the age of artificial intelligence.

DISCUSSION

The growing integration of artificial intelligence (AI) into higher education has generated significant scholarly interest. However, the long-term implications of these technologies for the professoriate remain contested and unevenly understood. Although existing literature frequently presents AI as a transformative force capable of enhancing teaching efficiency, research productivity, and institutional decision-making, the evidence supporting these claims remains fragmented across disciplines, institutional settings, and technological applications. Consequently, the relationship between AI and the academic profession should be interpreted cautiously rather than through deterministic assumptions of inevitable technological progress.

One major area of debate concerns the extent to which AI genuinely improves educational quality. Supporters of AI-driven pedagogy argue that adaptive learning systems, intelligent tutoring platforms, and learning analytics can personalize instruction and support student engagement. However, critics caution that many AI-supported educational systems remain heavily dependent on quantitative behavioral data that may not adequately capture deeper forms of learning, such as critical reasoning, creativity, reflective thinking, or disciplinary interpretation. Furthermore, evidence regarding the long-term effectiveness of AI-assisted learning environments remains inconsistent across educational contexts and disciplines. While some technology-intensive disciplines may benefit from automated feedback systems, humanities and socially interpretive disciplines may encounter greater limitations due to the contextual and subjective nature of knowledge production.

The integration of generative AI into academic work also raises unresolved questions regarding authorship, intellectual authenticity, and scholarly labor. Although AI tools may accelerate literature synthesis, coding assistance, and data analysis, increased efficiency does not necessarily guarantee stronger scholarly rigor or conceptual originality. Machine-generated outputs may reproduce existing biases, generate inaccurate information, or encourage superficial synthesis rather than critical interpretation. As a result, debates continue regarding the appropriate boundaries between AI-assisted support and independent scholarly contribution. Universities and academic publishers have begun developing AI usage guidelines, yet institutional policies remain inconsistent and continue to evolve rapidly.

Another unresolved tension concerns algorithmic governance and academic autonomy. Data-driven performance systems may improve institutional monitoring and administrative efficiency, but they may also intensify managerial forms of governance within universities. Increased reliance on publication metrics, predictive analytics, and performance dashboards could reshape academic priorities by encouraging measurable productivity over exploratory, interdisciplinary, or community-engaged scholarship. Such developments raise concerns regarding the potential reduction of complex academic work into simplified quantitative indicators. The extent to which AI-driven governance strengthens institutional accountability or reinforces surveillance-oriented management practices remains a debate in higher education research.

The transformation of faculty roles also presents contradictory implications. On one hand, AI technologies may reduce repetitive administrative tasks and allow academics to focus more on mentorship, creativity, and conceptual work. On the other hand, technological integration may intensify workload, create continuous digital adaptation pressures, and foster expectations for perpetual technological upskilling. Faculty members across institutions and disciplines may therefore experience AI integration differently depending on institutional infrastructure, disciplinary culture, technological access, and governance support systems. These uneven experiences complicate universal claims regarding the benefits or risks of AI adoption in higher education.

Additionally, substantial global inequalities remain embedded within AI integration processes. Universities with advanced technological infrastructure and financial resources may adopt AI-supported systems more rapidly than institutions operating within resource-constrained environments. Consequently, AI integration may unintentionally widen existing disparities in research capacity, digital access, and institutional competitiveness across regions and educational systems. Questions surrounding technological dependency, digital colonialism, and unequal access to AI infrastructure, therefore, require further scholarly attention.

The discussion presented in this chapter should therefore be understood as a conceptual interpretation of emerging developments rather than definitive empirical conclusions. While AI technologies undoubtedly influence contemporary higher education systems, their long-term institutional, pedagogical, and professional consequences remain dynamic, context-dependent, and contested. Future research must continue examining how AI integration affects academic labor, governance systems, pedagogical quality, disciplinary practices, and scholarly identity across diverse higher education environments.

Limitations

This chapter has several limitations that should be acknowledged. First, the study adopts a conceptual review approach, using structured narrative synthesis rather than empirical data collection. Consequently, the chapter does not provide primary evidence derived from interviews, surveys, ethnographic observation, or institutional case analysis. The arguments developed in this chapter, therefore, rely primarily on interpretation and synthesis of existing scholarly literature.

Second, the field of artificial intelligence in higher education is evolving rapidly. Technologies such as generative AI systems, adaptive learning platforms, and algorithmic governance tools continue to develop at a pace that often exceeds the speed of academic publication. As a result, some institutional practices, ethical concerns, and governance responses discussed in this chapter may continue to change significantly over time.

Third, the existing literature on AI in higher education remains uneven across disciplines, institutional contexts, and geographical regions. Much of the currently available research focuses on technologically advanced educational systems, particularly in Western, highly digitized institutional contexts. Consequently, the chapter may not fully capture the experiences of institutions operating within resource-constrained or technologically unequal environments.

Fourth, many existing studies on AI integration emphasize projected benefits, institutional experimentation, or emerging practices rather than long-term evidence regarding educational outcomes, faculty well-being, or governance consequences. Longitudinal empirical evidence examining the sustained impact of AI on academic labor, institutional structures, and scholarly identity remains relatively limited.

Finally, because the chapter synthesizes literature from multiple disciplinary traditions—including digital pedagogy, governance studies, educational technology, and sociology of higher education—some conceptual interpretations may remain open to alternative theoretical perspectives. Future research employing empirical, comparative, and interdisciplinary methodologies will therefore be necessary to further validate, refine, and extend the conceptual arguments presented in this chapter.

RECOMMENDATIONS AND SOLUTIONS

The integration of artificial intelligence (AI) into higher education presents both significant opportunities and complex institutional challenges. While AI technologies may enhance instructional efficiency, research productivity, and data-informed decision-making, their successful integration requires governance structures that preserve academic autonomy, ethical accountability, and human-centered educational values. Universities must therefore adopt balanced and context-sensitive strategies that support responsible technological innovation without reducing higher education to purely automated or metric-driven systems.

First, universities should strengthen faculty AI literacy and professional development initiatives. As AI technologies increasingly influence teaching, research, and academic administration, faculty members require ongoing training in digital pedagogy, generative AI systems, learning analytics, and ethical technology use. Professional development programs should move beyond technical training alone and include critical discussions regarding algorithmic bias, academic integrity, data governance, and responsible AI-assisted scholarship. Institutions such as the University of Michigan and the National University of Singapore have already introduced faculty development initiatives focused on generative AI and digital pedagogy, demonstrating the growing institutional recognition that technological adaptation requires continuous academic support and training.

Second, higher education institutions should establish transparent ethical governance frameworks for AI integration. Universities increasingly rely on AI-supported systems for teaching, assessment, student monitoring, research analytics, and institutional decision-making. Consequently, institutions must develop clear policies addressing data privacy, algorithmic accountability, authorship disclosure, academic integrity, and equitable access to technological resources. Governance frameworks should also ensure that faculty members remain actively involved in decisions related to AI adoption, evaluation systems, and institutional policy formation. Maintaining participatory governance structures is essential to prevent excessive dependence on surveillance-oriented management practices or purely quantitative performance metrics.

Third, universities should redesign assessment and teaching practices to align with AI-mediated learning environments. Traditional assessment models based primarily on standardized essays or take-home assignments may become increasingly vulnerable to AI-generated content. Educational institutions should therefore emphasize assessment approaches that evaluate analytical reasoning, critical reflection, creativity, and applied problem-solving. Oral presentations, collaborative projects, case-based analysis, reflective portfolios, and in-class discussions may provide more meaningful opportunities for students to demonstrate intellectual engagement beyond automated content generation. At the same time, institutions should encourage critical AI literacy among students by teaching them how to evaluate AI-generated information, recognize algorithmic limitations, and engage responsibly with digital technologies.

Fourth, universities should support interdisciplinary collaboration and responsible innovation in AI-related educational research. The challenges associated with AI integration extend across multiple fields, including education, computer science, sociology, psychology, ethics, and public policy. Interdisciplinary collaboration can therefore help institutions better understand the pedagogical, organizational, and ethical implications of AI adoption. Research centers and collaborative initiatives focused on AI in education may contribute to the development of more inclusive, transparent, and human-centered technological systems while ensuring that educational priorities remain central to innovation processes.

Fifth, institutions should address issues of digital inequality and technological accessibility. Universities with advanced technological infrastructure are often better positioned to adopt AI-supported systems than institutions operating in resource-constrained environments. Without careful planning, AI integration may therefore widen existing inequalities in educational access, research capacity, and institutional competitiveness. Universities and policymakers must ensure equitable access to digital infrastructure, technological resources, and faculty support systems so that AI adoption does not reinforce structural disparities within higher education systems.

Finally, universities should maintain human-centered pedagogical and governance principles throughout AI integration processes. Although AI technologies may improve efficiency and analytical capacity, they cannot fully replace the interpretive judgment, ethical reasoning, mentorship, and relational engagement provided by human academics. The role of professors as mentors, critical thinkers, and facilitators of intellectual inquiry remains central to the mission of higher education. Consequently, AI systems should function as supportive instruments that augment rather than diminish human scholarly expertise and academic creativity.

Overall, the responsible integration of AI in higher education requires more than the mere adoption of technology. Universities must combine ethical governance, faculty development, pedagogical innovation, interdisciplinary collaboration, and equitable institutional policies to ensure that AI technologies strengthen rather than undermine the intellectual and human foundations of academic life.

FUTURE RESEARCH DIRECTIONS

The rapid integration of artificial intelligence (AI) into higher education has generated significant interest among scholars, policymakers, and educators. While current research has explored several aspects of AI adoption in universities—such as adaptive learning systems, automated research tools, and data-driven governance—many questions remain unanswered. As AI technologies continue to evolve, future research must examine the long-term implications of these innovations for academic institutions, faculty roles, and knowledge production processes. Addressing these research gaps is essential for developing a deeper understanding of how AI can be responsibly integrated into higher education while preserving academic values and institutional integrity.

One important direction for future research is to conduct longitudinal studies examining the long-term effects of AI adoption on academic career trajectories and faculty evaluation systems. The increasing use of data analytics and algorithmic systems in academic governance has introduced new metrics for assessing faculty productivity, including publication counts, citation indices, grant acquisition rates, and teaching evaluation scores. While these metrics can provide measurable indicators of academic performance, their integration with AI-based analytics tools may reshape promotion and tenure processes within universities. Future studies should investigate whether AI-driven evaluation systems influence the criteria used for academic promotions, hiring decisions, and research funding allocation. Researchers may also explore how AI-supported performance analytics affect early-career scholars, interdisciplinary researchers, and scholars working in fields where traditional quantitative metrics may not fully capture scholarly impact.

Another significant area for future research concerns cross-cultural variations in AI adoption across global higher education systems. Universities around the world operate within diverse cultural, institutional, and regulatory contexts that shape how technological innovations are implemented. While some countries have advanced digital infrastructures and strong governmental support for AI research, others face challenges related to technological access, funding limitations, or regulatory constraints. Comparative studies examining AI adoption in universities across different regions can provide valuable insights into how institutional traditions, educational policies, and economic conditions influence the integration of AI technologies. Such research can help identify best practices and policy frameworks that support responsible AI adoption while addressing contextual challenges unique to specific educational systems.

Future research should also focus on the ethical implications of algorithmic governance in higher education institutions. As universities increasingly rely on AI-supported analytics platforms to monitor student engagement, evaluate faculty performance, and guide institutional decision-making, concerns have emerged regarding transparency, accountability, and fairness. Algorithmic systems may unintentionally reproduce biases present in historical data or prioritize measurable outcomes over qualitative aspects of academic work. Researchers should examine how algorithmic decision-making systems influence academic governance structures, faculty autonomy, and institutional accountability. Additionally, studies should examine how universities can design governance frameworks that ensure ethical oversight, transparency, and meaningful faculty participation in decisions regarding AI adoption.

The impact of generative AI on academic publishing and knowledge production represents another important area for future investigation. Generative AI tools capable of producing scholarly text, summarizing research findings, and assisting with data analysis are increasingly used by academics. While these tools can enhance research efficiency, they also raise complex questions about authorship, intellectual property, and scholarly credibility. For example, future research should examine whether AI-generated content should be explicitly disclosed in academic publications and how such contributions should be acknowledged within existing authorship guidelines. Furthermore, scholars should investigate how generative AI may influence peer-review processes, editorial practices, and the integrity of scholarly communication. Understanding these implications will help academic institutions and publishers develop appropriate standards and policies for AI-assisted scholarship.

Another critical research direction involves examining the pedagogical implications of human–AI collaboration in teaching and learning environments. As AI-powered educational technologies become more sophisticated, universities are increasingly experimenting with hybrid teaching models that combine human instruction with intelligent tutoring systems and adaptive learning platforms. Future studies should evaluate the effectiveness of these human–AI collaborative models in enhancing student engagement, critical thinking skills, and academic achievement. Experimental research designs could compare traditional teaching approaches with AI-supported learning environments to determine whether AI technologies genuinely improve learning outcomes or alter instructional methods without producing significant educational benefits.

Additionally, research should investigate how AI-supported educational technologies influence student learning behaviors and cognitive development. AI-driven platforms often provide instant feedback, automated recommendations, and personalized learning pathways. While these features can enhance learning efficiency, it is important to examine whether they also affect students' ability to develop independent problem-solving and critical reasoning skills. Scholars should explore how students interact with AI systems, how they interpret AI-generated feedback, and whether reliance on automated assistance affects their intellectual autonomy and creativity.

Another promising research area concerns the role of AI in supporting inclusive and equitable education. AI technologies have the potential to address educational inequalities by providing personalized learning support, language translation tools, and accessibility features for students with diverse learning needs. For example, AI-based speech recognition systems can assist students with disabilities, while translation technologies can support international students studying in multilingual academic environments. Future research should evaluate how AI tools can be designed and implemented to promote equitable access to educational opportunities. At the same time, scholars must examine potential risks associated with algorithmic bias and digital inequality that may arise if AI systems are trained on unrepresentative datasets or deployed in contexts with unequal technological access.

Research on faculty perceptions and attitudes toward AI adoption also represents an important area for further investigation. The successful integration of AI technologies in higher education depends not only on technological infrastructure but also on educators' willingness to adopt and use these tools. Studies should explore how faculty members perceive the benefits and challenges of AI technologies, how they adapt their teaching and research practices to technological change, and what institutional support they require to integrate AI effectively into their professional activities.

Another emerging research topic involves the psychological and professional impacts of AI on the academic workforce. As AI systems increasingly automate routine tasks and introduce new forms of performance monitoring, faculty members may experience changes in workload distribution, job expectations, and professional identity. Future research should examine how these transformations affect academic job satisfaction, career stability, and perceptions of professional autonomy. Understanding these dynamics will help universities develop policies that support faculty well-being while encouraging responsible technological innovation.

Finally, scholars should explore policy frameworks and governance models that guide responsible AI integration in higher education. Universities, governments, and international organizations are beginning to develop guidelines for the ethical use of AI in education. Comparative research examining these policy initiatives can provide valuable insights into effective governance strategies that balance technological advancement with ethical responsibility. Studies may also examine how international collaborations and global research networks can help develop shared standards for AI governance in higher education.

In conclusion, the rapid advancement of artificial intelligence presents numerous opportunities and challenges for the future of higher education. While existing research has provided valuable insights into the potential applications of AI in teaching, research, and governance, much remains to be explored. Future research must adopt interdisciplinary and international perspectives to understand better how AI technologies influence academic institutions, professional identities, and knowledge production processes. By addressing these emerging research questions, scholars can contribute to the development of responsible and sustainable approaches to AI integration that strengthen the intellectual foundations of higher education while embracing the transformative potential of technological innovation.

CONCLUSION

Artificial intelligence (AI) is increasingly reshaping higher education by influencing teaching practices, research processes, institutional governance, and the professional identity of the professoriate. The growing integration of generative AI systems, learning analytics platforms, predictive technologies, and AI-assisted research tools demonstrates that universities are entering a period of significant technological and organizational transformation. As academic environments become more digitally mediated, the traditional roles of professors as educators, researchers, and institutional contributors are being redefined through evolving forms of human–AI collaboration.

This chapter adopted a conceptual review approach, using structured narrative synthesis, to examine how AI integration contributes to pedagogical restructuring, faculty role transformation, governance pressures, and the adaptation of digital scholarly identity within higher education institutions. The analysis demonstrated that AI technologies may support instructional personalization, research efficiency, data-driven decision-making, and interdisciplinary collaboration. At the same time, the chapter highlighted that the consequences of AI integration remain complex, uneven, and context-dependent rather than universally beneficial.

The findings of this chapter suggest that the future impact of AI on higher education will depend significantly on institutional governance conditions and the extent to which universities maintain human-centered educational values. AI systems may improve efficiency and expand analytical capacity, but they cannot fully replace the interpretive judgment, ethical reasoning, mentorship, creativity, and relational engagement provided by human academics. Consequently, universities must ensure that technological adoption does not reduce education to purely automated or metric-driven processes. Human-centered pedagogy, critical inquiry, and intellectual autonomy must remain central to academic practice even within increasingly AI-supported educational environments.

The chapter also emphasizes the importance of institutional safeguards and ethical governance frameworks in guiding responsible AI integration. Universities will require transparent policies addressing data privacy, algorithmic accountability, authorship disclosure, academic integrity, and equitable access to technological resources. Faculty participation in AI governance processes will be particularly important to ensure that institutional decision-making does not become excessively surveillance-oriented or dominated by purely quantitative performance metrics. Similarly, ongoing faculty development initiatives related to digital literacy, AI ethics, and technology-supported pedagogy will remain necessary as academic work continues to evolve.

At the same time, several unresolved tensions continue to shape debates surrounding AI in higher education. Questions concerning algorithmic bias, academic labor precarity, intellectual ownership, overreliance on automated systems, and global inequalities in access to technology remain insufficiently resolved. The long-term implications of AI for disciplinary diversity, scholarly creativity, faculty autonomy, and institutional culture also remain uncertain. These tensions indicate that AI integration should not be interpreted as a linear, universally progressive transformation, but rather as an ongoing institutional negotiation shaped by governance choices, educational priorities, and social contexts.

Ultimately, the challenge facing universities is not simply whether AI technologies should be adopted, but how they should be integrated in ways that preserve the intellectual, ethical, and human foundations of higher education. The future professoriate will likely operate within hybrid academic environments characterized by continuous interaction between computational systems and human expertise. Ensuring that this transformation strengthens rather than undermines the core values of higher education will require critical governance, responsible institutional leadership, and sustained commitment to human-centered scholarship in the age of artificial intelligence.

REFERENCES

Bates, A. W. (2019). *Teaching in a digital age: Guidelines for designing teaching and learning* (2nd ed.). Tony Bates Associates Ltd., https://pressbooks.bccampus.ca/teachinginadigitalagev2/

Brynjolfsson, E., & McAfee, A. (2017). *Machine, platform, crowd: Harnessing our digital future*. W. W. Norton & Company. https://wwnorton.com/books/Machine-Platform-Crowd/

Castells, M. (2010). *The rise of the network society* (2nd ed.). Wiley-Blackwell., DOI: 10.1002/9781444319514

Crompton, H., Burke, D., & Gregory, K. (2023). Artificial intelligence in higher education: The state of the field. *International Journal of Educational Technology in Higher Education, 20*(1), 22. DOI: 10.1186/s41239-023-00392-8

Long, D. Y., & Aleven, V. (2025). Artificial intelligence in higher education: A systematic review of instructional implications. *Frontiers in Education, 10*. Advance online publication. DOI: 10.3389/feduc.2025.1648661

Marginson, S. (2016). *The dream is over: The crisis of Clark Kerr's California idea of higher education*. University of California Press., DOI: 10.1525/9780520966208

Selwyn, N. (2019). *Should robots replace teachers? AI and the future of education*. Polity Press. https://www.politybooks.com/bookdetail/?isbn=9781509528967

Wang, S., Wang, F., Zhu, Z., Wang, J., Tran, T., & Du, Z. (2024). Artificial intelligence in education: A systematic literature review. *Expert Systems with Applications, 252*, 124167. DOI: 10.1016/j.eswa.2024.124167

Williamson, B., & Eynon, R. (2020). Historical threads, missing links, and future directions in AI in education. *Learning, Media and Technology, 45*(3), 223–235. DOI: 10.1080/17439884.2020.1798995

Zawacki-Richter, O., Marín, V. I., Bond, M., & Gouverneur, F. (2019). Systematic review of AI applications in higher education. *International Journal of Educational Technology in Higher Education, 16*(39). Advance online publication. DOI: 10.1186/s41239-019-0171-0

KEY TERMS AND DEFINITIONS

Artificial Intelligence (AI): Artificial Intelligence refers to computational systems and algorithms designed to perform tasks that typically require human cognitive abilities, such as learning, reasoning, problem-solving, decision-making, and language processing. In higher education, AI technologies are used to support personalized learning, automate administrative tasks, assist research processes, and enhance academic decision-making through data analytics.

Academic Governance: Academic governance refers to the formal and informal structures, policies, and decision-making processes that guide the management and operation of universities and higher education institutions. It includes the roles of faculty, administrators, governing boards, and regulatory bodies in shaping institutional policies related to curriculum design, research priorities, faculty appointments, academic standards, and strategic planning.

Digital Pedagogy: Digital pedagogy refers to teaching and learning practices that integrate digital technologies, online platforms, and interactive tools to enhance educational engagement and knowledge acquisition. It emphasizes innovative instructional strategies, such as blended learning, online collaboration, multimedia instruction, and technology-supported assessment, to improve student learning outcomes.

Higher Education Transformation: Higher education transformation refers to the structural, pedagogical, and institutional changes occurring within universities as they adapt to technological innovation, globalization, changing labor market demands, and evolving societal expectations. This transformation often involves integrating digital technologies, interdisciplinary research approaches, new models of academic governance, and alternative modes of knowledge delivery.

Human–AI Collaboration: Human–AI collaboration refers to the cooperative interaction between human professionals and artificial intelligence systems to accomplish complex tasks more effectively. In academic contexts, this collaboration involves professors using AI tools to support teaching, research, data analysis, and administrative decision-making while maintaining human judgment, creativity, and ethical oversight.

Professoriate: The professoriate refers to the collective body of professors, lecturers, and academic scholars who are responsible for teaching, research, and service within higher education institutions. It represents the professional community that shapes intellectual inquiry, academic governance, and the advancement of knowledge within universities.

Scholarly Identity: Scholarly identity refers to the professional self-concept of academics shaped by their roles as researchers, educators, mentors, and contributors to intellectual communities. It encompasses values, expertise, research interests, teaching philosophy, and professional responsibilities that define an academic's position within the broader knowledge ecosystem.

Technological Change: Technological change refers to the development and adoption of new tools, systems, and innovations that transform social, economic, and institutional practices. In higher education, technological change includes the integration of artificial intelligence, digital learning platforms, big data analytics, and automation, which collectively influence how knowledge is created, disseminated, and evaluated.

Chapter 5
AI and the Academic Profession:
Navigating Careers in Higher Education

Hanh Le
http://orcid.org/0009-0007-8172-0809
University of the Cumberlands, USA

ABSTRACT

Artificial intelligence (AI) is reshaping higher education, influencing faculty roles, identities, and career trajectories. This chapter examines the impact of AI on recruitment, evaluation, tenure, promotion, and professional development. Drawing on literature from higher education studies, AI ethics, and the sociology of professions, it explores opportunities such as efficiency, transparency, and data-driven insights, alongside risks including bias, metric-driven cultures, and threats to autonomy and equity. A conceptual framework for the responsible integration of AI emphasizes transparency, human oversight, and alignment with institutional values. Comparative case studies from North America, Europe, and the Global South highlight successes, limitations, and lessons for achieving equitable and accountable academic careers.

INTRODUCTION

Artificial intelligence is starting to transform higher education in ways that go well beyond new instructional technologies or research tools. Its presence is becoming visible in the foundational systems that organize academic work and influence how academic careers unfold (Bagherimajd & Khajedad, 2025; Holmes et al., 2023). AI-supported platforms are now commonly used in hiring, promotion, and tenure

DOI: 10.4018/979-8-3373-8525-9.ch005

reviews, becoming a regular part of how academic careers are evaluated. They can track research activity, highlight strong candidates through predictive models, and help automate many administrative and evaluation tasks. Although these technologies can make processes more efficient and consistent, they also raise important questions about fairness, academic freedom, and the long-term vitality of scholarly work (Memarian & Doleck, 2023; Radanliev, 2025).

For many years, academic careers have been shaped by values such as professional autonomy, peer review, and shared decision-making (Braverman, 1974; Clark, 1983). In the past, hiring and promotion decisions were based largely on thoughtful human judgment of a candidate's teaching, research, and service. AI is also beginning to influence these decisions today. These tools can process large volumes of data, measure research impact, and even try to predict career paths. However, they cannot fully capture the complexity of academic work. Interdisciplinary projects or nontraditional careers may be overlooked, and AI systems can unintentionally repeat the biases found in the data they were trained on (Memarian & Doleck, 2023; Selwyn, 2022).

This chapter examines how AI is reshaping academic careers in three main areas: faculty hiring and appointments, evaluation and reward systems, and professional identity and career development. It uses research, theory, and global examples to show the benefits and risks of using AI in these processes. It also introduces a framework for responsible AI use that emphasizes fairness, strong human oversight, transparency, and alignment with institutional goals and professional standards (Bagherimajd & Khajedad, 2025; Radanliev, 2025). These principles are consistent with international guidance on trustworthy AI, including the UNESCO Recommendation on the Ethics of Artificial Intelligence (UNESCO, 2021) and the OECD AI Principles (OECD, 2019), both of which emphasize human-centered governance, accountability, transparency, and respect for human rights.

Drawing on research in higher education, AI ethics, and the sociology of professions, this chapter situates AI within the context of everyday academic work. It provides practical guidance for faculty, campus leaders, and policymakers as they navigate ongoing changes in how academic careers are shaped and supported. Rather than treating AI as a neutral tool or a discrete innovation, the chapter frames it as a sociotechnical development with far-reaching consequences for equity, professional autonomy, and the evolving identity of academic work (Le, 2025; Selwyn, 2022).

THE ACADEMIC PROFESSION IN THE AI ERA

Academic work has changed a great deal over time, shaped by new technologies, shifting expectations, and evolving ideas about what counts as meaningful scholarship. Universities have grown from small, independent scholarly communities into institutions increasingly guided by performance metrics, accountability standards, and administrative oversight (Braverman, 1974; Clark, 1983). Faculty roles once centered mainly on teaching, research, and service, and promotions were largely determined through peer review and professional judgment. Collegial governance and academic freedom were key principles that allowed professors to choose their research topics, design their courses, and participate in university life based on their own expertise rather than simply following administrative orders (Clark, 1983; Hackman & Oldham, 1976).

Higher education has, in recent decades, come under growing pressure to operate more efficiently, be more transparent, and show more precise results. Governments, accrediting bodies, and university administrators are increasingly focused on performance indicators, such as publication counts, citations, student evaluations, and success in securing research funding (Memarian & Doleck, 2023; Selwyn, 2022). In this environment, AI tools have gained popularity because they seem to help meet these expectations.

AI systems are increasingly used to assess research, assist with faculty hiring, manage workloads, and evaluate teaching. The rapid expansion of AI across higher education has prompted international organizations to call for governance frameworks that ensure AI remains aligned with educational values and public interests. UNESCO (2023) emphasizes that generative AI should support human agency, equity, and academic integrity, while the OECD AI Principles (2019) advocate for transparency, robustness, accountability, and human-centered implementation. They are often promoted as ways to improve consistency, reduce administrative work, and support data-driven decision-making (Bagherimajd & Khajedad, 2025; Holmes et al., 2023).

AI is increasingly being used across many areas of academia. Chatbots help with administrative communication; intelligent tutoring systems evaluate teaching effectiveness; bibliometric and scientometric tools track publication trends and research impact; and large language models support tasks such as content analysis and grant writing (Liang et al., 2024; UNESCO, 2023; Holmes et al., 2023). Additionally, predictive analytics are used to track collaboration patterns, identify promising scholars, and calculate the likelihood of tenure or promotion based on historical trends (Bai et al., 2023). In teaching, AI-powered analytics provide continuous feedback on student engagement, course design, and learning outcomes. This real-time information helps instructors adjust their teaching more easily and respond to student needs more effectively (Kukulska-Hulme & Ilic, 2025; Muncey, 2025).

At the same time, the use of AI in academic career decisions raises significant concerns. Relying too heavily on numbers can overlook essential aspects of scholarly work, such as taking intellectual risks, collaborating across disciplines, mentoring students, and engaging with communities (Le, 2025). Many AI tools can also reinforce existing inequalities since they are trained on historical data. This can put early-career faculty, women, scholars of color, and those at less-resourced institutions at a disadvantage (Memarian & Doleck, 2023; Radanliev, 2025). The lack of transparency in AI systems can exacerbate these issues—trust may erode when it's unclear how decisions are made or how different factors are weighed (Holmes et al., 2023; Selwyn, 2022).

Braverman's concept of deskilling brings these worries into sharp focus. The theory found that automation can quietly render workers' creative work obsolete. Likewise, in education, automation encourages students to continually refresh and adapt their skills (Le, 2025).

This is why strong governance is crucial, not optional. With clear oversight and active faculty involvement, AI can be directed to uphold academic freedom and professional judgment. Without these protections, the technology could change academic life in ways that are truly concerning.

AI IN FACULTY RECRUITMENT AND APPOINTMENT PROCESSES

Faculty recruitment and appointment sit at the core of academic life. Decisions about hiring shape who enters an institution, but they also influence its intellectual direction, disciplinary mix, and longer-term academic culture. For much of the twentieth century, these decisions were handled through explicitly human processes. Hiring committees read candidates' work closely, conduct in-person interviews, and rely on peer judgment to assess teaching, research, and service (Clark, 1983).

According to Bai et al. (2023), AI has become an essential role in faculty recruitment. Research shows that these systems can quickly and efficiently review applications by considering factors such as publications, citation counts, grant records, teaching evaluations, and patterns of research collaboration. From an institutional perspective, AI-assisted tools provide faster processing and more consistent assessment, helping to lighten the workload during the early stages of review. For initial screening, it's revolutionary.

AI-assisted hiring tools can be effective and beneficial, but they cannot eliminate significant risks. Because these systems learn from historical data, they may unintentionally reinforce established patterns, often favoring applicants from prestigious universities, well-funded fields, or historically overrepresented groups (Memarian & Doleck, 2023; Selwyn, 2022).

AI tools often focus on publications, citations, and grants as a straightforward measure. As a result, they may overlook important contributions that are harder to quantify, including mentoring students, community-based research, interdisciplinary work, and innovative teaching (Le, 2025). Over time, this can quietly narrow how institutions think about and define academic excellence.

These shifts aren't just about efficiency. When algorithms start shaping who moves forward, faculty can feel their own judgment slipping into the background, replaced by systems they can't fully see or question. Early-career scholars—especially those in new fields or from marginalized groups—often feel this most, since AI tends to reward familiar, traditional paths over creativity or social impact. And when the criteria aren't clear, trust fades fast, leaving both candidates and committees unsure about what actually matters.

This section examines how AI is increasingly used in hiring and faculty appointments. It explains why these tools are appealing, while also discussing the ethical and professional issues they raise. The section covers examples such as AI-based screening, AI-supported peer review, and prediction tools. It examines how they affect university decision-making, academic identity, and concerns about fairness and accountability. By considering both what these systems can do and the environments in which they are used, this discussion helps explain how academic career paths are changing and what protections are needed to make sure progress does not harm equity, diversity, or academic integrity.

Algorithmic Recruitment

For a long time, faculty hiring has been based on human-centered evaluation. This includes peer reviews, interviews, and careful review of a candidate's teaching, research, and service (Clark, 1983). These traditional approaches allowed committees to look beyond numbers and consider expert judgment. They could also assess qualities like creativity, intellectual ability, and potential for long-term success in academia.

In recent years, colleges and universities have increasingly begun to use AI-powered tools in hiring. These systems analyze multiple applicant profiles simultaneously using data such as publication records, collaboration networks, and written materials (Bai et al., 2023; Liang et al., 2024). By processing large amounts of information quickly and consistently, AI can help institutions identify strong candidates, reduce administrative workload, and support more data-informed hiring decisions.

AI-enhanced recruitment brings several notable benefits. Predictive models can efficiently screen large applicant pools, highlight individuals with strong research trajectories, and evaluate alignment with institutional priorities or strategic goals (Bagherimajd & Khajedad, 2025).

Even with their benefits, using AI in hiring brings real risks. Because these systems are trained on past data, they can unintentionally reproduce old patterns—such as favoring groups that have historically dominated top academic positions. As a result, women, scholars of color, and candidates from less well-known institutions may be placed at a disadvantage (Memarian & Doleck, 2023; Selwyn, 2022).

AI can also shape how candidates present themselves. As automated metrics become more influential, some scholars may feel pressured to focus on what the algorithm rewards—such as high citation counts, lots of publications, or certain "high-impact" journals. This can come at the expense of creativity, interdisciplinary work, or community-focused research (Le, 2025).

These factors could slowly narrow the range of academic perspectives and steer research toward a more uniform and constrained set of priorities. These dynamics together show how complicated and promising AI-assisted hiring can be. AI could worsen systemic injustices and change how students behave in ways that could undermine creativity and intellectual diversity, even as it could also make institutions more productive and more aware of candidate diversity. It is important to understand these conflicts in order to make hiring procedures that use AI in a responsible way while still following the rules of justice, academic integrity, and professional autonomy in higher education.

AI-Assisted Peer Review and Evaluation

The evaluation of academic quality has traditionally relied heavily on peer review. Hiring, promotion, and tenure decisions have historically been based on shared professional norms, disciplinary standards, and expert judgment (Clark, 1983; Peoples, 2021). However, AI-based tools have started to appear in these evaluation spaces more recently. Algorithmic systems now produce quantitative summaries of research productivity, citation influence, and publication visibility (Liang et al., 2024). Large language models (LLMs) extend this capacity by scanning research texts for features such as originality, thematic focus, methodological coherence, and relevance to departmental or institutional priorities (Puccio et al., 2025). Used in this way, AI functions as an additional source of information—one that can inform review processes but does not substitute for disciplinary expertise.

These developments have also impacted teaching evaluation. Automated assessment platforms, often integrated into Learning Tools Interoperability (LTI) environments, generate ongoing data about student engagement, participation patterns, and feedback trends (Ball, 2025; Kukulska-Hulme & Ilic, 2025). These systems can point to areas where instructors may benefit from support, surface patterns associated with effective teaching or suggest possible adjustments to course design. By shifting some evaluative work away from manual reporting and toward continuous analytics, AI tools may ease administrative pressures while offering timely feedback that can inform instructional practice (Muncey, 2025; WhizzBridge, 2025).

However, there are a number of problems with the growing use of AI in academic assessment. These concerns align with growing international discussions regarding responsible research assessment. The San Francisco Declaration on Research Assessment (DORA, 2012) and the Coalition for Advancing Research Assessment (CoARA, 2022) caution against excessive reliance on quantitative metrics and advocate broader recognition of diverse scholarly contributions. The integration of AI into evaluation processes may amplify existing metric-based biases if institutions fail to adopt more holistic assessment approaches. Scholarly endeavors like interdisciplinary experimentation, community-engaged scholarship, mentoring relationships, and service contributions may be obscured by an emphasis on quantitative indicators (Le, 2025; Selwyn, 2022). Concerns about transparency are also crucial. When evaluative outputs are generated by systems whose internal logic is not immediately apparent, it can be difficult for faculty to understand how decisions are made. This could jeopardize professional autonomy and undermine trust (Radanliev, 2025). When career advancement is closely tied to algorithmic metrics, academics may also feel pressured to prioritize measurable outcomes, such as citation counts or publication volume, at the expense of longer-term, exploratory research or intellectual risk-taking (Le, 2025). The breadth of topics studied and the diversity of scholarly contributions may eventually decline as a result of these pressures.

Together, these dynamics suggest that AI-assisted evaluation offers both important analytical advantages and substantial challenges. While these tools can boost productivity and improve access to data, they also bring up difficult questions about justice, transparency, and the values that guide academic judgment. As institutions continue to incorporate AI into their evaluation frameworks, careful consideration will be required to ensure that these systems enhance rather than restrict the application of scholarly judgment and professional responsibility.

AI and Tenure & Promotion

Tenure and promotion decisions are very important in a professor's career. They affect job security, how connected someone feels to their university, and future opportunities. As universities handle more data, many are starting to use AI tools to help with these decisions. These tools review past information, such as research, teaching, service, and collaboration, to estimate career progress (Bagherimajd & Khajedad, 2025; Bai et al., 2023). For example, AI might highlight faculty who are likely to meet promotion requirements, identify those who may be at risk of leaving, or help with planning future staffing needs. The main purpose of these tools is to support decisions, not to replace human judgment, which remains essential. At the same time, the use of AI in tenure and promotion raises serious ethical and equity-related questions. Because algorithmic models are trained on historical data, they often reflect the structural inequalities embedded in past academic systems. This concern is particularly important in light of ongoing reforms in responsible research assessment, which emphasize evaluating research quality, societal contribution, mentorship, and interdisciplinary engagement rather than relying primarily on bibliometric indicators (DORA, 2012; CoARA, 2022). Treating past disparities as neutral predictors of future performance may disadvantage women, early-career scholars, and faculty from underrepresented groups (Memarian & Doleck, 2023; Radanliev, 2025).

Global disparities in research funding, access to bibliometric databases, and AI infrastructure exacerbate these issues. Models calibrated to academic contexts with abundant resources may disadvantage institutions in the Global South systemically (Bagherimajd & Khajedad, 2025). In these instances, AI-mediated evaluation may reinforce existing hierarchies of opportunity and prestige rather than undermine them. To meet these challenges, we need to find the right balance between how sensitive human judgment is to context and how analytical AI is. One way to keep things fair, nuanced, and collaborative is to use human-in-the-loop methods, in which algorithmic outputs assist but don't make evaluative decisions (Holmes et al., 2023; Selwyn, 2022). Also, it's important to be open. It is necessary to educate faculty members about the evolution of metrics, their applications, and their relative importance in decision-making. To preserve academic freedom and professional autonomy, opportunities to question, contextualize, or improve algorithmic assessments remain crucial. When such safeguards are in place, universities may be better positioned to benefit from AI's analytical capabilities while maintaining the integrity of tenure and promotion procedures.

IMPACTS ON FACULTY IDENTITY AND PROFESSIONAL AUTONOMY

This section examines these issues by considering how algorithmic evaluation, predictive analytics, and AI-enabled teaching and research tools interact with faculty self-awareness, motivation, and discretion. It highlights the ethical, psychological, and professional challenges faced by academic staff in environments increasingly affected by algorithmic systems, addressing both the risks and the opportunities.

Redefining Academic Identity

In academic settings that use AI, scholars' views of their own work and professional identity are increasingly shaped by numbers and prediction tools (Le, 2025;

Memarian & Doleck, 2023). Because algorithms help determine which research is considered important or influential, some faculty feel pressure to focus on topics that perform well in citation counts or prediction models. As a result, exploratory research, new fields, or socially meaningful projects that do not fit easily into these systems may receive less attention (Selwyn, 2022).

Over time, this can create an academic culture where metrics matter more than curiosity and creativity. Braverman's (1974) idea of "deskilling" is still relevant, as professional judgment may be replaced by external evaluation systems. Faculty may begin adjusting their research to meet algorithmic standards rather than pursuing long-term intellectual goals or adhering to the values of their discipline.

AI has an impact on both research and education. Examples of AI-supported instructional analytics that currently generate ongoing data on student participation, learning behaviors, and course outcomes include intelligent tutoring systems, learning dashboards, and automated engagement reports (Ball, 2025; Kukulska-Hulme & Ilic, 2025). These tools can assist teachers by identifying patterns of difficulty and highlighting areas that may need additional support. Additionally, these systems create different kinds of pressure. When evaluations of teaching rely heavily on algorithmic indicators, educators may feel pushed to standardize their methods or design courses around what the system can measure most easily. This can reduce opportunities for innovative, personalized, or culturally responsive teaching, discourage experimentation, and limit the diversity of instructional approaches (Godwin-Jones, 2022). As a result, in increasingly data-driven academic environments, AI-mediated evaluation shapes not only the teaching decisions faculty make but also their understanding of their identities and roles as educators.

Autonomy and Motivation

Faculty motivation is strongly correlated with the structure of academic work and the degree of control individuals feel they have over their professional activities (Hackman & Oldham, 1976). When AI-driven assessment tools are used in performance reviews, this sense of balance could be upset. If the algorithms that underpin these systems are unclear or inadequately explained, faculty members may feel that their work is being assessed by mechanisms over which they have no real control or understanding. This could erode internal motivation.

Researchers describe this as algorithmic oversight fatigue—a gradual decline in engagement, satisfaction, and ownership that stems from constant monitoring, data tracking, and automated scoring (Le, 2025; Muncey, 2025). Over time, these pressures can make faculty feel more restricted by external expectations and less connected to the intellectual core of their work.

AI does not, however, inherently reduce autonomy. In fact, it can improve it when carefully planned and executed. Faculty can think more strategically about their research, teaching, and long-term career development when they have access to tools that provide clear, interpretable insights instead of strict judgments.

For example, AI-enabled mentoring platforms can identify trends in a researcher's work and recommend pertinent training, possible partners, or new lines of inquiry. In these situations, technology serves as a guide instead of a command. Teachers are still free to choose whether or how to use the data (Bagherimajd & Khajedad, 2025; Holmes et al., 2023). AI has the potential to be a helpful tool that enhances rather than diminishes academic agency if it is transparent and subject to strict human oversight.

Ethical Tensions

There are real ethical concerns when using AI to evaluate faculty. As Radanliev (2025) and others point out, AI systems need to be transparent, fair, and accountable. When algorithms work like "black boxes" and no one understands how decisions are made, faculty can lose trust in the process. If the rules for using AI aren't clear, people may feel as though machines—not humans—are making major career decisions. This can weaken the collaborative, peer-driven culture that academic evaluation has always relied on.

These issues also affect professional independence. Faculty may feel less control over their work and careers if they believe automated systems carry more weight than human judgment. Keeping people at the center of the process is essential for maintaining confidence, fairness, and a healthy academic community. This could push scholars to focus on meeting algorithm-driven metrics rather than exploring new ideas or unconventional research, thereby limiting creativity and intellectual diversity.

Finding the right balance between AI support and human oversight is key. AI can provide helpful insights, but human judgment must remain at the center. Clear guidelines, open communication about how AI is used, and chances for faculty to discuss or question AI-based decisions are critical. With these safeguards, institutions can protect academic freedom, support a range of scholarly work, and ensure that faculty evaluations remain fair and ethical.

EQUITY, DIVERSITY, AND INCLUSION IN AI-MEDIATED CAREERS

The growing use of artificial intelligence (AI) in faculty evaluation and career management is reshaping long-standing conversations about equity, diversity, and inclusion (EDI) in higher education. Although AI promises more consistent assessment practices, the ability to surface overlooked talent, and a reduction in some forms of human bias, these benefits are not guaranteed. Without intentional design and ethical safeguards, AI-driven systems can unintentionally reinforce the very inequities they aim to solve (Memarian & Doleck, 2023; Radanliev, 2025). Because recruitment, promotion, and tenure decisions determine who enters the academy, who advances, and whose work is valued, the stakes of algorithmic decision-making are especially high for historically marginalized groups.

Most AI evaluation tools draw on extensive datasets—publication metrics, citation patterns, grant records, teaching evaluations, and other performance indicators—to generate predictions about faculty success (Bai et al., 2023). These datasets are far from neutral. They reflect decades of unequal access to resources, uneven recognition of scholarly work, and systemic disadvantages linked to gender, race, geography, and institutional prestige (Selwyn, 2022). When AI systems learn from this data, they can unintentionally repeat these patterns—favoring candidates from elite universities, well-funded fields, or dominant demographic groups, while putting scholars in emerging disciplines, underrepresented communities, or resource-limited settings at a disadvantage.

This issue is even harder because the focus is on quantitative, metric-driven evaluation. Numbers and rankings frequently overlook the contributions that foster inclusivity in academic culture, such as mentoring students, cultivating interdisciplinary connections, engaging with communities, or advocating for marginalized groups (Le, 2025; Memarian & Doleck, 2023). Faculty who excel in these domains may find their contributions undervalued or overlooked in AI systems, perpetuating existing obstacles and constricting the definition of "academic excellence."

Global inequalities add another layer of complexity. Universities in the Global South often lack access to large bibliometric databases, advanced AI tools, or robust evaluation systems. As a result, their scholars may be underrepresented or mischaracterized in AI-driven assessments, widening the gap between academic communities in the Global North and Global South (Bagherimajd & Khajedad, 2025; Bai et al., 2023). Without context-sensitive adjustments, AI could marginalize diverse ways of knowing and limit recognition of scholarship worldwide.

Addressing these challenges requires a careful, human-centered approach. UNESCO's Recommendation on the Ethics of Artificial Intelligence (2021) identifies fairness, non-discrimination, inclusion, and cultural diversity as core requirements for AI governance. These principles are especially relevant in faculty evaluation systems, where algorithmic decisions can directly influence career opportunities and institutional representation. Transparent algorithms, meaningful human oversight, inclusive and context-aware metrics, and ongoing checks for bias are all crucial to ensure that AI supports—not undermines—equity, diversity, and inclusion (Memarian & Doleck, 2023; Radanliev, 2025). When used responsibly, AI can help universities spot inequities, widen participation, and create fairer career pathways. This section examines both the promise and the risks of AI-driven evaluation and offers strategies for leveraging technology to build more inclusive, equitable, and empowering academic environments for scholars everywhere.

Risks of Bias and Discrimination

Historical inequities in academic data can easily be carried over into AI-based evaluation systems if they aren't carefully examined. Metrics such as citation counts, bibliometric scores, and measures of research impact often reflect long-standing structural imbalances, thereby giving more visibility to scholars from elite universities, well-funded regions, and already dominant demographic groups (Memarian & Doleck, 2023; Selwyn, 2022). When AI tools for hiring, promotion, or tenure rely on these patterns, they can unintentionally repeat the same disparities—disadvantaging women, scholars of color, early-career researchers, and those working in underfunded or emerging fields. Instead of correcting inequities, AI can end up encoding them into automated decision-making.

Many of the most valuable aspects of academic work are also hard for AI to capture. Mentoring students, supporting colleagues, engaging with communities, and building interdisciplinary connections are all crucial for creating inclusive, vibrant academic environments. Yet these contributions rarely show up in the metrics AI uses (Le, 2025; Selwyn, 2022). As a result, faculty who dedicate time to these important relational and community-focused activities may find their work underrepresented or overlooked in AI-driven assessments. This not only skews our understanding of academic excellence but also risks weakening the practices that make institutions fairer, more collaborative, and more inclusive.

Global Disparities

AI is being adopted in higher education at very different rates around the world. These differences reflect unequal access to technology, funding, and digital infrastructure. Budget constraints and restricted access to research databases, analytics tools, and high-performance computing plague many Global South universities (Bagherimajd & Khajedad, 2025; Bai et al., 2023). As a result, the information used to assess scholars in these areas is frequently lacking. When AI systems use such data to assess the impact of research or academic performance, they may unintentionally disadvantage these scholars from the start.

Most AI tools are developed at affluent institutions, primarily in the Global North. They require widespread access to large archives of publications, standardized metrics, and robust digital systems. When these tools are used globally without alteration, they tend to favor researchers whose work is already widely visible in major databases. As a result, important contributions from underrepresented or emerging academic communities may be overlooked, incorrectly categorized, or undervalued.

These biases could worsen existing inequalities in recognition, career opportunities, and funding. Eventually, they influence the kinds of knowledge and voices that are recognized in global academia. To meet this challenge, more inclusive approaches to AI design and evaluation are required. By identifying different scholarly practices and adapting tools to local contexts, AI can be used to reduce rather than increase inequality in higher education.

Strategies for Equitable AI Integration

Reducing the risks that come with AI-based evaluation starts with using these tools in ways that are open, fair, and always grounded in human judgment. AI shouldn't be making decisions behind the scenes. Instead, universities should build systems that honor academic values and recognize the many different ways scholars contribute to their fields. A few practical steps can help institutions move in this direction:

Be open about how AI works

Universities should be clear and open about how their AI systems work—what data they rely on, which metrics they emphasize, and how results are produced (Radanliev, 2025). When faculty understand how an algorithm reaches its conclusions, they are better equipped to interpret, question, or challenge those outcomes. Transparency also helps reduce concerns about opaque "black box" decision-making and builds greater trust in the process.

Keep people at the center of decisions

AI should support, not replace, expert judgment. Faculty participation in hiring, promotion, and evaluation remains essential because it ensures that AI outputs are interpreted within the appropriate disciplinary and institutional context (Memarian & Doleck, 2023). Human oversight helps committees catch nuance, recognize non-traditional career paths, and correct any gaps or errors in algorithmic assessments.

Take a broad view of what success looks like

Numbers alone cannot reflect the full range of academic excellence. Institutions should combine quantitative metrics with qualitative indicators such as mentoring, community engagement, interdisciplinary work, leadership, and contributions to equity and inclusion (Le, 2025). This more holistic approach helps AI systems recognize the true diversity of academic work, rather than focusing only on what is easiest to measure.

Check regularly for bias

AI systems need ongoing monitoring to ensure they're not unintentionally disadvantaging certain groups. Regular audits should look at how evaluation tools affect faculty across gender, race, institution type, geographic region, and discipline (Radanliev, 2025). Continuous review helps keep AI aligned with institutional commitments to fairness and equity.

When AI is paired with ethical oversight, clear communication, and genuine faculty involvement, it can strengthen fairness in academic evaluation. Used thoughtfully, AI can broaden participation, reveal hidden biases, and support more inclusive career pathways across higher education.

AI-SUPPORTED FACULTY DEVELOPMENT AND WORKLOAD

Artificial intelligence (AI) is becoming an increasingly important part of higher education, offering new ways to support faculty growth, career development, and day-to-day work. Today's faculty juggle many responsibilities at once—research, teaching, mentoring, grant writing, service, and administrative tasks—all within limited time and energy. This growing workload often leads to stress, burnout, and fewer opportunities for thoughtful, reflective scholarship (Muncey, 2025). When used well, AI can help ease these pressures by automating routine tasks, offering data-informed insights, and providing personalized support that improves both efficiency and the quality of academic work.

AI tools can take over many repetitive administrative duties, such as scheduling, grading, curriculum planning, and compliance reporting. Recent UNESCO guidance on generative AI in education and research similarly highlights the potential of AI to reduce administrative burden and support professional development, while cautioning institutions to maintain human oversight and safeguard academic integrity (UNESCO, 2023). This allows faculty to spend more time on intellectually meaningful activities (Singh, 2025; WhizzBridge, 2025). With low-code and no-code tools, instructors can automate many course tasks without needing advanced technical skills. This frees up more time for mentoring students, doing research, and designing creative lessons (Singh, 2025). AI-powered chatbots can also answer common student questions, manage course logistics, and support communication in multiple languages, which greatly reduces everyday administrative work (WhizzBridge, 2025).

Beyond saving time, AI can also support faculty growth in meaningful ways. Tools like predictive analytics, machine learning, and AI-assisted curriculum design can help instructors find collaboration opportunities, identify areas for skill development, and improve teaching based on individual needs (Bagherimajd & Khajedad, 2025; Liang et al., 2024). Large language models can support the creation of flexible, student-centered courses, while AI analyses of research trends or teaching feedback can highlight new research areas and training opportunities. These insights can help faculty plan their careers more thoughtfully, explore new directions, and strengthen their teaching.

At the same time, increased reliance on AI raises important concerns. When automated systems take over tasks such as grading, content creation, or curriculum design, faculty may have fewer opportunities to exercise creativity, critical thinking, and professional judgment (Braverman, 1974; Le, 2025). To protect academic autonomy and the depth of scholarly work, it is essential that AI tools support, rather than replace, human expertise.

AI can also open the door to new forms of innovation in teaching and research. Writing assistants can help improve clarity and style in scholarly work, while AI-driven analytics can uncover patterns in student engagement or research impact that support more informed decision-making (Godwin-Jones, 2022). Technologies such as mobile-assisted language learning (MALL) platforms demonstrate how AI can create adaptive, personalized learning experiences and expand pedagogical possibilities (Kukulska-Hulme & Ilic, 2025).

Overall, AI presents both opportunities and challenges for faculty. It can reduce workload pressures, offer personalized professional development, and encourage innovation, but it must be implemented thoughtfully to avoid risks such as deskilling, loss of autonomy, or excessive standardization. When guided by human oversight, ethical governance, and alignment with institutional and disciplinary values, AI can become a powerful tool for supporting faculty development, managing workload demands, and sustaining professional engagement in higher education.

Personalized Career Support

AI-enabled professional development systems can analyze patterns in publications, teaching feedback, and scholarly networks to provide personalized guidance for faculty growth (Holmes et al., 2023; Liang et al., 2024). Using predictive analytics, these tools can suggest targeted training opportunities, mentorship options, or potential research collaborators that match a faculty member's changing career goals. By offering data-informed insights, AI helps academics make more thoughtful decisions about their research focus, teaching improvements, and service commitments. This support encourages more intentional, proactive career planning and helps faculty navigate their professional paths with greater clarity and confidence (Bagherimajd & Khajedad, 2025).

Reducing Administrative Burdens

Low-code and no-code technologies allow faculty to automate many time-consuming tasks—such as scheduling office hours, creating grade reports, organizing assignments, or preparing routine documents—without needing advanced programming skills (Singh, 2025). By simplifying these everyday processes, faculty can manage their courses more efficiently and reduce the mental effort involved in daily academic administration.

At the same time, AI-powered chatbots are becoming helpful partners in academic settings. These tools can quickly answer student questions, offer support in multiple languages, share course announcements, track deadlines, and assist with departmental communication (WhizzBridge, 2025). Because they operate around the clock and can handle large volumes of requests, chatbots reduce the need for faculty to respond to every logistical or administrative question themselves.

Together, these technologies significantly reduce routine work, easing workload pressures and reducing burnout. By automating administrative tasks, faculty gain more time and mental energy to focus on what matters most—research, innovative teaching, student mentoring, and scholarly collaboration. In this way, AI-enabled tools not only improve efficiency but also create better conditions for meaningful academic work and long-term professional growth.

Balancing Skill Development and Deskilling

AI can be very helpful in making academic work more efficient, but its growing use also brings challenges, especially when automation begins to replace faculty expertise. Relying too much on AI-based tests, auto-generated course materials, or automated grading can limit opportunities for reflection, creative course design, and careful teaching. These activities are essential for faculty development and high-quality education (Braverman, 1974; Le, 2025). When AI makes too many teaching decisions, instructors may lose chances to use their professional judgment, experiment with new ideas, and connect more deeply with students' learning.

These concerns show why AI should be used to support human expertise, not replace it. Universities should adopt AI in ways that strengthen faculty creativity and intellectual work. This includes keeping instructors actively involved in important tasks such as creating assessments, understanding student progress, and guiding the overall direction of a course.

Faculty development programs are key to maintaining this balance. With the right training, educators can use AI thoughtfully and responsibly—allowing automation to handle routine tasks while instructors remain fully engaged in teaching and learning.

Such programs may include workshops on AI literacy, guidance on protecting academic standards when using automated tools, and hands-on opportunities to combine AI insights with human teaching judgment (Le, 2025; Muncey, 2025). By building these skills, institutions can help faculty use AI effectively while preserving long-term growth, professional independence, and creativity.

Supporting Teaching and Research Innovation

AI has the potential to spark meaningful innovation in both teaching and research by offering deeper, data-informed insights into how students learn and how academic fields change over time. By examining patterns in student engagement, learning outcomes, and emerging research areas, AI tools can help faculty better understand instructional needs and disciplinary trends. This knowledge supports more informed, flexible, and creative academic decision-making.

For example, large language models can help instructors design dynamic, adaptable curricula that respond to student needs, evolving disciplines, or real-world contexts. Environment-specific curriculum generation (Liang et al., 2024) allows educators to adjust learning experiences as conditions change, encouraging more personalized and student-centered teaching approaches.

In language education, AI-enhanced mobile-assisted language learning (MALL) platforms offer new ways to support both student independence and instructor creativity. These tools can personalize practice activities, track learner progress, and provide immediate feedback, making language instruction more engaging while helping students take greater responsibility for their learning (Kukulska-Hulme & Ilic, 2025).

AI also supports innovation in research by improving scholarly communication. Intelligent writing assistants can help faculty strengthen their manuscripts by suggesting improvements in clarity, organization, and alignment with disciplinary conventions (Godwin-Jones, 2022). By easing parts of the writing process, these tools allow researchers to focus more on developing strong ideas and arguments.

Together, these technologies enhance faculty creativity and analytical capacity. They support more responsive teaching, clearer scholarly communication, and more innovative research practices across higher education.

CONCEPTUAL FRAMEWORK FOR RESPONSIBLE AI INTEGRATION

As AI becomes more embedded in faculty career processes—from hiring and promotion to teaching evaluation and professional development—it is essential for institutions to approach these tools with intention and care. Increased dependence on AI also increases the stakes. Without strong oversight, automated systems can unintentionally reproduce inequities, reduce faculty autonomy, and erode foundational academic values such as fairness, collegiality, and intellectual independence (Memarian & Doleck, 2023; Radanliev, 2025).

When used thoughtfully, AI can bring real advantages. It can offer deeper insights, reduce administrative strain, support stronger decision-making, and help faculty connect their professional goals with broader institutional priorities (Bagherimajd & Khajedad, 2025; Holmes et al., 2023). The challenge, of course, is finding the right balance—welcoming innovation without sacrificing equity, academic integrity, or the human judgment that higher education depends on.

To help strike that balance, this chapter introduces a three-part framework for using AI ethically and effectively in academic career systems. It centers on three key principles:

- Transparency and explainability
- Human-in-the-loop oversight
- Alignment with professional and institutional values

Grounded in AI ethics, organizational theory, and research on higher-education governance, this framework serves as both a guiding perspective and a practical roadmap. By prioritizing clarity, fairness, and sensitivity to context, it frames AI as a tool that enhances—rather than replaces—human expertise. Ultimately, the aim is to ensure that AI strengthens academic judgment, supports equitable career pathways, and reinforces the values that define higher education as a professional and intellectual community.

The framework proposed in this chapter aligns closely with internationally recognized AI governance frameworks. UNESCO's Recommendation on the Ethics of Artificial Intelligence (2021) emphasizes transparency, accountability, human oversight, fairness, and human rights protections. Similarly, the OECD AI Principles

(2019) advocate inclusive growth, transparency, robustness, accountability, and human-centered values. These principles provide a strong policy foundation for the responsible use of AI in academic career systems.

Transparency and Explainability

Transparency plays a key role in building trust in AI-supported evaluation systems. Faculty are more likely to feel comfortable with AI-generated outcomes when they understand how these tools interpret their research, teaching, and service work (Radanliev, 2025; Selwyn, 2022). Explainable AI (XAI) approaches help make this possible by shedding light on how decisions are made—showing which indicators matter, how different factors are weighed, and how final scores or recommendations are reached. When AI systems are open about how they work, they reduce uncertainty, ease concerns about hidden bias, and demonstrate an institution's commitment to ethical and responsible use.

Putting transparency into practice takes thoughtful design. Institutions can begin by clearly explaining how their AI models function and why certain criteria are used. User-friendly dashboards can make this information easier to understand by breaking evaluations into clear, accessible pieces. Just as important is creating opportunities for conversation. Feedback channels allow faculty to ask questions, provide context, or request corrections, ensuring that human judgment remains central to the evaluation process (Holmes et al., 2023; Memarian & Doleck, 2023). When these elements come together, AI becomes a transparent and accountable partner in academic evaluation—one that supports faculty expertise rather than acting as a hidden or unquestionable authority.

Human-in-the-Loop Oversight

AI is most helpful when it supports human expertise rather than replacing it. Even as universities begin using algorithmic tools to inform decisions, the most important parts of academic life—hiring, promotion, tenure, mentoring, and peer review—still rely on human judgment, discussion, and shared professional values (Le, 2025; Selwyn, 2022). Keeping humans involved helps ensure that the parts of faculty work that are hard to measure—such as mentoring, working across disciplines, or serving the community—are still recognized and valued, rather than overshadowed by simple numbers (Memarian & Doleck, 2023; Radanliev, 2025).

Strong human oversight doesn't happen on its own; it takes real effort. Faculty need to help shape the development of AI evaluation tools so that the criteria reflect disciplinary standards and professional expectations. Review committees also need training to carefully evaluate AI-generated information, paying attention to context and potential bias. Regular checks of AI systems help ensure their recommendations continue to align with the institution's mission, equity goals, and ethical standards (Bagherimajd & Khajedad, 2025; Holmes et al., 2023).

When these protections are in place, AI becomes a helpful partner instead of a limiting one. This approach keeps academic evaluation rooted in human judgment while still leveraging the analytical strengths AI can provide.

Alignment with Professional Values

Using AI in faculty evaluation should always be grounded in the core values of higher education, including academic freedom, shared governance, and support for professional growth (Le, 2025; Selwyn, 2022). For AI to truly support these principles, the measures it uses must reflect the full scope of academic work. This means looking beyond simple numbers like publication counts to also include teaching quality, mentoring, service, community involvement, and other contributions that help academic communities grow. Institutions also need to ensure that AI supports faculty skills rather than reducing them or pushing scholars to focus solely on rigid, metric-based measures of productivity (Braverman, 1974; Le, 2025).

A value-aligned approach to using AI starts with how academic work is evaluated. Universities can deliberately give more weight to forms of work that are often overlooked, such as mentoring students, interdisciplinary collaboration, equity efforts, and service roles. These activities are vital to institutional life, even if they are harder to measure. AI tools can also be more helpful when their insights are linked to personalized career development, allowing faculty to pursue paths that align with their interests and goals rather than feeling constrained by automated recommendations.

It is equally important to design AI systems that are flexible enough to work across different disciplines and institutional settings. Evaluation models should respect the varied norms, methods, and expectations of different fields, rather than applying a one-size-fits-all approach (Bagherimajd & Khajedad, 2025; Liang et al., 2024). When AI tools align with institutional missions and disciplinary cultures, universities can benefit from innovation while still preserving the human-centered values that define academic life.

CASE STUDIES OF AI IN FACULTY EVALUATION

The use of artificial intelligence (AI) in faculty evaluation varies widely across higher education systems worldwide. Its adoption has been shaped by variations in institutional goals, national policies, access to technology, and cultural expectations about academic work. Comparative case studies illustrate how AI is used in practice, highlighting both its potential benefits and the challenges it poses for managing academic careers (Bagherimajd & Khajedad, 2025; Memarian & Doleck, 2023). Examining examples from North America, Europe, and the Global South demonstrates that while AI can improve efficiency, transparency, and predictive accuracy, it also raises persistent concerns about fairness, bias, and the preservation of faculty autonomy.

North American Research Universities

Early and enthusiastic adopters of AI-enabled assessment tools are North American research-intensive universities. Algorithmic systems are now used by many universities to help manage work as faculty evaluations become more complex and data driven. Publication records, citation patterns, grant activities, teaching evaluations, student feedback, collaboration networks, and professional connections are just a few of the types of data these tools often examine. Universities want to use predictive analytics to better identify research potential and provide clear, data-based information to support promotion and tenure decisions (Bagherimajd & Khajedad, 2025).

A concrete example of AI-assisted faculty evaluation can be found at Pennsylvania State University. In 2025, Penn State issued guidance permitting the use of AI tools to summarize student feedback during promotion and tenure reviews. However, the guidance explicitly states that AI should not generate evaluative judgments and that faculty reviewers remain responsible for interpretation and decision-making (Penn State Faculty Affairs, 2025). The University of Florida's Faculty Excellence and Advancement initiative utilizes Academic Analytics to support faculty evaluation, promotion, and tenure processes while maintaining human review and governance mechanisms (University of Florida, 2025).

According to Muncey (2025), AI helps speed up review processes, allowing committees to handle large numbers of applicants and complete regular evaluations more quickly. By helping faculty and academic leaders consider possible career paths, interactive dashboards provide additional support. Also, these efficiencies bring real concerns. Many faculty worry that a strong focus on numbers, especially citation counts and grant success, can overshadow equally important parts of academic work that are harder to measure. Activities such as mentoring, interdisciplinary collaboration, community engagement, and service to the institution do not always fit neatly into quantitative models, which makes them more likely to be overlooked in AI-mediated evaluations (Selwyn, 2022).

To address these concerns, many North American institutions have implemented human-in-the-loop safeguards. Peer review committees remain central to interpreting AI-generated results, adding context to numerical indicators, and incorporating qualitative evidence to keep evaluations balanced and fair (Memarian & Doleck, 2023). Transparency efforts—such as explaining how AI models work, clarifying how metrics are weighted, and giving faculty opportunities to share narrative context—have also been essential for building trust and staying true to core academic values.

European Higher Education Institutions

European universities often take a more collaborative and inclusive approach when bringing AI into faculty evaluation, with a strong focus on shared governance and open academic dialogue. Rather than introducing algorithmic systems from the top down, institutions usually involve faculty from the start. Faculty work together to shape evaluation criteria that reflect disciplinary norms and institutional values, decide how different metrics should be balanced to avoid overemphasizing narrow indicators, and review AI-generated analyses before any decisions are finalized. In this approach, AI acts as a supportive advisor rather than a decision-maker.

The aim is to use data to support, not replace, thoughtful conversations among colleagues (Holmes et al., 2023; Memarian & Doleck, 2023). Evaluation committees treat AI-generated input as just one piece of a much larger review. They still consider many kinds of contributions—such as interdisciplinary projects, mentoring, community engagement, and service. This approach helps make sure all forms of academic work are valued. European case studies also show that using AI in this supportive way can build trust, increase transparency, and give faculty more freedom. Institutions benefit from enhanced efficiency while preserving the essential human judgment required for evaluation.

Cardiff University has implemented a Responsible Research Assessment Policy aligned with DORA principles, emphasizing evaluation criteria that go beyond traditional bibliometric indicators (Cardiff University, 2024). Similarly, the University of Bath has adopted responsible research assessment practices to reduce reliance on citation-based metrics and promote more holistic evaluation approaches (University of Bath, 2024). The University of Edinburgh established a Research Metrics Working Group to oversee the responsible use of metrics in academic evaluation and promotion processes (University of Edinburgh, 2024).

Consequently, faculty are more inclined to perceive AI as a beneficial tool rather than a threat to academic freedom. It's still hard to judge different academic fields fairly, especially those where standard measures like citation counts or journal impact factors don't capture the whole picture (Bagherimajd & Khajedad, 2025). Many European universities are working together in a sustained way to solve these problems. They regularly update their AI systems and consult with faculty to ensure they meet the needs of different fields and support more thorough evaluation processes. This regular participation encourages fair and thoughtful academic decision-making and helps avoid overreliance on a small number of metrics.

Asia and the Global South

In many parts of Asia and the Global South, the use of AI in faculty evaluation is shaped by real structural challenges. Limited digital infrastructure, uneven access to bibliometric databases, and the absence of standardized citation systems mean that universities often lack the data-rich environments found in institutions in more technologically advanced regions (Bagherimajd & Khajedad, 2025; Bai et al., 2023). As a result, faculty can be placed at a disadvantage when global benchmarks or data-heavy evaluation models are applied without considering local conditions, especially in emerging disciplines or under-resourced institutions.

To work within these constraints, many universities are beginning to adopt more context-sensitive approaches that balance innovation with local realities. Instead of relying on AI alone, many institutions combine AI insights with peer review and qualitative evaluation so that human judgment adds important context. Others adjust evaluation criteria to reflect regional priorities, disciplinary practices, and institutional goals rather than relying only on global metrics. In some cases, AI is also used to support professional development by helping faculty find training opportunities, potential collaborators, and areas to build new skills. Examples from across the region show that when AI is used thoughtfully and adapted to local needs, it can support faculty evaluation without increasing existing inequalities. These experiences highlight the value of flexible, context-aware approaches that enable AI to enhance academic work while respecting diverse institutional settings.

Cross-Case Lessons and Best Practices

Across different regions, a few shared principles consistently guide the effective and ethical use of AI in faculty evaluation. These shared principles closely mirror international AI governance standards established by UNESCO (2021) and the OECD (2019), suggesting growing global consensus around transparency, accountability, human oversight, and fairness as essential requirements for AI-enabled decision-making. Being open is one of the most crucial things. Institutions need to clearly communicate how their AI systems work, what data they use, and how evaluation results are produced. Teachers feel more confident and less uncertain when they understand the rationale behind the metrics and models being used (Radanliev, 2025).

Maintaining human judgment at the core of the process is equally crucial. AI should be a useful analytical partner, not a substitute for in-depth discussion or peer review. In addition to identifying blind spots or limitations in algorithmic assessments, human evaluators provide context and acknowledge contributions that defy numerical metrics and capabilities that AI cannot achieve independently (Le, 2025; Selwyn, 2022).

Equity also depends on the design of the metrics themselves. Because AI systems can unintentionally reproduce existing inequalities, institutions need to choose criteria that reflect disciplinary diversity, global differences, and nontraditional forms of scholarly work. More inclusive metrics help prevent AI from reinforcing disparities tied to geography, institutional resources, or academic norms (Bagherimajd & Khajedad, 2025; Bai et al., 2023).

Another key lesson is how much context matters. AI tools work best when they are not treated as one-size-fits-all solutions but instead adapted to local cultures, available resources, and disciplinary expectations. Using participatory design and culturally responsive approaches helps ensure that AI stays both effective and ethically grounded (Holmes et al., 2023).

Finally, ongoing monitoring is crucial. Regular audits, feedback loops, and iterative updates allow institutions to catch unintended consequences, correct bias, and keep systems aligned with their goals over time (Radanliev, 2025).

AI can be a real help in faculty evaluation when it's used with care. It can take on routine tasks, clarify the process, and offer useful insights for decision-making. The strongest approaches keep people actively involved, follow solid ethical principles, and protect fairness and academic freedom. With thoughtful use, AI can strengthen higher education while still honoring the human values that make it meaningful.

RECOMMENDATIONS FOR POLICY, PRACTICE, AND RESEARCH

To ensure AI truly supports fair, effective, and ethically grounded academic career management, institutions need to take a thoughtful, research-informed approach. Clear ethical guidelines and strong governance structures are an important place to start. Universities should be explicit about how AI can—and cannot—be used in faculty evaluation, with clear commitments to fairness, transparency, and accountability (Memarian & Doleck, 2023; Radanliev, 2025). A clear and well-defined policy can help to stop the misuse of AI. The contribution of faculties also helps clear, well-defined policies help prevent misuse and ensure AI systems are used responsibly. Faculty involvement is just as essential. Meaningful participation should happen at every stage of AI use—from helping design evaluation frameworks to serving in oversight and review roles. Faculty also need clear opportunities to question AI results, add context, or challenge decisions when required. This kind of engagement builds trust in AI systems while protecting academic autonomy and shared governance. Training and capacity building also play a key role. Both faculty and administrators benefit from opportunities to develop AI literacy, including learning how these systems work, where their limitations lie, and how bias can show up in automated decision-making (Bagherimajd & Khajedad, 2025; Holmes et al., 2023). When users understand AI more deeply, they are better prepared to interpret results critically rather than accepting them at face value.

Ongoing monitoring is equally essential. AI systems should be treated as evolving tools that need regular review, not as fixed solutions. Institutions should also align AI-supported evaluation systems with emerging responsible research assessment initiatives, including DORA and CoARA, which encourage broader recognition of research quality, societal impact, mentorship, and service contributions. Such alignment can help prevent AI systems from reinforcing narrow bibliometric definitions of academic excellence. Continuous audits, impact assessments, and feedback loops enable institutions to identify unintended consequences, address inequities, and refine systems over time, ensuring they remain aligned with institutional values and equity goals. At the same time, institutions need to balance efficiency with professional growth. AI should make academic work easier, not reduce the value of faculty expertise. Used thoughtfully, it can take on routine tasks and free up time for teaching, research, and mentoring, while still supporting human judgment and professional growth (Le, 2025; Singh, 2025). AI tools also need to fit the contexts in which they are used. Systems designed for well-funded institutions may not work as intended in settings with different resources, disciplines, or cultural norms. Adapting AI to local and regional realities helps avoid unfair outcomes and supports more balanced and equitable evaluation practices across higher education (Bai et al., 2023).

CONCLUSION

AI is changing academic work in noticeable ways. It can speed up tasks, improve transparency, and open up new opportunities for professional development. At the same time, its growing use raises concerns about fairness, faculty autonomy, and how academic work is judged. Tools such as automated hiring systems, AI-supported peer review, and promotion prediction models can be helpful, but they need close supervision. Without careful use, these tools may increase bias, focus too heavily on numbers, or ignore the creative and intellectual sides of academic work.

This chapter focuses on three guiding ideas for using AI responsibly in faculty evaluation: being clear about how AI systems work, keeping people involved in decisions, and making sure AI reflects institutional and professional values. Examples from North America, Europe, and the Global South show that institutions are responding to these challenges in different ways. Together, these cases highlight useful innovations and practical lessons for using AI in ways that respect local contexts. Using AI ethically and fairly is an ongoing process. Faculty must be actively involved in shaping these systems, and evaluation practices should be reviewed regularly to ensure they reflect local needs, disciplinary differences, and shared academic values. This ongoing engagement helps ensure that AI strengthens, rather than undermines, the values that define academic life.

When AI is positioned as a tool that supports—rather than replaces—human judgment, it can strengthen collegial decision-making and preserve the relational, nuanced qualities that define academic work. Balancing technological capabilities with professional autonomy enables universities to embrace AI while protecting the integrity, creativity, and long-term vitality of the academic profession (Le, 2025; Memarian & Doleck, 2023; Selwyn, 2022). In the end, thoughtful AI integration offers a path toward a more efficient, inclusive, and forward-looking academic environment—one that leverages technological innovation without sacrificing the core values that define higher education.

REFERENCES

Bagherimajd, K., & Khajedad, K. (2025). Designing a model of sustainable education based on artificial intelligence in higher education. *Computers and Education: Artificial Intelligence, 9*, 100439. Advance online publication. DOI: 10.1016/j.caeai.2025.100439

Bai, J., Marin, V., Jung, I., & Zawacki-Richter, O. (2023). Future Prospects of Artificial Intelligence in Education: A Preliminary Analysis of Educator Perspectives from Focus Groups in Japan, Spain, and Germany. *Ubiquity Proceedings, 3*(1). Advance online publication. DOI: 10.5334/uproc.74

Ball, J. (2025). *A Beginner's Guide to Learning Tools Interoperability (LTI) in Education*. Retrieved from https://www.atomicjolt.com/post/a-beginners-guide-to-learning-tools-interoperability-lti-in-education

Braverman, H. (1974). *Labor and monopoly capital*. Monthly Review Press. DOI: 10.14452/MR-026-03-1974-07_1

Cardiff University. (2024). *Responsible research assessment*. Retrieved from Cardiff University: https://www.cardiff.ac.uk/research/our-research-environment/integrity-and-ethics/responsible-research-assessment

Clark, B. R. (1983). *The higher education system: Academic organization in cross-national perspective*. University of California Press. DOI: 10.1525/9780520340725

CoARA. (2022). *Agreement on Reforming Research Assessment*. Retrieved from Coalition for Advancing Research Assessment: https://coara.eu/agreement/

DORA. (2012). *San Francisco Declaration on Research Assessment*. Retrieved from https://sfdora.org/read

Florida, U. o. (2025). *Faculty: Excellence and Advancement (FEA)*. Retrieved from University of Florida: https://aa.ufl.edu/policies--guidelines/tenure-and-promotion-information/fea/

Godwin-Jones, R. (2022). Partnering with AI: Intelligent writing assistance and instructed language learning. *Language Learning & Technology, 26*(2), 5–24. DOI: 10.64152/10125/73474

Hackman, J. R., & Oldham, G. R. (1976). Motivation through the design of work: Test of a theory. *Organizational Behavior and Human Performance, 16*(2), 250–279. DOI: 10.1016/0030-5073(76)90016-7

Holmes, W., Bialik, M., & Fadel, C. (2023). Artificial intelligence in education. *Data ethics: Building trust — How digital technologies can serve humanity*, 621-653. DOI: 10.58863/20.500.12424/4276068

Kukulska-Hulme, A., & Ilic, P. (2025). MALL in the Age of AI. *The Palgrave Encyclopedia of Computer-Assisted Language Learning*, 1-8. DOI: 10.1007/978-3-031-51447-0_323-1

Le, H. (2025). Design and Development Effective Learning AI Education: Navigating Deskilling in the Age of Intelligent Automation. In R. Zheng, *The Intersection of AI and Student Development in Learning* (p. 32). IGI Global.

Liang, W., Wang, S., Wang, H.-J., Bastani, O., Jayaraman, D., & Ma, Y. J. (2024). Environment Curriculum Generation via Large Language Models. *8th Annual Conference on Robot Learning*. Retrieved from https://eureka-research.github.io/eurekaverse/

Memarian, B., & Doleck, T. (2023). Fairness, Accountability, Transparency, and Ethics (FATE) in Artificial Intelligence (AI) and higher education: A systematic review. *Computers and Education: Artificial Intelligence*, *5*, 100152. Advance online publication. DOI: 10.1016/j.caeai.2023.100152

Muncey, N. (2025). *How AI can help lighten the educator workload and prevent burnout*. Retrieved from https://schoolai.com/blog/ai-lighten-educator-workload-prevent-burnout

OECD. (2019). *OECD Principles on Artificial Intelligence*. Retrieved from Paris: OECD Publishing: https://oecd.ai/en/ai-principles

Penn State Faculty Affairs. (2025). *Guidance for the optional use of AI in summarizing student feedback for faculty assessment*. Retrieved from Pennsylvania State University: https://facultyaffairs.psu.edu/guidance-for-the-optional-use-of-ai-in-summarizing-student-feedback-for-faculty-assessment

Peoples, K. (2021). *How to write a phenomenological dissertation: A step-by-step guide* (Vol. 56). SAGE.

Puccio, B., Castagna, F., Tucker, A., & Veltri, P. (2025). Towards medical AI misalignment: a preliminary study. https://doi.org//arXiv.2505.18212DOI: 10.48550

Radanliev, P. (2025). AI ethics: Integrating transparency, fairness, and privacy in education. *Applied Artificial Intelligence*, *39*(1), 2463722. Advance online publication. DOI: 10.1080/08839514.2025.2463722

Selwyn, N. (2022). The future of AI and education: Some cautionary notes. *European Journal of Education*, *57*(4), 620–631. DOI: 10.1111/ejed.12532

Singh, A. (2025). *Low-code/no-code for the education industry*. Retrieved from https://blog.tooljet.ai/modernize-education-using-low-code-no-code-platforms

UNESCO. (2021). *Recommendation on the Ethics of Artificial Intelligence*. Retrieved from Paris: UNESCO: https://unesdoc.unesco.org/ark:/48223/pf0000381137

UNESCO. (2023). *Guidance for Generative AI in Education and Research*. Retrieved from Paris: UNESCO: https://unesdoc.unesco.org/ark:/48223/pf0000386693

University of Bath. (2024). *Responsible research assessment*. Retrieved from https://www.bath.ac.uk/campaigns/responsible-research-assessment/

University of Edinburgh. (2024). *Responsible research assessment*. Retrieved from https://www.ed.ac.uk/research-cultures/home/responsible-research-assessment

WhizzBridge. (2025). *AI-chatbot development services: Custom, GPT-based, multilingual solutions*. Retrieved from https://www.whizzbridge.com/software/ai-chatbot-development-services

KEY TERMS AND DEFINITIONS

Faculty People who teach: do research, and provide service at a college or university.

Ethical Tension A situation where important values conflict: such as efficiency versus fairness or innovation versus privacy.

Human-in-the-Loop A process where humans are involved in checking and approving AI results.:

Faculty Evaluation Faculty members' work is being reviewed based on teaching: research, or service.

Research The invention or study of new ideas.:

Algorithmic Decision-Making The decision is based on a computer system.:

Academic Freedom The independence of faculty to teach: research, and share ideas without restriction.

Bias in AI Unfair results produced by an AI system:

Transparency How clearly an AI system shows what it does: what data it uses, and how it makes decisions.

Data Privacy Protecting personal and academic information from being misused or accessed without permission.:

Automation Using technology to carry out tasks with little or no human involvement.:

Institutional Policy Rules and guidelines created by an institution to direct how AI and other tools should be used.:

Chapter 6
Redefining Professorial Roles and Navigating AI Integration in Academic Careers

Stephanie Nicolas Pantelides
http://orcid.org/0000-0002-6917-3650
Frederick University, Cyprus

ABSTRACT

This chapter examines how artificial intelligence (AI) is reshaping the academic profession and professorial appointments in contemporary higher education. Situating AI within the historical evolution of academic evaluation—from peer judgment and collegial governance to metricization and algorithmic mediation—the chapter analyzes how AI-driven systems are transforming research, teaching, service, and faculty career pathways. Drawing on the sociology of professions, audit culture, and theories of algorithmic governance, it conceptualizes AI as a sociotechnical force that reconfigures professional authority, autonomy, and notions of academic merit. Particular attention is given to the implications of AI for faculty recruitment, promotion, and tenure, as well as for early-career academics and institutional equity. The chapter argues that while AI offers opportunities for efficiency and innovation, its integration requires robust governance frameworks to safeguard academic freedom, professional judgment, and inclusivity.

DOI: 10.4018/979-8-3373-8525-9.ch006

INTRODUCTION TO THE ACADEMIC PROFESSION IN THE AGE OF AI

Artificial intelligence (AI) is rapidly becoming a defining feature of contemporary higher education, shaping how knowledge is produced, disseminated, evaluated, and governed. While much of the early discourse on AI in universities focused primarily on teaching and learning innovations—such as adaptive learning systems, automated assessment platforms, and generative tools for instructional design—AI technologies are now increasingly embedded in broader institutional processes that directly affect the academic profession itself. Recruitment systems, workload management platforms, research analytics, citation databases, predictive evaluation tools, and learning analytics systems are becoming integral components of the infrastructures through which academic work is organized, monitored, and assessed.

This chapter argues that AI should not be understood merely as a neutral technological tool designed to improve efficiency. Rather, AI functions as a sociotechnical governance mechanism that reshapes professional authority, academic evaluation, institutional decision-making, and scholarly identity within higher education. The integration of AI into hiring, promotion, tenure, performance management, and institutional planning has profound implications for academic autonomy, professional legitimacy, equity, and the future organization of academic labor.

The academic profession has historically been organized around a relatively stable set of norms and practices, including peer review, collegial governance, disciplinary expertise, academic freedom, and professional autonomy (Altbach, 2000; Freidson, 2001). Professorial appointments and career progression traditionally relied on expert judgment exercised through disciplinary communities, departmental committees, and shared governance structures. Over the past several decades, however, these arrangements have been progressively reshaped by managerial reforms, audit cultures, performance-based funding systems, institutional rankings, and metric-driven accountability mechanisms that emphasize efficiency, visibility, and measurable outputs (Power, 1997; Shore & Wright, 2015).

AI-driven systems represent the latest—and arguably most consequential—phase in this historical transformation. They intensify trends toward datafication, quantification, and algorithmic governance by enabling increasingly sophisticated forms of monitoring, prediction, and evaluation. In research, AI tools automate literature discovery, data analysis, and scholarly writing support. In teaching, learning analytics platforms generate granular data on student engagement and instructional effectiveness. In administration, AI systems support workload allocation, grant management, and institutional planning. Most significantly for this chapter, AI-driven metrics and predictive systems are increasingly embedded in faculty recruitment, promotion, and tenure processes, shaping how academic merit, productivity, and professional value are defined and assessed (Hicks et al., 2015; Williamson & Eynon, 2020).

These developments raise important questions about the future of the academic profession. What happens to peer judgment and disciplinary expertise when algorithmic systems increasingly mediate academic careers? How do AI-driven metrics reshape notions of excellence, merit, impact, and scholarly legitimacy? What forms of inequality may emerge when AI systems privilege certain outputs, institutions, disciplines, or career trajectories over others? And how can universities and policymakers develop governance frameworks that harness the potential benefits of AI while protecting academic freedom, collegiality, and professional autonomy?

Although scholarship on AI in higher education has expanded rapidly, much of the literature continues to focus on pedagogy, instructional innovation, and student learning. Comparatively less attention has been paid to the implications of AI for professorial appointments, promotion systems, academic careers, and professional identity. This chapter addresses that gap by examining how algorithmic and data-driven systems increasingly influence the governance of academic work and the organization of the academic profession.

The originality of this chapter lies in its integration of the sociology of professions, audit culture, science and technology studies (STS), algorithmic governance, and AI ethics into a unified analytical framework for understanding the transformation of professorial roles in AI-mediated universities. By focusing specifically on academic appointments, career progression, and evaluation systems, the chapter extends current debates beyond classroom applications of AI and contributes to emerging scholarship on digital governance in higher education.

A central concern of this analysis is the growing reliance on data-driven and algorithmic systems in faculty hiring, promotion, and evaluation. Universities worldwide face increasing pressure to demonstrate accountability, competitiveness, productivity, and global visibility through rankings, performance indicators, and standardized benchmarks (Marginson & van der Wende, 2007). AI amplifies these pressures by enabling more advanced forms of measurement, prediction, and comparison. Bibliometric analytics, citation-based indicators, predictive profiling systems, and algorithmic recommendation tools promise efficiency and objectivity, yet they also risk narrowing definitions of academic value while reinforcing existing institutional, disciplinary, and geopolitical hierarchies (Espeland & Sauder, 2007; Müller & de Rijcke, 2017).

For early-career academics, these dynamics are particularly consequential. As AI-driven metrics increasingly shape hiring and promotion decisions, scholars may feel compelled to align their research, teaching, and service activities with what is most visible and measurable within algorithmic systems. This can discourage intellectual risk-taking, interdisciplinary scholarship, and forms of knowledge production that are less compatible with dominant digital infrastructures. Unequal access to AI-enhanced research tools and data infrastructures may also exacerbate disparities between well-resourced and under-resourced institutions, as well as between scholars across geographic and disciplinary contexts (Czerniewicz et al., 2021).

The implications of AI extend beyond individual careers to broader questions of governance and accountability. As algorithmic systems become increasingly influential in appointments and evaluation processes, issues of transparency, explainability, contestability, and institutional oversight become more pressing. Decisions that were once shaped primarily through collegial deliberation may now be partially delegated to opaque systems developed by external vendors or built on proprietary data models. This raises concerns about the erosion of shared governance, the redistribution of authority within universities, and academics' capacity to challenge AI-mediated decisions that affect their professional lives (Kitchin, 2017; Selwyn, 2019).

At the same time, it would be misleading to portray AI solely as a threat to the academic profession. When thoughtfully designed and responsibly governed, AI systems have the potential to reduce administrative burdens, support more inclusive hiring practices, enhance research collaboration, and improve access to institutional data for decision-making. The challenge lies in ensuring that AI enhances rather than undermines professional judgment, equity, and academic freedom. This requires robust ethical frameworks, transparent governance structures, and institutional policies that recognize the sociopolitical dimensions of AI adoption.

The purpose of this chapter, therefore, is not to advocate either for or against AI in higher education, but to provide a critical and nuanced analysis of how AI is reshaping the academic profession and professorial appointments. The chapter proceeds from the premise that the future of academic work is not technologically predetermined. Rather, it is shaped by decisions made by universities, policymakers, accreditation bodies, technology providers, and academic communities concerning how AI systems are designed, implemented, and governed.

The chapter proceeds in several stages. The next section outlines the conceptual and theoretical frameworks informing the analysis, drawing on the sociology of professions, audit culture, algorithmic governance, and AI ethics. This is followed by a historical overview tracing the evolution of academic evaluation from peer-based collegial judgment to data-driven and algorithmically mediated systems. Subsequent sections examine the transformation of professorial work in research, teaching, and service; analyze AI-driven appointments, promotion, and tenure systems; and explore the implications of AI-driven metrics for academic merit, professional identity, governance, and institutional policy. The chapter concludes by reflecting on how higher education institutions and academic communities can prepare for an AI-integrated future while preserving the core values of scholarly judgment, equity, and academic integrity.

CONCEPTUAL AND THEORETICAL FRAMEWORK

The integration of AI into higher education requires an interdisciplinary framework capable of addressing technological, organizational, ethical, and professional dimensions simultaneously. AI does not operate in isolation; it is embedded within institutional structures, governance systems, disciplinary norms, and broader sociotechnical environments. Understanding AI's influence on professorial work, appointments, and academic careers therefore requires drawing on complementary perspectives from the sociology of professions, audit culture, science and technology studies (STS), algorithmic governance, and AI ethics. Together, these frameworks provide analytical tools for understanding AI not simply as a technological innovation, but as a sociotechnical force that reshapes academic labor, professional authority, institutional governance, and evaluative practices.

Sociology of Professions: Autonomy, Expertise, and Jurisdiction

The sociology of professions conceptualizes academic work as a form of specialized knowledge labor governed by professional autonomy, disciplinary expertise, peer review, and collegial authority (Abbott, 1988; Freidson, 2001). Traditionally, academic appointments, promotions, and tenure decisions relied heavily on collegial judgment exercised within disciplinary communities. Professional legitimacy was grounded in peer recognition and scholarly expertise rather than external managerial control.

AI-mediated evaluation systems challenge these traditional arrangements in several ways. First, algorithmic systems codify, quantify, rank, and compare academic activities through standardized metrics and predictive analytics, potentially displacing nuanced forms of professional judgment (Williamson & Eynon, 2020). Second, AI redistributes evaluative authority from disciplinary communities toward data infrastructures, institutional management systems, and external technology vendors. Tasks historically performed by departmental committees or peer reviewers are increasingly mediated by algorithmic tools.

From this perspective, AI alters professional jurisdiction by reshaping who controls evaluation, expertise, and legitimacy within higher education institutions. The sociology of professions therefore provides an important framework for understanding how AI both reinforces and destabilizes traditional forms of academic authority, while also illuminating the resistance strategies and adaptive practices academics may adopt to preserve professional autonomy.

Audit Culture and Metricization

A complementary framework is the concept of audit culture, which examines the expansion of performance measurement, accountability systems, benchmarking, and quantitative evaluation in professional organizations (Power, 1997; Shore & Wright, 2015). Higher education has experienced decades of managerial reform emphasizing rankings, productivity indicators, citation metrics, grant income, and measurable institutional outputs.

AI intensifies these trends by enabling large-scale data analysis, predictive assessment, automated benchmarking, and increasingly granular forms of institutional oversight. Research productivity, teaching effectiveness, institutional visibility, and academic impact are now frequently evaluated through algorithmically mediated indicators and analytics platforms.

While these systems promise efficiency, comparability, and transparency, audit culture theory highlights several associated risks. Metrics-driven evaluation can narrow definitions of academic success by privileging outputs that are easily quantified while undervaluing interdisciplinary, critical, pedagogical, or locally relevant scholarship (Espeland & Sauder, 2007; Hicks et al., 2015). AI systems may also amplify existing institutional, disciplinary, and geographic inequalities by embedding historical biases into algorithmic evaluation frameworks.

By situating AI within audit culture, this chapter foregrounds enduring tensions between efficiency and professional judgment, accountability and autonomy, and standardization and intellectual diversity.

Algorithmic Governance and Sociotechnical Systems

The literature on algorithmic governance and sociotechnical systems provides a framework for understanding how AI mediates institutional authority and organizational decision-making (Kitchin, 2017; Mittelstadt et al., 2016). Algorithmic governance refers to the use of computational systems to monitor, classify, evaluate, predict, and regulate human activity within organizational settings.

In higher education, algorithmic systems increasingly influence faculty recruitment, publication visibility, workload allocation, teaching evaluation, institutional planning, and promotion trajectories. Importantly, these systems are not neutral technical instruments. They reflect institutional priorities, commercial interests, embedded assumptions about academic excellence, and broader political and economic logics.

From a sociotechnical perspective, AI systems are co-constituted with human practices, organizational cultures, institutional policies, and governance structures (Selwyn, 2019; Williamson, 2017). Decisions concerning which metrics to prioritize, how outputs are weighted, or how recommendation systems are designed are inherently social and political. Consequently, AI systems shape not only administrative processes but also professional norms, institutional power relations, and scholarly behavior.

This perspective allows the chapter to conceptualize AI as part of a broader ecology of academic governance in which technological systems interact dynamically with professional cultures, managerial objectives, and institutional structures.

AI Ethics and Professional Responsibility

Ethical frameworks for AI adoption emphasize fairness, accountability, transparency, explainability, and inclusivity in automated systems (Jobin et al., 2019; Mittelstadt, 2019). In academic contexts, these concerns are particularly significant because AI increasingly influences high-stakes decisions related to hiring, tenure, promotion, workload distribution, and scholarly recognition.

Algorithmic systems trained on historical academic data may reproduce and amplify existing inequalities related to gender, race, institutional prestige, discipline, geography, or publication practices. Metrics-based systems may disadvantage scholars working in under-resourced institutions, interdisciplinary fields, or disciplines with slower publication cycles.

Responsible AI governance therefore requires balancing technological innovation with professional values such as academic freedom, collegiality, intellectual diversity, inclusivity, and equitable participation. Ethical governance also involves ensuring transparency regarding how AI systems function, how decisions are derived, and how individuals may contest or appeal algorithmically influenced outcomes.

In this context, AI ethics intersects directly with questions of professional responsibility and institutional governance. The challenge is not simply technical accuracy, but whether AI systems align with the normative values and democratic traditions of higher education.

Conceptual Approach and Literature Selection

This chapter adopts a conceptual and interdisciplinary analytical approach rather than an empirical methodology. The analysis draws on scholarship from higher education studies, sociology of professions, science and technology studies, AI governance, digital labor studies, organizational sociology, and critical data ethics.

Sources were selected through thematic review of foundational and contemporary scholarship related to academic evaluation, algorithmic governance, faculty careers, audit culture, digitalization, and AI integration in higher education. Particular attention was given to literature published between 2023 and 2026, while also incorporating foundational theoretical works necessary for historical and conceptual grounding.

Integrating the Frameworks: A Multidimensional Lens

Taken together, these frameworks provide a multidimensional lens for understanding AI's impact on the academic profession. The sociology of professions highlights transformations in professional autonomy and jurisdiction; audit culture illuminates the growing centrality of metrics, accountability, and managerial oversight; algorithmic governance situates AI within broader sociotechnical systems of institutional control; and AI ethics foregrounds the normative and political implications of algorithmic decision-making.

By synthesizing these perspectives, the chapter conceptualizes AI not merely as a technological intervention but as a transformative force reshaping the social, organizational, political, and ethical dimensions of academic work. This conceptual foundation underpins the subsequent sections, which examine the historical evolution of academic evaluation, the transformation of professorial labor, the role of AI in appointments and promotion systems, and the governance challenges emerging within AI-mediated higher education.

HISTORICAL CONTEXT: FROM PEER JUDGMENT TO ALGORITHMIC MEDIATION

Understanding the contemporary impact of artificial intelligence (AI) on the academic profession requires situating it within the longer historical evolution of academic evaluation, professional authority, and institutional governance. Systems of faculty appointment, promotion, and recognition have never been static; rather, they have evolved in response to broader political, economic, technological, and organizational transformations.

What distinguishes the current moment is not simply the introduction of new technologies, but the progressive relocation of evaluative authority—from collegial peer judgment toward increasingly data-driven and algorithmically mediated systems. AI therefore represents both a continuation and an intensification of historical trends toward quantification, managerial governance, and digital oversight within higher education.

Peer Judgment, Collegial Governance, and Professional Authority

Historically, academic appointments and promotion decisions relied heavily on peer review, disciplinary expertise, and collegial governance structures. Faculty committees, external reviewers, and senior scholars assessed scholarly quality through professional judgment shaped by disciplinary norms, institutional culture, and shared understandings of intellectual contribution (Altbach, 2000; Abbott, 1988). These peer-based systems reflected what Freidson (2001) describes as professional autonomy, whereby the academic profession itself maintained authority over standards of quality, legitimacy, and expertise. Peer judgment served multiple functions: it ensured scholarly rigor, socialized academics into disciplinary cultures, and defined the boundaries of legitimate knowledge.

Importantly, collegial systems enabled contextualized evaluation. Committees could account for disciplinary differences, emerging research areas, teaching-intensive roles, institutional missions, and forms of scholarly contribution not easily reducible to numerical indicators. At the same time, these systems were not free from criticism. Peer-based evaluation could be opaque, slow, exclusionary, and vulnerable to favoritism, homophily, and informal power networks, often disadvantaging women, scholars from marginalized groups, and academics working outside dominant paradigms (Musselin, 2005). Such limitations would later be invoked to justify more standardized and quantitative approaches to academic evaluation.

The Emergence of Quantification and Bibliometric Indicators

Over time, higher education systems experienced increasing managerialization and metricization. The post–World War II expansion of universities created pressures for greater coordination, accountability, and comparability across institutions and disciplines.

It was within this context that bibliometrics, citation indexes, publication counts, rankings, and performance indicators gradually supplemented qualitative academic judgment. The development of citation indexing and bibliometric tools—most notably associated with Garfield's (1979) work—provided standardized mechanisms for assessing scholarly productivity and research influence.

Publication counts, journal impact factors, citation metrics, and grant indicators aligned closely with emerging national science policies and performance-based funding systems seeking measurable evidence of academic excellence and institutional productivity.

Initially, these quantitative indicators were intended to complement rather than replace peer judgment. Promotion and tenure committees generally considered bibliometric data alongside qualitative evaluations of research quality, teaching effectiveness, and service contributions. Nonetheless, the growing legitimacy of numerical indicators gradually reshaped academic norms and professional behavior, encouraging scholars to prioritize outputs visible within dominant databases, ranking systems, and publication infrastructures.

Audit Culture and the Managerial Turn in Higher Education

From the late twentieth century onward, higher education systems became increasingly shaped by managerial reforms emphasizing accountability, efficiency, transparency, benchmarking, and measurable performance. Governments, accreditation bodies, and funding agencies demanded demonstrable returns on public investment, leading to the proliferation of rankings, performance indicators, benchmarking exercises, and institutional audits (Power, 1997; Shore & Wright, 2015).

Within this audit culture, academic work was progressively reframed as a set of measurable outputs. Research productivity, grant income, student satisfaction, employability indicators, and institutional visibility became central to university reputation and resource allocation (Hazelkorn, 2015).

This managerial turn reduced the discretionary space traditionally occupied by collegial governance structures and normalized data-driven oversight within universities. Importantly, it also created institutional demand for increasingly sophisticated forms of measurement and analysis, laying essential groundwork for the later adoption of AI systems.

By the early twenty-first century, many universities had already incorporated institutional dashboards, research information systems, ranking platforms, and bibliometric databases into academic governance processes. AI emerged within this broader environment of digital managerialism rather than as a wholly separate development.

Digitalization and Early Algorithmic Systems

The expansion of digital infrastructures accelerated these transformations. Universities increasingly adopted analytics platforms, institutional dashboards, learning management systems, and bibliometric databases to monitor research productivity, teaching performance, and institutional activity in real time (Williamson, 2017).

Early algorithmic systems primarily focused on descriptive analytics: tracking publication outputs, automating citation counts, ranking journals, monitoring student evaluations, and generating institutional performance reports. Although these systems did not usually make decisions autonomously, they structured the informational environments within which decisions were made.

Importantly, these digital infrastructures were not neutral. The selection of indicators, dashboard designs, ranking methodologies, and weighting systems reflected institutional priorities and broader political-economic assumptions concerning academic excellence and productivity (Müller & de Rijcke, 2017). Research-intensive forms of academic work were frequently privileged, while teaching excellence, mentorship, collegiality, community engagement, and service activities often remained less visible within digital evaluation systems.

From Metrics to Predictive and Algorithmic Mediation

AI represents the latest stage in this historical evolution from peer judgment toward increasingly predictive and algorithmically mediated systems of academic governance.

Contemporary AI systems are capable not only of aggregating historical performance data but also of predicting future outcomes such as research impact, funding success, publication trajectories, teaching effectiveness, and career progression (Williamson & Eynon, 2020). AI tools can analyze publication networks, citation trajectories, co-authorship patterns, grant histories, and teaching analytics at scales beyond human capacity.

In some higher education systems, AI-supported platforms are already used to shortlist faculty candidates, identify "high-potential" researchers, benchmark institutional performance, flag perceived tenure risks, and support strategic hiring decisions. While these systems are generally framed as decision-support tools rather than autonomous decision-makers, their recommendations can significantly shape institutional outcomes, particularly within highly competitive and resource-constrained environments.

Recent developments across higher education systems also demonstrate uneven patterns of AI integration. Research-intensive universities in North America, Europe, and parts of Asia increasingly use AI-supported systems to monitor publication output, grant income, collaboration networks, and teaching analytics. In contrast, many institutions in lower-resource settings continue to rely primarily on traditional peer-review processes because of infrastructural, financial, and technological limitations.

This uneven integration demonstrates that AI adoption is not technologically inevitable. Rather, it reflects institutional priorities, governance models, funding structures, digital capacities, and broader geopolitical inequalities.

At the same time, AI-mediated evaluation raises important questions concerning professional authority, transparency, and accountability. When evaluative judgments rely on opaque predictive models trained on historical data, it becomes more difficult to contest, interpret, or explain decisions. Algorithmic mediation may obscure value judgments behind technical complexity while reducing opportunities for deliberation, contextual interpretation, and collegial appeal (Kitchin, 2017; Selwyn, 2019).

Continuity, Rupture, and the Significance of AI

Situating AI within this broader historical trajectory reveals both continuity and rupture. AI builds upon long-standing trends toward quantification, standardization, digitalization, and managerial oversight within higher education. Yet it also introduces new dynamics through predictive analytics, continuous monitoring, automated classification, and increasingly opaque forms of algorithmic mediation.

What distinguishes the contemporary moment is the scale, speed, predictive capacity, and infrastructural integration of AI systems. These technologies operate continuously across institutional boundaries, embedding evaluative assumptions in digital systems that may be difficult to scrutinize or challenge.

Crucially, AI intensifies enduring tensions within the academic profession: between autonomy and accountability, diversity and standardization, collegial judgment and managerial oversight, intellectual freedom and measurable performance.

Recognizing AI as part of a longer historical transformation underscores that its adoption is neither neutral nor inevitable. Rather, AI reflects institutional choices, governance regimes, political priorities, and professional negotiations concerning how academic work should be organized, evaluated, and rewarded.

This historical perspective provides the foundation for the subsequent sections of the chapter, which examine how AI reshapes research, teaching, service, faculty appointments, promotion systems, and professional identity within contemporary higher education.

TRANSFORMING PROFESSORIAL WORK: AI, ACADEMIC LABOR, AND THE RECONFIGURATION OF RESEARCH, TEACHING, AND SERVICE

The historical evolution from peer-based collegial judgment to metricization and algorithmic mediation, discussed in the previous section, provides important context for understanding how artificial intelligence (AI) is reshaping academic labor. AI-driven technologies do not emerge in isolation; they are layered onto existing digital infrastructures, managerial governance systems, and audit cultures that increasingly emphasize accountability, efficiency, visibility, and measurable performance. Consequently, AI does not simply introduce new tools into higher education. Rather, it reconfigures how research, teaching, service, and institutional governance are organized, evaluated, and recognized within the academic profession.

The transformation extends beyond questions of efficiency or automation. AI increasingly affects professional identity, workload expectations, career trajectories, and definitions of academic merit. Across research, teaching, and administrative work, AI systems influence what academics do, how their work is monitored, and which forms of labor become institutionally visible and rewarded.

Research and Scholarly Production

Historically, academic research was governed primarily through disciplinary expertise, peer review, and collegial judgment, with scholarly communities determining standards of originality, rigor, and contribution (Abbott, 1988; Freidson, 2001). Over time, bibliometrics, citation indicators, and institutional rankings introduced more quantitative forms of research evaluation. AI represents a further stage in this evolution by embedding computational intelligence directly into research production, dissemination, and evaluation.

AI-assisted systems are now widely used for literature discovery, citation analysis, language editing, predictive analytics, and research mapping. Machine learning–based recommendation systems can identify relevant scholarship, detect emerging research trends, and analyze collaboration networks at a scale previously impossible for individual scholars (Stokel-Walker, 2023). In data-intensive fields, AI tools accelerate data analysis and pattern recognition, expanding methodological possibilities and supporting large-scale interdisciplinary research.

Research analytics platforms increasingly monitor publication impact, citation visibility, collaboration patterns, grant performance, and institutional benchmarking. Universities often use AI-supported bibliometric systems to identify high-impact researchers and compare institutional performance against global rankings. While such systems may support strategic planning and research management, they also risk encouraging publication strategies oriented toward measurable visibility rather than intellectual originality or social relevance.

Generative AI tools further complicate scholarly practice by automating drafting, summarization, translation, coding assistance, and textual production. These developments raise significant questions concerning authorship, originality, intellectual property, scholarly integrity, and the boundaries between human and machine contribution in academic knowledge production.

Importantly, AI reshapes not only the evaluation of research outputs but also the research process itself. Earlier metric systems primarily assessed scholarly performance retrospectively after publication. AI systems increasingly intervene during the production process by shaping what literature is encountered, which topics appear promising, which journals are prioritized, and how research findings are framed and disseminated. This creates a subtle but important shift from retrospective evaluation toward real-time algorithmic mediation of scholarly work.

While AI can enhance productivity, collaboration, and access to information, it may also reinforce dominant paradigms and existing inequalities. Recommendation systems trained on historical publication and citation data tend to privilege already visible journals, methodologies, institutions, and research agendas, potentially marginalizing innovative, interdisciplinary, locally relevant, or critical scholarship (Müller & de Rijcke, 2017). In this sense, AI intensifies cumulative advantage dynamics already associated with metric-driven academic systems (Espeland & Sauder, 2007).

For early-career academics in particular, AI-mediated research environments may shape professional behavior in powerful ways. Scholars may increasingly align their research agendas with algorithmically visible trends and measurable indicators in order to maximize publication impact, funding opportunities, and career progression. Consequently, AI functions not merely as a technical infrastructure but also as a normative force influencing research priorities, scholarly visibility, and professional identity.

Teaching and Pedagogical Evaluation

Teaching has historically been one of the least standardized dimensions of academic work. Traditionally, teaching quality was assessed through peer observation, disciplinary norms, student feedback, and professional reflection. As managerial reforms expanded across higher education, student evaluations and standardized performance indicators became increasingly prominent—although often contested—mechanisms for assessing instructional effectiveness.

AI represents a further intensification of this trend through the growth of learning analytics, adaptive platforms, and data-driven pedagogical systems. AI-driven learning analytics platforms generate detailed data concerning student participation, engagement, assessment performance, progression patterns, and online learning behaviors (Siemens, 2013; Selwyn, 2019). In some institutions, these data are integrated into faculty teaching evaluations, workload systems, curriculum planning, and promotion processes.

This development reflects a broader shift from episodic teaching evaluation toward continuous pedagogical visibility, where instructional practices are increasingly monitored through digital infrastructures. Proponents argue that such systems can help identify learning difficulties, personalize instruction, and improve student outcomes. However, critics caution that quantified indicators cannot fully capture pedagogical quality, mentorship, intellectual development, or the relational and transformative dimensions of teaching.

Overreliance on analytics may privilege standardized instructional models that align with platform-generated indicators while undervaluing disciplinary diversity, critical pedagogy, and less measurable forms of educational engagement. AI-mediated teaching evaluation therefore challenges traditional notions of pedagogical autonomy by embedding assumptions about effective teaching within algorithmic systems. Importantly, AI systems do not simply measure teaching; they can shape pedagogical behavior. Instructors may feel pressure to adapt course structures, communication styles, or assessment strategies to align with metrics that improve engagement scores, retention rates, or platform-based indicators of success. As in research evaluation, the concern is not necessarily the replacement of academic judgment but its gradual displacement by algorithmic proxies and managerial oversight.

Administrative, Service, and Governance Work

Service and administrative work have traditionally been essential but comparatively undervalued dimensions of academic labor. Mentorship, committee participation, institutional governance, student advising, and community engagement have often relied on trust-based and qualitative recognition systems rather than standardized metrics.

AI systems are increasingly being integrated into scheduling, grant management, workload allocation, institutional reporting, resource planning, and performance management. These systems can automate routine administrative tasks and reduce some bureaucratic burdens, potentially freeing time for research and teaching activities.

At the same time, the platformization of academic labor has intensified forms of digital oversight and managerial surveillance. Universities increasingly operate through interconnected digital systems that translate academic activities into measurable data flows. AI-supported workload systems may standardize expectations regarding productivity, responsiveness, and efficiency, while simultaneously increasing institutional monitoring of academic behavior.

Importantly, many AI-driven workload and evaluation systems rely on standardized task categories and time-allocation assumptions that may inadequately capture invisible forms of academic labor, including mentoring, emotional support, diversity and inclusion work, and informal collegial contributions. Such forms of labor are often disproportionately undertaken by women and minoritized academics (Czerniewicz et al., 2021). Consequently, AI systems may reproduce or even intensify existing inequalities in the recognition and valuation of academic work. Where service activities become quantified through institutional dashboards or reporting systems, there is also a risk that academic service becomes increasingly instrumentalized.

Participation may be measured by numerical indicators—committee memberships, outreach activities, leadership roles, or administrative outputs—but these indicators may not adequately capture the quality, complexity, or institutional significance of such contributions.

AI, Academic Identity, and the Fragmentation of Professional Work

Historically, the academic profession was organized around a relatively integrated model of research, teaching, and service, unified through professional identity, disciplinary culture, and collegial governance. The expansion of audit culture and managerial reforms fragmented this model by introducing distinct performance indicators and accountability structures across different domains of academic work.

AI intensifies this fragmentation by enabling domain-specific optimization through multiple interconnected data systems. Research productivity, teaching effectiveness, service contributions, and institutional visibility may each be governed through separate algorithmic frameworks with different evaluative logics and performance expectations.

This fragmentation has important implications for professional identity and academic autonomy. Academics increasingly navigate competing algorithmic demands aligned with institutional priorities, rankings, funding pressures, and managerial objectives. The cumulative effect is a shift away from holistic professional judgment toward portfolio-based and continuously monitored forms of evaluation.

At the same time, AI should not be understood simply as a rupture with previous academic traditions. Rather, it represents an intensification of longer historical trends toward quantification, standardization, digitalization, and managerial governance in higher education. What distinguishes the current moment is the scale, speed, predictive capacity, and opacity of AI-mediated systems. These technologies can operate continuously across institutional boundaries while embedding evaluative assumptions that may remain difficult to contest or fully understand.

Implications for the Academic Profession

The transformation of research, teaching, administration, and service under AI has profound implications for the future of the academic profession. AI reshapes not only what academics do, but also how scholarly value, productivity, and professional legitimacy are defined and rewarded within universities.

By embedding institutional priorities and historical patterns into algorithmic systems, AI risks narrowing academic diversity while presenting itself as neutral and objective. Yet these outcomes are not technologically inevitable. As with earlier phases of metricization and audit culture, the effects of AI depend on governance structures, institutional choices, professional norms, and the capacity of academic communities to critically shape how technologies are adopted and evaluated.

Recognizing AI as part of a longer historical transformation allows universities and academic communities to assess more carefully which aspects of academic work should be enhanced, protected, or reimagined in an AI-integrated future. This analysis also sets the stage for the next section, which examines how AI directly influences faculty appointments, promotion, and tenure, where the stakes of algorithmic mediation become particularly visible and consequential.

AI IN PROFESSORIAL APPOINTMENTS, PROMOTION, AND TENURE

Artificial intelligence (AI) is increasingly integrated into the processes that determine faculty appointments, promotions, and tenure decisions, fundamentally reshaping academic career trajectories and institutional governance. Traditionally, professorial appointments and promotions were guided by collegial evaluation, peer review, and disciplinary norms grounded in professional expertise and shared governance structures. Although these systems emphasized qualitative judgment and contextual interpretation, AI introduces data-driven and algorithmically mediated forms of evaluation that promise efficiency, standardization, scalability, and predictive capability.

At the same time, AI-driven evaluation systems raise significant concerns regarding bias, transparency, accountability, professional autonomy, and the changing meaning of academic merit. Building on the historical and theoretical frameworks developed in earlier sections, this section examines how AI transforms faculty recruitment, promotion, tenure, and career progression, situating these developments within broader debates concerning academic governance, equity, audit culture, and professional identity.

AI in Faculty Recruitment

AI technologies are increasingly used to streamline and support academic recruitment processes. Applicant tracking systems (ATS), natural language processing (NLP) tools, bibliometric analytics, and machine learning algorithms can process large volumes of applications by analyzing CVs, publication records, citation patterns, teaching statements, grant histories, and other indicators of academic performance (Huang & Rust, 2021; Upadhyay & Khandelwal, 2018).

These systems often aggregate multiple forms of data into predictive profiles intended to estimate candidates' future scholarly productivity, funding potential, teaching effectiveness, or institutional "fit." Some universities have also experimented with AI-supported recommendation systems that identify candidates based on historical hiring trends, co-authorship networks, citation trajectories, and disciplinary productivity patterns (Williamson & Piattoeva, 2022).

AI-mediated recruitment offers several institutional advantages. Automated systems can reduce administrative workload, increase scalability for large applicant pools, standardize preliminary screening processes, and potentially reduce some forms of overt human subjectivity. In highly competitive hiring environments, AI systems are often presented as mechanisms for improving efficiency, consistency, and evidence-based decision-making.

However, these systems also introduce substantial ethical, professional, and organizational challenges.

First, algorithmic systems are only as unbiased as the data on which they are trained. Historical hiring data frequently reflect longstanding inequalities related to gender, race, geography, institutional prestige, discipline, and language. Consequently, AI recruitment systems may reproduce or amplify existing disparities by favoring candidates whose profiles resemble historically successful or institutionally privileged trajectories (Bogen & Rieke, 2018).

Second, the opacity of many AI systems complicates transparency and accountability. Candidates may be unable to understand how decisions were derived, which indicators were prioritized, or why particular applicants were advanced or excluded (Kitchin, 2017). This raises important concerns regarding procedural fairness, contestability, and due process in academic hiring.

Third, algorithmic recruitment systems may shift evaluative emphasis away from qualitative assessments of intellectual potential, originality, teaching philosophy, mentorship capacity, collegiality, and institutional contribution toward quantifiable indicators such as publication counts, citation metrics, grant acquisition, or institutional rankings.

A key tension therefore emerges between efficiency and professional judgment. While AI systems can process extensive datasets rapidly, hiring decisions in academia often require nuanced and context-sensitive evaluation that cannot easily be reduced to standardized metrics (Abbott, 1988; Freidson, 2001). Consequently, AI is best understood not as a replacement for human decision-making but as a supplementary infrastructure that shapes how evaluative judgments are organized and prioritized.

AI in Promotion and Tenure Evaluation

AI is also transforming promotion and tenure (P&T) processes, which have historically relied on peer review, external letters, teaching evaluations, service records, and institutional performance indicators (Altbach, 2000). Contemporary AI systems allow institutions to aggregate and analyze data across multiple domains of academic activity, generating increasingly detailed profiles of scholarly productivity, teaching effectiveness, grant income, professional service, and institutional engagement.

Predictive analytics systems may estimate future research impact, funding success, collaboration potential, or international visibility, thereby extending evaluation beyond retrospective assessment toward anticipatory forms of career governance.

These systems are often promoted as mechanisms for increasing consistency, standardization, and objectivity across departments and institutions (Hicks et al., 2015). AI can also identify patterns in career progression, benchmark faculty performance against institutional expectations, and assist administrators in monitoring tenure eligibility or productivity trajectories. Nevertheless, AI-mediated promotion and tenure systems raise several important concerns.

Algorithmic Bias and Disciplinary Inequality

Metrics-based evaluation systems may disadvantage scholars working in disciplines with lower publication or citation rates, including many humanities and social science fields. Interdisciplinary scholars, community-engaged researchers, and early-career academics may also be disadvantaged because algorithmic systems frequently privilege established publication patterns and cumulative citation visibility (Müller & de Rijcke, 2017).

Opacity and Explainability

Many AI systems function as "black boxes," producing rankings or predictive outputs without transparent explanation regarding how evaluations were calculated or weighted (Selwyn, 2019). This lack of explainability complicates appeals, remediation, and professional accountability.

Metricization of Academic Merit

AI-driven evaluation systems intensify the broader trend toward metricization discussed in earlier sections. Reliance on bibliometrics, citation indicators, altmetrics, and productivity dashboards risks reducing complex scholarly contributions to numerical proxies, potentially undervaluing creativity, mentorship, pedagogical innovation, collegiality, and public engagement (Espeland & Sauder, 2007).

Professional Autonomy and Collegial Governance

The integration of AI into promotion and tenure systems may shift evaluative authority away from collegial deliberation toward institutional management systems and algorithmic infrastructures. This transformation raises important questions regarding professional autonomy, academic freedom, and the future role of peer review within academic governance (Freidson, 2001; Power, 1997).

These developments are particularly consequential for early-career academics, who increasingly navigate professional environments shaped by digital visibility, strategic metric alignment, and algorithmically mediated evaluation systems. Familiarity with AI-driven indicators and data infrastructures may become as important for career progression as traditional forms of mentorship and collegial recognition (Czerniewicz et al., 2021).

Emerging Practices and Institutional Developments

Across higher education systems, universities and research organizations are experimenting with AI-supported approaches to recruitment, evaluation, and institutional management.

Examples include:

- AI-powered bibliometric dashboards used to monitor publication output, collaboration networks, citation impact, and grant success;
- Predictive hiring tools that identify candidates likely to achieve high research impact or funding success based on historical datasets and network analysis (Williamson & Piattoeva, 2022);
- Learning analytics systems that integrate teaching data into promotion dossiers and instructional evaluation frameworks (Siemens, 2013);
- Institutional benchmarking systems that compare faculty productivity across departments, disciplines, and international rankings.

These developments demonstrate AI's growing role in shaping academic careers and institutional priorities. At the same time, they underscore persistent tensions regarding transparency, disciplinary diversity, equity, and the preservation of collegial governance.

Importantly, AI adoption remains uneven across higher education systems. Research-intensive universities in well-resourced contexts are generally more likely to adopt AI-driven governance systems, while institutions with fewer technological and financial resources continue to rely more heavily on traditional peer-review mechanisms. This unevenness reflects broader global inequalities in digital infrastructure, institutional capacity, and access to data-driven technologies.

Equity, Diversity, and Inclusion in AI-Mediated Evaluation

AI-mediated evaluation systems have profound implications for equity, diversity, and inclusion within academic careers. Algorithms trained on historical academic data may encode and reproduce systemic inequalities by favoring candidates and career trajectories historically associated with institutional success (Bogen & Rieke, 2018).

Institutional prestige, publication language, disciplinary norms, geographic location, gender, race, and access to digital resources may become embedded within algorithmic outputs, thereby shaping opportunities for hiring, promotion, and recognition.

Ensuring equitable AI deployment requires several interconnected strategies:

1. **Bias Auditing**

Regular evaluation of AI systems is necessary to detect discriminatory patterns and unequal outcomes across demographic, disciplinary, and institutional categories.

2. **Transparency and Explainability**

Institutions should clearly communicate how AI systems operate, which indicators are used, and how evaluative weights are assigned.

3. **Human Oversight**

Peer review and collegial judgment must remain central to academic decision-making, with AI functioning as a support mechanism rather than a replacement for professional expertise.

4. **Inclusive Evaluation Frameworks**

Institutions should develop broader indicators of academic contribution that recognize mentorship, teaching innovation, interdisciplinary scholarship, community engagement, and public intellectual work (Crawford & Paglen, 2019).

By embedding equity considerations into AI-mediated evaluation systems, universities can potentially benefit from efficiency and analytical support while reducing the risks of exclusionary or discriminatory outcomes.

Implications for Professional Identity and Governance

AI's integration into recruitment, promotion, and tenure reshapes not only evaluation systems but also professional identity itself. Academics increasingly operate within environments where scholarly visibility, productivity, and professional recognition are mediated through algorithmic systems.

Professors must therefore navigate complex relationships between collegial norms, institutional expectations, and digital evaluation infrastructures. Understanding how AI systems define, measure, and reward academic value becomes increasingly important for career development and professional legitimacy.

At the institutional level, universities face growing pressure to develop governance structures that ensure AI complements rather than replaces professional judgment. Preserving academic freedom, transparency, accountability, and shared governance remains essential as algorithmic systems become more deeply embedded in academic careers (Williamson & Eynon, 2020; Kitchin, 2017).

AI should therefore be understood not merely as a technical innovation but as a sociopolitical actor within higher education, shaping power relations, resource allocation, institutional priorities, and professional hierarchies.

Summary

AI is rapidly reshaping faculty appointments, promotion, and tenure by introducing new forms of data-driven evaluation, predictive analytics, and algorithmic governance. While these systems offer opportunities for efficiency, standardization, and institutional coordination, they also raise critical concerns regarding bias, transparency, metricization, professional autonomy, and equity.

Understanding AI's influence on academic careers requires recognizing that algorithmic systems are not neutral instruments but infrastructures that shape how academic merit, productivity, and legitimacy are defined and rewarded. The next section explores how AI-driven metrics and analytics further reconfigure notions of academic value and scholarly excellence.

METRICS, MERIT, AND THE RECONFIGURATION OF ACADEMIC VALUE

The integration of artificial intelligence (AI) into higher education has profoundly altered how academic merit and scholarly value are defined, measured, and recognized. Historically, academic excellence was assessed primarily through qualitative mechanisms such as peer review, disciplinary recognition, mentorship, collegial reputation, and intellectual contribution (Freidson, 2001). Increasingly, however, AI-mediated systems evaluate academic work through quantitative indicators, predictive analytics, bibliometric profiling, and algorithmic ranking systems.

These developments are not merely technical adjustments to existing evaluation practices. AI-driven metrics actively reshape institutional definitions of excellence, influence academic behavior, and redefine the relationship between professional judgment and measurable performance. This section examines how AI reconfigures academic value, the implications for professional identity and scholarly labor, and the risks associated with increasingly metric-driven systems of governance.

From Peer Judgment to Quantitative Metrics

The evaluation of academic merit has evolved over several decades from predominantly peer-centered judgment toward increasingly metric-based forms of assessment. Bibliometric indicators such as publication counts, citation indexes, journal rankings, and impact factors were initially introduced to supplement expert review and provide standardized measures of scholarly influence (Hicks et al., 2015).

Over time, however, these metrics became increasingly central to decisions concerning hiring, promotion, tenure, funding, and institutional reputation. This development reflected broader processes of managerialization and audit culture within higher education (Power, 1997; Shore & Wright, 2015).

AI intensifies this trend by enabling algorithmic aggregation, predictive modeling, and continuous performance monitoring. Machine learning systems can combine multiple indicators—including citations, grant histories, co-authorship networks, altmetrics, institutional rankings, teaching evaluations, and collaboration patterns—to produce increasingly complex profiles of academic performance (Müller & de Rijcke, 2017).

Unlike earlier metric systems that primarily measured past outputs, AI systems increasingly predict future productivity, impact, and visibility. This predictive capacity extends evaluative logic beyond retrospective assessment toward anticipatory governance of academic careers.

Redefining Academic Merit

AI-driven metrics do more than measure academic work; they shape institutional understandings of what counts as valuable scholarship. Indicators increasingly function as de facto standards of excellence, influencing research agendas, publication strategies, teaching practices, and professional behavior.

Scholars may prioritize highly cited topics, high-impact journals, internationally visible collaborations, or grant-funded projects because these activities align with algorithmically recognized indicators of success (Espeland & Sauder, 2007).

This reconfiguration of academic value has several important consequences.

Narrowing of Research Agendas

AI-driven metrics may encourage research that is easily measurable, internationally visible, and likely to generate citations, potentially discouraging interdisciplinary, innovative, critical, or locally relevant scholarship that falls outside dominant bibliometric systems (Hicks et al., 2015).

Transformation of Professional Identity

Academic identity increasingly incorporates forms of metric literacy and data awareness. Professional success is no longer determined solely by intellectual contribution or teaching excellence but also by visibility within algorithmic evaluation systems and digital infrastructures (Williamson, 2017).

Commodification and Datafication of Scholarship

AI-driven metrics contribute to the broader datafication of academic labor by framing scholarly work as a series of measurable outputs rather than a holistic intellectual and professional endeavor (Crawford & Paglen, 2019).

Implications for Early-Career and Marginalized Scholars

Metric-driven evaluation systems have particularly significant implications for early-career academics and scholars working outside dominant institutional or disciplinary structures.

AI systems frequently rely on historical publication trajectories, citation networks, funding histories, and institutional visibility to assess scholarly impact or career potential. Early-career scholars, who may not yet possess extensive publication records or professional networks, risk being undervalued or overlooked within these systems (Czerniewicz et al., 2021).

Similarly, scholars from marginalized groups—including women, racial and ethnic minorities, scholars in under-resourced institutions, and academics in the Global South—may experience algorithmic disadvantage if historical inequalities become embedded within predictive models and evaluative infrastructures (Bogen & Rieke, 2018).

Without careful oversight and auditing, AI-mediated evaluation risks reproducing structural inequities while presenting itself as objective, neutral, and evidence-based.

Metrics and the Visibility of Academic Labor

AI systems also reshape which forms of academic labor become institutionally visible and rewarded. Traditional academic evaluation often included qualitative recognition of mentoring, curriculum development, governance participation, public scholarship, and community engagement.

By contrast, AI-mediated systems tend to privilege activities that can be easily quantified and digitally captured. Teaching quality may be reduced to student evaluation scores, completion rates, engagement metrics, or learning analytics indicators (Siemens, 2013; Williamson & Eynon, 2020).

Although such systems may improve accountability and institutional coordination, they also risk marginalizing forms of labor that are relational, collaborative, emotional, or difficult to measure.

Mentoring graduate students, supporting colleagues, participating in governance, conducting public scholarship, or engaging in diversity and inclusion work may remain undervalued because these activities are less visible within algorithmic infrastructures.

Consequently, AI systems not only evaluate academic work but also influence institutional perceptions of what kinds of work matter.

Balancing Quantitative and Qualitative Evaluation

Mitigating the risks associated with AI-driven evaluation requires balanced approaches that integrate quantitative indicators with qualitative professional judgment.

Several principles are particularly important:

1. **Multidimensional Evaluation**

Assessment systems should integrate diverse forms of scholarly contribution across research, teaching, mentorship, service, and societal engagement rather than relying narrowly on bibliometric indicators (Hicks et al., 2015).

2. **Transparency and Explainability**

Institutions should ensure that AI-generated evaluations are understandable, interpretable, and open to scrutiny (Mittelstadt et al., 2016).

3. **Human Oversight**

Peer review and collegial deliberation should remain central to academic decision-making, with AI functioning as a decision-support infrastructure rather than a replacement for professional judgment (Selwyn, 2019).

4. **Equity Auditing**

Algorithms and metrics should be regularly evaluated for discriminatory outcomes and structural bias across demographic, disciplinary, and institutional contexts (Jobin et al., 2019).

These strategies emphasize the importance of human–AI collaboration rather than technological substitution in academic evaluation.

Summary

AI-driven metrics are not neutral instruments of evaluation. They actively shape institutional definitions of academic excellence, scholarly productivity, and professional value.

By determining what counts as success and visibility, algorithmic systems influence research priorities, career trajectories, institutional hierarchies, and resource allocation. Although AI offers opportunities for efficiency, coordination, and data-informed decision-making, it also carries risks of narrowing intellectual diversity, reinforcing inequality, and reducing complex scholarly contributions to measurable indicators.

Balancing quantitative evaluation with qualitative professional judgment, transparency, inclusivity, and ethical governance is therefore essential for preserving the multidimensional character of academic work. These issues provide the foundation for the next section, which examines the broader ethical, governance, and policy challenges associated with AI-mediated academic systems.

ETHICAL, GOVERNANCE, AND POLICY CHALLENGES IN THE AI-MEDIATED ACADEMIC PROFESSION

The increasing integration of artificial intelligence (AI) into academic work, evaluation, and institutional governance raises substantial ethical, organizational, and policy challenges for higher education systems. As demonstrated in previous sections, AI systems are no longer peripheral administrative tools; they increasingly shape how academic merit is assessed, careers are advanced, institutional priorities are determined, and professional authority is exercised.

This section examines the ethical risks associated with AI-mediated academic systems, the governance dilemmas universities face, and the policy frameworks needed to ensure that AI adoption aligns with core academic values such as fairness, transparency, academic freedom, collegial governance, and professional autonomy.

Ethical Risks in AI-Mediated Academic Systems

AI systems are frequently presented as objective, efficient, and technologically neutral. However, extensive scholarship demonstrates that algorithms are socially situated and value-laden, reflecting the assumptions, priorities, and data environments from which they emerge (Kitchin, 2017; Mittelstadt et al., 2016).

In the context of academic careers and evaluation, several ethical concerns are particularly significant.

Algorithmic Bias

AI systems trained on historical academic data may reproduce and amplify existing inequalities related to gender, race, institutional prestige, geography, discipline, language, and publication practices (Bogen & Rieke, 2018; Jobin et al., 2019).

For example, citation-based systems may disadvantage scholars working in the humanities, interdisciplinary fields, or institutions outside dominant research centers. Predictive hiring models may privilege profiles resembling historically successful candidates, thereby reinforcing existing hierarchies and limiting diversity within the academic profession.

Opacity and Explainability

Many AI systems used in recruitment, promotion, workload management, and evaluation function as "black boxes," generating rankings or recommendations without transparent explanation of how decisions are produced (Selwyn, 2019).

For academics affected by these systems, lack of explainability limits opportunities to contest decisions, seek remediation, or understand how professional behavior is shaped by algorithmic infrastructures. This raises broader concerns regarding procedural justice, due process, and institutional accountability.

Data Privacy and Surveillance

AI systems increasingly rely on extensive data collection, including publication histories, digital communications, learning analytics, online engagement metrics, workload records, and performance indicators.

The aggregation of these data can create conditions of continuous monitoring and institutional surveillance, where academic activities become persistently quantified and evaluated (Williamson, 2017). Without clear safeguards, such systems may undermine trust, blur boundaries between accountability and intrusion, and weaken academic freedom.

Academic Freedom and Professional Autonomy

AI-mediated governance poses important challenges to academic freedom and professional autonomy, which have historically been central principles of the academic profession (Altbach, 2000; Freidson, 2001).

Although AI systems are often framed as neutral decision-support tools, their influence on hiring, promotion, research visibility, and institutional evaluation can subtly shape academic behavior.

When algorithmic systems define success through measurable outputs and predictive indicators, academics may increasingly optimize their work for visibility within digital infrastructures. This may discourage risky, critical, experimental, or unconventional scholarship in favor of outputs more likely to align with dominant metrics.

These dynamics reflect broader critiques of audit culture in which professional practice becomes shaped by anticipatory compliance with evaluative systems rather than autonomous scholarly judgment (Power, 1997; Shore & Wright, 2015).

Moreover, as evaluative authority becomes increasingly embedded within algorithmic systems, collegial governance structures may weaken. Decisions once negotiated through peer deliberation risk becoming centralized, standardized, and technocratically managed.

The core issue is therefore not simply whether AI systems are accurate, but whether they remain compatible with the normative foundations of academic self-governance.

Governance Challenges: Accountability and Oversight

The deployment of AI within academic governance creates complex questions regarding accountability, responsibility, and institutional oversight.

When AI systems influence hiring, promotion, or evaluation decisions, responsibility for outcomes may become difficult to locate. Accountability may be dispersed among software developers, institutional leaders, evaluators, administrators, and external vendors (Kitchin, 2017).

Effective governance therefore requires clearly defined institutional responsibilities concerning:

- who selects and configures AI systems;
- who monitors algorithmic performance and unintended consequences;
- who is accountable for biased or harmful outcomes;
- and how appeals and remediation processes are managed.

These challenges are particularly significant when universities rely on proprietary commercial platforms whose algorithms may resist transparency and external scrutiny (Crawford & Paglen, 2019).

Governance frameworks should therefore include:

- **Human-in-the-loop decision-making**, ensuring that final authority remains with academic professionals rather than automated systems;
- **Algorithmic auditing mechanisms** to identify bias, drift, or discriminatory outcomes;
- **Appeal and redress procedures** for individuals affected by AI-mediated decisions;
- **Institutional transparency policies** concerning data collection, system operation, and evaluative criteria.

Policy Frameworks for Responsible AI in Higher Education

In response to these ethical and governance challenges, universities require robust policy frameworks for the responsible integration of AI.

Such frameworks should align with emerging international ethical guidelines while also reflecting the specific norms and democratic traditions of higher education institutions (Jobin et al., 2019; UNESCO, 2021; UNESCO, 2023; OECD, 2024; European Commission, 2024). Several policy principles are particularly important.

Transparency

Institutions should clearly communicate where and how AI systems are used in recruitment, promotion, workload management, evaluation, and institutional governance. Faculty members should have access to understandable explanations concerning metrics, indicators, and algorithmic decision-support processes.

Equity and Inclusion

AI systems should be regularly audited for disparate impacts across gender, race, discipline, career stage, geography, and institutional type. Equity considerations should be embedded throughout system design, implementation, and review.

Proportionality

AI should only be used where it demonstrably enhances institutional processes and should not replace qualitative peer judgment in complex evaluative decisions.

Consent and Data Governance

Faculty members should be informed regarding what data are collected, how data are used, and how long information is retained. Data governance frameworks must respect privacy, intellectual ownership, and academic freedom.

Capacity Building and AI Literacy

Institutions should invest in AI literacy and governance competence among faculty members, academic leaders, and evaluators to enable informed participation in AI-mediated systems (Williamson & Eynon, 2020).

Toward Ethical–Professional Alignment

Ultimately, responsible AI governance requires alignment between technological systems and professional values.

AI should support—not redefine—the purposes of academic work. This requires resisting assumptions that efficiency necessarily equals excellence or that quantification automatically reflects quality.

A values-based approach recognizes that:

- academic merit is multidimensional and context-dependent;
- peer judgment remains essential for evaluating intellectual contribution;
- professional autonomy and academic freedom are foundational conditions for meaningful scholarship rather than obstacles to innovation.

Governance frameworks grounded in these principles can help institutions benefit from AI while safeguarding the integrity and democratic traditions of the academic profession.

Summary

The ethical, governance, and policy challenges associated with AI in higher education are neither peripheral nor temporary. As AI systems become embedded in professorial appointments, evaluation, and institutional governance, they reshape power relations, professional norms, and institutional accountability.

Addressing algorithmic bias, transparency, data governance, academic freedom, and institutional oversight is therefore essential for ensuring that AI enhances rather than undermines the academic profession.

The next section considers how universities and academics can prepare for evolving professional realities within increasingly AI-integrated higher education systems.

PREPARING FOR THE FUTURE ACADEMIC PROFESSION IN THE AGE OF ARTIFICIAL INTELLIGENCE

As artificial intelligence (AI) becomes increasingly embedded within higher education systems, the academic profession faces a period of profound institutional and professional transformation. The preceding sections have demonstrated that AI reshapes not only research, teaching, and service, but also the systems through which academic merit is evaluated, careers are advanced, and institutional authority is exercised.

Preparing for the future academic profession therefore requires strategic, institutional, and individual responses capable of balancing technological innovation with the preservation of core academic values such as equity, intellectual diversity, collegial governance, academic freedom, and professional autonomy.

Reconfiguring Academic Competencies and Professional Development

One of the most immediate implications of AI integration is the need to redefine academic competencies.

Beyond disciplinary expertise, future academics increasingly require forms of AI literacy, data awareness, and algorithmic understanding. These competencies do not imply that all academics must become technical AI specialists. Rather, academics should be capable of critically engaging with the systems that shape their work, evaluation, and professional opportunities (Williamson & Eynon, 2020).

Professional development initiatives should therefore include:

- understanding how AI-driven metrics and analytics operate;
- interpreting and contesting algorithmic evaluations;
- ethical decision-making in AI-mediated research and teaching;
- data governance, privacy, and intellectual property issues;
- responsible use of generative AI tools in scholarly and pedagogical contexts.

For early-career academics in particular, AI literacy is increasingly connected to professional survival within datafied academic environments. Without institutional support, unequal access to digital skills and AI infrastructures may deepen existing inequalities across institutions, disciplines, and geographic regions (Czerniewicz et al., 2021).

Institutional Strategies for Responsible AI Integration

Preparing for the future academic profession is not solely an individual responsibility; it is fundamentally an institutional governance challenge.

Universities must develop coherent strategies for AI adoption that align technological innovation with academic missions, professional norms, and public accountability.

Several institutional priorities are especially important.

Embedding AI Governance into Academic Leadership

AI-related decisions should involve academic leaders, faculty representatives, governance bodies, and professional communities rather than being delegated exclusively to IT units or external vendors. This helps ensure that disciplinary diversity and professional values shape AI implementation.

Developing Clear AI Policies

Institutions should establish transparent policies governing the use of AI in recruitment, promotion, evaluation, teaching, research, workload management, and student support. Such policies should clarify that AI functions as a decision-support mechanism rather than a replacement for peer judgment.

Investing in Inclusive Digital Infrastructure

Equitable access to AI tools, training, and data resources is essential to prevent the concentration of technological advantage within already well-resourced institutions or departments.

This issue is particularly important in global contexts characterized by significant digital inequalities.

Continuous Monitoring and Auditing

AI systems should be regularly evaluated for bias, accuracy, transparency, and unintended consequences. Governance frameworks must allow institutions to revise, suspend, or withdraw systems that undermine professional autonomy, equity, or academic integrity (Jobin et al., 2019).

Through these strategies, universities can move from reactive technological adoption toward deliberate and values-driven AI governance.

Implications for Early-Career and Precarious Academics

The future academic profession is increasingly characterized by precarity, competition, and institutional stratification—trends that AI may intensify if left unregulated. Early-career academics are particularly vulnerable to metric-driven evaluation systems emphasizing short-term productivity, digital visibility, citation performance, and predictive indicators of success. AI-driven hiring and promotion systems may disadvantage scholars whose work develops slowly, challenges dominant paradigms, prioritizes teaching or community engagement, or falls outside mainstream publication infrastructures. Preparing for the future, therefore, requires rethinking how institutions recognize diverse scholarly trajectories and career pathways. Mentorship programs, flexible tenure policies, multidimensional evaluation systems, and holistic promotion frameworks can help mitigate these risks. Importantly, universities must resist using AI primarily to optimize efficiency at the expense of intellectual diversity, human development, and collegial academic culture.

Reimagining Academic Value and Excellence

AI integration also invites broader reconsideration of what constitutes academic excellence.

As discussed in previous sections, algorithmic systems tend to privilege activities that are easily measurable, digitally visible, and institutionally comparable (Espeland & Sauder, 2007; Hicks et al., 2015). Preparing for the future academic profession, therefore, requires reaffirming pluralistic understandings of scholarly value, including:

- high-quality teaching and mentorship;
- interdisciplinary and socially engaged research;
- public scholarship and knowledge mobilization;
- institutional service and collegial contribution;
- diversity, equity, and inclusion work;
- critical and innovative scholarship that may not align with dominant metrics.

AI systems should be designed to support rather than constrain these diverse forms of academic labor. This may require context-sensitive indicators, narrative evaluation components, and mixed-method assessment frameworks that combine qualitative peer review with quantitative data.

Future Research Directions and Policy Agendas

The rapid evolution of AI within higher education underscores the need for continued research, institutional experimentation, and international policy coordination.

Several areas require further investigation:

- comparative studies of AI adoption across national higher education systems;
- longitudinal analyses of AI's effects on academic careers and institutional inequality;
- faculty perceptions of AI-mediated governance and evaluation;

- the implications of generative AI for authorship, pedagogy, and intellectual labor;
- the role of commercial technology providers in shaping academic governance.

From a policy perspective, collaboration among universities, governments, accreditation bodies, and professional associations will be essential.

Shared standards, ethical guidelines, transparency frameworks, and accountability mechanisms can help prevent fragmented or inequitable implementation across higher education systems (UNESCO, 2021).

Summary

Preparing for the future academic profession in the age of AI requires more than technological adaptation. It demands institutional reflexivity, ethical governance, professional renewal, and sustained commitment to the democratic values of higher education.

AI systems will continue to influence how academic work is organized, evaluated, and rewarded. The challenge for universities is to ensure that these technologies enhance rather than erode academic freedom, intellectual diversity, collegial governance, and equitable participation.

By investing in AI literacy, inclusive governance structures, multidimensional evaluation frameworks, and responsible institutional policies, higher education institutions can help shape academic careers that remain grounded in scholarly values while engaging critically and productively with technological change.

CONCLUSION: THE ACADEMIC PROFESSION AT A CROSSROADS

The academic profession stands at a critical crossroads. As this chapter has demonstrated, artificial intelligence (AI) is no longer a peripheral technological development within higher education but a structuring force reshaping academic work, evaluation, governance, and professional identity.

Across research, teaching, service, appointments, promotion, and tenure, AI systems increasingly influence how academic value is produced, measured, recognized, and rewarded. The integration of AI therefore presents higher education with a fundamental choice: whether algorithmic systems will quietly reconfigure academic careers according to logics of efficiency, prediction, and quantification, or whether universities will deliberately govern AI in ways that uphold the core values of scholarship, equity, collegiality, and academic freedom. This chapter has argued that AI's significance lies not simply in technological substitution but in the reconfiguration of professional authority and institutional governance. AI-mediated metrics, predictive analytics, and automated evaluation systems introduce new forms of epistemic and organizational power that increasingly operate alongside—and sometimes in tension with—traditional forms of peer review and collegial governance. Although these systems offer clear advantages in terms of scalability, consistency, and administrative efficiency, they also risk narrowing definitions of academic merit, reinforcing existing inequalities, and displacing contextual professional judgment with opaque algorithmic assessments (Espeland & Sauder, 2007; Kitchin, 2017).

A central insight of this chapter is that AI systems are not neutral. Algorithms encode assumptions concerning excellence, productivity, visibility, and professional potential, and these assumptions have material consequences for academic careers and institutional hierarchies. When embedded in hiring, promotion, and evaluation systems, AI may privilege particular disciplines, publication practices, institutional profiles, and forms of scholarly visibility while marginalizing others. Without careful oversight and governance, AI-driven systems risk reproducing and intensifying existing inequalities, particularly for early-career academics, scholars from underrepresented groups, and academics working in less resourced institutional contexts (Czerniewicz et al., 2021; Jobin et al., 2019).

At the same time, the chapter has emphasized that AI's transformative potential should not be dismissed. When responsibly designed and governed, AI systems can support innovative scholarship, enhance pedagogical practices, reduce administrative burden, improve institutional coordination, and provide richer forms of evidence for academic decision-making. The central challenge lies in ensuring that AI functions as a supportive infrastructure rather than a determinative authority. This requires recalibrating the relationship between human expertise and algorithmic systems while reaffirming the primacy of peer judgment, disciplinary knowledge, professional discretion, and democratic governance.

From a governance perspective, the chapter underscores the importance of transparency, accountability, and institutional responsibility. Universities must move beyond ad hoc or purely technocratic AI adoption toward coherent governance frameworks that clearly define where, how, and under what conditions AI systems are used. Human-in-the-loop processes, algorithmic auditing, transparent evaluation criteria, appeal mechanisms, and robust data governance policies are essential for safeguarding procedural justice, academic freedom, and professional autonomy.

The increasing reliance on commercial AI platforms also raises broader concerns regarding data ownership, intellectual property, institutional dependency, and the externalization of academic governance to private technology actors. Looking ahead, the future of the academic profession in the age of AI will depend on institutional reflexivity, collective action, and democratic governance. Individual academics can cultivate AI literacy and ethical awareness, but meaningful transformation requires coordinated engagement among universities, professional associations, accreditation bodies, policymakers, and technology providers. Shared standards for responsible AI governance—aligned with international ethical principles while grounded in the traditions of academic self-governance—will be critical for preventing fragmented, inequitable, or excessively managerial forms of implementation (UNESCO, 2021). This chapter also highlights important directions for future research.

Comparative analyses across national and institutional contexts are needed to understand how AI reshapes academic careers under different governance regimes. Longitudinal research can illuminate the cumulative effects of AI-mediated evaluation on intellectual diversity, professional autonomy, and academic inequality. Equally important are empirical studies examining how academics interpret, negotiate, resist, or adapt to AI systems within everyday institutional practice. Ultimately, the future of the academic profession is not technologically predetermined. AI has the potential either to intensify existing trends toward metricization, managerialism, surveillance, and precarity, or to support more transparent, inclusive, collaborative, and reflective forms of academic governance. The outcome will depend on the values, policies, governance structures, and professional choices that shape the integration of AI into higher education.

By approaching AI not merely as a tool for optimization but as a site of ethical, political, and professional deliberation, universities can help ensure that the evolution of the academic profession remains aligned with its foundational commitments to knowledge, critique, intellectual diversity, and the public good.

REFERENCES

Abbott, A. (1988). *The system of professions: An essay on the division of expert labor*. University of Chicago Press. DOI: 10.7208/chicago/9780226189666.001.0001

Altbach, P. G. (2000). *The changing academic workplace: Comparative perspectives*. Boston College Center for International Higher Education.

Bogen, M., & Rieke, A. (2018). *Help wanted: An examination of hiring algorithms, equity, and bias*. Upturn. Upturn Report

Crawford, K., & Paglen, T. (2019). Excavating AI: The politics of images in machine learning training sets. *International Journal of Communication*, *13*, 310–329.

Czerniewicz, L., Trotter, H., Haupt, G., & Newman, M. (2021). Digital inclusion and inequality in higher education. *Educational Technology Research and Development*, *69*(2), 1–5. DOI: 10.1007/s11423-021-09978-6

Espeland, W. N., & Sauder, M. (2007). Rankings and reactivity: How public measures recreate social worlds. *AJS; American Journal of Sociology*, *113*(1), 1–40. DOI: 10.1086/517897

European Commission. (2024). *Ethical guidelines on the use of artificial intelligence and data in teaching and learning for educators*. Publications Office of the European Union.

Freidson, E. (2001). *Professionalism: The third logic*. University of Chicago Press.

Garfield, E. (1979). *Citation indexing: Its theory and application in science, technology, and humanities*. Wiley.

Hazelkorn, E. (2015). *Rankings and the reshaping of higher education: The battle for world-class excellence* (2nd ed.). Palgrave Macmillan. DOI: 10.1057/9781137446671

Hicks, D., Wouters, P., Waltman, L., de Rijcke, S., & Rafols, I. (2015). Bibliometrics: The Leiden Manifesto for research metrics. *Nature*, *520*(7548), 429–431. DOI: 10.1038/520429a PMID: 25903611

Huang, M.-H., & Rust, R. T. (2021). A strategic framework for artificial intelligence in marketing. *Journal of the Academy of Marketing Science*, *49*(1), 30–50. DOI: 10.1007/s11747-020-00749-9

Jobin, A., Ienca, M., & Vayena, E. (2019). The global landscape of AI ethics guidelines. *Nature Machine Intelligence*, *1*(9), 389–399. DOI: 10.1038/s42256-019-0088-2

Kitchin, R. (2017). Thinking critically about and researching algorithms. *Information Communication and Society*, *20*(1), 14–29. DOI: 10.1080/1369118X.2016.1154087

Marginson, S., & van der Wende, M. (2007). *Globalisation and higher education* (OECD Education Working Papers No. 8). OECD Publishing. https://doi.org/DOI: 10.1787/19939019

Mittelstadt, B. D. (2019). Principles alone cannot guarantee ethical AI. *Nature Machine Intelligence*, *1*(11), 501–507. DOI: 10.1038/s42256-019-0114-4

Mittelstadt, B. D., Allo, P., Taddeo, M., Wachter, S., & Floridi, L. (2016). The ethics of algorithms: Mapping the debate. *Big Data & Society*, *3*(2), 1–21. DOI: 10.1177/2053951716679679

Müller, R., & de Rijcke, S. (2017). Thinking with indicators: Exploring the epistemic impacts of academic performance indicators in the life sciences. *Research Evaluation*, *26*(3), 157–168. DOI: 10.1093/reseval/rvx023

Musselin, C. (2005). Change or continuity in higher education governance? Lessons drawn from twenty years of reforms in Europe. *European Journal of Education*, *40*(1), 65–79. DOI: 10.1111/j.0141-8211.2005.00202.x

OECD. (2024). *OECD AI principles* (updated 2024 version). OECD Publishing.

Power, M. (1997). *The audit society: Rituals of verification*. Oxford University Press.

Selwyn, N. (2019). What's the problem with learning analytics? *Journal of Learning Analytics*, *6*(3), 11–19. DOI: 10.18608/jla.2019.63.3

Shore, C., & Wright, S. (2015). Governing by numbers: Audit culture, rankings and the new world order. *Social Anthropology*, *23*(1), 22–28. DOI: 10.1111/1469-8676.12098

Siemens, G. (2013). Learning analytics: The emergence of a discipline. *The American Behavioral Scientist*, *57*(10), 1380–1400. DOI: 10.1177/0002764213498851

Stokel-Walker, C. (2023). How AI is changing the research landscape. *Nature*, *614*(7949), 22–25. DOI: 10.1038/d41586-023-00210-5

UNESCO. (2021). *Recommendation on the ethics of artificial intelligence*. UNESCO Publishing.

UNESCO. (2023). *Guidance for generative AI in education and research*. UNESCO Publishing.

Upadhyay, A. K., & Khandelwal, K. (2018). Applying artificial intelligence: Implications for recruitment. *Strategic HR Review*, *17*(5), 255–258. DOI: 10.1108/SHR-07-2018-0051

Williamson, B. (2017). Big data in education: The digital future of learning, policy, and practice. *Sage (Atlanta, Ga.)*. Advance online publication. DOI: 10.4135/9781529714920

Williamson, B., & Eynon, R. (2020). Historical threads, missing links, and future directions in AI in education. *Learning, Media and Technology*, *45*(3), 223–235. DOI: 10.1080/17439884.2020.1798995

Williamson, B., & Piattoeva, N. (2022). Education governance and algorithmic accountability: Examining AI in policy and practice. *Learning, Media and Technology*, *47*(1), 1–18. DOI: 10.1080/17439884.2021.1990102

Chapter 7

Appointments of Professors in the Age of AI-Driven Hiring, Promotion, and Tenure in Higher Education: Appointment Legitimacy in Academic Careers

Ashraf Alam
http://orcid.org/0000-0001-6178-1187
Department of Education, National Institute of Technology Calicut, Kozhikode, India

ABSTRACT

This chapter examines professorial hiring, promotion, and tenure as legitimacy-critical sociotechnical regimes under AI-mediated evaluation. It shows how data-fication, commensuration, and dashboard governance reconstitute academic merit into machine-legible proxies, amplifying construct drift, proxy sovereignty, and automation bias unless bounded by appointment-grade constraints. Integrating professional jurisdiction, institutional logics, sociotechnical infrastructure, measurement-validity governance, and epistemic justice, it specifies due-process requirements for transparency, explainability, contestability, data minimization, and academic freedom. It proposes auditable governance controls and a capability-building roadmap so committees and leaders retain accountable peer judgment while modernizing evaluation.

DOI: 10.4018/979-8-3373-8525-9.ch007

1. INTRODUCTION

1.1 Purpose, Scope, and Legitimacy Anchor for AI-Mediated Appointments

This chapter constructs a conceptual-theoretical account of professorial hiring, promotion, and tenure under AI-mediated evaluation, treating *appointment legitimacy* as the primary quality criterion for career-affecting decisions. It defines legitimacy as a composite of *procedural integrity*, *substantive defensibility*, and *relational trustworthiness*, each of which must remain robust when evidence is rendered machine-legible and judgments are filtered through computational pipelines (Bai et al., 2025; Hüther & Krücken, 2013; Benson & Trower, 2012; Siekkinen et al., 2016). The scope spans the full appointment lifecycle, from recruitment architecture and shortlisting to hiring, probationary confirmation, promotion, tenure, leadership appointment, workload allocation, merit pay, and separation decisions. The chapter is designed for multi-sector readerships, including academics, policymakers, workforce-development professionals, and digital learning technologists, because professorial appointments now operate at the intersection of institutional governance, labor-market signaling, and platform-mediated reputational economies. Sections 2 through 6 each contain a table that crystallizes governance implications into portable decision artifacts without relying on figures, boxes, or appendices.

1.2 Core Problem Statement and High-Stakes Sociotechnical Risk Landscape

AI-enabled evaluation is not a neutral efficiency layer, it is an epistemic intervention that reshapes what counts as merit, how evidence is produced, and who controls judgment. When narrative dossiers are compressed into dashboards, and heterogeneous contributions are commensurated into comparable scores, appointment systems can drift toward *proxy sovereignty*, where measurable indicators acquire decision authority beyond their evidentiary warrant. A parallel hazard is *authority displacement*, where committees become validators of machine outputs rather than accountable deliberators applying discipline-specific standards. A third hazard is *governance drift*, in which default weights, hidden thresholds, and platform constraints silently harden into policy, narrowing excellence norms without explicit authorization (Aguilar-Smith & Gonzales, 2021; Liu et al., 2025; Karran et al., 2017). These risks are structurally amplified by applicant-volume pressures, time scarcity in committees, and reputational competition across global rankings ecosystems. The chapter treats these dynamics as predictable failure modes in high-stakes sociotechnical systems, requiring appointment-grade governance controls that preserve reasoned judgment, plural evidence, and contestable decision pathways.

1.3 Definitional Clarifications, Boundary Conditions, and Category-Error Controls

AI in appointment contexts is specified as an ensemble of systems that structure, rank, score, extract, summarize, or standardize career-relevant evidence, including *predictive analytics*, *recommender architectures*, *natural language processing* pipelines, and *generative models* that draft or compress evaluative texts. To prevent category errors, the chapter separates *automation* from *decision support*, and treats *measurement* as distinct from *judgment*, since judgment entails normative reasoning about rigor, contribution, fit, and institutional responsibility. It differentiates *transparency* as knowability of system use, *explainability* as intelligible reason-giving, and *contestability* as an operational capacity to challenge, correct, and appeal (Cadez et al., 2017; Tytherleigh et al., 2005; Flores & Rae Gomez, 2020; Alam & Mohanty, 2022). It also distinguishes consistency from fairness, and efficiency from legitimacy, because streamlined processes can still produce unjust exclusion or non-actionable rejection rationales. The chapter remains conceptual-theoretical, avoids vendor-specific appraisal, and relies on stylized institutional scenarios only to clarify mechanisms, governance implications, and design constraints in AI-mediated appointment regimes.

1.4 Conceptual Contribution Through Multi-Lens Theoretical Integration

The chapter offers an integrative architecture that connects professional jurisdiction, institutional legitimacy pressures, measurement regimes, and algorithmic infrastructures into a single analytic framework for appointment legitimacy. It deploys *professional jurisdiction* and *boundary work* to explain how evaluative authority is claimed, delegated, or displaced in committee-centered governance (Rainnie et al., 2013; Young, 2006; T. A. Heffernan, 2018). It uses *institutional logics* and legitimacy dynamics to explain why metric-centered systems diffuse and stabilize, especially under audit intensification and performance-contract cultures. It applies *sociotechnical infrastructure* thinking to show how data schemas, interoperability standards, and platform dependencies embed hidden governance, shaping what is visible, comparable, and actionable. It incorporates *measurement theory* constructs such as *construct validity*, *measurement invariance*, and *construct drift* to explain why standardized proxies can gradually redefine excellence (Seo et al., 2017; Langen, 2011; Rambe, 2024). It elevates *epistemic justice* as a first-order constraint, requiring recognition of multilingual scholarship, interdisciplinary translation labor, community-engaged contributions, mentoring intensity, and institutional citizenship that often resist machine-ready codification.

1.5 Guiding Questions and Sectional Progression Logic

The chapter advances five interlocking questions that structure the narrative across Sections 2 to 7. The first asks what changes when academic merit becomes computable, commensurable, and dashboard-governed, and which dimensions of excellence become systematically amplified or erased. The second asks how AI-mediated pipelines redistribute evaluative authority across committees, administrators, regulators, and vendors, and how *algorithmic governance* emerges at distinct decision points. The third asks which failure modes follow from proxy dominance, including automation bias, strategic gaming, and evidentiary monocultures, and how these failures propagate across the appointment lifecycle. The fourth asks what governance constraints must be treated as non-negotiable, including procedural fairness, contestability, privacy boundaries, and academic freedom protections. The fifth asks what capability architectures are required so committees retain evaluative competence under computational mediation. Section 2 constructs the theoretical scaffold, Section 3 specifies merit reconfiguration mechanisms, Sections 4 and 5 translate constraints into governance controls, Section 6 develops capability-building, and Section 7 synthesizes a future-facing legitimacy compact.

2. CONCEPTUAL FOUNDATIONS AND INTEGRATIVE THEORETICAL FRAMEWORK

2.1 Academic Profession as a Jurisdictional Field of Evaluative Authority

Professorial appointments operate within an *occupational jurisdiction* in which evaluative authority is a scarce resource, continuously negotiated through *boundary work*, *credential gatekeeping*, and the performative codification of "excellence" as an admissible status claim. In this jurisdictional field, committees function as legitimacy-producing assemblages that translate disciplinary epistemics into organizational decisions, while simultaneously managing *principal-agent* tensions between scholarly autonomy and managerial accountability (Defleur, 2007; Henry et al., 2017; Delucchi et al., 2024). AI-mediated pipelines intensify these dynamics by converting craft knowledge into machine-readable proxies, thereby risking *deprofessionalization* through the substitution of interpretive judgment with computational classification. The critical theoretical move is to treat appointment decisions as *normatively saturated* determinations that require reasoned justification, not merely procedural throughput (Berheide et al., 2022; Byrne et al., 2012; Crawford & Germov, 2015). This section prefigures the multi-lens synthesis consolidated in Table 1, where professional jurisdiction is positioned as a protective mechanism against proxy sovereignty, score deference, and silent policy drift in high-stakes academic career pathways.

2.2 Institutional Logics, Legitimacy Pressures, and Metricized Governance Ecologies

Appointments are shaped by competing *institutional logics* that cohabit uneasily within contemporary universities, a scholarly logic oriented toward epistemic contribution, a managerial logic oriented toward standardization and risk containment, a reputational-market logic oriented toward rank-positioning, and a regulatory logic oriented toward auditability and procedural defensibility. When these logics collide, institutions often resolve ambiguity through commensuration, because quantified signals travel across administrative layers with low interpretive friction (Tagg, 2012; Duffy, 2019; Maher & Tetreault, 2011; Alam & Mohanty, 2023a). This produces an *audit culture* in which comparability is reified as fairness, and visibility is mistaken for value. Under such conditions, AI-enabled evaluation becomes attractive as a coordination technology, yet it can harden into a governance substrate that silently reshapes what is rewarded (Amirtham S & Kumar, 2023; X. Xu et al., 2025; Kezar, 2012). Table 1 later specifies how legitimacy-seeking environments incentivize adoption cascades, even when measurement validity is weak or discipline-fit is compromised. A legitimacy-centered framework therefore treats diffusion, standardization, and KPI-cascades as causal antecedents of proxy dominance, not as neutral modernization.

2.3 Sociotechnical Infrastructures, Platform Dependencies, and Hidden Policy Encodings

Evaluation systems are best conceptualized as *sociotechnical infrastructures* that produce and stabilize "facts" about candidates through data schemas, interoperability standards, workflow automations, and platform-mediated visibility regimes. These infrastructures embed hidden governance because classification taxonomies, default weights, and threshold settings function as policy, even when no formal policy statement is issued (Murai & Foote, 2025; Culver et al., 2025; Anokhin, 2025). Platform dependency amplifies this effect through vendor-controlled update cycles, opaque feature drift, and constrained inspection of scoring logic, which collectively create a structural asymmetry between institutional accountability and technical controllability. In appointment contexts, infrastructural politics manifests as selective legibility, what can be parsed becomes what can be valued, what cannot be parsed becomes administratively marginal (Gioti, 2025; Caballero et al., 2025; Dorenkamp & Süß, 2017; Alam, 2023a). The conceptual correction is to treat dossiers, rubrics, and dashboards as *boundary objects* that coordinate actors while disciplining interpretive freedom. Table 1 situates infrastructure thinking as a safeguard lens that demands auditability, version governance, and provenance discipline to prevent silent algorithmic policy-making.

2.4 Measurement-Theoretic Integrity and Commensuration Politics in Merit Construction

Academic merit is a high-dimensional construct that resists single-score governance, which makes *measurement theory* indispensable for appointment legitimacy. The core risk is *construct underrepresentation*, where measurable outputs stand in for contribution depth, and *construct drift*, where the construct itself mutates to match what systems can score consistently (Deutsch & Yao, 2014; Han & Xie, 2026; Kim & Cooc, 2021). A second risk is failed *measurement invariance*, where cross-disciplinary comparability is asserted even though epistemic cultures differ in output forms, temporal horizons, authorship conventions, and validation standards. A third risk is commensuration politics, where plural goods are collapsed into one scale, producing proxy sovereignty and amplifying stratification through prestige signals. These dynamics necessitate governance that mandates triangulated evidence, discipline-calibrated rubrics, and explicit limits on proxy weight (Pham & Nguyen, 2020; Haviland et al., 2017; Solem & Foote, 2006; Alam, 2023b). Table 1 distills the principal theoretical optics needed to diagnose validity failure, authority displacement, and legitimacy erosion under AI-mediated appointment regimes.

Table 1. Theoretical Optics for Legitimate AI-Mediated Academic Appointments

Theoretical Optic	Conceptual Core Construct Set	Appointment System Phenomena Explained	Dominant Failure Mode Diagnosed	Governance Design Imperative
Professional Jurisdiction Theory	*Jurisdictional control, boundary work, credential authority, peer sovereignty*	How committees legitimize merit claims, how expertise boundaries are defended under computational mediation	Authority displacement through score deference and committee deskilling	Codify committee decision-rights, require reasoned overrides, preserve peer interpretive primacy
Institutional Logics and Legitimacy Theory	*Isomorphic diffusion, audit rationality, symbolic compliance, organizational legitimacy*	Why metricized AI adoption normalizes, how accountability pressures reshape appointment architectures	Governance drift through copied templates and unexamined comparability assumptions	Require local justification, periodic legitimacy reviews, explicit disciplinary fit criteria
Sociotechnical Infrastructure Theory	*Infrastructure-as-governance, platform dependency, classification politics, boundary objects*	How data schemas and platforms shape visibility, how defaults encode policy without deliberation	Hidden rule-making via opaque weights, thresholds, and provenance gaps	Mandate audit logs, version governance, provenance traceability, change-control protocols
Measurement and Validation Theory	*Construct validity, measurement invariance, reliability-fairness tradeoff, construct drift*	Why proxies misrepresent excellence, why cross-field ranking distorts merit, why signals drift over time	Proxy sovereignty, validity collapse, commensuration error	Enforce triangulation, discipline-calibrated rubrics, limits on proxy weight, validity stress-testing
Epistemic Justice Theory	*Testimonial justice, hermeneutical justice, recognition, epistemic pluralism*	Whose contributions become illegible, how interpretive resources bias evaluation toward dominant forms	Systematic undervaluation of mentoring, multilingual scholarship, community-engaged work	Build plural evidence standards, protected narrative space, context-sensitive evaluation rules

The integrated implication of Table 1 is that appointment legitimacy requires simultaneous control of epistemic validity, infrastructural opacity, and authority allocation, since failure in any one domain can cascade into unjust exclusion, non-actionable rejection rationales, and durable erosion of institutional trust. When commensuration tools are introduced without invariance constraints, the system shifts from evaluation to sorting, and when sorting becomes automated, committees risk becoming procedural endorsers rather than accountable deliberators. A legitimacy-preserving design therefore treats AI as bounded decision support, not as a substitutive adjudicator, and it operationalizes constraints through enforceable decision-rights, provenance governance, contestable reason-giving, and discipline-fit rubrics that resist proxy sovereignty.

2.5 Integrative Multi-Level Model

The chapter operationalizes an integrative model across three analytically separable levels that interact dynamically, a macro layer of regulatory architectures, funding incentives, accreditation pressures, and reputational markets, a meso layer of institutional governance, HR design, procurement rules, and assessment architectures, and a micro layer of committee deliberation, identity signaling, and candidate sensemaking under evaluative uncertainty (Rudick & Dannels, 2019; O'Meara & Terosky, 2010; Fagan-Wilen et al., 2006). The model treats appointment legitimacy as an outcome of coupled mechanisms, datafication produces visibility shifts, visibility shifts intensify commensuration, commensuration accelerates construct drift and strategic adaptation, while governance design moderates harm through contestability, provenance discipline, and accountable judgment (Stupnisky et al., 2017; Lumpkin, 2009; Peng & Wiggins, 2025; Alam, 2023c). The vocabulary introduced here, including *decision criticality*, *automation bias*, *function creep*, *proxy sovereignty*, *measurement invariance*, and *epistemic pluralism*, is used consistently across subsequent sections to prevent conceptual slippage. Table 1 already establishes how different theoretical optics map onto different failure modes, and this sub-section formalizes their integration as a coherent diagnostic and design grammar for appointment-grade governance under AI-mediated evaluation regimes.

3. AI-MEDIATED EVALUATION AND THE RECONFIGURATION OF ACADEMIC MERIT

3.1 AI as an Evidentiary Pipeline that Manufactures Evaluative Facts

AI-mediated appointments operate through an evidentiary pipeline that converts heterogeneous academic activity into machine-legible representations, thereby transforming lived scholarly practice into administratively portable signals. Datafication compresses complex work into categorical fields, timestamped traces, and derived indicators that travel through CV parsers, bibliometric dashboards, learning-analytics layers, and workflow platforms that privilege standardization over contextual nuance (Blackham, 2020; Kassab, 2025; Ceci, 2018). This pipeline behaves like a socio-epistemic filter, it foregrounds what is readily extractable, it backgrounded what is relational, tacit, and longitudinal, and it reorders committee attention through salience engineering. The dossier becomes less a narrative artifact and more a structured dataset, which intensifies *commensuration* and encourages interpretive shortcuts under time scarcity (K. Heffernan et al., 2022; Carey et al., 2020; Hollywood et al., 2020; Alam & Mohanty, 2024). The decisive shift is from deliberation over plural evidence to triage over ranked artifacts, a move that increases throughput but destabilizes legitimacy when interpretive authority is displaced from peer judgment to data schemas and scoring routines.

3.2 Measurement-Theoretic Integrity for Appointments under Computational Mediation

Appointments require measurement logic without succumbing to measurement absolutism, because academic merit is a high-dimensional construct with weak comparability across disciplines, career stages, and institutional missions. *Construct Validity* becomes the central integrity constraint, since proxy indicators can produce *construct underrepresentation* by capturing outputs while excluding contribution depth, epistemic risk-taking, and slow scholarship (O'Meara et al., 2017; Wolverton et al., 2005). *Measurement Invariance* is equally pivotal, because cross-field ranking presumes commensurability even when output formats, authorship norms, and validation regimes are structurally non-equivalent. The reliability-fairness tradeoff also becomes acute, because standardization can increase procedural consistency while amplifying systematic disadvantage through legibility gaps. Legitimate evaluation therefore requires multi-modal triangulation, explicit weighting rationales, and disciplined boundaries on proxy authority, rather than a monolithic composite score (Larson et al., 2019; Bhopal, 2022; Si, 2023). These tensions are crystallized in Table 2, which maps merit dimensions to signal archetypes, distortion pathways, legitimacy externalities, and appointment-grade countermeasures.

3.3 Metric Reactivity, Strategic Adaptation, and Proxy Sovereignty Under High Stakes

In high-stakes appointment ecologies, indicators become reactive, producing predictable strategic adaptation through *Goodhart's Law* and *Campbell's Law* dynamics that convert measurement into behavioral steering. When publication counts, citation velocity, venue prestige surrogates, and engagement traces are treated as decision-relevant, academic labor reorganizes around what is optimizable, not necessarily what is epistemically valuable. Generative systems intensify this reactivity by lowering the transaction costs of text production, narrative polishing, and rhetorical alignment, thereby accelerating performative compliance and amplifying the risk of synthetic plausibility overshadowing substantive contribution (Nir &

Zilberstein-Levy, 2006; McConnell, 2019; Lampman et al., 2016). The system-level outcome is *proxy sovereignty*, where the proxy ceases to be evidence and becomes a governing target, enabling institutional drift toward score-led sorting. Table 2 operationalizes this mechanism by specifying how signal archetypes can distort each merit dimension, and how countermeasures must be designed to restore interpretive accountability without collapsing into anti-analytic nostalgia.

Table 2. Merit Signals Across AI-Mediated Appointment Pipelines and Countermeasures

Merit Dimension	Machine-Legible Signal Archetypes	Interpretive Distortion Pathway	Legitimacy Externality	Appointment-Grade Countermeasure
Research Contribution	Output counts, citation velocity, venue-prestige surrogates, grant-density indices, network-centrality cues	Proxy substitution that collapses epistemic significance into popularity and platform visibility	Construct drift toward safely publishable, metric-conforming scholarship	Portfolio-based reading anchors, contribution narratives, explicit proxy-weight caps, discipline-calibrated adjudication rules
Teaching and Assessment Quality	Survey sentiment aggregates, LMS trace intensities, completion and retention proxies, engagement heatmaps	Reduction of pedagogy into behavioral telemetry, penalizing inclusive and high-support teaching	Misallocation of recognition, erosion of pedagogical pluralism, incentive misalignment	Authentic assessment evidence, structured teaching portfolios, context-adjusted interpretation protocols, privacy-bounded analytics
Mentoring and Supervision	Coauthorship adjacency, completion timelines, advisee placement traces, supervision load counts	Visibility bias that privileges measurable throughput over developmental care and scaffolding	Systematic undervaluation of relational labor, inequitable recognition of care-intensive roles	Mentoring dossiers, triangulated testimonies, workload-normalized evaluation, protected narrative space for developmental impact
Service and Institutional Citizenship	Committee membership tallies, meeting attendance logs, task completion timestamps	Quantification of presence over substantive governance labor and institutional stewardship	Underrecognition of invisible governance work, demoralization of institutional citizenship	Role-criticality grading, service-impact narratives, verified contribution records, safeguards against mere activity counting
Leadership and Capacity Building	Project milestone tracking, budget execution traces, program growth metrics, administrative productivity indicators	Performative managerialism that rewards legible outputs over durable capability building	Shift from academic leadership to operational throughput, legitimacy fatigue	Independent qualitative review, long-horizon impact documentation, accountability mapping, limits on productivity surveillance

The logic embedded in Table 2 is that each merit dimension has a distinct evidentiary ontology, which means appointment systems must resist one-size commensuration by pairing each signal family with tailored interpretive constraints and counterweights. Without such pairing, metric reactivity converts evaluation into optimization, and optimization gradually converts academic vocation into instrumentally rational production. Appointment-grade countermeasures therefore function as institutional guardrails that preserve plural evidence, stabilize *construct validity*, and maintain contestable, reasoned judgment under computational mediation, while still enabling administrative coordination and defensible process integrity.

3.4 Algorithmic Governance Across the Appointment Lifecycle and Decision Criticality

AI-mediated appointment systems instantiate *algorithmic governance* by embedding decision rules into screening pipelines, ranking interfaces, and composite scoring routines that shape who is seen, who is shortlisted, and whose dossier receives deliberative attention. Recruitment visibility can be steered by recommender logics and targeting mechanisms, shortlisting can be pre-structured by keyword matching and fit scoring, and promotion-tenure deliberation can be pre-framed by dashboards that prioritize bibliometric and funding surrogates (Solomon & du Plessis, 2023; Bodkin & Fleming, 2021; Ross et al., 2011). These systems introduce *automation bias* and *epistemic deferral*, especially when committees face cognitive load, compressed timelines, and high applicant volumes. Decision criticality therefore becomes the governance hinge, low-criticality use may support coordination, medium-criticality use may support traceable summarization, but high-criticality use such as exclusionary ranking requires maximal contestability, disclosure, and accountable override discipline (Richardson et al., 2021; Jolley et al., 2014; Mathews, 2018; Alam & Mohanty, 2023b). The risk, illustrated by the legitimacy externalities in Table 2, is that lifecycle embedding of proxies can reconfigure excellence norms without explicit authorization, turning committees into procedural ratifiers.

3.5 Rebundling Academic Work, Incentive Architectures, and Legitimacy-Preserving Design

AI-mediated evaluation can rebundle academic work by privileging what is easiest to record and compare, thereby shifting the incentive architecture of teaching, research, service, mentoring, and leadership toward machine-legible productivity. This rebundling functions like a policy lever, it can accelerate narrow output maximization, degrade institutional citizenship, and externalize relational labor into invisibility, producing a legitimacy gap that manifests as distrust, grievances, and chilled academic agency (Civera et al., 2025; Hartley & Jarvis, 2022; Åkerlind, 2005). A legitimacy-preserving design therefore requires an explicit evidence architecture that recognizes plural contributions, constrains proxy sovereignty, and maintains procedural due process through reason-giving and contestability. The operational principle is not anti-metric sentiment, it is disciplined *evidence pluralism* with validity governance, where each metric is treated as a bounded indicator rather than a decision surrogate (Cooray et al., 2014; Bülbül, 2021; Viefers et al., 2006). Table 2 provides a practical mapping for this architecture by showing how each merit dimension requires distinct counterweights, ensuring that AI-enabled modernization strengthens accountability while preserving professional autonomy and epistemic diversity.

4. ETHICS, EQUITY, ACADEMIC FREEDOM, AND PROFESSIONAL AUTONOMY AS GOVERNANCE CONSTRAINTS

4.1 Normative Foundations for Evaluating Evaluators Under High-Stakes Automation

Legitimate professorial appointments require a normative grammar that treats evaluation itself as an object of ethical scrutiny, because the evaluator is a powerholder and the candidate is a rights-bearing subject within a career-defining adjudicatory process. *Organizational Justice Theory* supplies the minimal architecture, *procedural justice* demands voice, neutrality, respectful treatment, and consistency, *distributive justice* demands outcomes that are defensible under plural standards of merit, and *interactional justice* demands dignitarian communication that does not reduce persons to scores (Mayer & Tikka, 2008; Blake, 2022; Harris et al., 2025). In AI-mediated regimes, these requirements intensify because model outputs can be perceived as ontologically authoritative, creating a legitimacy trap when committees defer to dashboards instead of producing reasons. This section therefore frames appointment legitimacy as reason-giving plus reviewability, with *accountability* anchored in identifiable decision-makers rather than in technical systems (Simmons et al., 2022; Broadbent et al., 2013; Foote, 2010; Alam & Mohanty, 2023c). The concrete governance implication, developed further in Table 3, is that evaluative modernization must be constrained by due-process design, not by throughput optimization, because efficiency without justificatory integrity is a structurally unstable equilibrium.

4.2 Algorithmic Fairness Meets Stratification, Intersectionality, and Merit Pluralism

Algorithmic fairness in appointments is not a single target, it is a set of partially incompatible constraints that must be selected, justified, and governed across stages, because the fairness criterion that protects one group under one base-rate structure can disadvantage another under a different distribution. When base rates differ across groups due to structural inequality, calibration and equalized error rates cannot generally be satisfied simultaneously, which makes hidden fairness defaults ethically indefensible (Teelken et al., 2021; T. Heffernan, 2022; Morley, 2005). The academic stratification substrate further complicates this because discipline hierarchies, language dominance, unequal access to funding, platform visibility asymmetries, caregiving burdens, and precarity produce patterned differences in output forms and timelines that are not reducible to individual merit. *Intersectionality* is therefore not a rhetorical overlay, it is a diagnostic necessity that detects compounded disadvantage across gender, caste, disability, geography, and contract type. A legitimacy-preserving design treats *merit pluralism* as a fairness strategy, enforcing evidence architectures that recognize multilingual scholarship, community-engaged contribution, mentoring intensity, and institutional citizenship, while preventing proxy sovereignty from converting stratification into apparently neutral ranking.

4.3 Transparency, Explainability, and Contestability as Due-Process Infrastructure

Transparency, explainability, and contestability should be treated as a coupled due-process infrastructure rather than as optional ethics add-ons, because each addresses a different failure mode in AI-mediated appointments. *Transparency* operationalizes knowability of tool use, scope, data sources, and decision role, preventing silent automation from becoming de facto policy (Subbaye & Vithal, 2017; Chang et al., 2014; Osei-Kofi, 2012). *Explainability* operationalizes intelligible reason-giving, enabling candidates to understand which standards were applied and which evidentiary deficits mattered, rather than receiving generic rejection text. *Contestability* operationalizes remedy, enabling correction of data errors, challenge of misclassification, and independent review when the evaluative pipeline malfunctions (Friedman et al., 2021; Takagi, 2018; Mabasa & Ngirande, 2015; Alam & Mohanty, 2023d). These constraints must be stage-calibrated by decision criticality, since exclusionary shortlisting has higher irreversibility than interview scheduling. Table 3 consolidates these constraints into appointment-grade requirements that can be translated into committee protocols, documentation discipline, and audit-ready governance without converting evaluation into mechanistic box-ticking.

Table 3. Ethical Constraints Translated into Appointment-Grade Governance Requirements Across Career-Defining Decisions

Ethical Constraint	Appointment-Specific Meaning	Minimum Governance Safeguard	Verifiability Checkpoint	Legitimacy Failure Prevented
Fairness and Non-Discrimination	Comparable standards without structural penalty, group-aware harm detection, discipline-fit protection	Pre-decision disparity screening, bias-impact reviews, controlled use of prestige proxies	Outcome distribution monitoring, subgroup error audits, documented mitigation steps	Discriminatory shortlisting, proxy-driven exclusion, stratification laundering
Transparency and Disclosure	Candidates and committees can know when AI mediated the process, what role it played, what data it used	Stage-wise AI use notice, tool registry, decision-role declaration for each pipeline step	Retained disclosure records, accessible process map, auditable tool configuration logs	Hidden automation, opaque thresholds, ungoverned policy drift
Explainability and Reason-Giving	Decisions are accompanied by intelligible academic-relevant rationales, not technical feature lists	Structured reason statements aligned to rubrics, bounded use of model rationales	Readability review, relevance validation, consistency checks across comparable cases	Non-actionable rejection, arbitrary rationalization, legitimacy deficit
Contestability and Remedy	Candidates can correct records, challenge inferences, request independent review, obtain timely resolution	Correction window, appeal pathway, independent review panel, documented resolution timelines	Logged appeals outcomes, turnaround tracking, evidence of corrective action	Due-process erosion, irreversible error propagation, procedural injustice
Data Minimization and Purpose Limitation	Only purpose-relevant data are processed, teaching traces and behavioral telemetry are not repurposed	Input minimization, retention limits, access controls, prohibition of secondary punitive uses	Access-log audits, retention compliance checks, purpose-bound processing attestations	Function creep, privacy harm, surveillance normalization

The operational insight of Table 3 is that legitimacy is produced when constraints are engineered into workflow, documentation, and decision rights, rather than appended as aspirational statements. Transparency without explainability creates informed opacity, explainability without contestability creates unchallengeable narratives, and contestability without minimization creates surveillance-based governance that overwhelms rights through data accumulation. Appointment-grade design therefore requires that committees treat model outputs as defeasible evidence, enforce structured deliberation that triangulates across modalities, and maintain override discipline with accountable reasoning records. When these constraints are coupled, AI can support administrative coordination and evidence organization without becoming an unreviewable adjudicator, thereby preventing score deference from displacing professional judgment. The constraints also create institutional learning loops, because appeal outcomes and disparity audits generate actionable signals for rubric recalibration, data pruning, and tool-scope reduction when legitimacy indicators deteriorate.

4.4 Data Governance, Privacy Boundaries, and Surveillance-Limiting Institutional Design

Data governance in AI-mediated appointments must be framed as a legitimacy infrastructure that prevents *function creep* and preserves academic personhood against ambient surveillance. Appointment systems increasingly ingest behavioral telemetry from learning platforms, productivity tools, and communication systems, yet the ethical boundary is that employment governance should not metastasize into omnipresent monitoring that chills inquiry and pedagogy (Pietilä, 2015; Macfarlane, 2007; Henningsson, 2025). *Privacy-by-Design* implies purpose limitation, minimization, retention discipline, access segmentation, and auditable logging, while *security-by-design* implies encryption, least-privilege permissions, and breach-resilient handling of dossiers and external letters. Governance must also address consent asymmetry, because faculty and candidates cannot meaningfully refuse data processing without career penalty, which converts nominal consent into coerced compliance. The actionable design requirement is a data taxonomy that classifies evidence by decision relevance, sensitivity, and permissible use, accompanied by enforceable prohibitions on secondary punitive repurposing of teaching traces (Ford, 2016; T. Wang et al., 2024; Machovcova et al., 2024). Table 3 already operationalizes minimization and purpose limitation, and this sub-section extends it into concrete boundary-setting that prevents telemetry-rich environments from becoming disciplinary apparatuses.

4.5 Academic Freedom, Professional Autonomy, and Generative Evaluation Text Ethics

Academic freedom and professional autonomy are legitimacy conditions for appointments, because knowledge production requires epistemic risk-taking, methodological heterogeneity, and pedagogical experimentation that cannot survive under pervasive scoring and surveillance. When AI-mediated monitoring becomes a background condition, the system can induce *chilling effects*, self-censorship, and *metric conformity*, narrowing research agendas and teaching strategies toward what is machine-legible rather than what is intellectually necessary (Lumpkin & Jones, 2023; George & Maguire, 2021). Professional autonomy is institutional rather than individualistic, it is enacted through shared governance, committee authority, and peer-accountable deliberation, which is why score deference is not merely a technical problem, it is a governance failure. Generative systems introduce additional ethics burdens in evaluative texts, because AI-assisted letters, summaries, and committee statements can produce standardized tonalities that erase context, amplify implicit bias through linguistic normalization, and create confidentiality leakage risks if sensitive materials touch external systems (Ooms et al., 2019; B. Li & Shen, 2022; Champlin & Knoedler, 2017). A legitimacy-preserving norm-set requires disclosure-of-assistance within committee processes, provenance discipline for summaries, and strict handling rules for confidential dossiers, with Table 3 serving as the enforceable backbone that keeps academic freedom compatible with accountable modernization.

5. INSTITUTIONAL GOVERNANCE AND POLICY DESIGN FOR RESPONSIBLE AI IN PROFESSORIAL PATHWAYS

5.1 Appointment-Grade AI as a Risk-Calibrated Governance Standard

Appointment-grade AI designates a governance tier for any computational system that materially influences career-affecting determinations, including hiring, confirmation, promotion, tenure, leadership appointment, and separation decisions. The category is defined by decision criticality, irreversibility, and reputational gravity, not by technical sophistication, because a simple ranking heuristic can be more harmful than an interpretable model if it silently drives exclusion (Finkelstein et al., 2017; McNaughtan et al., 2022; Taylor, 2025). The central construct is *defeasible decision support*, where algorithmic outputs remain contestable inputs into human judgment rather than dispositive verdicts. A legitimacy-preserving institution therefore formalizes decision-rights, allocates accountable authorities, and constrains automation through explicit scope boundaries that prevent proxy sovereignty (Chalmers, 2011; Nam et al., 2021; Jepsen et al., 2014). This standard also requires *procedural non-delegation* for high-stakes adjudication, meaning committees cannot outsource normative reasoning about rigor, contribution, and disciplinary fit. Table 4 later operationalizes this standard into a control architecture that binds policy, process, data, technology, and culture into an auditable governance substrate.

5.2 Three-Layer Governance Architecture for Sociotechnical Accountability

Responsible deployment of appointment-grade systems requires a three-layer architecture that couples normative commitments with procedural discipline and technical controls, because legitimacy failures typically emerge from misalignment between values, workflows, and infrastructure. The normative layer specifies *rights-adjacent constraints* such as contestability, reason-giving, and academic freedom protections, converting ethical commitments into enforceable decision constraints (Schmalz et al., 2019; Stupnisky et al., 2015; Mukhamejanova & Kuchumova, 2025). The procedural layer specifies committee protocols, documentation routines, and appeal pathways that turn evaluative deliberation into a reproducible, reviewable practice rather than an opaque craft susceptible to automation bias. The technical layer specifies data minimization, provenance traceability, access segmentation, audit logging, model version governance, and drift monitoring, preventing silent reparameterization from becoming implicit policy (Bull et al., 2025; DeZure et al., 2014; Bhardwaj, 2025). Governance becomes credible only when these layers are mutually reinforcing, because a transparent policy without logs is non-verifiable, and a robust technical stack without committee discipline is normatively unmoored. Table 4 provides the integrated control schema that prevents hidden thresholds and platform defaults from substituting for authorized evaluative standards.

5.3 Procurement, Vendor Governance, and Control-Matrix Operationalization

Procurement is evaluation policy by other means, because tool capabilities define what becomes legible, comparable, and administratively actionable within the appointment pipeline. Appointment-grade procurement therefore requires auditability, change-control, and accountability clauses that treat vendor opacity as a legitimacy risk rather than a commercial inconvenience (Cantwell, 2011; Hardy et al., 2018; Yin et al., 2024). Core requirements include documented model behavior boundaries, explicit update notifications, regression testing duties, data residency options where jurisdictionally necessary, retention limits, subcontractor disclosure, and institution-controlled exportability to reduce platform lock-in. Vendor governance also requires *assurance enforceability*, meaning the institution can pause or roll back deployment when drift or disparity indicators breach agreed thresholds (Guillaume & Apodaca, 2022; W. Xu & Poole, 2024; Sommersguter-Reichmann & Reichmann, 2025). These requirements must be translated into a control-matrix that committees and professional services can execute without technical mystification, and Table 4 provides that matrix as a portable governance artifact usable for tool registries, committee handbooks, and audit-ready compliance routines.

Table 4. Governance Control Matrix for Appointment-Grade AI System Stewardship

Control Domain	System Element Under Stewardship	Appointment-Critical Exposure Point	Operationalization Mechanism	Verification Artifact for Auditability
Policy Scope Governance	Allowed-use boundaries, decision-rights allocation, prohibited automation zones	Exclusionary screening, composite ranking, tenure risk scoring	Stage-wise permission registry, accountable owner assignment, explicit non-delegation rules for high-criticality decisions	Approved scope registry, signed decision-rights charter, recorded exceptions with justification
Procedural Deliberation Governance	Committee workflows, rubric application, reason-giving discipline	Shortlisting rationales, promotion-tenure deliberation, leadership appointment decisions	Structured deliberation protocol,ubric calibration sessions, documented override rationales, mandatory triangulation across evidence modalities	Reasoned decision record, override log with accountable sign-off, rubric calibration report
Data Provenance and Access Governance	Input datasets, dossier sources, identity attributes, telemetry boundaries	CV parsing, teaching analytics ingestion, external letter handling	Data minimization rules, provenance mapping, least-privilege access controls, retention schedules with deletion triggers	Provenance map, access-log report, retention compliance register, sensitive-data handling attestations
Model Assurance and Drift Governance	Model versions, thresholds, weights, feature pipelines, uncertainty handling	Annual review cycles, policy updates, platform feature changes	Version control, regression testing, disparity monitoring, drift detection thresholds tied to suspension triggers	Model change ledger, assurance test summary, drift-monitor dashboard export, remediation action log
Vendor Accountability Governance	Contractual obligations, update notifications, subcontractor ecosystem, exit pathways	Cloud processing of dossiers, proprietary scoring updates, cross-border processing risks	Auditability clauses, notification SLAs, subcontractor disclosure, portability and termination provisions	Executed vendor addendum, update notification archive, subcontractor list, exit plan documentation
Legitimacy and Culture Governance	Norms, incentives, training, professional identity safeguards	Automation bias in committees, metric conformity pressures, legitimacy disputes	Certification for committee roles, legitimacy monitoring instruments, protected narrative space for plural merit recognition	Training completion register, legitimacy climate pulse report, appeals trend analysis, governance review minutes

The governance logic captured in Table 4 is that legitimacy is produced through coupling, not through isolated safeguards, because proxy sovereignty emerges when policy permissions, committee routines, data pipelines, and vendor constraints drift out of alignment. A control-matrix becomes appointment-grade only when it yields concrete artifacts that can be inspected, challenged, and improved, such as decision records, override logs, provenance maps, and change ledgers, rather than relying on aspirational statements. This design also creates institutional learning loops, since drift-monitor exports, appeals trend analysis, and legitimacy climate pulses generate feedback that can recalibrate rubrics, tighten data boundaries, or narrow tool scope when harms accumulate. By keeping the committee as the accountable adjudicator while equipping it with auditable infrastructure, the institution avoids the false choice between modernization and autonomy, and instead secures a governed hybrid that is contestable, reviewable, and procedurally dignified.

5.4 Responsible Research Assessment as Institutional Policy

Responsible assessment in appointments requires an evidence architecture that treats merit as plural, temporally distributed, and disciplinarily heterogeneous, thereby resisting the managerial temptation to collapse excellence into a single commensurative index. A legitimacy-preserving institution operationalizes *portfolio-based evaluation* that integrates research contribution, teaching quality, mentoring intensity, service labor, and leadership capacity, while explicitly constraining the weight of prestige proxies and platform visibility signals (Porter et al., 2020; Morris & Laipple, 2015; Pandit, 2020). *Narrative CV* logic becomes an evaluative instrument, not a decorative text, when it is assessed through structured rubrics that reward contribution substance, epistemic risk-taking, methodological rigor, and societally relevant knowledge translation without demanding uniform output formats. This requires discipline-calibrated standards that respect epistemic pluralism, including field-specific timelines, authorship conventions, and validation regimes, thereby avoiding invalid comparability. Table 4 supports this shift by specifying how procedural deliberation governance and data provenance governance protect plural evidence from being overwritten by dashboard primacy. The result is an appointment system that is analytically literate yet normatively constrained, capable of modernization without epistemic monoculture.

5.5 Oversight, Assurance Cycles, and Change Management for Durable Legitimacy

Oversight must be institutionalized as a continuous assurance cycle rather than an episodic crisis response, because AI-mediated evaluation systems evolve through data drift, platform updates, and behavioral adaptation driven by metric incentives. Effective oversight therefore combines risk classification by decision criticality with periodic audits of disparity indicators, false negative patterns in screening, and construct drift in what the institution rewards over time (Herbert & Tienari, 2013; Zambrana et al., 2023). Accountability mapping must remain explicit, ensuring that committees, deans, HR, and professional services each hold defined responsibilities for documentation integrity, data boundary enforcement, and contestability pathways. Change management is not a communications exercise, it is legitimacy work that requires participatory governance, training-based capability building, and norm stabilization that protects academic freedom against surveillance creep and metric conformity. Resistance should be treated as diagnostic signal rather than obstruction, indicating where professional identity, epistemic standards, or procedural dignity are being compromised (Mgaiwa, 2023; Madison & Fahlman, 2021; Tian & Lu, 2017). Table 4 already specifies culture governance and legitimacy monitoring artifacts, and this sub-section extends them into a durable institutional operating model where modernization proceeds through governed increments, auditable controls, and reversible scope adjustments when legitimacy indicators deteriorate.

6. PROFESSIONAL DEVELOPMENT AND THE REDEFINITION OF PROFESSORIAL ROLES IN AI-MEDIATED UNIVERSITIES

6.1 Why Professional Development is a Structural Safeguard for Appointment Legitimacy

Professional development is not an auxiliary intervention in AI-mediated appointment systems, it is a structural safeguard that preserves evaluative competence, mitigates automation bias, and stabilizes legitimacy under computational mediation. When committees face dashboard primacy, compressed timelines, and high applicant volume, the risk is *epistemic deferral*, where members treat algorithmic summaries as authoritative rather than defeasible (Pineda & Salazar Morales, 2024; Bäker et al., 2020; Jacobs & Winslow, 2004). Capability building therefore functions as cognitive-institutional infrastructure, ensuring that deliberators can interrogate construct validity, detect proxy substitution, and articulate reasoned decisions that remain contestable and procedurally dignified. This requires more than generic AI literacy, it requires *evaluation literacy* grounded in *measurement theory*, *organizational justice*, and discipline-fit adjudication, as foreshadowed by Table 4 and operationalized in Table 5. The governance implication is that institutions cannot claim appointment-grade design without role-calibrated competencies that are certified, refreshed, and embedded into committee appointment procedures. In effect, professional development becomes a legitimacy technology that enables plural evidence architectures to function under real-world constraints.

6.2 Competency Architecture for the AI-Era Academic Profession

A competency architecture for the AI-era professoriate must be multi-domain, because academic roles now blend epistemic labor with governance participation, data stewardship, and risk-aware decision-making. AI literacy should be defined as situated competence, including uncertainty comprehension, error-mode anticipation, and critical understanding of model limitations, rather than tool fluency (Hearn & Burns, 2021; Yakoboski, 2016; Curnalia & Mermer, 2018). Evaluation literacy must include *construct validity reasoning*, *measurement invariance awareness*, rubric engineering, and triangulation design, so committees can resist commensuration shortcuts and proxy sovereignty. Integrity competence must cover disclosure norms for AI-assisted scholarly production, authorship accountability, and detection of synthetic plausibility that masquerades as epistemic contribution (Trendowski, 2023; Y. Li et al., 2013; Murgatroyd, 2025). Pedagogical competence must address assessment resilience, evidence of authentic learning, and interpretive caution in the use of learning analytics to avoid reductive governance of teaching. Governance competence must include procurement literacy, audit log interpretation, contestability pathway administration, and principled boundary setting against function creep. Table 5 later maps these competencies to stakeholder groups, learning modalities, tangible outputs, and legitimacy indicators, ensuring professional development is operational rather than aspirational.

6.3 Adult Learning, Transformative Professional Learning, and Threshold-Concept Engineering

Faculty development in AI-mediated universities requires an adult-learning architecture that treats professionals as autonomous meaning-makers embedded in disciplinary cultures, not as passive recipients of compliance training. *Andragogy* implies relevance, self-direction, and immediate applicability to appointment realities, such as rubric calibration, reason-giving, and appeal handling (Clark & d'Ambrosio, 2005; Pyke, 2013; T. Heffernan, 2021). *Transformative Learning Theory* becomes critical because AI-mediated evaluation challenges deep assumptions about objectivity, merit, and the epistemic status of metrics, requiring perspective shifts rather than surface skill acquisition. Communities of practice provide the social substrate for norm stabilization, enabling peer-to-peer calibration of evidence standards, integrity norms, and committee deliberation discipline across departments (Henningsson et al., 2018; Yang et al., 2024; McAlpine & Emmioğlu, 2015). A threshold-concept approach is especially powerful because constructs such as *construct validity*, *contestability*, *auditability*, and *function creep* are irreversible conceptual pivots that change evaluators' cognition and practice once internalized. Table 5 translates these learning theories into role-specific capability pathways, linking learning design to the concrete governance artifacts required for appointment legitimacy.

6.4 Learning Architecture by Stakeholder Group and Decision Criticality

A legitimacy-preserving learning architecture must be stakeholder-differentiated because decision exposure and accountability vary across early-career academics, committee members, academic leaders, and professional services personnel. Early-career academics require dossier literacy, disclosure competence, and navigational sensemaking to avoid identity foreclosure under metric conformity pressures, while maintaining epistemic risk-taking and methodological integrity (Murray, 2019; S. Wang & Jones, 2021; Bosanquet et al., 2017). Committee members require high-stakes training in procedural justice, rubric calibration, triangulation discipline, and documentation rigor, because their decisions are the institutional locus of accountable judgment. Academic leaders require sociotechnical governance competence, including risk classification by decision criticality, procurement stewardship, and escalation protocol design, so modernization remains bounded and auditable (Loomes et al., 2019; Sanz-Menéndez & Cruz-Castro, 2019; Tariq, 2024). Professional services staff require data governance competence, access-control administration, retention discipline, and audit-log literacy to prevent confidentiality breaches and function creep. Teaching-focused faculty require assessment design competence that produces authentic evidence resilient to inappropriate automation, while protecting inclusivity and learning equity. Table 5 provides an operational curriculum map that aligns stakeholder learning with tangible outputs, ensuring capability building translates into reproducible appointment-grade practice.

6.5 Career Trajectories, Role Reconfiguration, and Stratification Risks toward 2035

AI-mediated universities are likely to reconfigure academic career trajectories through new role clusters and new stratification vectors that must be governed rather than passively accepted. Emergent roles include assessment-integrity specialists, evaluation analytics stewards, AI governance fellows, pedagogical AI leads, and institutional evidence architects who translate plural merit into audit-ready portfolios (Chiang, 2025; L. Wang, 2022). While these roles can strengthen governance, they can also create a two-tier academic structure, where those with analytic capital, platform fluency, and institutional proximity gain reputational acceleration, while those engaged in mentoring-intensive, community-embedded, or slow scholarship become comparatively invisible. Another risk is committee deskilling, where reliance on summaries reduces reading depth, eroding disciplinary judgment and increasing score deference over time. A further risk is the rebalancing of academic labor toward measurable outputs, downgrading teaching, service, and institutional citizenship (Alakoum et al., 2024; Khairullah et al., 2025). Table 5 integrates these risks into capability pathways that protect plural roles, ensuring professional development functions as an equity instrument that resists stratification by legibility and platform access.

Table 5. Capability-Building Roadmap for Legitimate AI-Mediated Professorial Appointments

Stakeholder Cohort	Priority Competency Constellation	Learning Modality Architecture	Tangible Practice Outputs	Legitimacy Signal and Monitoring Indicator
Early-Career Academics	*Dossier literacy*, disclosure norms, portfolio design, reputational risk awareness, integrity-by-design habits	Mentoring dyads, scenario clinics, rubric walkthroughs, reflective practice loops	Appointment-ready portfolios, disclosure statements, evidence-mapping templates for plural contributions	Reduced uncertainty, fewer procedural disputes, improved clarity of evaluative expectations
Appointment Committee Members	*Procedural justice*, triangulation discipline, validity reasoning, automation-bias resistance, documentation rigor	Simulation-based deliberation labs, calibration workshops, certification pathways, peer-review rehearsals	Reasoned decision records, override logs with justification, calibrated rubric interpretations	Lower contestation rates, improved perceived fairness, consistent reason-giving quality
Academic Leaders and Deans	Risk classification by decision criticality, procurement literacy, accountability mapping, escalation protocol design	Policy studios, governance clinics, tabletop incident exercises, cross-functional review boards	Governed tool registry, risk-tiered use permissions, documented governance charters	Audit-ready compliance, controlled scope drift, fewer unreviewable high-criticality deployments
Professional Services and HR-IT	Data minimization, provenance mapping, access governance, retention discipline, assurance reporting literacy	SOP training, audit-log practicums, security drills, lifecycle governance workshops	Provenance maps, access-control reports, retention schedules, assurance dashboards	Reduced privacy incidents, improved traceability, verified compliance with purpose limitation
Teaching-Focused Faculty	Authentic assessment design, analytics interpretation restraint, learning-evidence quality, inclusivity preservation	Communities of practice, assessment redesign sprints, peer observation cycles, feedback analytics clinics	Redesigned assessments, evidence portfolios, interpretation protocols for telemetry	Improved evidence quality, reduced reductive scoring, higher equity in learning evaluation

The operational synthesis of Table 5 is that legitimacy is sustained when capability-building is engineered as a reproducible institutional system that produces inspectable artifacts, not merely trained individuals. Each stakeholder cohort must generate tangible outputs that feed appointment-grade governance, such as reasoned decision records, provenance maps, and governed tool registries, thereby converting learning into auditable practice. The roadmap also functions as an anti-stratification mechanism by equipping those engaged in mentoring, teaching, and institutional citizenship with portfolio architectures that make plural merit legible without collapsing it into a single score. When these capabilities are institutionalized, committees can interpret AI-generated summaries as defeasible, leaders can prevent scope drift through risk-tiered permissions, and professional services can enforce purpose limitation and retention discipline. In this way, professional development becomes a legitimacy infrastructure that stabilizes academic freedom, preserves professional autonomy, and enables computational modernization without converting appointments into unreviewable algorithmic sorting.

7. CONCLUSION

7.1 Integrative Synthesis of the Appointment-Legitimacy Argument Under AI Mediation

This chapter has treated AI-mediated professorial appointments as a high-stakes sociotechnical governance domain in which legitimacy is produced through coupled control of evidentiary validity, authority allocation, and rights-adjacent procedural integrity. The central proposition is that computational mediation transforms the epistemic substrate of appointments, converting plural scholarly practice into machine-legible signals that can intensify *commensuration*, accelerate *construct drift*, and induce *proxy sovereignty* unless bounded by appointment-grade constraints. The integrative framework has shown that legitimacy failure is rarely a single-point defect, it is a cascade that begins with selective legibility, proceeds through dashboard primacy and automation bias, and culminates in non-actionable reason-giving, inequitable sorting, and erosion of professional autonomy. The normative architecture specified that *procedural justice*, *contestability*, *data minimization*, and academic freedom protections are not optional values, they are structural requirements for career-affecting adjudication. The governance and capability-building logics specified that modernization can be compatible with autonomy only when committees remain accountable adjudicators, evidence remains plural and discipline-calibrated, and infrastructures remain auditable, provenance-traceable, and resistant to silent policy drift.

7.2 Core Conceptual Takeaways with Cross-Sector Actionability

The most actionable takeaway is that appointments must be governed as legitimacy-critical determinations rather than as throughput-optimization problems, which means AI can be admitted only as bounded decision support that remains defeasible, reviewable, and contestable. A second takeaway is that responsible assessment and responsible AI are analytically inseparable because both govern the evidentiary ontology of merit, determining which contributions become visible, comparable, and institutionally rewarded. A third takeaway is that fairness cannot be reduced to a single metric constraint, because appointments operate on structurally unequal baselines, discipline-specific epistemics, and intersecting identity pressures that require plural evidence architectures and explicit limits on proxy authority. A fourth takeaway is that procurement and infrastructure are governance, because data schemas, default thresholds, and platform dependencies silently encode policy unless controlled through change governance, audit logs, and accountable decision-rights. A fifth takeaway is that professional development is a structural safeguard, because evaluation literacy, validity reasoning, and procedural justice competence are the only durable counterweights to automation bias, score deference, and function creep in telemetry-rich institutions.

7.3 Future-Facing Agenda for Governed Modernization and Institutional Resilience

A forward agenda requires institutions to treat appointment-grade governance as a resilience architecture that can withstand model drift, strategic adaptation, and reputational-market volatility without sacrificing academic freedom or plural epistemic cultures. Conceptual development should further refine constructs such as *merit pluralism*, *evidentiary provenance*, *algorithmic contestability*, and *jurisdictional non-delegation*, translating them into operational decision-rights and enforceable process guarantees. Institutional design should prioritize risk-tiered AI use permissions, evidence triangulation mandates, disciplined reason-giving standards, and independent review pathways that prevent irreversible exclusion through opaque ranking. Workforce-development strategy should formalize role-calibrated capability pathways so committees, leaders, and professional services can interpret model outputs as defeasible artifacts rather than authoritative verdicts, while maintaining privacy boundaries and purpose limitation against surveillance normalization. The durable endpoint is not maximal automation, it is legitimate modernization, an institutional settlement in which computational tools enhance coordination and evidence organization, yet the conditions of knowledge creation, epistemic risk-taking, and dignitarian career pathways remain protected through auditable governance, plural evidence standards, and accountable peer judgment.

REFERENCES

Aguilar-Smith, S., & Gonzales, L. D. (2021). A study of community college faculty work expectations: Generous educators and their managed generosity. *Community College Journal of Research and Practice*, *45*(3), 184–204. DOI: 10.1080/10668926.2019.1666062

Åkerlind*, G. S. (2005). Postdoctoral researchers: roles, functions and career prospects. *Higher Education Research & Development*, *24*(1), 21-40. DOI: 10.1080/0729436052000318550

Alakoum, A., Nica, E., & Abiad, M. (2024). Revolutionizing faculty performance evaluation: The future role of AI in higher education. *Journal of Self-Governance and Management Economics*, *12*(1), 25–49. DOI: 10.22381/jsme12120242

Alam, A. (2023a). The secret sauce of student success: Cracking the code by navigating the path to personalized learning with educational data mining. In *2023 2nd International Conference on Smart Technologies and Systems for Next Generation Computing (ICSTSN)* (pp. 1-8). IEEE. DOI: 10.1109/ICSTSN57873.2023.10151558

Alam, A. (2023b). Media multitasking with M-learning technology in real-time classroom learning: Analysing the dynamics in formal educational settings for the future of E-learning in India. In *2023 2nd International Conference on Smart Technologies and Systems for Next Generation Computing (ICSTSN)* (pp. 1-6). IEEE. DOI: 10.1109/ICSTSN57873.2023.10151509

Alam, A. (2023c). Leveraging the power of 'modeling and computer simulation' for education: An exploration of its potential for improved learning outcomes and enhanced student engagement. In *2023 International Conference on Device Intelligence, Computing and Communication Technologies (DICCT)* (pp. 445-450). IEEE. DOI: 10.1109/DICCT56244.2023.10110159

Alam, A., & Mohanty, A. (2022). Facial analytics or virtual avatars: competencies and design considerations for student-teacher interaction in AI-powered online education for effective classroom engagement. In *International Conference on Communication, Networks and Computing* (pp. 252-265). Cham: Springer Nature Switzerland. DOI: 10.1007/978-3-031-43145-6_21

Alam, A., & Mohanty, A. (2023a). Learning on the move: a pedagogical framework for state-of-the-art mobile learning. In *International Conference on Data Management, Analytics & Innovation* (pp. 735-748). Singapore: Springer Nature Singapore. DOI: 10.1007/978-981-99-1414-2_52

Alam, A., & Mohanty, A. (2023b). From bricks to clicks: The potential of big data analytics for revolutionizing the information landscape in higher education sector. In *International Conference on Data Management, Analytics & Innovation* (pp. 721-732). Singapore: Springer Nature Singapore. https://doi.org/DOI: 10.1007/978-981-99-1414-2_51

Alam, A., & Mohanty, A. (2023c). Developing 'happiness engineering' subject for the schools in India: Designing the pedagogical framework for a sustainable happiness curriculum. *Qubahan Academic Journal*, *3*(4), 1–20. DOI: 10.48161/qaj.v3n4a145

Alam, A., & Mohanty, A. (2023d). Implications of virtual reality (VR) for school teachers and instructional designers: An empirical investigation. *Cogent Education*, *10*(2), 2260676. DOI: 10.1080/2331186X.2023.2260676

Alam, A., & Mohanty, A. (2024). Framework of Self-Regulated cognitive engagement (FSRCE) for sustainable pedagogy: A model that integrates SRL and cognitive engagement for holistic development of students. *Cogent Education*, *11*(1), 2363157. DOI: 10.1080/2331186X.2024.2363157

Amirtham, S. N., & Kumar, A. (2023). The underrepresentation of women in STEM disciplines in India: A secondary analysis. *International Journal of Science Education*, *45*(12), 1008–1031. DOI: 10.1080/09500693.2023.2179901

Anokhin, I. (2025). Towards academic leadership: literature review on the advancement of foreign-born faculty in the US higher education sector. *Perspectives: Policy and Practice in Higher Education*, 1-13. DOI: 10.1080/13603108.2025.2540312

Bai, Q., Nam, B. H., English, A. S., Marshall, R. C., & Tian, X. (2025). Mental health and early career adaptation challenges of Chinese returnees and Korean ambitionists among the STEAM doctoral cohorts in the post-pandemic academic job market. *Compare: A Journal of Comparative Education*, *55*(6), 1030–1050. DOI: 10.1080/03057925.2024.2352831

Bäker, A., Muschallik, J., & Pull, K. (2020). Successful mentors in academia: Are they teachers, sponsors and/or collaborators? *Studies in Higher Education*, *45*(4), 723–735. DOI: 10.1080/03075079.2018.1544235

Benson, R. T., & Trower, C. A. (2012). Data, leadership, and catalyzing culture change. *Change: The magazine of higher learning, 44*(4), 27-34. DOI: 10.1080/00091383.2012.691862

Berheide, C. W., Watanabe, M., Falci, C., Borland, E., Bates, D. C., & Anderson-Hanley, C. (2022). Gender, type of higher education institution, and faculty work-life integration in the United States. *Community Work & Family*, *25*(4), 444–463. DOI: 10.1080/13668803.2020.1776220

Bhardwaj, A. (2025). Faculty Tenure in US Academic Medical Institutions: A Critical Review of Controversy and Debate. *Advances in Medical Education and Practice*, *16*, 569–576. DOI: 10.2147/AMEP.S508439 PMID: 40206578

Bhopal, K. (2022). Academics of colour in elite universities in the UK and the USA: The 'unspoken system of exclusion'. *Studies in Higher Education*, *47*(11), 2127–2137. DOI: 10.1080/03075079.2021.2020746

Blackham, A. (2020). Unpacking precarious academic work in legal education. *The Law Teacher*, *54*(3), 426–442. DOI: 10.1080/03069400.2020.1714276

Blake, D. J. (2022). Gendered and racialized career sacrifices of women faculty accepting dual-career offers. *Journal of Women and Gender in Higher Education*, *15*(2), 113–133. DOI: 10.1080/26379112.2022.2067168

Bodkin, C. P., & Fleming, C. J. (2021). Supporting women scholars' paths to academia: An examination of family-friendly policies of public affairs doctoral programs. *Journal of Public Affairs Education*, *27*(3), 301–325. DOI: 10.1080/15236803.2019.1694385

Bosanquet, A., Mailey, A., Matthews, K. E., & Lodge, J. M. (2017). Redefining 'early career' in academia: A collective narrative approach. *Higher Education Research & Development*, *36*(5), 890–902. DOI: 10.1080/07294360.2016.1263934

Broadbent, K., Troup, C., & Strachan, G. (2013). Research staff in Australian universities: is there a career path?. *Labour & Industry: a journal of the social and economic relations of work, 23*(3), 276-295. DOI: 10.1080/10301763.2013.839082

Bülbül, S. (2021). Glass ceiling in academia revisited: Evidence from the higher education system of Turkey. *International Journal of Sociology*, *51*(2), 87–104. DOI: 10.1080/00207659.2021.1881872

Bull, S., Cooper, A., Laidlaw, A., Milne, L., & Parr, S. (2025). 'You certainly don't get promoted for just teaching': Experiences of education-focused academics in research-intensive universities. *Studies in Higher Education*, *50*(2), 239–255. DOI: 10.1080/03075079.2024.2333946

Byrne, M., Chughtai, A. A., Flood, B., & Willis, P. (2012). Job satisfaction among accounting and finance academics: Empirical evidence from Irish higher education institutions. *Journal of Higher Education Policy and Management*, *34*(2), 153–167. DOI: 10.1080/1360080X.2012.662740

Caballero, K., Harland, T., Wald, N., & Mula-Falcón, J. (2025). The impact of evaluation and accountability on academic careers. *European journal of higher education, 15*(2), 323-339. DOI: 10.1080/21568235.2024.2331116

Cadez, S., Dimovski, V., & Zaman Groff, M. (2017). Research, teaching and performance evaluation in academia: The salience of quality. *Studies in Higher Education, 42*(8), 1455–1473. DOI: 10.1080/03075079.2015.1104659

Cantwell, B. (2011). Academic in-sourcing: International postdoctoral employment and new modes of academic production. *Journal of Higher Education Policy and Management, 33*(2), 101–114. DOI: 10.1080/1360080X.2011.550032

Carey, J. M., Carman, K. R., Clayton, K. P., Horiuchi, Y., Htun, M., & Ortiz, B. (2020). Who wants to hire a more diverse faculty? A conjoint analysis of faculty and student preferences for gender and racial/ethnic diversity. *Politics, Groups & Identities, 8*(3), 535–553. DOI: 10.1080/21565503.2018.1491866

Ceci, S. J. (2018). Women in academic science: Experimental findings from hiring studies. *Educational Psychologist, 53*(1), 22–41. DOI: 10.1080/00461520.2017.1396462

Chalmers, D. (2011). Progress and challenges to the recognition and reward of the scholarship of teaching in higher education. *Higher Education Research & Development, 30*(1), 25–38. DOI: 10.1080/07294360.2011.536970

Champlin, D. P., & Knoedler, J. (2017). Contingent labor and higher education. *Review of Political Economy, 29*(2), 232–248. DOI: 10.1080/09538259.2017.1316054

Chang, H., Longman, K. A., & Franco, M. A. (2014). Leadership development through mentoring in higher education: A collaborative autoethnography of leaders of color. *Mentoring & Tutoring, 22*(4), 373–389. DOI: 10.1080/13611267.2014.945734

Chiang, L. C. (2025). Doctoral qualifications matter in the competitive faculty job market: The perspectives of university senior administrators and their implications. *Studies in Higher Education, 50*(10), 1–15. DOI: 10.1080/03075079.2025.2522740

Civera, A., Horta, H., Meoli, M., & Paleari, S. (2025). Academically inbred presidents and university performance. *Studies in Higher Education*, •••, 1–16. DOI: 10.1080/03075079.2025.2483885

Clark, R. L., & d'Ambrosio, M. B. (2005). Recruitment, retention, and retirement: Compensation and employment policies for higher education. *Educational Gerontology, 31*(5), 385–403. DOI: 10.1080/03601270590921663

Cooray, A., Verma, R., & Wright, L. (2014). Does a gender disparity exist in academic rank? Evidence from an Australian university. *Applied Economics*, *46*(20), 2441–2451. DOI: 10.1080/00036846.2014.904496

Crawford, T., & Germov, J. (2015). Using workforce strategy to address academic casualisation: A University of Newcastle case study. *Journal of Higher Education Policy and Management*, *37*(5), 534–544. DOI: 10.1080/1360080X.2015.1079394

Culver, K. C., Kezar, A., & Koren, E. R. (2025). Faculty, Academic Careers, and Environments (FACE) Framework: A Guide to Faculty Work for Research, Practice, and Policy. *The Journal of Higher Education*, •••, 1–33. DOI: 10.1080/00221546.2025.2466421

Curnalia, R. M., & Mermer, D. (2018). Renewing our commitment to tenure, academic freedom, and shared governance to navigate challenges in higher education. *The Review of Communication*, *18*(2), 129–139. DOI: 10.1080/15358593.2018.1438645

Defleur, M. L. (2007). Raising the Question# 5 What Is Tenure and How Do I Get It? *Communication Education*, *56*(1), 106–112. DOI: 10.1080/03634520601081263

Delucchi, M., Dadzie, R. B., Dean, E., & Pham, X. (2024). What's that smell? Bullshit jobs in higher education. *Review of Social Economy*, *82*(1), 1–22. DOI: 10.1080/00346764.2021.1940255

Deutsch, F. M., & Yao, B. (2014). Gender differences in faculty attrition in the USA. *Community Work & Family*, *17*(4), 392–408. DOI: 10.1080/13668803.2014.885880

DeZure, D., Shaw, A., & Rojewski, J. (2014). Cultivating the next generation of academic leaders: Implications for administrators and faculty. *Change*, *46*(1), 6–12. DOI: 10.1080/00091383.2013.842102

Dorenkamp, I., & Süß, S. (2017). Work-life conflict among young academics: Antecedents and gender effects. *European Journal of Higher Education*, *7*(4), 402–423. DOI: 10.1080/21568235.2017.1304824

Duffy, A. (2019). A delicate balance: How postsecondary education dance faculty in the United States perceive themselves negotiating responsibilities expected for tenure. *Research in Dance Education*, *20*(1), 73–84. DOI: 10.1080/14647893.2018.1523382

Fagan-Wilen, R., Springer, D. W., Ambrosino, B., & White, B. W. (2006). The support of adjunct faculty: An academic imperative. *Social Work Education*, *25*(1), 39–51. DOI: 10.1080/02615470500477870

Finkelstein, M. J., Conley, V. M., & Schuster, J. H. (2017). Whither the faculty? *Change*, *49*(4), 43–51. DOI: 10.1080/00091383.2017.1357099

Flores, L. A., & Rae Gomez, L. (2020). Disciplinary containment: Whiteness and the academic scarcity narrative. *Communication and Critical/Cultural Studies*, *17*(2), 236–242. DOI: 10.1080/14791420.2020.1770818

Foote, K. E. (2010). Creating a community of support for graduate students and early career academics. *Journal of Geography in Higher Education*, *34*(1), 7–19. DOI: 10.1080/03098260902954087

Ford, L. E. (2016). Two steps forward, one step back? Strengthening the foundations of women's leadership in higher education. *Politics, Groups & Identities*, *4*(3), 499–512. DOI: 10.1080/21565503.2016.1170705

Friedman, D. B., Yelton, B., Corwin, S. J., Hardin, J. W., Ingram, L. A., Torres-McGehee, T. M., & Alberg, A. J. (2021). Value of peer mentorship for equity in higher education leadership: A school of public health focus with implications for all academic administrators. *Mentoring & Tutoring*, *29*(5), 500–521. DOI: 10.1080/13611267.2021.1986795

George, R., & Maguire, M. (2021). Academics 'staying on'post retirement age in English university departments of education: Opportunities, threats and employment policies. *British Journal of Educational Studies*, *69*(4), 453–470. DOI: 10.1080/00071005.2020.1814951

Gioti, L. (2025). Neoliberal higher education restructuring, job satisfaction and professional development of academics. *Studies in the Education of Adults*, •••, 1–21. DOI: 10.1080/02660830.2025.2451453

Guillaume, R. O., & Apodaca, E. C. (2022). Early career faculty of color and promotion and tenure: The intersection of advancement in the academy and cultural taxation. *Race, Ethnicity and Education*, *25*(4), 546–563. DOI: 10.1080/13613324.2020.1718084

Han, S., & Xie, J. (2026). Facing inequalities in academia: Understanding Chinese early-career academics' identity formation. *Higher Education Research & Development*, •••, 1–17. DOI: 10.1080/07294360.2026.2615301

Hardy, A., McDonald, J., Guijt, R., Leane, E., Martin, A., James, A., Jones, M., Corban, M., & Green, B. (2018). Academic parenting: Work–family conflict and strategies across child age, disciplines and career level. *Studies in Higher Education*, *43*(4), 625–643. DOI: 10.1080/03075079.2016.1185777

Harris, R., Mate-Sanchez-Val, M., & Ruiz Marín, M. (2025). Gender disparities in promotions and exiting in UK Russell Group universities. *Applied Economics*, *57*(31), 4441–4457. DOI: 10.1080/00036846.2024.2361384

Hartley, K., & Jarvis, D. S. (2022). Let nine universities blossom: Opportunities and constraints on the development of higher education in China. *Higher Education Research & Development*, *41*(5), 1542–1556. DOI: 10.1080/07294360.2021.1915963

Haviland, D., Alleman, N. F., & Cliburn Allen, C. (2017). 'Separate but not quite equal': Collegiality experiences of full-time non-tenure-track faculty members. *The Journal of Higher Education*, *88*(4), 505–528. DOI: 10.1080/00221546.2016.1272321

Hearn, J. C., & Burns, R. (2021). Contingent faculty employment and financial stress in public universities. *The Journal of Higher Education*, *92*(3), 331–362. DOI: 10.1080/00221546.2020.1851570

Heffernan, K., Hazzan, A. A., & Dauenhauer, J. (2022). Promoting age-friendly organizational culture through lifelong learning programs in higher education: Experience and insights from faculty. *Educational Gerontology*, *48*(6), 260–272. DOI: 10.1080/03601277.2022.2033929

Heffernan, T. (2021). Academic networks and career trajectory: 'There's no career in academia without networks'. *Higher Education Research & Development*, *40*(5), 981–994. DOI: 10.1080/07294360.2020.1799948

Heffernan, T. (2022). Sexism, racism, prejudice, and bias: A literature review and synthesis of research surrounding student evaluations of courses and teaching. *Assessment & Evaluation in Higher Education*, *47*(1), 144–154. DOI: 10.1080/02602938.2021.1888075

Heffernan, T. A. (2018). Approaches to career development and support for sessional academics in higher education. *The International Journal for Academic Development*, *23*(4), 312–323. DOI: 10.1080/1360144X.2018.1510406

Henningsson, M. (2025). Organizing the Swedish academic career 1955–2020: Reforms and recurring problems in national policy discussion1. *Nordic Journal of Studies in Educational Policy*, *11*(2), 147–160. DOI: 10.1080/20020317.2024.2401183

Henningsson, M., Jörnesten, A., & Geschwind, L. (2018). Translating tenure track into Swedish: Tensions when implementing an academic career system. *Studies in Higher Education*, *43*(7), 1215–1226. DOI: 10.1080/03075079.2016.1239704

Henry, F., Dua, E., Kobayashi, A., James, C., Li, P., Ramos, H., & Smith, M. S. (2017). Race, racialization and Indigeneity in Canadian universities. *Race, Ethnicity and Education*, *20*(3), 300–314. DOI: 10.1080/13613324.2016.1260226

Herbert, A., & Tienari, J. (2013). Transplanting tenure and the (re) construction of academic freedoms. *Studies in Higher Education*, *38*(2), 157–173. DOI: 10.1080/03075079.2011.569707

Hollywood, A., McCarthy, D., Spencely, C., & Winstone, N. (2020). 'Overwhelmed at first': The experience of career development in early career academics. *Journal of Further and Higher Education, 44*(7), 998–1012. DOI: 10.1080/0309877X.2019.1636213

Hüther, O., & Krücken, G. (2013). Hierarchy and power: A conceptual analysis with particular reference to new public management reforms in German universities. *European Journal of Higher Education, 3*(4), 307–323. DOI: 10.1080/21568235.2013.850920

Jacobs, J. A., & Winslow, S. E. (2004). The academic life course, time pressures and gender inequality. *Community Work & Family, 7*(2), 143–161. DOI: 10.1080/1366880042000245443

Jepsen, D. M., Sun, J. J. M., Budhwar, P. S., Klehe, U. C., Krausert, A., Raghuram, S., & Valcour, M. (2014). International academic careers: Personal reflections. *International Journal of Human Resource Management, 25*(10), 1309–1326. DOI: 10.1080/09585192.2013.870307

Jolley, M. R., Cross, E., & Bryant, M. (2014). A critical challenge: The engagement and assessment of contingent, part-time adjunct faculty professors in United States community colleges. *Community College Journal of Research and Practice, 38*(2-3), 218–230. DOI: 10.1080/10668926.2014.851969

Karran, T., Beiter, K., & Appiagyei-Atua, K. (2017). Measuring academic freedom in Europe: A criterion referenced approach. *Policy Reviews in Higher Education, 1*(2), 209–239. DOI: 10.1080/23322969.2017.1307093

Kassab, M. (2025, June). Navigating Academic Careers in Software Engineering: An Empirical Study of Faculty and Postdoctoral Roles. In *Proceedings of the 33rd ACM International Conference on the Foundations of Software Engineering* (pp. 936-946). DOI: 10.1145/3696630.3727250

Kezar, A. (2012). Spanning the great divide between tenure-track and non-tenure-track faculty. *Change, 44*(6), 6–13. DOI: 10.1080/00091383.2012.728949

Khairullah, S. A., Harris, S., Hadi, H. J., Sandhu, R. A., Ahmad, N., & Alshara, M. A. (2025, February). Implementing artificial intelligence in academic and administrative processes through responsible strategic leadership in the higher education institutions. In *Frontiers in Education* (Vol. 10, p. 1548104). Frontiers Media SA. DOI: 10.3389/feduc.2025.1548104

Kim, G. M., & Cooc, N. (2021). Asian Americans and Pacific Islanders in academe: Race and gender through the tenure pipeline from 1993-2017. *Race, Ethnicity and Education, 24*(3), 338–356. DOI: 10.1080/13613324.2020.1753675

Lampman, C., Crew, E. C., Lowery, S. D., & Tompkins, K. (2016). Women faculty distressed: Descriptions and consequences of academic contrapower harassment. *Journal about Women in Higher Education, 9*(2), 169–189. DOI: 10.1080/19407882.2016.1199385 PMID: 28239435

Langen, J. M. (2011). Evaluation of adjunct faculty in higher education institutions. *Assessment & Evaluation in Higher Education, 36*(2), 185–196. DOI: 10.1080/02602930903221501

Larson, L. R., Duffy, L. N., Fernandez, M., Sturts, J., Gray, J., & Powell, G. M. (2019). Getting started on the tenure track: Challenges and strategies for success. *SCHOLE: A Journal of Leisure Studies and Recreation Education, 34*(1), 36-51. DOI: 10.1080/1937156X.2019.1589804

Li, B., & Shen, Y. (2022). Publication or pregnancy? Employment contracts and childbearing of women academics in China. *Studies in Higher Education, 47*(4), 875–887. DOI: 10.1080/03075079.2020.1817888

Li, Y., Li, J., & Sun, Y. (2013). Young faculty job perceptions in the midst of Chinese higher education reform: The case of Zhejiang University. *Asia Pacific Journal of Education, 33*(3), 273–294. DOI: 10.1080/02188791.2013.787388

Liu, Y., Qin, H., & Li, H. (2025). Competing for research grants: Institutional resource inequality and early-career academics' research agenda setting. *Studies in Higher Education, 50*(10), 2157–2177. DOI: 10.1080/03075079.2025.2544232

Loomes, S., Owens, A., & McCarthy, G. (2019). Patterns of recruitment of academic leaders to Australian universities and implications for the future of higher education. *Journal of Higher Education Policy and Management, 41*(2), 137–152. DOI: 10.1080/1360080X.2019.1565296

Lumpkin, A. (2009, July). Follow the yellow brick road to a successful professional career in higher education. In *The Educational Forum* (Vol. 73, No. 3, pp. 200-214). Taylor & Francis Group. DOI: 10.1080/00131720902991251

Lumpkin, A., & Jones, S. J. (2023). Toughest job in higher education: Chairs' responsibilities. *International Journal of Leadership in Education*, •••, 1–22. DOI: 10.1080/13603124.2023.2290144

Mabasa, F. D., & Ngirande, H. (2015). Perceived organisational support influences on job satisfaction and organisational commitment among junior academic staff members. *Journal of Psychology in Africa, 25*(4), 364–366. DOI: 10.1080/14330237.2015.1078102

Macfarlane, B. (2007). Defining and rewarding academic citizenship: The implications for university promotions policy. *Journal of Higher Education Policy and Management*, *29*(3), 261–273. DOI: 10.1080/13600800701457863

Machovcova, K., Kováts, G., Mudrak, J., Cidlinská, K., & Zabrodska, K. (2024). (Dis) continuities in academic middle management career trajectories: A longitudinal qualitative study. *Journal of Higher Education Policy and Management*, *46*(2), 200–217. DOI: 10.1080/1360080X.2023.2276589

Madison, G., & Fahlman, P. (2021). Sex differences in the number of scientific publications and citations when attaining the rank of professor in Sweden. *Studies in Higher Education*, *46*(12), 2506–2527. DOI: 10.1080/03075079.2020.1723533

Maher, F. A., & Tetreault, M. K. T. (2011). Long-term transformations: Excavating privilege and diversity in the academy. *Gender and Education*, *23*(3), 281–297. DOI: 10.1080/09540253.2010.491790

Mathews, K. (2018). Growing our own: Cultivating faculty leadership. *Change*, *50*(3-4), 88–92. DOI: 10.1080/00091383.2018.1509617

Mayer, A. L., & Tikka, P. M. (2008). Family-friendly policies and gender bias in academia. *Journal of Higher Education Policy and Management*, *30*(4), 363–374. DOI: 10.1080/13600800802383034

McAlpine, L., & Emmioğlu, E. (2015). Navigating careers: Perceptions of sciences doctoral students, post-PhD researchers and pre-tenure academics. *Studies in Higher Education*, *40*(10), 1770–1785. DOI: 10.1080/03075079.2014.914908

McConnell, K. F. (2019). Teaching and learning in an age of precarity: Toward a pedagogy of the transitory. *Communication Education*, *68*(2), 252–258. DOI: 10.1080/03634523.2019.1569248

McNaughtan, J., Eicke, D., Thacker, R., & Freeman, S. (2022). Trust or self-determination: Understanding the role of tenured faculty empowerment and job satisfaction. *The Journal of Higher Education*, *93*(1), 137–161. DOI: 10.1080/00221546.2021.1935601

Mgaiwa, S. J. (2023). Job satisfaction among university academics: Do academic rank and age make a difference? *Cogent Education*, *10*(2), 2230395. DOI: 10.1080/2331186X.2023.2230395

Morley, L. (2005). Opportunity or exploitation? Women and quality assurance in higher education. *Gender and Education*, *17*(4), 411–429. DOI: 10.1080/09540250500145106

Morris, T. L., & Laipple, J. S. (2015). How prepared are academic administrators? Leadership and job satisfaction within US research universities. *Journal of Higher Education Policy and Management*, *37*(2), 241–251. DOI: 10.1080/1360080X.2015.1019125

Mukhamejanova, D., & Kuchumova, G. (2025). Faculty perspectives on the changing research and teaching career tracks of academics at private universities in Kazakhstan. *Studies in Higher Education*, *50*(12), 2700–2715. DOI: 10.1080/03075079.2024.2426533

Murai, E., & Foote, K. (2025). Non-tenure track faculty in US geography: Strategies for support. *Journal of Geography in Higher Education*, •••, 1–18. DOI: 10.1080/03098265.2025.2569363

Murgatroyd, S. J. (Ed.). (2025). *Strategic Choices and Leadership Change in Higher Education Institutions*. IGI Global., DOI: 10.4018/979-8-3373-2081-6

Murray, D. S. (2019). The precarious new faculty majority: Communication and instruction research and contingent labor in higher education. *Communication Education*, *68*(2), 235–245. DOI: 10.1080/03634523.2019.1568512

Nam, B. H., Love, A., & Marshall, R. C. (2021). Entering into global academia: US academic hegemony and former Korean elite athletes' faculty appointment in higher education. *Journal of Further and Higher Education*, *45*(4), 481–496. DOI: 10.1080/0309877X.2020.1784399

Nir, A. E., & Zilberstein-Levy, R. (2006). Planning for academic excellence: Tenure and professional considerations. *Studies in Higher Education*, *31*(5), 537–554. DOI: 10.1080/03075070600922725

O'Meara, K., Kuvaeva, A., & Nyunt, G. (2017). Constrained choices: A view of campus service inequality from annual faculty reports. *The Journal of Higher Education*, *88*(5), 672–700. DOI: 10.1080/00221546.2016.1257312

O'Meara, K., & Terosky, A. L. (2010). Engendering faculty professional growth. *Change*, *42*(6), 44–51. DOI: 10.1080/00091383.2010.523408

Ooms, W., Werker, C., & Hopp, C. (2019). Moving up the ladder: Heterogeneity influencing academic careers through research orientation, gender, and mentors. *Studies in Higher Education*, *44*(7), 1268–1289. DOI: 10.1080/03075079.2018.1434617

Osei-Kofi, N. (2012). Junior faculty of color in the corporate university: Implications of neoliberalism and neoconservatism on research, teaching and service. *Critical Studies in Education*, *53*(2), 229–244. DOI: 10.1080/17508487.2012.672326

Pandit, K. (2020). Mentoring graduate students in an era of faculty career restructuring. *Journal of Geography in Higher Education*, *44*(3), 335–349. DOI: 10.1080/03098265.2020.1771548

Peng, L., & Wiggins, L. M. (2025). What Do Employers Want?: Tracking Changes in the Academic Librarian Job Market Through A Study of US Full-Time Job Advertisements. *Journal of Library Administration*, *65*(6-7), 761–782. DOI: 10.1080/01930826.2025.2525731

Pham, H. T., & Nguyen, C. H. (2020). Academic staff quality and the role of quality assurance mechanisms: The Vietnamese case. *Quality in Higher Education*, *26*(3), 262–283. DOI: 10.1080/13538322.2020.1761603

Pietilä, M. (2015). Tenure track career system as a strategic instrument for academic leaders. *European Journal of Higher Education*, *5*(4), 371–387. DOI: 10.1080/21568235.2015.1046466

Pineda, P., & Salazar Morales, D. (2024). Managerialism, accreditation and insecure academic employment across different higher education traditions. *Studies in Higher Education*, *49*(11), 2080–2103. DOI: 10.1080/03075079.2023.2289087

Porter, C. J., Moore, C. M., Boss, G. J., Davis, T. J., & Louis, D. A. (2020). To be Black women and contingent faculty: Four scholarly personal narratives. *The Journal of Higher Education*, *91*(5), 674–697. DOI: 10.1080/00221546.2019.1700478

Pyke, J. (2013). Women, choice and promotion or why women are still a minority in the professoriate. *Journal of Higher Education Policy and Management*, *35*(4), 444–454. DOI: 10.1080/1360080X.2013.812179

Rainnie, A., Goods, C., Bahn, S., & Burgess, J. (2013). The challenges of working in Australian academia: An introduction. *Labour & Industry: a journal of the social and economic relations of work*, *23*(3), 191-199. DOI: 10.1080/10301763.2013.839080

Rambe, P. (2024). Research excellence and productivity for global impact at an African university. *Studies in Higher Education*, *49*(8), 1397–1424. DOI: 10.1080/03075079.2023.2265931

Richardson, J., Suseno, Y., & Wardale, D. (2021). The paradoxical management of casual academics: An Australian case study. *Higher Education Research & Development*, *40*(2), 370–385. DOI: 10.1080/07294360.2020.1756749

Ross, J. I., Richards, S. C., Newbold, G., Jones, R. S., Lenza, M., Murphy, D. S., Hogan, R., & Curry, G. D. (2011). Knocking on the ivory tower's door: The experience of ex-convicts applying for tenure-track university positions. *Journal of Criminal Justice Education*, *22*(2), 267–285. DOI: 10.1080/10511251003778982

Rudick, C. K., & Dannels, D. P. (2019). "Yes, and..." continuing the scholarly conversation about contingent labor in higher education. *Communication Education*, *68*(2), 259–263. DOI: 10.1080/03634523.2019.1572198

Sanz-Menéndez, L., & Cruz-Castro, L. (2019). University academics' preferences for hiring and promotion systems. *European Journal of Higher Education*, *9*(2), 153–171. DOI: 10.1080/21568235.2018.1515029

Schmalz, D. L., Parr, M. G., Powell, G. M., Bricker, K. S., & Dustin, D. L. (2019). Post-tenure pathways: Individualized careers in higher education. *SCHOLE: A Journal of Leisure Studies and Recreation Education, 34*(1), 52-61. DOI: 10.1080/1937156X.2019.1589809

Seo, G. E., Hedayati Mehdiabadi, A., & Huang, W. (2017). Identifying core competencies to advance female professors' careers: An exploratory study in United States academia. *Journal of Further and Higher Education*, *41*(6), 741–759. DOI: 10.1080/0309877X.2016.1177167

Si, J. (2023). No other choices but involution: Understanding Chinese young academics in the tenure track system. *Journal of Higher Education Policy and Management*, *45*(1), 53–67. DOI: 10.1080/1360080X.2022.2115332

Siekkinen, T., Pekkola, E., & Kivistö, J. (2016). Recruitments in Finnish universities: Practicing strategic or pathetic HRM? *Nordic Journal of Studies in Educational Policy*, *2016*(2-3), 32316. DOI: 10.3402/nstep.v2.32316

Simmons, C. A., Weiss, E. L., & Schwartz, S. L. (2022). Job satisfaction indicators for tenure and non-tenure track social work faculty: Similar but not equal. *Social Work Education*, *41*(2), 175–194. DOI: 10.1080/02615479.2020.1808608

Solem, M. N., & Foote, K. E. (2006). Concerns, attitudes, and abilities of early-career geography faculty. *Journal of Geography in Higher Education*, *30*(2), 199–234. DOI: 10.1080/03098260600717299

Solomon, S., & du Plessis, M. (2023). Temporary academics in South African higher education institutions: Their lived precarity experiences. *Journal of Psychology in Africa*, *33*(5), 522–529. DOI: 10.1080/14330237.2023.2258001

Sommersguter-Reichmann, M., & Reichmann, G. (2025). Institutional corruption in higher education: diving into indicator-based funding and employment conditions in Austrian universities. *Policy Reviews in Higher Education*, 1-18. DOI: 10.1080/23322969.2025.2489953

Stupnisky, R. H., Hall, N. C., Daniels, L. M., & Mensah, E. (2017). Testing a model of pretenure faculty members' teaching and research success: Motivation as a mediator of balance, expectations, and collegiality. *The Journal of Higher Education, 88*(3), 376–400. DOI: 10.1080/00221546.2016.1272317

Stupnisky, R. H., Weaver-Hightower, M. B., & Kartoshkina, Y. (2015). Exploring and testing the predictors of new faculty success: A mixed methods study. *Studies in Higher Education, 40*(2), 368–390. DOI: 10.1080/03075079.2013.842220

Subbaye, R., & Vithal, R. (2017). Gender, teaching and academic promotions in higher education. *Gender and Education, 29*(7), 926–951. DOI: 10.1080/09540253.2016.1184237

Tagg, J. (2012). Why does the faculty resist change? Change. *Change, 44*(1), 6–15. DOI: 10.1080/00091383.2012.635987

Takagi, K. (2018). Accommodating project-based professionals in higher education institutions in Japan. *Journal of Higher Education Policy and Management, 40*(3), 272–286. DOI: 10.1080/1360080X.2018.1462434

Tariq, M. U. (Ed.). (2024). *AI-Driven Learning and Engagement in Higher Education*. IGI Global., DOI: 10.4018/979-8-3693-4074-5

Taylor, Z. (2025). Professional ghosting and bureaucratic kindness: Institutional communication with applicants to tenure-track academic staff positions in student affairs and/or higher education. *Journal of Higher Education Policy and Management, 47*(2), 129–153. DOI: 10.1080/1360080X.2024.2433303

Teelken, C., Taminiau, Y., & Rosenmöller, C. (2021). Career mobility from associate to full professor in academia: Micro-political practices and implicit gender stereotypes. *Studies in Higher Education, 46*(4), 836–850. DOI: 10.1080/03075079.2019.1655725

Tian, M., & Lu, G. (2017). What price the building of world-class universities? Academic pressure faced by young lecturers at a research-centered University in China. *Teaching in Higher Education, 22*(8), 957–974. DOI: 10.1080/13562517.2017.1319814

Trendowski, T. (2023). Delayed promotion to full professor in physical education teacher education. *International Journal of Kinesiology in Higher Education, 7*(4), 285–295. DOI: 10.1080/24711616.2022.2152510

Tytherleigh*, M. Y., Webb, C., Cooper, C. L., & Ricketts, C. (2005). Occupational stress in UK higher education institutions: A comparative study of all staff categories. *Higher education research & development, 24*(1), 41-61. DOI: 10.1080/0729436052000318569

Viefers, S. F., Christie, M. F., & Ferdos, F. (2006). Gender equity in higher education: Why and how? A case study of gender issues in a science faculty. *European Journal of Engineering Education, 31*(1), 15–22. DOI: 10.1080/03043790500429948

Wang, L. (2022). Newbie or experienced: An empirical study on faculty recruitment preferences at top national HEIs in China. *Studies in Higher Education, 47*(4), 783–798. DOI: 10.1080/03075079.2020.1804849

Wang, S., & Jones, G. A. (2021). Competing institutional logics of academic personnel system reforms in leading Chinese Universities. *Journal of Higher Education Policy and Management, 43*(1), 49–66. DOI: 10.1080/1360080X.2020.1747958

Wang, T., Yu, L., Wang, W., & Dai, K. (2024). Employees in change: An exploration of academics' perceived employee-organisation relationship in the reform of the tenure-track system in China. *Studies in Higher Education, 49*(11), 2066–2079. DOI: 10.1080/03075079.2023.2288940

Wolverton, M., Ackerman, R., & Holt, S. (2005). Preparing for leadership: What academic department chairs need to know. *Journal of Higher Education Policy and Management, 27*(2), 227–238. DOI: 10.1080/13600800500120126

Xu, W., & Poole, A. (2024). 'Academics without publications are just like imperial concubines without sons': The 'new times' of Chinese higher education. *Journal of Education Policy, 39*(6), 861–878. DOI: 10.1080/02680939.2023.2288339

Xu, X., Arshad, M. A., He, Y., Liu, H., Chen, Q., & Yang, J. (2025). From skilled workers to smart talent: AI-driven workforce transformation in the construction industry. *Buildings (Basel, Switzerland), 15*(14), 2552. DOI: 10.3390/buildings15142552

Yakoboski, P. J. (2016). Adjunct views of adjunct positions. *Change, 48*(3), 54–59. DOI: 10.1080/00091383.2016.1170553

Yang, X., Cai, X. L., & Li, T. S. (2024). Does the tenure track influence academic research? An empirical study of faculty members in China. *Studies in Higher Education, 49*(3), 476–492. DOI: 10.1080/03075079.2023.2238767

Yin, Z., Jiang, X., & Tong, P. (2024). Why do they leave? University personnel system reforms in China and the impacts on academic staff turnover. *Journal of Higher Education Policy and Management, 46*(5), 463–483. DOI: 10.1080/1360080X.2024.2307738

Young, P. (2006). Out of balance: Lecturers' perceptions of differential status and rewards in relation to teaching and research. *Teaching in Higher Education, 11*(2), 191–202. DOI: 10.1080/13562510500527727

Zambrana, R. E., Carvajal, D., & Townsend, J. (2023). Institutional penalty: Mentoring, service, perceived discrimination and its impacts on the health and academic careers of Latino faculty. *Ethnic and Racial Studies*, *46*(6), 1132–1157. DOI: 10.1080/01419870.2022.2160651 PMID: 37719448

Chapter 8
Academic Promotion in Cambodian Public Universities:
Challenges and Moving Forward

Rany Sam
http://orcid.org/0000-0003-3266-5974
National University of Battambang, Cambodia

Sereyrath Em
http://orcid.org/0000-0002-6803-195X
National University of Chea Sim Kamchaymear, Cambodia

Sinath No
http://orcid.org/0009-0001-1644-8702
National University of Battambang, Cambodia

Sopheak Sam
http://orcid.org/0009-0009-2362-8611
University of Heng Samrin Thbongkhmum, Cambodia

Channorak Ngo
http://orcid.org/0009-0002-0017-7212
National Mean Chey University, Cambodia

Ry Hour
http://orcid.org/0009-0002-6488-4370
National University of Battambang, Cambodia

Mardy Serey
http://orcid.org/0009-0002-1049-7324
Svay Rieng University, Cambodia

Morin Tieng
http://orcid.org/0009-0000-1564-3381
National University of Battambang, Cambodia

Bora Phan
http://orcid.org/0009-0008-0931-1530
National University of Chea Sim Kamchaymear, Cambodia

Vuthea Da
http://orcid.org/0009-0003-3185-0999
National University of Battambang, Cambodia

DOI: 10.4018/979-8-3373-8525-9.ch008

ABSTRACT

This chapter examines the academic promotion system in Cambodian public universities, highlighting national and institutional challenges that hinder merit-based career advancement. Despite rapid expansion in higher education, promotion practices remain inconsistent, with unclear criteria, limited research capacity, and centralized decision-making processes constraining academic development within specialized, relevant ministries and the Council of Ministers. Heavy teaching workloads, insufficient funding, and weak research support further limit faculty productivity and progression. Drawing on comparative insights and policy analysis, the chapter argues for a more transparent, standardized, and performance-oriented promotion framework. It proposes practical reforms, including clearer evaluation criteria, strengthened research infrastructure, and decentralized yet accountable governance mechanisms, to enhance fairness, motivation, and institutional quality in Cambodia's public higher education sector.

INTRODUCTION

Background of the study

Higher education is widely regarded as a primary driver of Cambodia's human, social, and economic development (Phan, 2015; Heng et al., 2023; Sok & Bunry, 2024a). As Cambodia aspires to move from a lower-middle-income economy to a high-income economy by 2050, the role of public universities in producing both qualified human resources and high-quality research becomes evident (Royal Government of Cambodia, 2023; World Bank, 2024). The efficacy of social, economic, and human development, however, is always tied to the quality and motivation of academic staff. The classification of Cambodian public university lecturers as state civil servants is an accurate characterization that has historically stifled the development of independent scholarship.

The adoption of the Royal Decree concerning professorship titles in Cambodia in 2013 was interpreted as a turning point for developing national education policies and aligning Cambodian educational criteria to the standards adopted in other countries through regional development cooperation under the AUN (Heng & Heng, 2023; Chiv et al., 2025; Sam et al., 2025a). This involved establishing a hierarchical system based on achievement in teaching, research, and community service. However, even with a clear policy, the transition from a "teaching-focused" civil service to a "research-active" professorship has experienced challenges.

The Cambodian higher education sector faces a range of major challenges that affect its efficiency and responsiveness to labor market needs. Specifically, the promotion system exemplifies, in many ways, the greater tensions within the state. The modernization of higher education is necessitated by the need for faster scientific discovery, greater openness in research, and international cooperation. Modernization should, however, be undertaken cautiously to ensure a proper balance between competitiveness and the integrity of academia, intellectual property rights, and access to education (Saraite Sariene et al., 2020; Sam et al., 2025b). On the other hand, the promotion process seems to be anchored in a political settlement characterized by centralization and a lack of transparency (Kelsall, 2022).

The faculty functions on a point of tension. Professors who come back from abroad with their doctoral degrees tend to face tension related to the idea of "brain return." Under the strained budget system, professors have heavy workloads meant to supplement small salaries, which limit their time for research. Such an imbalance makes it difficult for them to function in merit-based environments (Ros & Oleksiyenko, 2018; Sam et al., 2026). This scenario underscores the contradiction between the high standards set by the 2013 decree.

Herein lies an analysis of the dynamics at play. The discussion begins with a dissection of the policy setting, particularly as embodied by the policies spelled out in the Royal Decree of 2013 and subsequent regulations. The purpose of the analysis will be to explain, in detail, why the advancement of academia remains such a complex and contentious issue in Cambodia and the steps that must be taken to update an important component of its higher education structure (Royal Government of Cambodia, 2013).

Research Problem

Although Cambodia formally introduced a professorial ranking system through the Royal Decree on Professorial Titles in 2013 and began its large-scale implementation in 2023, the scholarly analysis of how academic promotion is carried out in Cambodian public universities remains limited. Existing studies have focused primarily on the opportunities, significance, and challenges associated with professorial titles, while comparatively little attention has been given to the broader institutional, governance, and structural factors that shape promotion outcomes (Heng & Heng, 2023; Heng et al., 2023; Chin et al., 2023).

Academic promotion is implemented within a higher education system characterized by centralized governance, limited institutional autonomy, constrained research capacity, heavy teaching workloads, and weak incentive mechanisms (Sok & Bunry, 2024a; Heng et al., 2023). These conditions raise important concerns regarding the effectiveness, fairness, and sustainability of a merit-based promotion system. Furthermore, the dual status of academics as both civil servants and scholars creates competing expectations and accountabilities, complicating the evaluation of academic performance and professional advancement (Sok & Bunry, 2024b).

Given Cambodia's aspiration to strengthen research productivity and transition toward a knowledge-based economy by 2050, a critical examination of its academic promotion system is both timely and necessary (Royal Government of Cambodia, 2025; World Bank, 2024). This study therefore investigates the policy framework, implementation challenges, and future directions of academic promotion in Cambodian public universities. Despite the ambitious policy framework established by the 2013 Royal Decree on Professorial Titles, implementing a merit-based academic promotion system in Cambodian public universities remains fraught with challenges. A substantial gap persists between the government's vision of fostering a research-active, performance-oriented professoriate and the structural, governance, and economic realities that faculty members face.

Several interrelated challenges have emerged. First, although the decree identifies research productivity as a core criterion for promotion, many public universities still lack the infrastructure needed to support meaningful research. These limitations include inadequate research funding, limited access to international scholarly databases, limited laboratory facilities, and insufficient provision of protected research time for faculty members (Heng et al., 2023; Chiv et al., 2025; Sam et al., 2026). Second, the dual status of academics as state civil servants and university scholars creates conflicting accountability structures. Promotion processes remain embedded within seniority-based bureaucratic systems and centralized approval mechanisms involving ministries and the Council of Ministers, often limiting the role of institutional peer review and merit-based assessment (Heng & Heng, 2023; Un et al., 2017).

Third, the widespread practice of moonlighting, including additional teaching at private universities and private tutoring, reflects the economic realities faced by many academics whose salaries remain relatively low. While such activities provide supplementary income, they substantially reduce the time and intellectual capacity available for research and scholarly publication (Heng et al., 2023). Fourth, the absence of transparent, digitized, and evidence-based evaluation systems has contributed to perceptions of opacity, patronage, and inconsistency in the application of promotion criteria across institutions and academic disciplines (Heng & Heng, 2023; Chin et al., 2023).

As a result, academic promotion often functions more as a symbolic, state-conferred honor than as a predictable, evidence-based mechanism for career advancement, academic excellence, and the development of research capacity. Emerging evidence suggests relatively low rates of successful promotion, underrepresentation of women in senior academic ranks, and growing concerns about predatory publishing and proxy writing as strategies used to satisfy publication requirements (Heng & Heng, 2023; Heng et al., 2024). These challenges extend beyond administrative concerns and have significant implications for Cambodia's ambition to develop a competitive higher education system and a knowledge-based economy within the ASEAN region.

Accordingly, this study seeks to address the following central problem: Why does a well-intentioned merit-based academic promotion policy struggle to translate into effective practices in Cambodian public universities, and what institutional, governance, and structural reforms are required to bridge the gap between policy aspirations and implementation realities?

Research Objectives

This study aims to do the following:

- Examine the policy, legal, and institutional frameworks governing academic promotion in Cambodian public universities, with particular emphasis on the implementation of the 2013 Royal Decree on Professorial Titles and related ministerial regulations.
- The structural, governance, and institutional challenges affecting the implementation of academic promotion policies, including research capacity, teaching workload, institutional autonomy, evaluation mechanisms, and administrative procedures, should be analyzed.
- Assess the extent to which the current academic promotion system supports merit-based career advancement and academic excellence within Cambodian public universities.
- Policy and institutional reforms should be proposed to enhance the transparency, effectiveness, accountability, and sustainability of academic promotion practices in Cambodia.

Research Questions

This study seeks to answer the following questions:

- What policy, legal, and institutional frameworks currently govern academic promotion in Cambodian public universities?
- What structural, governance, and institutional factors influence the implementation of academic promotion policies in Cambodian public universities?
- To what extent does the current academic promotion system reflect the principles of meritocracy, transparency, and academic excellence?

- What policy and institutional reforms are needed to strengthen the effectiveness, fairness, and sustainability of academic promotion practices in Cambodia?

Research Methodology

The researchers employed document analysis (Creswell & Creswell, 2018) as the primary methodological approach to examine policy documents, research articles, and other pertinent materials concerning the conferral of professorial titles within Cambodia's education sector. The corpus of reviewed materials included policy frameworks, royal decrees, official proclamations, press releases, and other relevant publications from the Ministry of Education, Youth and Sport, as well as scholarly articles and online resources. This comprehensive document review was undertaken to elucidate the procedural mechanisms, opportunities, and challenges associated with implementing the professorial ranking system in Cambodia. In addition to these secondary sources, the present article draws substantially on the professional experience, contextual knowledge, and subject-matter expertise of the authors, who have conducted extensive research and engaged in scholarly work on higher education in Cambodia from 2000 to 2026. The triangulation of documentary evidence with the authors' experiential and empirical insights reinforces the rigor, depth, and credibility of the analysis presented herein (Denzin & Lincoln, 2011).

Scope and Limitations

This study is based exclusively on documentary evidence and secondary data. Therefore, the findings reflect policy intentions and published evidence rather than the lived experiences of faculty members. Future studies may employ interviews, surveys, or mixed-methods approaches to examine how academic promotion policies are implemented and perceived across Cambodian public universities.

FINDINGS

THE POLICY, LEGAL, AND INSTITUTIONAL FRAMEWORKS OF GOVERNING ACADEMIC PROMOTION IN CAMBODIAN PUBLIC UNIVERSITIES

The promotion process in Cambodian academia is a complex system involving royal decrees, subdecrees, and ministerial regulations. These policies aim to turn the sector into a system of academics by standardizing it after the period of postwar reconstruction. However, the implementation of such policies highlights some complexities involved in building the state. The foundation of Cambodia's contemporary academic promotion system is the March 2013 Royal Decree (Preah Reach Kret) No. NS/RKT/0313/214. The decree laid out, for the first time, three-tier academic titles: Assistant Professor, Associate Professor, and Professor. Higher education degrees have historically transformed the professoriate from a broad, informal label for any teacher into a formalized, highly regulated title. Through mandates regarding certain types of research output, peer-reviewed journals, and high qualification standards, current laws limit the use of titles to those recognized as experts in their fields (Hermanowicz, 2022). As Cambodia aspires to monetize the titles, the 2013 Decree sought to link them to specific criteria.

The decree requires that candidates for these positions meet a high standard (Heng & Heng, 2023; Smith et al., 2025). For example, the title of an assistant professor requires a PhD and several years of teaching and publishing in an academic field. The differences between associate and full professors continue to build on this rigor by considering not only the quantity of research produced but also the consequences of the work and academic leadership roles (Smith et al., 2025). The hope was that this would indicate Cambodia's commitment to the international academic community and support the "standardization" of faculty in the ASEAN region.

Following the Royal Decree, the Ministry of Education, Youth and Sport (MoEYS) and other relevant ministries (including the Ministry of Health) issued Prakas (ministerial letters), which explained the criteria for evaluation. Point systems that award separate points for scholarly research papers, as well as for required teaching and administrative time, usually form part of workload or promotion policies. The purpose of using these approaches is to quantify academic activity and comply with educational institutions' regulations (Spivakovsky et al., 2022; Rushforth & Hammarfelt, 2023). The tools used to measure academic activities include the GPA, success rate, standardized tests, and impact factors such as the h-index. The educational institutions that collect and analyze the above information (Spivakovsky et al., 2022) use information systems. These laws prescribed the "points" assigned to publications and the required hours for teaching and administrative work at the university. Nevertheless, the process remains centralized. Universities are responsible for the initial screening, but the decision to confer the titles of Associate Professor and Professor is made by the Council of Ministers and issued as a royal decree for each individual. This suggests that the state honors the symbolic nature of the academic title, but political and bureaucratic intervention can restrict academic promotion.

Table 1 summarizes the principal legal, policy, and scholarly documents that collectively shape Cambodia's professorial promotion system. The evolution of these documents illustrates a gradual transition from strengthening national research capacity toward establishing a comprehensive merit-based framework for academic promotion. Early policies focused primarily on developing research infrastructure and institutional capacity, while subsequent regulations introduced formal procedures for evaluating and awarding professorial titles. More recent strategic plans, subdecrees, and implementation guidelines demonstrate the government's continued efforts to strengthen governance, improve research quality, and modernize higher education in line with regional and international standards. In parallel, recent scholarly publications have provided important evidence concerning the opportunities, implementation challenges, governance issues, and policy reforms required to enhance the effectiveness and credibility of Cambodia's academic promotion system. Together, these policy instruments and academic studies provide a legal, institutional, and conceptual foundation for understanding the development of professorial titles in Cambodian public universities (Royal Government of Cambodia, 2026).

Table 1. Existing policies, papers, and regulations related to professorships

Category	Policy/Document	Year	Main Purpose	Contribution to Academic Promotion
Policy	Policy on Research and Development in the Education Sector (MoEYS, 2010)	2010	Establish national research priorities for the education sector.	Provides the initial policy foundation to strengthen the research culture in higher education.
	Master Plan for Research and Development in the Education Sector (MoEYS, 2011)	2011	Develop research capacity and institutional research management.	Supports research development as a prerequisite for future academic promotion.
Royal Decree	Royal Decree on Professorial Titles	2013	Establish the national professorial ranking system (Assistant Professor, Associate Professor, Professor).	Serves as the principal legal framework governing academic promotion in Cambodia.
Ministerial Regulation (Prakas)	Proclamation on the Selection and Appointment of Professorial Titles in the Education Sector (MoEYS, 2020)	2020	Define eligibility requirements, evaluation procedures, and appointment mechanisms.	Operationalizes the implementation of the Royal Decree through standardized assessment procedures.
Research Articles	Implementing professorial titles, Chet et al. (2023)	2023	Examines the significance of implementing professorial titles.	Highlights the importance of academic promotion in improving the quality of higher education.
	Chin et al. (2023)	2023	Explores the relationship between professorial titles and research productivity.	Demonstrates how promotion can strengthen research performance and academic excellence.

continued on following page

Table 1. Continued

Category	Policy/Document	Year	Main Purpose	Contribution to Academic Promotion
	Heng & Heng (2023)	2023	Investigates opportunities and implementation challenges.	Identifies institutional, governance, and policy barriers affecting promotion.
	Heng et al. (2023)	2023	Examines Cambodia's research ecosystem.	Explains structural constraints affecting research productivity and promotion readiness.
	Heng & Heng (2024)	2024	Reviews opportunities, challenges, and future implications of professorial titles.	Provides updated evidence supporting reform of Cambodia's academic promotion system.
Strategic Policy	Education Strategic Plan 2024–2028 (MoEYS, 2024a)	2024	Strengthen the quality of higher education, research, and innovation.	Aligns academic promotion with national higher education reform priorities.
Guideline	Guidelines for Quality Management of Doctoral Training (MoEYS, 2024b)	2024	Improve the quality of doctoral education and research supervision.	Enhances the quality of future candidates eligible for professorial promotion.
Sub-Decree	Sub-Decree on the National Council for Granting Professorial Titles	2025	Establish the National Council responsible for evaluating professorial appointments.	Strengthens national governance and quality assurance in academic promotion.
	Sub-Decree on the Organization and Functioning of the General Secretariat of the National Committee for the Conferment of Professorial Titles	2026	Define the administrative structure supporting the National Committee.	Improves coordination and administrative management of the promotion process.

Shifts in Promotion Criteria: From Civil Service to Merit-based Systems

The move toward more formalized promotion criteria in Cambodia is a story of change. For a large portion of the 1980s and 1990s, the central focus of the higher education system was "reconstruction," reconstituting the intellectual capital that was destroyed under the Khmer Rouge. During this time, the faculty were treated as part of the civil service. Promotion followed the Law on the Common Statute of Civil Servants, which was based on seniority, hierarchy, and state loyalty. In this model of "civil service," promotion could be automatically based on time-in-grade or contingent on the assumption of administrative leadership roles within the university or the ministry.

The shift toward a "merit-based" system started in the mid-2000s as part of a broader movement toward public administrative reform (Heng et al., 2023; Heng & Heng, 2023). The state believed that the old system based on seniority would not be a suitable workforce for an economy that required specialists and innovators. The 2013 Decree was an indication of this recognition. The decree sought to overlay an already civil servant bureaucracy with a more meritocratic hierarchy. The 2013 policy and decree have resulted in a "dual identity" for academics in Cambodia, who are state employees bound by civil-service rules and regulations and independent scholars expected to compete in a global marketplace of ideas.

The adoption of merit-based criteria has established "research" as a prerequisite for professional standing. However, the process is not yet complete. In many public universities, "merit" for promotion is often equated with "institutional loyalty". Although the formal criteria specify publications, the informal or "politically settled" process at the university suggests that those with connections or who are part of management are better positioned to access expedited applications (Kelsall et al., 2022; Dressel, 2024). The strain between the "rational-legal" mandate of the decree and the "neo-patrimonial" reality of the institution remains evident in the Cambodian context.

A Comparative Study of National Policy Promotion Guidelines and Institutional Policy Promotion Guidelines

There is a large gap between the perceived and the practical gap between national-level policy aspirations and institution-level promotion policy. At the national level, MoEYS has attempted to establish a unified standard and ensure that a "Professor" at the Royal University of Phnom Penh (RUPP) has the same meaning as a "Professor" at the University of Health Sciences (UHS). The impetus to "standardize" reflects a desire to adopt a regional quality assurance standard, the ASEAN Ministers of Education Organization, but at the institutional level, this standardization is inconsistent. Public universities in Cambodia operate with different degrees of autonomy (Sok & Bunry, 2024). At some universities, such as the Royal University of Agriculture and the Institute of Technology of Cambodia, internal committees provide more rigorous peer review than other institutions do. University promotion processes across many areas are dependent on clearance from higher ministries, which limits the freedom of action and expression within universities. Centralized management, in most cases, leaves the university with only an advisory role, while all final decisions regarding recruitment and promotions are made externally (Liu & Yan, 2019). This leads to bottlenecks because national standards cannot be applied, as the central authority lacks the disciplinary capacity to assess the research specified in the application across all fields.

Additionally, the "national" guidelines can be criticized as "one-size-fits-all". The application of these guidelines can vary across public universities. Variability can occur both in the interpretations of different institutions and across disciplines. An illustrative example is the requirement for "international publications," which can be easier to accommodate in the natural sciences, where more established journals exist, than in "Cambodian"-specific social research, where the aim is for any audience or impact to be local (Kayashima & Asada, 2024). As a result, it has been much more common for some institutions to "mimic" or apply the national guidelines on paper but to apply the guidelines loosely, to meet the particular context of the institutional culture, or as a way to protect faculty who have had longstanding appointments but may not meet the new standards for research qualifications. This phenomenon, often referred to as "isomorphic mimicry" or "liberal mimicry", describes a capability trap in which developing organizations adopt the external aesthetics and rhetoric of "best practices" to project legitimacy rather than building the functional capacity to implement them (Andrews et al., 2017). Existing Cambodian studies have largely examined the introduction of professorial titles and their potential benefits but have paid limited attention to the governance, institutional, and structural constraints that affect the implementation of academic promotion.

STRUCTURAL AND INSTITUTIONAL CONDITIONS OF CAREER DEVELOPMENT

The state of promotional processes in Cambodia is not just policy-based; the barriers to advancement are also structural and institutional. For meritocracy to work, faculty need the opportunity to meet the prerequisites set before them. In Cambodia, the opportunity to perform is limited by a lack of research resources, heavy workloads, and weak infrastructure for assessing scholarships.

Research Capacity and the Shortage of Academic Infrastructure

Although the 2013 Royal Decree mandated research as a condition of promotion, it failed to develop the infrastructure required to undertake that research. Most Cambodian public universities were created as teaching universities and, as research schools, remain relatively young. Academic infrastructure shortages remain perhaps the single most significant barrier to academic development (Heng et al., 2023; Chiv et al., 2025).

Cambodia has actively transitioned from fragmented, project-based research toward a coordinated national ecosystem by officially establishing the **National Research Foundation (NRF)** and the **National Research Fund** as dedicated trust. The rationale behind these organizations was to serve as the primary source of funding and administration, ensuring the centralization of resources, both within and outside the nation, to facilitate innovation and research (Chiv et al., 2025; Igiri et al., 2021). Such a structure reflects a phenomenon known as "research neocolonialism," whereby reliance on donors from the Global North forces researchers from the Global South to conduct studies aligned with expatriates' interests, thereby ignoring local problems (Cameron et al., 2025). This dependence on external funding leads to an "asymmetry" in faculty conducting research for promotion because only those with international networks or those working in "donor-friendly" fields (e.g., public health, climate change) can or will undertake the research to receive promotion.

Second, physical and digital infrastructure is lacking. Many faculty members have low-speed internet, a laboratory, and, most importantly, continued access to subscription-based digital libraries (Heng et al., 2023). While some faculty conduct research, researchers from Cambodia are at a distinct disadvantage when they are trying to publish in global journals without access to the latest thinking in global research. Access to these infrastructures is pivotal to faculty research self-efficacy. When institutions do not provide resources such as protected research time, funding, or mentorship, faculty members' research self-efficacy declines rapidly. Even highly interested academics struggle with the "publish or perish" cycle when they face excessive workloads and inadequate infrastructure (Hu & Gill, 2000). This leads to a "compliance culture" in which faculty may resort to and publish in very poor "predatory" journals to meet promotion article requirements rather than contribute meaningful knowledge to the discipline.

Effects of Heavy Teaching Workload and the Economic Reality of Academic Performance

The reality of being an academic in Cambodia is a strong disincentive to promotion. The state provides a base salary to faculty as civil servants, but this wage is insufficient to support a middle-class lifestyle. This disconnect creates a "financial constraint" that limits the time available to conduct research and to provide the services necessary to advance an academic career.

Faculty moonlighting, such as taking on extra teaching at private universities or providing private tutoring, is a widespread but heavily scrutinized practice in higher education (Maeda et al., 2025; Heng et al., 2023). This is because it is an important source of additional income; however, it is related to policies concerning conflicts of interest and conflicts of commitment in institutions (Maeda et al., 2025). Although it can be perceived as unethical in basic education, it is acceptable in higher education. When a professor spends 20 to 30 hours teaching at multiple campuses, there is no remaining "cognitive surplus" available to do scholarly work. "Job responsibility" and workload are consistently offered as the main causes of job dissatisfaction among educators in the region (Oblina, 2021).

It creates a catch-22: a faculty member needs to do research to get promoted; to do research, they need time; to have time, they need a higher salary and to teach less; but a higher salary usually comes only after promotion. Additionally, the financial bump for reaching the rank of assistant or associate professor is often marginal relative to income from extra teaching or consultancy work (Fudickar et al., 2018). Accordingly, many high-performing academics, especially those with degrees earned abroad, see "consultancy" for NGOs or international agencies as preferable to the exhausting, low-reward work of pursuing formal academic promotion. Ultimately, the "brain drain" that occurs at the university, when the best minds are present in the body but their intellectual efforts are sold elsewhere, can seriously depress the growth of a robust internal academic culture.

Limitations in Data Management and Evidence-based Evaluation

A functioning promotion system requires evidence-based, transparent evaluation. Within Cambodian universities and the MoEYS, there are clear challenges to data management and the systemic ability to track faculty performance. For many years, faculty records were kept in paper files, making it impossible to verify teaching hours, publication records, or service contributions over multiple years.

There is no centralized or digitized system for academic administration, which makes the entire promotion process seem like a matter of random selection. In many academic institutions, promotion processes involve long waiting times and lack transparency. It must be considered that the promotion file goes through multiple steps, including departmental committee reviews, peer reviews, and evaluation before the dean of colleges and the provosts' committee members (Williams-Jones, 2026). In addition, without any transparency in the process, trust in the system suffers. When there is no clear data-driven feedback on why an application was declined or delayed, faculty members are more likely to conclude that the outcome was due to "patronage" or "not knowing the right people" rather than to fail to meet criteria that were (or were not) made clear to them.

Furthermore, the measurement and assessment of innovation and research quality represent crucial weaknesses in the management structure of academia in Cambodia. Although the government has taken steps to stimulate research, the limitations associated with inadequate funding, limited faculty expertise, and an evaluative approach that prioritizes compliance over the development of a vibrant research culture stand out (Chiv et al., 2025). The term "quality" is subjective and therefore poses a challenge to measuring the success or failure of research endeavors. In the absence of reliable external data and owing to continued dependence on peer reviews, evaluation panels have been known to use indicators such as "the number of pages in the report" and the reputation of the university attended by a nominee as proxies for quality. Academic success measures, which are subjective in nature, pose a significant barrier to the growth of emerging scholars, particularly female scholars, because most of them lack sufficient social capital to navigate complex academic reward structures (Llorens et al., 2021). Unless academic promotion, curriculum, and evaluation systems transition to more "objective" and data-driven interventions, possibly through modern digital tracking software and AI-assisted screening, the system will remain administratively dysfunctional.

Thus, the current academic promotion system in Cambodia is characterized by an elaborate legal framework that is increasingly at odds with the structural and economic realities of its faculty. While the Royal Decree of 2013 created a "meritocratic" future, these structural "bottlenecks"—funding, workload, and an absence of data—will need to be addressed in the academic promotion system moving forward, not simply as a "symbolic" exercise but as an instrument of academic excellence.

Comparative Analysis: Cambodia vs. ASEAN Systems

Table 2 compares the academic promotion systems of Cambodia with those of Malaysia, Thailand, and Vietnam, highlighting important similarities and differences in terms of governance, evaluation mechanisms, institutional autonomy, research expectations, and transparency. Although Cambodia has established a comprehensive legal framework through the 2013 Royal Decree and subsequent ministerial regulations, its promotion system remains considerably more centralized than those of neighboring ASEAN countries are. In contrast, Malaysia and Thailand have delegated greater responsibility for promotion decisions to universities while maintaining national quality assurance through external peer review and standardized evaluation criteria. Although it has retained a centralized governance model, Vietnam has progressively strengthened institutional autonomy and international research expectations as part of its higher education reforms.

The comparison suggests that Cambodia's principal challenge is not the absence of policy but the effective implementation of existing regulations. Several regional practices could inform future reforms, including greater institutional autonomy, transparent evaluation procedures, broader use of external peer reviewers, digital management systems, and stronger investment in research capacity. Rather than replicating another country's model, Cambodia could adopt a hybrid approach that preserves national quality assurance while empowering universities to conduct rigorous peer review and evidence-based evaluation. Such reforms would enhance the credibility, efficiency, and international recognition of Cambodia's professorial promotion system and support the country's ambition to develop a competitive knowledge-based higher education sector.

Table 2. Comparative Analysis of Academic Promotion Systems in Selected ASEAN Countries

Dimension	Cambodia	Malaysia	Thailand	Vietnam	Lessons for Cambodia
Governance Structure	Highly centralized under ministries and the Council of Ministers	Semicentralized with considerable university autonomy	Shared governance between universities and national agencies	Centralized with increasing institutional decentralization	Gradually decentralize promotion decisions while maintaining national quality standards.
Academic Employment Status	Predominantly civil servant system	University employment with performance-based contracts	Mixed system of civil servants and university employees	Civil servant-based with ongoing reforms	Shift from seniority toward performance-oriented academic careers.
Primary Promotion Criteria	Academic qualifications, years of service, publications, and administrative experience	Teaching, research, supervision, leadership, external funding, and service	Teaching effectiveness, research quality, publications, community engagement	Research productivity, teaching performance, publications, and academic qualifications	Develop a balanced evaluation system that values teaching, research, leadership, and community service equally.
Research Expectations	Emerging research culture with limited international publications	Strong expectation of Scopus/Web of Science publications	Increasing emphasis on international publications and research impact	Rapidly increasing publication and international collaboration requirements	Expand research funding, mentorship, and international collaboration opportunities.
Evaluation Mechanism	Ministry-led review with centralized approval	University committees supported by external peer reviewers	Institutional peer review combined with national oversight	Institutional review followed by ministerial approval	Introduce greater use of independent external peer review to improve objectivity.

continued on following page

Table 2. Continued

Dimension	Cambodia	Malaysia	Thailand	Vietnam	Lessons for Cambodia
Transparency of Promotion Process	Limited transparency and feedback	Clearly, published promotion guidelines and evaluation rubrics	Formalized procedures with applicant feedback	Improving through administrative reforms and digitalization	Increase transparency through standardized criteria and applicant feedback mechanisms.
Institutional Autonomy	Limited autonomy in promotion decisions	High institutional autonomy	Moderate institutional autonomy	Moderate autonomy under national regulation	Grant universities greater responsibility while preserving national oversight.
Role of External Reviewers	Limited and inconsistent	Mandatory external assessment for senior promotion	Frequently used for senior academic appointments	Increasing use of national and international reviewers	Expand independent peer-review systems to strengthen academic credibility.
Digitalization of Promotion System	Predominantly manual and paper-based	Integrated digital academic management systems	Partial digitalization across universities	Expanding electronic management systems	Develop a national online academic promotion platform.
Internationalization	Developing alignment with ASEAN standards	Strong alignment with global university rankings and accreditation	Regional collaboration through ASEAN networks	Increasing international collaboration and publication requirements	Strengthen global research collaboration and international benchmarking.
Overall Strength	Strong legal framework but implementation challenges	Mature, performance-oriented promotion system	Balanced governance with institutional flexibility	Rapid modernization supported by government reforms	Integrate governance reform, research investment, and institutional autonomy to improve implementation.

CHALLENGES: GOVERNANCE, CENTRALIZATION, AND DECISION-MAKING PROCESSES

The general state administration setting, as well as the civil service system, heavily influences the management of academic promotions in Cambodia. Unlike many other Western models that confer degrees through their respective university senates or boards, the Cambodian system operates primarily under a centralized model. Such an order derives from the country's history, in which, after the postconflict reconstruction period, the state needed to introduce uniformity in qualifications and control the rapidly developing higher education system (Milton & Barakat, 2016). However, such centralization creates a complex interplay between bureaucracy and meritocracy in academia, leading to red tape and a lack of institutional autonomy. Table 3 summarizes the principal challenges affecting the implementation of Cambodia's professorial ranking system. Although the Royal Decree on Professorial Titles established a merit-based framework for academic promotion, its implementation continues to face substantial governance, institutional, and structural constraints. The most significant challenges include limited research capacity, insufficient institutional support, centralized administrative procedures, inconsistent evaluation criteria, inadequate incentives, and limited transparency throughout the promotion process. Together, these factors create a considerable gap between policy intentions and practical implementation, making academic promotion a lengthy and highly bureaucratic process rather than a predictable mechanism for recognizing academic excellence. Consequently, strengthening research infrastructure, improving governance transparency, increasing institutional autonomy, and modernizing evaluation procedures are essential for ensuring that professorial titles genuinely reflect scholarly achievement and contribute to the development of high education development in Cambodia.

Table 3. Challenges Related to the Awarding of Professorships

No.	Challenge	Explanation	Implications for Academic Promotion
1	Quality of Research Publications	Many applicants face difficulties meeting publication requirements due to limited research funding, inadequate mentoring, restricted access to international journals, and increasing risks of predatory publishing.	Limits research productivity and weakens the credibility of merit-based promotion.
2	Promotion Criteria and Evaluation Standards	Existing criteria emphasize publications and years of service, but evaluation standards remain inconsistent across disciplines and institutions. The balance between teaching, research, leadership, and community service is not always clearly defined.	Creates inconsistencies in promotion decisions and reduces perceptions of fairness.
3	Research Infrastructure and Institutional Support	Public universities often lack sufficient research grants, laboratories, digital libraries, research assistants, protected research time, and opportunities for international collaboration.	Prevents faculty from meeting promotion requirements despite possessing academic potential.
4	Centralized Assessment and Administrative Procedures	Promotion decisions require multiple levels of review involving universities, specialized ministries, the National Committee for Professorial Titles, the Council of Ministers, and Royal approval. This lengthy process increases bureaucracy and delays decisions.	Reduces institutional autonomy and discourages qualified academics from pursuing promotion.
5	Limited Incentives and Career Benefits	Financial rewards and career advancement associated with professorial titles remain relatively modest compared with additional income from private teaching, consultancy, and external projects.	Weakens motivation to invest time in research and long-term academic career development.
6	Transparency and Accountability	Promotion procedures, committee deliberations, and evaluation feedback are often insufficiently transparent, while digital monitoring systems remain underdeveloped.	Creates perceptions of favoritism, inconsistency, and reduced trust in the promotion system.
7	Institutional Autonomy versus Government Control	Although universities conduct preliminary evaluations, final decisions remain centralized under government authorities, limiting universities' authority over academic personnel decisions.	Restricts institutional flexibility and slows responsiveness to disciplinary needs.

The Role of Specialized Ministries and the Council of Ministers

The system of promotion in Cambodian universities is highly centralized and administered by the central government, not by individual universities. Teachers are considered servants of the government, and there is a very strict system for promotion from one rank to another. The Ministry of Education, Youth and Sport (MoEYS) is the primary regulator for most higher education institutions unless the institution is under a specialized ministry, such as the Ministry of Health, the Ministry of Agriculture, Forestry and Fishing, or the Ministry of Labor and Vocational Training. These ministries regulate universities within their respective domains, requiring significant interministerial coordination, often nested within the Council of Ministers.

The Council of Ministers is the most important body in the conferral of academic titles, at least for associate and full professors. As the 2013 Royal Decree indicates, while the evaluation process starts with a university committee and then at the ministry level, the final academic titles of Associate Professor and Full Professor must be issued by a Royal Decree (Kret) or a Sub-decree (Anukret), signed by the Council of Ministers and ultimately the King. "The involvement of the elite level of the executive branch in the process of awarding an academic title highlights the symbolic or political importance attached to academic titles in Cambodia. " This is because in such cases, a professorship title is more than just a recognition of achievements in one's profession; rather, it becomes an honor bestowed by the state (Heng & Heng, 2023).

This statement accurately reflects the predominant form of governance in Southeast Asia. Despite past attempts to achieve independence among universities, national governments in the region continue to rely on developmentalism. This approach underscores centralization, quality control, and strict adherence to economic priorities at the cost of academic independence (Ratanawijitrasin, 2015). By retaining control of the appointment process, the central government ensures that academic promotion aligns with national strategic priorities, as identified in the Pentagonal Strategy, which identifies human capital as one of its priority pillars for national growth. However, the signatures required from high-level politics often create an administrative "loop" of bureaucratic approval that can take considerable time to resolve. In many cases, academic promotion applications are likely to spend years in bureaucratic limbo as it moves from the university committee to the technical department within the ministry and eventually to the Council of Ministers (Field, 2021). All of these often lead to the fatigue of an active researcher who simply wants timely acknowledgment of their considerable contributions to academia.

Centralized Authority versus Institutional Autonomy in Appointments

There is a fundamental contradiction inherent in the relationship between centralized state authority and the autonomy that public universities seek. In Cambodia, many public agencies, including higher education institutions and technical colleges, operate as public administrative institutions (PAIs), thereby becoming semiautonomous bodies with greater autonomy than regular line ministries do (Sok & Bunry, 2024). However, these higher education institutions lack autonomy over staffing decisions and appointments. These decisions still lie mainly in the hands of the ministers and at the national level.

Owing to limited institutional autonomy, universities' ability to define promotion paths on the basis of their institutional mission or strengths is compromised. For example, an institute that focuses on technical education, including engineering programs, would need different criteria from a liberal arts institute. Both would still have to adhere to the nationally imposed standardization policies defined in the Royal Decree of 2013. Standardization policy may disconnect institutional goals from faculty motivations since the university has very little control over appointments and promotions (Przytuła et al., 2025). The limited influence of universities on personnel management undermines the authority of the university leadership and the internal academic senate. Faculty may feel more accountable to the central ministry than to their own university community.

The centralizing trend in Cambodia is largely justified on the grounds of avoiding “title inflation” and nepotism, both of which are real concerns in systems with weak institutional safeguards. The state believes that a centralized process prevents variation in standards throughout the country. In Audit Culture, the effects of managerial and accounting approaches on higher education are explored. It states that the audit culture pushes universities and educators to focus on the measurable aspect of research rather than its inherent importance (Gao & Wang, 2024). In this context, academic promotion is treated as administrative paperwork rather than as a peer-review system that assesses the academic value of a scholar's intellectual output. In addition, the central governance of higher education systems is not flexible enough to respond to globalization. The lack of institutional freedom may prevent universities from attracting elite academics or conducting the successful international collaborations required to promote academics in line with current market demands (Gül et al., 2010).

Transparency and Accountability in Selection Committees

The validity of the academic promotion process largely depends on the accountability of selection committees. In Cambodia, such selection committees tend to be dominated by representatives from ministries and universities, as well as professors. However, nonacademic committee members, particularly those who do not produce scholarly output themselves and hold low ranks, can create inequalities between the evaluator and the evaluated parties. The tendency of high-ranking academic bureaucrats to prioritize seniority and organizational commitment over ongoing scholarly work is one example of the tensions within academia between professional and managerial functions (Vellamo et al., 2022).

Transparency is often compromised by a lack of clear feedback in the faculty promotion process. Candidates who have been denied promotions often feel that the reason for the denial is not convincing enough, thus giving rise to suspicions of bias or patronage in the promotion process. Patronage and clientelist networks, as well as social capital, often trump democratic principles in Southeast Asia, according to many academics, who point out that this is a result of the long history of hierarchical obligations in the region (Dressel, 2024).

Furthermore, the responsibilities of selection committees in the promotion process are hindered by inadequate information management systems. Applications are often processed with printed copies, making tracing and auditing extremely challenging. Self-reported publication records and the absence of a single database for research validation create the ground for issues related to fact-checking. Such an environment encourages fraudulent behavior, including paper padding, inflated citation indices, and predatory publishing. Therefore, verifying information by linking profiles is necessary for committee members (Kurysheva et al., 2023). Switching from traditional models of governance and decision-making to a more contemporary format, in which information management is digitized and supported by clear evidence, leads to the implementation of transparent and traceable processes (Hanisch et al., 2023). In other words, automation, performance assessment through metrics, and systematic monitoring help to avoid any form of manipulation. Otherwise, the promotion system remains a black box that operates according to unknown criteria.

MOVING FORWARD: STRATEGIES FOR REFORM AND MODERNIZATION

In addressing the issues of structure and governance discussed above, Cambodia should embark on a total modernization of the faculty evaluation process. It is inevitable that changing from a system in which administration is based on seniority to one based on merit entails a series of steps. To successfully modernize faculty evaluations, it is crucial that the rewards provided to faculty members align with the institution's core competencies and ensure transparency and fairness in the process (Lee et al., 2023).

Standardizing Transparent and Performance-Oriented Evaluation Criteria

In stage one of modernization, the emphasis is on developing strong evaluation criteria. While the 2013 Royal Decree laid down the basic framework for implementing a merit-based promotion system, there are still areas that require attention regarding the criteria for "research" and "society contribution". The next steps should include implementing discipline-based criteria for evaluating a scholar's contribution to the academic community. For example, for a STEM professor, journal publications and patents are the criteria used (O'Sullivan et al., 2020).

To modernize these standards for academic promotion, changes must also be made for a fundamental shift from quantity to quality. The current system's emphasis on counting pages or counting publications can unintentionally lead faculty to publish in verminous or predatory journals to reach a threshold. When responsible metrics are applied in the promotion process, the focus shifts from quantitative measures to the intrinsic worth, importance, and novelty of the scholar's research (Rushforth & Hammarfelt, 2023). This will involve the use of international indexing databases (Scopus and/or Web of Science) to assess journal quality or a traditional peer-review process with external experts from within or outside the region.

To be more transparent, the entire promotion process should be digitalized. One way to do this is with a national portal for academic promotion. This proposed electronic portal facilitates candidate portfolio submissions and enables them to track their applications instantly. The benefit here is that it eliminates the inefficiencies associated with manually handling these documents and creates an audit trail that documents the steps taken by the selection panels. Government transparency in the promotion process is key to organizational accountability. Once the criteria for promotion and the selection process are clearly outlined, this will ensure that only those who deserve the promotion receive it for their hard work (Jahija, 2025).

Strengthening Research Support and Incentive Mechanisms

An effective academic promotion system based on merit cannot function alone; rather, it must be built upon a sound scientific environment. The greatest obstacle to fulfilling promotion requirements in Cambodia is not a lack of ability but rather a lack of time and resources. The government and universities must come together to build the scholarly infrastructure needed for success. This can look like competitive internal grants, access to international e-libraries, and the development of research labs and centers.

Financial incentives also need to be realigned to promote promotions. Currently, the salary bump from an academic promotion pales in comparison to the earnings faculty can earn from "moonlighting" or private consulting. Promotion goals must also be paired with a significant increase in base salary and benefits to alleviate the faculty's need to teach to exhaustion. Moreover, universities need to create a system that relieves researchers and professors at the pinnacle of their academic careers in terms of teaching duties. Mentoring is important because it helps young researchers cope with the demands of their jobs, such as by allowing them to publish more papers, while older professors focus on higher-level scholarly research. Taken together, these aspects help develop a university's research reputation (Sarabipour et al., 2023).

Finally, the promotion system could do a better job of embedding national or international collaboration and studying abroad. Faculty who return from doctoral studies abroad can often possess a battery of research skills that are oppressed by the home institution's lack of infrastructure. Criteria for promotion should consider academic collaborations through professional networks, copublications with scholars from other countries, and participation in international conferences and workshops to interact with fellow professionals. Academicians who have studied abroad are important for Cambodia because they are key human resources for promoting research within the country (Sok & Bunry, 2024).

Decentralizing Governance and Strengthening Institutional Leadership

The sustainability of the academic promotion system is contingent upon the shift from a centrally run system to one that promotes autonomy with accountability. Although the central authority will continue to set and enforce these standards, the role of the university should be to assess and recommend candidates for promotion. This empowerment of academic leaders can serve as a catalyst for an ownership culture within organizations, transforming passive adherence to bureaucracy into active collaboration and cohesion with the organization's goals (Wang & Yang, 2021; Wang, 2025).

Decentralization requires granting the University Senates and Faculty Promotion Committees the right to conduct objective peer reviews. These entities should be entrusted with developing promotional recommendations, while the Ministry's responsibility needs to shift from being the one who "approves" to the one who "reviews." This means that the Ministry should focus on ensuring adherence to the country's criteria for conducting an objective peer review rather than evaluating individual candidates separately. Although decentralization is often implemented in the higher education sector to provide universities with greater freedom to develop curricula and conduct research according to local needs, it should be noted that decentralized management does not guarantee positive outcomes (Kameshwara et al., 2020).

Of course, decentralization should include championed accountability mechanisms to ensure that standards remain meaningful. For example, an independent body should audit a university's promotion process, and universities should publish annual performance reports on their academic staff. Through an ongoing analysis of various databases, including attendance records, graduation rates, and standardized test results, ministries of education can pinpoint specific schools or areas that need targeted funding, consultancy, or educational solutions (Wang, 2025). The combination of independence and responsibility helps Cambodia create an adaptive promotion system that enables its universities to perform excellently for the nation.

CONCLUSION AND RECOMMENDATIONS

Conclusion

While the introduction of professorial titles represents a significant milestone in the modernization of higher education, the system's success depends on whether promotion serves as a genuine mechanism for recognizing academic excellence rather than merely an administrative exercise. Achieving this transformation requires a comprehensive reform agenda encompassing governance, research funding, institutional autonomy, digitalization, and transparent evaluation mechanisms. If implemented effectively, academic promotion can serve as a strategic instrument to strengthen Cambodia's research capacity and support the nation's aspiration to become a knowledge-based economy by 2050.

Academic promotion at public universities in Cambodia marked a critical stage in the country's educational modernization process. Going beyond the civil servant approach, which focuses more on longevity, academic promotion in Cambodia is gradually evolving into a meritocratic system in which research output, effective teaching, and productive academic involvement take precedence. The Royal Decree issued in 2013 regarding professorial titles highlights an important policy direction with great promise; however, its implementation faces several barriers. This chapter shows how the main impediment to development is the gap between policy intentions and institutional compliance and engagement. A lack of adequate research capacity, combined with the heavy teaching burden placed on researchers and governmental centralization, results in a situation in which acquiring titles becomes more important than acquiring knowledge (Heng et al., 2023; Chiv et al., 2025). The reform of promotion in Cambodia is a shift from degree-based qualifications to performance-based assessments of competence. Faced with significant constraints, including low research output compared with their Southeast Asian counterparts and limited research capacity, the reform addresses Cambodia's overarching goal of making its universities drivers of the knowledge economy (Kinias et al., 2025). Apart from improving the evaluation criteria, the reform also requires considerable investment in research, realigning incentives, and a principled approach to redefining university autonomy. Allowing universities in Cambodia to be autonomous in academic promotion and investing in the infrastructure necessary to support the faculty are integral to initiating the reforms.

Recommendations

Table 4 presents strategic policy recommendations to strengthen Cambodia's professorial promotion system by addressing the governance, institutional, and structural challenges identified throughout this study. These recommendations emphasize four interconnected priorities: enhancing the quality and transparency of evaluation criteria, strengthening research capacity and institutional support, modernizing governance through digitalization and greater institutional autonomy, and establishing sustainable incentive and accountability mechanisms. Collectively, these reforms seek to transform academic promotion from a predominantly administrative process into a transparent, evidence-based, and performance-oriented system that rewards scholarly excellence while supporting Cambodia's long-term goal of developing a competitive knowledge-based economy. Successful implementation will require strong collaboration among the Royal Government of Cambodia, the Ministry of Education, Youth and Sport, specialized ministries, public universities, and the wider academic community.

continued on following page

Table 4. Continued

Table 4. Policy Recommendations for Strengthening the Awarding of Professorial Titles in Cambodian Public Universities

No.	Policy Recommendation	Rationale	Expected Outcomes
1	Strengthen evaluation criteria using international standards	Revise the promotion criteria to align with ASEAN and international best practices while maintaining relevance to Cambodia's higher education context.	Greater consistency, fairness, and international recognition of professorial titles.
2	Adopt transparent and evidence-based assessment mechanisms	Develop standardized evaluation rubrics that emphasize research quality, teaching effectiveness, academic leadership, innovation, and community engagement rather than relying primarily on seniority or publication counts.	Improved transparency, accountability, and confidence in promotion decisions.
3	Invest in research infrastructure and funding	Expand competitive research grants, digital libraries, laboratories, research centers, and international database subscriptions to support scholarly productivity.	Increased research output and improved faculty readiness for promotion.
4	Strengthen faculty capacity development	Provide continuous professional development, research mentoring, academic writing training, grant-writing support, and international collaboration opportunities.	Higher research competence and stronger academic leadership.
5	Improve incentive and reward systems	Increase financial incentives, salary progression, research awards, workload reductions, and recognition associated with professorial promotion.	Greater motivation to pursue research excellence and academic advancement.
6	Digitalize the promotion management system	Develop a national electronic promotion platform to manage applications, monitor progress, verify publications, and provide applicants with timely feedback.	Increased efficiency, transparency, and reduced administrative delays.
7	Increase institutional autonomy with external quality assurance	Delegate greater responsibility for academic evaluation to universities while maintaining national oversight through independent external review and quality assurance mechanisms.	Faster promotion decisions while preserving academic standards and accountability.
8	Strengthen research integrity and publication ethics	Introduce clear policies addressing predatory journals, plagiarism, proxy authorship, and research misconduct, supported by ethics training and publication verification systems.	Enhanced credibility and integrity of Cambodia's academic promotion system.
9	Expand the professorial system across the higher education sector	Gradually extend standardized professorial ranking to qualified private higher education institutions under nationally consistent quality standards.	Improved quality assurance and academic competitiveness across Cambodia's higher education system.
10	Establish continuous monitoring and policy evaluation	Regularly assess promotion outcomes, faculty satisfaction, gender equity, research productivity, and institutional performance to inform future policy revisions.	Evidence-based policy improvement and sustainable modernization of the promotion system.

REFERENCES

Andrews, M., Pritchett, L., & Woolcock, M. (2017). Looking like a state: The seduction of isomorphic mimicry. In *Building state capability: Evidence, analysis, action* (pp. 57–76). Oxford University Press., DOI: 10.1093/acprof:oso/9780198747482.003.0003

Cameron, L. M., Kovalchuk, S., D'Angelo, S. M., & Igodoe, A. A. (2025). Localizing the education development research agenda in the Global South: The case of GPE KIX. *International Journal of Educational Development, 113*, 103207. DOI: 10.1016/j.ijedudev.2025.103207

Chet, C., Thou, R., Sok, S., & Rath, S. (2023). Significance of Professorship Implementation at Higher Education Institutions (HEIs) in Cambodia. *Insight: Cambodia Journal of Basic and Applied Research, 5*(1), 4–7. DOI: 10.61945/cjbar.2023.5.1.edi

Chin, P., Em, S., & Phann, S. (2023). Enhancing research knowledge and productivity through professorship titles in Cambodia: Striking a balance. *Journal As-Salam, 7*(2), 133–143. DOI: 10.37249/assalam.v7i2.653

Chiv, S., Hong, K., Meak, C., Sam, R., Tieng, M., Yoeng, H., & Serey, M. (2025). Enhancing research on academic research capacity in Cambodian higher education institutions. *Discover Education, 4*(1), 283. Advance online publication. DOI: 10.1007/s44217-025-00723-z

Creswell, J. W., & Creswell, J. D. (2018). *Research design: Qualitative, quantitative, and mixed methods approaches* (5th ed.). SAGE Publications.

Denzin, N. K., & Lincoln, Y. S. (2011). *The SAGE handbook of qualitative research* (4th ed.). SAGE Publications.

Dressel, B. (2024). *Courts and politics in Southeast Asia*. Cambridge University Press., DOI: 10.1017/9781108770088

Field, S. (2021). Seven ways to get a grip on running a successful promotions process. *Canadian Medical Education Journal, 12*(3), 147–150. DOI: 10.36834/cmej.71638 PMID: 34249200

Fudickar, R., Hottenrott, H., & Lawson, C. (2018). What's the price of academic consulting? Effects of public- and private-sector consulting on academic research. *Industrial and Corporate Change, 27*(4), 699–722. DOI: 10.1093/icc/dty007

Gao, Y., & Wang, X. (2024). When policy meets practice: Evaluating the Breaking Five-Only policy through academic production in China. *Publications / MDPI*, *12*(4), 44. DOI: 10.3390/publications12040044

Gül, H., Gül, S. S., Kaya, E., & Alican, A. (2010). Main trends in the world of higher education, internationalization, and institutional autonomy. *Procedia: Social and Behavioral Sciences*, *9*, 1878–1884. DOI: 10.1016/j.sbspro.2010.12.417

Hanisch, M., Goldsby, C. M., Fabian, N. E., & Oehmichen, J. (2023). Digital governance: A conceptual framework and research agenda. *Journal of Business Research*, *162*, 113777. DOI: 10.1016/j.jbusres.2023.113777

Heng, K., Hamid, M. O., & Khan, A. (2023). Research engagement of academics in the Global South: The case of Cambodian academics. *Globalisation, Societies and Education*, *21*(3), 322–337. DOI: 10.1080/14767724.2022.2040355

Heng, K., & Heng, K. (2023). The implementation of the professorial ranking system in Cambodia: Opportunities and challenges. *Cambodian Journal of Educational Research*, *3*(2), 62–77. DOI: 10.62037/cjer.2023.03.02.04

Heng, K., & Heng, K. (2024). Professorial Titles in the Education Sector in Cambodia: Opportunities, Challenges, and Implications. *Cambodian Journal of Education and STEM*, *2*(1). Advance online publication. DOI: 10.62219/cjes.2024218

Hermanowicz, J. C. (2022). Professors. In Ritzer, G. (Ed.), *The Blackwell encyclopedia of sociology*. Wiley-Blackwell., DOI: 10.1002/9781405165518.wbeosp105.pub3

Hu, Q., & Gill, T. G. (2000). IS faculty research productivity: Influential factors and implications. [IRMJ]. *Information Resources Management Journal*, *13*(2), 15–25. DOI: 10.4018/irmj.2000040102

Igiri, B. E., Okoduwa, S. I. R., Akabuogu, E. P., Okoduwa, U. J., Enang, I. A., Idowu, O. O., Abdullahi, S., Onukak, I. E., Onuruka, C. C., Christopher, O. P. O., Salawu, A. O., Chris, A. O., & Onyemachi, D. I. (2021). Focused research on the challenges and productivity of researchers in Nigerian academic institutions without funding. *Frontiers in Research Metrics and Analytics*, *6*, 727228. Advance online publication. DOI: 10.3389/frma.2021.727228 PMID: 34805734

Jahija, J. (2025). Recruiting public personnel: A comparative approach. *International Journal of Civil Service Reform and Practice*, *13*(1), 73–84. DOI: 10.56289/ijcsrp.186

Kameshwara, K. K., Sandoval-Hernandez, A., Shields, R., & Dhanda, K. R. (2020). A false promise? Decentralization in education systems across the globe. *International Journal of Educational Research*, *104*, 101669. DOI: 10.1016/j.ijer.2020.101669

Kayashima, N., & Asada, S. R. (2024). Introduction: Development of universities in Southeast Asia and the impacts of study abroad. In N. Kayashima, M. Sugimura, K. Kuroda, & Y. Kitamura (Eds.), *Impacts of study abroad on higher education development* (Sustainable Development Goals Series, pp. 1–17). Springer. https://doi.org/DOI: 10.1007/978-981-97-0775-1_1

Kelsall, T., Schulz, N., Ferguson, W. D., Hau, M. V., Hickey, S., & Levy, B… (2022). Political Settlements and Development. https://doi.org/DOI: 10.1093/oso/9780192848932.001.0001

Kinias, I., Papasolomou, I., & Thrassou, A. (2025). Educating family businesses in Asia: The FAB multicountry project case. *Journal of Asia Business Studies*. Advance online publication. DOI: 10.1108/JABS-01-2025-0028

Kurysheva, A., van Rijen, H. V. M., Stolte, C., & Dilaver, G. (2023). Validity, acceptability, and procedural issues of selection methods for graduate study admissions in the fields of science, technology, engineering, and mathematics: A mapping review. *International Journal of STEM Education, 10*(1), 55. DOI: 10.1186/s40594-023-00445-4

Lee, M., Volpe Horii, C., Austin, A. E., Avery, L., DeSanctis, M., Finkelstein, N., & Schaal, B. (2023). An instructional-workforce framework for coordinated change in undergraduate education. *Change: The Magazine of Higher Learning*, *55*(1), 54–63. DOI: 10.1080/00091383.2023.2151809

Liu, W., & Yan, W. (2019). The internal governance model in Chinese universities: An international comparative analysis. *Journal of Applied Research in Higher Education, 11*(3), 428–438. DOI: 10.1108/JARHE-09-2018-0200

Llorens, A., Tzovara, A., Bellier, L., Bhaya-Grossman, I., Bidet-Caulet, A., Chang, W. K., Cross, Z. R., Dominguez-Faus, R., Flinker, A., Fonken, Y., Gorenstein, M. A., Holdgraf, C., Hoy, C. W., Ivanova, M. V., Jimenez, R. T., Jun, S., Kam, J. W. Y., Kidd, C., Marcelle, E., & Dronkers, N. F. (2021). Gender bias in academia: A lifetime problem that needs solutions. *Neuron, 109*(13), 2047–2074. DOI: 10.1016/j.neuron.2021.06.002 PMID: 34237278

Maeda, M., Soeung, S., & Chim, V. (2025). Teachers' side jobs in Cambodia: Who engages, work trends, motives, and impacts. *Compare: A Journal of Comparative Education*, •••, 1–19. DOI: 10.1080/03057925.2025.2587639

Milton, S., & Barakat, S. (2016). Higher education as the catalyst of recovery in conflict-affected societies. *Globalisation, Societies and Education*, *14*(3), 403–421. DOI: 10.1080/14767724.2015.1127749

MoEYS. (2010). Policy on research development in the education sector. https://data.opendevelopmentcambodia.net/dataset/policy-on-research-development-in-the-education-sector

MoEYS. (2011). Master plan for research development in the education sector 2011–2015. https://planipolis.iiep.unesco.org/index.php/en/2011/master-plan-research-development-education-sector-2011-2015-5220

MoEYS. (2020). Proclamation on the selection and appointment of professorial titles in the education sector.

MoEYS. (2024a). Education strategic plan 2024–2028. https://www.nepcambodia.org/documents/education-strategic-plan-esp-2024-2028-kh/

MoEYS. (2024b). Guidelines for quality management of doctoral training at higher education institutions under the supervision of the Ministry of Education, Youth and Sport.

O'Sullivan, S., Friebe, M., Tonti, W., Hartnett, M., Castro, M., Pozzo, M. I., & Nilsiam, Y. (2020). Surveyed the impact of intellectual property training in STEM education on innovation, research, and development. *The Journal of World Intellectual Property*, *23*(5-6), 658–678. DOI: 10.1111/jwip.12167

Oblina, A. C., Linh, T. P., & Phuong, H. T. M. (2021). *Job Satisfaction of Basic Education Teachers in Southeast Asia: Key Issues and Policy Recommendations.* VNU Journal of Science Education Research., DOI: 10.25073/2588-1159/vnuer.4438

Phan, S. (2015). *Envisioning a higher education system for the 21st century: Cambodia.* University of British Columbia cIRcle. https://doi.org/DOI: 10.14288/1.0166746

Przytuła, S., Sułkowski, Ł., & Kulikowski, K. (2025). Introduction. In *Human resource management in higher education institutions: An international perspective* (pp. 1–6). Routledge., DOI: 10.4324/9781003458425-1

Ratanawijitrasin, S. (2015). The evolving landscape of South–East Asian higher education and the challenges of governance. In Curaj, A., Matei, L., Pricopie, R., Salmi, J., & Scott, P. (Eds.), *The European higher education area* (pp. 271–290). Springer., DOI: 10.1007/978-3-319-20877-0_15

Ros, V., & Oleksiyenko, A. (2018). Policy misalignments and development challenges in the Cambodian academic profession: Insights from public university lecturers. *Higher Education Policy*, *31*(1), 19–35. DOI: 10.1057/s41307-017-0043-y

Royal Government of Cambodia. (2013). *Royal Decree No. NS/RKT/0313/214 on professorial titles (Preah Reach Kret).* Royal Government of Cambodia.

Royal Government of Cambodia. (2023). *Pentagonal Strategy–Phase I for growth, employment, equity, efficiency, and sustainability: Building the foundation toward realizing Cambodia Vision 2050*. Royal Government of Cambodia. https://asset.cambodia.gov.kh/mptc/2023/08/EN-PENTAGONAL-STRATEGY-PHASE-I.pdf

Royal Government of Cambodia. (2025). *Subdecree no. 244 on the organization and functioning of the General Secretariat of the National Council for Sustainable Development* (Subdecree No. 244). https://data.opendevelopmentcambodia.net/en/dataset/subdecree-no-244-on-the-organization-and-functioning-of-the-general-secretariat-of-the-national-co/resource/1e5f1860-05fe-4ab9-802c-700c2ae1ad17?view_id=64a5a8d8-f52d-4791-be3f-d45a45a9abc2

Royal Government of Cambodia. (2026). *Sub-Decree on the Organization and Functioning of the General Secretariat of the National Committee for the Conferment of Professorial Titles*.

Rushforth, A., & Hammarfelt, B. (2023). The rise of responsible metrics as a professional reform movement: A collective action frames account. *Quantitative Science Studies*, *4*(4), 879–897. DOI: 10.1162/qss_a_00280

Sam, R., Serey, M., Ry, H., Sarith, C., Tieng, M., & Yoeng, H. (2025b). Academic Accreditation and Evaluation in Cambodian Higher Education Institutions: Development, Challenges, and Opportunities. In Lytras, M., & erban, A. (Eds.), *Academic Accreditation and Evaluation in Higher Education: Practices, Experiences, and Quality Assurance* (pp. 241–262). IGI Global Scientific Publishing., DOI: 10.4018/979-8-3693-5608-1.ch010

Sam, R., Tieng, M., Yoeng, H., Sarith, C., Serey, M., & Sam, S. (2025a). Enhancing Research for Academicians in Cambodian Higher Education Institutions: A Policy Perspective. In Mdikana, A. (Ed.), *Enhancing Research for Academicians in Higher Education* (pp. 225–248). IGI Global Scientific Publishing., DOI: 10.4018/979-8-3693-4496-5.ch012

Sam, R., Voeun, N., Vando, P., Vet, K., No, S., Hour, R., Em, S., Sou, S., Phuong, S., & Da, V. (2026). Leadership-Driven Faculty Collaboration and Research Capacity Building in ASEAN: Insights From Cambodia. In Sam, R. (Ed.), *Implementing Research Management Policies in ASEAN Higher Education Institutions* (pp. 189–214). IGI Global Scientific Publishing., DOI: 10.4018/979-8-3373-3291-8.ch007

Sarabipour, S., Niemi, N. M., Burgess, S. J., Smith, C. T., Bisson Filho, A. W., Ibrahim, A., & Clark, K. (2023). The faculty-to-faculty mentorship experience: A survey on challenges and recommendations for improvements. Proceedings of the Royal Society B: Biological Sciences, Article 20230983. https://doi.org/DOI: 10.1098/rspb.2023.0983

Saraite Sariene, L., Caba Pérez, C., & López Hernández, A. M. (2020). Expanding the actions of Open Government in higher education sector: From web transparency to Open Science. *PLoS One*, *15*(9), e0238801. DOI: 10.1371/journal.pone.0238801 PMID: 32915833

Smith, J., Poe, J., & Skop, E. (2025). Cultivating Faculty-Driven Reform of Promotion to Full Professor Structures to Reward and Regard the Scholarship of Engagement. *Journal of Participatory Research Methods*, *6*(5). Advance online publication. DOI: 10.35844/001c.153975

Sok, S., & Bunry, R. (2024a). Higher education development and study abroad experiences of faculty in Cambodia. In Kayashima, N., Sugimura, M., Kuroda, K., & Kitamura, Y. (Eds.), *Impacts of study abroad on higher education development* (pp. 223–241). Springer., DOI: 10.1007/978-981-97-0775-1_12

Sok, S., & Bunry, R. (2024b). Higher Education in Cambodia. In Symaco, L. P., & Hayden, M. (Eds.), *International Handbook on Education in Southeast Asia. Springer International Handbooks of Education*. Springer., DOI: 10.1007/978-981-16-8136-3_47-1

Spivakovsky, A., Vinnyk, M., Poltoratskyi, M., Tarasich, Y., & Omelchuk, S. (2022). Information technologies for measuring the qualitative and quantitative indicators of higher education institutions' work. *Information Technologies and Learning Tools*, *89*(3), 190–208. DOI: 10.33407/itlt.v89i3.4895

Vellamo, T., Kosonen, J., Siekkinen, T., & Pekkola, E. (2022). Bureaucratic, professional and managerial power in university tenure track recruitment. In E. Forsberg, L. Geschwind, S. Levander, & W. Wermke (Eds.), *Peer review in an era of evaluation* (pp. 301–321). Palgrave Macmillan. https://doi.org/DOI: 10.1007/978-3-030-75263-7_16

Wang, C. J., & Yang, I. H. (2021). Why and how does empowering leadership promote proactive work behavior? An examination with a serial mediation model among hotel employees. *International Journal of Environmental Research and Public Health*, *18*(5), 2386. DOI: 10.3390/ijerph18052386 PMID: 33804442

Wang, Y. (2025). Artificial intelligence in student management systems to enhance academic performance monitoring and intervention. *Scientific Reports*, *15*(1), 35122. DOI: 10.1038/s41598-025-19159-4 PMID: 41062725

Williams-Jones, B. (2026). *The committee of eternal deliberation: Institutional satire from inside the university*. BrynStorming Project, École de santé publique de l'Université de Montréal. https://doi.org/DOI: 10.71781/34524

World Bank. (2024). Cambodia's systematic country diagnostic update. World Bank Group. https://www.worldbank.org/en/country/cambodia/publication/cambodia-systematic-country-diagnostic-update

Keywords and Definitions

Academic Promotion Academic promotion is the formal process through which university faculty members advance from one academic rank to another and is based on established criteria for teaching: research, scholarly publications, academic service, and professional achievements. In Cambodian public universities, academic promotion is governed by the Royal Decree on Professorial Titles and related ministerial regulations, which provide pathways from Assistant Professors to Associate Professors and Professors. Academic promotion serves as a mechanism for recognizing academic excellence, encouraging professional development, and strengthening institutional capacity in teaching and research.

Professorial Ranking System The professorial ranking system is a structured hierarchy of academic titles used to recognize the qualifications, experience, and scholarly contributions of university academics. In Cambodia, the system consists of three main ranks: Assistant Professor, Associate Professor, and Professor. Established through the 2013 Royal Decree on Professorial Titles, the system aims to promote merit-based career advancement, improve research productivity, and align Cambodian higher education with regional and international academic standards.

Merit-Based Promotion Merit-based promotion refers to an advancement system in which academic ranks are awarded on the basis of demonstrated performance: achievements, and competencies rather than solely on seniority or administrative position. Criteria commonly include research publications, teaching effectiveness, academic leadership, community service, and professional contributions. In the Cambodian context, merit-based promotion represents a shift from the traditional civil-service model toward a performance-oriented system that fosters academic excellence, accountability, and competitiveness within public universities.

Research capacity Research capacity refers to the ability of individual academic and higher education institutions to conduct: manage, disseminate, and utilize research effectively. It encompasses human resources, research skills, funding availability, infrastructure, access to scholarly resources, and institutional support mechanisms. Strong research capacity is essential for academic promotion because research outputs, publications, and scholarly contributions constitute key criteria for advancement. In Cambodia, limited research funding, inadequate infrastructure, and heavy teaching workloads continue to constrain the research capacity of public universities.

Institutional Autonomy Institutional autonomy refers to the degree of independence granted to higher education institutions in managing academic: administrative, financial, and personnel affairs. This includes authority over faculty recruitment, promotion, curriculum development, and research activities. Greater institutional autonomy is often associated with improved responsiveness, innovation, and accountability. In Cambodian public universities, academic promotion remains highly centralized within government ministries, creating ongoing debates over the balance between state oversight and university self-governance.

Governance in Higher Education Governance in higher education refers to the structures: processes, policies, and decision-making mechanisms through which universities and higher education systems are managed and regulated. It involves the roles of government agencies, university leadership, academic committees, and other stakeholders in shaping institutional operations and academic standards. Effective governance promotes transparency, accountability, efficiency, and quality assurance. In Cambodia, governance plays a critical role in academic promotion, as promotion decisions are shaped by centralized administrative procedures, ministerial oversight, and national policy frameworks.

Chapter 9
Datafying the Professoriate:
AI, Metrics, and the Changing Nature of Academic Work

Rahul Dattu Gangurde
http://orcid.org/0009-0005-9599-0063
Government Law College, Mumbai, India

Sanjana Bharadwaj
http://orcid.org/0000-0003-1371-7572
NALSAR University of Law, India

ABSTRACT

The integration of data-driven systems and artificial intelligence in higher education is reshaping academic work in significant ways. This chapter examines how datafication and metric-based evaluation reconfigure the labour, priorities, and identity of the professoriate in India. Drawing on qualitative interviews with 80 faculty members, it shows that administrative demands and performance metrics increasingly dominate academic life, reducing time for sustained research. While AI is widely used for teaching-related efficiency, its impact on research remains limited. The findings also reveal growing inequalities across career stages, particularly affecting early-career and contractual faculty. The chapter argues that datafication restructures academic work by privileging measurable outputs over intellectual autonomy.

DOI: 10.4018/979-8-3373-8525-9.ch009

INTRODUCTION

Globalization, the market orientation of higher education, various accountability processes, and digital technologies have led to significant changes worldwide. Universities—long known as places for critical questioning, knowledge creation, and societal transformation—are increasingly subjected to data-driven schemes of performance evaluation, institutional ranking, auditing, and assessment. This move has resulted in the creation of the so-called "measured university" in which academic work is increasingly assessed in measurable rather than intellectual, pedagogical, or social ways (Sutton, 2017). This reshaped academic world gave rise to what is now known as the "quantified professoriate": an aspect of university life that exists today. Academic value is increasingly restricted to "metrics assemblages", which quantify publication, citations, the h-index, grants, impact factors, and performance (Burrows, 2012). Academic identity is thus in a permanent state of evaluation, comparison, and appraisal.

With the quantified professoriate, the quantified university provides a telling indication of broader trends within neoliberal platforms of governance, the university's increasing commercialization, and the conversion of the campus into a competitive, market-oriented space. In such contexts, it has been noted that the relationships among accountability, quantitative indicators, and audit procedures are becoming increasingly entangled in efforts to "make academic results explicit and measurable and thus somehow transposable". Academic performance is no longer limited to intellectual output or the effectiveness of teaching and learning; it must deliver measurable results to ensure that the institution is perceived as good and maintains its position on ranking tables. In the academic world, quantification becomes a leading paradigm, and it can compromise traditional values such as collegiality, mentoring, academic freedom, and public scholarship.

These global developments have affected the higher education system in India. The spheres of education and social guidance, community involvement, and knowledge for the wider public have always been significant for Indian universities. However, the Academic Performance Indicators (API) of the University Grants Commission (UGC) and the Academic and Research Score (ARS) were in stark contrast with the current systems. The objective of these systems is to improve transparency and accountability by establishing performance measures for recruitment, promotion, and career advancement (Akhter et al., 2020; Luthra et al., 2022). Even then, a growing body of scholarly insurgency challenges these frameworks on various grounds, including their tendency to foster administrative overload, a mechanistic understanding of academic work, and rigid bureaucratization (Kanagaraj, 2019; Kulkarni & Rajas, 2025). The results of this phenomenon, in which publications, conference presentations, and recorded achievements are sought, often come at the cost of quantity. This tendency to invariably favor quantity over quality leads to "quality deprivation through quality assessment" (Akhter et al., 2020).

These aspects have been greatly accentuated with the introduction of the National Institutional Ranking Framework (NIRF). The NIRF has been designed to assess universities on the five benchmarks of research output, teaching and learning, outreach and inclusivity, and peer review and has triggered a race for all Indian universities (Mondal, 2024). There is increasing alignment between the university's strategic goals and the criteria governments use to rank it; faculty members' work can serve as a tool for branding and positioning the university. Many institutions have become primarily involved in publishing academic papers, in which academic work is often judged by the number of publications rather than by its quality or societal significance (Jose & Koley, 2026; Pant & Bhadoria, 2025).

The emergence of digital governance and artificial intelligence has further complicated this complex situation. Transformation and innovation, powered by technology and AI-enabled learning, are central themes of the NEP 2020, which underscores their importance as key drivers of the educational revolution (Peerzada et al., 2024; Toppo, 2025). Academic institutions are increasingly implementing AI-powered solutions to support various functions, such as evaluation, learning analytics, management, and support. While these technologies hold promise for increased efficiency and personalization, they also create new models of surveillance and monitoring, as well as algorithmic governance. This phenomenon is called "digital Taylorism" by researchers, as academic work is increasingly quantifiable, optimizable, and managerially overseeable (Mustaqeem, 2025; Woodcock, 2018).

On the basis of the findings of this investigation, it is clear that these developments are not merely policy shifts to be written off on paper but rather phenomena that impact daily experiences in school. Academicians at various universities in India report a considerable increase in administrative work, much of which is time-consuming. Other activities and duties, such as admissions, examinations, compliance with accreditation standards, reporting requirements, committee work, and institutional paperwork, can also compete with research and teaching efforts. Many respondents described these roles as barriers to academic achievement rather than as opportunities for it. Administrative growth represents the administrative structuring of academic work and busy work replacing investigation.

Similarly, the implementation of AI in higher education institutions has increased expectations for policy outcomes that are far from the results achieved. Mostly, professors use AI to help them reduce the burden of teaching and administration rather than to support their research activities. Participants reported using AI to create lecture materials, summarize content, write routine communications, and optimize classroom activities. Such applications increase research productivity but do not significantly increase research scholars' productivity or creativity. AI appears to be a supplementary resource in an already overstrained academic field, merely reinforcing the existing "labor pattern" rather than causing large structural change.

Within the academic workforce, there is a variable distribution of the influence of metrics-based governance. Amidst an increasingly competitive world, early-career academics face heavy pressure in terms of publication, professional identity construction, and career progression. Contractual faculty members experience a variety of problems, compounded by job insecurity and a lack of institutional support. Furthermore, formal rationality in the form of a performance norm may be akin to informal institutional behavior. The participants noted that there is still preferential treatment, networking advantages, and the continued existence of social hierarchy, including caste, which can still impact opportunities for becoming noticed, moving forward, and career progression. Therefore, quantification is not a destructive practice of eradicating inequality but rather one that operates in complex ways alongside prevailing patterns of privilege.

Given this situation, this article explores the interplay between API-ARS and NIRF, their roles in transforming academic work and professional identity, and the impact of AI on governance in higher education in India. The authors argue, however, that rather than being perceived as individual policy tools, these developments can be understood as interrelated technologies of governance that affect the everyday experiences of academics. On the basis of qualitative data collected from a group of faculty members from different universities in India, this paper argues that academic labor has undergone significant change because of datafication, assessment through metrics, and the incorporation of AI. All these forces help to produce what we can call a quantified professoriate, a professoriate defined in measurable terms, through administrative performance, through visibility, and through continual evaluation. This change raises key questions about academic freedom, the creation of knowledge, the autonomy of professionals, and the broader goals of higher education in an ever-expanding university form.

LITERATURE REVIEW

In the increasingly quantified age of academic life in Indian universities, performance indicators, rankings, and electronic governance and management systems shape both the professional identity and the career trajectory of academics as well as the educational value of an institution (Burrows, 2012; Peacock et al., 2023). This shift reflects a broader shift to "neoliberal modes of governance in academia beyond centralized state control" (Bristow et al., 2019), in which academic pursuits are increasingly regulated, monitored, held accountable, and evaluated according to market principles. The incorporation of academic performance indicators (APIs), national institutional ranking framework (NIRF) evaluations, and innovative artificial intelligence (AI)-based governance systems has created new paradigms of academic labor, institutional efficacy, and knowledge generation in India. Although they are often seen as independent policy interventions, these policies work together to enable a "measured university" in which the value of academic work becomes increasingly defined through quantitative indicators.

Underpinning this transition is the institutionalization of performance assessment through the Academic Performance Indicator (API) and the Academic and Research Score (ARS) of a performance-based system, as per the University Grants Commission (UGC). The introduction of these systems aimed to simplify and standardize the recruitment and promotion process by assigning academics into measurable categories such as teaching, professional development, and research productivity (Akhter et al., 2020; Kanagaraj, 2019; Samanta et al., 2022). Empirical research shows that there is a strong relationship between API scores and teaching-related activities, a relationship that is far weaker with performance scores and substantive research production (Samanta et al., 2022). Supportive people view these frameworks as the basis for professional incentives and accountability, whereas oppositional people argue that they have institutionalized an audit-and-compliance culture that focuses on numerical accumulation rather than intellectual depth (Kulkarni & Rajas, 2025; Luthra et al., 2021). Indeed, the focus on publication metrics, conference participation, and documentation often leads to a "cookie-cutter" approach to scholarly work, as described by Akhter et al. (2020) as "quality deprivation through quality assessment". Thus, academic work increasingly estranges itself from its social, ethical, and transformational dimensions, limiting it to mere bureaucratic performance indicators (Kanagaraj, 2019; Sutton, 2017).

Many institutional ranking systems have proliferated. The Ministry of Education has introduced the National Institutional Ranking Framework (NIRF) as an important ranking system that uses "data and information" on research output, teaching quality, inclusivity, outreach, and institutional reputation as parameters (Mondal, 2024). The NIRF has increased international recognition and openness among Indian institutions, but researchers have raised concerns about its unintended consequences. The trend of counting and announcing the number of publications, citation counts, and ranking institutions has given rise to practices such as self-citation, padding journal articles, and prioritizing publication quantity over quality (Kumar et al., 2019; Pant & Bhadoria, 2025). As the rank-order measurement of institutional reputation grows in a market-driven higher education system, critics say that rankings increasingly portray institutions as rivals. Under these circumstances, some institutions have used incentive systems associated with publication occasions and journal rankings, turning research into a productivity endeavor (Jose & Koley, 2026). The ranking methodology has been criticized for providing special treatment to schools that are historically grounded and have adequate resources; therefore, it continues to lead to inequalities in higher education and thus narrows the scope of regional schools emerging from place to place (Pant & Bhadoria, 2025).

The implementation of the National Education Policy (NEP) 2020 ushered in a new era of change, introducing digitalization in education, learning, and institutional management through artificial intelligence (AI). AI applications in education are used in teaching and learning, including learning management systems, AI-powered prediction tools, automated assessment systems, and smart tutors, which help to streamline processes and personalize education (Toppo, 2025; Kumari, 2026). Some of the instruments used in teacher training aim to enhance data-informed decision-making and practice more broadly. This extends to the academic sphere, with many students and professors now turning to AI-powered tools to aid their research, summarize content, and perform academic support tasks, thereby indicating a shift toward digital transformation in academia (Anagha, 2026).

In HEG, the issues of equality and autonomy, as well as academic subjectivity, are linked to the application of AI. Academic experts worry that AI-driven educational systems could exacerbate the uneven distribution of educational opportunities, potentially caused by biases in AI algorithms, differences in access to educational technology, and the use of digital monitoring systems (Mustaqeem, 2025).

As data analytics plays an increasing role, it is fertile ground for the development of a form of "digital Taylorism," defined by technological boosts to surveillance, evaluation, and the optimization of academic labor (Dwivedi et al., 2019). As such, AI is experienced not only as a means of instruction but also as a developing governance technology that extends the audit culture into hitherto uncharted territory in academia.

India's holistic AI governance framework, including through NITI Aayog's initiative #AIforAll, positions AI as a key enabler of India's development, competitiveness, and technical excellence (Bhalla et al., 2023; Sidam Madhuar, 2026). While stressing ethical AI governance, workforce reskilling, and inclusive innovation, these policies also reveal the extent to which AI governance is woven into the overall architecture of informational capitalism, where data become a core input for value generation and economic and institutional integration (Joshi, 2024). A lack of engagement with local sociocultural contexts and a technologically deterministic approach to policy narratives, with a greater emphasis on innovation than on critical engagement, have been identified as concerns (Marda, 2018; Than et al., 2021). The challenge is to ensure that AI governance regimes are compatible with principles such as social justice, fairness, accountability, and transparency to avoid exacerbating inequalities and surveillance.

This study provides evidence that the here-quantified professoriate is an important restructuring of academic activities in Indian universities. The combination of

API scores, institutional rankings, and AI governance has resulted in a quantitative, data-driven, and precise approach to defining academic identity—thus institutional legitimacy—in an increasingly precise way. They provide greater transparency, accountability, and efficiency but might also signal more fundamental issues in academic freedom and intellectual innovation in higher education and the university's broader social aspirations. The foremost challenges of higher education in India are not only the ways to quantify academic productivity but also the relationships among technological innovation, institutional accountability, the reproduction of scholarly autonomy and critical inquiry, and the upholding of educational standards in today's data-driven academic culture.

2.1 Research methodology

Purposive sampling was used to recruit 80 faculty members from central, state, and private universities, representing different professional segments (early career faculty, mid-career faculty, and senior faculty) and job types (permanent faculty and contractual faculty), to ensure diversity across institutions and job types. Semistructured interviews were conducted using a predesigned interview schedule that included five themes: administrative burden, evaluation mechanisms, pressure for research and publications, and the impact of AI on academic tasks and career advancement. The interviews were conducted online for 3 months each, lasting half an hour to an hour. All the respondents were given detailed information about the objectives of the study, voluntary participation, confidentiality, and the ability to withdraw from the study at any time before participation. Informed consent was obtained and proper for the recording and transcription process prior to the meeting. During the research, values related to the anonymity, confidentiality, and safe management of the data obtained were strictly respected. Data analysis was conducted using the thematic analysis approach proposed by Braun and Clarke. This process included initial familiarization with transcripts, followed by open coding; thematic grouping was then followed by the development of inductive codes, which were grouped into larger themes. These topics were then revised through an iterative process. Coding was conducted in multiple stages to ensure consistency and coherence across the transcripts, thereby improving the reliability of the analytics. The data reported in the results are percentages based on a denominator of the total sample (N = 80), unless otherwise indicated. Percentages have been calculated using the specific subgroup count (e.g., the number of early-career faculty or contractual faculty) as the denominator for subgroup analyses. The percentages are relative, meaning that they are intended only to illustrate how participants' experiences and perceptions are distributed, not to make statistical generalizations.

DATAFICATION AND THE RECONFIGURATION OF ACADEMIC WORK

The concept of datafication is associated with the transformation of social practices into quantifiable information, therefore enabling its monitoring and assessment. This in the academic world has had a great influence on the structure and evaluation of academic activities. Viktor Mayer-Schoenberger and Kenneth Cukier suggest that through datafication, it is possible to reduce actions in a measurable form; thus, they can be compared and regulated. According to this logic, in academia, there is an increasing reliance on measures such as the number of publications, citation indices, impact factors and other ranking mechanisms. Academic labor is thereby reinstitutionalized as a system of measurable products in which intellectual labor is institutionalized when and only when it is exposed in data-driven paradigms.

The phenomenon of datafication is intricately linked to the framework that Marilyn Strathern articulates, which she calls "audit culture" (Strathern, 2000). The culture of audits instigates systems of incomplete review and responsibility, where academic practices become subject to standardized measures and routine evaluations. As Strathern argues, these systems do not simply perform performance assessment; rather, they proactively transform performance through necessitating people to match their performance with measurable metrics. To further this claim, Wendy Nelson Espeland and Michael Sauder explain how rankings and metrics can be used as tools of governance, which change behavior by applying comparative and competitive pressures (Espeland & Sauder, 2007). In this context, researchers initiate the procedure of internalizing metrics, thus putting a structure around their research choices and professional priorities, with a perspective on future assessments.

The Indian system of higher education is a very striking example of an exaggerated form of this change. Quantification has become an institutionalized form of governance with regulatory frameworks that are based upon metrics, notably the Academic Performance Indicator (API) system and national ranking systems, including the National Institutional Ranking Framework (NIRF). Such systems have faculty members record their academic contributions on a regular basis, hence tying performance to outcomes such as promotions, incentives and the reputation of the institution in general. As a result, academic activities are being more organized around measurable criteria, as opposed to incorporating wider intellectual or social objectives (Meho, 2025). Modern studies on the governance of higher education in India have increasingly focused on developing measures, institutional frameworks, and assessments facilitated by technological change. With the creation of the National Institutional Ranking Framework, performance measurement through indicators such as research output, teaching quality, and institutional perception has been institutionalized as part of national policy frameworks. In addition, recruitment, promotion, and career development have been tied to quantifiable outcomes, such as publications and contributions to the institution, as expressed in the faculty assessment models set by the University Grants Commission, most notably the Academic Performance Indicator (API). By establishing a system of accountability, standardization, and outcome-based assessments, the National Education Policy 2020 has been built on recent progress. The establishment of new organizational systems such as the National Research Foundation and digital credit systems accompanies this effort. Moreover, the growing literature on artificial intelligence in the educational setting indicates increased attention to issues of governance, ethical considerations, and institutional policy. This discussion highlights the rapid adoption of AI tools and emphasizes that regulatory frameworks should accompany this adoption to guide their use in academic settings. Studies on the ethical implications of artificial intelligence and the institutional leadership that would govern its application reveal significant deficiencies in institutional preparedness, particularly in openness, accountability, and the integration of relevant curricula. The collection of these bodies of literature suggests that the convergence of regulatory metrics, policy-based assessment, and technological management is gradually endorsing contemporary higher education. However, such further developments are often covered in ways that do not necessarily connect with broader contexts. This chapter contributes to the current body of scholarship by discussing the overlaps among these processes and their consequences for the repositioning of academic labor, institutional practices, and career trajectories within the Indian higher education context.

These developments can be interpreted by studying academic capitalism, such as the writings of Sheila Slaughter and Gary Rhoades (Slaughter & Rhoades, 2004). It is argued that higher education is becoming more market oriented and that efficiency, productivity, and competitiveness are the key organizing concepts. Dataafication in these respects may be viewed as one of the primary processes by which such logics are leveraged and academic work is made into measurable units that are subject to assessment in institutional and global regimes.

The consequences of this change extend much farther than the changes in procedures, and the implications of the change are structural. Datafication alters the climate of academic work in terms of its fundamentals, reassigning time, placing an emphasis on quantifiable goods and transforming professional identity. Academic profession that is traditionally associated with autonomy and stringent research is becoming deeply ingrained into a system of metric governance when performance is questioned and measured constantly. In the Indian context, in which such systems coexist with a preexisting institutional hierarchy and unequal distribution of resources, datafication is not simply the standardization of academic work. It interacts with existing inequalities, leading to complex and often controversial development of the academic profession.

DISCUSSION

Institutional expansion of administrative labor

The transformation of academic activities under the conditions of datafication is vividly evident in the increase in the number of administrative tasks of higher education establishments. The tasks once thought peripheral to the academic profession-processing of admissions, the administration of exams, the creation and evaluation of academic work, and the oversight of compliance-related reports have become core aspects of the faculty workload. The characteristics of the mentioned responsibilities are defined by their ongoing character, systematization, and close association with the institutional requirements that regulate data production and reporting. Therefore, academic activities are increasingly organized in the context of the creation and maintenance of institutional information, which is not merely based on pedagogical and research practices (Plekhanov et al., 2023).

The empirical results of this research support the observed structural change. Much of the administrative work was found to constitute a large percentage of the working time, as a considerable proportion of the respondents indicated that administrative work has taken more of their working time than research work has. The organization of admissions, the administration of the exams, and the preparation of documentation for the institutional audit were regularly identified as serious burdens on faculty efforts. In addition, mandatory gatherings, which tend to be procedural and redundant, further divide academic time and thus limit the time to longer intellectual work. The aggregate impact is the redistribution of academic resources by shifting attention to activities that are predetermined by the needs set by the administration rather than intensive research activities.

Such expansion has a complex relationship with the general tenets of audit culture, as explained by Marilyn Strathern, whereby accountability is maintained by means of unrelenting documents and verification cycles (Strathern, 2023). As structures that are subjected to metrics, universities have to be perpetually fed with data to show the compliance, performance, and reputation of the institute. Administrative work here is not just auxiliary to the system but a part of it. Faculty members become central participants in the production, authentication and reproduction of such data flows; therefore, administrative duties are incorporated into the very fabric of academic work.

Institutional practices that accentuate standardization and documentation further institutionalize the proceduralisation of academic life. Moreover, reporting systems and compliance activities are platforms where data are reviewed, validated and translated into institutional measures (Stvilia et al., 2024). Despite these processes being supposed to foster transparency and accountability, they are perceived as being too cumbersome and inefficient by their participants, with little impact on academic progress. The emphasis on procedural compliance over substantive investigation reflects a larger change where the value of academic activities is measured more by their written expression than by their intellectual soundness.

In this context, the growth of administrative labor cannot be regarded as a casual byproduct of institutional growth. Data-based governance systems enable structural production and necessitate continuous measurement, reporting, and verification. Wendy Nelson Espeland and Michael Sauder demonstrate the fundamental transformations that quantification has brought to the behavior of organizations by instituting incentives that would foster visibility and comparability (Espeland & Sauder, 2007). In the case of institutions of higher learning, this is expressed through an increased administrative workload on the academic workforce whereby faculty members devote more and more of their time to the activities that justify the existence of metrics-based systems of evaluation. What has been born of this is a renegotiated intellectual role where administration is not just an add-on to the business of educational institutions in the contemporary world.

METRICS, EVALUATION SYSTEMS, AND ACADEMIC BEHAVIOR

The increasing reliance on metrics in higher education has dramatically altered how academic performance is assessed as well as the conceptualization and implementation of academic work. The measurement of the number of publications, citation indices and journal rankings, particularly those listed in Scopus and Web of Science, has grown to occupy a central position in institutional evaluation systems. These indicators in the context of India, through performance frameworks similar to the API and promotion criteria, are intricately incorporated into academic careers, thus creating a relationship between measurable products and professional development (Stvilia et al., 2024). Here, evaluation is not just an external mechanism, which is applied once the knowledge has been produced, but an active process that predetermines the circumstances under which the knowledge will be produced.

This transformation is emphasized in the scholarly study of quantification. Wendy Nelson Espeland and Michael Sauder argue that metrics are devices of governance that create settings of comparison that trigger behavioral change (Espeland & Sauder, 2007). Academic involvement initiates the procedure of foreseeing evaluation, thus fitting their approaches to those that are measurable and worthy of appreciation. This anticipatory orientation is strongly reflected in the empirical findings of this study.

A significant percentage of the respondents—64 of 80—pointed out that they were under continuous pressure to be published in indexed journals. This pressure affects not only official periods of evaluation but also the routine involved in academic decision-making. According to one of the mid-career faculty members, the main factor has changed to the importance of what one has researched to the first question as to whether it will be accepted in a Scopus-indexed journal. These reactions indicate that publication is becoming viewed as a requirement for institutional viability instead of a logical byproduct of scholarly research.

The effects of metrics are directly proportional to the choice of research methodology. A considerable percentage of the respondents, in particular, 42 out of the 80, were aware that pressures of time limitations and expectations of performance influence them to study the subjects who have more chances of achieving quick results of publication. This often involves choosing areas in which the publication trend has been identified, in lieu of working on complex or context-driven questions that might take a long time to develop. This dilemma was described by one of the young scholars, who said that he had started to think about what would be published the fastest, as opposed to what deserved detailed research. The shift of curiosity-driven research to choosing strategically important topics is an example of how metric systems influence the course of scholarly inquiry.

The trends in cooperation also explain different types of strategic adaptations. Approximately 57 percent of the respondents said that they occasionally use co-authorship practices to increase the output of publications in limited timeframes. Collaboration continues to be a fundamental aspect of scholarly endeavors; however, its use to meet metrics signals a broader reconfiguration of academic standards (Stvilia et al., 2024). Similarly, many respondents emphasized the trend of reducing research into smaller and publishable units. Such an approach allows the production of several outputs, but it can harm the consistency of scholarly works. As one of the scholars noted, there is pressure to produce more papers but not to focus on improving their quality.

The identified changes in behavior suggest a deeper change in the nature of academic production. Measures are used to evaluate the research not only after its completion but also to fundamentally impact its structure, direction and pace. The visibility and measurability of knowledge production increase when quantifiable outputs are used to define academic success. Studies similar to the known publication channels are more likely to gain significance. Conversely, interdisciplinary, critical or context-specific work can be deprioritized because of its uncertainty in compliance with metric requirements.

The functionality of such metric-based systems is best realized when analyzed within the framework of normal institutional practices, such as API scores, PBAS documentation, and CAS-based promotion processes. The faculty consistently illustrated that calculating API scores leads to career development, particularly in terms of promotions and eligibility for higher academic levels. Notably, a respondent in his mid-career remarked as follows: "The need to obtain the requisite API score as indicated is increasingly determined not on the basis of a compilation of a comprehensive academic contribution but rather on the need to have the desired API score documented. Similarly, the efforts to maintain detailed PBAS accounts were described as an ongoing administrative process. One participant explained that instead of doing the acts, we spend more time writing about what we did on the computer, which is then verified and checked for later review. This pressure is compounded by the effects of national ranking frameworks, such as the NIRF, which force institutions to translate the ranking criteria into internal measures, including publication output and citation metrics. One of the young faculty members said, *"We are pressured as a scholar to increase our publication output, as this will lead to higher rankings*; the pressure is not necessarily indirect—but rather directly built in to our duties and obligations. The analysis of these institutional practices helps to identify how national policy systems are implemented at the micro level. This procedure brings the structure of everyday academic operations into direct association with recruitment, promotion, and professional sustainability.

Metrics, in turn, are not only unbiased assessment tools but also regulatory schemes that fundamentally transform the way things are conducted in academia. They include activities such as redirecting the focus of research, unifying scholarly practices, and redefining the meaning of valuable knowledge. The product is a form of intellectual activity that increasingly conforms to the requirements of quantification where the production of knowledge is closely bound to the standards of its evaluation.

AI IN ACADEMIC WORK

The integration of AI in education has been described as a groundbreaking development with the potential to revolutionize the education sector across teaching and learning. The use of AI in education has been described as a game changer that can transform the educational landscape from the student to the professor. In contrast to what is often discussed in Indian higher education, when viewed through this lens, the success of an integrated approach has been far from consistent. Numerous institutional limitations have hampered this process. AI is mostly used to streamline workflows, enabling teachers to manage their already overloaded workloads amid a rapidly evolving landscape of metric-driven, administrative burdens rather than to transform their thinking. The findings of this investigation suggest that compared with AI capabilities, the contextual discourses that define academic labor have a greater effect on the functional outcomes of AI use.

In the present study, 80 respondents were interviewed; 46.25% (37 faculty members) reported using AI-based tools in their work. The patterns that emerged in the responses were either pedagogical or administrative uses of artificial intelligence; the use of artificial intelligence was not targeted at research-oriented, in-depth work. A vast majority (78%) of people who used AI-based tools said they relied on them for lecture note-taking and/or summarizing readings, creating outlines for lectures, breaking down content and making it more accessible to learners, and/or organizing lecture material more effectively. Expert 1 respondents reported that artificial intelligence mainly came into play in the scheduling of lectures in the context of working across multiple classes and short time slots. These results indicate that AI is largely valued for its ability to ease the burden of day-to-day education and streamline procedures for educational institutions with high operational needs.

In contrast, the use of AI in the research sector has been limited. Of the 37 participants who reported using AI tools, only 11—approximately 30 percent—stated that they used them for research-related tasks. The main application areas of artificial intelligence in this group were processing and basic writing (literature summarization, language editing and formatting, writing support). Very few participants mentioned the use of AI for conceptual thinking, methodological design, the creation of theory, or substantive analytical interpretation. According to one of the higher-ranking faculty members, "The human touch in creating meaningful research by providing directions on how to draft and structure it is where AI is lacking: 'It cannot replace intellectual involvement and the sense of time. This dichotomy highlights a crucial distinction between the tangible influence of AI on academic tasks and its conceptual transformation: while AI can undoubtedly enhance the efficiency of academic activities, it does not necessarily revolutionize the nature of academic research.

It is important to understand the meaning of this limited use of AI in the institutional context of higher education. Most (52/80) responded that AI was assisting them in being more efficient as teachers and in administrative duties but not in the quality or depth of research. Such perceptions are deeply connected to stress stemming from rising administrative demands and the shift toward outcome-based assessments. The lecturer is confronted with several disjointed time tables related to lecturing, examination responsibilities, checking, institutional reporting, and other continuous evaluation activities. Under these conditions, AI is mostly used in areas where a quick increase in efficiency is clear, not in activities that require long-term thought and academic rigor.

Figure 1. AI Usage and Impact on Academic Work (n = 80)

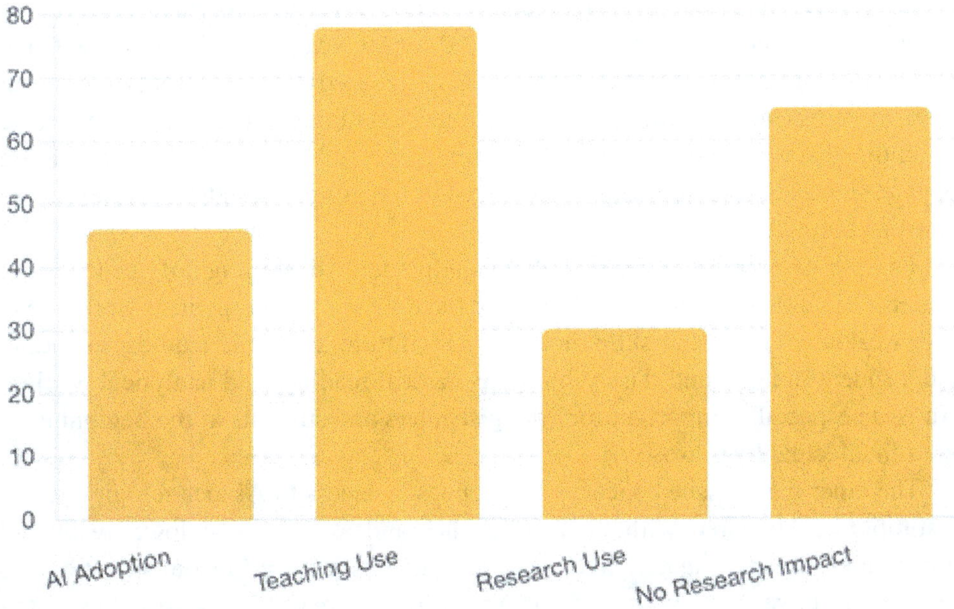

As shown in Figure 2, these differences are well expressed. This is primarily focused on related activities within the teaching space (78 percent) and in research (30 percent); the use of AI is slightly lower in content creation (63 percent) and even lower in children's activities (59 percent). Moreover, a sizable portion of the respondents (65 percent) indicated that AI had a minimal, if any, negative effect on the quality of research. These findings extend the dominant discourses that position AI as a transformative capacity for the production of knowledge. They say that, at the moment, AI is only being used by institutions to adapt and by academics to address an ever-increasing workload, not to alter the structures of academic work.

Concurrently, the implementation of AI in education presents a series of ethical and institutional challenges that transcend efficiency. An important issue is authorship and academic honesty. Perceptions of originality and academic contribution are threatened by the ability of the generative AI system to generate summaries, literature reviews, lecture material, and even entire written drafts. Many felt that there was a lack of understanding of what AI can do, what it can create, and how AI-writing tools can diminish overall engagement. The problem is not only traditional concerns about plagiarism but also broader concerns about the impact on independent work in essays and the undermining of IP rights.

A strong positive relationship between such concerns and the growing use of AI-detection software and algorithmic monitoring systems within academic institutions is found. Institutions are increasingly implementing systems to recognize AI-generated articles and monitor academic work. These developments fit into new modalities of policing in the academic world, where text production is subjected to even closer algorithmic scrutiny. Participants expressed concerns about the risk that these systems could produce false accusations, creating mistrust, and engendering a 'continual surveillance culture'. AI, therefore, extends the scope of audit culture beyond publications and institutional rankings to writing, evaluation, and academic conversation.

The use of AI raises concerns about the gradual "deskilling" of academic research. While AI can significantly reduce the time spent on repetitive work, it can also weaken some of the skills necessary for future academic studies, including independent thought and theory-building, critical reading, and analytical writing. An issue especially important for young scholars and students at the beginning of their intellectual lives arose.

The other major issue concerns differences in access to AI technologies across institutions. Compared with their colleagues and associates at lower-resourced universities, the investigators may be faculty members at well-resourced private or prestigious universities, who are frequently afforded greater access to sophisticated artificial intelligence technologies, robust digital infrastructure, and comprehensive institutional training programs. The inequalities in funding, language, and institutional hierarchy and the precarity of contracts typify the complex and unequal terrain of higher education in India. AI technologies are also highly accessible to some students and less so to others, risking an even greater impact on existing academic inequalities. AI is not neutral or socially neutral; instead, it is interwoven with existing structures of institutionalized privilege and exclusion.

This expansion of algorithmic governance to academic contexts includes the growing presence of AI in peer review, editorial evaluations, and institutional assessments. AI-powered tools are being increasingly used to assess manuscripts, analyze writing styles, gauge article visibility, and manage academic publications. How these are developed helps shape an academic culture that increasingly focuses on data-driven approaches, ideas, and ways of making things that produce machine-readable outputs, are highly visible, and can be quantified in terms of their effects. For these reasons, the academic practices of scholars might gradually become oriented toward alignment with institutional norms, algorithmic preferences, and digital forms of recognition.

THE MARGINALIZATION OF RESEARCH

One of the most notable effects of datafication and metric-based governance in higher education is the gradual sidelining of research as the key element of academic work. Although research is officially recognized as a core academic activity, its practical significance appears to be increasingly diminished in regard to the routine activities of institutions. The empirical evidence provided in this research shows a steady trend according to which clashing demands hamper in-depth involvement in research, specifically administrative duties and performance-based evaluation frameworks.

A significant majority (57 out of 80) of participants reported that nonacademic duties have had a detrimental effect on their ability to conduct meaningful, long-term research. The expansion of administrative roles, which includes admission processes, examination requirements and documentation related to compliance, undermines the time spent in academics. Unlike pedagogical or administrative duties, research requires long periods of dedicated mental activity. However, participants always highlighted the difficulties of such continuity in the existing institutional structures. A faculty member noted that *"Research requires long spurts of focused time, but our timetables are broken up with a variety of administrative work scattered all over the day"*. This extension is seen not only as an increase in workload but also as a complete change in academic time. The expression of one of the respondents is *"My routine activity is no longer shaped around teaching or research, but rather it is dictated by timelines to submit reports, hold meetings, and compliance requirements."* The other faculty member would note that *"Even when I am engaged in research activities, the ongoing administrative tasks in the background do not allow me to fully settle into my concentration"*. The given descriptions clarify that the intensification of the administration, in addition to burning out time resources, also undermines the intellectual engagement process, making long-term intellectual activity increasingly challenging.

This discontinuous time fragmentation itself is a direct cause of a change in research methods. Another important percentage of the reactionaries, 42 out of the 80, tended to prefer quick publications rather than more serious and long-term projects. An emphasis on producing measurable outcomes in limited time frames facilitates the transition to less lengthy, less complex research projects that can be completed and circulated in a short amount of time. This shift was described plainly by an early-career academic: "The years of commitment to a single idea are no longer affordable. The fact that the modernity of outputs necessitates the repetition of outputs every year emphasizes the impact of time on not only the speed but also the depth and goals of academic research.

This tendency is empowered by the influence of assessment systems that are based on metrics. In a case where the performance of academics is strictly connected with the number of publications and indexed outputs, it is more likely that the goal of research will be closer to the ideals of productivity than to inquiry. Members of the faculty are more likely to choose projects that are better suited to generate publishable products within limited time constraints, and they tend to avoid those projects that may need much fieldwork, an interdisciplinary team or critical analysis. This repositioning highlights a circularity where research is largely valued on the basis of its quantifiable outcomes over the quality of its research.

The amounts of time allocation data (see Figure 2) presented earlier predetermine a structural framework of these experiences. The fairly high administrative load (38 percent of faculty time) and the relatively small share (21 percent) of research highlight the peripheral role of research in the academic workforce. It is not only a matter of personal time management but also institutional values wherein conformity, paperwork, and performance indicators are valued over long-term academic activity.

The cumulative effect of these changes leads to a new composition of academic labor, in which research ceases to be the primary organizing principle. Instead, it is among many competing demands and is often pushed to the background by administrative and evaluative demands. The academic role shifts from that of a researcher engaged in the ongoing creation of knowledge to that of an administrator who must cope with numerous, often fragmented tasks.

This change has far-reaching consequences for the nature of knowledge production. The imposition of time constraints, quantitative indicators, and administrative requirements on research activities significantly limits the possibility of critical, innovative, and contextually oriented scholarship. This marginalization of research is, therefore, not an isolated issue of an individual perspective but rather a systemic problem that greatly affects the quality and direction of academic research. This process indicates a radical restructuring of the higher education sector, in which the imperatives of data-driven governance retune the parameters of what can be considered valuable academic work.

The patterns identified above are summarized in Table 1.

Table 1. Marginalization of Research Under Metric Governance and Administrative Intensification

Dimension	Empirical Findings	Illustrative Evidence	Analytical Implication
Decline in Sustained Research Engagement	57/80 respondents (71%) reported reduced ability to engage in long-term research	"Research needs uninterrupted time, which is no longer available"	Research is structurally constrained by competing institutional demands
Time Fragmentation	Majority reported fragmented schedules due to administrative tasks and meetings	"The day is broken into small tasks; there is no continuity for research"	Intellectual work is disrupted by procedural and administrative pressures
Shift to Quick Publications	42/80 respondents (52%) prioritize shorter, publishable outputs over long-term projects	"You cannot spend years on one idea anymore"	Emphasis on output frequency over depth and originality
Metric-Driven Topic Selection	Over half reported choosing research topics based on publishability and indexing potential	Preference for "safe" and trending topics	Knowledge production becomes aligned with evaluative metrics
Reduced Research Time (Structural)	Research accounts for only 21% of total academic time (see Figure 2)	Administrative work dominates (38%)	Institutional priorities displace research as core activity
Impact on Research Quality	Respondents noted decline in depth, innovation, and critical inquiry	"More papers, but not necessarily better research"	Quantification leads to standardization and dilution of scholarship
Overall Trend	Research increasingly subordinated to administrative and evaluative demands	Consistent across institutions and career stages	Research is no longer the central axis of academic work

Table 1 shows a conceptual representation of the way in which administrative growth and metric pressure cause a cascading effect, which ultimately can be used to marginalize research in the context of academic work. Academic identity is increasingly incorporated into the recruiting, promotion, and recognition standards of institutional evaluation systems. The trends above are interrelated with the contexts of academic careers in institutions, as well as with the workload and research practice environments. Recruitment is increasingly focusing on candidates with indexed journal publications whose advancement and career development are based on the number of publications, citation indices, and institutional contributions. These criteria are critical for deciding whether contracts will be renewed and whether the professors under the contract are employed; thus, the process of quantifying production is essential. This is particularly true for those in their early years of employment in academic institutions, who are still developing their careers. Datafication coordinates the dynamics of academic entries, advancements and protection, which is not limited to the scholarship sphere. In turn, career structures based on productivity rather than intellectual inquiry and not necessarily aligned with workload imperatives can be said to drive the marginalization of research.

PRECARITY, CAREER STAGE, AND UNEQUAL PRESSURES

The implications of datafication and governance driven by metrics manifest unevenly throughout the academic labor force. Instead, they interact with established institutional hierarchies to create different pressures depending on the stage of their career and their employment status. The evidence collected empirically in this paper shows that recent early-career academics and those on a contractual basis are most affected by these pressures, hence demonstrating how data-driven structures contribute to labor stratification in higher education.

A particularly vulnerable group of people in this regard are those individuals at the formative phases of their educational careers. A high percentage of respondents (24 out of 28), or 86 percent, reported that they were under much pressure to produce and often lacked mentoring or institutional support. Academic careers are increasingly dependent on the fulfillment of set measure performance, such as having publications in repositories and provable research output in limited time limits. In parallel, 19 out of 28 early-career respondents (68 percent) noted that they had difficulty accessing informal educational networks, which play a key role in supporting collaborative efforts, publication prospects, and careers. According to one of the respondents, there is a need to perform immediately; nevertheless, there is a very inadequate indication of how to maneuver the system. This interaction between high expectations and low support conditions is a delicate situation in which academics in their early careers must quickly adjust to the standards of the metrics.

Another clear example of the difference in the impact of the two systems is the difference between contractual and permanent faculty. Of the respondents whose obligations were under the terms of the contract, 29 out of 34 (85 percent) said that they felt pressure to produce and perform and that these pressures were commonly linked to the renewal of the contract and their retention in the company. On the other hand, interestingly, whereas permanent faculty members are also exposed to metric-based evaluation systems, a considerable majority, namely, 38 of 46 (82 percent), reported that the perception of job security can be used to reduce the intensity of these pressures. One contractual faculty member commented, in our case, that the publications are not only a promotion but also a question of survival. This difference highlights the role of metrics as mechanisms of discipline that also have a greater impact on those who are in more precarious situations. A contractual faculty member remarked, "*Publications are not just for promotion; they decide whether I keep my job.*"

This ambiguity in terms of employment increases the dependence on measurable aspects as one of the validation of professions. Scholars in contractual jobs and those who are still in their early years of practice have a high internalization of evaluative standards. This tendency makes them plan their studies and teaching practices around measurable deliverables, whereby they become institutionalized. This often causes strategic behavior, which includes the maximization of quantity compared with quality, research choice in accordance with its publication prospects, and academic behavior in close accord with institutional rules. These trends can be described only as the reaction to the circumstances dictated by structural forces and not by individual preferences.

The results included here are consistent with a wealth of analyses of scholarly labor that emphasize the stratifying nature of performance-based models. Sheila Slaughter and Gary Rhoades argue that an increasing market orientation in higher education institutions creates a type of labor in the academy that is varied and with unequal security, autonomy and recognition. These dynamics are reinforced through the process of datafication, which incorporates the element of evaluation into quantifiable models and thus makes it easier to regulate and compare people at different levels of hierarchy.

The consequences of such stratification go much further than individual experiences and impact the structure of academic labor itself. The state of heightened strain and lack of independence among certain categories of academics significantly undermines the ability to produce equitable knowledge. Early-stage faculty and those on contractual arrangements may be left in need of necessitating them to concentrate on quick outputs instead of engaging in long-term academic development, thus limiting the ability to be innovative and engage in critical discussion. Moreover, the relative isolation of permanent faculty could reinforce existing hierarchies, thus impacting mentorship and collegial relationships and the allocation of institutional power.

The overall impact is a stratified academic labor force, where data-driven assessment mechanisms exacerbate and reproduce existing inequities. Here, datafication is not a neutral process of standardization. Instead, it functions as an organizing device that redistributes risk, exacerbates precarity, and sorts academic labor by career level and status. The resulting system places the greatest performance stress on those with the lowest institutional security, thus only reinforcing institutional inequalities in the prevailing state of academic affairs.

ACADEMIC IDENTITY UNDER DATAFICATION

The transformations brought about by datafication and governor-by-metrics modalities extend past the organizational framework of academic labor, even when the very character of the professoriate is altered. Academic careers have traditionally been founded on the values of intellectual independence, rigorous research, and the process of lifelong engagement with knowledge; however, the vocabulary of performance, productivity, and quantifiable results is now taking over. According to the results of this study, it is not only structural but also very experiential change that determines how researchers see their roles, motivations, and professional aspirations.

One such theme that emerges regularly in the interviews is the replacement of the scholar by what can be termed an incremental responsive metric performer. The faculty members are also planning their professional actions with more emphasis on evaluation and thus are not emphasizing intellectual affairs but rather orienting their actions on their measurements in the institution. One of the respondents said, "We are no longer students; we are under constant examination, performers. These kinds of sensibility declare a greater internalization of the logic of metrics, according to which the value of scholarly work resides in its relevance within the apparatus of assessment and not in the sense that the scholar is making meaningful contributions to the body of knowledge.

The emotional aspects of this transition are rather significant and are always present in the stories of the respondents. The faculty members reported having experiences that were marked by exhaustion, frustration and a growing lack of connection to the intellectual aspect of their professional activities. Such inflexible emphasis on quantifiable results, together with administrative responsibilities and limited opportunities to engage in contemplative participation, creates a general feeling of continuous evaluation. According to one of the faculty members, it is a system that rewards visibility, as opposed to thought, and accordingly, it was a concise summation of the tension between institutional requirements and the traditional ideals of scholarship. These descriptions suggest that there is a growing gap between the demands imposed on academics and their perceptions of what is considered to be good scholarly practice.

The decrease in intellectual independence is a pivotal issue. External measures and institutional requirements increasingly affect decisions related to the topics of research, the strategies of publications and pedagogies. This restriction constrains the ability of scholars to undertake independent studies, particularly those that are outside mainstream evaluative frameworks. It has a stronger effect on early-career and contractual faculty whose career sustainability often depends on strict adherence to performance indicators. In this case, autonomy becomes contingent rather than intrinsic.

Academic identity shift can be conceptualized under the concept of audit culture as elaborated by Marilyn Strathern, whereby evaluative systems not only transform practices in institutions but also influence perceptions of self. Simultaneously, Wendy Nelson Espeland and Michael Sauder explain how, after the institutionalization of metrics, individuals adopt them, thereby mediating behavior and reconstituting professional norms. In academia, it results in an identity that is more compliant and performance oriented and has measurable productivity.

The cumulative effect is a reworking of the essence of scholarly work itself. The role of the professoriate is becoming more clearly defined by its efforts to produce knowledge and critical discourse rather than by its capacity to satisfy institutionalized metrics and maintain visibility in a data-driven paradigm. Intellectual inquiry does not disappear but is instead recontextualized within a narrow, often fragmented professional situation. Academic identity is formed as a site where structural pressures are internalized and negotiated and, at times, actively opposed.

With these developments, there is increased scrutiny of the future of academic life. The opportunity for continued intellectual stimulation is gradually curtailed in an environment where performance, visibility, and output are valued over other factors. Academic identity transformation in the environment of datafication is not just an issue of professional adjustment; it is an indication of broader alterations in the values and priorities on which higher education is based.

RESULTS

When considered collectively, the outcome of this research reveals a clear trend: datafication and AI-mediated systems do not exist as separate phenomena but as interdependent systems that can profoundly transform academic labor. This change covers aspects such as the redistribution of workloads, behavioral orientation, technology use, and institutional hierarchies. What emerges is the redefinition of the role of academics, which is a shift in the context of the production and valuation of knowledge.

This change is based on the growth of administrative labor, which is a basic structural basis. These empirical data indicate that there is a steady increase in duties such as duties related to admissions, examination, compliance and institutional meetings, which are occupying a substantial amount of faculty time. Such growth is not a mere coincidence; instead, it is closely tied to the requirements of data-driven governance, which relies upon a cycle of documentation, reporting and verification. The resulting effect is a fall apart from academic time, and the longer the time of research is, the more difficult it becomes. In this context, the research efforts are replaced by administrative tasks, both in terms of time provision and in terms of priorities in the institutional setting.

Within such a narrow frame, metric-based systems of evaluation drastically change academic behavior. The pressure to produce measurable outcomes, the most obvious of which are published articles in indexed journals, is an incentive to encourage the effective recalibration of faculty members. The consistency of research decision-making, partnering behavior, and publication activity with the ratio of quantifiable indicators and evaluative standards becomes sharper. Wendy Nelson Espeland and Michael Sauder suggest that quantification constitutes a mechanism of governance, a mechanism that goes beyond the assessment of activities to actively reorganize them. This claim is supported by the findings of this study, which illustrate that metrics can affect not only the evaluation of research but also its general direction and organization.

The role of artificial intelligence here is enlightening. To achieve a radical change in academic activities, artificial intelligence is primarily used as a compensatory tool to assist faculty in coping with the requirements presented by an increased workload. This tool has been applied mainly in educational settings, where its ability to reduce the time taken in normal preparatory activities is highly efficient. However, this effectiveness does not increase research involvement. On the other hand, the time saved is often redirected toward administration or other institutional responsibilities. Artificial intelligence, then, is applied to reinforce existing patterns and not to confront them and in line with the general logic of datafication, which values efficiency and productivity over intellectual depth.

The net effect of these processes is the marginalization of research to a backburner. According to the data, a significant proportion of the respondents report a decreased capacity to conduct research projects that are lengthy and long term, as well as the emergence of the tendency to create shorter, more easily printable works. Research personality is becoming increasingly fragmented and time bounded and is largely driven by a desire to achieve measurements rather than by a determination to engage in a prolonged investigation. This change in research emphasis off the main stream of academic activity is indicative of a more general reorganization of institutional priorities, where a concern with quantifiable productivity is given greater priority than with intellectual contributions.

The above changes do not occur in the same proportion across the academic workforce. This study clarifies the role of datafication in enhancing existing disparities, particularly in terms of career stage and employment. Early career faculty members and those with contractual agreements are under increased pressure to deliver performance metrics in an environment that is marked by limited resources and job insecurity. Permanent faculty, on the other hand, although still under the pressures of evaluation systems, achieve a relatively high level of insulation. The unequal distribution of risk and responsibility is a prime illustration of the stratifying effects of academic capitalism as outlined by Sheila Slaughter and Gary Rhoades, whereby institutional logics produce diverse forms of academic labor. This is enhanced by such dynamics of datafication when factors such as evaluation are incorporated into measurable systems that can be unevenly distributed across hierarchies.

Taken together, the findings can be explained by the system of audit culture developed by Marilyn Strathern. The audit culture phenomenon cultivates systems of unending control and responsibility, thus altering institutional practices and personal behaviors. This can be seen in the Indian system of higher education, where administrative procedures, metric assessment, and technology work together to control academic activities. Academic faculty is thus placed within a regulatory framework that emphasizes the value of visibility, comparability and performance measures.

The main contribution of the study is that datafication and artificial intelligence are not just a series of improvements in the field of academic efficiency but also a complete reorganization of the system of academic labor. An increase in administrative duties reduces the time devoted to research activity, and metrics considerably change academic behavior. Artificial intelligence presumably eases workload overload, but it does not lead to a change in intellectual practices. Moreover, differences are compounded because people are exposed to different amounts of evaluative pressure. The subsequent outcome is a shift whereby research is no longer the central point of academic activities but an aspect of a larger picture where the important consideration is measurement and adherence to standards.

These findings have crucial implications: technology- and data-based reforms in the context of higher education must be framed in the context of institutional structures. Without a careful analysis of the structural basis of academic labor, the introduction of measurements and artificial intelligence can only increase but not reduce existing stressors. The development of academic activities, in turn, represents not only the introduction of new technologies but also the creation of a system of government where the measurable comes to determine what is increasingly valued.

It must be acknowledged that any system of evaluation based on metrics and artificial intelligence lacks an inherent capacity to harm academic efforts. Theoretically, metric systems have the potential to enhance transparency, enable comparability across institutions, and instigate the application of organized criteria for recruitment, promotion, and the distribution of resources. Similarly, artificial intelligence has the potential to enhance research activities by streamlining data analysis, synthesizing literature, and encouraging interdisciplinary exploration. However, as the discussion shows, in practice, the tools do not work as intended by the theory on which they are based. Instead of encouraging the spirit of true accountability, metric-based systems tend to foster a culture of compliance-focused thinking, where academic activity is oriented not toward the development of substantive inquiry but toward reaching such evaluation or compliance targets. In a similar vein, the use of artificial intelligence is substantially instrumental and efficiency oriented, benefiting faculty in handling contemporary workloads rather than enhancing the breadth or depth of research undertakings. This divergence between the idealized potential of these tools and their actualization within specific organizational and regulatory conditions underscores the need to explore not only the intended purpose of these systems but also their operational dynamics within these contexts.

CONSIDERATIONS FOR POLICY AND PRACTICE

The findings of this study highlight why a reevaluation of institutional approaches in the context of higher education, specifically where datafication, metrics-driven assessment, and the incorporation of artificial intelligence are rapidly revamping academic activities, is urgently needed. These implications include assessment systems, workload arrangements, technology management, and institutional support arrangements.

a. Assessment Reform

Current assessment systems that rely mostly on quantifiable data such as publication rates and journal placement in indices require a comprehensive review. Institutions must take a step toward more just models of assessment, which capture the qualitative nature of academic work, including originality, social relevance and contributions to the field of pedagogy. This overemphasis might result in a prioritization of amount over richness, thereby limiting the scope of knowledge production. A better evaluation system should be based on peer review, contextual assessment, and discipline-specific criteria and thus should protect the primacy of intellectual quality over simple numerical values.

b. Redistribution of workload

The differentiation in the growth of administrative functions requires a systematic redistribution of academic functions. Universities must thoroughly evaluate the extent and character of administrative responsibilities delegated to faculty members, especially those associated with compliance and documentation requirements. The outsourcing of the daily administrative tasks to the specialized support staff, coupled with the rationalization of the requirements of the procedure, are ways of reclaiming the precious time that could be spent on the research and intellectual activities. Clear workload policies defining the differences between the teaching, research, and administrative roles are necessary and are the basis of maintaining a viable academic environment.

c. Governance of Artificial Intelligence in Academic Institutions

The growing use of AI tools in academia highlights the need to develop institutional policies to balance efficiency with academic integrity ideals. Universities must be urged to avoid adopting AI on an ad hoc basis but rather design and adopt detailed policies that will guide the right use of AI in the fields of teaching, research and evaluation. Such frameworks should interact with the issues related to transparency, authorship, and ethical usage but also consider the possibility of artificial intelligence as a supportive tool. Notably, the implementation of artificial intelligence should not be viewed as an alternative to addressing such root institutional issues as the presence of too much work; instead, its role should be discussed within the framework of overall institutional change.

d. Mentorship and Organizational Support

The disproportionate effects of metric-based systems on early-career and contractual faculty can be explained by the need to enhance the mentorship system. Institutions should ensure that they develop formal mentoring programs to facilitate research development, enhance publication strategies, and promote professionalism. Research funding and institutional guidance can help alleviate the stresses on early-career academics by helping them access cohort networks openly. Moreover, however, there is an acute need to ensure that evaluation systems take into account differences in career levels and working conditions, thereby making the expectations in question fair and context dependent.

CONCLUSION

The findings in this chapter suggest that academic development in Indian universities is more than just administrative modernity or technological sophistication. Rather, it connotes a deeper restructuring of the university through intertwined processes of datafication, metric governance, audit culture, and AI integration. The increasing regulation of academic labor is achieved through processes of visibility, quantification, documentation, and continuous assessment, which are changing the production of knowledge and the profile of scholars. There are many administrative burdens, including an increasing volume of compliance paperwork, accreditation requirements, institution rankings and evaluations, and time-consuming tasks that take up a large amount of faculty time. Moreover, there is a measurement-driven evaluation system that focuses on output in publications, citations, and measurable indicators. This emphasis creates a more academic atmosphere, closer to the institutional corpus and less attuned to intellectual curiosity, disciplinary engagement, or the longevity of inquiry. The introduction of AI has thus far largely reinforced these trends, as it primarily provides a tool to improve administrative efficiency and support teaching further but not a breakthrough for research innovation. The impact of such developments is evident in the careers of early-career and contractual faculty, where ingrained inequalities in the institutional hierarchy, social networks, caste, and access to resources continue to shape opportunities and recognition in the academic arena. This leads to a world in which academic institutions are increasingly under pressure, sliced up, and constantly evaluated and in which professional status and recognition are precariously linked to performance and institutional visibility. The chapter argues that this may have the unintended impact of prioritizing measurable, productive output over the depth of ideas in higher education institutions if there is no critical rethinking of emerging quantified governance. This marked change is poised to make academics not independent knowledge makers but into perpetual performers in an increasingly flat and sprawling austerity regime of audit and accountability.

REFERENCES

Akhter, Y., Ahmed, M., & Yadav, S. K. (2020). Quality deprivation through quality assessment: the academic score system in Indian higher education. In *University of Patras* (pp. 6–28). DOI: 10.26220/aca.3438

Braun, V., & Clarke, V. (2006). Using thematic analysis in psychology. *Qualitative Research in Psychology*, *3*(2), 77–101. DOI: 10.1191/1478088706qp063oa

Bristow, A., Robinson, S., & Ratle, O. (2019). Academic Arrhythmia: Disruption, Dissonance, and Conflict in the Early-Career Rhythms of CMS Academics. *Academy of Management Learning & Education*, *18*(2), 241–260. DOI: 10.5465/amle.2017.0340

Burrows, R. (2012). Living with the h-index? Metric assemblages in the contemporary academy. *The Sociological Review*, *60*(2), 355–372. DOI: 10.1111/j.1467-954X.2012.02077.x

Burrows, R. (2012). Living with the H-Index? Metric Assemblages in the Contemporary Academy. *The Sociological Review*, *60*(2), 355–372. DOI: 10.1111/j.1467-954X.2012.02077.x

Espeland, W. N., & Sauder, M. (2007). Rankings and reactivity: How public measures recreate social worlds. *AJS; American Journal of Sociology*, *113*(1), 1–40. DOI: 10.1086/517897

Jose, P., & Koley, M. (2026). *Doctoral education and the Political Economy of Private Universities in India*. DOI: 10.31235/osf.io/xyv4c_v1

Joshi, D. (2024). AI governance in India – law, policy and political economy. *Communication Research and Practice*, *10*(3), 328–339. DOI: 10.1080/22041451.2024.2346428

Kanagaraj, K. (2019). ACADEMIC PERFORMANCE INDICATORS AND THE QUALITY OF RESEARCH IN HIGHER EDUCATION INSTITUTIONS IN INDIA: A STUDY OF UNIVERSITY TEACHERS' OPINIONS. *International Journal of Advance Research and Innovative Ideas in Education*, *5*(5), 267–274. https://ijariie.com/AdminUploadPdf/ACADEMIC_PERFORMANCE_INDICATORS_AND_THE_QUALITY_OF_RESEARCH_IN_HIGHER_EDUCATION_INSTITUTIONS_IN_INDIA__A_STUDY_OF_UNIVERSITY_TEACHERS'_OPINIONS_ijariie10846.pdf

. Kulkarni, Dr. V., & Rajas, S. (2025). PERCEPTION OF UNIVERSITY TEACHERS ABOUT ACADEMIC PERFORMANCE INDICATOR (API) IN EDUCATION SYSTEM. *ANANYAŚĀSTRAM An International Multidisciplinary Journal (A Unique Treatise of Knowledge), 1*(2), 33–40. DOI: 10.64328/aimjv01i02074

Luthra, A., Singh, K., & Singh, S. (2021). Academic performance indicator as performance management tool: Employees perception and factors governing to its acceptance and rejection in Indian educational institute. *International Journal of Strategic Business Alliances*, *7*(1), 1–1. DOI: 10.1504/IJSBA.2022.120076

Luthra, A., Singh, K., & Singh, S. (2022). Academic performance indicator as performance management tool: Employees' perception and factors governing to its acceptance and rejection in Indian educational institutes. *International Journal of Strategic Business Alliances*, *7*(1), 23–23. DOI: 10.1504/IJSBA.2022.120076

Mayer-Schönberger, V., & Cukier, K. (2013). *Big Data: A Revolution That Will Transform How We Live, Work, and Think.* John Murray.

Meho, L. I. (2025). Measuring research performance in higher education: Metrics, rankings, and institutional behavior. *Research Evaluation*, *34*(2), 145–160.

Meho, L. I. (2025). Gaming the metrics: Bibliometric anomalies in global university rankings and the research integrity risk index (RI2). *Scientometrics*, *130*(11), 6683–6726. Advance online publication. DOI: 10.1007/s11192-025-05480-2

Mondal, D. (2024). Research Performance Analysis of Five Key Parameters of Top 20 Indian Universities: An Evaluation. *Journal of Data Science Informetrics and Citation Studies*, *3*(2), 216–222. DOI: 10.5530/jcitation.3.2.22

Mustaqeem, M. (2025). The Digital Pandit: Artificial Intelligence in Indian Higher Education: A critical inquiry into transformation, equity and ethics. *International Journal of Applied Research, 11*(9), 403–407. DOI: 10.22271/allresearch.2025.v11.i9e.13309

National Institutional Ranking Framework. (2023). *Methodology for Ranking of Higher Educational Institutions in India*. Ministry of Education, Government of India.

Pant, J., & Bhadoria, A. S. (2025). Challenges of National Institute's Ranking Framework (NIRF). *Journal of Medical Evidence*, *6*(1), 81–82. DOI: 10.4103/JME.JME_34_25

Peacock, V., Bruun, M. K., Dungey, C., & Shapiro, M. (2023). *Surveillance.* Open Encyclopedia of Anthropology., DOI: 10.29164/23surveillance

Peerzada, R. A., Sharma, A., Gurumurthy, A. A., & Gurumurthy, A. A. (2024). Interrogating "light but tight" model of education: Saffron neoliberalism and India's new education policy. *Human Geographies, 18*(3), 345–357. DOI: 10.1177/19427786241265426

Plekhanov, A., Trunova, E., & Volkova, N. (2023). Administrative burden and academic productivity: Evidence from higher education institutions. *Higher Education Policy, 36*(2), 275–295.

Plekhanov, D., Franke, H., & Netland, T. H. (2023). Digital transformation: A review and research agenda. *European Management Journal, 41*(6), 821–844. DOI: 10.1016/j.emj.2022.09.007

Slaughter, S., & Rhoades, G. (2004). *Academic Capitalism and the New Economy: Markets, State, and Higher Education*. Johns Hopkins University Press.

Slaughter, S., & Rhoades, G. (2004). *Academic Capitalism and the New Economy: Markets, State, and Higher Education*. Johns Hopkins University Press.

Strathern, M. (Ed.). (2000). *Audit Cultures: Anthropological Studies in Accountability, Ethics, and the Academy*. Routledge.

Strathern, M. (2000). *Audit Cultures: Anthropological Studies in Accountability, Ethics, and the Academy*. Routledge.

Strathern, M. (2023). Audit and accountability in higher education: Revisiting audit culture. *Journal of the Royal Anthropological Institute, 29*(1), 1–18. DOI: 10.1111/1467-9655.t01-2-00001

Strathern, M. (2023). *Property, Substance, and Effect: Anthropological Essays on Persons and Things*. HAU Books.

Stvilia, B., Gibradze, L., & Jansen, B. J. (2024). Academic metrics and research productivity: A systematic review. *Journal of Informetrics, 18*(1), 101–120.

Stvilia, B., Pang, Y., Lee, D. J., & Gunaydin, F. (2024). Data quality assurance practices in research data repositories: A systematic literature review. *Journal of the Association for Information Science and Technology, 76*, 238–261. DOI: 10.1002/asi.24948

Sutton, P. (2017). Lost souls? The demoralization of academic labor in the measured university. *Higher Education Research & Development, 36*(3), 625–636. DOI: 10.1080/07294360.2017.1289365

Toppo, P. K. (2025). ARTIFICIAL INTELLIGENCE AND THE NATIONAL EDUCATION POLICY (NEP) 2020: A QUALITATIVE EXPLORATION OF INTEGRATION, OPPORTUNITIES, AND CHALLENGES. *International Journal of Advanced Research, 13*(10), 1218–1221. DOI: 10.21474/IJAR01/22015

University Grants Commission. (2018). *UGC Regulations on Minimum Qualifications for Appointment of Teachers and Other Academic Staff in Universities and Colleges and Measures for the Maintenance of Standards in Higher Education.* Government of India.

Woodcock, J. (2018). Digital Labor in the University: Understanding the Transformations of Academic Work in the UK. *tripleC Communication Capitalism & Critique Open Access Journal for a Global Sustainable Information Society, 16*(1), 129–142. DOI: 10.31269/triplec.v16i1.880

KEY TERMS AND DEFINITIONS

Academic Capitalism: This framework defines how institutions of higher education and tertiary institutions are progressively adjusting their operational activities to adopt a market-driven, more production-centered approach and to employ quantifiable outputs and results in their organizational operations.

Administrative Intensification: The expansion and consolidation of bureaucratic and compliance-oriented duties in academic undertakings have resulted in a significant redistribution of time, shifting the focus of conduct and intent toward research and intellectual pursuits.

Audit Culture: A system that is characterized by continuous evaluation and accountability, where corporate actions in the field of scholarship are exposed to the same metrics, documentation, and verification, thus altering institutional procedures and professionalism.

Datafication: A change in scholarly activities, such as teaching, research, and administration, into measurable units eases their measurement, comparison, and control in institutions.

Metric-Based Governance: A system of institutions in which academic performance is largely evaluated in terms of quantifiable factors such as publications, citations, and rankings, thus influencing both behaviors and decision-making processes.

Chapter 10
Digitalization, AI, and the Changing Social Contract of the Professoriate

Mustafa Kayyali
http://orcid.org/0000-0003-3300-262X
Maaref University of Applied Sciences, Syria

ABSTRACT

This chapter examines how digitalization and artificial intelligence are reshaping the social contract of the professoriate in contemporary higher education. The academic profession has long been built around a delicate balance of autonomy, intellectual responsibility, institutional service, and public trust. Yet the growing presence of AI-driven systems, data analytics, automated assessment, digital teaching platforms, and performance-based monitoring is altering how professors teach, research, publish, collaborate, and are evaluated. Rather than treating AI as a purely technical innovation, the chapter considers it as a force that quietly reorganizes academic labor, authority, and identity. It explores the tensions between efficiency and freedom, transparency and surveillance, innovation and precarity. Ultimately, the chapter argues that universities must rethink the social contract of academic work so that technological transformation strengthens, rather than weakens, the human, ethical, and scholarly foundations of the professoriate.

INTRODUCTION

The professoriate has always stood at the center of a delicate social arrangement. Professors are not merely employees who deliver lectures, publish papers, attend meetings, and satisfy institutional procedures. At their best, they are custodians of

DOI: 10.4018/979-8-3373-8525-9.ch010

knowledge, critics of society, mentors of future generations, and participants in the slow, sometimes untidy, work of intellectual civilization. The university, in return, has traditionally granted them a degree of autonomy that is unusual in most professions: the freedom to ask difficult questions, to challenge accepted truths, to teach with judgment, to pursue research whose value may not be immediately visible, and to serve society through expertise rather than obedience. This arrangement has never been perfect. It has always been shaped by politics, funding pressures, bureaucratic demands, disciplinary hierarchies, and unequal access to academic privilege. Yet, despite its imperfections, the social contract of the professoriate has rested on a powerful idea: that society benefits when scholars are given enough trust, time, and independence to think deeply on its behalf.

Today, that contract is being quietly rewritten. The rewriting is not taking place through one dramatic reform, nor through a single policy document that openly declares the end of the old academic order. It is happening through platforms, dashboards, learning management systems, citation metrics, automated assessment tools, AI-assisted writing, predictive analytics, digital surveillance, online teaching environments, institutional ranking systems, and increasingly sophisticated forms of data-driven governance. Digitalization and artificial intelligence are not simply adding new instruments to academic life; they are changing the conditions under which academic life is imagined, measured, valued, and controlled (Schneider, 2023). What once appeared as a set of helpful tools has become part of a wider transformation in the meaning of academic work itself.

The university has, of course, never been outside technology. The printed book, the laboratory, the library catalogue, the computer, the internet, and the digital database have all changed scholarly practice in profound ways. What distinguishes the current moment is not merely the presence of new tools, but the speed, scale, and administrative logic through which these tools are being embedded into university systems. Digitalization has made academic activity more visible, traceable, comparable, and quantifiable. Artificial intelligence adds another layer: it does not only store or transmit information; it interprets, predicts, ranks, recommends, generates, and increasingly participates in decisions that were once considered matters of human judgment. In this sense, AI does not simply assist the professoriate. It enters the space of academic judgment itself (Aithal & Aithal, 2023).

This transformation raises uncomfortable questions. What happens to academic autonomy when teaching, research, and service are continuously translated into data points? What becomes of professorial authority when AI systems can generate lectures, summarize literature, grade assignments, suggest research directions, detect "productivity gaps," and predict student performance? How does the role of the professor change when institutions begin to value what can be counted more than what can be understood? And perhaps most importantly, who benefits from this new arrangement, and who becomes vulnerable within it?

These questions matter because the professoriate is already under pressure from several directions. Many academics face heavier workloads, shorter contracts, intensified publication expectations, growing administrative demands, and reduced time for serious intellectual reflection (Hostler, 2023). In some institutions, the ideal of the professor as an independent scholar has slowly been replaced by the image of the professor as a measurable performer: productive, responsive, visible, competitive, digitally available, and constantly evaluated. Digital systems often promise to make academic work more efficient, but efficiency can become a subtle language of compression. More can be expected in less time. More students can be reached with fewer resources. More outputs can be demanded because digital tools supposedly make them easier to produce. The result is not always liberation. Sometimes, it is acceleration disguised as innovation.

Artificial intelligence intensifies this tension. On one hand, AI offers genuine possibilities for academic enrichment. It can support personalized learning, assist with literature discovery, improve accessibility, reduce repetitive tasks, enhance feedback, facilitate multilingual communication, and open new pathways for research. It can help professors manage certain burdens and create more inclusive learning environments. It would be simplistic, even dishonest, to portray AI only as a threat. For many academics, AI may become a valuable intellectual companion, a practical assistant, or a bridge toward forms of teaching and research that were previously difficult to imagine.

On the other hand, the adoption of AI within higher education is not neutral. Technologies carry assumptions about what counts as quality, intelligence, productivity, evidence, and success (Block, 2022). When AI systems are designed around measurable indicators, they may privilege what is easy to process over what is educationally meaningful. When automated tools enter evaluation processes, they may reinforce existing biases while appearing objective. When AI-generated content becomes common, questions of authorship, originality, intellectual labor, and scholarly integrity become more difficult to settle. When universities rely on predictive analytics, students and professors may both become subjects of anticipatory judgment: categorized not by what they have done, but by what the system predicts they are likely to do.

The changing social contract of the professoriate must therefore be understood not only as a technological issue, but as an ethical, institutional, and cultural one. The central problem is not whether professors should use AI. They already do, directly or indirectly, and the use will only expand (Fitria, 2023). The deeper question is whether AI will be integrated into higher education in ways that strengthen the academic profession or weaken its most important foundations. Will it give professors more room for mentoring, creativity, and critical inquiry, or will it narrow their role into managing platforms and meeting algorithmic expectations? Will it support academic freedom, or will it introduce new forms of surveillance and behavioral control? Will it democratize knowledge, or will it deepen inequalities between well-resourced institutions and those struggling to keep pace?

The concept of the social contract is useful here because it reminds us that academic work is never merely private labor. Professors serve students, institutions, disciplines, professions, communities, and wider publics. Their authority depends on trust: trust that they pursue knowledge with integrity, that they teach with care, that they evaluate fairly, that they speak honestly, and that they contribute to society in ways that may not always produce immediate economic return. In exchange, society and institutions are expected to protect the conditions that make such work possible. These include academic freedom, reasonable security, intellectual space, collegial governance, respect for expertise, and recognition of forms of labor that cannot be fully captured by metrics.

Digitalization and AI disturb this contract because they introduce new actors into the relationship between professor, university, student, and society. Platforms mediate teaching. Metrics mediate reputation. Algorithms mediate visibility. Automated systems mediate evaluation. Corporate technology providers, data infrastructures, and external ranking mechanisms increasingly shape internal academic priorities. The professor is no longer working only within the university; the professor is working within a dense digital architecture that quietly organizes attention, behavior, and value. The danger is not that technology will replace professors in a simple, mechanical sense. The greater danger is that technology may redefine the professor's work so deeply that the older language of vocation, judgment, and intellectual responsibility begins to sound outdated.

Yet this chapter does not begin from nostalgia. The older academic contract was not equally generous to all. Many early-career academics, adjunct instructors, women scholars, Global South researchers, and scholars outside dominant languages and institutions have long experienced the professoriate as precarious, hierarchical, and uneven. A renewed social contract should not aim to restore a romantic past. Rather, it should ask what kind of academic profession is worth building in an AI-mediated university. Such a contract must protect human judgment without rejecting technological support. It must embrace innovation without surrendering academic values to platform logic. It must recognize productivity without reducing intellectual life to performance indicators. It must defend autonomy while also acknowledging accountability to students, communities, and society.

This chapter therefore explores digitalization and AI as forces that are reshaping the academic profession at the level of labor, identity, authority, and institutional trust. It examines how professors are being repositioned within systems of algorithmic governance, how academic autonomy is being renegotiated, and how the meaning of professorial purpose is changing in universities increasingly organized around data and automation. The argument developed here is that the professoriate does not simply need technical training for the age of AI. It needs a new social settlement: one that defines what should remain human, what may be responsibly automated, what must be democratically governed, and what values universities are unwilling to sacrifice.

In the end, the future of the professoriate will not be determined by AI alone. It will be determined by the choices universities make about AI: who designs it, who controls it, who benefits from it, who is harmed by it, and what forms of academic life it is allowed to reshape. The question, then, is not whether the professoriate will change. It already is changing. The real question is whether that change will produce a thinner, faster, more monitored academic profession, or a wiser, more humane, and more publicly responsive one.

THE PROFESSORIATE AT A TURNING POINT: DIGITALIZATION, AI, AND INSTITUTIONAL CHANGE

The professoriate is standing at a strange and demanding threshold. For a long time, academic life appeared to move according to rhythms that were recognizably slow: semesters, peer review cycles, sabbaticals, research projects that matured over years, doctoral supervision that unfolded through patience rather than speed, and scholarly conversations that often took decades to gain shape. The university was never static, of course. It changed with politics, markets, wars, demographic shifts, funding structures, student movements, and intellectual revolutions (Schwab, 2026). Yet there remained a certain image of the professor as a person whose authority came from depth, accumulated judgment, disciplinary memory, and the ability to dwell with difficult questions longer than most institutions could tolerate. That image has not disappeared, but it is now under pressure from forces that do not speak the old language of scholarly patience. Digitalization and artificial intelligence have entered higher education not merely as tools, but as organizing logics. They are changing the texture of academic work from the inside.

At first glance, digital transformation in universities may seem practical, even ordinary. Learning management systems help organize courses. Online libraries widen access to knowledge. Video conferencing connects scholars across continents (Verma & Dwivedi, 2023). Digital assessment platforms reduce paperwork. AI tools support literature searches, language editing, data analysis, feedback generation, and administrative coordination. No serious observer can deny the usefulness of these developments. In many places, they have opened doors that were previously closed. A professor in an under-resourced institution can now access archives, lectures, databases, and scholarly networks that once required travel, privilege, or institutional wealth. Students with disabilities can benefit from assistive technologies. Multilingual learners can receive support that makes academic participation less intimidating. Research collaboration can move across borders with a speed that would have seemed almost magical a generation ago.

And yet, usefulness is not the same as innocence. Technologies arrive carrying habits of thought. They quietly teach institutions what to value. They reward some behaviors and make others invisible. A digital platform does not simply host teaching; it reshapes the way teaching is planned, monitored, archived, and evaluated. A citation database does not simply record scholarly influence; it participates in defining whose influence counts. An AI writing assistant does not merely polish language; it unsettles long-standing assumptions about authorship, originality, and intellectual labor (Rodrigues, 2025). Predictive analytics do not simply identify risk; they create new categories of suspicion, intervention, and institutional control. The professoriate, then, is not only adopting technologies. It is being repositioned by them.

This repositioning is subtle, which makes it more difficult to resist or even name. Rarely does a university announce that it is reducing academic judgment to measurable behavior. Instead, it introduces dashboards for transparency, workload models for fairness, analytics for student success, digital records for quality assurance, AI-assisted systems for efficiency, and performance metrics for accountability. Each measure may sound reasonable in isolation. Who would oppose transparency? Who would reject student support? Who would argue against efficiency when academic staff are already exhausted? The problem begins when these instruments accumulate and form an atmosphere. The professor gradually becomes more visible to the institution, but not always more understood. Visibility can be a strange kind of shadow. The more one is tracked, the less one may be trusted.

Academic work has always involved accountability, and rightly so. Professors are not sacred figures floating above institutional responsibility (Beale & Easton, 2026). They teach students who deserve care and seriousness. They conduct research that must meet ethical and scholarly standards. They receive public or private resources that require justification. Still, the new accountability differs from older forms because it is increasingly mediated by data systems that favor what can be counted quickly. Course engagement, publication frequency, grant capture, student satisfaction scores, online responsiveness, research impact indicators, and platform activity can all become signs of academic value (Sharif Nia et al, 2023). These signs are not useless. Some of them can reveal patterns that deserve attention. Yet when they become dominant, they risk producing a flattened portrait of the academic person: productive but not necessarily wise, active but not necessarily thoughtful, visible but not necessarily transformative.

Here lies one of the deeper tensions of the present moment. The professoriate is being asked to become more innovative, more flexible, more digitally fluent, more student-centered, more globally connected, and more productive, often without a corresponding expansion of time, security, or institutional trust. AI is then introduced as the solution to pressures that institutions themselves have intensified. It will save time, we are told. It will streamline tasks. It will help professors cope. Sometimes it does. But there is a trap hidden in this promise. When technology makes work faster, institutions may not allow the saved time to become reflective time (McDiarmid & Zhao, 2023). They may simply raise expectations. More feedback. More publications. More online presence. More reports. More availability. More proof that one is doing enough. The academic day stretches, not because the clock has changed, but because digital work has weakened the boundary between presence and absence.

The professor's office, once a physical space with a door, has become dispersed across email, messaging platforms, virtual classrooms, shared documents, institutional portals, research networks, and algorithmic profiles. The scholar is never entirely away. There is always something to answer, upload, revise, approve, check, monitor, or document. Even silence can begin to look like negligence in a system that equates responsiveness with responsibility. This is not a minor inconvenience. It changes the inner climate of academic work. The mind becomes crowded. The professor may still appear productive, perhaps more productive than before, but the deeper forms of thinking — the kind that require boredom, wandering, uncertainty, even temporary uselessness — become harder to protect (Kwiek & Roszka, 2024).

Figure 1. Digital Pressures Reshaping the Professoriate

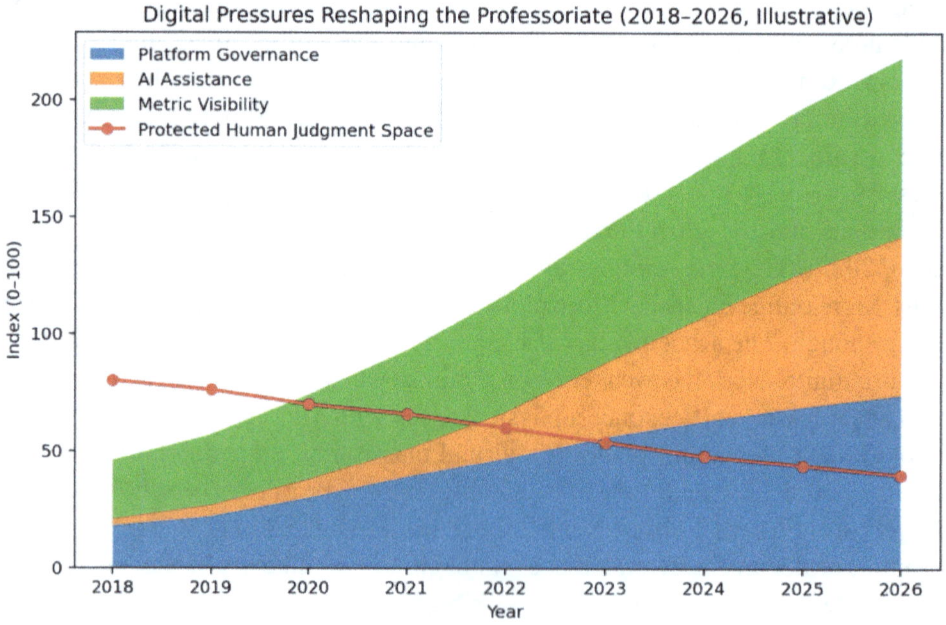

Artificial intelligence intensifies this condition because it does not merely digitize existing tasks; it begins to participate in cognitive and evaluative activities. AI can draft texts, summarize articles, generate lesson plans, produce quiz questions, classify student performance, recommend readings, evaluate patterns in research productivity, and assist institutional decision-making (Almaqtari et al, 2026). These capacities challenge the older distinction between human intellectual work and technical support. If a machine can generate a lecture outline, what is the professor's distinctive contribution? If an AI system can provide instant feedback to students, what becomes of pedagogical care? If algorithms can evaluate research trends, identify "high-impact" topics, or suggest promising collaborations, does scholarly curiosity become increasingly guided by predictive calculation?

The answer is not simple. It would be lazy to say that AI diminishes the professor by default. In some cases, it may do the opposite. It may release academics from dull routines, widen their imaginative range, and help them experiment with new forms of teaching and research. A professor using AI critically may become more capable, not less. The danger lies elsewhere: in the possibility that institutions will mistake AI-supported output for intellectual growth, or assume that because certain tasks can be automated, the human labor behind them no longer deserves recognition (Aliyu, 2026). The professor may not be replaced outright; a cruder future is possible, where professors remain in place but their work is progressively redefined around supervision of automated systems, compliance with data regimes, and continuous adaptation to tools they did not choose.

This is why the phrase "turning point" matters. The professoriate is not facing a simple technological upgrade. It is confronting a reorganization of authority. In the traditional academic model, authority rested, at least ideally, on expertise, peer judgment, disciplinary standards, and institutional autonomy. Under digital and AI-driven conditions, authority becomes more distributed and, at times, more opaque. Platform designers shape pedagogical possibilities. Data analysts influence institutional priorities. Ranking systems affect research strategies (Edu, 2025). Software vendors define the architecture of academic interaction. AI models trained on vast but uneven datasets begin to mediate language, visibility, and knowledge production. The professor still acts, but within a field increasingly structured by non-academic actors.

This shift has consequences for academic identity. Professors have often understood themselves through a combination of roles: teacher, researcher, mentor, critic, colleague, public intellectual, disciplinary contributor. Digitalization adds new roles that are less romantic but increasingly unavoidable: content manager, data producer, platform user, online moderator, digital assessor, compliance agent, personal brand curator, AI supervisor. These roles do not simply add tasks; they alter the symbolic meaning of academic labor. The professor is encouraged to become measurable, searchable, responsive, and marketable. Even reputation becomes platformed. A scholar's intellectual life is scattered across databases, profiles, rankings, repositories, and metrics that may travel farther than the work itself.

One might ask whether this is entirely new. Haven't professors always been shaped by institutional expectations? Haven't universities always had mechanisms of control? Yes, certainly. The past should not be cleaned up too neatly. Academic freedom has always existed alongside hierarchy, exclusion, patronage, bureaucracy, and competition. Many professors, especially those outside elite institutions or secure appointments, have never enjoyed the full dignity promised by the classical idea of the professoriate (Rhoades, 2024). Yet the present transformation has a distinctive quality because it combines managerial pressure with technological intimacy. The institution no longer only evaluates outputs at intervals; it can observe processes continuously. It no longer only asks what has been produced; it can monitor how, when, and through which channels academic work unfolds. That is a different kind of power.

Institutional change in the age of AI is also uneven. Wealthy universities may frame digital transformation as innovation, while poorer institutions may experience it as dependency (Mohamed Hashim et al, 2022). A well-funded professor may use AI to enhance research capacity; an overburdened lecturer may be required to use the same technology to handle impossible teaching loads. In elite settings, AI may support experimentation. In fragile systems, it may justify austerity. The same tool can mean enrichment in one context and extraction in another. This unevenness should trouble any serious discussion of the future professoriate. There is no single academic profession. There are professoriates — plural, stratified, geographically uneven, linguistically diverse, and differently exposed to technological disruption.

The Global South, in particular, faces a complicated bargain. Digitalization can help scholars bypass certain barriers of access, visibility, and collaboration. It can also deepen dependence on platforms, databases, and AI systems designed elsewhere, often in dominant languages and according to assumptions that do not fully reflect local realities. If AI becomes a major mediator of scholarly communication, whose knowledge will it amplify? Whose accents, archives, questions, and epistemologies will it misrecognize? A professor working in Arabic, Turkish, Swahili, or Bahasa Indonesia may encounter AI not only as a tool but as a linguistic and cultural filter. The danger is not only exclusion; it is translation into someone else's intellectual grammar.

Universities must therefore approach AI not as an administrative shortcut, but as a matter of academic governance. Decisions about AI adoption should not be left entirely to technology offices, procurement departments, or external vendors (Rainy & Chowdhury, 2022). Professors need a voice in shaping how these systems enter teaching, research, evaluation, hiring, promotion, and student support. Students, too, must be included, because they are not merely users of digital systems; they are subjects within them. Ethical governance should ask difficult questions before harm becomes normal. What data are collected? Who owns them? How are AI tools audited? Can professors challenge algorithmic judgments? Are automated systems being used to support academic freedom or quietly discipline it? What happens when efficiency conflicts with care?

The professoriate's turning point is, in this sense, moral as much as technological. The issue is not whether professors will use AI. They will, and many already do. The deeper issue is whether they will remain authors of academic change or become objects of it. A profession that surrenders its language to metrics may eventually struggle to defend its soul. A university that treats digitalization as destiny may forget that technology should serve educational purposes, not define them. There is still time to choose differently, though not unlimited time.

The future professor will need new competencies, certainly: digital literacy, AI awareness, data ethics, adaptive pedagogy, and the ability to work across human-machine environments (Al-Abdullatif, 2025). But the older virtues are not obsolete. Judgment. Integrity. Patience. Courage. Intellectual hospitality. The ability to sit with ambiguity. The willingness to tell students that not every answer should be instant, not every thought should be optimized, and not every form of knowledge can be compressed into a dashboard. These virtues may become more valuable precisely because they are less easily automated.

The professoriate is not ending. That claim is too theatrical. But it is being unsettled, and the settlement that follows is not predetermined. Digitalization and AI may narrow academic life into a regime of speed, surveillance, and measurable output (Dunleavy & Margetts, 2025). They may also help build a more open, responsive, and intellectually generous university. The difference will depend on institutional choices, professional courage, and the willingness to defend the human purposes of higher education in a time when the machine is becoming very good at imitating its surface. What must not happen is sleepwalking. The social contract of the professoriate is being revised line by line, sometimes in policy, sometimes in code, sometimes in the quiet normalization of new expectations. Professors, universities, and societies must read those lines carefully before signing their names to them.

FROM ACADEMIC AUTONOMY TO ALGORITHMIC ACCOUNTABILITY

Academic autonomy has never been a simple gift handed to professors by generous institutions. It has always been negotiated, defended, interrupted, and sometimes quietly withdrawn (Berlinerblau, 2025). Still, for much of the modern history of the university, the professoriate has been associated with a particular kind of freedom: the freedom to think beyond immediate usefulness, to pursue questions whose value may not be obvious to administrators or markets, to teach according to disciplinary judgment, and to participate in the slow making of knowledge without being entirely absorbed by external demands. This autonomy did not mean absence of responsibility. On the contrary, it carried a heavy burden. The professor was expected to be accountable to truth, to students, to the scholarly community, to ethical standards, and to society's longer intellectual needs. Yet the form of that accountability was largely professional and collegial. It relied on peer review, academic standards, disciplinary reputation, public trust, and the assumption that scholarly judgment cannot be fully governed from the outside.

That older arrangement is now being reworked by a new language: metrics, dashboards, analytics, indicators, performance scores, algorithmic recommendations, digital traces, predictive models. Accountability has become increasingly computational. It no longer waits patiently for annual reviews, departmental discussions, peer assessments, or the gradual recognition of intellectual contribution. It appears in real time. It accumulates in databases. It travels across platforms. It follows the professor through publication indexes, student evaluation systems, learning management platforms, research assessment exercises, grant-tracking tools, plagiarism detectors, workload allocation models, and institutional ranking mechanisms. The academic is not simply evaluated after the fact; academic behavior is continuously rendered into data, and that data begins to speak with a strange authority of its own.

The transition from academic autonomy to algorithmic accountability is not always dramatic. It rarely announces itself as a philosophical shift in the nature of the university. It arrives under respectable banners: transparency, quality assurance, efficiency, fairness, evidence-based management, student success, research excellence. These are not empty ideals. Universities should be transparent. Students deserve good teaching. Research quality matters. Public resources require responsible stewardship. The difficulty is that the instruments used to secure these values may slowly redefine them (Voorn, 2023). Once academic work is reorganized around what can be measured, the immeasurable becomes vulnerable. It does not disappear immediately; it simply becomes harder to defend.

Figure 2. Waterfall: From Academic Autonomy to Algorithmic Accountability

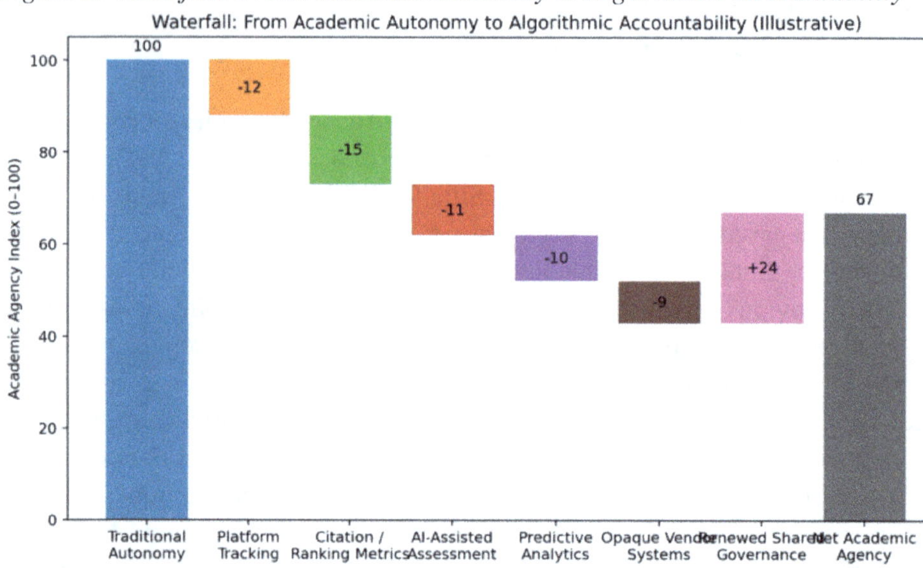

A professor may spend months helping a struggling doctoral student find intellectual confidence. Where does that appear? A scholar may reject a fashionable research trend because it seems shallow, even though pursuing it would increase publication output. How is that counted? A teacher may redesign a course to provoke deeper thinking rather than higher satisfaction scores, knowing that students sometimes resist difficulty before they appreciate it. What metric captures that kind of pedagogical courage? A senior academic may protect a junior colleague from institutional harm, mediate conflict, or build a culture of intellectual generosity in a department exhausted by competition. These forms of labor hold universities together, but they often leave faint digital footprints. Algorithmic systems are not naturally hostile to such work, but they are often poorly equipped to perceive it.

The danger, then, is not only surveillance. It is misrecognition. Algorithmic accountability may look at the professor and see only the measurable remainder of a much larger vocation (Cooper et al, 2022). It may mistake frequency for commitment, speed for competence, visibility for influence, and volume for intellectual seriousness. A professor who publishes constantly in indexed outlets may appear more valuable than one who writes slowly but reshapes a field. A lecturer who answers messages at midnight may appear more responsive than one who establishes healthy boundaries and teaches students responsibility. A course with high online engagement may appear more successful than a course that unsettles students into genuine reflection. Numbers do not lie in a simple sense. But they can tell the wrong truth.

Academic autonomy becomes fragile when institutional trust is replaced by permanent verification (Moodley, 2025). The professor is increasingly asked to prove, document, upload, report, justify, and evidence nearly every dimension of work. Some documentation is necessary, of course. The university cannot function through vague declarations of good intention. Yet when documentation expands beyond reason, it creates a culture in which doing the work and proving the work become two competing occupations. The academic writes reports about teaching instead of improving teaching. The researcher feeds databases instead of reading deeply. The supervisor records mentoring activity instead of having time to mentor well. Slowly, a peculiar inversion occurs: evidence of work becomes almost as important as the work itself.

Artificial intelligence strengthens this inversion by making measurement more sophisticated and less visible. Earlier forms of academic accountability were often crude: publication counts, student surveys, promotion committees, grant totals. AI-enabled systems promise richer analysis. They can detect patterns, compare performance, predict outcomes, recommend interventions, and identify risk (Diameh et al, 2025). In principle, this could support better institutional decisions. A university might use analytics to identify unreasonable workloads, discover hidden inequalities, support students before they fail, or recognize undervalued forms of teaching labor. There is nothing inherently wrong with using data to see what human perception might miss. The problem begins when such systems are treated not as partial instruments but as neutral arbiters.

Algorithms are built from choices. Choices about data, categories, weightings, proxies, thresholds, and desired outcomes. These choices are rarely innocent. If an institution defines good teaching through student satisfaction, platform engagement, completion rates, and assessment turnaround time, then AI systems trained on these assumptions will reproduce that definition with impressive confidence. If research excellence is tied to citation performance, journal ranking, grant income, and international visibility, then algorithmic tools will privilege scholars already advantaged by language, geography, discipline, funding, and network position. The algorithm may appear objective because it does not frown, flatter, or gossip. But objectivity is not achieved simply by removing the human face from judgment. Sometimes bias becomes harder to challenge precisely because it has been dressed in technical clothing.

This has significant implications for professorial appointments and advancement. Hiring, promotion, tenure, contract renewal, and performance review are increasingly influenced by quantified profiles. Citation scores, h-indexes, altmetrics, teaching ratings, research impact data, grant histories, and digital visibility can become shorthand for academic worth (Taherdoost, 2025). Committees may still deliberate, but their deliberation begins under the shadow of numbers that seem difficult to ignore. A candidate with strong metrics enters the room already glowing. Another with slower, less measurable forms of contribution enters already diminished. The human evaluators may insist they are using judgment, and perhaps they are. Yet metrics frame the imagination. They tell evaluators where to look first and what to doubt.

This framing effect can reshape academic behavior long before formal evaluation occurs. Professors learn to anticipate the algorithmic gaze. They choose research topics with citation potential. They divide studies into publishable fragments. They design courses with satisfaction surveys in mind. They cultivate online profiles, track their visibility, optimize keywords, and adjust intellectual risk according to measurable reward. This does not mean academics become cynical. Many remain deeply committed to knowledge and students. But systems teach habits. When survival depends on indicators, even principled scholars begin to negotiate with them. A young academic on a temporary contract may not have the luxury of ignoring metrics. A professor in a peripheral institution may need international visibility to be taken seriously (Jiang et al, 2025). A scholar writing in a language outside the dominant academic marketplace may feel compelled to reshape thought for discoverability. Autonomy is not destroyed by a single command; it is narrowed by incentives that become hard to refuse.

The moral complexity here should not be underestimated. Academic autonomy has sometimes been misused. It has protected laziness, elitism, unaccountable teaching, exclusionary networks, and resistance to necessary reform. Some professors invoke freedom when what they really seek is insulation from criticism. Students have suffered under poor supervision, outdated pedagogy, and arrogant forms of authority. Institutions have a legitimate responsibility to ask whether academics are fulfilling their duties. Accountability, in this sense, is not the enemy of autonomy. It is part of its ethical condition. A professor who serves no one but personal preference cannot claim the dignity of academic freedom without emptying it of meaning.

The difficulty is to distinguish accountability that strengthens academic responsibility from accountability that reduces academic life to managed performance. The first is dialogic. It asks for reasons, context, evidence, and reflection. It recognizes the diversity of disciplines, the unpredictability of research, the complexity of teaching, and the uneven conditions under which professors work. The second is extractive. It collects data, ranks bodies, standardizes judgment, and rewards compliance with visible indicators. The first treats professors as ethical agents. The second treats them as units of output. The difference may sound abstract, but it is felt in daily life: in whether a professor is trusted to exercise judgment, or merely instructed to satisfy a dashboard.

Algorithmic accountability also changes the relationship between professors and students (Cooper et al, 2022). Digital platforms can record attendance, participation, submission times, feedback cycles, assessment patterns, and even forms of engagement that once belonged to the private rhythm of learning. AI tools may flag students as at risk, classify their writing as suspicious, recommend interventions, or evaluate their emotional and cognitive engagement. Professors may be asked to act on these signals. Sometimes this helps. A student who is quietly disappearing from a course may be noticed sooner. But there is also a danger that pedagogical relationships become mediated by suspicion and prediction. The student is no longer only encountered as a person in formation, but as a profile of probabilities. The professor, too, becomes accountable for responding to those probabilities correctly.

This predictive environment can create a subtle redistribution of responsibility. If an AI system identifies a risk and the professor does not intervene, is the professor negligent? If the system fails to identify a student in difficulty, who is responsible? If automated feedback is available, must the professor provide more, faster, and in greater detail than before? If AI can generate personalized learning pathways, does human teaching become judged against machine scalability? These questions show how algorithmic accountability can expand obligations without clarifying authority. Professors may be held responsible for systems they did not design, data they cannot fully inspect, and predictions they may not trust.

The issue becomes even sharper when institutions use digital systems to monitor professors themselves. Teaching analytics, email responsiveness, online course activity, grading speed, student feedback sentiment, research productivity, collaboration networks, and public engagement can all be transformed into performance signals. Not all monitoring is malicious. Some of it may be intended to support quality or identify areas for development. Yet the line between support and surveillance is thin, and it is often crossed without ceremony. Support asks, "What do you need to do this work well?" Surveillance asks, "Why are you not matching the expected pattern?" One invites conversation. The other produces anxiety.

Anxiety is becoming an underdiscussed feature of the digital university (Pesántez-Avilés et al, 2024). Professors are expected to appear competent in systems that constantly change, to adapt to tools introduced with minimal consultation, to satisfy students whose expectations have been shaped by instant digital services, and to remain productive in research environments saturated with competitive measurement. AI adds a fresh unease: the fear of being outpaced, replaced, exposed, or rendered obsolete. Some of this fear is exaggerated, but not all of it. The real threat may not be replacement by machines but degradation of professional authority through machine-mediated control. The professor remains employed, perhaps, but with less discretion, less privacy, less time, and less confidence that scholarly judgment will prevail over administrative analytics.

A humane university would not respond to this concern by rejecting data altogether. That would be too easy, and frankly, not very convincing. Data can reveal inequities that tradition hides. It can show patterns of student exclusion, workload imbalance, publication bias, and institutional neglect. It can help universities act more responsibly. But data must be placed inside a wider culture of interpretation. Numbers should provoke questions, not close them. Algorithms should support judgment, not impersonate it. Dashboards should be beginnings of dialogue, not instruments of verdict. The professoriate does not need a return to unexamined autonomy; it needs a richer, more democratic form of accountability, one that respects professional judgment while refusing complacency.

Such accountability would require transparency in algorithmic systems used for academic evaluation. Professors should know what data are collected, how they are interpreted, who has access, and how decisions are influenced (Ghamrawi et al, 2024). They should have the right to challenge algorithmic assessments, especially when those assessments affect employment, promotion, workload, or reputation. Institutions should avoid using single metrics as proxies for complex academic value. They should recognize disciplinary difference: the rhythm of philosophy is not the rhythm of biomedical science; the labor of studio teaching cannot be measured like the labor of large-scale online instruction; community-engaged scholarship may not produce immediate citation rewards but may carry profound public meaning. Any system that ignores these differences will punish intellectual diversity while claiming administrative fairness.

The professoriate itself must also participate more actively in shaping the terms of accountability. It is not enough to complain after systems are installed. Academic staff need to be involved in procurement decisions, AI governance committees, ethics reviews, workload model design, promotion criteria, and digital policy formation. This involvement should not be symbolic. A token professor on a technology committee cannot protect academic values if decisions have already been made elsewhere. The social contract of the professoriate in the AI age requires shared governance with actual teeth: the authority to question, delay, revise, and reject systems that undermine educational integrity.

At the heart of this debate lies a deceptively simple question: what kind of accountability is worthy of a university? If accountability means making professors legible to systems of control, then academic autonomy will continue to shrink beneath the weight of technical compliance. If accountability means sustaining trust through thoughtful evidence, peer judgment, ethical responsibility, and public purpose, then autonomy can be renewed rather than abandoned. The professoriate should not be free from answerability. No profession that shapes minds and knowledge deserves that kind of exemption. But professors must remain answerable in ways appropriate to the nature of their work.

Academic work is not a set of mechanical outputs. It is interpretive, relational, uncertain, and often slow (Turcotte & Holmes, 2024). It involves failure, revision, disagreement, and the courage to resist premature clarity. Algorithmic systems, by contrast, tend to prefer patterns, predictions, and comparability. The challenge is not to choose one world against the other, but to prevent the second from colonizing the first. A university that cannot distinguish between measurable performance and intellectual responsibility may become efficient while losing its depth. It may produce reports, rankings, and optimized workflows, yet forget why professors were granted autonomy in the first place.

Table 1. Digital and AI Mechanisms Reshaping the Professoriate

AI / Digital Mechanism	How It Reshapes Academic Work	Potential Benefit	Social-Contract Risk
Learning Management Analytics	Makes teaching activity visible through clicks, submissions, engagement traces, and feedback cycles	Can identify students needing support and improve course design	May turn teaching into continuous surveillance and reduce trust
Citation and Impact Metrics	Translates scholarly influence into comparable indicators and dashboards	Can reveal visibility, reach, and collaboration patterns	May privilege volume, English-language dominance, and easily measured outputs
Generative AI Assistants	Support drafting, summarizing, translation, feedback, and content preparation	Can reduce repetitive labor and widen access to academic communication	May blur authorship, originality, and recognition of intellectual labor
Predictive Student Analytics	Classifies students by risk level and recommends interventions	Can support earlier and more targeted student assistance	May create anticipatory judgment and shift responsibility onto professors

continued on following page

Table 1. Continued

AI / Digital Mechanism	How It Reshapes Academic Work	Potential Benefit	Social-Contract Risk
Automated Assessment Tools	Score, classify, or provide feedback on student work	Can speed up formative feedback in large classes	May weaken pedagogical care and over-standardize judgment
Workload Dashboards	Represent academic labor through visible tasks, time, outputs, and responsiveness	Can expose workload inequality if designed fairly	May normalize permanent verification and invisible digital labor
Vendor Platform Ecosystems	Embed teaching, assessment, communication, and analytics in external infrastructures	Can improve interoperability and service delivery	May transfer academic governance to non-academic actors

The movement from academic autonomy to algorithmic accountability is therefore one of the defining tensions of the AI-mediated university. It is not wholly negative, nor is it comfortably benign. It is a contested passage. Along the way, institutions will decide whether professors are trusted professionals or monitored operators, whether data serve judgment or replace it, whether accountability deepens academic responsibility or merely disciplines academic behavior. These decisions will shape not only the future of professorial work, but the moral architecture of higher education itself. The university must be careful here. Very careful. Once autonomy is traded for the smooth convenience of algorithmic control, it may not be easily recovered.

AI, WORKLOAD, AND THE RECONFIGURATION OF ACADEMIC LABOR

The arrival of artificial intelligence in higher education is often narrated through the language of relief. AI will save time. AI will reduce repetitive tasks. AI will help professors grade faster, prepare materials more efficiently, summarize articles, manage communication, personalize instruction, and perhaps even recover some of the intellectual space that has been steadily eaten away by bureaucracy (Shah, 2023). There is something tempting in this promise, especially for academics whose working lives have become increasingly crowded, fragmented, and strangely breathless. The modern professor is rarely only a teacher or researcher. The role has stretched into a many-armed creature: lecturer, supervisor, grant writer, curriculum designer, reviewer, committee member, data reporter, pastoral adviser, public communicator, compliance officer, platform manager, and, on difficult days, emotional shock absorber for an institution that has forgotten how much human strain it quietly exports to its staff.

So, when AI appears and says, in effect, "Let me carry some of this," the offer is not trivial. It may even feel merciful.

Yet the question of workload in the age of AI is more complicated than the cheerful rhetoric of efficiency admits. Technologies that promise to reduce labor often end up reorganizing it. They remove certain tasks, yes, but they also create new ones. They accelerate some processes while raising expectations elsewhere. They simplify particular operations while adding fresh layers of oversight, training, troubleshooting, ethical negotiation, and institutional reporting. Academic labor does not merely shrink under AI; it is redistributed, reclassified, intensified, and sometimes made less visible. This is the paradox at the heart of the AI-mediated university: the tools that seem designed to save academic time may also participate in the further colonization of that time.

The professoriate has already been living through a long workload crisis. Before AI entered the conversation with its polished confidence, academic work had been expanding under the combined pressure of mass higher education, competitive research cultures, audit regimes, international rankings, student satisfaction frameworks, precarious employment, and digital availability (Nelson, 2024). More students, more publications, more grant applications, more administrative forms, more emails, more online systems, more evidence of impact, more proof of quality, more responsiveness to institutional priorities that change faster than any curriculum can reasonably absorb. The university has developed a talent for adding tasks without removing old ones. Every reform arrives with a new template. Every innovation requires a report. Every strategy produces a committee. Every committee produces minutes, action plans, indicators, follow-up meetings, and, naturally, another spreadsheet.

AI enters this already crowded landscape. It does not arrive in an empty room. It arrives in a room where people are tired.

This matters because the effects of AI on academic workload depend heavily on the institutional conditions into which it is inserted. In a humane environment, AI could genuinely reduce unnecessary burden. It could help professors draft routine correspondence, generate first versions of administrative documents, organize literature, support inclusive teaching materials, provide preliminary feedback, translate basic texts, and identify students who need timely assistance. Used carefully, it might clear away some of the clerical fog that surrounds academic life. It might allow professors to return, however partially, to the more meaningful dimensions of their work: thinking with students, reading slowly, designing better questions, mentoring with attention, and conducting research that does not have to be squeezed between two urgent emails and a malfunctioning institutional portal.

But institutions do not always use efficiency to create breathing space. Often, they use it to justify expansion. If AI can help a professor grade faster, perhaps class sizes can grow. If AI can generate feedback, perhaps students can expect more frequent responses. If AI can assist with research summaries, perhaps publication expectations can rise. If AI can draft reports, perhaps reporting cycles can become more frequent. If AI can make online teaching materials easier to produce, perhaps every course must now include richer digital content, multimedia resources, automated quizzes, analytics-based interventions, weekly updates, and individualized learning pathways (Meron & Araci, 2023). The time supposedly saved is quietly reabsorbed by the institution. Nothing is gained except speed.

This pattern is not new. Digitalization has already taught academics that convenience can become compulsion. Email was supposed to make communication easier; it also made academics permanently reachable. Learning management systems were supposed to organize teaching; they also made teaching continuously auditable. Online meetings were supposed to reduce travel; they also multiplied meetings because the friction of gathering people disappeared. Digital submission systems were supposed to streamline assessment; they also made feedback cycles more visible, comparable, and administratively monitorable. In each case, the tool solved a problem and produced another one, often less dramatic but more invasive. AI may follow the same path unless universities make deliberate choices about limits.

The reconfiguration of academic labor is especially visible in teaching. AI can assist in lesson planning, question generation, rubric design, translation, accessibility support, and student feedback. These capacities are valuable, particularly for academics teaching large classes or working across languages and diverse student needs. Still, teaching is not simply content preparation plus assessment. It is an interpretive and relational practice. A professor reads a room, senses hesitation, notices when silence means confusion rather than reflection, adjusts examples, responds to unexpected questions, and carries the ethical weight of judging student work with fairness and care. AI can support parts of this process, but it can also tempt institutions to disassemble teaching into manageable fragments: content delivery, engagement tracking, automated feedback, performance analytics, intervention alerts. Once fragmented, teaching becomes easier to standardize and redistribute.

Figure 3. AI Tools: Workload Relief vs Autonomy Risk

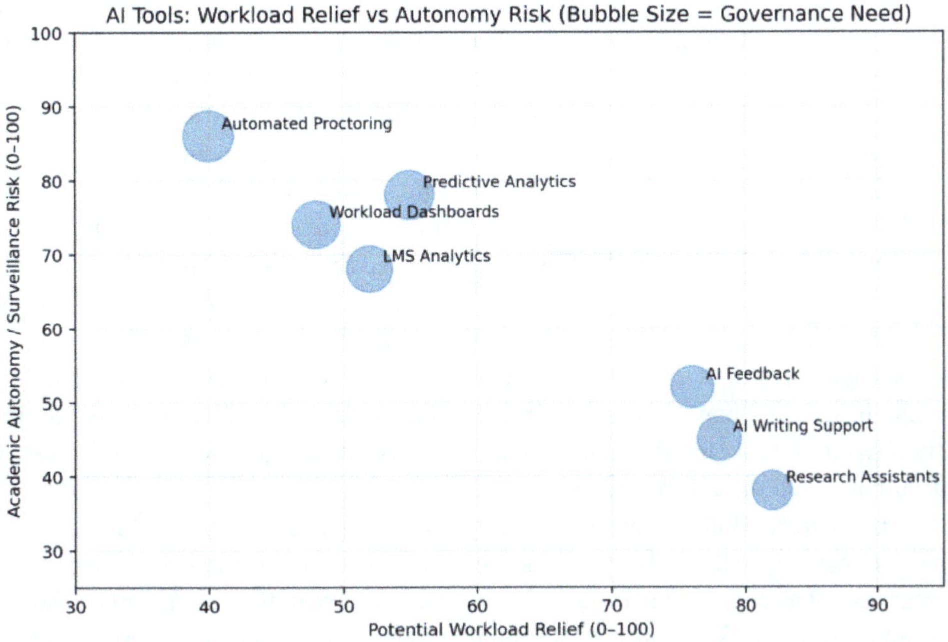

The professor may then become less a teacher in the older sense and more a coordinator of learning systems. This is not automatically degrading. Some coordination is pedagogically intelligent. Yet when taken too far, it can hollow out academic labor. The professor becomes the person who supervises platforms, checks AI-generated materials, responds to alerts, validates automated feedback, and ensures compliance with digital quality standards (Yarram & Yallavula, 2022). The visible work appears efficient; the invisible work expands. Someone must check the accuracy of AI-generated content. Someone must correct bias. Someone must explain to students when machine feedback is wrong or shallow. Someone must redesign assessments because students also use AI. Someone must update academic integrity policies, attend training sessions, reassure anxious colleagues, and negotiate the strange new boundary between acceptable assistance and dishonest outsourcing. That someone is often the professor.

AI also changes research labor in similarly ambivalent ways. It can accelerate literature mapping, detect patterns in large datasets, support coding, generate summaries, assist with language refinement, and expand the capacity of researchers who lack large teams. For scholars working outside dominant English-speaking contexts, AI may offer linguistic support that makes publication more accessible (Gualdrón et al, 2025). This should not be dismissed. There is a democratic possibility here, though it remains fragile and uneven. Yet research acceleration has its own dangers. When AI makes certain stages of research faster, the scholarly system may come to expect faster output. The slow craft of inquiry may be treated as inefficiency. Reading may become scanning. Interpretation may become extraction. Writing may become production. The old academic vice of "publish or perish" could mutate into something even more restless: generate, optimize, circulate, repeat.

This does not mean AI destroys scholarship. It means scholarship must defend its slower organs. A literature review is not only a summary of existing texts; it is an apprenticeship in judgment. Writing is not only the final packaging of thought; it is one of the ways thought discovers itself. Data analysis is not only pattern detection; it requires theoretical sensitivity, doubt, contextual intelligence, and the ability to know when a result is elegant but empty. If AI takes over the mechanical parts of research, scholars may have more time for conceptual work. That would be a gift. But if AI-driven acceleration trains institutions to value only the volume and velocity of outputs, then the gift becomes a leash.

Administrative labor may be the area where AI appears most immediately attractive (Pennathur et al, 2024). Few academics are romantically attached to repetitive paperwork. The endless forms, reports, templates, accreditation documents, meeting summaries, progress updates, ethics applications, and compliance narratives drain energy from the intellectual core of the profession. AI can help draft, summarize, format, and organize such material. In principle, this could reduce a significant burden. But again, the institutional appetite for documentation is rarely satisfied by easier production. When reports become easier to generate, more reports may be requested. When data become easier to analyze, more indicators may be demanded. When administrative language becomes easier to produce, bureaucratic expectations may become more elaborate, not less. AI may not end academic bureaucracy; it may make bureaucracy smoother, faster, and more difficult to contest because its burdens are hidden behind automation.

There is also the matter of emotional labor, a dimension of academic workload that is persistently underestimated. Professors do not only transfer knowledge. They absorb uncertainty. They guide students through failure, confusion, ambition, family pressure, financial hardship, mental fatigue, and sometimes despair. They support colleagues, manage conflict, soothe institutional anxieties, and carry the quiet ache of caring about people within systems that often reward measurable outputs more than human presence. AI may assist with student support, but it cannot take responsibility for another person's becoming. It cannot replace the trust built when a student feels seen by a teacher who remembers their struggle, understands their hesitation, and knows when to push and when to pause. If universities imagine AI as a substitute for this form of labor, they misunderstand both teaching and care.

At the same time, professors should not be forced into a heroic model of endless availability simply because human care matters. That is another trap. The language of vocation has too often been used to justify exploitation. Because professors care, they answer late messages. Because they care, they take on extra supervision. Because they care, they rewrite feedback, support distressed students, review manuscripts without recognition, mentor junior colleagues, attend unpaid events, and accept institutional overload as moral duty. AI may help reduce some pressures, but only if universities also confront the deeper culture that treats academic devotion as an infinite resource. A professor is not a machine powered by purpose. Fatigue is real. Burnout is not a weakness of character. It is often a rational response to irrational expectations.

The unequal distribution of AI's workload effects deserves particular attention. Senior academics may use AI as a discretionary tool, choosing when and how it supports their work (Bosman et al, 2025). Early-career scholars, adjunct faculty, and precariously employed lecturers may experience AI differently: as another expectation, another competency to prove, another system to master, another source of comparison. Those with secure positions may be praised for thoughtful resistance to AI excess; those on short contracts may not have the freedom to resist. They may be required to adopt tools, produce more materials, manage larger classes, or demonstrate digital innovation to remain employable. The same technology that enhances autonomy for one group may intensify dependency for another.

Disciplinary differences matter too. AI may be easily integrated into some fields and more awkwardly into others. A professor in computer science, business analytics, or biomedical research may encounter AI as an extension of existing methods, while a professor in philosophy, literature, history, or the arts may face deeper questions about authorship, interpretation, and originality. Studio-based teaching, clinical education, laboratory supervision, fieldwork, and community-engaged scholarship all involve embodied, situated, and relational forms of labor that do not translate neatly into automated workflows. A uniform institutional AI policy may therefore produce unfairness by treating unlike forms of academic work as though they were equivalent.

Global inequality complicates the picture further. In well-resourced universities, AI tools may come with training, technical support, ethical guidelines, data protection, and integration into broader academic development. In underfunded institutions, professors may be expected to adopt free or poorly supported tools on their own, often without clarity about privacy, reliability, or intellectual property. Scholars in less dominant languages may rely on AI systems that handle their linguistic contexts unevenly (Dovchin, 2024). Researchers with limited access to premium databases may use AI as a bridge, but also risk depending on tools whose outputs reflect the biases of more powerful knowledge systems. Once again, AI does not simply reduce workload; it redistributes advantage.

The reconfiguration of academic labor also touches the meaning of expertise. If AI can produce a syllabus, generate a lecture, summarize a book, draft an article, and respond to student questions, then the professor's expertise may appear less visible to outsiders. This is dangerous because AI often imitates the surface of expertise without possessing its depth. It can sound confident while missing context, nuance, and responsibility. The professor's labor may shift toward verification: checking, correcting, contextualizing, and ethically framing machine outputs. Verification is labor. It requires expertise, not less of it. Yet institutions may fail to recognize this because checking looks less productive than creating. The professor who carefully audits AI-generated materials may appear slower than the one who simply distributes them. The careful academic becomes, perversely, the inefficient academic.

This is where workload and academic integrity intersect. AI has made it easier for students to produce polished work without fully engaging in the learning process. Professors must now redesign assessments, clarify acceptable use, detect misuse, teach ethical AI literacy, and avoid creating cultures of suspicion that damage trust (Shawkey, 2026). This is heavy work. It is not merely technical; it is pedagogical and moral. A poorly designed response to AI cheating can turn classrooms into policing environments. A naïve response can make assessment meaningless. Professors are caught between vigilance and generosity, between protecting standards and recognizing that AI is now part of the intellectual environment students inhabit. That balancing act takes time, thought, and emotional steadiness.

Universities often respond to such complexity by offering training. Training is useful, but training can also become a ritual substitute for structural change. A workshop on AI tools does not solve workload overload. A webinar on prompt engineering does not fix casualized labor. A policy document on responsible AI does not create time for professors to redesign courses properly. Professional development becomes meaningful only when paired with workload recognition, institutional support, and realistic expectations. Otherwise, it becomes one more task added to the pile, decorated with the vocabulary of empowerment.

What, then, would a more humane approach look like? It would begin by refusing to treat AI as a magical solvent for academic overload. Universities would ask not only what AI can do, but which tasks should exist in the first place (Spivakovsky et al, 2023). Some administrative work should not be automated; it should be abolished. Some reporting requirements should not be made easier; they should be questioned. Some teaching expectations should not be scaled through AI; they should be matched with proper staffing. Some research pressures should not be accelerated; they should be moderated. AI governance must therefore be linked to workload governance. Otherwise, technology will polish the machinery of overwork rather than challenge it.

A responsible institution would also make AI-related labor visible. Time spent learning tools, checking outputs, redesigning assessments, supporting students in AI-rich environments, protecting data privacy, and participating in ethical governance should be recognized in workload models. It is not extra. It is now part of academic labor. The old categories of teaching, research, and service may no longer be sufficient unless they are revised to include digital and AI-mediated responsibilities. Without such recognition, professors will carry an expanding shadow workload: necessary, time-consuming, intellectually demanding, and institutionally invisible.

The professoriate, for its part, must cultivate a more discriminating relationship with AI. Not rejection. Not surrender. Something more adult than both. Professors need to learn where AI can genuinely help, where it distorts, where it saves time, where it creates hidden work, and where it threatens the educational relationship. They must also resist the shame of slowness. In an AI-saturated environment, slowness may become a scholarly virtue when it protects thought from becoming mere output. The professor who takes time to read carefully, question assumptions, and respond humanely is not obsolete. That professor may be preserving the university's endangered center.

The reconfiguration of academic labor is still unfolding. Its final shape has not been determined. AI may become a tool that helps restore proportion to academic life, removing drudgery and supporting better teaching and research (Wilstic, 2025). It may also become an engine of intensification, making professors faster, more measurable, more available, and more exhausted. The difference will not lie in the technology alone. It will lie in institutional ethics, labor policy, shared governance, and the courage to say that not every saved minute should be converted into another obligation.

Academic work has always contained a certain excess, a portion that refuses neat accounting: the conversation after class, the half-formed idea in the margin, the patient reading of a student's clumsy but sincere draft, the years spent chasing a question that may not yield quick reward. AI can assist the profession, but it must not be allowed to erase this excess in the name of efficiency. The professoriate does not need to become anti-technological to defend itself. It needs to insist that technology should make academic labor more thoughtful, not merely more productive; more humane, not simply more scalable; more intellectually alive, not just easier to monitor. That insistence may sound modest. In the present climate, it is almost radical.

TOWARD A RENEWED SOCIAL CONTRACT FOR THE ACADEMIC PROFESSION

A renewed social contract for the academic profession cannot begin with technology. That may sound odd in a chapter concerned with digitalization and artificial intelligence, but it is precisely the point. If universities begin with the tool, they will almost certainly end with the tool's logic: efficiency, scale, speed, prediction, optimization, and measurable output. These are not worthless aims. A university that refuses efficiency altogether becomes wasteful; a university that ignores data becomes blind in certain ways; a university that treats AI as a passing distraction risks leaving both professors and students unprepared for the world already forming around them (Borgman & Brand, 2022). Still, the academic profession cannot be rebuilt around technical possibility alone. The first question should not be, "What can AI do for universities?" It should be: what kind of university is worth protecting, and what kind of professoriate can sustain it?

The old social contract of the professoriate rested, at least in principle, on a mutual promise. Society and institutions granted professors a measure of autonomy because their work served purposes that could not be reduced to immediate utility. Professors were expected to teach with seriousness, conduct research with integrity, preserve disciplinary knowledge, challenge intellectual complacency, mentor younger minds, and contribute to public understanding. In return, they required academic freedom, institutional trust, reasonable security, and enough time to think beyond the next report, meeting, or measurable target. This contract was never fully honored. It excluded many, privileged some, and often spoke the language of freedom while tolerating hierarchy, precarity, and invisible labor. Yet its central insight remains valuable: knowledge work requires conditions of trust.

The AI-mediated university tests this insight. It asks whether professors can remain trusted intellectual agents in institutions increasingly organized around platforms, dashboards, analytics, automated systems, and externally visible indicators. It asks whether academic freedom can survive in an environment where so much work is documented, tracked, compared, and translated into evidence. It asks whether professorial judgment will be strengthened by AI or quietly displaced by it. These are not abstract anxieties. They are already present in the everyday life of academic staff: in automated plagiarism systems, student evaluation dashboards, citation metrics, research performance tools, online teaching records, institutional ranking pressures, and the creeping expectation that every activity must leave a digital trace.

A renewed social contract must therefore insist on a simple but easily forgotten principle: AI should serve academic judgment, not replace it. This does not mean romanticizing professors as if human judgment were always wise, fair, or ethically sound. Professors can be biased. Departments can be narrow. Peer review can be conservative. Academic cultures can protect mediocrity as easily as excellence (Berg & Seeber, 2025). The human element is not automatically virtuous. Yet replacing imperfect judgment with opaque systems does not solve the problem; it may merely hide it behind technical elegance. Algorithms may rank, classify, detect, recommend, and predict, but they do not carry responsibility in the human sense. They do not understand the moral consequences of their classifications. They do not know what it feels like to misjudge a student, to reject a promising scholar, to flatten a field's complexity into a performance score, or to confuse linguistic polish with intellectual depth.

For this reason, the new contract must be built around shared governance of technology. Professors cannot be treated as end-users of systems chosen elsewhere. They must participate in decisions about AI adoption, data collection, digital assessment, academic integrity, workload allocation, hiring, promotion, and student analytics. This participation must be substantive, not decorative. Too often, institutional consultation happens after the architecture has already been built. A committee is formed, a policy is circulated, a few concerns are noted, and the system proceeds almost unchanged. That is not governance; it is choreography. If AI is going to reshape teaching, research, evaluation, and academic identity, then professors must have the authority to question, redesign, delay, or reject systems that undermine the deeper purposes of higher education.

The renewed contract must also confront workload honestly. Universities often speak of AI as a tool for reducing burden, but the history of digitalization teaches a more sobering lesson (George, 2024). Tools that save time often create new obligations. Email made communication easier and also made academics perpetually reachable. Learning platforms organized courses and also made teaching more continuously visible. Online meetings reduced travel and then multiplied meetings. AI may draft faster, summarize faster, classify faster, and provide feedback faster, but unless institutions deliberately protect the time supposedly saved, that time will be consumed by higher expectations. More students. More feedback. More reports. More outputs. More responsiveness. More innovation. More proof.

Here, the contract must be blunt: efficiency gains should not automatically become workload expansion. If AI reduces administrative effort, professors should regain time for mentoring, research, reading, course design, intellectual experimentation, and rest. Rest should not be treated as an embarrassment in academic life. It is part of thought's ecology. Exhausted professors may still produce, but production is not the same as insight. A university that burns through its scholars while praising innovation has misunderstood its own mission. The academic profession cannot be renewed if it remains built on permanent overextension.

A fair social contract must also make invisible labor visible. Much professorial work is not easily captured by metrics: mentoring students, supporting distressed colleagues, maintaining academic standards, reviewing manuscripts, building departmental culture, advising early-career researchers, translating institutional demands into workable practices, and performing the quiet emotional labor that keeps educational communities from becoming cold machines. AI may alter some of this labor, but it will not abolish it. In fact, it may intensify it. Professors will need to teach students how to use AI ethically, redesign assessments, interpret algorithmic outputs, challenge machine errors, protect academic integrity, and help learners distinguish generated fluency from genuine understanding. This is real work. It takes time. It requires expertise. It should be recognized in workload models, promotion criteria, and institutional planning.

The question of academic freedom must also be revisited with new seriousness (Reichman, 2025). In the past, academic freedom was often imagined primarily as protection from political interference, censorship, institutional retaliation, or disciplinary orthodoxy. These threats remain real. Yet the digital university introduces softer forms of constraint. A professor may not be openly silenced, yet their work may be nudged, ranked, monitored, incentivized, or made invisible by systems that privilege certain outputs over others. Research topics may be chosen because they are more fundable, more citable, more aligned with institutional priorities, or more likely to perform well in algorithmic environments. Teaching may be adjusted to protect student satisfaction scores. Public engagement may be shaped by platform visibility. Freedom is not only violated when someone forbids speech. It can also be eroded when the conditions of professional survival quietly punish intellectual risk.

A renewed contract should protect the right to scholarly slowness. This may sound almost quaint, but it is becoming crucial. AI accelerates nearly everything: writing, searching, summarizing, designing, comparing, responding. Acceleration has benefits, but the university cannot become a place where every form of thought is expected to match machine tempo. Some ideas need years. Some arguments need to fail before they mature. Some books must be read without an extractive purpose. Some conversations with students cannot be rushed into outcomes. The professoriate must defend forms of intellectual labor that do not look efficient at first glance. Not every delay is laziness. Sometimes delay is depth taking its own inconvenient shape.

The renewed social contract must also be global in imagination. AI and digitalization do not affect all professors equally. In wealthy universities, AI may appear as an opportunity for experimentation, supported by training, infrastructure, legal guidance, and technical staff (McGrath et al, 2023). In under-resourced institutions, it may arrive as pressure without support. Professors may be expected to use tools they did not choose, in languages poorly served by dominant models, under policies copied from contexts that do not resemble their own. Scholars working outside English, outside elite databases, or outside powerful research networks may find that AI amplifies existing inequalities while pretending to democratize knowledge. A genuine contract cannot be written only for the comfortable professor in the well-funded institution. It must include the precarious lecturer, the early-career scholar, the adjunct teacher, the researcher in a fragile system, the academic working in a minoritized language, and the professor whose institutional reality is defined more by scarcity than abundance.

This global dimension also demands epistemic humility. AI systems are trained on uneven knowledge worlds. They absorb dominant languages, dominant archives, dominant styles of reasoning, and dominant assumptions about what counts as legitimate knowledge. If universities allow these systems to shape scholarship uncritically, they may reinforce an already narrow map of intellectual authority. Professors must be empowered to challenge not only the outputs of AI, but the knowledge hierarchies embedded in its design. The future university should not become a place where all thought is translated into the grammar of a few powerful platforms. Academic diversity is not a decorative slogan. It is the condition under which knowledge remains alive.

Students occupy a central place in this renewed contract. The professoriate cannot defend its own autonomy while ignoring students' changing realities. Students are entering universities in a world saturated with AI-generated content, algorithmic recommendations, automated communication, and digital distraction. They need more than access to tools. They need intellectual formation. They need to learn how to question outputs, trace assumptions, recognize bias, use AI without surrendering agency, and understand why original thinking still matters when machines can produce convincing text in seconds. The professor's role becomes more important here, not less. In an age of abundant generation, the professor must teach discernment. In an age of instant answers, the professor must protect the value of better questions.

Yet professors cannot carry this responsibility alone. Institutions must avoid turning every AI-related challenge into an individual burden placed on already overloaded staff (Ashfaq, 2025). Academic integrity cannot be preserved only through the vigilance of exhausted teachers. AI literacy cannot depend only on a few enthusiastic innovators. Data ethics cannot be left to scattered workshops. Universities need coherent policies, proper staffing, technical support, legal safeguards, and pedagogical resources. They must also create spaces where professors and students can speak honestly about AI without fear, shame, or moral panic. The classroom cannot become a battlefield between suspicious teachers and evasive students. It must become a site of negotiated responsibility.

The renewed social contract must therefore balance trust and accountability. Professors should be trusted, but not exempt from scrutiny. Institutions should be accountable, but not permitted to govern through opaque surveillance. Students should be supported, but not reduced to predictive profiles. AI should be used, but not worshipped. Data should inform, but not dominate. This balance will not emerge by accident. It requires policy, culture, dialogue, and, perhaps above all, restraint. Universities must learn to say no to certain uses of AI even when they are technically possible. Not every possible automation is educationally wise. Not every measurable activity is worth measuring. Not every prediction should guide intervention. Not every efficiency should be pursued.

One of the most urgent elements of the new contract is transparency. Professors and students should know when AI systems are being used, what data are being collected, how decisions are influenced, and what rights individuals have to challenge automated or semi-automated judgments (Morison & McInerney, 2025). Hidden systems corrode trust. A university that monitors without clarity teaches suspicion. A university that uses AI in evaluation without explanation undermines the moral legitimacy of its own decisions. Transparency does not solve every problem, but secrecy makes nearly every problem worse.

The contract should also affirm that the professoriate remains a public profession. Professors are not only employees of universities; they are contributors to society's capacity for thought. Their work matters because societies need people who can interpret evidence, preserve memory, criticize power, educate citizens, imagine alternatives, and resist the flattening of public life into slogans and metrics. AI may support these tasks, but it cannot assume their ethical burden. A society that weakens the professoriate in the name of efficiency may later discover that it has damaged one of the few professions trained to think beyond the immediate noise of the present.

A renewed social contract, then, is not a nostalgic plea for the old university. The old university had its exclusions, its arrogance, its silences. The task is not restoration. It is reconstruction. The academic profession must become more open, more ethically aware, more technologically literate, more globally attentive, and more honest about its own inequalities. At the same time, it must refuse the reduction of academic life to platform behavior, productivity scores, and algorithmic legibility. It must defend the human density of teaching and scholarship: the hesitation before judgment, the care behind criticism, the stubbornness of difficult truth, the generosity of mentorship, the private discipline of reading, the public courage of speaking when convenience advises silence.

The future of the professoriate will not be decided by AI itself. It will be decided by the agreements universities make around AI: who controls it, who questions it, who benefits from it, who is burdened by it, and which values remain non-negotiable. The professoriate is not asking to stand outside change (Okulicz-Kozaryn et al, 2026). It cannot. Nor should it. But it must insist on being more than raw material for institutional optimization. Professors are not merely content providers, data producers, compliance actors, or human supervisors of automated systems. They are, when the profession is allowed to breathe properly, custodians of intellectual responsibility.

That responsibility is now being tested. The renewed social contract must say, with care but without hesitation, that digital transformation is acceptable only when it deepens the university's human purposes. AI should help professors teach better, not make teaching more mechanical. It should support research, not turn inquiry into accelerated output. It should illuminate inequities, not harden them into algorithmic destiny. It should reduce meaningless burden, not expand institutional appetite. It should widen access to knowledge, not impose a single technological grammar on the world's intellectual diversity.

Table 2. Roadmap for a Renewed Social Contract of the Professoriate

Phase	Focus	Key Actions	Evidence / Deliverables
Phase 1	Academic Values Audit	Define which aspects of teaching, research, mentoring, authorship, and judgment must remain human-led	Academic values statement; AI use boundary map
Phase 2	Participatory Governance	Create shared AI governance involving professors, students, IT, legal teams, and institutional leaders	AI governance committee; consultation records; decision rights
Phase 3	Workload Recognition	Recognize time spent learning AI tools, verifying outputs, redesigning assessment, and teaching AI literacy	Revised workload model; AI-related labor categories
Phase 4	Transparent Accountability	Disclose what data are collected, how analytics are used, and how algorithmic judgments can be challenged	Data transparency policy; appeal and audit procedures
Phase 5	Professional Development	Move beyond tool training toward AI ethics, pedagogy, authorship, bias, accessibility, and academic freedom	Professional development plan; faculty resource hub
Phase 6	Review and Renewal	Evaluate AI impact on autonomy, workload, student learning, academic freedom, and equity	Annual social-contract review; improvement roadmap

Perhaps the most important clause of this renewed contract is also the simplest: the university must remain a place where human judgment matters. Not because humans are flawless. They are not. But because education, scholarship, and public knowledge require responsibility, and responsibility cannot be automated. The professoriate's future depends on whether universities remember this before the machinery becomes too smooth, too convenient, and too deeply embedded to question.

CONCLUSION

Digitalization and artificial intelligence have brought the professoriate to a moment of serious reckoning. The issue is no longer whether universities will become digital, nor whether AI will enter teaching, research, administration, and academic evaluation. That threshold has already been crossed. The more urgent question is what kind of academic profession will emerge from this transformation. Will the professor become a platform-managed knowledge worker, constantly measured, optimized, and compared? Or will the professoriate be reimagined as a more ethically grounded, technologically capable, and socially responsive profession, one that uses digital tools without allowing them to define the meaning of academic life?

This chapter has argued that the rise of AI in higher education is not simply a matter of innovation. It is a renegotiation of the social contract between professors, universities, students, and society. For decades, perhaps even centuries, the professoriate has been sustained by a fragile agreement: society grants scholars a degree of autonomy because their work serves purposes larger than immediate efficiency. Professors are expected to teach truthfully, research rigorously, mentor responsibly, challenge intellectual complacency, and contribute to the public good. In return, they require trust, protection, time, institutional support, and freedom from excessive interference. This balance has always been imperfect, and in many contexts it has been unevenly distributed. Still, it remains one of the moral foundations of higher education.

AI unsettles this foundation because it changes how academic work is seen. What can be digitized can often be tracked; what can be tracked can be measured; what can be measured can be compared; and what can be compared can be governed from a distance. This sequence may appear administrative, even harmless, but its consequences are profound. When the work of professors is increasingly translated into data, the university may begin to confuse visibility with value. A professor's intellectual influence may be reduced to citation counts, student evaluations, learning analytics, publication volume, grant income, platform engagement, and other measurable indicators. These indicators are not meaningless, but they are incomplete. They can illuminate certain aspects of academic activity while casting others into shadow.

Some of the most important dimensions of professorial work resist easy measurement. The slow conversation that changes a student's confidence. The difficult book that takes years to mature. The ethical judgment exercised in supervising fragile research. The courage to ask unpopular questions. The invisible labor of mentoring junior colleagues. The careful refusal to simplify a complex truth. The intellectual patience required to teach students not only what to think, but how to live with uncertainty. These are not decorative elements of academic life. They are central to it. If AI-driven universities become too captivated by what can be instantly counted, they risk weakening the very qualities that make the professoriate valuable.

At the same time, resistance alone is not enough. It would be unwise to treat AI as an external enemy standing at the gates of the university. AI is already inside the institution, and it brings real possibilities. It can reduce repetitive administrative burdens, assist with research organization, support students with diverse learning needs, improve access to knowledge, enable multilingual academic communication, and help professors identify students who may otherwise disappear quietly into failure. Used wisely, AI may restore time for the human parts of academic work rather than erode them. It may allow professors to focus less on mechanical tasks and more on interpretation, guidance, creativity, and care. The problem, then, is not AI itself. The problem is the governance of AI, the values embedded in its use, and the institutional imagination that surrounds it.

A renewed social contract for the professoriate must therefore avoid two extremes. The first is technological surrender: the belief that whatever can be automated should be automated, and that academic work must adapt itself without question to the logic of efficiency, prediction, and optimization. This view is dangerous because it mistakes technical capacity for educational wisdom. The second extreme is defensive nostalgia: the belief that the professoriate can preserve its identity by refusing technological change altogether. This, too, is inadequate. The older university was not pure, fair, or free from bureaucracy. Many of its traditions excluded voices, protected privilege, and ignored forms of labor that did not fit dominant academic models. The future cannot simply be a return to the past.

What is needed instead is a more mature settlement. Universities must decide, deliberately and publicly, which aspects of academic work should be supported by AI and which must remain governed by human judgment. They must establish transparent policies for algorithmic decision-making, data ownership, academic evaluation, AI-assisted authorship, student surveillance, and automated assessment. Professors should not be passive users of systems designed elsewhere. They must be involved in shaping the ethical, pedagogical, and scholarly conditions under which these systems operate. The professoriate cannot remain outside technological governance, because technological governance is now part of academic governance itself.

This requires a shift in institutional culture. Too often, digital transformation is introduced as a managerial project: faster systems, better dashboards, more efficient workflows, stronger analytics, more competitive outputs. These goals may have their place, but they are not enough. A university is not a factory of credentials, nor a content-delivery company, nor a ranking machine. It is a human institution built around inquiry, formation, disagreement, memory, and imagination. Its technologies should serve these purposes. When they do not, the institution must have the courage to slow down and ask why.

The professoriate, too, must rethink its own responsibilities. Academic autonomy cannot mean isolation from accountability. Professors cannot reject scrutiny while asking society to preserve their freedom. In the age of AI, academic freedom must be paired with technological literacy, ethical awareness, and a renewed commitment to public trust. Professors need to understand how AI systems work, where their limits lie, how bias can enter their outputs, and how students may be affected by their use. They must also model intellectual honesty in a time when text, images, data, and even scholarly arguments can be generated with astonishing speed. The professor's role as a guardian of integrity becomes more important, not less.

Students will also encounter the professoriate differently in AI-mediated universities. They may receive automated feedback before meeting a teacher. They may interact with chatbots, adaptive platforms, and AI tutors as part of their ordinary learning experience. This does not eliminate the need for professors. It clarifies it. In a world overflowing with generated information, students need human educators who can help them distinguish knowledge from noise, confidence from truth, fluency from understanding, and convenience from wisdom. The professor of the future may be less a gatekeeper of information and more a guide through intellectual abundance. That role is demanding. It requires judgment, humility, empathy, and depth.

The changing social contract must also address inequality. Digitalization and AI do not affect all professors equally. Well-resourced universities may use AI to enhance teaching and research, while underfunded institutions may experience it as another pressure to do more with less. Senior academics may enjoy the freedom to experiment, while precarious faculty may be monitored more closely through digital performance systems. Scholars in dominant languages may benefit from AI visibility, while others may be misread, marginalized, or poorly represented by systems trained on uneven data. A serious social contract cannot speak only for elite institutions. It must consider the global professoriate, including those working under conditions of scarcity, political pressure, linguistic exclusion, and unstable employment.

For this reason, the future of the professoriate cannot be left to market forces, software vendors, or administrative enthusiasm alone. It must be shaped through shared governance, ethical regulation, and sustained academic dialogue. Professors, students, institutional leaders, policymakers, and technology developers all have a role to play. But the voice of the professoriate is especially important because professors understand, from within, the texture of academic work: its visible duties and hidden burdens, its public outputs and private struggles, its intellectual joys and quiet disappointments. Any AI strategy that ignores this lived reality will be shallow, no matter how advanced its technology appears.

Ultimately, the question raised by digitalization and AI is not only what professors will do, but what society still expects professors to be. If professors are valued only as producers of measurable outputs, then AI will likely accelerate a narrow and impoverished model of academic professionalism. If, however, professors are recognized as interpreters, critics, mentors, researchers, ethical agents, and public intellectuals, then AI may become part of a richer academic future. The distinction matters. Technology can enlarge a profession, but it can also hollow it out.

The chapter closes with a simple but demanding claim: the professoriate must not allow its social contract to be rewritten silently. The changes now unfolding in higher education are too consequential to be treated as technical adjustments. They touch the meaning of academic freedom, the dignity of scholarly labor, the relationship between knowledge and power, and the kind of university society wishes to sustain. AI can assist the professoriate, but it cannot replace the moral imagination at the heart of academic life. It can generate language, but it cannot assume responsibility. It can process information, but it cannot care about truth. It can predict patterns, but it cannot decide what kind of future higher education ought to serve.

That decision remains human. And it is precisely there, in that difficult human responsibility, that the professoriate still matters.

REFERENCES

Aithal, P. S., & Aithal, S. (2023). Optimizing the use of artificial intelligence-powered GPTs as teaching and research assistants by professors in higher education institutions: A study on smart utilization. [IJMTS]. *International Journal of Management, Technology, and Social Sciences*, *8*(4), 368–401. DOI: 10.47992/IJMTS.2581.6012.0326

Al-Abdullatif, A. M. (2025). Auditing AI literacy competency in K–12 education: The role of awareness, ethics, evaluation, and use in human–machine cooperation. *Systems*, *13*(6), 490. DOI: 10.3390/systems13060490

Aliyu, M. O. (2026). *Artificial intelligence, scholastic development, and academic proficiency of graduate students in Memorial University*. Newfoundland and Labrador.

Almaqtari, J. W., Alramada, E., & Alsabry, A. (2026). An Overview and Impact Analysis of AI Tools in Academic Research, Learning, and Educational Performance. *Sana'a University Journal of Applied Sciences and Technology*, *4*(2), 1665–1681. DOI: 10.59628/jast.v4i2.1921

. Ashfaq, D. M. S. (2025). Artificial Intelligence and the Future of the Professoriate: A Study of the Impact of AI on Faculty Roles and Responsibilities.

Beale, J., & Easton, C. (Eds.). (2026). *The future of education: Reimagining its aims and responsibilities*. Oxford University Press. DOI: 10.1093/9780197669761.001.0001

Berg, M., & Seeber, B. K. (2025). *The slow professor: Challenging the culture of speed in the academy*. University of Toronto Press.

Berlinerblau, J. (2025). *As Professors Lay Dying: Selecting a College Amidst an Educational Crisis*. Simon and Schuster.

Block, F. (2022). Technology and productivity: A critique of aggregate indicators. *Journal of Post Keynesian Economics*, *45*(1), 1–23. DOI: 10.1080/01603477.2022.2029491

Borgman, C. L., & Brand, A. (2022). Data blind: Universities lag in capturing and exploiting data. *Science*, *378*(6626), 1278–1281. DOI: 10.1126/science.add2734 PMID: 36548403

. Bosman, J. P., Van Petegem, W., De Laet, T., & Tshuma, N. (2025). How to select the right AI tool for the job? An Autonomy-values framework for educational AI with a focus on academic advising. Ubiquity Proceedings, 6(1).

Cooper, A. F., Moss, E., Laufer, B., & Nissenbaum, H. (2022, June). Accountability in an algorithmic society: relationality, responsibility, and robustness in machine learning. In *Proceedings of the 2022 ACM conference on fairness, accountability, and transparency* (pp. 864-876). DOI: 10.1145/3531146.3533150

Diameh, J. T., Oluwatobi, B. T., Daniels, C., Sunday, O. E., Nelson, C. A., & Quaye, M. (2025). Integrating AI-driven predictive analytics in project risk management to optimize decision-making and performance efficiency. *Int. J. Eng. Technol. Res. Manag*, *9*, 373–389.

Dovchin, S. (2024). Artificial Intelligence in Applied Linguistics: A double-edged sword. *Australian Review of Applied Linguistics*, *47*(3), 410–417. DOI: 10.1075/aral.24145.dov

Dunleavy, P., & Margetts, H. (2025). Data science, artificial intelligence and the third wave of digital era governance. *Public Policy and Administration*, *40*(2), 185–214. DOI: 10.1177/09520767231198737

Edu, N. (2025). The influence of international rankings on higher education reforms and institutional strategies. *International Journal of Innovative Social Sciences & Humanities Research*, *13*(1), 273–280.

Fitria, T. N. (2023). The use of artificial intelligence in education (AIED): Can AI replace the teacher's role? *Epigram*, *20*(2), 165–187. DOI: 10.32722/epi.v20i2.5711

George, A. S. (2024). Technology tension in schools: Addressing the complex impacts of digital advances on teaching, learning, and wellbeing. [PUMRJ]. *Partners Universal Multidisciplinary Research Journal*, *1*(3), 49–65.

Ghamrawi, N., Shal, T., & Ghamrawi, N. A. (2024). Exploring the impact of AI on teacher leadership: Regressing or expanding? *Education and Information Technologies*, *29*(7), 8415–8433. DOI: 10.1007/s10639-023-12174-w

Gualdrón, E. O., Duque, M., Javakhishvili, M., Bartoszak, M., Watkins, L. G., Montero-Zamora, P., Alpysbekova, A., Vo, D. H., Lee, S. W., Acaf, Y., Bochkina, E., & Schwartz, S. J. (2025). Creating an Internationally Equitable Playing Field for Publishing in English-Language Scholarly Journals. *Journal of Scholarly Publishing*, *56*(4), 840–869. DOI: 10.3138/jsp-2024-0104

Hostler, T. J. (2023). The invisible workload of open research. *Journal of Trial and Error*, *4*(1), 21–36. DOI: 10.36850/mr5

Jiang, X., Li, M., & Zhang, Z. (2025). 'Bridging borders in academia': The motivations, barriers, and strategies of Global North scholars in Chinese higher education research. *Higher Education*, •••, 1–23. DOI: 10.1007/s10734-025-01558-1

Kwiek, M., & Roszka, W. (2024). Once highly productive, forever highly productive? Full professors' research productivity from a longitudinal perspective. *Higher Education*, *87*(3), 519–549. DOI: 10.1007/s10734-023-01022-y

McDiarmid, G. W., & Zhao, Y. (2023). Time to rethink: Educating for a technology-transformed world. *ECNU Review of Education*, *6*(2), 189–214. DOI: 10.1177/20965311221076493

McGrath, C., Pargman, T. C., Juth, N., & Palmgren, P. J. (2023). University teachers' perceptions of responsibility and artificial intelligence in higher education-An experimental philosophical study. *Computers and Education: Artificial Intelligence*, *4*, 100139. DOI: 10.1016/j.caeai.2023.100139

Meron, Y., & Araci, Y. T. (2023). Artificial intelligence in design education: Evaluating ChatGPT as a virtual colleague for post-graduate course development. *Design Science*, *9*, e30. DOI: 10.1017/dsj.2023.28

Mohamed Hashim, M. A., Tlemsani, I., & Duncan Matthews, R. (2022). A sustainable university: Digital transformation and beyond. *Education and Information Technologies*, *27*(7), 8961–8996. DOI: 10.1007/s10639-022-10968-y PMID: 35340534

Moodley, M. (2025). Exploring academic freedom, institutional autonomy, and public accountability in the global landscape of private higher education. *South African Journal of Higher Education*, *39*(4), 165–178. DOI: 10.20853/39-4-7516

Morison, J., & McInerney, T. (2025). When should a computer decide?: Judicial decision-making in the age of automation, algorithms and generative artificial intelligence. In *Research handbook on judging and the judiciary* (pp. 54–87). Edward Elgar Publishing. DOI: 10.4337/9781788978743.00009

Nelson, R. (2024). *Academic identity in the age of AI: Higher education and the digital revolution*. Emerald Group Publishing.

Okulicz-Kozaryn, W., Artyukhov, A., & Artyukhova, N. (2026). Will AI Replace Us? Changing the University Teacher Role. *Societies (Basel, Switzerland)*, *16*(1), 32. DOI: 10.3390/soc16010032

Pennathur, P. R., Boksa, V., Pennathur, A., Kusiak, A., & Livingston, B. A. (2024). The future of office and administrative support occupations in the era of artificial intelligence: A state of the art review and future research directions. *International Journal of Industrial Ergonomics*, *104*, 103665. DOI: 10.1016/j.ergon.2024.103665

Pesántez-Avilés, F., Cárdenas-Tapia, J., Torres-Toukoumidis, A., & Vintimilla, S. (2024, January). Understanding academic anxiety in the digital age: An exploratory analysis among university students and the influence of new technologies. In International Conference on Information Technology & Systems (pp. 279-289). Cham: Springer Nature Switzerland. DOI: 10.1007/978-3-031-54256-5_26

Rainy, T. A., & Chowdhury, A. R. (2022). The Role Of Artificial Intelligence In Vendor Performance Evaluation Within Digital Retail Supply Chains: A Review Of Strategic Decision-Making Models. *American Journal of Scholarly Research and Innovation*, *1*(01), 220–248. DOI: 10.63125/96jj3j86

Reichman, H. (2025). *Understanding academic freedom*. JHU Press. DOI: 10.56021/9781421450940

Rhoades, G., Hohl, E., Shermer, E. T., Berry, J., Worthen, H., Alker, G., & Park, J. (2024). *Contingent faculty and the remaking of higher education: A labor history*. University of Illinois Press.

Rodrigues, T. V. (2025). *Distant Writing and The Epistemology of Authorship: On Creativity*. Delegation, And Plagiarism in The Age Of AI.

Schneider, T. (2023). *Digitalization and Artificial Intelligence*. Springer Books. DOI: 10.1007/978-3-658-40383-6

Schwab, K. (2026). *Universities, Professors, and Students in the Intelligent Age: A Call for Systems Change*. Schwab Academy.

Shah, P. (2023). *AI and the Future of Education: Teaching in the Age of Artificial Intelligence*. John Wiley & Sons.

Sharif Nia, H., Marôco, J., She, L., Khoshnavay Fomani, F., Rahmatpour, P., Stepanovic Ilic, I., Mohammad Ibrahim, M., Muhammad Ibrahim, F., Narula, S., Esposito, G., Gorgulu, O., Naghavi, N., Pahlevan Sharif, S., Allen, K.-A., Kaveh, O., & Reardon, J. (2023). Student satisfaction and academic efficacy during online learning with the mediating effect of student engagement: A multi-country study. *PLoS One*, *18*(10), e0285315. DOI: 10.1371/journal.pone.0285315 PMID: 37792853

Shawkey, J. G. (2026). Beyond AI Tools: Professors Addressing Ethical AI Detection in Faith-Based Academia (Doctoral dissertation, Charleston Southern University).

Spivakovsky, O. V., Omelchuk, S. A., Kobets, V. V., Valko, N. V., & Malchykova, D. S. (2023). Institutional policies on artificial intelligence in university learning, teaching and research. *Information Technologies and Learning Tools*, *97*(5), 181–202. DOI: 10.33407/itlt.v97i5.5395

Taherdoost, H. (2025). *Maximizing Research Impact: Practical Strategies for Enhancing Research Visibility*. Taylor & Francis. DOI: 10.4324/9781003604785

Turcotte, P. L., & Holmes, D. (2024). Vanishing academics: On the importance of speed and becoming-imperceptible. *Nursing Inquiry*, *31*(2), e12619. DOI: 10.1111/nin.12619 PMID: 38062860

Verma, S., & Dwivedi, U. (2023). Optimizing digital knowledge repositories: Leveraging electronic resources in university libraries for enhanced academic advantages. *Perspectives in Social Work*, *37*(03), 112–132.

Voorn, B. (2023). Professional managers, public values? The delicate balance between corporatization and stewardship to society. *Public Management Review*, *25*(8), 1498–1516. DOI: 10.1080/14719037.2022.2026691

. Wilstic, D. E. (2025). AI in Education: Leveraging Artificial Intelligence to Combat Academic Malpractice in Higher Education.

Yarram, V. K., & Yallavula, R. (2022). Adaptive Machine Learning Driven Compliance Scoring Models for Automated Risk Detection, Quality Validation of AI-Generated Content in Regulated Industries. *International Journal of Emerging Research in Engineering and Technology*, *3*(1), 116–126. DOI: 10.63282/3050-922X.IJERET-V3I1P112

KEY TERMS AND DEFINITIONS

Academic Autonomy: the professional freedom of professors to teach, research, question, and judge according to disciplinary expertise and ethical responsibility.

AI-Mediated Academic Labor: teaching, research, assessment, administration, and mentoring reshaped by AI tools, automation, and digital workflows.

Algorithmic Accountability: accountability systems shaped by dashboards, metrics, analytics, and AI-based evaluation rather than only collegial or peer judgment.

Digital Governance: the use of platforms, data systems, dashboards, and institutional technologies to organize, monitor, and evaluate academic work.

Human Judgment in Higher Education: the irreplaceable role of professors in interpretation, care, ethical decision-making, intellectual formation, and scholarly responsibility.

Invisible Academic Workload: essential but poorly measured labor such as mentoring, emotional support, assessment redesign, AI verification, and academic integrity work.

Social Contract of the Professoriate: the implicit agreement through which professors receive autonomy and trust in exchange for teaching, research, mentoring, public service, and intellectual responsibility.

Chapter 11
The Impact of AI on Academic Freedom, Institutional Governance, and Professional Autonomy

Shivendu Kumar Rai
http://orcid.org/0000-0001-8240-1884
Tecnia Institute of Advanced Studies, India

Kumari Pallavi
http://orcid.org/0000-0003-3534-6899
Galgotias University, India

Indrani Bhattacharjee
Tecnia Institute of Advanced Studies, India

Sandaboina Shivakumar
KL Business School, Koneru Lakshmaiah Education Foundation (Deemed to be University), India

Arjune Selvam
http://orcid.org/0000-0003-0854-1728
Christ University, India

Ramesh Pettela
http://orcid.org/0000-0002-2661-8779
Aditya University, India

Veena Rani
http://orcid.org/0009-0004-0456-9517
Rajagiri School of Engineering and Technology, India

ABSTRACT

AI is transforming education in various ways, as this chapter shows. It examines how algorithmic systems affect research, policy, curriculum, faculty evaluation, and student assessment. This chapter examines how academic administration

DOI: 10.4018/979-8-3373-8525-9.ch011

and institutional governance are increasingly using generative AI tools, AI-driven analytics, and automated decision systems. We examine monitoring, algorithmic bias, openness, intellectual freedom, and the erosion of researchers' and teachers' professional judgement. Academic autonomy is examined in relation to automated performance evaluation, predictive analytics, and AI-assisted monitoring systems. The chapter also discusses university AI ethics and regulation. New ideas include participatory governance models, explainable AI, and human-centered AI frameworks. Balancing technological advancement with ethical governance principles can help universities ensure that AI supports academic honesty, institutional responsibility, and professional independence.

INTRODUCTION

An essential restructuring of the processes of knowledge generation, regulation, and validation is signaled by the interaction between Academic Freedom (AF) and the growing impact of AI in education. Algorithmic systems are increasingly influencing the traditional human-centered paradigm of academic agency as institutions utilize AI-driven technologies for research, teaching, and administration. While this progression could lead to new innovations, it also raises serious concerns about responsibility, autonomy, and epistemic justice. Long seen as a bedrock principle of universities, AF ensures that researchers are free to pursue knowledge without undue influence from vested interests in power, money, or other institutions. It is a cornerstone of democratic discourse and the generation of new knowledge, as Jeffrey C. Sun stresses, since it safeguards AF and professional independence (Sun, 2025).

New governance mechanisms shaped by data, algorithms, and predictive models are emerging with AI's arrival in the academy. These mechanisms have the potential to subtly restrict or redirect academic practices. The shift from "Academic Freedom" to "Algorithmic Agency" suggests a change in power dynamics, as algorithms increasingly control access to information, establish evaluation systems, and influence educational decision-making. Although AI has the potential to improve administrative processes and student achievement, it also raises serious ethical and epistemological questions, according to researchers. Open and remote learning using AI enhances accessibility and customization but also raises concerns about research integrity and intellectual autonomy.

A virtue ethics framework is proposed by C. Prinsloo and colleagues as a means to balance the promise of AI with the need to uphold fairness, AF, and responsibility (Prinsloo et al., 2025). In this view, AI-enhanced classrooms should prioritize developing students' moral character alongside their technical competence. The concept of algorithmic agency builds on this discussion by recognizing AI systems as more than tools; they are active participants in knowledge generation. In their "Interactive Theory of AI in Academic Knowledge Production," Amal and M. Amayreh argue that under dialogic and interpretive frameworks, human and machine intelligence co-create knowledge. But this rethinking necessitates a thorough investigation into the honesty, authorship, and prejudice of algorithmically controlled epistemic processes.

In addition to these theoretical developments, empirical research has shown that AI tools, such as adaptive learning platforms and generative writing systems, are transforming assessment and education. While these strategies can enhance language accuracy and information organization, they often stifle creativity and critical thinking when used mindlessly (Han, 2025). AF ideals intersect directly with the challenges posed by algorithmic authorship regarding intellectual property and the boundaries of human creativity. In addition, we need to reevaluate the philosophical parts of education in this age of AI. N. Quoc and Le-Thi Kim Nhung worry that students' moral agency and creativity would be eroded as a result of education's commercialization and uniformity. There is general unease about how algorithmic systems generate knowledge, and this criticism aligns with it.

In conclusion, the fundamental issue with AI-enhanced education is how to take advantage of technology's potential while preserving human liberty and ethical responsibility; this is illustrated by the connection between AF and algorithmic agency(Ajmal, 2025). This paper situates the discussion within the broader discourse on knowledge governance and argues that reforming institutions and reimagining the ethical and epistemological underpinnings of academic life in the algorithmic age are just as important as technological advancements to the future of education.

Academic Freedom and Professional Autonomy

Colleges and universities have come a long way from their humble beginnings as 19th-century bastions of AF to the research-focused institutions of the 20th century and, finally, the controlled, entrepreneurial institutions of the 21st(Chattopadhyay, 2025). Universities are under increasing pressure to respond to market signals, comply with government regulations, and meet public demands, all of which erode the traditional academic independence of instructors, a defining feature of academia. The philosophical bedrock of academia is the idea of academic independence.

The primary goal of a university is to provide an environment where students are free to ask whatever questions they want. University research, in contrast to the short-sightedness of politics and the market, serves society's long-term interests best when it is unfettered and unhindered by outside forces. Since they are places of study, universities are perpetually springboards for fresh perspectives and criticisms(Chikane, 2026). Education and research are rooted in inquiry. The state often dislikes, even in a democratic setting, when colleges criticize its policies and try to rally public opinion. Universities have a double duty in participating in public discourse: they must serve and critique, be both providers and consumers of services, and be both active in and demanded by society.

University Autonomy and Academic Freedom

The success of a university depends on the quality of its faculty and students. Consequently, AF needs to be understood in the larger context of the university's system of governance, which includes both the market and the state. (Bowen, William G., 2015) highlight the link between autonomous thinking and professional obligations, which include the need to maintain professional standards and to penalise those who fail to do so, along with the limitations on academic autonomy imposed by institutional mandates. AF is not guaranteed by university autonomy on its own. AF depends on university leadership, faculty involvement in governance, and the active engagement of professors to execute the institution's mandate.

The AF of the faculty would dictate the academic output of a university if it were autonomous, not subject to market or state pressures, and received full public funding. In terms of evaluating academic work, this is the same as a bottom-up approach. AF of thought and expression may endure outside of the confines of academic engagement when universities are subject to market pressures or national or international accrediting or rating agencies(Bernasconi, 2025). The reason behind this is that academics are compelled to match their teaching and research with the important goals of the universities. This is typically the case for a top-tier university that competes on a global basis, which means that ranking criteria and their weightings must be followed.

Accountability and institutional autonomy are indivisible aspects of AF. The traditional character of university governance institutions presents unique challenges to AF, which we must understand. There are many different levels of operation and ways in which a university interacts with its internal and external environments(Ramlo, 2025). Due to the autonomy exhibited by faculty members, who are seen as experts in their respective fields across departmental levels, authority is spread out, making the vertical structure of power relatively weak. Constructing consensus is more difficult in higher education institutions due to their horizontal authority structures, which are defined by a large number of senior personnel. Therefore, participatory governance is compatible with AF and open scientific advocacy. There is still a lack of clarity regarding the optimal level and scope of faculty involvement in university administration.

Establishing Accountability in the University System

The key question is who is responsible to whom, for what goals, to whom, how, and with what consequences, given the interconnectedness of AF and responsibility. All public policy tools inevitably strive to institutionalize accountability, and the regulation of academic activities and the administration of higher education institutions is no exception. Previous studies have shown that there are essentially two kinds of accountability: internal and external(Waddington et al., 2024). At one end of the spectrum, we have measures of internal accountability, such as self-awareness; at the other end, we have measures of peer accountability; and, finally, on the far right, we have measures of external accountability in various forms. The goal of governance reform, mostly through financial and legislative means, has been to make universities and their faculty more answerable to outside parties, including the state, society, students, and, eventually, the market. Here, we'll examine worldwide policy revisions and assess the impact they've had on the NEP.

AI Technologies in Higher Education

More and more people are interested in creating computer systems that can think, solve problems, and make decisions like humans as a result of advancements in computing power(Wang, Youmei, Chenchen Liu, 2021). Aiming toward human-level cognition, AI is defined by researchers as a computer-based system that exhibits human-like behavior and can perform tasks such as thinking, learning, and self-correction. Computational intelligence, machine intelligence, and artificial intelligence are all terms for the same concept. Speech recognition, chess, Intelligent Personal Assistants (IPAs), poetry, and illness diagnosis are just a few of the areas where academics have been working on AI implementations in the last few decades (Yang et al., 2021)(Chen, Xie, Zou, et al., 2020).

One of the most exciting new areas of cutting-edge educational technology is AI. Thanks to AI technology, learners are no longer limited by time or place. With the convenience of mobile devices, they can access materials, practice, and gain knowledge whenever they choose. AI learning systems, meanwhile, may tailor their instructional support and supplemental materials to each learner's unique circumstances (Liu et al., 2019). The main application domains of AIEd were found to be profiling and prediction, evaluation and assessment, adaptive systems and personalization, and Intelligent Tutoring Systems (ITSs), according to a literature review by (Zawacki-Richter et al., 2019) covering the years 2007–2018.

By analyzing each student's unique learning characteristics and circumstances, ITS can, for instance, provide personalized learning interfaces and materials (Chen, Xie, & Hwang, 2020). Based on students' current status, it can also choose instructional strategies and methodologies, providing timely coaching and appropriate support to improve learning efficacy (Huang & Chen, 2016). By taking into account each student's emotional and mental conditions, the adaptive learning model has the potential to improve educational outcomes and help students who aren't doing as well as others complete their coursework in intelligent, adaptive online learning environments (Hwang et al., 2020). In an effort to build user learning models, some researchers have turned to big data analysis on massive amounts of data collected from educational and learning systems.

Technology Acceptance Model (TAM)

Researchers first proposed the TAM to study how people respond to new technology. TAM emphasizes the use of technology, whether it's consumers' intention to use it or their actual use. When people see technology as useful, they are more inclined to embrace it and keep a positive attitude toward it (Dávideková,. On the flip side, customers are more likely to embrace new technologies if they perceive them as easy to use and have the potential to boost productivity. People will stick with what they know or find a way around less-complicated alternatives if the technologies are difficult to use, even if they have great potential.

The importance of teachers' perspectives about the use of new technologies in the classroom on their adoption behavior has been shown by research (Ifinedo, 2020). Educators' goals and actions in relation to incorporating new technologies into their teaching practices have been the subject of much research using the TAM (Scherer, 2018). The degree to which educators believe they can effectively use new technology in the classroom is a strong predictor of how they will feel about and act toward these tools. According to current research, teachers' positive or negative views toward technology adoption will shape their attitudes and actions in this area.

In addition, studies have shown that users' concerns about the technology's "Ease of Use" decrease as they become more familiar with it, which may influence their perceptions of the technology's usability and their attitudes toward embracing it. With the rapid development of technology, establishing Smart Learning Environments (SLEs) has become a popular and crucial goal for teachers. This highlights the crucial role that educators play in incorporating AI into classroom practices (Kinshuk, 2016). Accordingly, using the TAM, this study sought to understand how educators feel, what they think, and what they plan to do regarding the incorporation of AI into the curriculum.

Self-Efficacy (SE)

A person's SE in the context of information technology is often defined as their confidence in their own abilities to use that technology to complete a specific task. Some studies have shown that SE alters people's opinions about technology adoption and affects how users perceive its utility. One definition of teacher self-efficacy is faith in one's own abilities. A key component of integrating technology into education, this has the potential to improve students' learning. According to the study's findings, teachers with higher levels of SE were more likely to successfully integrate teaching into their professional development. For example, in flipped classroom activities, attitudes towards the use of technology are influenced by university teachers' SE (Lai et al., 2018).

Anxiety (AN)

People's fear and nervousness about new technology is the root cause of AN. Adverse emotions experienced by users as a result of AN and other new technologies may have a negative impact on their attitudes and sense of self-efficacy, according to the research (Cazan & Cocorad, 2016). AN has a negative effect on both students' and teachers' attitudes toward mobile technology, and research has shown that this effect is proportional to the degree to which users experience anxiety. Educators' attitudes toward using technology in the classroom are influenced by their AN, according to the research. The adoption attitudes of educators are shaped by their views regarding the incorporation of technology into education (Clark-gordon et al., 2019).

Impact of AI on Academic Freedom

Modern academics cannot escape the pervasive influence of AI, which is changing the face of many areas, including teaching, research, and administration. Data analysis, Personalized learning, and predictive modeling are among its many applications. AF, or the ability of scholars to pursue knowledge without undue restrictions, has been at the center of a heated controversy over the introduction of AI into educational institutions. AI biases, potential censorship, and general control of information dissemination are all topics covered in this discussion. Examining the impact of AI systems on the independence and credibility of academic work is crucial as these technologies mediate academic activities more and more (Mann et al., 2025).

Research Autonomy and AI

Research autonomy and artificial intelligence interact in complex ways. AI offers unmatched resources for processing, uncovering patterns, massive information, and speeding up discoveries in a variety of domains. Because they allow for rapid hypothesis testing and simulation, AI-driven models have revolutionized domains such as materials research and genetics (Kirkham, 2021). There are issues with using AI in research. One big worry is that AI can introduce or reinforce biases in research findings. If the data used to train an AI system had biases from the past, those biases could find their way into the AI's analysis and recommendations. The problem becomes more pronounced in fields like the humanities and social sciences where findings may be influenced by individual perspectives or cultural norms. Conflicts of interest, in which commercial goals influence research agendas and outcomes, may also emerge from relying on proprietary AI tools developed by private firm.

Censorship and Content Moderation in AI

The use of AI for content filtering has far-reaching consequences for the dissemination of scholarly information. The use of AI algorithms to identify hate speech is on the rise, with the goal of filtering disinformation, monitoring and controlling online content, and eliminating other harmful elements. While maintaining the material's quality and integrity is the goal, these strategies could inadvertently limit meaningful intellectual discourse. The elimination or restriction of important scholarly contributions could be due to AI-driven moderation algorithms' inability to distinguish between damaging content and critical conversation. Misguided AI laws, warns the Organization for Security and Cooperation in Europe (OSCE), might stifle legitimate speech by imposing unintended restrictions. Academics' ability to conduct open and critical research is hampered by the secrecy of AI decision-making algorithms, making it more difficult for them to challenge or appeal material removal decisions.

AI Bias and Its Effects on Academic Freedom

When AI systems are biased, they compromise the objectivity and inclusivity of research and conversation, which in turn threatens AF(Alhafidh, 2025). Without proper evaluation, AI models trained on biased datasets could perpetuate prejudice and worsen existing inequalities through their skewed predictions. When AI approaches are used to assess student performance, provide learning materials, or even predict academic success, this becomes particularly problematic in educational settings. According to Shweta Singh, developers of AI systems may unwittingly incorporate their own society's viewpoints into these systems, leading to biased outputs that reflect and reinforce societal prejudices. She stresses the importance of AF and critical thinking and argues that scholars must ensure that AI development and application are done ethically. Without strict regulation and a commitment to fairness, AI systems have the potential to diminish the diversity of opinion essential to robust scholarly debate.

Impact on Institutional Governance

Assuming there are few cross-jurisdictional spillovers, decentralising public good funding and delivery has the potential to improve public service provision governance in three main ways: by making better use of allocated resources, by making government officials more accountable and reducing corruption, and by making it easier to recoup costs(Moodley et al., 2025). Having local administrations that are at least somewhat democratic is essential for the three interdependent pillars of governance.

Efficiency Allocative

A key theoretical argument in favor of decentralization is that it can improve the efficiency of distribution.

> *Products and services offered by decentralized government systems are unique to each region. Beyond the uniform levels usually associated with national provision, decentralized provision improves economic welfare by tailoring products and services to the particular preferences and situations of its members. This argument boils down to this: different jurisdictions will have different ideal levels of production for a "Local" public benefit, since people's tastes and budgets differ. (Oates 1999, 1121-22)*

Subnational administrations, being closer to the people than the federal government, are believed to have more insight into the needs of individual communities, according to this line of thinking. Therefore, they are considered more able to deal with changes in the demand for products and services. Secondly, changes in the demand for and the costs of providing public goods are best handled by subnational governments. By encouraging competition among subnational institutions, decentralization is thought to increase the likelihood that governments will meet the needs of the local populace.

It is believed that when subnational governments compete with one another, a variety of local public goods are produced(Ültanır et al., 2025). People show their preferences for these goods by moving to jurisdictions that match them, a phenomenon known as "Voting with their feet." This puts tax income at risk while pressuring subnational governments to listen to their citizens and tailor service delivery appropriately. It is believed that this "Voting with feet" will increase the likelihood that governments will fulfil citizens' wishes, leading to a more efficient allocation of resources. Private companies and NGOs may play an important role in providing alternatives to government agencies in areas where people are unable to easily leave, such as many developing and transitioning nations.

Accountability

Government corruption and increased accountability are two goals that proponents of decentralization argue would be achieved(Hao, 2025). People believe that local governments are more in tune with people's needs than the federal government because they are closer to the people. People who are apprehensive of corruption may move to other jurisdictions or providers as a result of the subsequent rivalry among subnational governments that provide public goods. This is seen as a form of government discipline. When a small group colludes to harm the larger group, it's called corruption. Theoretically, greater legitimacy and consensus in the selection of public services should result from shifting duties to smaller groups closer to the people.

Vigilance, cooperation, and adherence to regulations governing public sector integrity are expected to be enhanced by this(Li et al., 2025). In cases when public services are financed by the distribution of tax instruments or the collection of user fees, this becomes especially relevant. Optimal levels of social homogeneity and social capital, and, by extension, the propensity to cooperate at the local level, become important questions in pluralistic or socially fractionalized states.

Cost Recovery

Families are more likely to be prepared to pay for services if they are more responsive to demand, which can be achieved through decentralization. Households are more likely to support and invest in services that meet their requirements, according to the argument. Here we see the antithesis of allocative efficiency in action. Local cost-sharing or cost recovery, along with transparency and suitably balanced supply and demand, can provide the informational base and incentives for efficient local oversight. The latter may help reduce information leaks and asymmetries, which can hinder cost recovery and allocative efficiency, and is thus an important part of any thorough anti-corruption effort.

Influence on Media Content

The people who decide what appears in the media are not limited to journalists. When looking at how different variables affect respondents' topic selections, the survey shows both agreement and disagreement(Nygren et al., 2015). Engagement with the public, journalistic interests, and editorial practices of the media firm are the fundamental features that are consistent throughout all three nations. Not to mention, there are notable differences,

- Compared to their Swedish colleagues, Russian and Polish journalists place a far higher value on the political loyalty of media conglomerates and powerful politicians outside of the media.
- Compared to Sweden, Poland and Russia have a far higher perception of the influence that advertisers have.

Reporters in Sweden claim that the government has almost no influence. Perceptions of the effect of advertisers and external corporations are lower than in Poland and Russia, but nevertheless noticeable(Tabacu, 2025). This might be a result of the combined effects of increased participation in today's online culture, more market competition, and "Market-Driven Journalism." Still, there are major differences in how the journalists perceive the changing effect. In some cases, discrepancies are more difficult to explain,

- Polish journalists are being heavily monetized. Commercials and owners are having an ever-increasing impact. This is related to the increasing influence of other departments within the media company and other business organizations. From the perspective of the journalists themselves, the impact of politicians and journalists is nearly identical.
- In Sweden, the political clout is dwindling. As the power of owners and advertisers continues to expand, other parts of the media company are also becoming more influential. Almost the same amount of weight is given to journalists' opinions.
- When asked about their influence in Russia, the vast majority of journalists surveyed said it was increasing. The influence of other parts of the media company and its owners is positively connected with this expanding effect. There is a wide gap in opinion among Russian journalists on the subject of the influence of politics on media content, even though this gap is narrowing.

Power dynamics are relevant to the effect on media content. When looking at the dynamics of power change, it is common to see one group gain power while other groups lose ground. In a similar vein, the results from Poland and Sweden show that empowering journalists has the opposite effect on owners(Painsi et al., 2025), other parts of the media company, and marketers. Journalists in these countries feel their power dwindling as owners and markets gain more control over media content.

Russia does not have this kind of legislation. Corporate, owner, audience, and private enterprise perceptions of journalists' enhanced influence are strongly correlated. The only one that stands out is political influence, which is seen as slightly on the rise but is unrelated to journalists' sway. This might be because Russian journalists believe their influence grows when the country's media apparatus as a whole is strong in contrast to the political system. The impact of journalists and their audiences is highly correlated in both Poland and Russia(Colonna, 2026). This shows that journalists in Poland and Russia see public opinion as a tool to further their own influence, especially in more conventional forms of political influence. According to journalists working in Sweden's media system, their personal impact is diminished by external forces.

Human-Centered AI in Education

Technology in education is distinct from more traditional forms of technology. When it comes to teaching and interacting with people, educational technology must prioritize a human-centered approach. Therefore, AI-powered learning spaces should put people's feelings and the results they achieve first, not just performance(Yang et al., 2021). The implications of smart learning environments for current technology, modern learning platforms, and educational communities should prompt a discussion of ethics and standards.

Precision Education

Similar to precision medicine, precision education is based on a set of principles (Kuch, Declan, Matthew Kearnes, 2020)(Yang, 2021). Obama, the former president of the United States, instituted precision medicine. Since people differ greatly in their living circumstances, genetic composition, and ways of life, he discussed the problems with a universal approach (Lin et al., 2021). The four-stage implementation of precision medicine is thus recommended: Assessment, prognosis, treatment, and rehabilitation. From these four procedures, the core idea of targeted instruction is formed. Inadequate academic performance and learning difficulties are only two of the many difficulties and risks that individuals may face when pursuing an education. Therefore, the four steps of prediction, diagnosis, therapy, and prevention can be used to investigate and discuss students' learning behaviors, environments, and strategies.

Table 1. Research Topics of Precision Education

Policy and Governance	Practice and Technology
Consider the effects of precision education on new arenas of learning, such as computer programming, AR/VR, MOOCs, eBooks, and robots.	Assessment of student participation, learning styles, and conduct.
Precision education's ethical and other challenges,	The creation of assessment and evaluation strategies for targeted instruction.
Curriculum development and the creation of precise education tools.	Improving prediction models and making predictions about kids' academic performance.
Developing methods of instruction and exercises for precision education.	Teachers' roles in promoting wellness and avoiding illness.
Using precision education to study the key factors impacting students' academic performance	Data analytics, including text, video, image, and speech analytics, for personalised instruction.
Looking at how precision instruction affects students' academic performance once teachers intervene.	Data visualisation, including simulations and dashboards, for accurate instruction.

Technology, precise education, policy, all-encompassing government, and practice are the topics covered in Table 1. Due to differences in learning and teaching approaches, pedagogical models will evolve. A digital platform will bring about many qualitative transformations (Quadir et al., 2020). Although the methods differ, the platform stays the same. A teacher's value lies in their ability to employ strategies and educational methods with discernment. Students' learning outcomes and the development of their learning methods can be enhanced through the use of pedagogical models and technologies to design all-encompassing learning experiences (Tempelaar et al., 2021). Assessments and analytics for learning also need to be considered (Alyahyan & Düştegör, 2020). As AI is integrated, smart learning analytics and evaluations will need to be developed. To accomplish the aims of precision education, the appropriateness requirements must be met.

Analytics of Smart Learning

Smart learning analytics research focuses on identifying at-risk students and providing timely interventions using big data and AI. Improving both teacher effectiveness and student achievement is the ultimate goal. If we want to improve the quality of instruction, identify which students are struggling with which subjects, and understand how best to use the material, we need to look into smart learning analytics. Using intelligent learning analytics, teachers can monitor their students' progress and adjust lesson plans based on students' understanding levels. Students are given the tools they need to take charge of their own learning with smart learning analytics. They can see how they stack up against their classmates, take tests to make sure they're on track academically, and teachers can use the data to pinpoint where their students lack fundamental knowledge and study skills.

Students can benefit from intelligent learning analytics because they provide better insights into their progress and the steps they need to take to reach their educational goals, allowing for more personalized and self-directed skill and knowledge acquisition. With the use of smart learning analytics, students may decide for themselves whether or not to authorize the gathering and use of their data, which helps protect their privacy.

Smart Assessment

Understanding and measuring students' learning outcomes through an efficient grading policy, gauging their learning behaviors through suitable learning tactics, and identifying their learning difficulties are all part of intelligent assessment research. Teachers can use this data to tailor their lessons to each student's unique strengths, weaknesses, and learning style (Lu et al., 2018). The correlation between learning efficacy and learning patterns can be better understood with the use of learning pattern classification and learning efficacy prediction tools (Wong et al., 2019). Based on students' study habits, they may be offered prompt guidance. Improving students' educational achievement could be as simple as defining and assessing their attention, motivation, and engagement, and then designing learning activities that boost these qualities.

Improving smart assessment can be done by incorporating an examination mechanism into the smart evaluation system and by enhancing the evaluation of students' learning activities, such as reflection, pre-class previews, oral presentations, specialized themes, assignments, and program writing. In this model, teachers provide course materials, AI summarises those materials to extract key ideas, and then the system figures out how to test those ideas by creating exam questions and reference answers on its own (Kurdi et al., 2020). Cloze, multiple-choice, fill-in-the-blank, essay, and short-answer forms are all possible for test questions (Das, Bidyut, 2017).

By comparing students' answers to reference solutions for short-answer questions, the system can automatically provide scores and feedback using deep learning. Textbooks and presentation slides are provided by educators to help with effective evaluation. The system creates a knowledge map by extracting key concepts from the textbook and applying natural language processing text summarisation algorithms. Every node in the knowledge map represents a basic idea, and every edge shows the relationship between two nodes in context.

To determine whether a user has grasped a crucial idea, the system automatically generates test questions and reference answers using the principal notions represented by the knowledge map nodes. If students submit written responses, the system can compare them to reference answers, use deep learning to rate them, and then provide feedback. Compared with those who only review the content, students who engage in repeated testing and practice are better able to retain information, understand key concepts more deeply, and perform at a higher level.

Emerging Themes

As a result of changes in the European and global economies, a number of governance issues arise both inside and between EHEA member states. Public funding for higher education is under scrutiny in many countries, which has multiple consequences, including the rise of private providers and the push for publicly funded institutions to become more commercial and diversify their income(Middlehurst & Teixeira, 2012). Potential institutional tensions between academic and business interests, and systemic concerns about new regulatory frameworks that could undermine existing quality assurance or accountability systems, could have far-reaching effects on governance in the not-too-distant future.

Governance and the selection of competent governors will be hindered by the increasing complexity of university operations, regardless of whether conflict is the main worry or not(Azevedo & Best, 2025). The real issue for governance is to turn this conflict into a positive force rather than a negative one, as tensions have intensified due to the confluence of institutions becoming more open to outside influences and the internal need to moderate diverse interests. In light of increasing demand for higher education, mass participation frameworks, and lifelong learning, as well as resource and funding constraints, the trend towards enhanced institutional differentiation and systemic diversity is expected to worsen.

Mergers and acquisitions, whether private sector driven or prompted by state or system-level coordination, will shape the environment, as will institutional efforts to form consortia and networks, such as public-private partnerships(Ardito, 2025). 'Disruptive Innovation' predictions at the systemic and institutional levels may become applicable when Information and Communication Technology (ICT) innovations are integrated into these changes, such as more online and distant learning options and the emergence of new providers offering higher education in novel formats, possibly more adaptable and cheaper.

Technological progress has far-reaching effects on the workings of government; with the ease with which data can be gathered and shared through management information systems and performance indicators, the cause of openness and responsibility can be advanced. Enhanced management competence within institutions and related governance acumen are required to effectively understand and interpret data, as trends in system guidance through performance monitoring are predicted to rise.

Among the many challenges in governance, four stand out; some are already under investigation, but they need further attention in both theoretical and practical realms.

The first problem has multiple possible interpretations and concerns networks. To start, new arrangements in higher education show that old boundaries are being reshaped, blurred, crossed, or dissolved. Because they call into doubt the efficacy of preexisting frameworks of governance that apply to particular industries, national governments, institutions, or individuals, these structural changes have implications for governance(Mouta et al., 2025). People in particular occupations that involve dynamic, non-hierarchical planning and cybernetic deliberation and execution of public policy through horizontally structured networks might also benefit from the idea.

Another similar view is that policy networks, including those in Europe and elsewhere, as well as many national, regional, and municipal organizations, are responsible for developing and implementing higher education policies. Here, in the murky territory between the state and civil society, policy networks form, including the informal contacts necessary for effective policymaking. The authors argue that policy network analysis provides a theoretical basis for studying how multi-level governance affects the practice and policy of higher education. Because they raise both theoretical and practical questions about the role of governance in higher education, the several ways in which networks have been interpreted in terms of their structures, processes, and relationships with reference to governance provide promising directions for further research.

Another issue concerns relationships, which are significant in procedural and structural settings. A large portion of the policy literature focuses on the formal framework of connections between various groups, agents, and systems. De Boer and colleagues call the changing power dynamics between institutions and governments "The doing of governance," and it is crucial to explore micro-level relationships, such as those between the Rector and the Board, to improve these assessments (Tripathi, 2025). Recent studies on "Governing body effectiveness" in the United Kingdom and "Excellent" governance in Australia focus more on the dynamics of governance, whereas older studies on accountability frameworks and relationships deal with power and trust directly.

An insightful personal comment on the dynamics of power in institutional governance is offered in a new study from the Higher Education Policy Institute. The author draws from the experiences of an institutional leader. Given the prevalence of competing ideals, ethical dilemmas, the need to prioritise interests, and finite resources in governance talks, participants can anticipate an ever-increasing level of complexity in the field. Relationship, value, and interest dynamics, along with the 'Efficiency' of government, constitute a third obstacle(Omodan, 2025). Again, there are several facets to the subject. Previous study focused on one aspect: the extent to which higher education governance systems may be implemented with integrity, with a focus on the public life standards advocated for and, more especially, the UK's Good Governance Standard for Public Services.

They contend that the evidence is not clear. What constitutes 'effective' governance with respect to particular values is an important question to ask in light of impending problems like the commercialization of some university activities, possible ethical dilemmas with managing transnational education and international research partnerships, and dangers to academic freedom in different European countries. It has been noted that the most academically accomplished institutions in the UK do not exhibit the characteristics of good governance that are promoted by the present "corporate-hierarchical" model of institutional leadership.

To evaluate the real conditions and rhetoric surrounding governance reviews in European higher education, more thorough investigations into the effectiveness of governance in relation to academic performance are necessary. A recent study that examined governance through academics' perceptions of changing work practices and internal governance structures shed some light on this issue. Last but not least, there is the question of how to ensure that universities' economic and non-economic aspects are balanced, with ramifications for institutional governance. The view that institutions constitute a separate type of economic structure has been overshadowed by the tendency to see them as quasi-economic entities. In addition, we should not lose sight of the fact that higher education is more than just a hierarchical framework.

While the two names are often used interchangeably, the latter has grown more common in recent years, universities are more like institutions with a clear purpose than just any old organization. Focusing on the institution rather than its larger social function diminishes the importance of higher education's history, tradition, norms, and path-dependency and narrows one's view of the institution's scope and legitimacy. Funds are essential for the advancement of higher education institutions' operations. Still, they're capable of doing it in quite different ways. Transforming into a business that provides academic services while doing away with the institutional component is one possible approach. Finding a happy medium between responding to immediate social and economic needs and responding to market signals is possible without sacrificing the university's long-term mission. HE may face costs, difficulties, and gains as a result of its response to social and economic issues.

Expanding on earlier studies, we argue that institutions of higher learning, like nonprofits, may differ from for-profits not only in legal constraints but also in the goals and aspirations of their upper-level management. There is a wide range of goals and leadership styles among the administrators and faculty of universities and colleges due to the unique nature of these organizations. There will be a certain type of leadership and management that will keep that bias alive in higher education administrations as they become increasingly aligned with corporate models.

CONCLUSION

AI is having a profound effect on AF, professional autonomy, and institutional governance in higher education. The customization, efficiency, and decision-making help offered by AI technologies are undeniable. However, there are concerns about algorithmic bias, surveillance, loss of professional autonomy, and government centralization that accompany these technologies. To preserve academic ideals while leveraging technological breakthroughs, educational institutions should establish AI frameworks that are human-centered and ethically grounded. Reconciling accountability, transparency, professional autonomy, and academic integrity with AI-driven transformation is crucial for the future of higher education.

REFERENCES

Ajmal, M. (2025). From Academic Freedom To Algorithmic Agency : Knowledge Governance In Ai-Enhanced Education. *Journal of Management Science Research Review*, 1036–1058.

Alhafidh, F. (2025). The Use of AI and Academic Freedom in Higher Education. *Journal of Academic Freedom*, 0–1.

Alyahyan, E., & Düştegör, D. (2020). Predicting academic success in higher education: Literature review and best practices. *International Journal of Educational Technology in Higher Education*, *17*(1), 3. Advance online publication. DOI: 10.1186/s41239-020-0177-7

Ardito, C. G. (2025). AI at the knowledge gates : Institutional policies and hybrid configurations in universities and publishers. *AI at the Knowledge Gates : Institutional Policies and Hybrid Configurations in Universities and Publishers*, *7*(August), 1–16. DOI: 10.3389/fcomp.2025.1608276

Azevedo, L., & Best, E. (2025). Institutional Policies on Artificial Intelligence in Higher Education : Frameworks and Best Practices for Faculty. *New Directions for Adult and Continuing Education*, *2025*(188), 70–78. DOI: 10.1002/ace.70013

Bernasconi, A. (2025). Latin America : Weak academic freedom within strong university autonomy. *Global Constitutionalism*, 96–117. DOI: 10.1017/S204538172400011X

Bowen, W.G., and E. M. T. (2015). Locus of authority: The evolution of faculty roles in the governance of higher education. *Locus of Authority: The Evolution of Faculty Roles in the Governance of Higher Education.*, 1–4.

Cazan, A., & Cocorad, E. (2016). Computers in Human Behavior Computer anxiety and attitudes towards the computer and the internet with Romanian high-school and university students t a. *Computers in Human Behavior*, *55*, 2013–2015. DOI: 10.1016/j.chb.2015.09.001

Chattopadhyay, S. A. U. M. E. N. (2025). ACADEMIC FREEDOM, INSTITUTIONAL AUTONOMY AND INSTITUTIONALISING ACCOUNTABILITY : A REFLECTION ON THE NATIONAL EDUCATION POLICY 2020 SAUMEN CHATTOPADHYAY Volume 4, 2020 THE JMC REVIEW. *ACADEMIC FREEDOM, INSTITUTIONAL AUTONOMY AND INSTITUTIONALISING ACCOUNTABILITY : A REFLECTION ON THE NATIONAL EDUCATION POLICY 2020 SAUMEN CHATTOPADHYAY Volume 4, 2020 THE JMC REVIEW, November.*

Chen, X., Xie, H., & Hwang, G. (2020). Computers and Education : Arti fi cial Intelligence A multi-perspective study on Arti fi cial Intelligence in Education : grants, conferences, journals, software tools, institutions, and researchers. *Computers and Education: Artificial Intelligence*, *1*(August), 100005. DOI: 10.1016/j.caeai.2020.100005

Chen, X., Xie, H., Zou, D., & Hwang, G. (2020). Computers and Education : Arti fi cial Intelligence Application and theory gaps during the rise of Arti fi cial Intelligence in Education. *Computers and Education: Artificial Intelligence*, *1*(August), 100002. DOI: 10.1016/j.caeai.2020.100002

Chikane, R. (2026). Rhodes Must Fall and the incongruence of academic freedom and decoloniality. *Globalisation, Societies and Education*, *7724*(3), 641–657. DOI: 10.1080/14767724.2024.2341103

Clark-gordon, C. V., Bowman, N. D., Hadden, A., Frisby, B., Hadden, A., & Frisby, B. (2019). College instructors and the digital red pen: An exploratory study of factors influencing the adoption and non-adoption of digital written feedback technologies. *Computers & Education*, *128*, 414–426. DOI: 10.1016/j.compedu.2018.10.002

Colonna, L. (2026). Artificial Intelligence in Education (AIED): Towards More Effective Regulation. *Artificial Intelligence in Education (AIED): Towards More Effective Regulation*, 161–181. DOI: 10.1017/err.2025.10039

Das, B., & Majumder, M. (2017, December). Das, Bidyut, and M. M. (2017). Factual open cloze question generation for assessment of learner ' s knowledge. *International Journal of Educational Technology in Higher Education*, *14*(1), 24. Advance online publication. DOI: 10.1186/s41239-017-0060-3

Dávideková, M., Mjartan, M., & Greguš, M.Dávideková. (2017). ScienceDirect Utilization of Virtual Reality in Education of Employees in Slovakia. *Procedia Computer Science*, *113*, 253–260. DOI: 10.1016/j.procs.2017.08.365

Han, Y. (2025). Beyond the Algorithm : Reconciling Generative AI and Human Agency in Academic Writing Education. *International Journal of Learning and Teaching*, *11*(1), 39–42. Advance online publication. DOI: 10.18178/ijlt.11.1.39-42

Hao, Z. (2025). Institutional Autonomy in Relation to Academic Freedom, the Role of the Government and the Need for Higher Education as a Federation. *European Review (Chichester, England)*, *33*(S1), 70–85. DOI: 10.1017/S1062798725000146

Huang, J., & Chen, Z. (2016). The Research and Design of Web-based Intelligent Tutoring System. *International Journal of Multimedia and Ubiquitous Engineering*, *11*(6), 337–348. DOI: 10.14257/ijmue.2016.11.6.30

Hwang, G., Sung, H., Chang, S., & Huang, X. (2020). Computers and Education : Arti fi cial Intelligence A fuzzy expert system-based adaptive learning approach to improving students ' learning performances by considering affective and cognitive factors. *Computers and Education: Artificial Intelligence, 1*(August), 100003. DOI: 10.1016/j.caeai.2020.100003

Ifinedo, A. (2020). This is a self-archived version of an original article. This version may differ from the original in pagination and typographic details. Copyright : Rights : Rights url. *Computers & Education, 103760*. Advance online publication. DOI: 10.1016/j.compedu.2019.103760

Kinshuk. (2016). Evolution Is not enough : Revolutionizing Current Learning Environments to Smart Learning Environments. *International Journal of Artificial Intelligence in Education*, 561–581. DOI: 10.1007/s40593-016-0108-x

Kirkham, R. (2021). Industrial Limitations on Academic Freedom in Computer Science. *Industrial Limitations on Academic Freedom in Computer Science*, 1–15.

Kuch, D., Kearnes, M., & Gulson, K. (2020). The promise of precision: datafication in medicine, agriculture and education. Policy Studies, 41(5), 527-546.

Kurdi, G., Leo, J., Parsia, B., Sattler, U., & Al-Emari, S. (2020). A Systematic Review of Automatic Question Generation for Educational Purposes. *International Journal of Artificial Intelligence in Education, 30*(1), 121–204. DOI: 10.1007/s40593-019-00186-y

Lai, H., Hsiao, Y., & Hsieh, P. (2018). Computers & Education The role of motivation, ability, and opportunity in university teachers ' continuance use intention for fl ipped teaching. *Computers & Education, 124*(November 2017), 37–50. DOI: 10.1016/j.compedu.2018.05.013

Li, M., Xie, Q., Enkhtur, A., Meng, S., Chen, L., Yamamoto, B. A., & Murakami, M. (2025). A framework for developing university policies on generative AI governance: A cross-national comparative study. *A Framework for Developing University Policies on Generative AI Governance: A Cross-National Comparative Study*, 1–47.

Lin, H., Tu, Y., Hwang, G., & Huang, H. (2021). From Precision Education to Precision Medicine : Factors Affecting Medical Staff ' s Intention to Learn to Use AI Applications in Hospitals. *Journal of Educational Technology & Society, 24*, 123–137.

Liu, K., Cao, Y., Hu, Y., & Wei, L. (2019). Application status and development of big data in medical education in China. *Medical Data Mining, 2*(3), 118–125. DOI: 10.53388/mdm2018023

Lu, O. H. T., Huang, A. Y. Q., Huang, J. C. H., Lin, A. J. Q., & Yang, S. J. H. (2018). Applying Learning Analytics for the Early Prediction of Students ' Academic Performance in Blended Learning. *Journal of Educational Technology & Society*, *21*, 220–232.

Mann, S. P., Aboy, M., Seah, J. J., Lin, Z., Luo, X., Rodger, D., Zohny, H., Minssen, T., Savulescu, J., & Earp, B. D. (2025). *AI and the Future of Academic Peer Review*. AI and the Future of Academic Peer Review.

Middlehurst, R., & Teixeira, P. N. (2012). Governance Within the EHEA : Dynamic Trends, Common Challenges, and National Particularities. *Governance Within the EHEA : Dynamic Trends, Common Challenges, and National Particularities*, 527–551. DOI: 10.1007/978-94-007-3937-6

Moodley, M., Tourism, G., & Africa, S. (2025). Exploring academic freedom, institutional autonomy, and public accountability in the global landscape of private higher education. *South African Journal of Higher Education*, *39*(4), 165–178. DOI: 10.20853/39-4-7516

Mouta, A., María, E., Sánchez, T., María, A., & Llorente, P. (2025). Comprehensive professional learning for teacher agency in addressing ethical challenges of AIED : Insights from educational design research. In *Education and Information Technologies* (Vol. 30, Issue 3). Springer US. DOI: 10.1007/s10639-024-12946-y

Nygren, G., Dobek-ostrowska, B., & Anikina, M. (2015). Professional autonomy. *Professional Autonomy*, *36*, 79–95.

Omodan, B. I. (2025). Redefining the role of supervisors in the era of artificial intelligence : Implications for hybrid postgraduate research governance implications for hybrid postgraduate research governance. *Cogent Education*, *12*(1), 2536534. Advance online publication. DOI: 10.1080/2331186X.2025.2536534

Painsi, P. W., Leitner, K., & Rybnicek, R. (2025). The impact of institutional autonomy on higher education institutions in Europe. *Science and Public Policy, December 2024*, 236–253.

Prinsloo, C., Ramashego, S. M., Learning, D., Visagie, R. G., Tjano, N., Support, S., & Africa, S. (2025). BALANCING ACADEMIC FREEDOM AND RESEARCH INTEGRITY THROUGH VIRTUE ETHICS IN THE USE OF AI IN OPEN DISTANCE. *South African Journal of Higher Education*, *39*(4), 236–262. DOI: 10.20853/39-4-7523

Quadir, B., Chen, N., & Isaias, P. (2020). Analyzing the educational goals, problems and techniques used in educational big data research from 2010 to 2018. *Interactive Learning Environments, 4820*. Advance online publication. DOI: 10.1080/10494820.2020.1712427

Ramlo, S. (2025). Examining Views about Academic Freedom at Institutions of Higher Education in the US. *Innovative Higher Education, 51*(2), 711–732. DOI: 10.1007/s10755-025-09845-6

Scherer, R. (2018). University of Oslo, Faculty of Educational Sciences, Department of Teacher Education and SC. *Computers & Education.*

Sun, J. C. (2025). *Academic Freedom in US Higher Education : Rights Emergent from the Law and the Profession*. Encyclopedia.

Tabacu, A. E. (2025). REGULATORY FRAMEWORK FOR THE USE OF ARTIFICIAL INTELLIGENCE IN EUROPEAN HIGHER EDUCATION. *Jurídicas, 21*(1), 124–152. DOI: 10.17981/juridcuc.21.1.2025.07

Tempelaar, D., Rienties, B., & Nguyen, Q. (2021). The Contribution of Dispositional Learning Analytics to Precision Education. *Journal of Educational Technology & Society, 24*, 109–122.

Tripathi, P. (2025). RESEARCH PAPERS AI IN CLASSROOMS : IMPACT ON TEACHER. *AI in Classrooms: Impact on Teacher Identity and Autonomy.", 20*(4).

Ültanır, Y. G., Author, C., & Gürcan, Y. (2025). Autonomy and Academic Freedom in Universities : Country Examples Based on Types of Governance. *Higher Education Governance and Policy, 6*, 68–86. DOI: 10.55993/hegp.1584027

Waddington, D. I., Maxwell, B., Maclean, T., Mcdonough, K., Waddington, D. I., Maxwell, B., Maclean, T., Mcdonough, K., & Waddington, D. I. (2024). theory and practice How free are classroom teachers ? Understanding teacher academic freedom in the United States and Canada academic freedom in the United States and Canada. *Theory and Practice How Free Are Classroom Teachers ? Understanding Teacher Academic Freedom in the United States and Canada Academic Freedom in the United States and Canada*. DOI: 10.1080/13540602.2024.2422859

Wang, Y., Liu, C., & Tu, Y. F. (2021). Factors affecting the adoption of AI-based applications in higher education. Educational technology & society, 24(3), 116-129.

Wong, J., Khalil, M., Baars, M., De Koning, B. B., & Paas, F. (2019). Computers & Education Exploring sequences of learner activities in relation to self- regulated learning in a massive open online course. *Computers & Education, 140*(February), 103595. DOI: 10.1016/j.compedu.2019.103595

Yang, S. J. H. (2021). Guest Editorial : Precision Education - A New Challenge for AI in Education. *Journal of Educational Technology & Society*, *24*, 105–108.

Yang, S. J. H., Ogata, H., Matsui, T., & Chen, N. (2021). Computers and Education : Arti fi cial Intelligence Human-centered arti fi cial intelligence in education : Seeing the invisible through the visible. *Computers and Education: Artificial Intelligence*, *2*(January), 100008. DOI: 10.1016/j.caeai.2021.100008

Zawacki-Richter, O., Marín, V. I., Bond, M., & Gouverneur, F. (2019). Systematic review of research on artificial intelligence applications in higher education – where are the educators? *International Journal of Educational Technology in Higher Education*, *16*(1), 39. Advance online publication. DOI: 10.1186/s41239-019-0171-0

Chapter 12
Future Scenarios for the Professoriate and Higher Education:
Leadership in 2035

Sinath No
http://orcid.org/0009-0001-1644-8702
National University of Battambang, Cambodia

Mai Meta
http://orcid.org/0009-0007-2192-6848
National University of Battambang, Cambodia

Sam Sopheak
http://orcid.org/0009-0009-2362-8611
University of Heng Samrin Thboung Khmom (UHSK), Cambodia

Toem Tet
http://orcid.org/0009-0000-3057-3262
National of Battambang University, Cambodia

ABSTRACT

The analysis of 2035 for professors and education leadership is undertaken in this chapter using futures studies, with scenario planning being the focus. A crisis in the academic paradigm, the development of a "research precariat," and the decline of the Humboldtian vision of the scholarly-citizen are recognized. Based on an assessment of present trends, including generative AI, academic de-bundling, and the diffusion of the knowledge authority, four scenarios are derived, namely, the Augmented AI Academy, the Global Knowledge Network, the Corporate Integration

DOI: 10.4018/979-8-3373-8525-9.ch012

of Vocational Education, and the Resilient Human-Centric Organization. These scenarios bring about distinct challenges for the professoriate and its leadership that would require a transition from bureaucratic management toward ecosystem leadership and anticipatory governance. The implications of this foresight exercise indicate a possible evolution in the value proposition of the professoriate, from knowledge diffusion to validation and social innovation by 2035.

1. INTRODUCTION

Higher education is operating in an environment marked by rapid technological change, intensified public scrutiny, uneven global development, and rising expectations that universities demonstrate social value. In this context, educational leadership can no longer be understood primarily as the administration of a bounded campus. The problem must be analysed as one of governing an ecosystem that is shaped by such developments as digitalization, artificial intelligence, changes in the labour market, participation in the public sphere, and the prospect of uncertainty. What leadership qualities do we need in our institutions of higher learning by 2035? In this chapter, we will analyse professor positions in the field of artificial intelligence with respect to recruitment, selection, retention, evaluation, and skill needs, as well as examine the possible future influence of new technologies and organizational structures on professorial career paths in academia until 2035.

The recent years have witnessed the swift introduction of AI technology in universities around the world. According to UNESCO (2024), more than 60% of the universities use AI technology in classroom teaching or examination processes or administration. However, at the same time, the OECD (2023) is witnessing increasing job insecurity among scholars. The current chapter is a conceptual literature review based on an integrative analysis of scholarly articles and primary documents covering the period of 2019 to 2026. This review examines six trend clusters that have an impact on higher education management: digital institutionalization, GenAI governance, third missions and social innovations, doctoral growth and diversified careers, anticipatory governance, and human-centric resilience. The aim is not to test a causal model, but to identify the strongest recurring themes and derive an analytically coherent leadership framework for 2035. This chapter seeks to situate these transformations in a future orientation.

The following are the research questions addressed in this paper:

1. What is the importance of the evolution of the professoriate to our understanding of the present structural crisis and our future possibilities by 2035?

2. Which futures thinking approaches work well when considering the future of universities after the digital age?
3. What scenarios are possible for the professoriate and institutional governance in the next ten years?
4. What are the critical leadership capabilities required by institutions by 2035?

In parallel, the objectives of this research project are:

1. Deconstruct the current "crisis" of the professoriate by examining the transition from vocation-based paradigms to the gig economy and unbundled academic roles.
2. Synthesize emerging global phenomenon, including digital transformation, social innovation and demographic shifts, into an integrated futures frame.
3. Create four foresight scenarios demonstrating the possible futures in higher education. Provide actionable solutions concerning leadership and policies for the year 2035.
4. Which practical recommendations would be made to address leadership issues in 2035?

2. LITERATURE REVIEW

2.1 The Historical Trajectory and Current Crisis of the Professoriate

The historical trajectory of the professoriate has shifted from the Humboldtian ideal of the 19th century unification of research and teaching to its current state of fragmentation and precarity. During the mid-20th century, the "Golden Age" of the professoriate served to enshrine tenure as a safeguard for academic freedom and a mechanism for social mobility. However, during the late 20th and early 21st centuries, the tenure system has slowly been dismantled by a neoliberal managerialism that privileges market-like measurement in place of academic freedom.

The "research precariat" constitutes one of the prominent symptoms associated with the present-day crisis where researchers are either postdoctoral researchers or academic labourers working under fixed-term tenure track contracts without the promise of future job security (OECD, 2021). The research precariat has transformed the career trajectory of the professoriate from a predictable "ladder" to a precarious "gig economy" where junior scholars often must seek external funding in order to only cover their wages (Roumbanis, 2018). In this context, a culture of "symbolic violence" is established in which behaviours are legitimatized market like behaviour and the instability of the current career system is understood as a normative rationality of practice (Roumbanis, 2018).

In addition to the professoriate's sentiment toward a career, there is also the now growing sentiment among doctoral students regarding traditional faculty roles, particularly in high need fields like engineering and computing. Research is showing that many PhD students, who were excited to pursue an academic career, are now dissuaded themselves by the "toxic" culture associated with review, the stress of writing applications for grants and the normative pressures of junior faculty life (McGee et al., 2019). This evidence suggests that the current model of faculty is increasingly understood as a relic and unappealing for the next generation of knowledge producers.

The crisis is also characterized by a particularized gendered and racialized context. The myth of the "meritocracy," which often conceals structural oppression, has gender and precariousness as processes that are interrelated to one another, especially when looking at the experiences of minority women and academic mothers (Zheng, 2018). The COVID-19 pandemic only highlighted the dichotomy between neoliberal productivity and the need for caregiving, resulting in discourses on how there should be a decentring of masculinity in academic career paths (Bowyer et al., 2022).

Figure 1. Evolution of the professoriate from the Humboldtian academic model toward AI-augmented and ecosystem-oriented higher education structures by 2035.

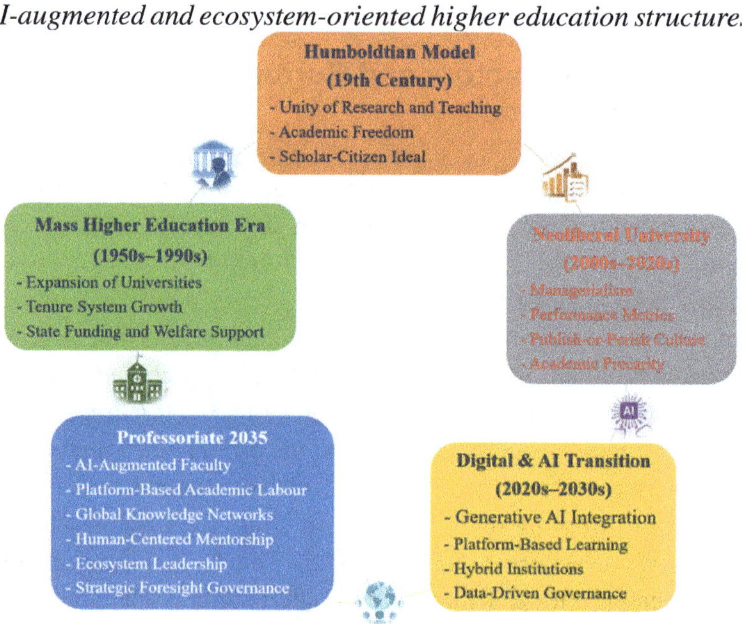

2.2 Theoretical Frameworks for Future Studies in Higher Education

To help understand the complexity of 2035, academics have been resorting more and more to "futures thinking" and "strategic foresight" in relation to various theoretical perspectives that do not adhere to linear forecasts anymore. Such perspectives made it possible to analyse what is known as "wicked" problems related to the future of education (such as climate change, biodiversity decline, rapid urbanization, etc.) (IPCC, 2023). Scenario planning as methodology provided an opportunity to utilize the potential of "signals of change" and break through the institutional inertia to develop new archetypes of the university.

Another significant theoretical prism for understanding the topic is that of the "post digital condition"; digital technology is not anymore considered separate from social and physical reality, but rather something that constitutes the "ecosystem" of "modernity" in the field of higher education (Alenezi, 2023). Whereas the "digital transformation" would perhaps have been previously viewed as a technical transformation, what we see now is an ontological transformation in terms of knowledge co-creation and co-production (Traxler et al., 2021). Under the post digital condition, the function of the university is approached via the "Quadruple/ Quintuple Helix Model" approach toward theorization of knowledge creation in collaboration (Morawska, 2021).

Then comes the theory of intersectionality, focusing on the issues of technological mediation from the perspectives of fairness and algorithmic governance. Since more and more universities depend on algorithms in their management and educational practices, it is possible that the results will reflect existing social inequalities, which can also be considered biased representations of social structures (Ovalle et al., 2023).

Additionally, leadership theory has been moving toward "Change Leadership for Sustainability or the practice by leaders of fostering identity, perspective, and agency around intergenerational well-being within a multitude of spheres (Novy et al., 2021). In this way, developing specific competencies - systems thinking and emotional intelligence - to support agents of change who must lead in complex social-environmental systems holds importance (Novy et al., 2021). Finally, there is emerging interest in "servant leadership" as a model in nurturing work engagement and extra-role behaviours in non-profit organization and educational settings, as it stands in contrast to all the top-down narratives of managerialism (Mer et al., 2024).

2.3 Expanding Trends in Global Educational Leadership

A series of macro trends is reshaping the practice of educational leadership. Industry 4.0-related digitalization is one of the most consequential drivers because it compels institutions to redesign not only delivery formats but also strategy, governance, staffing, and credential structures. Educational leaders are therefore under pressure to build "digital institutions" that can operate across blended, modular, and globally networked learning environments rather than simply digitizing existing campus routines (Trí et al., 2021; Alenezi, 2023). This is not only confined to micro-credentials and nano-degrees but also the "unbundling" of degrees into skills (Alenezi, 2023). The implication for leaders is that they should no longer be focused on running an institution on-site but instead create a "digital institution" able to cater for globalization (Alenezi, 2023).

Furthermore, the advent of generative artificial intelligence has hastened this paradigm shift by changing the modes of instruction, evaluation, support for students, and expertise perception. Even though there is a likelihood of increased efficiency and innovation in learning due to the use of generative artificial intelligence, challenges such as academic fraud, breach of privacy, excessive reliance on proprietary software, and the impairment of analytical skills exist. In view of this, the response by the leadership ought to focus on AI literacy, assessment reform, and institutional management rather than banning (Rudolph et al., 2024). AI literacy needs to be cultivated in educators and learners by the leadership to ensure that technological application is based on humanitarian values (Rudolph et al., 2024). This problem becomes increasingly complex when addressing developing countries eager to exploit the advantages of IR 4.0 without being worried about falling behind (Trí et al., 2021).

The growing evaluation of universities according to their social innovation and regional development is becoming more prominent in the modern world. The above approach brings into consideration that there is a paradigm shift from universities as knowledge creators in isolation to universities collaborating with other partners such as communities in solving socio-economic problems (Morawska, 2021). The above trend is evident in new trends in urbanization and revival of rural areas, where universities are the catalysts of high-quality regional development (Chen et al., 2021).

Taking into consideration all of these trends together, it can be concluded that the most significant challenge for educational leaders in 2035 will be the combination of the advantages of technological efficiency and humanism (Sarrico, 2022). Anticipatory governance, competitive intelligence, individual resilience, and socially and environmentally responsible innovations are expected to be viewed as the competencies of successful leaders (Molotoks et al., 2020). The implementation of technological advancements is very important for an organization, but so are maintaining academic integrity, fostering the well-being of employees, earning public trust, and developing value-based innovations (Madureira et al., 2021).

Table 1. Expanding Trends in Global Educational Leadership Toward 2035

Trend cluster	Core development	Leadership implication by 2035
IR 4.0 and digital institutionalization	The transition of higher education to platform-based, blended, and data-driven institutional ecosystems has started.	Institutions will need to create digital institutions rather than simply digitizing their existing processes.
Generative AI and critical AI literacy	The advent of GenAI will affect learning and teaching, assessment, learner support, research, and institutional governance.	There is a need for ethical governance of AI, assessment redesign, and AI literacy.
Third mission and social innovation	Universities are now expected to help with regional development, social innovation, and overcoming issues within communities.	Leaders need to bring education and research together with social involvement and value generation.
PhD growth and careers	There has been an increase in participation in PhD studies, although career options for academics have become restricted and diverse.	Leaders need to open up PhD opportunities and appreciate non-teaching and hybrid academic positions.
Anticipatory governance and competitive intelligence	Uncertainty demands a culture of strategic foresight and horizon scanning.	Leadership needs to expand access to PhDs and value non-teaching roles in academia.
Human-centred resilience and circular innovation	Academic life is subject to workload stress, precarity, inequality, and ecological transformation.	Leaders need to integrate education and scholarship with social engagement and value creation.

Leadership implication is not just increased competition for faculty positions but the realization of the necessity of having a larger ecology of career options for PhDs outside of academia. In parallel, widening global insecurity, including persistent food insecurity in many regions, underscores that higher education futures are being shaped within unequal and unstable social conditions rather than within a single universal trajectory (Sarrico, 2022). This indicates the increased need for the 2035 professoriate to expand the framework of careers to consider non-faculty roles. Given that, "Doctoral participation has expanded significantly, while career destinations have become more diverse and academic employment remains constrained."

These trends will mean that 2035 will be a period of tension between technology-focused efficiencies and human-centered values of work. The leadership would have to grapple with the "GenAI Paradox," where the ability to access information undermines the unchallengeable position of the professor (Rudolph et al., 2024). The performance of the organization would rely on whether educational colleges have the ability to build "stress adaptation and resilience" among its professors (Ross et al., 2023) but would proactively work to ensure that it moves towards a "circular innovation" model, which encompasses the social and ecological considerations for value creation (Suchek et al., 2021).

Despite growing scholarship on AI, digital transformation, and higher education reform, limited research has integrated these developments into a comprehensive foresight-oriented framework examining how the professoriate and institutional leadership may evolve simultaneously by 2035. This chapter addresses that gap by combining futures studies, strategic foresight, and scenario planning to conceptualize multiple trajectories for academic work and institutional governance.

3. METHODS

3.1 Strategic Foresight and Scenario Planning Methodology

Exploring the future of the professoriate and leadership in higher education in 2035 requires a methodological approach that surpasses conventional linear forecasting. Strategic foresight is utilized as the main methodology, and is differentiated from simple horizon scanning as it employs sense making and strategy development in relation to the future, rather than simply identifying future technologies (Cuhls, 2019). Horizon scanning is one component of "things to come," but strategic foresight goes one step further in integrating signals in an active process centered on creating long-term strategic decision-making (Cuhls, 2019). This strategy foresight approach, which will be used in this research, is modified to cope with the current uncertainties and instabilities in the international higher education landscape.

In this study, the investigation is structured based on the recognition and analysis of "megatrends." Megatrends can be described as major social, economic, political, ecological, and technological trends which usually influence human behaviour (OECD, 2018). The megatrends analysed in this study include trends such as the evolution of digital demand and enabling technologies, and they serve as the primary drivers in the future scenarios (OECD, 2018). Identifying the more complex dimensions of these drivers supports the development of futures in which higher education might engage over the next ten years. This is particularly useful in socio-environmental systems analysis because of the complex interaction between technological advancement and diverse human agency (Elsawah et al., 2020).

The scenario planning piece of the study helps develop discrete, internally consistent narratives about the future. Unlike predictions, scenarios are useful stories that challenge prevailing mental models and privileged assumptions about the professoriate and academic leadership (Chalmers & Armour, 2019). Using current trajectories of consideration, such as rapidly developing artificial intelligence integration and decentralized knowledge networks, support a continuous anticipatory governance approach to the study. The methodological choice supports rigorous creative thinking and offers exposure beyond gratuitous speculation about systemic changes that are actively underway globally, reshaping our economy and society.

3.2 Selection of Expert Panels and Delphi Technique Application

The 2035 scenarios were constructed and validated through the Delphi technique. This is a widely adopted method for collecting expert data and deriving a consensus opinion on complex real-world problems (Chalmers & Armour, 2019). The Delphi process is particularly appropriate for identifying consensus in the absence of empirical data about the future in disciplines and fields of practice, as it proceeds in a structured fashion using multiple iterations of structured questionnaires (Chalmers & Armour, 2019). This study used a three-round Delphi process to validate the scenarios and articulate the leadership competencies appropriate for each future. Choosing the expert panel was a vital part of the methodology to support a multidisciplinary perspective. The panel consisted of 60 people who represented sectors of senior university administrators, educational technologists, labour economists and digital ethics experts. The collective input from these sectors is important for drawing from the multiple perspectives needed to tackle the complex challenges of the Fourth Industrial Revolution from engineering, management and the social sciences (Horváth & Szabó, 2019). The panel also included experts from established multinational institutions and lesser-known educational providers to balance the assessment of forces and barriers contributing to institutional change (Horváth & Szabó, 2019).

Participants were selected through purposive sampling based on expertise in higher education leadership, educational technology, labour economics, digital governance, AI ethics, and futures studies. Experts were required to possess at least five years of professional or research experience related to higher education transformation or policy. The study adopted a three-round Delphi process, and consensus was considered achieved when more than 75% of participants demonstrated convergence regarding the plausibility and significance of the identified future drivers. Ethical procedures included anonymization of responses and voluntary participation throughout all rounds.

In the iterative rounds, experts were asked to provide to contextualize the plausibility of the drivers, for example, generative AI and block chain credentialing, and the impact drivers on higher education and academic success. The process also facilitated "social learning," where experts were able to refine their view based on the anonymized feedback from the group. Participation was important for establishing and improving the credibility of the research findings since it captures a diverse range of perspectives and experiences without requiring a superficial consensus

(Brito et al., 2018). The compiled scenarios ultimately reflect a synthesized expert view of the biggest opportunities and realistic assessments of impact for universities in 2035 (Dwivedi et al., 2019).

3.3 Data Analysis and Scenario Construction Framework

After the data collection phase, a multi-criteria approach was employed for data analysis and to structure the complex collection of data from the Delphi rounds and literature review. To support robust scenario building in the research, the "back casting," process was used to define a desirable or plausible future and then work backwards to determine the systemic change and policy interventions required to realize the defined future. This approach enables organizations to think holistically about implementation action and integrates future needs into organizational decision-making today (Mendoza et al., 2017).

A central lens for analysis in this study was the conceptualization of organizational resiliency as a meta-capability, which has been decomposed into three, successive stages; anticipation, coping, and adapting. In the analysis, attention was directed to how higher education institutions build organizational "capabilities" to navigate unexpected events and plan for successful futures acting in a complex and uncertain context (Duchek, 2020). By mapping the resilience stages of adaptation and coping onto the constructed scenarios, the research can identify the organizational structures that are more likely to thrive, or abject to failure in 2035.

The final construction of the research finding was also guided by the "Industry 4.0" framework that reflects the integration of digital twins, the Internet of Things (IoT), and autonomous decision-making (Chen et al., 2023). The findings also focused on how these technological drivers interact with social innovation to change the management functions and delivery of education (Morrar & Arman, 2017). This was done by conducting an expert review during the final phase to ensure that the scenarios had taken into consideration all aspects of digital literacy, personal identification, and online communication, which are expected to be very important in the future of cyber communications (Zvereva, 2023).

4. FINDINGS

4.1 Scenario One: The AI-Augmented and Hyper-Personalized Academy

2035 is the period when there will be an "AI Augmented Academy," where artificial intelligence moves from being marginal to becoming part of the cognitive processes of the academy (Dwivedi et al., 2019). According to empirical evidence, artificial intelligence can provide opportunities for both human enhancement as well as replacement of humans in certain situations within intellectual and social settings (Dwivedi et al., 2019). In such an altered academic landscape, the conventional position of the teacher as the main source of information transmission has been overtaken by artificial intelligence that can provide customized lessons based on the unique cognitive attributes of students.

In education, digital twins of learners and their surroundings permit real-time evaluation and prediction that gives the faculty the ability to act with great precision (Chen et al., 2023). However, this is, to an extent, also a product of managerial desire for more control, apart from real-time performance evaluation and monitoring, which is resisted by the middle management and employees who may not want to be assessed in such a manner (Horváth & Szabó, 2019). In this scenario, the role of the professor has shifted to "epistemic validator" and high-level mentor, positioned more humanly and personally where humans are much more important (and figuratively rich), in comparison to tasks that machines cannot yet replicate.

The socio-economic implications for this approach, should it be implemented, would be immense. According to organizations that have already adopted such technology as AI and block chains, their efficiency rate in operations has been increased by up to 25% (Setyadi et al., 2025). In Scenario One, this approach allows the academy to cope with large and varied cohorts of students using fewer resources.

During this time, the AI-Augmented Academy will still have significant challenges in digital ethics issues and the "prestige paradox". In this scenario, leaders will need to navigate a malleable, but ongoing tension between algorithms that are perceived as more efficient in governance and the need to maintain its intellectual integrity. The new " AI-augmented elite faculty model" of 2035 is able to use AI solutions to manage thousands of students, but this could still create a "two-tier" system of human-only instruction contrasted with AI-only instruction for a larger swath of the population.

4.2 Scenario Two: The Decentralized Global Knowledge Network

The second scenario entertains the concept of a "Decentralized Global Knowledge Network" in which the centralized structure of higher education institutions disappears and is supplanted by a Web 3.0-based ecosystem. In this case, the use of block chain is key in the education system since it enables creation of a data structure with security capabilities such as encryption and decentralization, which create trust in educational transactions (Wenhua et al., 2023). In this emerging education setting, there is no monopoly by individual or traditional universities in terms of knowledge possession. When reputation for quality knowledge is established, such knowledge gets traded in the context of Decentralized Autonomous Organizations (DAOs) or series of platforms called the metaverse (Sutikno & Aisyahrani, 2023).

This move towards metaversity involves using NFTs to prove authenticity for college degrees and certificates, giving the learners the power to own and disseminate an array of electronic portfolios (Sutikno & Aisyahrani, 2023). Under the decentralization model, there is the "unbundling" of the professoriate. Scholars become independent actors or "knowledge contractors," selling knowledge and credentials to several institutions rather than a single institution. This is an "Uber-ization" of the professoriate, but is made real through the use of smart contracts to execute automatic enforcement of the terms of the transaction agreed by untrusted parties; the professoriate's role is diminished (Mnasri et al., 2025) .

Although Web 3.0, on the other hand, has decentralization or the distribution of network as its characteristic, it also faces many security risks that are associated with it. Infringement and privacy leaks are key security concerns in the digital economy (Chen et al., 2022). Block chain systems, furthermore, are also subject to unique risks such as Sybil and Double-spending attacks that could challenge the credibility of any decentralized academic credentials (Iqbal & Matulevičius, 2021). In this scenario, leadership moves from institutional management and governance to "ecosystem curation," which includes mastering the governance of the platform and fostering trust in a trust-less environment (Wenhua et al., 2023).

The decentralized model also implies a different understanding of a campus. The physical nature of a "campus" is replaced by a digital world in which the people meet through virtual or augmented realities, interacting and collaborating in ways never previously imagined using all manner of devices. This is particularly attractive to Generation Z and the subsequent generations, who are interested in customized digital environments, embodied representations of presence navigating the metaversity through avatars (Periyasami & Periyasamy, 2022). For the professor, this implies traversing a global educational marketplace, where reputation and encomium are assessed algorithmically and impact metrics are certified in the block chain.

4.3 Scenario 3: The Corporate-Integrated and Vocational Model

Scenario 3 is described as a "Corporate-Integrated and Vocational Model," in which the boundaries between higher education and the industrial sector have become porous. Such a scenario is driven by existing and projected requirements imposed by the Fourth Industrial Revolution and this development is expected to present significant technological and organizational challenges to companies (Horváth & Szabó, 2019). In this new future scenario, universities are merely the R&D and specialized training arms of large firms and industries. According to Shamzzuzoha et al., (2022), members of academia are considered "industry-academic hybrids," and their loyalty is divided between the industry and the university since they focus on research that is evaluated based on economic or environmental benefits.

The burgeoning drive toward this model is inspired by the demand for "smart" systems and the pragmatic adoption of wireless intelligent technologies in sectors such as agriculture and manufacturing (Karunathilake et al., 2023). As industry moves toward sustainable development and the closure of energy and materials loops, it needs a work force skilled in highly specific vocational competencies (Weishaupt & Quiceno-Soto, 2026). By 2035, institutions begin to prioritize the need for these skills often by way of centers of excellence in vocational education (Shamzzuzoha et al., 2022). In some ways, this represents a movement away from the Humboldtian idea of "knowledge for its own sake" and a turn toward a more pragmatic focus regarding national interest and economic development (Aganbegyan, 2022).

Leadership in this context is indicative of a CEO model, in which university presidents are drawn from other sectors based on their ability to steward cross-sector partnerships and generate corporate funding. The concern becomes one of the "accelerated growth of investment in fixed and human capital" to narrow the gap between institutions and the needs of the advanced global economy (Aganbegyan, 2022). There is a danger that this model will "hollow out" the humanities and social sciences as funding will tend to be targeted toward those issues, which have immediate application to industry.

The vocational shift also relates to the structure of the academic work force. Multinational enterprises are often able to exert larger driving forces and face fewer barriers to adopting these new models than do small and medium-sized institutions (Horváth & Szabó, 2019). This creates a stratified patchwork in which some universities become central and corporate for global educational capital while others are less differentiated in a fiercely competitive vocationalized market. The responsibility of the professor migrates to "competence-based training," indicative of constructivist pedagogy and a process of learning that favours "what you can do" over "what you know" (Vare et al., 2019).

4.4 Scenario Four: The Resilient Human-Centric and Value-Driven Institution

The final scenario, "Resilient Human-Centric and Value-Driven Institution," arises as a response to the humanization of the AI-augmented and corporate scenarios. In this future, universities see themselves as sanctuaries of human agency, ethical reflection and sustainable development. This scenario is fundamentally centred on the idea of organizational resilience that allows institutions to manage unexpected events and engender future success through sensing and adapting to change (Duchek,

2019). In this future, the professoriate is appreciated as a community of "human-centered intellectual guides' doing the deep, transformative learning that we're told AI cannot do.

An abiding theme of this scenario is also based on the United Nations Sustainable Development Goals (SDG) commitment to the deserted university experience. Research has shown that for many regions maintaining a stable course is a key driver for 'sustainability', also that a great deal of progress will have occurred by 2030 (Škokić et al., 2025). By 2035 the resilient institution has built these goals into all aspects of its operations and curriculum with a view to education for sustainability (ESD) and other forms of employment related to green innovation and enterprise. Here the role of the professor is to enable students to "engender a rounder sense of purpose" to develop competences that equip with a capacity to engage and navigate a cheaper and ethical relational landscape in the 21st century (Vare et al., 2019). Digital ethics is fundamentally important in the scenario. Education is more technologized, and we must modernize and codify traditional moral principles to allow effective communications through cyberspace (Zvereva, 2023). Leadership is focused on "anticipatory governance" to utilize strategic foresight to defend an institution's core values from the uncertainly of the market in a resilient institution.

The scenario has something to say about the "slow-education" movement too; in this case a premium model of human-to-human engagement. While high-tech tools are at play, they are subordinate to pedagogical agendas of instilling critical thinking and social responsibility. There is no indication of an institution's value being supported by its efficiency or its corporate affiliations, or any other support, but assistance for a "restoration of the safety of the people", and enhancing societal well-being (Aganbegyan, 2022).

Each of the four scenarios highlights different combinations of efficiency, power, market and humanity-based perspectives. The first scenario focuses on efficiency and customization; the second scenario focuses on power and platform learning; the third scenario is focused on efficiency and the market for labour while the fourth scenario concentrates on humanity-based perspectives such as ethics and sustainability.

Table 2. Comparative Characteristics of the Four Future Scenarios

Scenario	Core Characteristics	Role of the Professor	Leadership Model	Major Risks
AI-Augmented Academy	AI-integrated teaching, personalized learning, automation of assessment and administration	Epistemic validator, mentor, AI-assisted educator	Data-driven and anticipatory governance	Over-reliance on AI, algorithmic bias, two-tier education
Decentralized Global Knowledge Network	Block chain credentials, Web 3.0, met averse learning, distributed platforms	Independent knowledge contractor	Ecosystem curation and platform governance	Credential insecurity, fragmentation, academic instability
Corporate-Integrated Vocational Model	Strong industry partnerships, workforce-oriented education, vocational specialization	Industry-academic hybrid and competence trainer	CEO-style strategic management	Commercialization of education, marginalization of humanities
Resilient Human-Centric Institution	Ethical governance, sustainability, human flourishing, community engagement	Transformative mentor and human-cantered intellectual guide	Resilience-based and values-driven leadership	Financial sustainability pressures, slower technological adaptation

5. DISCUSSION

5.1 Redefining Academic Identity and Career Paths

The road to 2035 calls for a complete rethinking of the academic identity model, moving away from the conventional model of the "scholar-citizen" of the 20th century. According to recent research, academics are undergoing changes in their career paths from being a sustainable profession to being a "gig worker" because of losing tenure positions, which has caused academic precarity (Boocock, 2025). This emerging gig economy identity is not solely an economic shift, but represents a reconstitution of the intellectual labor workforce. The "unbundling" of faculty in higher education is at the forefront of this trajectory, where the professor identity, historically entire with teaching, research, and service acting as identity markers, is being disassembled into functional roles with discrete identifiers (i.e., teaching designers, assessment specialists, research contractors).

Thus, the competencies required from those on the professoriate are evolving at a rapid pace. The reality is that critical thinking skills, communication skills, and emotional intelligence shall be valued highly before long since AI will take care of delivering knowledge (Muzam, 2022). By 2035, the knowledge worker (i.e., the professor) shall have to glorify the "practice of epistemic validation" which refers to a process by which a student navigates the complexities of true vs. fake knowledge with multiple layers of AI chatbots involved. What happens as a result is the creation of a "prestige paradox" since the prestige of institutions rests entirely upon a smaller number of elite faculty members.

In the case of professors, work would take place through "Digital Twins" in a simulation environment of AI-powered assessment and teaching (Hazrat et al., 2023). Within this setting, the academic field in 2035 would no longer focus on the institutional rigors and categories but instead become community-oriented and globally distributed. The "Uber-ization" of the professoriate creates flexibility and adaptive programming, yet simultaneously threatens the nature of the robust academic community and shared governance that marks college and university systems.

The psychological consequences of the dismantling of the traditional professor role should not be ignored. The "human-centric" model (Scenario Four) gives us the potential for a counter-narrative, where the professoriate is reclaimed as a new kind of "intellectual shaman" high-touch, transformative moments of human connection not replicable by machines (Carayannis & Morawska, 2022). In this model, a professors career path will be defined by the quality of mentorship and ability to propel "flourishing" in students, versus the traditional measures of publication load and teaching load.

5.2 Transformative Leadership Skills for the Life in 2035

Leadership will also have to move in 2035 into formation models of "ecosystem curation," opposed to being governed by bureaucratic managerialism from the early 21st century. It is predicted that the future complexity of higher education organizations will emerge from either decentralized systems or corporate-oriented vocational systems, thus making transformative leadership essential for effective governance of fractured systems and resources (Baroudi & Lytras, 2024).

Anticipatory governance means that we use strategic foresight as a form of continuous and ongoing institutional resilience. Leaders need to foresee the impending "Society 5.0," which refers to the upcoming period where humanity will be at the centre of innovative advancements within the organization (Carayannis & Morawska, 2022). The forethought would entail the need for comprehensive knowledge about the socio-technical forces behind the change, including the use of 6G technology and AI-based cognitive systems (You et al., 2020). Consequently, the leaders must be aware of the future to effectively address the conflict between the efficiency of AI and the inefficiency of deep learning.

Emotional intelligence will emerge as a fundamental strategic asset. As technical tasks are automated, leaders anticipate that their role will shift to managing the anxiety of precarious workforces and providing a "belonging" experience on a decentralized or virtual campus. Research shows clearly that the psychological well-being of both teachers and students will be one of the major considerations for future leaders, since they must adopt "flourishing" as an indicator of success (Huppert & So, 2013). It means developing a resilient culture that embraces optimism and healthy relationships even when facing challenges around the world.

Fourthly, talent ecosystems will have to be curated by the leaders. The future university is expected to run under the "Quintuple Helix" model where private and public viewpoints are considered in government, industry, civil society, and environment (Carayannis & Morawska, 2022). Thus, leaders are expected to engage in cross-sector partnerships and ethical oversight of AI. Leaders will need to integrate those who manage cross-sector partnerships and ethics with those who will coordinate these diverse stakeholders, while maintaining the institutional mission of public good. The ability to coordinate diverse stakeholder orientation, in particular, is significant for the sunrise economies including India, where the National Education Policy, 2020 already emphasizes "holistic", "multidisciplinary", and "research" oriented progress as the foundation for "future growth" (Aithal & Aithal, 2020).

A strong Global South example can already be observed in India's National Education Policy (NEP) 2020, which emphasizes multidisciplinary learning, digital transformation, flexible curricula, and research-oriented development as foundations for future national growth (Aithal & Aithal, 2020). This demonstrates how developing countries are attempting to align technological modernization with broader socio-economic and educational reform agendas.

5.3 Socio-Economic Implications and the Digital Divide in Future Scenarios

The risk of moving toward the 2035 scenarios involves significant socio-economic implications particularly with respect to the overall acute risk of a "two-tier" global higher education system, with one tier being elite institutions providing high-tech, high-face time education of a "premium" type and another tier which is a mass-market delivery, almost entirely on AI automation, and low-cost. The divide concerns not just digital connectivity but "relational readiness" that is, societal readiness to apply artificial intelligence to emotionally demanding contexts such as education (Mahajan, 2025). Nonetheless, an overreliance on institutions may result in the suppression of independent critical thinking and lead to the loss of human discretion in both teaching and evaluation. Over-automation may therefore create new ethical and intellectual vulnerabilities within higher education systems.

The information described above presents a considerable gap in how countries are ready for the "relational" side of AI. Countries with larger R&D capacity, such as the United States and China, who produce vast amounts of relevant research, are nonetheless behind other countries, such as Singapore and Japan, in their frameworks of "symbolic trust" and "emotional safety" (Mahajan, 2025). From the perspective of higher education, this implies that in 2035, the Digital Divide will be increasingly defined by the ability of organizations to sustain the "human touch." Therefore, when learners or other actors from less-endowed backgrounds find themselves in an environment dominated by AI, social disparities may be further entrenched, thus hindering social mobility (J & K, 2024).

In addition, there is a phenomenon called a spatial siphon effect, according to which urban centers or technological regions have a tendency to pull labour and other resources out of poorer rural and peri-urban areas (Zhou et al., 2023). Therefore, what is formed is an economic map of precariousness for the students and academics. Solving the problem and moving towards the future with equal access for all requires deliberate efforts aimed at strengthening governance capabilities and including poor communities into global knowledge networks (Li, 2025). Otherwise, Scenario Two will reinforce inequality.

The publish-or-perish mentality, coupled with the fact that AI is easily capable of creating data sets, poses risks to the validity of academic literature (Wilson & Burleigh, 2025). Thus, prospective leaders in academia will need to put in place stringent measures to ensure that their research work is sound. In addition, the concepts of Planetary Health or Ecological Civilization suggest that in the year 2035, there will be a need to achieve sustainable economic development in the institutions (Secretariat, 2025). In this case, the University of the Future will not only be the source of knowledge but will need to lead the world into a sustainable future (Whitmee et al., 2015).

6. CONCLUSION AND RECOMMENDATIONS

Ultimately, the future of the professoriate and leadership and higher education in 2035 is not a singular path that we can decide or conjure up, but multiple and competing scenarios. Moreover, the "crisis" of the present time in which we currently experience tenure erosion, artificial intelligence, and the shifting global powers, is the fuel for transformational change. Whether the academy becomes a hyper-personalized AI embraced space, a decentralized network of independent scholars, a corporate workplace in a vocational hub, or a resilient institution based on human engagement, will depend on the decisions made by today's leaders and policymakers.

The findings from this research highlight that "institutional resilience" and "human agency" must remain the focus of a more equitable future model. Unbundled professoriate, while providing cost savings, is likely to dilute the intellectual and social glue, which assures that the university functions as a public good.

For Governments and National Policymakers

As per the revolutionary National Education Policy 2020 of India, incorporating flexible structures enabling different study fields to connect and promote development and research-oriented learning (Aithal & Aithal, 2020).

It is not just about putting money into hardware; it needs emotional intelligence skills of its citizens as well as using artificial intelligence ethically in order to be involved in shaping the future knowledge economy (Mahajan, 2025).

The development of science and technology should be included within the framework of national security and economy policies in order to stay ahead in the era of Industry 4.0/5.0 (Lenchuk, 2022).

For Higher Education Institutions

Make use of anticipatory governance as a tool that will help move from crisis response to proactive "ecosystem curation" which emphasizes innovations for human beings (Carayannis & Morawska, 2022).

Understand the fragmented nature of the faculty position and chart a sustainable career development strategy for the different faculty positions (like teaching designers and research contractors).

Develop measures of success that consider both mental well-being and flourishing, and offer a more thorough assessment than mere ranking would (Huppert & So, 2013).

Develop policies on addressing the abuse of generative AI, and establish a mechanism to promote research integrity (Wilson & Burleigh, 2025).

To the Professoriate

Academics have to develop "skill mixes that combine deep disciplinary knowledge with digital literacy and emotional intelligence" (Hazrat et al., 2023)

Given the transformation into decentralized expertise, scholars should get involved while adhering to professional and ethical standards of the discipline.

The university in 2035 may be a hybrid of these scenarios, adjusting pace and adaptation of automation, efficiency and the irreplaceable work of humans as mentors of the craft. The institution that succeeds will be the one that takes advantage of the technological imperative to increase access and personalization, while fiercely defending the "human-centered" center of education. By building the "future-literate" leadership and academic identity in higher education adaptable and resilient to accede to the horizons of 2035.

REFERENCES

Aganbegyan, A. G. (2022). Two challenges of coronavirus pandemic: Decline in mortality and transitioning to sustainable social and economic growth. *Economic Revival of Russia*, *71*(1), 14–30. DOI: 10.37930/1990-9780-2022-1-71-14-30

Aithal, P. S., & Aithal, S. (2020). Analysis of the Indian National Education Policy 2020 towards achieving its objectives. *International Journal of Management, Technology, and Social Sciences*, *5*(2), 19–41. DOI: 10.47992/IJMTS.2581.6012.0102

Aithal, P. S., & Aithal, S. (2020). Implementation strategies of higher education part of National Education Policy 2020 of India towards achieving its objectives. *International Journal of Management, Technology, and Social Sciences*, *5*(2), 283–325. DOI: 10.47992/IJMTS.2581.6012.0119

Alenezi, M. (2023). Digital learning and digital institution in higher education. *Education Sciences*, *13*(1), 88. DOI: 10.3390/educsci13010088

Baroudi, S., & Lytras, M. D. (2024). *Transformative leadership and sustainable innovation in education: Interdisciplinary perspectives*. Emerald Publishing Limited. https://zu.elsevierpure.com/en/publications/transformative-leadership-and-sustainable-innovation-in-education-2/

Boocock, A. (2025). Neoliberalism and atomised, disaggregated Gig Academy workers: A challenge for HR professionals in the Higher Education sector? *Research in Post-Compulsory Education*, *30*(2), 390–409. DOI: 10.1080/13596748.2025.2502256

Bowyer, D., Deitz, M., Jamison, A., Taylor, C. E., Gyengési, E., Ross, J. M., Hammond, H., Ogbeide, A. E., & Dune, T. (2022). Academic mothers, professional identity and COVID-19: Feminist reflections on career cycles, progression and practice. *Gender, Work and Organization*, *29*(3), 889–905. https://pmc.ncbi.nlm.nih.gov/articles/PMC8652649/. DOI: 10.1111/gwao.12750

Brito, M. M. D., Evers, M., & Almoradie, A. (2018). Participatory flood vulnerability assessment: A multi-criteria approach. *Hydrology and Earth System Sciences*, *22*(1), 373–390. DOI: 10.5194/hess-22-373-2018

Carayannis, E. G., & Morawska, J. (2022). The futures of Europe: Society 5.0 and Industry 5.0 as driving forces of future universities. *Journal of the Knowledge Economy*, *13*(4), 3446–3471. DOI: 10.1007/s13132-021-00854-2

Chalmers, J., & Armour, M. (2019). The Delphi technique. In Liamputtong, P. (Ed.), *Handbook of research methods in health social sciences*. Springer., DOI: 10.1007/978-981-10-5251-4_99

Chen, C., Zhang, L., Li, Y., Liao, T., Zhao, S., Zheng, Z., Huang, H., & Wu, J. (2022). When digital economy meets Web 3.0: Applications and challenges. *IEEE Open Journal of the Computer Society*, *3*, 233–246. https://www.computer.org/csdl/journal/oj/2022/01/09931409/1HOt7HrC2U8. DOI: 10.1109/OJCS.2022.3217565

Chen, H. M., Shao, H., Deng, X., Wang, L., & Wang, X. (2023). Comprehensive survey of the landscape of digital twin technologies and their diverse applications. *Computer Modeling in Engineering & Sciences*, *137*(1), 1–44. DOI: 10.32604/cmes.2023.027834

Chen, M., Zhou, Y., Huang, X., & Ye, C. (2021). The integration of new-type urbanization and rural revitalization strategies in China: Origin, reality and future trends. *Land (Basel)*, *10*(2), 207. DOI: 10.3390/land10020207

Cuhls, K. (2019). Horizon scanning in foresight – Why horizon scanning is only a part of the game. *Futures & Foresight Science*, *1*(1–2), e23. https://ideas.repec.org/a/wly/fufsci/v2y2020i1ne23.html

Duchek, S. (2020). Organizational resilience: A capability-based conceptualization. *Business Research*, *13*(1), 215–246. DOI: 10.1007/s40685-019-0085-7

Dwivedi, Y. K., Hughes, L., Ismagilova, E., Aarts, G., Coombs, C., Crick, T., Duan, Y., Dwivedi, R., Edwards, J. S., Eirug, A., Galanos, V., Ilavarasan, P. V., Janssen, M., Jones, P., Kar, A. K., Kizgin, H., Kronemann, B., Lal, B., Lucini, B., & Williams, M. D. (2019). Artificial intelligence (AI): Multidisciplinary perspectives on emerging challenges, opportunities, and agenda for research, practice and policy. *International Journal of Information Management*, *57*, 101994. DOI: 10.1016/j.ijinfomgt.2019.08.002

Elsawah, S., Hamilton, S. H., Jakeman, A. J., Rothman, D. S., Schweizer, V., Trutnevyte, E., Carlsen, H., Drakes, C., Frame, B., Fu, B., Guivarch, C., Haasnoot, M., Kemp-Benedict, E., Kok, K., Kosow, H., Ryan, M., & van Delden, H. (2020). Scenario processes for socio-environmental systems analysis of futures: A review of recent efforts and a salient research agenda for supporting decision making. *The Science of the Total Environment*, *729*, 138393. DOI: 10.1016/j.scitotenv.2020.138393

Hazrat, M., Hassan, N., Chowdhury, A. A., Rasul, M., & Taylor, B. (2023). Developing a skilled workforce for future industry demand: The potential of digital twin-based teaching and learning practices in engineering education. *Sustainability (Basel)*, *15*(23), 16433. DOI: 10.3390/su152316433

Horváth, D., & Szabó, R. Z. (2019). Driving forces and barriers of Industry 4.0: Do multinational and small and medium-sized companies have equal opportunities? *Technological Forecasting and Social Change*, *146*, 119–132. DOI: 10.1016/j.techfore.2019.05.021

Huppert, F. A., & So, T. T. C. (2013). Flourishing across Europe: Application of a new conceptual framework for defining well-being. *Social Indicators Research*, *110*(3), 837–861. DOI: 10.1007/s11205-011-9966-7

Intergovernmental Panel on Climate Change (IPCC). (2023). Summary for policymakers. In *Climate change 2023: Synthesis report*. Cambridge University Press., DOI: 10.1017/9781009325844.001

Iqbal, M., & Matulevičius, R. (2021). Exploring Sybil and double-spending risks in blockchain systems. *IEEE Access : Practical Innovations, Open Solutions*, *9*, 76153–76177. DOI: 10.1109/ACCESS.2021.3081998

J, M. H., & K, L. (2024). Social impacts of AI in India: A societal perspective on adoption and inclusion. *International Journal of Scientific Research in Engineering and Management, 8*(4). https://doi.org/DOI: 10.55041/IJSREM37144

Karunathilake, E. M. B. M., Le, A. T., Heo, S., Chung, Y. S., & Mansoor, S. (2023). The path to smart farming: Innovations and opportunities in precision agriculture. *Agriculture*, *13*(8), 1593. DOI: 10.3390/agriculture13081593

Lenchuk, E. B. (2022). Science and technology development as a strategic national priority of Russia. *Economic Revival of Russia*, *71*(1), 58–65. DOI: 10.37930/1990-9780-2022-1-71-58-65

Li, J. (2025). Factors influencing national public health governance capacity: Based on NCA and fsQCA. *Frontiers in Public Health*, *13*, 1628677. DOI: 10.3389/fpubh.2025.1628677

Madureira, L., Popovič, A., & Castelli, M. (2021). Competitive intelligence: A unified view and modular definition. *Technological Forecasting and Social Change*, *173*, 121086. DOI: 10.1016/j.techfore.2021.121086

Mahajan, P. (2025). AI–family integration index (AFII): Benchmarking a new global readiness for AI as family. *Research Square* [Preprint]. https://doi.org/DOI: 10.21203/rs.3.rs-6577279/v1

McGee, E. O., Naphan-Kingery, D., Mustafaa, F. N., Houston, S., Botchway, P. K., & Lynch, J. M. (2019). Turned off from an academic career: Engineering and computing doctoral students and the reasons for their dissuasion. *International Journal of Doctoral Studies*, *14*, 203–226. DOI: 10.28945/4250

Mendoza, J. M. F., Sharmina, M., Gallego-Schmid, A., Heyes, G., & Azapagic, A. (2017). Integrating backcasting and eco-design for the circular economy: The BECE framework. *Journal of Industrial Ecology*, *21*(3), 526–544. https://e-space.mmu.ac.uk/618498/1/Manuscript_ID_16_JIE_5273_REV3_FINAL_University_library_s_gateway.pdf. DOI: 10.1111/jiec.12590

Mer, A., Kumar, V., Verma, V. K., De, T., & Mathew, J. (2024). A review of predictors and outcomes of work engagement in nonprofit organizations. *Social Sciences & Humanities Open*, *10*, 101083. DOI: 10.1016/j.ssaho.2024.101083

Mnasri, M., Jmal Maâlej, A., & Jmaiel, M. (2025). A systematic literature review on security testing of Ethereum smart contracts. *Blockchain: Research and Applications*, *7*(2), 100314. DOI: 10.1016/j.bcra.2025.100314

Molotoks, A., Smith, P., & Dawson, T. P. (2020). Impacts of land use, population, and climate change on global food security. *Food and Energy Security*, *9*(1), e261. https://kclpure.kcl.ac.uk/portal/en/publications/impacts-of-land-use-population-and-climate-change-on-global-food-/. DOI: 10.1002/fes3.261

Morawska, J. (2021). The role of universities in social innovation within the quadruple/quintuple helix model: Practical implications from Polish experience. *Journal of the Knowledge Economy*, *13*(4), 3000–3022. DOI: 10.1007/s13132-021-00804-y

Morrar, R., & Arman, H. (2017). The fourth industrial revolution (Industry 4.0): A social innovation perspective. *Technology Innovation Management Review*, *7*(11), 12–20. https://timreview.ca/sites/default/files/article_PDF/Morrar_et_al_TIMReview_November2017.pdf. DOI: 10.22215/timreview/1117

Muzam, J. (2022). The challenges of modern economy on the competencies of knowledge workers. *Journal of the Knowledge Economy*, *14*(3), 1886–1903. DOI: 10.1007/s13132-022-00979-y

Novy, J. W., Banerjee, B., & Matson, P. A. (2021). A core curriculum for sustainability leadership. *Sustainability (Basel)*, *13*(19), 10557. DOI: 10.3390/su131910557

Organisation for Economic Co-operation and Development (OECD). (2018). *Analysing megatrends to better shape the future of tourism* (OECD Tourism Papers No. 2018/02). OECD Publishing. https://doi.org/DOI: 10.1787/23071672

Organisation for Economic Co-operation and Development (OECD). (2021). *Reducing the precarity of academic research careers* (OECD Science, Technology and Industry Policy Papers No. 113). OECD Publishing. https://doi.org/DOI: 10.1787/23074957

Ovalle, A., Subramonian, A., Gautam, V., Gee, G. C., & Chang, K. (2023). Factoring the matrix of domination: A critical review and reimagination of intersectionality in AI fairness. In *Proceedings of the 2023 ACM Conference on Fairness, Accountability, and Transparency (FAccT '23)* (pp. 643–655). Association for Computing Machinery. https://www.lsv.uni-saarland.de/wp-content/uploads/2023/12/Ovalle-et-al.-2023-Factoring-the-Matrix-of-Domination-A-Critical-Rev.pdf

Periyasami, S., & Periyasamy, A. P. (2022). Metaverse as future promising platform business model: Case study on fashion value chain. *Businesses*, *2*(4), 386–402. DOI: 10.3390/businesses2040033

Ross, P. M., Scanes, E., & Locke, W. (2023). Stress adaptation and resilience of academics in higher education. *Asia Pacific Education Review*, *24*(4), 889–903. DOI: 10.1007/s12564-023-09829-1

Roumbanis, L. (2018). Symbolic violence in academic life: A study on how junior scholars are educated in the art of getting funded. *Minerva*, *56*(4), 397–418. DOI: 10.1007/s11024-018-9364-2

Rudolph, J., Ismail, F. M. M., & Popenici, . A. D. (2024). Higher education's generative artificial intelligence paradox: The meaning of chatbot mania. *Journal of University Teaching & Learning Practice*, *21*(2). Advance online publication. DOI: 10.53761/54fs5e77

Sarrico, C. S. (2022). The expansion of doctoral education and the changing nature and purpose of the doctorate. *Higher Education*, *84*(6), 1293–1311. DOI: 10.1007/s10734-022-00946-1

Setyadi, A., Soekotjo, S., Lestari, S. D., Pawirosumarto, S., & Damaris, A. (2025). Trends and opportunities in sustainable manufacturing: A systematic review of key dimensions from 2019 to 2024. *Sustainability (Basel)*, *17*(2), 789. DOI: 10.3390/su17020789

Shamzzuzoha, A., Chavira, P. C., Kekäle, T., Kuusniemi, H., & Jovanovski, B. (2022). Identified necessary skills to establish a center of excellence in vocational education for green innovation. *Cleaner Environmental Systems*, *6*, 100100. DOI: 10.1016/j.cesys.2022.100100

Škokić, V., Jelić, P., & Jerković, I. (2025). The role and contribution of sustainable development goals as a transformative framework in higher education: A case study of the University of Split. *WORLD (Oakland, Calif.)*, *6*(1), 22. DOI: 10.3390/world6010022

Suchek, N., Fernandes, C., Kraus, S., Filser, M., & Sjögrén, H. (2021). Innovation and the circular economy: A systematic literature review. *Business Strategy and the Environment, 30*(8), 3686–3702. https://ideas.repec.org/a/bla/bstrat/v30y2021i8p3686-3702.html. DOI: 10.1002/bse.2834

Sutikno, T., & Aisyahrani, A. I. B. (2023). Non-fungible tokens, decentralized autonomous organizations, Web 3.0, and the metaverse in education: From university to metaversity. [EduLearn]. *Journal of Education and Learning, 17*(1), 1–10. DOI: 10.11591/edulearn.v17i1.20657

Traxler, J., Connor, S., Hayes, S., & Jandrić, P. (2021). Futures studies, mobilities, and the postdigital condition: Contention or complement? *Postdigital Science and Education, 3*(3), 834–854. DOI: 10.1007/s42438-021-00245-5

Trí, N. M., Hoàng, P. D., & Dũng, N. T. (2021). Impact of the industrial revolution 4.0 on higher education in Vietnam: Challenges and opportunities. *Linguistics and Culture Review, 5*(S3), 1–15. DOI: 10.21744/lingcure.v5nS3.1350

UNESCO. (2025, September 2). *UNESCO survey: Two-thirds of higher education institutions have or are developing guidance on AI use*. UNESCO. https://www.unesco.org/en/articles/unesco-survey-two-thirds-higher-education-institutions-have-or-are-developing-guidance-ai-use

Vare, P., Arro, G., Hamer, A. D., Gobbo, G. D., De Vries, G., Farioli, F., Kadji-Beltran, C., Kangur, M., Mayer, M., Millican, R., Nijdam, C., Réti, M., & Zachariou, A. (2019). Devising a competence-based training program for educators of sustainable development: Lessons learned. *Sustainability (Basel), 11*(7), 1890. DOI: 10.3390/su11071890

Weishaupt, T., & Quiceno-Soto, G. (2026). Skills development in sustainable energy transitions: A systematic map and critical review of the drivers and barriers. *Energy Research & Social Science, 134*, 104576. DOI: 10.1016/j.erss.2026.104576

Wenhua, Z., Qamar, F., Abdali, T. N., Hassan, R., Jafri, S. T. A., & Nguy n, Q. N. (2023). Blockchain technology: Security issues, healthcare applications, challenges and future trends. *Electronics (Basel), 12*(3), 546. DOI: 10.3390/electronics12030546

Whitmee, S., Haines, A., Beyrer, C., Boltz, F., Capon, A., Dias, B. F. D. S., Ezeh, A., Frumkin, H., Gong, P., Head, P., Horton, R., Mace, G. M., Marten, R., Myers, S. S., Nishtar, S., Osofsky, S. A., Pattanayak, S. K., Pongsiri, M. J., Romanelli, C., & Yach, D. (2015). Safeguarding human health in the Anthropocene epoch: Report of The Rockefeller Foundation–Lancet Commission on planetary health. *Lancet, 386*(10007), 1973–2028. DOI: 10.1016/S0140-6736(15)60901-1

Wilson, A. C., & Burleigh, C. (2025). Research integrity in the era of generative artificial intelligence. *Journal of Educational Research and Practice*, *15*(1), 2054. DOI: 10.5590/JERAP.2025.15.2054

You, X., Wang, C., Huang, J., Gao, X., Zhang, Z., Wang, M., Huang, Y., Zhang, C., Jiang, Y., Wang, J., Zhu, M., Sheng, B., Wang, D., Pan, Z., Zhu, P., Yang, Y., Liu, Z., Zhang, P., Tao, X., & Liang, Y. (2020). Towards 6G wireless communication networks: Vision, enabling technologies, and new paradigm shifts. *Science China. Information Sciences*, *64*(1), 1–74. DOI: 10.1007/s11432-020-2955-6

Zheng, R. (2018). Precarity is a feminist issue: Gender and contingent labor in the academy. *Hypatia*, *33*(2), 235–255. DOI: 10.1111/hypa.12401

Zhou, X., Du, M., & Dong, H. (2023). RETRACTED: Spatial and temporal effects of China's digital economy on rural revitalization. *Frontiers in Energy Research*, *11*, 1061221. DOI: 10.3389/fenrg.2023.1061221

Zvereva, E. (2023). Digital ethics in higher education: Modernizing moral values for effective communication in cyberspace. *Online Journal of Communication and Media Technologies*, *13*(3), e202313. DOI: 10.30935/ojcmt/13033

KEY TERMS AND DEFINITIONS

Professoriate: The group of faculty members who are professors and other members of the teaching staff at universities and colleges generally brought together by the shared responsibility of teaching, doing research, and rendering services to the institution.

Strategic Foresight: A methodical approach to thinking about the future, recognizing possible forces of change, and developing scenarios based on them.

Unbundling: The process of breaking down a holistic service (like that provided by a professor) into its component parts, each of which can be performed by someone else, or in some instances, even by technology itself.

Society 5.0: A concept originating from Japan designed as a human-centered social system that balances economic development with a solution to social problems, through a service that greatly integrates cyberspace and physical space.

Industry 5.0: A social production model that emphasizes "human-machine partnership" with a focus on sustainability, human-centeredness, and resilience in ways that extend beyond the pure efficiency of Industry 4.0.

Digital Twin: A virtual representation, or digital equivalent, of a physical object, process or system (for example, a classroom or a lab), to enable simulation, monitoring, and training.

Epistemic Validation: The process of determining whether information is true or reliable, and the source of that information; an increasingly important skill in a time where AI can generate plausible but incorrect "facts."

Anticipatory Governance: A collection of rules, norms, and institutions which allows for the application of foresight to minimize risk and enhance the capacity of a system toreact early in the trajectory of potential events.

Quintuple Helix Model: An innovation framework that combines five subsystems of education, economy, environment, government, and civil society to encourage sustainable development.

Prestige Paradox: A state in which the programmatic and brand value of an institution is extremely high, yet the traditional structures that create that prestige (e.g. tenured faculty) are feeling diminished or replaced by precarious faculty.

Compilation of References

. Ashfaq, D. M. S. (2025). Artificial Intelligence and the Future of the Professoriate: A Study of the Impact of AI on Faculty Roles and Responsibilities.

. Bosman, J. P., Van Petegem, W., De Laet, T., & Tshuma, N. (2025). How to select the right AI tool for the job? An Autonomy-values framework for educational AI with a focus on academic advising. Ubiquity Proceedings, 6(1).

. Gbadamosi, G. G. (2025). Unequal Academy: The Struggle and Challenges of Token Black Academics in the United Kingdom. "Unequal Academy: The Struggle and Challenges of Token Black Academics in the UK".

. Hutson, J. (2025). From Prohibition to Preparation: Reframing Academic Integrity in the Age of AI. MRS Journal of Arts, Humanities and Literature, 2(11).

. Keen, J. (2025). Human Agency in Algorithmic Universities: Student Leadership and Ethical Governance in AI-Mediated Universities.

. Kulkarni, Dr. V., & Rajas, S. (2025). PERCEPTION OF UNIVERSITY TEACHERS ABOUT ACADEMIC PERFORMANCE INDICATOR (API) IN EDUCATION SYSTEM. *ANANYAŚĀSTRAM An International Multidisciplinary Journal (A Unique Treatise of Knowledge), 1*(2), 33–40. DOI: 10.64328/aimjv01i02074

. Lado, M. J. (2025). Data Modeling and Process Analysis: Essential for Technology Analysts and AI Experts: How Can Diagrams Solve Challenges in AI and Process Analysis?. Amazon Digital Services LLC-Kdp, 2025.

. Muhammed-Mikaaeel, A. A., Hassan, S. K., & Salman, K. O. (2025). EXPLORING CONSIDERABLE FACTORS TOWARDS CHOOSING A GOOD RESEARCH-ABLE LEGAL TOPIC.

. Nelson, R. (2025). Academic Identity in the AI Era. AI-Powered Pedagogy and Curriculum Design: Practical Insights for Educators.

. Schwartz, R. (2022). Towards a standard for identifying and managing bias in artificial intelligence.

. Wilstic, D. E. (2025). AI in Education: Leveraging Artificial Intelligence to Combat Academic Malpractice in Higher Education.

. Youvan, D. C. (2024). Amplification Through Progression: From Analog Signals to Artificial Intelligence.

Abbott, A. (1988). *The system of professions: An essay on the division of expert labor*. University of Chicago Press. DOI: 10.7208/chicago/9780226189666.001.0001

Aganbegyan, A. G. (2022). Two challenges of coronavirus pandemic: Decline in mortality and transitioning to sustainable social and economic growth. *Economic Revival of Russia*, *71*(1), 14–30. DOI: 10.37930/1990-9780-2022-1-71-14-30

Aguilar-Smith, S., & Gonzales, L. D. (2021). A study of community college faculty work expectations: Generous educators and their managed generosity. *Community College Journal of Research and Practice*, *45*(3), 184–204. DOI: 10.1080/10668926.2019.1666062

Aithal, P. S., & Aithal, S. (2020). Analysis of the Indian National Education Policy 2020 towards achieving its objectives. *International Journal of Management, Technology, and Social Sciences*, *5*(2), 19–41. DOI: 10.47992/IJMTS.2581.6012.0102

Aithal, P. S., & Aithal, S. (2020). Implementation strategies of higher education part of National Education Policy 2020 of India towards achieving its objectives. *International Journal of Management, Technology, and Social Sciences*, *5*(2), 283–325. DOI: 10.47992/IJMTS.2581.6012.0119

Aithal, P. S., & Aithal, S. (2023). Optimizing the use of artificial intelligence-powered GPTs as teaching and research assistants by professors in higher education institutions: A study on smart utilization. [IJMTS]. *International Journal of Management, Technology, and Social Sciences*, *8*(4), 368–401. DOI: 10.47992/IJMTS.2581.6012.0326

Ajmal, M. (2025). From Academic Freedom To Algorithmic Agency : Knowledge Governance In Ai-Enhanced Education. *Journal of Management Science Research Review*, 1036–1058.

Åkerlind*, G. S. (2005). Postdoctoral researchers: roles, functions and career prospects. *Higher Education Research & Development, 24*(1), 21-40. DOI: 10.1080/0729436052000318550

Akhter, Y., Ahmed, M., & Yadav, S. K. (2020). Quality deprivation through quality assessment: the academic score system in Indian higher education. In *University of Patras* (pp. 6–28). DOI: 10.26220/aca.3438

Al-Abdullatif, A. M. (2025). Auditing AI literacy competency in K–12 education: The role of awareness, ethics, evaluation, and use in human–machine cooperation. *Systems*, *13*(6), 490. DOI: 10.3390/systems13060490

Alakoum, A., Nica, E., & Abiad, M. (2024). Revolutionizing faculty performance evaluation: The future role of AI in higher education. *Journal of Self-Governance and Management Economics*, *12*(1), 25–49. DOI: 10.22381/jsme12120242

Alalaq, A. S. (2025). AI Tools for Data and Academic Content Analysis. *Authorea Preprints*.

Alam, A. (2023a). The secret sauce of student success: Cracking the code by navigating the path to personalized learning with educational data mining. In *2023 2nd International Conference on Smart Technologies and Systems for Next Generation Computing (ICSTSN)* (pp. 1-8). IEEE. DOI: 10.1109/ICSTSN57873.2023.10151558

Alam, A. (2023b). Media multitasking with M-learning technology in real-time classroom learning: Analysing the dynamics in formal educational settings for the future of E-learning in India. In *2023 2nd International Conference on Smart Technologies and Systems for Next Generation Computing (ICSTSN)* (pp. 1-6). IEEE. DOI: 10.1109/ICSTSN57873.2023.10151509

Alam, A., & Mohanty, A. (2022). Facial analytics or virtual avatars: competencies and design considerations for student-teacher interaction in AI-powered online education for effective classroom engagement. In *International Conference on Communication, Networks and Computing* (pp. 252-265). Cham: Springer Nature Switzerland. DOI: 10.1007/978-3-031-43145-6_21

Alam, A., & Mohanty, A. (2023a). Learning on the move: a pedagogical framework for state-of-the-art mobile learning. In *International Conference on Data Management, Analytics & Innovation* (pp. 735-748). Singapore: Springer Nature Singapore. DOI: 10.1007/978-981-99-1414-2_52

Alam, A., & Mohanty, A. (2023b). From bricks to clicks: The potential of big data analytics for revolutionizing the information landscape in higher education sector. In *International Conference on Data Management, Analytics & Innovation* (pp. 721-732). Singapore: Springer Nature Singapore. https://doi.org/DOI: 10.1007/978-981-99-1414-2_51

Alam, A. (2023c). Leveraging the power of 'modeling and computer simulation' for education: An exploration of its potential for improved learning outcomes and enhanced student engagement. In *2023 International Conference on Device Intelligence, Computing and Communication Technologies (DICCT)* (pp. 445-450). IEEE. DOI: 10.1109/DICCT56244.2023.10110159

Alam, A., & Mohanty, A. (2023c). Developing 'happiness engineering' subject for the schools in India: Designing the pedagogical framework for a sustainable happiness curriculum. *Qubahan Academic Journal*, *3*(4), 1–20. DOI: 10.48161/qaj.v3n4a145

Alam, A., & Mohanty, A. (2023d). Implications of virtual reality (VR) for school teachers and instructional designers: An empirical investigation. *Cogent Education*, *10*(2), 2260676. DOI: 10.1080/2331186X.2023.2260676

Alam, A., & Mohanty, A. (2024). Framework of Self-Regulated cognitive engagement (FSRCE) for sustainable pedagogy: A model that integrates SRL and cognitive engagement for holistic development of students. *Cogent Education*, *11*(1), 2363157. DOI: 10.1080/2331186X.2024.2363157

Alenezi, H., Alenezi, A., Alshahrani, A., & Alenezi, M. (2025). The quiet transformation of higher education in the AI era. PMC, Article PMC12438950. https://pmc.ncbi.nlm.nih.gov/articles/PMC12438950/

Alenezi, M. (2023). Digital learning and digital institution in higher education. *Education Sciences*, *13*(1), 88. DOI: 10.3390/educsci13010088

Alhafidh, F. (2025). The Use of AI and Academic Freedom in Higher Education. *Journal of Academic Freedom*, 0–1.

Ali, W., & Ali, W. (2022). How to Improve Productivity through a Goal-Oriented Approach? Journal of Economics, Management &. *Business Administration (London)*, *1*(1), 55–67.

Aliyu, M. O. (2026). *Artificial intelligence, scholastic development, and academic proficiency of graduate students in Memorial University*. Newfoundland and Labrador.

Almaqtari, J. W., Alramada, E., & Alsabry, A. (2026). An Overview and Impact Analysis of AI Tools in Academic Research, Learning, and Educational Performance. *Sana'a University Journal of Applied Sciences and Technology*, *4*(2), 1665–1681. DOI: 10.59628/jast.v4i2.1921

Altbach, P. G. (2000). *The changing academic workplace: Comparative perspectives*. Boston College Center for International Higher Education.

Altbach, P. G. (2015). *Global perspectives on higher education.* Johns Hopkins University Press.

Altbach, P. G., Gumport, P. J., & Berdahl, R. O. (2000). *American higher education in the twenty-first century: Social, political, and economic challenges* (2nd ed.). Johns Hopkins University Press., https://www.worldcat.org/title/american-higher-education-in-the-twenty-first-century-social-political-and-economic-challenges/oclc/42682899

Altbach, P. G., & Knight, J. (2007). The internationalization of higher education: Motivations and realities. *Journal of Studies in International Education, 11*(3-4), 290–305. DOI: 10.1177/1028315307303542

Altbach, P. G., Reisberg, L., & Rumbley, L. E. (2009). *Trends in global higher education: Tracking an academic revolution.* UNESCO Institute for Higher Education and Brill.

Alyahyan, E., & Düştegör, D. (2020). Predicting academic success in higher education: Literature review and best practices. *International Journal of Educational Technology in Higher Education, 17*(1), 3. Advance online publication. DOI: 10.1186/s41239-020-0177-7

Amirtham, S. N., & Kumar, A. (2023). The underrepresentation of women in STEM disciplines in India: A secondary analysis. *International Journal of Science Education, 45*(12), 1008–1031. DOI: 10.1080/09500693.2023.2179901

Andoniou, C. (2025). Rewiring Education for a Super-Smart Society: Cognitive Integrity, AI Ethics, and the Future of Knowledge. *Computing&AI Connect, 2*(1), 1–10. DOI: 10.69709/CAIC.2025.112122

Andrews, M., Pritchett, L., & Woolcock, M. (2017). Looking like a state: The seduction of isomorphic mimicry. In *Building state capability: Evidence, analysis, action* (pp. 57–76). Oxford University Press., DOI: 10.1093/acprof:oso/9780198747482.003.0003

Anokhin, I. (2025). Towards academic leadership: literature review on the advancement of foreign-born faculty in the US higher education sector. *Perspectives: Policy and Practice in Higher Education*, 1-13. DOI: 10.1080/13603108.2025.2540312

Ardito, C. G. (2025). AI at the knowledge gates : Institutional policies and hybrid configurations in universities and publishers. *AI at the Knowledge Gates : Institutional Policies and Hybrid Configurations in Universities and Publishers, 7*(August), 1–16. DOI: 10.3389/fcomp.2025.1608276

Arimoto, A. (2009). Changing academic profession in the world from 1992 to 2007. In *The changing academic profession over 1992–2007: International, comparative, and quantitative perspectives* (RIHE International Publication Series No. 12, pp. 1–25). Research Institute for Higher Education, Hiroshima University.

Avramović, A. (2024). Great expectations: Change and continuity in academic roles and tasks. *Scandinavian Journal of Public Administration, 28*(1), 45–67. DOI: 10.58235/sjpa.2024.13153

Azevedo, L., & Best, E. (2025). Institutional Policies on Artificial Intelligence in Higher Education : Frameworks and Best Practices for Faculty. *New Directions for Adult and Continuing Education, 2025*(188), 70–78. DOI: 10.1002/ace.70013

Bagherimajd, K., & Khajedad, K. (2025). Designing a model of sustainable education based on artificial intelligence in higher education. *Computers and Education: Artificial Intelligence, 9*, 100439. Advance online publication. DOI: 10.1016/j.caeai.2025.100439

Bai, J., Marin, V., Jung, I., & Zawacki-Richter, O. (2023). Future Prospects of Artificial Intelligence in Education: A Preliminary Analysis of Educator Perspectives from Focus Groups in Japan, Spain, and Germany. *Ubiquity Proceedings, 3*(1). Advance online publication. DOI: 10.5334/uproc.74

Bai, Q., Nam, B. H., English, A. S., Marshall, R. C., & Tian, X. (2025). Mental health and early career adaptation challenges of Chinese returnees and Korean ambitionists among the STEAM doctoral cohorts in the post-pandemic academic job market. *Compare: A Journal of Comparative Education, 55*(6), 1030–1050. DOI: 10.1080/03057925.2024.2352831

Bäker, A., Muschallik, J., & Pull, K. (2020). Successful mentors in academia: Are they teachers, sponsors and/or collaborators? *Studies in Higher Education, 45*(4), 723–735. DOI: 10.1080/03075079.2018.1544235

Ball, J. (2025). *A Beginner's Guide to Learning Tools Interoperability (LTI) in Education.* Retrieved from https://www.atomicjolt.com/post/a-beginners-guide-to-learning-tools-interoperability-lti-in-education

Baroudi, S., & Lytras, M. D. (2024). *Transformative leadership and sustainable innovation in education: Interdisciplinary perspectives.* Emerald Publishing Limited. https://zu.elsevierpure.com/en/publications/transformative-leadership-and-sustainable-innovation-in-education-2/

Bates, A. W. (2019). *Teaching in a digital age: Guidelines for designing teaching and learning* (2nd ed.). Tony Bates Associates Ltd., https://pressbooks.bccampus.ca/teachinginadigitalagev2/

Bauer, E., Greisel, M., Kuznetsov, I., Berndt, M., Kollar, I., Dresel, M., Fischer, M. R., & Fischer, F. (2023). Using natural language processing to support peer-feedback in the age of artificial intelligence: A cross-disciplinary framework and a research agenda. *British Journal of Educational Technology*, *54*(5), 1222–1245. DOI: 10.1111/bjet.13336

Beale, J., & Easton, C. (Eds.). (2026). *The future of education: Reimagining its aims and responsibilities*. Oxford University Press. DOI: 10.1093/9780197669761.001.0001

Beer, D. (2017). The social power of algorithms. *Information Communication and Society*, *20*(1), 1–13. DOI: 10.1080/1369118X.2016.1216147

Beer, D. (2022). *The tensions of algorithmic thinking: Automation, intelligence and the politics of knowing*. Policy Press.

Benson, R. T., & Trower, C. A. (2012). Data, leadership, and catalyzing culture change. *Change: The magazine of higher learning, 44*(4), 27-34. DOI: 10.1080/00091383.2012.691862

Benzecry, G., & Smith, D. J. (2024). A Critical Analysis of Academia. Available at *SSRN* 4803139.

Berg, M., & Seeber, B. K. (2025). *The slow professor: Challenging the culture of speed in the academy*. University of Toronto Press.

Berheide, C. W., Watanabe, M., Falci, C., Borland, E., Bates, D. C., & Anderson-Hanley, C. (2022). Gender, type of higher education institution, and faculty work-life integration in the United States. *Community Work & Family*, *25*(4), 444–463. DOI: 10.1080/13668803.2020.1776220

Berlinerblau, J. (2025). *As Professors Lay Dying: Selecting a College Amidst an Educational Crisis*. Simon and Schuster.

Bernasconi, A. (2025). Latin America : Weak academic freedom within strong university autonomy. *Global Constitutionalism*, 96–117. DOI: 10.1017/S204538172400011X

Bhardwaj, A. (2025). Faculty Tenure in US Academic Medical Institutions: A Critical Review of Controversy and Debate. *Advances in Medical Education and Practice*, *16*, 569–576. DOI: 10.2147/AMEP.S508439 PMID: 40206578

Bhat, J. (2023). Automating Higher Education Administrative Processes with AI-Powered Workflows. *International Journal of Emerging Trends in Computer Science and Information Technology*, *4*(4), 147–157. DOI: 10.63282/3050-9246.IJETCSIT-V4I4P116

Bhopal, K. (2022). Academics of colour in elite universities in the UK and the USA: The 'unspoken system of exclusion'. *Studies in Higher Education*, *47*(11), 2127–2137. DOI: 10.1080/03075079.2021.2020746

Binns, R. (2018). Fairness in machine learning: Lessons from political philosophy. *Proceedings of the 1st Conference on Fairness, Accountability and Transparency*, 149–159. DOI: 10.1145/3278721.3278775

Blackham, A. (2020). Unpacking precarious academic work in legal education. *The Law Teacher*, *54*(3), 426–442. DOI: 10.1080/03069400.2020.1714276

Blake, D. J. (2022). Gendered and racialized career sacrifices of women faculty accepting dual-career offers. *Journal of Women and Gender in Higher Education*, *15*(2), 113–133. DOI: 10.1080/26379112.2022.2067168

Block, F. (2022). Technology and productivity: A critique of aggregate indicators. *Journal of Post Keynesian Economics*, *45*(1), 1–23. DOI: 10.1080/01603477.2022.2029491

Bodkin, C. P., & Fleming, C. J. (2021). Supporting women scholars' paths to academia: An examination of family-friendly policies of public affairs doctoral programs. *Journal of Public Affairs Education*, *27*(3), 301–325. DOI: 10.1080/15236803.2019.1694385

Bogen, M., & Rieke, A. (2018). Help wanted: An examination of hiring algorithms, equity, and bias. Upturn. https://www.upturn.org/reports/2018/hiring-algorithms/

Bogen, M., & Rieke, A. (2018). *Help wanted: An examination of hiring algorithms, equity, and bias*. Upturn. Upturn Report

Bong, Y., Yunus, S., Weerawarna, R., Senkerik, R., Tan, R., Masood, T., ... & Camilleri, V. (2025). Universities' role in the artificial intelligence innovation system for sustainable development.

Boocock, A. (2025). Neoliberalism and atomised, disaggregated Gig Academy workers: A challenge for HR professionals in the Higher Education sector? *Research in Post-Compulsory Education*, *30*(2), 390–409. DOI: 10.1080/13596748.2025.2502256

Borenstein, J., & Howard, A. (2021). Emerging challenges in AI and the need for AI ethics education. *Professional Ethics Report*, *34*(1), 61–65. https://www.semanticscholar.org/paper/Emerging-challenges-in-AI-and-the-need-for-AI-Borenstein-Howard/c463e0a0b9a4c53ad6a90d5254. DOI: 10.1007/s43681-020-00002-7 PMID: 38624388

Borgman, C. L. (2015). *Big data, little data, no data: Scholarship in the networked world*. MIT Press. DOI: 10.7551/mitpress/9963.001.0001

Borgman, C. L., & Brand, A. (2022). Data blind: Universities lag in capturing and exploiting data. *Science*, *378*(6626), 1278–1281. DOI: 10.1126/science.add2734 PMID: 36548403

Bosanquet, A., Mailey, A., Matthews, K. E., & Lodge, J. M. (2017). Redefining 'early career' in academia: A collective narrative approach. *Higher Education Research & Development*, *36*(5), 890–902. DOI: 10.1080/07294360.2016.1263934

Bowen, W.G., and E. M. T. (2015). Locus of authority: The evolution of faculty roles in the governance of higher education. *Locus of Authority: The Evolution of Faculty Roles in the Governance of Higher Education.*, 1–4.

Bowyer, D., Deitz, M., Jamison, A., Taylor, C. E., Gyengési, E., Ross, J. M., Hammond, H., Ogbeide, A. E., & Dune, T. (2022). Academic mothers, professional identity and COVID-19: Feminist reflections on career cycles, progression and practice. *Gender, Work and Organization*, *29*(3), 889–905. https://pmc.ncbi.nlm.nih.gov/articles/PMC8652649/. DOI: 10.1111/gwao.12750

Braun, V., & Clarke, V. (2006). Using thematic analysis in psychology. *Qualitative Research in Psychology*, *3*(2), 77–101. DOI: 10.1191/1478088706qp063oa

Braverman, H. (1974). *Labor and monopoly capital*. Monthly Review Press. DOI: 10.14452/MR-026-03-1974-07_1

Bristow, A., Robinson, S., & Ratle, O. (2019). Academic Arrhythmia: Disruption, Dissonance, and Conflict in the Early-Career Rhythms of CMS Academics. *Academy of Management Learning & Education*, *18*(2), 241–260. DOI: 10.5465/amle.2017.0340

Brito, M. M. D., Evers, M., & Almoradie, A. (2018). Participatory flood vulnerability assessment: A multi-criteria approach. *Hydrology and Earth System Sciences*, *22*(1), 373–390. DOI: 10.5194/hess-22-373-2018

Broadbent, K., Troup, C., & Strachan, G. (2013). Research staff in Australian universities: is there a career path?. *Labour & Industry: a journal of the social and economic relations of work, 23*(3), 276-295. DOI: 10.1080/10301763.2013.839082

Brynjolfsson, E., & McAfee, A. (2017). *Machine, platform, crowd: Harnessing our digital future*. W. W. Norton & Company. https://wwnorton.com/books/Machine-Platform-Crowd/

Buch-Hansen, H., Nesterova, I., & Nielsen, P. (2025). Envisioning an academia for degrowth transformations. *Globalizations*, *22*(6), 1050–1067. DOI: 10.1080/14747731.2025.2480527

Bülbül, S. (2021). Glass ceiling in academia revisited: Evidence from the higher education system of Turkey. *International Journal of Sociology*, *51*(2), 87–104. DOI: 10.1080/00207659.2021.1881872

Bull, S., Cooper, A., Laidlaw, A., Milne, L., & Parr, S. (2025). 'You certainly don't get promoted for just teaching': Experiences of education-focused academics in research-intensive universities. *Studies in Higher Education*, *50*(2), 239–255. DOI: 10.1080/03075079.2024.2333946

Burrows, R. (2012). Living with the h-index? Metric assemblages in the contemporary academy. *The Sociological Review*, *60*(2), 355–372. DOI: 10.1111/j.1467-954X.2012.02077.x

Byrne, M., Chughtai, A. A., Flood, B., & Willis, P. (2012). Job satisfaction among accounting and finance academics: Empirical evidence from Irish higher education institutions. *Journal of Higher Education Policy and Management*, *34*(2), 153–167. DOI: 10.1080/1360080X.2012.662740

Caballero, K., Harland, T., Wald, N., & Mula-Falcón, J. (2025). The impact of evaluation and accountability on academic careers. *European journal of higher education, 15*(2), 323-339. DOI: 10.1080/21568235.2024.2331116

Cadez, S., Dimovski, V., & Zaman Groff, M. (2017). Research, teaching and performance evaluation in academia: The salience of quality. *Studies in Higher Education*, *42*(8), 1455–1473. DOI: 10.1080/03075079.2015.1104659

Cameron, L. D. (2024). The making of the "good bad" job: How algorithmic management manufactures consent through constant and confined choices. *Administrative Science Quarterly*, *69*(2), 458–514. DOI: 10.1177/00018392241236163

Cameron, L. M., Kovalchuk, S., D'Angelo, S. M., & Igodoe, A. A. (2025). Localizing the education development research agenda in the Global South: The case of GPE KIX. *International Journal of Educational Development*, *113*, 103207. DOI: 10.1016/j.ijedudev.2025.103207

Cantwell, B. (2011). Academic in-sourcing: International postdoctoral employment and new modes of academic production. *Journal of Higher Education Policy and Management*, *33*(2), 101–114. DOI: 10.1080/1360080X.2011.550032

Carayannis, E. G., & Morawska, J. (2022). The futures of Europe: Society 5.0 and Industry 5.0 as driving forces of future universities. *Journal of the Knowledge Economy*, *13*(4), 3446–3471. DOI: 10.1007/s13132-021-00854-2

Cardiff University. (2024). *Responsible research assessment*. Retrieved from Cardiff University: https://www.cardiff.ac.uk/research/our-research-environment/integrity-and-ethics/responsible-research-assessment

Carey, J. M., Carman, K. R., Clayton, K. P., Horiuchi, Y., Htun, M., & Ortiz, B. (2020). Who wants to hire a more diverse faculty? A conjoint analysis of faculty and student preferences for gender and racial/ethnic diversity. *Politics, Groups & Identities*, *8*(3), 535–553. DOI: 10.1080/21565503.2018.1491866

Castells, M. (2010). *The rise of the network society* (2nd ed.). Wiley-Blackwell., DOI: 10.1002/9781444319514

Cazan, A., & Cocorad, E. (2016). Computers in Human Behavior Computer anxiety and attitudes towards the computer and the internet with Romanian high-school and university students t a. *Computers in Human Behavior*, *55*, 2013–2015. DOI: 10.1016/j.chb.2015.09.001

Ceci, S. J. (2018). Women in academic science: Experimental findings from hiring studies. *Educational Psychologist*, *53*(1), 22–41. DOI: 10.1080/00461520.2017.1396462

Chalmers, D. (2011). Progress and challenges to the recognition and reward of the scholarship of teaching in higher education. *Higher Education Research & Development*, *30*(1), 25–38. DOI: 10.1080/07294360.2011.536970

Chalmers, J., & Armour, M. (2019). The Delphi technique. In Liamputtong, P. (Ed.), *Handbook of research methods in health social sciences*. Springer., DOI: 10.1007/978-981-10-5251-4_99

Champlin, D. P., & Knoedler, J. (2017). Contingent labor and higher education. *Review of Political Economy*, *29*(2), 232–248. DOI: 10.1080/09538259.2017.1316054

Chang, H., Longman, K. A., & Franco, M. A. (2014). Leadership development through mentoring in higher education: A collaborative autoethnography of leaders of color. *Mentoring & Tutoring*, *22*(4), 373–389. DOI: 10.1080/13611267.2014.945734

Chattopadhyay, S. A. U. M. E. N. (2025). ACADEMIC FREEDOM, INSTITUTIONAL AUTONOMY AND INSTITUTIONALISING ACCOUNTABILITY : A REFLECTION ON THE NATIONAL EDUCATION POLICY 2020 SAUMEN CHATTOPADHYAY Volume 4, 2020 THE JMC REVIEW. *ACADEMIC FREEDOM, INSTITUTIONAL AUTONOMY AND INSTITUTIONALISING ACCOUNTABILITY : A REFLECTION ON THE NATIONAL EDUCATION POLICY 2020 SAUMEN CHATTOPADHYAY Volume 4, 2020 THE JMC REVIEW, November.*

Chen, C., Zhang, L., Li, Y., Liao, T., Zhao, S., Zheng, Z., Huang, H., & Wu, J. (2022). When digital economy meets Web 3.0: Applications and challenges. *IEEE Open Journal of the Computer Society*, *3*, 233–246. https://www.computer.org/csdl/journal/oj/2022/01/09931409/1HOt7HrC2U8. DOI: 10.1109/OJCS.2022.3217565

Chen, H. M., Shao, H., Deng, X., Wang, L., & Wang, X. (2023). Comprehensive survey of the landscape of digital twin technologies and their diverse applications. *Computer Modeling in Engineering & Sciences*, *137*(1), 1–44. DOI: 10.32604/cmes.2023.027834

Chen, H., Van Reyk, D., & Oliver, B. G. (2025). The use of AI large language models by university students for assignment preparation. *Advances in Physiology Education*, *49*(2), 517–525. DOI: 10.1152/advan.00181.2024 PMID: 40131177

Chen, M., Zhou, Y., Huang, X., & Ye, C. (2021). The integration of new-type urbanization and rural revitalization strategies in China: Origin, reality and future trends. *Land (Basel)*, *10*(2), 207. DOI: 10.3390/land10020207

Chen, X., Xie, H., & Hwang, G. (2020). Computers and Education : Arti fi cial Intelligence A multi-perspective study on Arti fi cial Intelligence in Education : grants, conferences, journals, software tools, institutions, and researchers. *Computers and Education: Artificial Intelligence*, *1*(August), 100005. DOI: 10.1016/j.caeai.2020.100005

Chen, X., Xie, H., Zou, D., & Hwang, G. (2020). Computers and Education : Arti fi cial Intelligence Application and theory gaps during the rise of Arti fi cial Intelligence in Education. *Computers and Education: Artificial Intelligence*, *1*(August), 100002. DOI: 10.1016/j.caeai.2020.100002

Chet, C., Thou, R., Sok, S., & Rath, S. (2023). Significance of Professorship Implementation at Higher Education Institutions (HEIs) in Cambodia. *Insight: Cambodia Journal of Basic and Applied Research*, *5*(1), 4–7. DOI: 10.61945/cjbar.2023.5.1.edi

Chiang, L. C. (2025). Doctoral qualifications matter in the competitive faculty job market: The perspectives of university senior administrators and their implications. *Studies in Higher Education*, *50*(10), 1–15. DOI: 10.1080/03075079.2025.2522740

Chih, W.-H., Ghasemaghaei, M., & Hassan, S. (2024). Will artificial intelligence drive the advancements in higher education? A tri-phased exploration. *Technological Forecasting and Social Change*, *201*, 123254. Advance online publication. DOI: 10.1016/j.techfore.2024.123254

Chikane, R. (2026). Rhodes Must Fall and the incongruence of academic freedom and decoloniality. *Globalisation, Societies and Education*, *7724*(3), 641–657. DOI: 10.1080/14767724.2024.2341103

Chin, P., Em, S., & Phann, S. (2023). Enhancing research knowledge and productivity through professorship titles in Cambodia: Striking a balance. *Journal As-Salam*, *7*(2), 133–143. DOI: 10.37249/assalam.v7i2.653

Chiv, S., Hong, K., Meak, C., Sam, R., Tieng, M., Yoeng, H., & Serey, M. (2025). Enhancing research on academic research capacity in Cambodian higher education institutions. *Discover Education*, *4*(1), 283. Advance online publication. DOI: 10.1007/s44217-025-00723-z

Ciasullo, A., Santoianni, F., & Manfredini, A. (2026). Rethinking Human Agency in AI-Mediated Education. *Journal of Inclusive Methodology and Technology in Learning and Teaching*, *6*(1).

Civera, A., Horta, H., Meoli, M., & Paleari, S. (2025). Academically inbred presidents and university performance. *Studies in Higher Education*, •••, 1–16. DOI: 10.1080/03075079.2025.2483885

Clark, B. R. (1987). The academic life: Small worlds, different worlds. Carnegie Foundation for the Advancement of Teaching. https://eric.ed.gov/?id=ED299902

Clark, B. R. (1983). *The higher education system: Academic organization in cross-national perspective*. University of California Press. DOI: 10.1525/9780520340725

Clark-gordon, C. V., Bowman, N. D., Hadden, A., Frisby, B., Hadden, A., & Frisby, B. (2019). College instructors and the digital red pen: An exploratory study of factors influencing the adoption and non-adoption of digital written feedback technologies. *Computers & Education*, *128*, 414–426. DOI: 10.1016/j.compedu.2018.10.002

Clark, R. L., & d'Ambrosio, M. B. (2005). Recruitment, retention, and retirement: Compensation and employment policies for higher education. *Educational Gerontology*, *31*(5), 385–403. DOI: 10.1080/03601270590921663

CoARA. (2022). *Agreement on Reforming Research Assessment.* Retrieved from Coalition for Advancing Research Assessment: https://coara.eu/agreement/

Coeckelbergh, M. (2023). Narrative responsibility and artificial intelligence: How AI challenges human responsibility and sense-making. *AI & Society*, *38*(6), 2437–2450. DOI: 10.1007/s00146-021-01375-x

Colonna, L. (2026). Artificial Intelligence in Education (AIED): Towards More Effective Regulation. *Artificial Intelligence in Education (AIED): Towards More Effective Regulation*, 161–181. DOI: 10.1017/err.2025.10039

Connell, R. (2007). *Southern theory: The global dynamics of knowledge in social science*. Allen & Unwin.

Cooper, A. F., Moss, E., Laufer, B., & Nissenbaum, H. (2022, June). Accountability in an algorithmic society: relationality, responsibility, and robustness in machine learning. In *Proceedings of the 2022 ACM conference on fairness, accountability, and transparency* (pp. 864-876). DOI: 10.1145/3531146.3533150

Cooray, A., Verma, R., & Wright, L. (2014). Does a gender disparity exist in academic rank? Evidence from an Australian university. *Applied Economics*, *46*(20), 2441–2451. DOI: 10.1080/00036846.2014.904496

Crawford, K., & Paglen, T. (2019). Excavating AI: The politics of images in machine learning training sets. *International Journal of Communication*, *13*, 310–329.

Crawford, T., & Germov, J. (2015). Using workforce strategy to address academic casualisation: A University of Newcastle case study. *Journal of Higher Education Policy and Management*, *37*(5), 534–544. DOI: 10.1080/1360080X.2015.1079394

Creswell, J. W., & Creswell, J. D. (2018). *Research design: Qualitative, quantitative, and mixed methods approaches* (5th ed.). SAGE Publications.

Crompton, H., Burke, D., & Gregory, K. (2023). Artificial intelligence in higher education: The state of the field. *International Journal of Educational Technology in Higher Education*, *20*(1), 22. DOI: 10.1186/s41239-023-00392-8

Cuhls, K. (2019). Horizon scanning in foresight – Why horizon scanning is only a part of the game. *Futures & Foresight Science*, *1*(1–2), e23. https://ideas.repec.org/a/wly/fufsci/v2y2020i1ne23.html

Culver, K. C., Kezar, A., & Koren, E. R. (2025). Faculty, Academic Careers, and Environments (FACE) Framework: A Guide to Faculty Work for Research, Practice, and Policy. *The Journal of Higher Education*, •••, 1–33. DOI: 10.1080/00221546.2025.2466421

Curnalia, R. M., & Mermer, D. (2018). Renewing our commitment to tenure, academic freedom, and shared governance to navigate challenges in higher education. *The Review of Communication, 18*(2), 129–139. DOI: 10.1080/15358593.2018.1438645

Czerniewicz, L., Trotter, H., Haupt, G., & Newman, M. (2021). Digital inclusion and inequality in higher education. *Educational Technology Research and Development, 69*(2), 1–5. DOI: 10.1007/s11423-021-09978-6

Das, B., & Majumder, M. (2017, December). Das, Bidyut, and M. M. (2017). Factual open cloze question generation for assessment of learner ' s knowledge. *International Journal of Educational Technology in Higher Education, 14*(1), 24. Advance online publication. DOI: 10.1186/s41239-017-0060-3

Dávideková, M., Mjartan, M., & Greguš, M.Dávideková. (2017). ScienceDirect Utilization of Virtual Reality in Education of Employees in Slovakia. *Procedia Computer Science, 113*, 253–260. DOI: 10.1016/j.procs.2017.08.365

Davidson, S. (2024). The economic institutions of artificial intelligence. *Journal of Institutional Economics, 20*, e20. DOI: 10.1017/S1744137423000395

Deem, R., & Brehony, K. J. (2005). Management as ideology: The case of 'new managerialism' in higher education. *Oxford Review of Education, 31*(2), 217–235. DOI: 10.1080/03054980500117827

Deem, R., Hillyard, S., & Reed, M. (2007). *Knowledge, higher education, and the new managerialism: The changing management of UK universities.* Oxford University Press., DOI: 10.1093/acprof:oso/9780199265909.001.0001

Defleur, M. L. (2007). Raising the Question# 5 What Is Tenure and How Do I Get It? *Communication Education, 56*(1), 106–112. DOI: 10.1080/03634520601081263

Delucchi, M., Dadzie, R. B., Dean, E., & Pham, X. (2024). What's that smell? Bullshit jobs in higher education. *Review of Social Economy, 82*(1), 1–22. DOI: 10.1080/00346764.2021.1940255

Denzin, N. K., & Lincoln, Y. S. (2011). *The SAGE handbook of qualitative research* (4th ed.). SAGE Publications.

Deutsch, F. M., & Yao, B. (2014). Gender differences in faculty attrition in the USA. *Community Work & Family, 17*(4), 392–408. DOI: 10.1080/13668803.2014.885880

DeZure, D., Shaw, A., & Rojewski, J. (2014). Cultivating the next generation of academic leaders: Implications for administrators and faculty. *Change, 46*(1), 6–12. DOI: 10.1080/00091383.2013.842102

Diameh, J. T., Oluwatobi, B. T., Daniels, C., Sunday, O. E., Nelson, C. A., & Quaye, M. (2025). Integrating AI-driven predictive analytics in project risk management to optimize decision-making and performance efficiency. *Int. J. Eng. Technol. Res. Manag, 9*, 373–389.

Diamond, R. M., & Adam, B. E. (Eds.). (2023). *The disciplines speak I: Rewarding the scholarly, professional, and creative work of faculty*. Taylor & Francis. DOI: 10.4324/9781003447764

Donoghue, R. (2025). Freedom under algorithms: How unpredictable and asocial management erodes free choice. *Frontiers in Artificial Intelligence, 8*, 1582085. DOI: 10.3389/frai.2025.1582085 PMID: 40860718

DORA. (2012). *San Francisco Declaration on Research Assessment*. Retrieved from https://sfdora.org/read

Dorenkamp, I., & Süß, S. (2017). Work-life conflict among young academics: Antecedents and gender effects. *European Journal of Higher Education, 7*(4), 402–423. DOI: 10.1080/21568235.2017.1304824

Dovchin, S. (2024). Artificial Intelligence in Applied Linguistics: A double-edged sword. *Australian Review of Applied Linguistics, 47*(3), 410–417. DOI: 10.1075/aral.24145.dov

Dressel, B. (2024). *Courts and politics in Southeast Asia*. Cambridge University Press., DOI: 10.1017/9781108770088

Duchek, S. (2020). Organizational resilience: A capability-based conceptualization. *Business Research, 13*(1), 215–246. DOI: 10.1007/s40685-019-0085-7

Duffy, A. (2019). A delicate balance: How postsecondary education dance faculty in the United States perceive themselves negotiating responsibilities expected for tenure. *Research in Dance Education, 20*(1), 73–84. DOI: 10.1080/14647893.2018.1523382

Dunleavy, P., & Margetts, H. (2025). Data science, artificial intelligence and the third wave of digital era governance. *Public Policy and Administration, 40*(2), 185–214. DOI: 10.1177/09520767231198737

Dwivedi, Y. K., Hughes, L., Ismagilova, E., Aarts, G., Coombs, C., Crick, T., Duan, Y., Dwivedi, R., Edwards, J. S., Eirug, A., Galanos, V., Ilavarasan, P. V., Janssen, M., Jones, P., Kar, A. K., Kizgin, H., Kronemann, B., Lal, B., Lucini, B., & Williams, M. D. (2019). Artificial intelligence (AI): Multidisciplinary perspectives on emerging challenges, opportunities, and agenda for research, practice and policy. *International Journal of Information Management, 57*, 101994. DOI: 10.1016/j.ijinfomgt.2019.08.002

Edu, N. (2025). The influence of international rankings on higher education reforms and institutional strategies. *International Journal of Innovative Social Sciences & Humanities Research, 13*(1), 273–280.

Elsawah, S., Hamilton, S. H., Jakeman, A. J., Rothman, D. S., Schweizer, V., Trutnevyte, E., Carlsen, H., Drakes, C., Frame, B., Fu, B., Guivarch, C., Haasnoot, M., Kemp-Benedict, E., Kok, K., Kosow, H., Ryan, M., & van Delden, H. (2020). Scenario processes for socio-environmental systems analysis of futures: A review of recent efforts and a salient research agenda for supporting decision making. *The Science of the Total Environment, 729*, 138393. DOI: 10.1016/j.scitotenv.2020.138393

Enders, J., & de Weert, E. (2009). Towards a T-shaped profession: Academic work and career in the knowledge society. In *The changing face of academic life: Analytical and comparative perspectives* (pp. 251–272). Palgrave Macmillan., DOI: 10.1057/9780230242166_13

Espeland, W. N., & Sauder, M. (2007). Rankings and reactivity: How public measures recreate social worlds. *AJS; American Journal of Sociology, 113*(1), 1–40. DOI: 10.1086/517897

European Commission. (2021). Proposal for a regulation on artificial intelligence (AI Act). https://digital-strategy.ec.europa.eu/en/library/proposal-regulation-laying-down-harmonised-rules-artificial-intelligence

European Commission. (2024). *Ethical guidelines on the use of artificial intelligence and data in teaching and learning for educators*. Publications Office of the European Union.

Fagan-Wilen, R., Springer, D. W., Ambrosino, B., & White, B. W. (2006). The support of adjunct faculty: An academic imperative. *Social Work Education, 25*(1), 39–51. DOI: 10.1080/02615470500477870

Field, S. (2021). Seven ways to get a grip on running a successful promotions process. *Canadian Medical Education Journal, 12*(3), 147–150. DOI: 10.36834/cmej.71638 PMID: 34249200

Finkelstein, M. J., Conley, V. M., & Schuster, J. H. (2017). Whither the faculty? *Change, 49*(4), 43–51. DOI: 10.1080/00091383.2017.1357099

Fitria, T. N. (2023). The use of artificial intelligence in education (AIED): Can AI replace the teacher's role? *Epigram, 20*(2), 165–187. DOI: 10.32722/epi.v20i2.5711

Flores, L. A., & Rae Gomez, L. (2020). Disciplinary containment: Whiteness and the academic scarcity narrative. *Communication and Critical/Cultural Studies, 17*(2), 236–242. DOI: 10.1080/14791420.2020.1770818

Florida, U. o. (2025). *Faculty: Excellence and Advancement (FEA)*. Retrieved from University of Florida: https://aa.ufl.edu/policies--guidelines/tenure-and-promotion-information/fea/

Floridi, L., Cowls, J., Beltrametti, M., Chatila, R., Chazerand, P., Dignum, V., Luetge, C., Madelin, R., Pagallo, U., Rossi, F., Schafer, B., Valcke, P., & Vayena, E. (2018). AI4People—An ethical framework for a good AI society: Opportunities, risks, principles, and recommendations. *Minds and Machines*, *28*(4), 689–707. DOI: 10.1007/s11023-018-9482-5 PMID: 30930541

Foote, K. E. (2010). Creating a community of support for graduate students and early career academics. *Journal of Geography in Higher Education*, *34*(1), 7–19. DOI: 10.1080/03098260902954087

Ford, L. E. (2016). Two steps forward, one step back? Strengthening the foundations of women's leadership in higher education. *Politics, Groups & Identities*, *4*(3), 499–512. DOI: 10.1080/21565503.2016.1170705

Freidson, E. (2001). *Professionalism: The third logic*. University of Chicago Press.

Friedman, D. B., Yelton, B., Corwin, S. J., Hardin, J. W., Ingram, L. A., Torres-McGehee, T. M., & Alberg, A. J. (2021). Value of peer mentorship for equity in higher education leadership: A school of public health focus with implications for all academic administrators. *Mentoring & Tutoring*, *29*(5), 500–521. DOI: 10.1080/13611267.2021.1986795

Fudickar, R., Hottenrott, H., & Lawson, C. (2018). What's the price of academic consulting? Effects of public- and private-sector consulting on academic research. *Industrial and Corporate Change*, *27*(4), 699–722. DOI: 10.1093/icc/dty007

Gao, Y., & Wang, X. (2024). When policy meets practice: Evaluating the Breaking Five-Only policy through academic production in China. *Publications / MDPI*, *12*(4), 44. DOI: 10.3390/publications12040044

Garfield, E. (1979). *Citation indexing: Its theory and application in science, technology, and humanities*. Wiley.

George, A. S. (2024). Technology tension in schools: Addressing the complex impacts of digital advances on teaching, learning, and wellbeing. [PUMRJ]. *Partners Universal Multidisciplinary Research Journal*, *1*(3), 49–65.

George, R., & Maguire, M. (2021). Academics 'staying on'post retirement age in English university departments of education: Opportunities, threats and employment policies. *British Journal of Educational Studies*, *69*(4), 453–470. DOI: 10.1080/00071005.2020.1814951

Ghamrawi, N., Shal, T., & Ghamrawi, N. A. (2024). Exploring the impact of AI on teacher leadership: Regressing or expanding? *Education and Information Technologies*, *29*(7), 8415–8433. DOI: 10.1007/s10639-023-12174-w

Gibbs, P. (2022). Self-Deception and the Duty of the Truth-Teller in the University–A Values Perspective. In *Trusting in Higher Education: A multifaceted discussion of trust in and for higher education in Norway and the United Kingdom* (pp. 173–183). Springer International Publishing.

Gioti, L. (2025). Neoliberal higher education restructuring, job satisfaction and professional development of academics. *Studies in the Education of Adults*, •••, 1–21. DOI: 10.1080/02660830.2025.2451453

Godwin-Jones, R. (2022). Partnering with AI: Intelligent writing assistance and instructed language learning. *Language Learning & Technology*, *26*(2), 5–24. DOI: 10.64152/10125/73474

Goyanes, M., Domínguez-Díaz, A., Jordá, B., & de-Marcos, L. (2025). Gender gap in citations, h-index, and representation: Examining the highly cited authors across continents and disciplines in Google Scholar. *PLoS One*, *20*(11), e0334690. DOI: 10.1371/journal.pone.0334690 PMID: 41231907

Gualdrón, E. O., Duque, M., Javakhishvili, M., Bartoszak, M., Watkins, L. G., Montero-Zamora, P., Alpysbekova, A., Vo, D. H., Lee, S. W., Acaf, Y., Bochkina, E., & Schwartz, S. J. (2025). Creating an Internationally Equitable Playing Field for Publishing in English-Language Scholarly Journals. *Journal of Scholarly Publishing*, *56*(4), 840–869. DOI: 10.3138/jsp-2024-0104

Guillaume, R. O., & Apodaca, E. C. (2022). Early career faculty of color and promotion and tenure: The intersection of advancement in the academy and cultural taxation. *Race, Ethnicity and Education*, *25*(4), 546–563. DOI: 10.1080/13613324.2020.1718084

Gül, H., Gül, S. S., Kaya, E., & Alican, A. (2010). Main trends in the world of higher education, internationalization, and institutional autonomy. *Procedia: Social and Behavioral Sciences*, *9*, 1878–1884. DOI: 10.1016/j.sbspro.2010.12.417

Hackman, J. R., & Oldham, G. R. (1976). Motivation through the design of work: Test of a theory. *Organizational Behavior and Human Performance*, *16*(2), 250–279. DOI: 10.1016/0030-5073(76)90016-7

Hanisch, M., Goldsby, C. M., Fabian, N. E., & Oehmichen, J. (2023). Digital governance: A conceptual framework and research agenda. *Journal of Business Research*, *162*, 113777. DOI: 10.1016/j.jbusres.2023.113777

Han, S., & Xie, J. (2026). Facing inequalities in academia: Understanding Chinese early-career academics' identity formation. *Higher Education Research & Development*, •••, 1–17. DOI: 10.1080/07294360.2026.2615301

Han, Y. (2025). Beyond the Algorithm : Reconciling Generative AI and Human Agency in Academic Writing Education. *International Journal of Learning and Teaching*, *11*(1), 39–42. Advance online publication. DOI: 10.18178/ijlt.11.1.39-42

Hao, Z. (2025). Institutional Autonomy in Relation to Academic Freedom, the Role of the Government and the Need for Higher Education as a Federation. *European Review (Chichester, England)*, *33*(S1), 70–85. DOI: 10.1017/S1062798725000146

Hardy, A., McDonald, J., Guijt, R., Leane, E., Martin, A., James, A., Jones, M., Corban, M., & Green, B. (2018). Academic parenting: Work–family conflict and strategies across child age, disciplines and career level. *Studies in Higher Education*, *43*(4), 625–643. DOI: 10.1080/03075079.2016.1185777

Harris, R., Mate-Sanchez-Val, M., & Ruiz Marín, M. (2025). Gender disparities in promotions and exiting in UK Russell Group universities. *Applied Economics*, *57*(31), 4441–4457. DOI: 10.1080/00036846.2024.2361384

Hartley, K., & Jarvis, D. S. (2022). Let nine universities blossom: Opportunities and constraints on the development of higher education in China. *Higher Education Research & Development*, *41*(5), 1542–1556. DOI: 10.1080/07294360.2021.1915963

Hartung, T., Hoffmann, S., & Whaley, P. (2025). Assessing risk of bias in toxicological studies in the era of artificial intelligence. *Archives of Toxicology*, *99*(8), 3065–3090. DOI: 10.1007/s00204-025-03978-5 PMID: 40615561

Hartz, R. (2024). Demeaning, depriving, and isolating the academic subject: A case study of the degradation of professional autonomy. *Management Learning*, *55*(5), 703–719. DOI: 10.1177/13505076231207938

Hashem, R., Ali, N., El Zein, F., Fidalgo, P., & Khurma, O. A. (2024). AI to the rescue: Exploring the potential of ChatGPT as a teacher ally for workload relief and burnout prevention. *Research and Practice in Technology Enhanced Learning*, •••, 19.

Haviland, D., Alleman, N. F., & Cliburn Allen, C. (2017). 'Separate but not quite equal': Collegiality experiences of full-time non-tenure-track faculty members. *The Journal of Higher Education*, *88*(4), 505–528. DOI: 10.1080/00221546.2016.1272321

Hazelkorn, E. (2015). *Rankings and the reshaping of higher education: The battle for world-class excellence* (2nd ed.). Palgrave Macmillan. DOI: 10.1057/9781137446671

Hazrat, M., Hassan, N., Chowdhury, A. A., Rasul, M., & Taylor, B. (2023). Developing a skilled workforce for future industry demand: The potential of digital twin-based teaching and learning practices in engineering education. *Sustainability (Basel), 15*(23), 16433. DOI: 10.3390/su152316433

Hearn, J. C., & Burns, R. (2021). Contingent faculty employment and financial stress in public universities. *The Journal of Higher Education, 92*(3), 331–362. DOI: 10.1080/00221546.2020.1851570

Heffernan, K., Hazzan, A. A., & Dauenhauer, J. (2022). Promoting age-friendly organizational culture through lifelong learning programs in higher education: Experience and insights from faculty. *Educational Gerontology, 48*(6), 260–272. DOI: 10.1080/03601277.2022.2033929

Heffernan, T. (2021). Academic networks and career trajectory: 'There's no career in academia without networks'. *Higher Education Research & Development, 40*(5), 981–994. DOI: 10.1080/07294360.2020.1799948

Heffernan, T. (2022). Sexism, racism, prejudice, and bias: A literature review and synthesis of research surrounding student evaluations of courses and teaching. *Assessment & Evaluation in Higher Education, 47*(1), 144–154. DOI: 10.1080/02602938.2021.1888075

Heffernan, T. A. (2018). Approaches to career development and support for sessional academics in higher education. *The International Journal for Academic Development, 23*(4), 312–323. DOI: 10.1080/1360144X.2018.1510406

Heng, K., Hamid, M. O., & Khan, A. (2023). Research engagement of academics in the Global South: The case of Cambodian academics. *Globalisation, Societies and Education, 21*(3), 322–337. DOI: 10.1080/14767724.2022.2040355

Heng, K., & Heng, K. (2023). The implementation of the professorial ranking system in Cambodia: Opportunities and challenges. *Cambodian Journal of Educational Research, 3*(2), 62–77. DOI: 10.62037/cjer.2023.03.02.04

Heng, K., & Heng, K. (2024). Professorial Titles in the Education Sector in Cambodia: Opportunities, Challenges, and Implications. *Cambodian Journal of Education and STEM, 2*(1). Advance online publication. DOI: 10.62219/cjes.2024218

Henkel, M. (2007). Shifting boundaries and the academic profession. In Kogan, M., & Teichler, U. (Eds.), *Key challenges to the academic profession* (pp. 93–122). UNESCO/International Centre for Higher Education Research.

Henningsson, M. (2025). Organizing the Swedish academic career 1955–2020: Reforms and recurring problems in national policy discussion1. *Nordic Journal of Studies in Educational Policy, 11*(2), 147–160. DOI: 10.1080/20020317.2024.2401183

Henningsson, M., Jörnesten, A., & Geschwind, L. (2018). Translating tenure track into Swedish: Tensions when implementing an academic career system. *Studies in Higher Education, 43*(7), 1215–1226. DOI: 10.1080/03075079.2016.1239704

Henry, F., Dua, E., Kobayashi, A., James, C., Li, P., Ramos, H., & Smith, M. S. (2017). Race, racialization and Indigeneity in Canadian universities. *Race, Ethnicity and Education, 20*(3), 300–314. DOI: 10.1080/13613324.2016.1260226

Herbert, A., & Tienari, J. (2013). Transplanting tenure and the (re) construction of academic freedoms. *Studies in Higher Education, 38*(2), 157–173. DOI: 10.1080/03075079.2011.569707

Hermanowicz, J. C. (2022). Professors. In Ritzer, G. (Ed.), *The Blackwell encyclopedia of sociology*. Wiley-Blackwell., DOI: 10.1002/9781405165518.wbeosp105.pub3

Hicks, D., Wouters, P., Waltman, L., de Rijcke, S., & Rafols, I. (2015). Bibliometrics: The Leiden Manifesto for research metrics. *Nature, 520*(7548), 429–431. DOI: 10.1038/520429a PMID: 25903611

Hollywood, A., McCarthy, D., Spencely, C., & Winstone, N. (2020). 'Overwhelmed at first': The experience of career development in early career academics. *Journal of Further and Higher Education, 44*(7), 998–1012. DOI: 10.1080/0309877X.2019.1636213

Holmes, W., Bialik, M., & Fadel, C. (2023). Artificial intelligence in education. *Data ethics: Building trust — How digital technologies can serve humanity*, 621-653. DOI: 10.58863/20.500.12424/4276068

Horváth, D., & Szabó, R. Z. (2019). Driving forces and barriers of Industry 4.0: Do multinational and small and medium-sized companies have equal opportunities? *Technological Forecasting and Social Change, 146*, 119–132. DOI: 10.1016/j.techfore.2019.05.021

Hostler, T. J. (2023). The invisible workload of open research. *Journal of Trial and Error, 4*(1), 21–36. DOI: 10.36850/mr5

Huang, J., & Chen, Z. (2016). The Research and Design of Web-based Intelligent Tutoring System. *International Journal of Multimedia and Ubiquitous Engineering, 11*(6), 337–348. DOI: 10.14257/ijmue.2016.11.6.30

Huang, M.-H., & Rust, R. T. (2021). A strategic framework for artificial intelligence in marketing. *Journal of the Academy of Marketing Science, 49*(1), 30–50. DOI: 10.1007/s11747-020-00749-9

Hu, H., Zhou, Q., & Hashim, H. (2025). Negotiating identity in the age of ChatGPT: Non-native English researchers' experiences with AI-assisted academic writing. *Humanities & Social Sciences Communications, 12*(1), 1–11. DOI: 10.1057/s41599-025-05351-4

Huppert, F. A., & So, T. T. C. (2013). Flourishing across Europe: Application of a new conceptual framework for defining well-being. *Social Indicators Research, 110*(3), 837–861. DOI: 10.1007/s11205-011-9966-7

Hu, Q., & Gill, T. G. (2000). IS faculty research productivity: Influential factors and implications. [IRMJ]. *Information Resources Management Journal, 13*(2), 15–25. DOI: 10.4018/irmj.2000040102

Hüther, O., & Krücken, G. (2013). Hierarchy and power: A conceptual analysis with particular reference to new public management reforms in German universities. *European Journal of Higher Education, 3*(4), 307–323. DOI: 10.1080/21568235.2013.850920

Hwang, G., Sung, H., Chang, S., & Huang, X. (2020). Computers and Education : Arti fi cial Intelligence A fuzzy expert system-based adaptive learning approach to improving students ' learning performances by considering affective and cognitive factors. *Computers and Education: Artificial Intelligence, 1*(August), 100003. DOI: 10.1016/j.caeai.2020.100003

Ifinedo, A. (2020). This is a self-archived version of an original article. This version may differ from the original in pagination and typographic details. Copyright : Rights : Rights url. *Computers & Education, 103760*. Advance online publication. DOI: 10.1016/j.compedu.2019.103760

Igiri, B. E., Okoduwa, S. I. R., Akabuogu, E. P., Okoduwa, U. J., Enang, I. A., Idowu, O. O., Abdullahi, S., Onukak, I. E., Onuruka, C. C., Christopher, O. P. O., Salawu, A. O., Chris, A. O., & Onyemachi, D. I. (2021). Focused research on the challenges and productivity of researchers in Nigerian academic institutions without funding. *Frontiers in Research Metrics and Analytics, 6*, 727228. Advance online publication. DOI: 10.3389/frma.2021.727228 PMID: 34805734

Intergovernmental Panel on Climate Change (IPCC). (2023). Summary for policymakers. In *Climate change 2023: Synthesis report*. Cambridge University Press., DOI: 10.1017/9781009325844.001

Iqbal, M., & Matulevičius, R. (2021). Exploring Sybil and double-spending risks in blockchain systems. *IEEE Access : Practical Innovations, Open Solutions, 9*, 76153–76177. DOI: 10.1109/ACCESS.2021.3081998

J, M. H., & K, L. (2024). Social impacts of AI in India: A societal perspective on adoption and inclusion. *International Journal of Scientific Research in Engineering and Management, 8*(4). https://doi.org/DOI: 10.55041/IJSREM37144

Jacobs, J. A., & Winslow, S. E. (2004). The academic life course, time pressures and gender inequality. *Community Work & Family, 7*(2), 143–161. DOI: 10.1080/1366880042000245443

Jahija, J. (2025). Recruiting public personnel: A comparative approach. *International Journal of Civil Service Reform and Practice, 13*(1), 73–84. DOI: 10.56289/ijcsrp.186

JAYARON, B. (2024). Educators' academic insights on artificial intelligence: Challenges and opportunities. Electronic Journal of eLearning.

Jepsen, D. M., Sun, J. J. M., Budhwar, P. S., Klehe, U. C., Krausert, A., Raghuram, S., & Valcour, M. (2014). International academic careers: Personal reflections. *International Journal of Human Resource Management, 25*(10), 1309–1326. DOI: 10.1080/09585192.2013.870307

Jiang, X., Li, M., & Zhang, Z. (2025). 'Bridging borders in academia': The motivations, barriers, and strategies of Global North scholars in Chinese higher education research. *Higher Education*, •••, 1–23. DOI: 10.1007/s10734-025-01558-1

Jobin, A., Ienca, M., & Vayena, E. (2019). The global landscape of AI ethics guidelines. *Nature Machine Intelligence, 1*(9), 389–399. DOI: 10.1038/s42256-019-0088-2

Jolley, M. R., Cross, E., & Bryant, M. (2014). A critical challenge: The engagement and assessment of contingent, part-time adjunct faculty professors in United States community colleges. *Community College Journal of Research and Practice, 38*(2-3), 218–230. DOI: 10.1080/10668926.2014.851969

Jose, P., & Koley, M. (2026). *Doctoral education and the Political Economy of Private Universities in India*. DOI: 10.31235/osf.io/xyv4c_v1

Joshi, D. (2024). AI governance in India – law, policy and political economy. *Communication Research and Practice, 10*(3), 328–339. DOI: 10.1080/22041451.2024.2346428

Jung, J., & Horta, H. (2019). Changing academic profession in East Asia: Responses to a common challenge. In J. Jung, H. Horta, & A. Yonezawa (Eds.), *The changing academic profession in international and comparative perspectives* (pp. 45–62). Springer. https://doi.org/DOI: 10.1007/978-981-13-9621-2_3

Kameshwara, K. K., Sandoval-Hernandez, A., Shields, R., & Dhanda, K. R. (2020). A false promise? Decentralization in education systems across the globe. *International Journal of Educational Research, 104*, 101669. DOI: 10.1016/j.ijer.2020.101669

Kanagaraj, K. (2019). ACADEMIC PERFORMANCE INDICATORS AND THE QUALITY OF RESEARCH IN HIGHER EDUCATION INSTITUTIONS IN INDIA: A STUDY OF UNIVERSITY TEACHERS' OPINIONS. *International Journal of Advance Research and Innovative Ideas in Education, 5*(5), 267–274. https://ijariie.com/AdminUploadPdf/ACADEMIC_PERFORMANCE_INDICATORS_AND_THE_QUALITY_OF_RESEARCH_IN_HIGHER_EDUCATION_INSTITUTIONS_IN_INDIA__A_STUDY_OF_UNIVERSITY_TEACHERS'_OPINIONS_ijariie10846.pdf

Karran, T., Beiter, K., & Appiagyei-Atua, K. (2017). Measuring academic freedom in Europe: A criterion referenced approach. *Policy Reviews in Higher Education, 1*(2), 209–239. DOI: 10.1080/23322969.2017.1307093

Karunathilake, E. M. B. M., Le, A. T., Heo, S., Chung, Y. S., & Mansoor, S. (2023). The path to smart farming: Innovations and opportunities in precision agriculture. *Agriculture, 13*(8), 1593. DOI: 10.3390/agriculture13081593

Kassab, M. (2025, June). Navigating Academic Careers in Software Engineering: An Empirical Study of Faculty and Postdoctoral Roles. In *Proceedings of the 33rd ACM International Conference on the Foundations of Software Engineering* (pp. 936-946). DOI: 10.1145/3696630.3727250

Kayashima, N., & Asada, S. R. (2024). Introduction: Development of universities in Southeast Asia and the impacts of study abroad. In N. Kayashima, M. Sugimura, K. Kuroda, & Y. Kitamura (Eds.), *Impacts of study abroad on higher education development* (Sustainable Development Goals Series, pp. 1–17). Springer. https://doi.org/DOI: 10.1007/978-981-97-0775-1_1

Kelsall, T., Schulz, N., Ferguson, W. D., Hau, M. V., Hickey, S., & Levy, B... (2022). Political Settlements and Development. https://doi.org/DOI: 10.1093/oso/9780192848932.001.0001

Kezar, A. (2012). Spanning the great divide between tenure-track and non-tenure-track faculty. *Change, 44*(6), 6–13. DOI: 10.1080/00091383.2012.728949

Khairullah, S. A., Harris, S., Hadi, H. J., Sandhu, R. A., Ahmad, N., & Alshara, M. A. (2025, February). Implementing artificial intelligence in academic and administrative processes through responsible strategic leadership in the higher education institutions. In *Frontiers in Education* (Vol. 10, p. 1548104). Frontiers Media SA. DOI: 10.3389/feduc.2025.1548104

Kim, G. M., & Cooc, N. (2021). Asian Americans and Pacific Islanders in academe: Race and gender through the tenure pipeline from 1993-2017. *Race, Ethnicity and Education*, *24*(3), 338–356. DOI: 10.1080/13613324.2020.1753675

Kinias, I., Papasolomou, I., & Thrassou, A. (2025). Educating family businesses in Asia: The FAB multicountry project case. *Journal of Asia Business Studies*. Advance online publication. DOI: 10.1108/JABS-01-2025-0028

Kinshuk. (2016). Evolution Is not enough : Revolutionizing Current Learning Environments to Smart Learning Environments. *International Journal of Artificial Intelligence in Education*, 561–581. DOI: 10.1007/s40593-016-0108-x

Kirkham, R. (2021). Industrial Limitations on Academic Freedom in Computer Science. *Industrial Limitations on Academic Freedom in Computer Science*, 1–15.

Kitchin, R. (2017). Thinking critically about and researching algorithms. *Information Communication and Society*, *20*(1), 14–29. DOI: 10.1080/1369118X.2016.1154087

Kogan, M., & Teichler, U. (Eds.). (2007). Key challenges to the academic profession. UNESCO Forum on Higher Education, Research and Knowledge. https://www.academia.edu/75785262/Key_Challenges_to_the_Academic_Profession

Koukaras, C., Hatzikraniotis, E., Mitsiaki, M., Koukaras, P., Tjortjis, C., & Stavrinides, S. G. (2025). Revolutionising educational management with AI and wireless networks: A framework for smart resource allocation and decision-making. *Applied Sciences (Basel, Switzerland)*, *15*(10), 5293. DOI: 10.3390/app15105293

Kuch, D., Kearnes, M., & Gulson, K. (2020). The promise of precision: datafication in medicine, agriculture and education. Policy Studies, 41(5), 527-546.

Kukulska-Hulme, A., & Ilic, P. (2025). MALL in the Age of AI. *The Palgrave Encyclopedia of Computer-Assisted Language Learning*, 1-8. DOI: 10.1007/978-3-031-51447-0_323-1

Kumar, R. (2023). Faculty members' use of artificial intelligence to grade student papers: A case of implications. *International Journal for Educational Integrity*, *19*(1), 9. DOI: 10.1007/s40979-023-00130-7

Kurdi, G., Leo, J., Parsia, B., Sattler, U., & Al-Emari, S. (2020). A Systematic Review of Automatic Question Generation for Educational Purposes. *International Journal of Artificial Intelligence in Education*, *30*(1), 121–204. DOI: 10.1007/s40593-019-00186-y

Kurysheva, A., van Rijen, H. V. M., Stolte, C., & Dilaver, G. (2023). Validity, acceptability, and procedural issues of selection methods for graduate study admissions in the fields of science, technology, engineering, and mathematics: A mapping review. *International Journal of STEM Education*, *10*(1), 55. DOI: 10.1186/s40594-023-00445-4

Kwiek, M., & Roszka, W. (2024). Once highly productive, forever highly productive? Full professors' research productivity from a longitudinal perspective. *Higher Education*, *87*(3), 519–549. DOI: 10.1007/s10734-023-01022-y

Lai, H., Hsiao, Y., & Hsieh, P. (2018). Computers & Education The role of motivation, ability, and opportunity in university teachers ' continuance use intention for fl ipped teaching. *Computers & Education*, *124*(November 2017), 37–50. DOI: 10.1016/j.compedu.2018.05.013

Lampman, C., Crew, E. C., Lowery, S. D., & Tompkins, K. (2016). Women faculty distressed: Descriptions and consequences of academic contrapower harassment. *Journal about Women in Higher Education*, *9*(2), 169–189. DOI: 10.1080/19407882.2016.1199385 PMID: 28239435

Langen, J. M. (2011). Evaluation of adjunct faculty in higher education institutions. *Assessment & Evaluation in Higher Education*, *36*(2), 185–196. DOI: 10.1080/02602930903221501

Larson, L. R., Duffy, L. N., Fernandez, M., Sturts, J., Gray, J., & Powell, G. M. (2019). Getting started on the tenure track: Challenges and strategies for success. *SCHOLE: A Journal of Leisure Studies and Recreation Education*, *34*(1), 36-51. DOI: 10.1080/1937156X.2019.1589804

Le, H. (2025). Design and Development Effective Learning AI Education: Navigating Deskilling in the Age of Intelligent Automation. In R. Zheng, *The Intersection of AI and Student Development in Learning* (p. 32). IGI Global.

Lee, M., Volpe Horii, C., Austin, A. E., Avery, L., DeSanctis, M., Finkelstein, N., & Schaal, B. (2023). An instructional-workforce framework for coordinated change in undergraduate education. *Change: The Magazine of Higher Learning*, *55*(1), 54–63. DOI: 10.1080/00091383.2023.2151809

Leisyte, L. (2014). Changing academic identities in the context of a managerial university – Bridging the duality between professions and organizations: Evidence from the US and Europe. In Fumasoli, T., Goastellec, G., & Kehm, B. M. (Eds.), *The relevance of academic work in comparative perspective* (pp. 69–88). Springer., DOI: 10.1007/978-3-319-06185-6_5

Lenchuk, E. B. (2022). Science and technology development as a strategic national priority of Russia. *Economic Revival of Russia*, *71*(1), 58–65. DOI: 10.37930/1990-9780-2022-1-71-58-65

Li, M., Xie, Q., Enkhtur, A., Meng, S., Chen, L., Yamamoto, B. A., & Murakami, M. (2025). A framework for developing university policies on generative AI governance: A cross-national comparative study. *A Framework for Developing University Policies on Generative AI Governance: A Cross-National Comparative Study*, 1–47.

Liang, W., Wang, S., Wang, H.-J., Bastani, O., Jayaraman, D., & Ma, Y. J. (2024). Environment Curriculum Generation via Large Language Models. *8th Annual Conference on Robot Learning*. Retrieved from https://eureka-research.github.io/eurekaverse/

Li, B., & Shen, Y. (2022). Publication or pregnancy? Employment contracts and childbearing of women academics in China. *Studies in Higher Education*, *47*(4), 875–887. DOI: 10.1080/03075079.2020.1817888

Li, J. (2025). Factors influencing national public health governance capacity: Based on NCA and fsQCA. *Frontiers in Public Health*, *13*, 1628677. DOI: 10.3389/fpubh.2025.1628677

Lin, H., Tu, Y., Hwang, G., & Huang, H. (2021). From Precision Education to Precision Medicine : Factors Affecting Medical Staff ' s Intention to Learn to Use AI Applications in Hospitals. *Journal of Educational Technology & Society*, *24*, 123–137.

Liu, K., Cao, Y., Hu, Y., & Wei, L. (2019). Application status and development of big data in medical education in China. *Medical Data Mining*, *2*(3), 118–125. DOI: 10.53388/mdm2018023

Liu, W., & Yan, W. (2019). The internal governance model in Chinese universities: An international comparative analysis. *Journal of Applied Research in Higher Education*, *11*(3), 428–438. DOI: 10.1108/JARHE-09-2018-0200

Liu, Y., Qin, H., & Li, H. (2025). Competing for research grants: Institutional resource inequality and early-career academics' research agenda setting. *Studies in Higher Education*, *50*(10), 2157–2177. DOI: 10.1080/03075079.2025.2544232

Li, Y., Li, J., & Sun, Y. (2013). Young faculty job perceptions in the midst of Chinese higher education reform: The case of Zhejiang University. *Asia Pacific Journal of Education*, *33*(3), 273–294. DOI: 10.1080/02188791.2013.787388

Llorens, A., Tzovara, A., Bellier, L., Bhaya-Grossman, I., Bidet-Caulet, A., Chang, W. K., Cross, Z. R., Dominguez-Faus, R., Flinker, A., Fonken, Y., Gorenstein, M. A., Holdgraf, C., Hoy, C. W., Ivanova, M. V., Jimenez, R. T., Jun, S., Kam, J. W. Y., Kidd, C., Marcelle, E., & Dronkers, N. F. (2021). Gender bias in academia: A lifetime problem that needs solutions. *Neuron*, *109*(13), 2047–2074. DOI: 10.1016/j.neuron.2021.06.002 PMID: 34237278

Long, D. Y., & Aleven, V. (2025). Artificial intelligence in higher education: A systematic review of instructional implications. *Frontiers in Education*, *10*. Advance online publication. DOI: 10.3389/feduc.2025.1648661

Loomes, S., Owens, A., & McCarthy, G. (2019). Patterns of recruitment of academic leaders to Australian universities and implications for the future of higher education. *Journal of Higher Education Policy and Management*, *41*(2), 137–152. DOI: 10.1080/1360080X.2019.1565296

Luckin, R., Holmes, W., Griffiths, M., & Forcier, L. B. (2016). Intelligence unleashed: An argument for AI in education. Pearson. https://www.pearson.com/content/dam/one-dot-com/one-dot-com/global/Files/efficacy-and-research/reports/Intelligence-Unleashed-v14-WEB.pdf

Lumpkin, A. (2009, July). Follow the yellow brick road to a successful professional career in higher education. In *The Educational Forum* (Vol. 73, No. 3, pp. 200-214). Taylor & Francis Group. DOI: 10.1080/00131720902991251

Lumpkin, A., & Jones, S. J. (2023). Toughest job in higher education: Chairs' responsibilities. *International Journal of Leadership in Education*, •••, 1–22. DOI: 10.1080/13603124.2023.2290144

Lu, O. H. T., Huang, A. Y. Q., Huang, J. C. H., Lin, A. J. Q., & Yang, S. J. H. (2018). Applying Learning Analytics for the Early Prediction of Students ' Academic Performance in Blended Learning. *Journal of Educational Technology & Society*, *21*, 220–232.

Luthra, A., Singh, K., & Singh, S. (2021). Academic performance indicator as performance management tool: Employees perception and factors governing to its acceptance and rejection in Indian educational institute. *International Journal of Strategic Business Alliances*, *7*(1), 1–1. DOI: 10.1504/IJSBA.2022.120076

Mabasa, F. D., & Ngirande, H. (2015). Perceived organisational support influences on job satisfaction and organisational commitment among junior academic staff members. *Journal of Psychology in Africa*, *25*(4), 364–366. DOI: 10.1080/14330237.2015.1078102

Macfarlane, B. (2007). Defining and rewarding academic citizenship: The implications for university promotions policy. *Journal of Higher Education Policy and Management*, *29*(3), 261–273. DOI: 10.1080/13600800701457863

Macháček, M., & Melecký, A. (2025). To be a professor: Academic mobility and publishing performance. *PLoS One*, *20*(11), e0336133. DOI: 10.1371/journal.pone.0336133 PMID: 41248149

Machajewski, S. (2026). *The Learn-It-All Educator: A Guidebook for Training Brains*. Not Replacing Them with AI.

Machovcova, K., Kováts, G., Mudrak, J., Cidlinská, K., & Zabrodska, K. (2024). (Dis) continuities in academic middle management career trajectories: A longitudinal qualitative study. *Journal of Higher Education Policy and Management*, *46*(2), 200–217. DOI: 10.1080/1360080X.2023.2276589

Madison, G., & Fahlman, P. (2021). Sex differences in the number of scientific publications and citations when attaining the rank of professor in Sweden. *Studies in Higher Education*, *46*(12), 2506–2527. DOI: 10.1080/03075079.2020.1723533

Madureira, L., Popovič, A., & Castelli, M. (2021). Competitive intelligence: A unified view and modular definition. *Technological Forecasting and Social Change*, *173*, 121086. DOI: 10.1016/j.techfore.2021.121086

Maeda, M., Soeung, S., & Chim, V. (2025). Teachers' side jobs in Cambodia: Who engages, work trends, motives, and impacts. *Compare: A Journal of Comparative Education*, •••, 1–19. DOI: 10.1080/03057925.2025.2587639

Mahajan, P. (2025). AI–family integration index (AFII): Benchmarking a new global readiness for AI as family. *Research Square* [Preprint]. https://doi.org/DOI: 10.21203/rs.3.rs-6577279/v1

Maher, F. A., & Tetreault, M. K. T. (2011). Long-term transformations: Excavating privilege and diversity in the academy. *Gender and Education*, *23*(3), 281–297. DOI: 10.1080/09540253.2010.491790

Mann, S. P., Aboy, M., Seah, J. J., Lin, Z., Luo, X., Rodger, D., Zohny, H., Minssen, T., Savulescu, J., & Earp, B. D. (2025). *AI and the Future of Academic Peer Review*. AI and the Future of Academic Peer Review.

Marginson, S., & van der Wende, M. (2007). *Globalisation and higher education* (OECD Education Working Papers No. 8). OECD Publishing. https://doi.org/DOI: 10.1787/19939019

Marginson, S. (2016). Globalization in higher education. In Marginson, S. (Ed.), *The good, the bad, and the ugly* (pp. 15–40). Routledge., DOI: 10.4324/9781003207528-2

Marginson, S. (2016). *The dream is over: The crisis of Clark Kerr's California idea of higher education*. University of California Press.

Marginson, S. (2016). The worldwide trend to higher participation in higher education: Dynamics of social stratification in inclusive systems. *Journal of Education Policy*, *31*(5), 601–623. DOI: 10.1080/02680939.2016.1171646

Mathews, K. (2018). Growing our own: Cultivating faculty leadership. *Change*, *50*(3-4), 88–92. DOI: 10.1080/00091383.2018.1509617

Ma, Y. (2025). AI, Education, and Academic Publishing in between Knowledge Capitalism and Socialism. *Beijing International Review of Education*, *7*(4), 351–374. DOI: 10.1177/25902547251390638

Mayer, A. L., & Tikka, P. M. (2008). Family-friendly policies and gender bias in academia. *Journal of Higher Education Policy and Management*, *30*(4), 363–374. DOI: 10.1080/13600800802383034

Mayer-Schönberger, V., & Cukier, K. (2013). *Big Data: A Revolution That Will Transform How We Live, Work, and Think*. John Murray.

McAlpine, L., & Emmioğlu, E. (2015). Navigating careers: Perceptions of sciences doctoral students, post-PhD researchers and pre-tenure academics. *Studies in Higher Education*, *40*(10), 1770–1785. DOI: 10.1080/03075079.2014.914908

McConnell, K. F. (2019). Teaching and learning in an age of precarity: Toward a pedagogy of the transitory. *Communication Education*, *68*(2), 252–258. DOI: 10.1080/03634523.2019.1569248

McDiarmid, G. W., & Zhao, Y. (2023). Time to rethink: Educating for a technology-transformed world. *ECNU Review of Education*, *6*(2), 189–214. DOI: 10.1177/20965311221076493

McGee, E. O., Naphan-Kingery, D., Mustafaa, F. N., Houston, S., Botchway, P. K., & Lynch, J. M. (2019). Turned off from an academic career: Engineering and computing doctoral students and the reasons for their dissuasion. *International Journal of Doctoral Studies*, *14*, 203–226. DOI: 10.28945/4250

McGeorge, D. (2023). *The ChatGPT revolution: How to simplify your work and life admin with AI*. John Wiley & Sons.

McGrath, C., Pargman, T. C., Juth, N., & Palmgren, P. J. (2023). University teachers' perceptions of responsibility and artificial intelligence in higher education-An experimental philosophical study. *Computers and Education: Artificial Intelligence*, *4*, 100139. DOI: 10.1016/j.caeai.2023.100139

McInnis, C. (2009). Traditions of academic professionalism and shifting academic identities. In Barnett, R., & Di Napoli, R. (Eds.), *Academic and professional identities in higher education: The changing frame of UK and US academics* (pp. 1–14). Routledge.

McNaughtan, J., Eicke, D., Thacker, R., & Freeman, S. (2022). Trust or self-determination: Understanding the role of tenured faculty empowerment and job satisfaction. *The Journal of Higher Education*, *93*(1), 137–161. DOI: 10.1080/00221546.2021.1935601

Meho, L. I. (2025). Gaming the metrics: Bibliometric anomalies in global university rankings and the research integrity risk index (RI2). *Scientometrics*, *130*(11), 6683–6726. Advance online publication. DOI: 10.1007/s11192-025-05480-2

Meho, L. I. (2025). Measuring research performance in higher education: Metrics, rankings, and institutional behavior. *Research Evaluation*, *34*(2), 145–160.

Memarian, B., & Doleck, T. (2023). Fairness, Accountability, Transparency, and Ethics (FATE) in Artificial Intelligence (AI) and higher education: A systematic review. *Computers and Education: Artificial Intelligence*, *5*, 100152. Advance online publication. DOI: 10.1016/j.caeai.2023.100152

Mendoza, J. M. F., Sharmina, M., Gallego-Schmid, A., Heyes, G., & Azapagic, A. (2017). Integrating backcasting and eco-design for the circular economy: The BECE framework. *Journal of Industrial Ecology*, *21*(3), 526–544. https://e-space.mmu.ac.uk/618498/1/Manuscript_ID_16_JIE_5273_REV3_FINAL_University_library_s_gateway.pdf. DOI: 10.1111/jiec.12590

Mer, A., Kumar, V., Verma, V. K., De, T., & Mathew, J. (2024). A review of predictors and outcomes of work engagement in nonprofit organizations. *Social Sciences & Humanities Open*, *10*, 101083. DOI: 10.1016/j.ssaho.2024.101083

Meron, Y., & Araci, Y. T. (2023). Artificial intelligence in design education: Evaluating ChatGPT as a virtual colleague for post-graduate course development. *Design Science*, *9*, e30. DOI: 10.1017/dsj.2023.28

Mgaiwa, S. J. (2023). Job satisfaction among university academics: Do academic rank and age make a difference? *Cogent Education*, *10*(2), 2230395. DOI: 10.1080/2331186X.2023.2230395

Middlehurst, R., & Teixeira, P. N. (2012). Governance Within the EHEA : Dynamic Trends, Common Challenges, and National Particularities. *Governance Within the EHEA : Dynamic Trends, Common Challenges, and National Particularities*, 527–551. DOI: 10.1007/978-94-007-3937-6

Milton, S., & Barakat, S. (2016). Higher education as the catalyst of recovery in conflict-affected societies. *Globalisation, Societies and Education*, *14*(3), 403–421. DOI: 10.1080/14767724.2015.1127749

Mittelstadt, B. D. (2019). Principles alone cannot guarantee ethical AI. *Nature Machine Intelligence*, *1*(11), 501–507. DOI: 10.1038/s42256-019-0114-4

Mittelstadt, B. D., Allo, P., Taddeo, M., Wachter, S., & Floridi, L. (2016). The ethics of algorithms: Mapping the debate. *Big Data & Society*, *3*(2), 1–21. DOI: 10.1177/2053951716679679

Mnasri, M., Jmal Maâlej, A., & Jmaiel, M. (2025). A systematic literature review on security testing of Ethereum smart contracts. *Blockchain: Research and Applications*, *7*(2), 100314. DOI: 10.1016/j.bcra.2025.100314

MoEYS. (2010). Policy on research development in the education sector. https://data.opendevelopmentcambodia.net/dataset/policy-on-research-development-in-the-education-sector

MoEYS. (2011). Master plan for research development in the education sector 2011–2015. https://planipolis.iiep.unesco.org/index.php/en/2011/master-plan-research-development-education-sector-2011-2015-5220

MoEYS. (2020). Proclamation on the selection and appointment of professorial titles in the education sector.

MoEYS. (2024a). Education strategic plan 2024–2028. https://www.nepcambodia.org/documents/education-strategic-plan-esp-2024-2028-kh/

MoEYS. (2024b). Guidelines for quality management of doctoral training at higher education institutions under the supervision of the Ministry of Education, Youth and Sport.

Mohamed Hashim, M. A., Tlemsani, I., & Duncan Matthews, R. (2022). A sustainable university: Digital transformation and beyond. *Education and Information Technologies*, *27*(7), 8961–8996. DOI: 10.1007/s10639-022-10968-y PMID: 35340534

Molotoks, A., Smith, P., & Dawson, T. P. (2020). Impacts of land use, population, and climate change on global food security. *Food and Energy Security*, *9*(1), e261. https://kclpure.kcl.ac.uk/portal/en/publications/impacts-of-land-use-population-and-climate-change-on-global-food-/. DOI: 10.1002/fes3.261

Mondal, D. (2024). Research Performance Analysis of Five Key Parameters of Top 20 Indian Universities: An Evaluation. *Journal of Data Science Informetrics and Citation Studies*, *3*(2), 216–222. DOI: 10.5530/jcitation.3.2.22

Mondal, H., Marndi, G., Behera, J. K., & Mondal, S. (2023). ChatGPT for teachers: Practical examples for utilizing artificial intelligence for educational purposes. *Indian Journal of Vascular and Endovascular Surgery*, *10*(3), 200–205. DOI: 10.4103/ijves.ijves_37_23

Monteiro-Krebs, L., Zaman, B., Geerts, D., & Caregnato, S. E. (2023). Every word you say: Algorithmic mediation and implications of data-driven scholarly communication. *AI & Society*, *38*(2), 1003–1012. DOI: 10.1007/s00146-022-01468-1

Moodley, M. (2025). Exploring academic freedom, institutional autonomy, and public accountability in the global landscape of private higher education. *South African Journal of Higher Education*, *39*(4), 165–178. DOI: 10.20853/39-4-7516

Morawska, J. (2021). The role of universities in social innovation within the quadruple/quintuple helix model: Practical implications from Polish experience. *Journal of the Knowledge Economy*, *13*(4), 3000–3022. DOI: 10.1007/s13132-021-00804-y

Morison, J., & McInerney, T. (2025). When should a computer decide?: Judicial decision-making in the age of automation, algorithms and generative artificial intelligence. In *Research handbook on judging and the judiciary* (pp. 54–87). Edward Elgar Publishing. DOI: 10.4337/9781788978743.00009

Morley, L. (2005). Opportunity or exploitation? Women and quality assurance in higher education. *Gender and Education*, *17*(4), 411–429. DOI: 10.1080/09540250500145106

Morley, L. (2014). *Academic women in neoliberal times*. Palgrave Macmillan.

Morrar, R., & Arman, H. (2017). The fourth industrial revolution (Industry 4.0): A social innovation perspective. *Technology Innovation Management Review*, *7*(11), 12–20. https://timreview.ca/sites/default/files/article_PDF/Morrar_et_al_TIMReview_November2017.pdf. DOI: 10.22215/timreview/1117

Morris, T. L., & Laipple, J. S. (2015). How prepared are academic administrators? Leadership and job satisfaction within US research universities. *Journal of Higher Education Policy and Management*, *37*(2), 241–251. DOI: 10.1080/1360080X.2015.1019125

Mouta, A., María, E., Sánchez, T., María, A., & Llorente, P. (2025). Comprehensive professional learning for teacher agency in addressing ethical challenges of AIED : Insights from educational design research. In *Education and Information Technologies* (Vol. 30, Issue 3). Springer US. DOI: 10.1007/s10639-024-12946-y

Mukhamejanova, D., & Kuchumova, G. (2025). Faculty perspectives on the changing research and teaching career tracks of academics at private universities in Kazakhstan. *Studies in Higher Education*, *50*(12), 2700–2715. DOI: 10.1080/03075079.2024.2426533

Mulenga, R., & Shilongo, H. (2024). Academic integrity in higher education: Understanding and addressing plagiarism. *Acta Pedagogia Asiana*, *3*(1), 30–43. DOI: 10.53623/apga.v3i1.337

Muller, J. (2018). *The tyranny of metrics*. Princeton University Press.

Müller, R., & de Rijcke, S. (2017). Thinking with indicators: Exploring the epistemic impacts of academic performance indicators in the life sciences. *Research Evaluation*, *26*(3), 157–168. DOI: 10.1093/reseval/rvx023

Muncey, N. (2025). *How AI can help lighten the educator workload and prevent burnout*. Retrieved from https://schoolai.com/blog/ai-lighten-educator-workload-prevent-burnout

Murai, E., & Foote, K. (2025). Non-tenure track faculty in US geography: Strategies for support. *Journal of Geography in Higher Education*, •••, 1–18. DOI: 10.1080/03098265.2025.2569363

Murgatroyd, S. J. (Ed.). (2025). *Strategic Choices and Leadership Change in Higher Education Institutions*. IGI Global., DOI: 10.4018/979-8-3373-2081-6

Murray, D. S. (2019). The precarious new faculty majority: Communication and instruction research and contingent labor in higher education. *Communication Education*, *68*(2), 235–245. DOI: 10.1080/03634523.2019.1568512

Musselin, C. (2005). Change or continuity in higher education governance? Lessons drawn from twenty years of reforms in Europe. *European Journal of Education*, *40*(1), 65–79. DOI: 10.1111/j.0141-8211.2005.00202.x

Musselin, C. (2018). New forms of competition in higher education. *Socio-economic Review*, *16*(3), 657–683. DOI: 10.1093/ser/mwy033

Mustaqeem, M. (2025). The Digital Pandit: Artificial Intelligence in Indian Higher Education: A critical inquiry into transformation, equity and ethics. *International Journal of Applied Research, 11*(9), 403–407. DOI: 10.22271/allresearch.2025.v11.i9e.13309

Mutua, S. N. (2025). Decolonizing Knowledge Production: Barriers and Strategies for African Scholars in Academic Publishing. *Multidisciplinary Journal of Technical University of Mombasa*, *4*(1), 93–104. DOI: 10.48039/mjtum.v4i1.92

Muzam, J. (2022). The challenges of modern economy on the competencies of knowledge workers. *Journal of the Knowledge Economy*, *14*(3), 1886–1903. DOI: 10.1007/s13132-022-00979-y

Nam, B. H., Love, A., & Marshall, R. C. (2021). Entering into global academia: US academic hegemony and former Korean elite athletes' faculty appointment in higher education. *Journal of Further and Higher Education*, *45*(4), 481–496. DOI: 10.1080/0309877X.2020.1784399

National Institutional Ranking Framework. (2023). *Methodology for Ranking of Higher Educational Institutions in India*. Ministry of Education, Government of India.

Nelson, R. (2024). *Academic identity in the age of AI: Higher education and the digital revolution*. Emerald Group Publishing.

Nir, A. E., & Zilberstein-Levy, R. (2006). Planning for academic excellence: Tenure and professional considerations. *Studies in Higher Education*, *31*(5), 537–554. DOI: 10.1080/03075070600922725

Noble, S. U. (2018). *Algorithms of oppression: How search engines reinforce racism*. NYU Press. DOI: 10.18574/nyu/9781479833641.001.0001

Novy, J. W., Banerjee, B., & Matson, P. A. (2021). A core curriculum for sustainability leadership. *Sustainability (Basel)*, *13*(19), 10557. DOI: 10.3390/su131910557

Nygren, G., Dobek-ostrowska, B., & Anikina, M. (2015). Professional autonomy. *Professional Autonomy*, *36*, 79–95.

O'Meara, K., Kuvaeva, A., & Nyunt, G. (2017). Constrained choices: A view of campus service inequality from annual faculty reports. *The Journal of Higher Education*, *88*(5), 672–700. DOI: 10.1080/00221546.2016.1257312

O'Meara, K., & Terosky, A. L. (2010). Engendering faculty professional growth. *Change*, *42*(6), 44–51. DOI: 10.1080/00091383.2010.523408

O'Sullivan, S., Friebe, M., Tonti, W., Hartnett, M., Castro, M., Pozzo, M. I., & Nilsiam, Y. (2020). Surveyed the impact of intellectual property training in STEM education on innovation, research, and development. *The Journal of World Intellectual Property*, *23*(5-6), 658–678. DOI: 10.1111/jwip.12167

Oblina, A. C., Linh, T. P., & Phuong, H. T. M. (2021). *Job Satisfaction of Basic Education Teachers in Southeast Asia: Key Issues and Policy Recommendations.* VNU Journal of Science Education Research., DOI: 10.25073/2588-1159/vnuer.4438

OECD. (2019). *OECD Principles on Artificial Intelligence*. Retrieved from Paris: OECD Publishing: https://oecd.ai/en/ai-principles

OECD. (2021). *Bridging the artificial intelligence divide: Policy options*. OECD Publishing., DOI: 10.1787/6e5f6549-

OECD. (2024). *OECD AI principles* (updated 2024 version). OECD Publishing.

Okulicz-Kozaryn, W., Artyukhov, A., & Artyukhova, N. (2026). Will AI Replace Us? Changing the University Teacher Role. *Societies (Basel, Switzerland)*, *16*(1), 32. DOI: 10.3390/soc16010032

Oleksiyenko, A., & Chan, S. J. (2020). Internationalization and the academic profession in Asia: Continuity and change. *Higher Education*, *80*(2), 215–230. DOI: 10.1007/s10734-019-00477-2

Omodan, B. I. (2025). Redefining the role of supervisors in the era of artificial intelligence : Implications for hybrid postgraduate research governance implications for hybrid postgraduate research governance. *Cogent Education*, *12*(1), 2536534. Advance online publication. DOI: 10.1080/2331186X.2025.2536534

Ooms, W., Werker, C., & Hopp, C. (2019). Moving up the ladder: Heterogeneity influencing academic careers through research orientation, gender, and mentors. *Studies in Higher Education*, *44*(7), 1268–1289. DOI: 10.1080/03075079.2018.1434617

Organisation for Economic Co-operation and Development (OECD). (2018). *Analysing megatrends to better shape the future of tourism* (OECD Tourism Papers No. 2018/02). OECD Publishing. https://doi.org/DOI: 10.1787/23071672

Organisation for Economic Co-operation and Development (OECD). (2021). *Reducing the precarity of academic research careers* (OECD Science, Technology and Industry Policy Papers No. 113). OECD Publishing. https://doi.org/DOI: 10.1787/23074957

Osei-Kofi, N. (2012). Junior faculty of color in the corporate university: Implications of neoliberalism and neoconservatism on research, teaching and service. *Critical Studies in Education*, *53*(2), 229–244. DOI: 10.1080/17508487.2012.672326

Ovalle, A., Subramonian, A., Gautam, V., Gee, G. C., & Chang, K. (2023). Factoring the matrix of domination: A critical review and reimagination of intersectionality in AI fairness. In *Proceedings of the 2023 ACM Conference on Fairness, Accountability, and Transparency (FAccT '23)* (pp. 643–655). Association for Computing Machinery. https://www.lsv.uni-saarland.de/wp-content/uploads/2023/12/Ovalle-et-al.-2023-Factoring-the-Matrix-of-Domination-A-Critical-Rev.pdf

Oyedokun, T. T. (2025). Navigating the dynamics of present-day academic libraries: An in-depth analysis of strategies, challenges, and emerging trends. *IFLA Journal, 51*(2), 470–489. DOI: 10.1177/03400352241291907

Painsi, P. W., Leitner, K., & Rybnicek, R. (2025). The impact of institutional autonomy on higher education institutions in Europe. *Science and Public Policy, December 2024*, 236–253.

Pandit, K. (2020). Mentoring graduate students in an era of faculty career restructuring. *Journal of Geography in Higher Education, 44*(3), 335–349. DOI: 10.1080/03098265.2020.1771548

Pant, J., & Bhadoria, A. S. (2025). Challenges of National Institute's Ranking Framework (NIRF). *Journal of Medical Evidence, 6*(1), 81–82. DOI: 10.4103/JME.JME_34_25

Peacock, V., Bruun, M. K., Dungey, C., & Shapiro, M. (2023). *Surveillance.* Open Encyclopedia of Anthropology., DOI: 10.29164/23surveillance

Pedró, F. (2009). Continuity and change in the academic profession in European countries. *Higher Education in Europe, 34*(3-4), 393–405. DOI: 10.1080/03797720903356594

Peerzada, R. A., Sharma, A., Gurumurthy, A. A., & Gurumurthy, A. A. (2024). Interrogating "light but tight" model of education: Saffron neoliberalism and India's new education policy. *Human Geographies, 18*(3), 345–357. DOI: 10.1177/19427786241265426

Peng, L., & Wiggins, L. M. (2025). What Do Employers Want?: Tracking Changes in the Academic Librarian Job Market Through A Study of US Full-Time Job Advertisements. *Journal of Library Administration, 65*(6-7), 761–782. DOI: 10.1080/01930826.2025.2525731

Penn State Faculty Affairs. (2025). *Guidance for the optional use of AI in summarizing student feedback for faculty assessment.* Retrieved from Pennsylvania State University: https://facultyaffairs.psu.edu/guidance-for-the-optional-use-of-ai-in-summarizing-student-feedback-for-faculty-assessment

Pennathur, P. R., Boksa, V., Pennathur, A., Kusiak, A., & Livingston, B. A. (2024). The future of office and administrative support occupations in the era of artificial intelligence: A state of the art review and future research directions. *International Journal of Industrial Ergonomics*, *104*, 103665. DOI: 10.1016/j.ergon.2024.103665

Peoples, K. (2021). *How to write a phenomenological dissertation: A step-by-step guide* (Vol. 56). SAGE.

Periyasami, S., & Periyasamy, A. P. (2022). Metaverse as future promising platform business model: Case study on fashion value chain. *Businesses*, *2*(4), 386–402. DOI: 10.3390/businesses2040033

Pesántez-Avilés, F., Cárdenas-Tapia, J., Torres-Toukoumidis, A., & Vintimilla, S. (2024, January). Understanding academic anxiety in the digital age: An exploratory analysis among university students and the influence of new technologies. In International Conference on Information Technology & Systems (pp. 279-289). Cham: Springer Nature Switzerland. DOI: 10.1007/978-3-031-54256-5_26

Pham, H. T., & Nguyen, C. H. (2020). Academic staff quality and the role of quality assurance mechanisms: The Vietnamese case. *Quality in Higher Education*, *26*(3), 262–283. DOI: 10.1080/13538322.2020.1761603

Phan, S. (2015). *Envisioning a higher education system for the 21st century: Cambodia*. University of British Columbia cIRcle. https://doi.org/DOI: 10.14288/1.0166746

Pietilä, M. (2015). Tenure track career system as a strategic instrument for academic leaders. *European Journal of Higher Education*, *5*(4), 371–387. DOI: 10.1080/21568235.2015.1046466

Pineda, P., & Salazar Morales, D. (2024). Managerialism, accreditation and insecure academic employment across different higher education traditions. *Studies in Higher Education*, *49*(11), 2080–2103. DOI: 10.1080/03075079.2023.2289087

Plekhanov, A., Trunova, E., & Volkova, N. (2023). Administrative burden and academic productivity: Evidence from higher education institutions. *Higher Education Policy*, *36*(2), 275–295.

Plekhanov, D., Franke, H., & Netland, T. H. (2023). Digital transformation: A review and research agenda. *European Management Journal*, *41*(6), 821–844. DOI: 10.1016/j.emj.2022.09.007

Porter, C. J., Moore, C. M., Boss, G. J., Davis, T. J., & Louis, D. A. (2020). To be Black women and contingent faculty: Four scholarly personal narratives. *The Journal of Higher Education*, *91*(5), 674–697. DOI: 10.1080/00221546.2019.1700478

Power, M. (1997). *The audit society: Rituals of verification*. Oxford University Press.

Prinsloo, C., Ramashego, S. M., Learning, D., Visagie, R. G., Tjano, N., Support, S., & Africa, S. (2025). BALANCING ACADEMIC FREEDOM AND RESEARCH INTEGRITY THROUGH VIRTUE ETHICS IN THE USE OF AI IN OPEN DISTANCE. *South African Journal of Higher Education, 39*(4), 236–262. DOI: 10.20853/39-4-7523

Przytuła, S., Sułkowski, Ł., & Kulikowski, K. (2025). Introduction. In *Human resource management in higher education institutions: An international perspective* (pp. 1–6). Routledge., DOI: 10.4324/9781003458425-1

Puccio, B., Castagna, F., Tucker, A., & Veltri, P. (2025). Towards medical AI misalignment: a preliminary study. https://doi.org//arXiv.2505.18212DOI: 10.48550

Pyke, J. (2013). Women, choice and promotion or why women are still a minority in the professoriate. *Journal of Higher Education Policy and Management, 35*(4), 444–454. DOI: 10.1080/1360080X.2013.812179

Quadir, B., Chen, N., & Isaias, P. (2020). Analyzing the educational goals, problems and techniques used in educational big data research from 2010 to 2018. *Interactive Learning Environments, 4820*. Advance online publication. DOI: 10.1080/10494820.2020.1712427

Radanliev, P. (2025). AI ethics: Integrating transparency, fairness, and privacy in education. *Applied Artificial Intelligence, 39*(1), 2463722. Advance online publication. DOI: 10.1080/08839514.2025.2463722

Rainnie, A., Goods, C., Bahn, S., & Burgess, J. (2013). The challenges of working in Australian academia: An introduction. *Labour & Industry: a journal of the social and economic relations of work, 23*(3), 191-199. DOI: 10.1080/10301763.2013.839080

Rainy, T. A., & Chowdhury, A. R. (2022). The Role Of Artificial Intelligence In Vendor Performance Evaluation Within Digital Retail Supply Chains: A Review Of Strategic Decision-Making Models. *American Journal of Scholarly Research and Innovation, 1*(01), 220–248. DOI: 10.63125/96jj3j86

Rambe, P. (2024). Research excellence and productivity for global impact at an African university. *Studies in Higher Education, 49*(8), 1397–1424. DOI: 10.1080/03075079.2023.2265931

Ramlo, S. (2025). Examining Views about Academic Freedom at Institutions of Higher Education in the US. *Innovative Higher Education, 51*(2), 711–732. DOI: 10.1007/s10755-025-09845-6

Rao, S. (2025). Universities in Ruins or on the Cusp of Renewal? Dark Academia, Global Data, Liberal Arts, and the Coming AI Shock. *INNOVAPATH, 1*(9), 7–7. DOI: 10.63501/s9xyhj53

Ratanawijitrasin, S. (2015). The evolving landscape of South–East Asian higher education and the challenges of governance. In Curaj, A., Matei, L., Pricopie, R., Salmi, J., & Scott, P. (Eds.), *The European higher education area* (pp. 271–290). Springer., DOI: 10.1007/978-3-319-20877-0_15

Reichman, H. (2025). *Understanding academic freedom*. JHU Press. DOI: 10.56021/9781421450940

Rhoades, G., Hohl, E., Shermer, E. T., Berry, J., Worthen, H., Alker, G., & Park, J. (2024). *Contingent faculty and the remaking of higher education: A labor history*. University of Illinois Press.

Richardson, J., Suseno, Y., & Wardale, D. (2021). The paradoxical management of casual academics: An Australian case study. *Higher Education Research & Development, 40*(2), 370–385. DOI: 10.1080/07294360.2020.1756749

Rider, S. (2022). Autonomy for Whom? Governance of What? The Rationality of Academic Freedom. In *Academic Freedom in the European Context: Legal, Philosophical and Institutional Perspectives* (pp. 117–148). Springer International Publishing. DOI: 10.1007/978-3-030-86931-1_6

Rodrigues, T. V. (2025). *Distant Writing and The Epistemology of Authorship: On Creativity*. Delegation, And Plagiarism in The Age Of AI.

Rony, M. K. K., Parvin, M. R., Wahiduzzaman, M., Debnath, M., Bala, S. D., & Kayesh, I. (2024). "I wonder if my years of training and expertise will be devalued by machines": Concerns about the replacement of medical professionals by artificial intelligence. *SAGE Open Nursing, 10*, 23779608241245220. DOI: 10.1177/23779608241245220 PMID: 38596508

Rosenberg, B. (2023). *"Whatever it is, I'm against it": Resistance to change in higher education*. Harvard Education Press.

Ross, J. I., Richards, S. C., Newbold, G., Jones, R. S., Lenza, M., Murphy, D. S., Hogan, R., & Curry, G. D. (2011). Knocking on the ivory tower's door: The experience of ex-convicts applying for tenure-track university positions. *Journal of Criminal Justice Education, 22*(2), 267–285. DOI: 10.1080/10511251003778982

Ross, P. M., Scanes, E., & Locke, W. (2023). Stress adaptation and resilience of academics in higher education. *Asia Pacific Education Review, 24*(4), 889–903. DOI: 10.1007/s12564-023-09829-1

Ros, V., & Oleksiyenko, A. (2018). Policy misalignments and development challenges in the Cambodian academic profession: Insights from public university lecturers. *Higher Education Policy*, *31*(1), 19–35. DOI: 10.1057/s41307-017-0043-y

Roumbanis, L. (2018). Symbolic violence in academic life: A study on how junior scholars are educated in the art of getting funded. *Minerva*, *56*(4), 397–418. DOI: 10.1007/s11024-018-9364-2

Royal Government of Cambodia. (2013). *Royal Decree No. NS/RKT/0313/214 on professorial titles (Preah Reach Kret)*. Royal Government of Cambodia.

Royal Government of Cambodia. (2023). *Pentagonal Strategy–Phase I for growth, employment, equity, efficiency, and sustainability: Building the foundation toward realizing Cambodia Vision 2050*. Royal Government of Cambodia. https://asset .cambodia.gov.kh/mptc/2023/08/EN-PENTAGONAL-STRATEGY-PHASE-I.pdf

Royal Government of Cambodia. (2025). *Subdecree no. 244 on the organization and functioning of the General Secretariat of the National Council for Sustainable Development* (Subdecree No. 244). https://data.opendevelopmentcambodia. net/en/dataset/ subdecree-no-244-on-the-organization-and-functioning-of-the-general-secretariat-of-the-national-co/resource/1e5f1860-05fe-4ab9-802c-700c2ae1ad17?view_ id=64a5a8d8-f52d-4791-be3f-d45a45a9abc2

Royal Government of Cambodia. (2026). *Sub-Decree on the Organization and Functioning of the General Secretariat of the National Committee for the Conferment of Professorial Titles*.

Rudick, C. K., & Dannels, D. P. (2019). "Yes, and…" continuing the scholarly conversation about contingent labor in higher education. *Communication Education*, *68*(2), 259–263. DOI: 10.1080/03634523.2019.1572198

Rudolph, J., Ismail, F. M. M., & Popenici, . A. D. (2024). Higher education's generative artificial intelligence paradox: The meaning of chatbot mania. *Journal of University Teaching & Learning Practice*, *21*(2). Advance online publication. DOI: 10.53761/54fs5e77

Rushforth, A., & Hammarfelt, B. (2023). The rise of responsible metrics as a professional reform movement: A collective action frames account. *Quantitative Science Studies*, *4*(4), 879–897. DOI: 10.1162/qss_a_00280

Russell, S., & Norvig, P. (2021). *Artificial intelligence: A modern approach* (4th ed.). Pearson., https://aima.cs.berkeley.edu/

Sam, R., Serey, M., Ry, H., Sarith, C., Tieng, M., & Yoeng, H. (2025b). Academic Accreditation and Evaluation in Cambodian Higher Education Institutions: Development, Challenges, and Opportunities. In Lytras, M., & erban, A. (Eds.), *Academic Accreditation and Evaluation in Higher Education: Practices, Experiences, and Quality Assurance* (pp. 241–262). IGI Global Scientific Publishing., DOI: 10.4018/979-8-3693-5608-1.ch010

Sam, R., Tieng, M., Yoeng, H., Sarith, C., Serey, M., & Sam, S. (2025a). Enhancing Research for Academicians in Cambodian Higher Education Institutions: A Policy Perspective. In Mdikana, A. (Ed.), *Enhancing Research for Academicians in Higher Education* (pp. 225–248). IGI Global Scientific Publishing., DOI: 10.4018/979-8-3693-4496-5.ch012

Sam, R., Voeun, N., Vando, P., Vet, K., No, S., Hour, R., Em, S., Sou, S., Phuong, S., & Da, V. (2026). Leadership-Driven Faculty Collaboration and Research Capacity Building in ASEAN: Insights From Cambodia. In Sam, R. (Ed.), *Implementing Research Management Policies in ASEAN Higher Education Institutions* (pp. 189–214). IGI Global Scientific Publishing., DOI: 10.4018/979-8-3373-3291-8.ch007

Sanz-Menéndez, L., & Cruz-Castro, L. (2019). University academics' preferences for hiring and promotion systems. *European Journal of Higher Education*, *9*(2), 153–171. DOI: 10.1080/21568235.2018.1515029

Sarabipour, S., Niemi, N. M., Burgess, S. J., Smith, C. T., Bisson Filho, A. W., Ibrahim, A., & Clark, K. (2023). The faculty-to-faculty mentorship experience: A survey on challenges and recommendations for improvements. Proceedings of the Royal Society B: Biological Sciences, Article 20230983. https://doi.org/DOI: 10.1098/rspb.2023.0983

Saraite Sariene, L., Caba Pérez, C., & López Hernández, A. M. (2020). Expanding the actions of Open Government in higher education sector: From web transparency to Open Science. *PLoS One*, *15*(9), e0238801. DOI: 10.1371/journal.pone.0238801 PMID: 32915833

Sarrico, C. S. (2022). The expansion of doctoral education and the changing nature and purpose of the doctorate. *Higher Education*, *84*(6), 1293–1311. DOI: 10.1007/s10734-022-00946-1

Scherer, R. (2018). University of Oslo, Faculty of Educational Sciences, Department of Teacher Education and SC. *Computers & Education*.

Schleck, J. (2022). *Dirty knowledge: Academic freedom in the age of neoliberalism*. U of Nebraska Press. DOI: 10.2307/j.ctv21v2b0c

Schmalz, D. L., Parr, M. G., Powell, G. M., Bricker, K. S., & Dustin, D. L. (2019). Post-tenure pathways: Individualized careers in higher education. *SCHOLE: A Journal of Leisure Studies and Recreation Education, 34*(1), 52-61. DOI: 10.1080/1937156X.2019.1589809

Schneider, T. (2023). *Digitalization and Artificial Intelligence*. Springer Books. DOI: 10.1007/978-3-658-40383-6

Schuster, J. H., & Finkelstein, M. J. (2006). *The American faculty: The restructuring of academic work and careers*. Johns Hopkins University Press.

Schwab, K. (2026). *Universities, Professors, and Students in the Intelligent Age: A Call for Systems Change*. Schwab Academy.

Selwyn, N. (2019). Should robots replace teachers? AI and the future of education. Polity Press. https://eric.ed.gov/?id=ED599636

Selwyn, N. (2019). *Should robots replace teachers? AI and the future of education*. Polity Press. https://www.politybooks.com/bookdetail/?isbn=9781509528967

Selwyn, N. (2022). Education and technology: Critical approaches. Bloomsbury Academic. https://www.bloomsbury.com/uk/education-and-technology-9781350145559/

Selwyn, N. (2019). What's the problem with learning analytics? *Journal of Learning Analytics*, *6*(3), 11–19. DOI: 10.18608/jla.2019.63.3

Selwyn, N. (2022). The future of AI and education: Some cautionary notes. *European Journal of Education*, *57*(4), 620–631. DOI: 10.1111/ejed.12532

Seo, G. E., Hedayati Mehdiabadi, A., & Huang, W. (2017). Identifying core competencies to advance female professors' careers: An exploratory study in United States academia. *Journal of Further and Higher Education*, *41*(6), 741–759. DOI: 10.1080/0309877X.2016.1177167

Setyadi, A., Soekotjo, S., Lestari, S. D., Pawirosumarto, S., & Damaris, A. (2025). Trends and opportunities in sustainable manufacturing: A systematic review of key dimensions from 2019 to 2024. *Sustainability (Basel)*, *17*(2), 789. DOI: 10.3390/su17020789

Shah, P. (2023). *AI and the Future of Education: Teaching in the Age of Artificial Intelligence*. John Wiley & Sons.

Shamzzuzoha, A., Chavira, P. C., Kekäle, T., Kuusniemi, H., & Jovanovski, B. (2022). Identified necessary skills to establish a center of excellence in vocational education for green innovation. *Cleaner Environmental Systems*, *6*, 100100. DOI: 10.1016/j.cesys.2022.100100

Sharif Nia, H., Marôco, J., She, L., Khoshnavay Fomani, F., Rahmatpour, P., Stepanovic Ilic, I., Mohammad Ibrahim, M., Muhammad Ibrahim, F., Narula, S., Esposito, G., Gorgulu, O., Naghavi, N., Pahlevan Sharif, S., Allen, K.-A., Kaveh, O., & Reardon, J. (2023). Student satisfaction and academic efficacy during online learning with the mediating effect of student engagement: A multi-country study. *PLoS One*, *18*(10), e0285315. DOI: 10.1371/journal.pone.0285315 PMID: 37792853

Shawkey, J. G. (2026). Beyond AI Tools: Professors Addressing Ethical AI Detection in Faith-Based Academia (Doctoral dissertation, Charleston Southern University).

Shore, C., & Wright, S. (2015). Audit culture revisited: Rankings, ratings, and the reassembling of society. *Current Anthropology*, *56*(4), 421–444. https://www.jstor.org/stable/2661148. DOI: 10.1086/681534

Shore, C., & Wright, S. (2015). Governing by numbers: Audit culture, rankings and the new world order. *Social Anthropology*, *23*(1), 22–28. DOI: 10.1111/1469-8676.12098

Siekkinen, T., Pekkola, E., & Carvalho, T. (2020). Change and continuity in the academic profession: Finnish universities as living labs. *Higher Education*, *80*(5), 931–948. DOI: 10.1007/s10734-019-00422-3

Siekkinen, T., Pekkola, E., & Kivistö, J. (2016). Recruitments in Finnish universities: Practicing strategic or pathetic HRM? *Nordic Journal of Studies in Educational Policy*, *2016*(2-3), 32316. DOI: 10.3402/nstep.v2.32316

Siemens, G. (2013). Learning analytics: The emergence of a discipline. *The American Behavioral Scientist*, *57*(10), 1380–1400. DOI: 10.1177/0002764213498851

Si, J. (2023). No other choices but involution: Understanding Chinese young academics in the tenure track system. *Journal of Higher Education Policy and Management*, *45*(1), 53–67. DOI: 10.1080/1360080X.2022.2115332

Simmons, C. A., Weiss, E. L., & Schwartz, S. L. (2022). Job satisfaction indicators for tenure and non-tenure track social work faculty: Similar but not equal. *Social Work Education*, *41*(2), 175–194. DOI: 10.1080/02615479.2020.1808608

Singh, A. (2025). *Low-code/no-code for the education industry*. Retrieved from https://blog.tooljet.ai/modernize-education-using-low-code-no-code-platforms

Škokić, V., Jelić, P., & Jerković, I. (2025). The role and contribution of sustainable development goals as a transformative framework in higher education: A case study of the University of Split. *WORLD (Oakland, Calif.)*, *6*(1), 22. DOI: 10.3390/world6010022

Slaughter, S., & Leslie, L. L. (1997). *Academic capitalism: Politics, policies, and the entrepreneurial university*. Johns Hopkins University Press.

Slaughter, S., & Rhoades, G. (2004). *Academic Capitalism and the New Economy: Markets, State, and Higher Education*. Johns Hopkins University Press.

Smith, J., Poe, J., & Skop, E. (2025). Cultivating Faculty-Driven Reform of Promotion to Full Professor Structures to Reward and Regard the Scholarship of Engagement. *Journal of Participatory Research Methods*, *6*(5). Advance online publication. DOI: 10.35844/001c.153975

Sok, S., & Bunry, R. (2024a). Higher education development and study abroad experiences of faculty in Cambodia. In Kayashima, N., Sugimura, M., Kuroda, K., & Kitamura, Y. (Eds.), *Impacts of study abroad on higher education development* (pp. 223–241). Springer., DOI: 10.1007/978-981-97-0775-1_12

Sok, S., & Bunry, R. (2024b). Higher Education in Cambodia. In Symaco, L. P., & Hayden, M. (Eds.), *International Handbook on Education in Southeast Asia. Springer International Handbooks of Education*. Springer., DOI: 10.1007/978-981-16-8136-3_47-1

Solem, M. N., & Foote, K. E. (2006). Concerns, attitudes, and abilities of early-career geography faculty. *Journal of Geography in Higher Education*, *30*(2), 199–234. DOI: 10.1080/03098260600717299

Solomon, S., & du Plessis, M. (2023). Temporary academics in South African higher education institutions: Their lived precarity experiences. *Journal of Psychology in Africa*, *33*(5), 522–529. DOI: 10.1080/14330237.2023.2258001

Sommersguter-Reichmann, M., & Reichmann, G. (2025). Institutional corruption in higher education: diving into indicator-based funding and employment conditions in Austrian universities. *Policy Reviews in Higher Education*, 1-18. DOI: 10.1080/23322969.2025.2489953

Spivakovsky, A., Vinnyk, M., Poltoratskyi, M., Tarasich, Y., & Omelchuk, S. (2022). Information technologies for measuring the qualitative and quantitative indicators of higher education institutions' work. *Information Technologies and Learning Tools*, *89*(3), 190–208. DOI: 10.33407/itlt.v89i3.4895

Spivakovsky, O. V., Omelchuk, S. A., Kobets, V. V., Valko, N. V., & Malchykova, D. S. (2023). Institutional policies on artificial intelligence in university learning, teaching and research. *Information Technologies and Learning Tools*, *97*(5), 181–202. DOI: 10.33407/itlt.v97i5.5395

Stokel-Walker, C. (2023). How AI is changing the research landscape. *Nature, 614*(7949), 22–25. DOI: 10.1038/d41586-023-00210-5

Strathern, M. (2023). Audit and accountability in higher education: Revisiting audit culture. *Journal of the Royal Anthropological Institute*, *29*(1), 1–18. DOI: 10.1111/1467-9655.t01-2-00001

Strathern, M. (2023). *Property, Substance, and Effect: Anthropological Essays on Persons and Things*. HAU Books.

Strathern, M. (Ed.). (2000). *Audit Cultures: Anthropological Studies in Accountability, Ethics, and the Academy*. Routledge.

Stupnisky, R. H., Hall, N. C., Daniels, L. M., & Mensah, E. (2017). Testing a model of pretenure faculty members' teaching and research success: Motivation as a mediator of balance, expectations, and collegiality. *The Journal of Higher Education, 88*(3), 376–400. DOI: 10.1080/00221546.2016.1272317

Stupnisky, R. H., Weaver-Hightower, M. B., & Kartoshkina, Y. (2015). Exploring and testing the predictors of new faculty success: A mixed methods study. *Studies in Higher Education*, *40*(2), 368–390. DOI: 10.1080/03075079.2013.842220

Stvilia, B., Gibradze, L., & Jansen, B. J. (2024). Academic metrics and research productivity: A systematic review. *Journal of Informetrics*, *18*(1), 101–120.

Stvilia, B., Pang, Y., Lee, D. J., & Gunaydin, F. (2024). Data quality assurance practices in research data repositories: A systematic literature review. *Journal of the Association for Information Science and Technology*, *76*, 238–261. DOI: 10.1002/asi.24948

Subbaye, R., & Vithal, R. (2017). Gender, teaching and academic promotions in higher education. *Gender and Education*, *29*(7), 926–951. DOI: 10.1080/09540253.2016.1184237

Sublime, J. (2024). The AI race: Why current neural network-based architectures are a poor basis for artificial general intelligence. *Journal of Artificial Intelligence Research*, *79*, 41–67. DOI: 10.1613/jair.1.15315

Suchek, N., Fernandes, C., Kraus, S., Filser, M., & Sjögrén, H. (2021). Innovation and the circular economy: A systematic literature review. *Business Strategy and the Environment*, *30*(8), 3686–3702. https://ideas.repec.org/a/bla/bstrat/v30y2021i8p3686-3702.html. DOI: 10.1002/bse.2834

Sun, J. C. (2025). *Academic Freedom in US Higher Education : Rights Emergent from the Law and the Profession*. Encyclopedia.

Sutikno, T., & Aisyahrani, A. I. B. (2023). Non-fungible tokens, decentralized autonomous organizations, Web 3.0, and the metaverse in education: From university to metaversity. [EduLearn]. *Journal of Education and Learning*, *17*(1), 1–10. DOI: 10.11591/edulearn.v17i1.20657

Sutton, P. (2017). Lost souls? The demoralization of academic labor in the measured university. *Higher Education Research & Development*, *36*(3), 625–636. DOI: 10.1080/07294360.2017.1289365

Tabacu, A. E. (2025). REGULATORY FRAMEWORK FOR THE USE OF ARTIFICIAL INTELLIGENCE IN EUROPEAN HIGHER EDUCATION. *Jurídicas*, *21*(1), 124–152. DOI: 10.17981/juridcuc.21.1.2025.07

Tagg, J. (2012). Why does the faculty resist change? Change. *Change*, *44*(1), 6–15. DOI: 10.1080/00091383.2012.635987

Taherdoost, H. (2025). *Maximizing Research Impact: Practical Strategies for Enhancing Research Visibility*. Taylor & Francis. DOI: 10.4324/9781003604785

Takagi, K. (2018). Accommodating project-based professionals in higher education institutions in Japan. *Journal of Higher Education Policy and Management*, *40*(3), 272–286. DOI: 10.1080/1360080X.2018.1462434

Tang, K. H. D. (2024). Implications of artificial intelligence for teaching and learning. *Acta Pedagogia Asiana*, *3*(2), 65–79. DOI: 10.53623/apga.v3i2.404

Tariq, M. U. (Ed.). (2024). *AI-Driven Learning and Engagement in Higher Education*. IGI Global., DOI: 10.4018/979-8-3693-4074-5

Taylor, Z. (2025). Professional ghosting and bureaucratic kindness: Institutional communication with applicants to tenure-track academic staff positions in student affairs and/or higher education. *Journal of Higher Education Policy and Management*, *47*(2), 129–153. DOI: 10.1080/1360080X.2024.2433303

Teelken, C., Taminiau, Y., & Rosenmöller, C. (2021). Career mobility from associate to full professor in academia: Micro-political practices and implicit gender stereotypes. *Studies in Higher Education*, *46*(4), 836–850. DOI: 10.1080/03075079.2019.1655725

Teichler, U. (2017). The changing academic profession. In *International higher education* (pp. 12–14). Springer., https://www.scribd.com/document/862316594/Teichler-Academic-Profession

Teixeira, P., & Korytkowski, P. (2022). The marketization of higher education: Continuity and change in the neoliberal era. *Higher Education Policy*, *35*(1), 1–20. DOI: 10.1057/s41307-021-00247-8

Tempelaar, D., Rienties, B., & Nguyen, Q. (2021). The Contribution of Dispositional Learning Analytics to Precision Education. *Journal of Educational Technology & Society*, *24*, 109–122.

Tian, M., & Lu, G. (2017). What price the building of world-class universities? Academic pressure faced by young lecturers at a research-centered University in China. *Teaching in Higher Education*, *22*(8), 957–974. DOI: 10.1080/13562517.2017.1319814

Tight, M. (2021). The neoliberal-turn and the marketization of higher education: The UK experience. *Higher Education*, *82*(4), 711–726. DOI: 10.1007/s10734-020-00619-0 PMID: 33776079

Toppo, P. K. (2025). ARTIFICIAL INTELLIGENCE AND THE NATIONAL EDUCATION POLICY (NEP) 2020: A QUALITATIVE EXPLORATION OF INTEGRATION, OPPORTUNITIES, AND CHALLENGES. *International Journal of Advanced Research*, *13*(10), 1218–1221. DOI: 10.21474/IJAR01/22015

Traxler, J., Connor, S., Hayes, S., & Jandrić, P. (2021). Futures studies, mobilities, and the postdigital condition: Contention or complement? *Postdigital Science and Education*, *3*(3), 834–854. DOI: 10.1007/s42438-021-00245-5

Trendowski, T. (2023). Delayed promotion to full professor in physical education teacher education. *International Journal of Kinesiology in Higher Education*, *7*(4), 285–295. DOI: 10.1080/24711616.2022.2152510

Trí, N. M., Hoàng, P. D., & Dũng, N. T. (2021). Impact of the industrial revolution 4.0 on higher education in Vietnam: Challenges and opportunities. *Linguistics and Culture Review*, *5*(S3), 1–15. DOI: 10.21744/lingcure.v5nS3.1350

Tripathi, P. (2025). RESEARCH PAPERS AI IN CLASSROOMS : IMPACT ON TEACHER. *AI in Classrooms: Impact on Teacher Identity and Autonomy.", 20*(4).

Turcotte, P. L., & Holmes, D. (2024). Vanishing academics: On the importance of speed and becoming-imperceptible. *Nursing Inquiry*, *31*(2), e12619. DOI: 10.1111/nin.12619 PMID: 38062860

Tytherleigh*, M. Y., Webb, C., Cooper, C. L., & Ricketts, C. (2005). Occupational stress in UK higher education institutions: A comparative study of all staff categories. *Higher education research & development, 24*(1), 41-61. DOI: 10.1080/0729436052000318569

Ültanır, Y. G., Author, C., & Gürcan, Y. (2025). Autonomy and Academic Freedom in Universities : Country Examples Based on Types of Governance. *Higher Education Governance and Policy*, *6*, 68–86. DOI: 10.55993/hegp.1584027

UNESCO. (2021). *Recommendation on the Ethics of Artificial Intelligence*. Retrieved from Paris: UNESCO: https://unesdoc.unesco.org/ark:/48223/pf0000381137

UNESCO. (2021). *Recommendation on the ethics of artificial intelligence*. UNESCO Publishing.

UNESCO. (2023). *Guidance for Generative AI in Education and Research*. Retrieved from Paris: UNESCO: https://unesdoc.unesco.org/ark:/48223/pf0000386693

UNESCO. (2023). *Guidance for generative AI in education and research*. UNESCO Publishing.

UNESCO. (2025, September 2). *UNESCO survey: Two-thirds of higher education institutions have or are developing guidance on AI use*. UNESCO. https://www.unesco.org/en/articles/unesco-survey-two-thirds-higher-education-institutions-have-or-are-developing-guidance-ai-use

University Grants Commission. (2018). *UGC Regulations on Minimum Qualifications for Appointment of Teachers and Other Academic Staff in Universities and Colleges and Measures for the Maintenance of Standards in Higher Education*. Government of India.

University of Bath. (2024). *Responsible research assessment*. Retrieved from https://www.bath.ac.uk/campaigns/responsible-research-assessment/

University of Edinburgh. (2024). *Responsible research assessment*. Retrieved from https://www.ed.ac.uk/research-cultures/home/responsible-research-assessment

Upadhyay, A. K., & Khandelwal, K. (2018). Applying artificial intelligence: Implications for recruitment. *Strategic HR Review*, *17*(5), 255–258. DOI: 10.1108/SHR-07-2018-0051

Usher, M., Barak, M., & Erduran, S. (2025). What role should higher education institutions play in fostering AI ethics? Insights from science and engineering graduate students. *International Journal of STEM Education*, *12*(1), 51. DOI: 10.1186/s40594-025-00567-x

Uttl, B. (2024). Student evaluation of teaching (SET): Why the emperor has no clothes and what we should do about it. *Human Arenas*, *7*(2), 403–437. DOI: 10.1007/s42087-023-00361-7

Välimaa, J., & Nokkala, T. (2014). The Finnish academic profession: Continuity and change in a changing world. In Fumasoli, T., Goastellec, G., & Kehm, B. M. (Eds.), *The academic profession in Europe: New tasks and new challenges* (pp. 125–144). Springer., DOI: 10.1007/978-3-319-01028-1_7 van den Hoonaard, D. K. (2025). Doing it right? Interpretive research in an era of research ethics review. In *Handbook of Interpretive Research Methods in the Social Sciences* (pp. 456–470). Edward Elgar Publishing. DOI: 10.4337/9781803926391.00038

Van Dis, E. A. M., Bollen, J., Zuidema, W., van Rooij, R., & Bockting, C. L. (2023). ChatGPT: Five priorities for research. *Nature, 614*(7947), 224–226. DOI: 10.1038/d41586-023-00288-7 PMID: 36737653

Vare, P., Arro, G., Hamer, A. D., Gobbo, G. D., De Vries, G., Farioli, F., Kadji-Beltran, C., Kangur, M., Mayer, M., Millican, R., Nijdam, C., Réti, M., & Zachariou, A. (2019). Devising a competence-based training program for educators of sustainable development: Lessons learned. *Sustainability (Basel), 11*(7), 1890. DOI: 10.3390/su11071890

Vellamo, T., Kosonen, J., Siekkinen, T., & Pekkola, E. (2022). Bureaucratic, professional and managerial power in university tenure track recruitment. In E. Forsberg, L. Geschwind, S. Levander, & W. Wermke (Eds.), *Peer review in an era of evaluation* (pp. 301–321). Palgrave Macmillan. https://doi.org/DOI: 10.1007/978-3-030-75263-7_16

Verma, S., & Dwivedi, U. (2023). Optimizing digital knowledge repositories: Leveraging electronic resources in university libraries for enhanced academic advantages. *Perspectives in Social Work, 37*(03), 112–132.

Viefers, S. F., Christie, M. F., & Ferdos, F. (2006). Gender equity in higher education: Why and how? A case study of gender issues in a science faculty. *European Journal of Engineering Education, 31*(1), 15–22. DOI: 10.1080/03043790500429948

Voorn, B. (2023). Professional managers, public values? The delicate balance between corporatization and stewardship to society. *Public Management Review, 25*(8), 1498–1516. DOI: 10.1080/14719037.2022.2026691

Waddington, D. I., Maxwell, B., Maclean, T., Mcdonough, K., Waddington, D. I., Maxwell, B., Maclean, T., Mcdonough, K., & Waddington, D. I. (2024). theory and practice How free are classroom teachers ? Understanding teacher academic freedom in the United States and Canada academic freedom in the United States and Canada. *Theory and Practice How Free Are Classroom Teachers ? Understanding Teacher Academic Freedom in the United States and Canada Academic Freedom in the United States and Canada.* DOI: 10.1080/13540602.2024.2422859

Wallbank, A. J. (2022). Academic writing and student identity: Helping learners write in an age of massification, metrics and consumerism. In *Student support services* (pp. 203–222). Springer Nature Singapore. DOI: 10.1007/978-981-16-5852-5_10

Wang, Y., Liu, C., & Tu, Y. F. (2021). Factors affecting the adoption of AI-based applications in higher education. Educational technology & society, 24(3), 116-129.

Wang, C. J., & Yang, I. H. (2021). Why and how does empowering leadership promote proactive work behavior? An examination with a serial mediation model among hotel employees. *International Journal of Environmental Research and Public Health, 18*(5), 2386. DOI: 10.3390/ijerph18052386 PMID: 33804442

Wang, L. (2022). Newbie or experienced: An empirical study on faculty recruitment preferences at top national HEIs in China. *Studies in Higher Education, 47*(4), 783–798. DOI: 10.1080/03075079.2020.1804849

Wang, S., & Jones, G. A. (2021). Competing institutional logics of academic personnel system reforms in leading Chinese Universities. *Journal of Higher Education Policy and Management, 43*(1), 49–66. DOI: 10.1080/1360080X.2020.1747958

Wang, S., Wang, F., Zhu, Z., Wang, J., Tran, T., & Du, Z. (2024). Artificial intelligence in education: A systematic literature review. *Expert Systems with Applications, 252*, 124167. DOI: 10.1016/j.eswa.2024.124167

Wang, T., Yu, L., Wang, W., & Dai, K. (2024). Employees in change: An exploration of academics' perceived employee-organisation relationship in the reform of the tenure-track system in China. *Studies in Higher Education, 49*(11), 2066–2079. DOI: 10.1080/03075079.2023.2288940

Wang, Y. (2025). Artificial intelligence in student management systems to enhance academic performance monitoring and intervention. *Scientific Reports, 15*(1), 35122. DOI: 10.1038/s41598-025-19159-4 PMID: 41062725

Weishaupt, T., & Quiceno-Soto, G. (2026). Skills development in sustainable energy transitions: A systematic map and critical review of the drivers and barriers. *Energy Research & Social Science, 134*, 104576. DOI: 10.1016/j.erss.2026.104576

Wenhua, Z., Qamar, F., Abdali, T. N., Hassan, R., Jafri, S. T. A., & Nguy n, Q. N. (2023). Blockchain technology: Security issues, healthcare applications, challenges and future trends. *Electronics (Basel), 12*(3), 546. DOI: 10.3390/electronics12030546

Whitmee, S., Haines, A., Beyrer, C., Boltz, F., Capon, A., Dias, B. F. D. S., Ezeh, A., Frumkin, H., Gong, P., Head, P., Horton, R., Mace, G. M., Marten, R., Myers, S. S., Nishtar, S., Osofsky, S. A., Pattanayak, S. K., Pongsiri, M. J., Romanelli, C., & Yach, D. (2015). Safeguarding human health in the Anthropocene epoch: Report of The Rockefeller Foundation–Lancet Commission on planetary health. *Lancet, 386*(10007), 1973–2028. DOI: 10.1016/S0140-6736(15)60901-1

WhizzBridge. (2025). *AI-chatbot development services: Custom, GPT-based, multilingual solutions*. Retrieved from https://www.whizzbridge.com/software/ai-chatbot-development-services

Williams-Jones, B. (2026). *The committee of eternal deliberation: Institutional satire from inside the university*. BrynStorming Project, École de santé publique de l'Université de Montréal. https://doi.org/DOI: 10.71781/34524

Williamson, B. (2017). Big data in education: The digital future of learning, policy, and practice. *Sage (Atlanta, Ga.)*. Advance online publication. DOI: 10.4135/9781529714920

Williamson, B. (2019). The hidden architecture of higher education: Building a big data infrastructure for the 'smarter university'. *International Journal of Educational Technology in Higher Education*, *16*(1), 50. DOI: 10.1186/s41239-019-0174-1

Williamson, B., & Eynon, R. (2020). Historical threads, missing links, and future directions in AI in education. *Learning, Media and Technology*, *45*(3), 223–235. DOI: 10.1080/17439884.2020.1798995

Williamson, B., & Piattoeva, N. (2022). Education governance and algorithmic accountability: Examining AI in policy and practice. *Learning, Media and Technology*, *47*(1), 1–18. DOI: 10.1080/17439884.2021.1990102

Wilson, A. C., & Burleigh, C. (2025). Research integrity in the era of generative artificial intelligence. *Journal of Educational Research and Practice*, *15*(1), 2054. DOI: 10.5590/JERAP.2025.15.2054

Wolverton, M., Ackerman, R., & Holt, S. (2005). Preparing for leadership: What academic department chairs need to know. *Journal of Higher Education Policy and Management*, *27*(2), 227–238. DOI: 10.1080/13600800500120126

Wong, J., Khalil, M., Baars, M., De Koning, B. B., & Paas, F. (2019). Computers & Education Exploring sequences of learner activities in relation to self- regulated learning in a massive open online course. *Computers & Education*, *140*(February), 103595. DOI: 10.1016/j.compedu.2019.103595

Woodcock, J. (2018). Digital Labor in the University: Understanding the Transformations of Academic Work in the UK. *tripleC Communication Capitalism & Critique Open Access Journal for a Global Sustainable Information Society*, *16*(1), 129–142. DOI: 10.31269/triplec.v16i1.880

World Bank. (2024). Cambodia's systematic country diagnostic update. World Bank Group. https://www.worldbank.org/en/country/cambodia/publication/cambodia-systematic-country-diagnostic-update

World Bank. (2025). Artificial intelligence revolution in higher education. https://www.worldbank.org/en/region/lac/publication/ia-educacion-superior-inteligencia-artificial16(1)

Xu, W., & Poole, A. (2024). 'Academics without publications are just like imperial concubines without sons': The 'new times' of Chinese higher education. *Journal of Education Policy*, *39*(6), 861–878. DOI: 10.1080/02680939.2023.2288339

Xu, X., Arshad, M. A., He, Y., Liu, H., Chen, Q., & Yang, J. (2025). From skilled workers to smart talent: AI-driven workforce transformation in the construction industry. *Buildings (Basel, Switzerland)*, *15*(14), 2552. DOI: 10.3390/buildings15142552

Xu, Z. (2022). Human judges in the era of artificial intelligence: Challenges and opportunities. *Applied Artificial Intelligence*, *36*(1), 2013652. DOI: 10.1080/08839514.2021.2013652

Yakoboski, P. J. (2016). Adjunct views of adjunct positions. *Change*, *48*(3), 54–59. DOI: 10.1080/00091383.2016.1170553

Yamada, K. (2026). Structural failures in AI safety: A cross-system comparative analysis with educational impact observations. Available at *SSRN* 6285340. DOI: 10.2139/ssrn.6285340

Yang, S. J. H. (2021). Guest Editorial : Precision Education - A New Challenge for AI in Education. *Journal of Educational Technology & Society*, *24*, 105–108.

Yang, S. J. H., Ogata, H., Matsui, T., & Chen, N. (2021). Computers and Education : Arti fi cial Intelligence Human-centered arti fi cial intelligence in education : Seeing the invisible through the visible. *Computers and Education: Artificial Intelligence*, *2*(January), 100008. DOI: 10.1016/j.caeai.2021.100008

Yang, X., Cai, X. L., & Li, T. S. (2024). Does the tenure track influence academic research? An empirical study of faculty members in China. *Studies in Higher Education*, *49*(3), 476–492. DOI: 10.1080/03075079.2023.2238767

Yarram, V. K., & Yallavula, R. (2022). Adaptive Machine Learning Driven Compliance Scoring Models for Automated Risk Detection, Quality Validation of AI-Generated Content in Regulated Industries. *International Journal of Emerging Research in Engineering and Technology*, *3*(1), 116–126. DOI: 10.63282/3050-922X.IJERET-V3I1P112

Yin, Z., Jiang, X., & Tong, P. (2024). Why do they leave? University personnel system reforms in China and the impacts on academic staff turnover. *Journal of Higher Education Policy and Management*, *46*(5), 463–483. DOI: 10.1080/1360080X.2024.2307738

Young, P. (2006). Out of balance: Lecturers' perceptions of differential status and rewards in relation to teaching and research. *Teaching in Higher Education*, *11*(2), 191–202. DOI: 10.1080/13562510500527727

You, X., Wang, C., Huang, J., Gao, X., Zhang, Z., Wang, M., Huang, Y., Zhang, C., Jiang, Y., Wang, J., Zhu, M., Sheng, B., Wang, D., Pan, Z., Zhu, P., Yang, Y., Liu, Z., Zhang, P., Tao, X., & Liang, Y. (2020). Towards 6G wireless communication networks: Vision, enabling technologies, and new paradigm shifts. *Science China. Information Sciences*, *64*(1), 1–74. DOI: 10.1007/s11432-020-2955-6

Zambrana, R. E., Carvajal, D., & Townsend, J. (2023). Institutional penalty: Mentoring, service, perceived discrimination and its impacts on the health and academic careers of Latino faculty. *Ethnic and Racial Studies*, *46*(6), 1132–1157. DOI: 10.1080/01419870.2022.2160651 PMID: 37719448

Zawacki-Richter, O., Marín, V. I., Bond, M., & Gouverneur, F. (2019). Systematic review of research on artificial intelligence applications in higher education – where are the educators? International Journal of Educational Technology in Higher Education, 16, 39. , Article 50. DOI: 10.1186/s41239-019-0171-06(1)

Zawacki-Richter, O., Marín, V. I., Bond, M., & Gouverneur, F. (2019). Systematic review of AI applications in higher education. *International Journal of Educational Technology in Higher Education*, *16*(39). Advance online publication. DOI: 10.1186/s41239-019-0171-0

Zhao, D. (2025). The impact of AI-enhanced natural language processing tools on writing proficiency: An analysis of language precision, content summarization, and creative writing facilitation. *Education and Information Technologies*, *30*(6), 8055–8086. DOI: 10.1007/s10639-024-13145-5

Zheng, R. (2018). Precarity is a feminist issue: Gender and contingent labor in the academy. *Hypatia*, *33*(2), 235–255. DOI: 10.1111/hypa.12401

Zhou, X., Du, M., & Dong, H. (2023). RETRACTED: Spatial and temporal effects of China's digital economy on rural revitalization. *Frontiers in Energy Research*, *11*, 1061221. DOI: 10.3389/fenrg.2023.1061221

Zvereva, E. (2023). Digital ethics in higher education: Modernizing moral values for effective communication in cyberspace. *Online Journal of Communication and Media Technologies*, *13*(3), e202313. DOI: 10.30935/ojcmt/13033

About the Contributors

Rany Sam has been a dedicated civil servant with the Cambodian Ministry of Education, Youth, and Sport since 2007. Since 2017, he has served as the Vice-Rector of the National University of Battambang (NUBB), a prominent public university in northwest Cambodia. In this capacity, he oversees the Graduate School, Faculty of Arts, Humanities, and Education, the Institute of Foreign Languages, and the Confucius Institute. Previously, he served as Director of the Institute of Foreign Languages from 2010 to 2017. He has served as the Director of the Confucius Institute at NUBB in Cambodia since 2019. Dr. Sam is an active member of several academic organizations, including the Southeast Asia Research Academy (SEARA), the Society of Transnational Academic Researchers (STAR) as a country director, and Responsible Borneo (REBORN). He earned his PhD in Education from the School of Educational Studies at the University of Science Malaysia in 2016. Additionally, he completed diplomas in public administration, leadership, and innovation programs at the Royal School of Administration in Cambodia in 2017 and 2022. He holds a Bachelor's and Master's degree in Law (LL.B. and LL.M.) from the Royal University of Law and Economics, completed in 2004 and 2007, respectively. Dr. Sam has authored approximately 100 academic papers and book chapters. He serves as project coordinator for multiple initiatives, including Erasmus+ Capacity Building in Higher Education, Korean ODA, USAID, and the World Bank-funded Higher Education Improvement Project (HEIP). His editorial roles include associate editor of Frontiers in Education (Higher Education) and Frontiers in Political Science, as well as editor for IGI Global book chapters. He has peer-reviewed over 100 manuscripts and book chapters published by leading academic publishers, including Springer Nature, Sage, Taylor & Francis, and Routledge. His research interests encompass legal studies, public policy and administration, educational history and cooperation, educational leadership and management, and various social research areas. His email address is samrany82@gmail.com or sam.rany@nubb.edu.kh, and his mobile phone number is +855 (92) 646-680.

***

Ashraf Alam is currently serving as an Assistant Professor in the Department of Education at NIT Calicut, Kerala, India. He has been recognised among the *World's Top 2% Scientists* by Stanford University and Elsevier. He earned his Ph.D. from IIT Kharagpur, where his research engaged with foundational concerns in educational policy, curriculum design, educational technology, philosophy of education, innovation in education, educational administration, governance, and pedagogical transformation. His academic contributions include more than 95 Scopus-indexed publications and over 100 conference presentations delivered at national and international academic forums. His work has appeared in reputed research publication platforms including Elsevier, Springer, Taylor & Francis, CRC Press, Routledge, Atlantis Press, Springer Nature, Palgrave Macmillan, and IEEE. His work is grounded in a transdisciplinary orientation that draws from educational sciences, digital pedagogy, curriculum theory, learning analytics, sustainability education, instructional design, artificial intelligence, ethics of technology, and socio-technical studies. Dr. Ashraf's scholarship strives to interrogate and expand the boundaries of educational thought by examining the epistemological, ethical, and social dimensions of digital and post-digital pedagogies. His work critically engages with the changing nature of knowledge production, learner agency, pedagogical mediation, and institutional transformation in technologically saturated educational environments. He is particularly invested in advancing inclusive digital learning, gamified instructional strategies, AI-mediated educational ecosystems, and ethically governed technology integration in education. His research agenda is animated by the pursuit of design-oriented, ethically attuned, and contextually responsive frameworks that can support meaningful educational reform. Through his work, he seeks to contribute to the development of pedagogical models that are not only technologically innovative but also socially just, epistemically inclusive, developmentally sensitive, and aligned with the broader goals of sustainable and human-centred education.

Sanjana Bharadwaj is a doctoral researcher in Law at NALSAR University of Law, Hyderabad, where she has been pursuing her Ph.D. She holds an LL.M. from NALSAR University of Law, with a strong academic foundation in constitutional law, international law, and governance studies. Her research engages with critical issues at the intersection of law, language, identity, and global justice. She has contributed to Scopus-indexed scholarship, including work on linguistic rights and minority protections, as well as constitutional responses to humanitarian crises such as the Rohingya issue. Her publication in the Journal of Asian and African Studies examines the concept of linguistic genocide and its implications within Indian legal frameworks, while her work in Novum Jus critically analyses constitutional failures in India and Myanmar. In addition to her research, she has served as an editor for academic volumes including Reimagining Constitutionalism in the Indian Context and Technology, AI & Law, reflecting her engagement with contemporary debates in constitutional theory and legal technology. Her work adopts an interdisciplinary and critical approach, contributing to emerging scholarship on rights, governance, and structural inequality.

Indrani Bhattacharjee, an alumnus of IIM Indore, is an ace academician with over 24 years of teaching and research experience at both under-graduate and post-graduate level. With a Master's degree in Management, a Doctoral degree in the field of Finance and a IIM Bangalore certification on MOOCs, currently she is associated as Professor (Finance & Entrepreneurship) with Institute of Management Studies, Ghaziabad (University Courses Campus). She is the recipient of BEST PH.D THESIS AWARD in 2008 and has delivered key-note addresses, published cases and research papers, edited books in the area of her discipline and chaired national and international conferences. Her current research area is Business Finance, Sustainable Finance and ESG practices.

Da Vuthea has been a committed civil servant under the Cambodian Ministry of Education, Youth, and Sport since 2013. He is currently serving at the National University of Battambang as a Director of the Research and Development Center and University-Industry Cooperation Officer, where he contributes to strengthening institutional research capacity and fostering collaboration between academia and industry. Prior to this role, he served at the National University of Meanchey in several academic and leadership positions, including Vice Dean of the Faculty of Agriculture and Director of Graduate Programs. In these capacities, he played a key role in academic program development, postgraduate education management, and institutional administration. He also served as a lecturer in higher education for many years, contributing to teaching, curriculum development, and student mentorship. Before entering the higher education sector, Dr. Da Vuthea gained valuable experience working with national and international organizations. His roles included Branch Director at Buddhism for Development, Team Leader in a cooperative development program, Provincial Trainer at CEDAC, Data Entry Officer at the World Food Programme (WFP), and Community Facilitator in a human rights organization. These experiences strengthened his expertise in project management, community development, and organizational leadership. Dr. Da Vuthea holds a PhD in Educational Management from the National University of Battambang (NUBB), a Master's degree in Accounting and Finance from the National Meanchey University (NMU), and a Bachelor's degree in Fisheries Science from the Kampong Cham

National School of Agriculture (KCNSA). In addition, he has completed several professional training programs in public administration, innovation, and research methodology, including certifications from the Royal School of Administration and the Education, Research, and Innovation Center in Cambodia. His professional and research interests include research methodology, higher education management, community development, Social Science, finance, and economics. He has actively participated in academic and institutional initiatives aimed at improving education quality and promoting research engagement in Cambodia.

Sereyrath Em is a Cambodian government teacher of English with a higher education degree, a university lecturer, and an educational researcher with over 20 years of experience in teaching, instructing, and lecturing. In addition, he holds three master's degrees: an MA in TESOL, an MA in Education, and an MBA, and he holds two doctoral degrees: a PhD in Educational Science and a PhD in Educational Administration. Moreover, he is also working hard toward his third PhD in Cooperative Education at Suranaree University of Technology, Thailand. Besides, he was a former editor at the Cambodian Journal of Educational Research (CJER) and is the founder and editor-in-chief of the Cambodian Journal of Educational and Social Sciences (CJESS). Additionally, he is also a reviewer and an editor for Frontiers in Education and Psychology, where he has contributed 35 scholarly pieces so far. Likewise, he is also an editor for IGI Global, where he has edited three books entitled Cultural and Political Impacts on Educational Leadership in ASEAN, Digital Leadership and Innovation in ASEAN Education, and Student Enrollment and Retention Strategies to Reduce Dropout in Higher Education. Noticeably, he also serves as a reviewer for many other well-known journals and publishers such as Cogent Education, MDPI, Taylor & Francis, Springer Nature, and Palgrave Macmillan, among other Scopus-indexed outlets. So far, he has published around 100 scholarly pieces in highly reputable journals and publishers. In January 2026, he was accepted to pursue a Doctor of Laws (LL.D.) at Paññāsāstra University of Cambodia (PUC), Phnom Penh, Cambodia, and has been taking the courses since then.

Rahul Gangurde is a legal academic and researcher whose scholarship engages with constitutional rights, public policy, and the political economy of welfare in India. His doctoral research focuses on healthcare rights and the dynamics of privatisation within the Indian health sector, examining the implications for access, regulation, and state responsibility. He is an alumnus of the Indian Law Society's ILS Law College, and is currently associated with Asia's oldest law college, Government Law College. Dr. Gangurde has published in several academic journals and edited volumes, and maintains wide-ranging intellectual interests reflected in his work as a voracious reader and interdisciplinary scholar. His research is marked by a critical engagement with rights discourse, institutional design, and socio-legal method.

Hour Ry is the Dean in the Faculty of Business Administration and Tourism of the National University of Battambang (NUBB), a public university in northwest Cambodia, which he joined in 2008. He received his Master's Degree in Business from Chamroeun University of Poly-Technology, Cambodia in 2006. In 2003, he graduated with Bachelor's degree of Science in Mathematics at the Royal University of Phnom Penh (RUPP). Currently, in 2025, Mr. Hour Ry serves as the Head of Procurement at the Second Higher Education Improvement Project (HEIP2) of NUBB, which is funded by World Bank's Cambodia Higher Education Improvement Project. He currently serves as Project Manager for the Official Development Assistance (ODA) South Korea Project in Cambodia at The National University of Battambang (NUBB), in cooperation with Duksung Women's University, and is supported by the Government of the Republic of Korea. The project name is "Establishment of a sustainable win-win model through the opening of the Department of International Trade And SCM at National University of Battambang and the Strengthening of cooperation with the local community In Cambodia". Mr. Hour Ry also serve as project Coordinator in Erasmus+ Project including Smart City Asian Learning Network (SCALe), Geomatics for Disaster Risk Reduction (GeoDRR). From 2018 to 2024, Mr Hour Ry served as the NUBB the Head of Procurement at NUBB for the World Bank-funded Higher Education Improvement Project (HEIP). From 2013 to 2016, Mr Hour Ry served as the NUBB Procurement Officer for the World Bank-funded Higher Education Quality and Capacity Improvement Project (HEQCIP).

Hanh Le is a passionate researcher and accomplished Full Stack Software Developer with deep expertise in software development, data analytics, data science, and cloud computing. She holds a Ph.D. in Information Technology and a Master's in Computer Science, bringing both academic rigor and a solution-driven mindset to her work. With extensive experience in front-end and back-end development, she specializes in scalable, database-driven applications that support evidence-based decision-making. Dr. Le has led transformative tech initiatives across healthcare, law enforcement, and retail, translating complex needs into high-performing systems. She values interdisciplinary collaboration, believing that impactful innovation often arises at the intersection of fields. Her blend of technical skill, research excellence, and collaborative spirit continues to drive progress in academia and industry alike.

Meta Mai completed a bachelor's degree in Civil Engineering at the National University of Battambang (2019-2024). Now pursuing a master's degree in Civil Engineering at Peter the Great St. Petersburg Polytechnic University in Russia.

Channorak Ngo is a distinguished Cambodian educator and higher education administrator who currently serves as the Vice Rector of the National Meanchey University (NMU) — a leading public higher education institution located in the northwestern region of Cambodia. In this leadership position, he plays a vital role in guiding the university's strategic direction, academic development, and institutional governance. Mr. Channorak began his professional career in education in 2007, dedicating himself to advancing the quality, accessibility, and relevance of higher education in Cambodia. Over nearly two decades of public service, he has contributed significantly to academic administration, curriculum enhancement, and institutional development. As Vice Rector, he is responsible for supervising both the academic and administrative affairs of all five faculties within NMU, ensuring that teaching, research, and community engagement are effectively aligned with national education policies and international standards. In addition to his administrative responsibilities, Mr. Channorak also serves as a Public Financial Officer (Roechetey Kar) at NMU, overseeing the university's financial management, budgeting, and expenditure planning. His efforts have been instrumental in promoting financial transparency, accountability, and good governance, thereby strengthening NMU's reputation as one of Cambodia's most credible and progressive public universities. Academically, Mr. Channorak is deeply committed to educational research, innovation, and leadership development. He is currently pursuing a Doctor of Philosophy (Ph.D.) in Education, specializing in Curriculum and Instruction at the National Institute of Education (NIE). His doctoral research focuses on curriculum design, innovative pedagogy, and the integration of modern teaching approaches that enhance student learning outcomes and institutional effectiveness. Mr. Channorak's educational background demonstrates both diversity and academic depth. He holds a Master's Degree in Tourism Management (November 2005), a Higher Bachelor's Degree (Bachelor +1) in Economics and Information Technology (October 2007), and a Bachelor's Degree in Tourism from the National Institute of Management (NIM) (October 2002). Earlier in his academic journey, he completed his High School Diploma at 10 January 1979 High School in Siem Reap in August 1998. Throughout his professional journey, Mr. Ngo Channorak has exemplified outstanding leadership, integrity, and vision in promoting educational excellence, institutional reform, and sustainable community development. His work at NMU reflects a balanced approach that integrates academic rigor, administrative efficiency, and social responsibility. Mr. Channorak continues to be a driving force in shaping Cambodia's higher education landscape — fostering innovation, mentoring young scholars, and building collaborative educational partnerships that contribute to national and regional development. His professional philosophy centers on lifelong learning, ethical leadership, and education as a catalyst for social transformation and progress.

Sinath No Currently serves as the Head of the Civil Engineering Department in the Faculty of Science and Technology, (NUBB).Have begun higher education journey in Russia, where earned a Bachelor of Technics and Technology in the field of Construction from Voronezh State University of Architecture and Civil Engineering in 2010. Following bachelor's degree, pursued a graduate master's degree in Civil and Industrial Engineering, specializing in "Effective and Economy Composite Structures" at the same university, which completed in late 2012.In 2018, has successfully defended Professional Engineer certification (No. 0005343PE/ Bldg.) and was honored with the title and decoration of Gold Medal by the Asian Engineering Register (AER). The professional excellence was further recognized in 2019 when was conferred the honorary title of a member of the Asian Federation of Engineering Organizations. This expertise, coupled with commitment to education and professional development, makes a prominent figure in the field of civil engineering in Cambodia. Tel: (+855) 12543334 E-Mail: no.sinath@nubb.edu.kh

Kumari Pallavi is currently serving as an Assistant Professor in the Department of Mass Communication, bringing with her over five years of teaching experience. She has been associated with Galgotias University since 2021 and actively contributes to academic and administrative responsibilities, including serving as the department-level IQAC coordinator and PhD coordinator. Her academic interests primarily lie in Development Communication and Intercultural Communication, along with areas such as Communication Research, Advertising, and Mass Communication Theories. Dr. Pallavi holds a Ph.D. in Mass Communication from Tezpur University, Assam, along with an M.Phil from Mahatma Gandhi Antarrashtriya Hindi Vishwavidyalaya (Wardha), an M.A. in Mass Communication from Makhanlal Chaturvedi National University of Journalism and Communication, Bhopal (where she was a Gold Medalist), and a B.A. (Hons.) in Journalism and Mass Communication from Patna Women's College, Patna University. Her research contributions include publications on green marketing, development communication among the Tharu community, media literacy, gender portrayal in media, and multiculturalism in new media. She has also enhanced her practical media skills through certification courses in audio production, video production, and photojournalism. Additionally, she has successfully qualified the UGC NET in Mass Communication and Journalism multiple times between 2013 and 2016, reflecting her strong academic foundation and commitment to excellence in teaching and research.

Pawan Pant is working as an Assistant Professor of Management at the University School of Business, Chandigarh University, Mohali, Punjab. He has published two research papers, one national and one international journal. He has 10 years of teaching experience and worked as an Assistant Manager (Purchase) at Pacific Industries Ltd., Udaipur (Rajasthan) for one year. His area of specialization is Economics. email: pawanpant04@gmail.com.

Stephanie Nicolas Pantelides is a cognitive psychologist and Visiting Lecturer in the Department of Psychology and Social Sciences at Frederick University, Cyprus. Her research focuses on spatial cognition, spatial memory, navigation, multisensory integration, and the relationship between visual and linguistic representations of space. She earned her Bachelor's, Master's, and Ph.D. in Psychology from the University of Cyprus. Before joining Frederick University, she conducted postdoctoral research at the University of Cyprus and taught at several higher education institutions in Cyprus. Dr. Pantelides has published in international peer-reviewed journals and is actively engaged in teaching, research, and student mentorship.

Ramesh Pettela is presently working as an Associate Professor of English at Aditya University, Surampalem, Andhra Pradesh, India. He was awarded a Ph.D. in English from Acharya Nagarjuna University, Guntur, A.P., in 2016. He has 27 years of full-time teaching experience across IIITs, universities and autonomous institutions as a Professor and Head of the Department. A prolific academic, Dr. Ramesh has published extensively in reputed journals including Scopus, SCI and UGC and has presented numerous papers at national and international forums. He has successfully submitted research projects exceeding 45 lakhs funded by agencies such as ICSSR and AICTE and holds a patent for his research work. Beyond the classroom, he is a certified communication and soft skills trainer with global credentials from APSCHE, JNTU-A, EFLU, Cambridge University (UK) and ETS (USA), and is an approved trainer for GRE, IELTS, TOEFL and CRT programs. He has served as a resource person at national level conferences and seminars. He is an active member of professional bodies including ELTAI and MISTE and contributes to curriculum development as a Board of Studies member for several autonomous institutions. He is also the author of the insightful books English for Educators: Easy Methods and Techniques and ELT and Theories of Knowledge, reflecting his passion for empowering learners through effective language training.

Bora Phan Project Coordinator at CRM/InnerCHANGE/Sunrise Program (USA Organization) 2003-2012. Director at KCC Children's Home from 2013-2015. Founder of Peace Family and Development Organization, 2015 till now. Founder peace pre-kindergarten. Co-founder SSVP Cambodia 2004-2026. Professional skills in peacebuilding and conflict reconciliation, entrepreneurship, and education science, Ph.D. Bona Mary University board member (BMU) and Peace Bridges Organization (PBO) board member, Education Psychometric Attribute, Ph.D. Lecture at the National University of Cheasim Kamchaymear (NUCK) based on Research Methodology, Organizational Behaviors.

Shivendu Kumar Rai is working as a Head of Department in the Tecnia Institute of Advanced Studies, Rohini, New Delhi. Before that, he worked as Assistant Professor at Galgotias University, Greater Noida and as Acting Dean and assistant Professor, Faculty of Professional Studies, Department of Journalism and Mass Communication, Rama University, Kanpur (U.P.) He has done Graduation in Mass Media (2011) from Jamia Millia Islamia Central University, and Post-Graduation & M.Phil in Mass Communication (2013 & 2014) from Makhanalal Chaturvedi National University of Journalism and Communication, Bhopal.& Ph.D. (2020) in Mass Communication from Mahatma Gandhi International Hindi University, Wardha (Maharashtra). He has qualified UGC- NET examination twice in 2018 and 2019. He worked as a Doctorate Research Fellow at Indian Council of Social Science Research, New Delhi in PhD Research Topic Project "Changes In the Communication Strategies of Political Parties: Special Reference to tribal areas of Sonbhadra". Dr. Shivendu Kumar Rai has published 35 full-length research papers in reputed UGC Listed/ Peer Review Research Journals. He has attended 55 Seminars/ Workshops/Conferences/FDP etc. His area of expertise is Communication for Development, New Media Communication Research, and Political Communication.

Veena Rani is an Assistant Professor in the Department of Computer Science and Business Systems at Rajagiri School of Engineering and Technology. She completed her Bachelor of Technology in Information Technology in 2010 and went on to earn her Master of Technology in Computer Science and Engineering in 2014. With a strong academic background and a passion for teaching, she is dedicated to fostering innovation and technical excellence among students. Her areas of interest include computer science applications, emerging technologies, and interdisciplinary approaches that integrate business systems with computing solutions.

Reetika Ranjan is an academic and researcher based at Christ University, India. With a strong foundation in the humanities and social sciences, her work explores contemporary cultural and pedagogical shifts. At Christ University, she is known for her student-centric teaching methods and commitment to fostering critical thinking. Her research often bridges traditional knowledge systems with modern educational practices, reflecting a deep engagement with India's evolving academic landscape.

Reetika actively contributes to curriculum development and interdisciplinary dialogue within her institution. Her scholarly pursuits and dedication to mentorship mark her as an emerging voice in Indian higher education, shaping future thinkers and practitioners.

Sam Sopheak has been a lecturer at the University of Heng Samrin Thboung Khmom (UHSK), Cambodia, since 2023. He holds a bachelor's degree in sociology from the Royal University of Phnom Penh (2012) and a master's degree in education from the University of Cambodia (2022). He is currently a doctoral student at the Pedagogical University of Russia.

Arjune Selvam is an Assistant Professor in the School of Business and Management at CHRIST (Deemed to be University), Yeshwanthpur Campus, Bangalore. He holds a PhD in Entrepreneurship from SASTRA Deemed to be University (JRF) and is UGC-NET qualified in Management. He completed his MBA in HR and Marketing from PSNA College of Engineering and Technology and B.E. in Electronics and Instrumentation Engineering from M. Kumarasamy College of Engineering. His research interests include entrepreneurship, technology adoption, and digital entrepreneurship. He has published in ABDC-indexed journals and presented papers at Scopus-indexed international conferences.

Serey Mardy is an Associate Professor at Svay Rieng University in Cambodia, where he also serves as the Head of the International Relations Office. He is a distinguished scholar with a diverse academic background, holding a dual PhD in Agricultural Economics from the Vietnam National University of Agriculture and in Public Administration from Sandigan Colleges, Inc. in the Philippines. His research interests are centered around rural and agricultural development, with a particular focus on agricultural economics. Dr. Mardy is a prolific author, with numerous publications in academic journals and contributions to scholarly books. His work has been cited by researchers globally, and he is actively involved in the academic community as an editor and reviewer for several journals. At Svay Rieng University, he has been a faculty member since 2008, contributing to the Department of Rural Development within the Faculty of Agriculture. His multifaceted expertise and dedication to research and international collaboration make him a significant figure in Cambodian higher education.

Sandaboina Shivakumar is an accomplished academician, researcher, and author with over 13 years of distinguished experience in the fields of Finance and Accounting. He is currently serving as an Assistant Professor in the Department of Commerce (Finance & Accounting) at KL Deemed to be University, Guntur. He holds a Ph.D. in Commerce from Mahatma Gandhi University, Nalgonda, and is qualified in AP & TS SET (Commerce) and TS-TET. Dr. Shivakumar has consistently demonstrated academic excellence throughout his educational journey. Dr. Shivakumar has made significant contributions to research and academia, having published over 25 research papers in reputed national and international journals, including UGC CARE-listed journals, and presented numerous papers at conferences. He has also authored textbooks on Human Resource Management and Principles of Management and Organizational Behavior catering to undergraduate and postgraduate students. A recognized scholar, he serves as a reviewer and editorial board member for several international journals and has contributed book chapters indexed in Scopus. His research interests span financial markets, accounting practices, and emerging business models.Dr. Shivakumar has received multiple prestigious awards, including the Dr. Sarvepalli Radhakrishnan Shiksha Ratna Award, Yuva Acharya Award, and several "Best Faculty Awards" from national and international institutions, recognizing his excellence in teaching, research, and academic leadership. Beyond teaching and research, he actively mentors students across B.Com, BBA, M.Com, and MBA programs, guiding them in academic projects and career development. He has organized numerous academic and cultural events and has been a resource person at various institutions, contributing to knowledge dissemination and academic collaboration. With a strong commitment to innovation in pedagogy, research excellence, and student empowerment, Dr. Shivakumar continues to contribute significantly to the academic community and the advancement of commerce and management education.

Ranjit Singha is a Doctorate Research Fellow at Christ (Deemed to be University) and holds a prestigious membership in the American Psychological Association (APA). With a strong background in Research and Development, he has significantly contributed to various fields such as Mindfulness, Addiction Psychology, Women Empowerment, UN Sustainable Development Goals, and Data Science. With over 15 years of experience in Administration, Teaching, and Research, both in Industry and Higher Education Institutions (HEI), Mr Ranjit has established himself as a seasoned professional. Mr Ranjit is dedicated to research and teaching endeavours, primarily focusing on mindfulness and compassion-based interventions. His work in these areas aims to promote well-being and foster positive change in individuals and communities.

Surjit Singha is an Associate Professor, PhD Research Guide, and Research Faculty at Kristu Jayanti (Deemed to be University). His expertise spans CSR, sustainability, entrepreneurship, policy studies, and emerging interdisciplinary domains. He serves as an editor and reviewer for international journals and actively collaborates across disciplines. His research emphasizes evidence-based insights with strong practical and societal impact, and he is open to international research collaboration and academic mobility. With an impressive academic portfolio, Dr. Singha has published over 160+ articles, book chapters, and textbooks, including 130+ SCOPUS-indexed publications. He also holds two US Copyrights and two Patents, demonstrating his dedication to innovation and originality. Additionally, he has successfully completed two fully funded minor research projects from Kristu Jayanti (Deemed to be University). As a research mentor, Dr. Singha has guided numerous students and young scholars toward academic excellence. His academic qualifications include a PhD, M.Phil, and MBA (Distinction) from Christ University, M.Com, BBM from Kristu Jayanti College (Bangalore University), and PGDHE (Higher Education) from IGNOU (Central University). He is also a UGC-NET (Commerce) qualifier and serves as an Examiner for International Baccalaureate (IB).

Toem Tet currently serves as of the Head The Pheam phsoath primiry school .Have begun higher education in cambodia,where earned a Bachelor in the field of applied Mathematics from Khemarak Unibersity 2020 Folling bachelor's degree' pursued a graduate master degree in the fied of applied mathematics from Khemarak Unibersity 2023, specializing in applied Mathematics.

Tieng Morin is a distinguished figure in the realm of higher education, serving as Vice Rector at the National University of Battambang, Cambodia, since 2007. In this capacity, he oversees crucial departments including the Faculty of Business Administration and Tourism, Faculty of Social and Rural Development, Document Center, and Student Affairs Office. Mr. Morin's academic journey was shaped by his pursuit of excellence, culminating in the attainment of a Master of Business Administration degree from the esteemed University Utara Malaysia in 2002. His scholarly interests primarily revolve around research themes in higher education, reflecting his commitment to advancing the educational landscape. Through his leadership and scholarly endeavors, Mr. Morin continues to make profound contributions to the field, leaving an enduring impact on both his institution and the wider academic community.

Pinnika Syam Yadav is a distinguished researcher and academician specializing in business and marketing analytics. Currently serving as an Assistant Professor at Christ University, he has established himself as a leading figure in research and education. His scholarly work spans advanced areas of marketing analytics, predictive modeling, and data-driven decision-making, contributing valuable insights to both academia and industry. Dr. Yadav has successfully guided and awarded Ph.D. scholars, reflecting his dedication to mentoring and advancing research excellence. His innovative approach and extensive knowledge continue to inspire young researchers, positioning him as a catalyst for progress in the field.

Index

A

C

D

E

F

G

H

I

K

M

P

R

S

T

www.ingramcontent.com/pod-product-compliance
Lightning Source LLC
LaVergne TN
LVHW061526290926
849162LV00004B/684